INTERNATIONAL TRADE LAW STATUTES AND CONVENTIONS 2019–2021

International Trade Law Statutes and Conventions 2019–2021 presents all the key legislation for international trade law in one student-friendly volume. Developed in response to feedback from both lecturers and students, the book:

- provides an up-to-date, fully comprehensive collection of current legislation
- is curated to align with international trade law courses
- is an un-annotated text, conforming to regulations so that it can be used during exams
- features a clear and attractive text design, detailed table of contents, and multiple indices to provide ease of reference and navigation.

Ideal for coursework, exam use, and general reference work, this is the perfect companion for anyone studying this important and fast-moving area of law.

Indira Carr is Emeritus Professor of Law at the University of Surrey. She writes extensively on international trade law, corruption, and information technology law. Carr edits *Information and Communications Technology Law* and co-edits *Asian Philosophy*. Both journals are published by Taylor & Francis.

Jae Sundaram is Senior Lecturer in Law at the University of Buckingham. A dual-qualified lawyer, he has published scholarly articles in the law of world trade, modern armed-conflict, and commercial conflict, and is the author of the monograph *Pharmaceutical Patent Protection and World Trade Law.*

INTERNATIONAL TRADE LAW STATUTES AND CONVENTIONS 2019–2021

Indira Carr and Jae Sundaram

Routledge
Taylor & Francis Group
LONDON AND NEW YORK

First published 2021
by Routledge
2 Park Square, Milton Park, Abingdon, Oxon OX14 4RN

and by Routledge
605 Third Avenue, New York, NY 10158

Routledge is an imprint of the Taylor & Francis Group, an informa business

British Library Cataloguing-in-Publication Data
A catalogue record for this book is available from the British Library

Library of Congress Cataloging-in-Publication Data
A catalog record has been requested for this book

ISBN: 978-0-367-64663-9 (hbk)
ISBN: 978-0-367-64662-2 (pbk)
ISBN: 978-1-003-12571-6 (ebk)

Typeset in Bembo
by Deanta Global Publishing Servies, Chennai, India

OUTLINE CONTENTS

DETAILED CONTENTS – CHRONOLOGICAL

DETAILED CONTENTS – ALPHABETICAL

ACKNOWLEDGEMENTS

The publishers and editors thank the following organisations for their permission to reproduce the materials listed:

Comité Maritime International (CMI Rules for Electronic Bills of Lading, 1990; CMI Rules for Sea Waybills, 1990, The York-Antwerp Rules, 2004, York-Antwerp Rules, 2016)

OTIF (Uniform Rules Concerning the Contract of International Carriage by Rail (CIM 1999))

UNCITRAL (UNCITRAL Arbitration Rules, 1976; UNCITRAL Conciliation Rules, 1980; UNCITRAL Model Law on Electronic Commerce, 1996, as amended 1998; UNCITRAL Model Law on Electronic Signatures, 2001; UNCITRAL Model Law on International Commercial Arbitration, 1985; UNCITRAL Model Law on International Commercial Conciliation, 2002; UNCITRAL Model Law on International Commercial Mediation and International Settlement Agreements resulting from Mediation, 2018)

UNIDROIT (UNIDROIT Principles of International Commercial Contracts, 2010)

Convention on the Recognition and Enforcement of Foreign Arbitral Awards (New York, 1958) (the "New York Convention")

United Nations Convention on Contracts for the International Sale of Goods (Vienna, 1980) (CISG)

Convention on the Limitation Period in the International Sale of Goods (New York, 1974)

United Nations Convention on the Carriage of Goods by Sea (Hamburg, 1978) (the "Hamburg Rules")

United Nations Conventions on International Bills of Exchange and International Promissory Notes (New York, 1988)

United Nations Conventions on Contracts for the International Sale of Goods (Vienna, 1980) (CISG)

United Nations Convention on the Liability of Operators of Transport Terminals in International Trade (Vienna, 1991)

United Nations Conventions on the Use of Electronics Communications in International Contracts (New York, 2005)

United Nations Conventions on Contracts for the International Carriage of Goods Wholly or Partly by Sea (New York, 2008) (the "Rotterdam Rules")

PREFACE

The study of International Trade Law requires access to a wide range of materials, many of which are not easily accessible, and the purpose of this book is to provide students with those documents to which they are likely to be referred in courses on this subject. We have provided extracts from statutes and conventions, all of which have been reproduced in their amended and updated form. In the Statutes section we have included the Consumer Rights Act, 2015, and the Enterprise Act, 2016, and in the final section on Rules and Model Laws the 2016 version of the York-Antwerp Rules, the amendments to the UNIDROIT Principles of International Commercial Contracts, 2010, introduced by the UNIDROIT Principles of International Commercial Contracts, 2016, and the UNCITRAL Model Law on International Commercial Mediation and International Settlement Agreement resulting from Mediation, 2018 (amending the UNCITRAL Model Law on International Commercial Conciliation, 2002) are included.

The collection is necessarily highly selective as the potential range of material is very wide; nevertheless we believe we have selected the documents which a student is likely to come across in any standard course on International Trade Law. We also believe that the materials in this collection will be of use to students following courses on commercial law and carriage of goods. We hope that this will provide a convenient and relatively inexpensive method of access to materials which might otherwise not be easily available.

The collection is divided into five sections: Statutes, Statutory Instruments, European Union Materials, Conventions, and Rules and Model Law. The material in Sections I to IV are arranged chronologically and in Section V alphabetically. The material is printed in its amended form, but we have not indicated the source of these amendments and the text is printed as amended even if that amendment is not yet in force. Sections which have been omitted or repealed are noted.

The collection contains material available to us up to 30 September 2020.

Indira Carr
Jae Sundaram

Section I

STATUTES

Bills of Exchange Act 1882

Part I Preliminary

1 [Omitted].

2 Interpretation of terms

In this Act, unless the context otherwise requires –

'Acceptance' means an acceptance completed by delivery or notification.

'Action' includes counter claim and set off.

'Banker' includes a body of persons whether incorporated or not who carry on the business of banking.

'Bankrupt' includes any person whose estate is vested in a trustee or assignee under the law for the time being in force relating to bankruptcy.

'Bearer' means the person in possession of a bill or note which is payable to bearer.

'Bill' means bill of exchange, and 'note' means promissory note.

'Delivery' means transfer of possession, actual or constructive, from one person to another.

'Holder' means the payee or indorsee of a bill or note who is in possession of it, or the bearer thereof.

'Indorsement' means an indorsement completed by delivery.

'Issue' means the first delivery of a bill or note, complete in form to a person who takes it as a holder.

'Person' includes a body of persons whether incorporated or not.

'Postal operator' has the meaning given by section 27 of the Postal Services Act 2011.

'Value' means valuable consideration.

'Written' includes printed, and 'writing' includes print.

Part II Bills of exchange

Form and interpretation

3 Bill of exchange defined

(1) A bill of exchange is an unconditional order in writing, addressed by one person to another, signed by the person giving it, requiring the person to whom it is addressed to pay on demand or at a fixed or determinable future time a sum certain in money to or to the order of a specified person, or to bearer.
(2) An instrument which does not comply with these conditions, or which orders any act to be done in addition to the payment of money, is not a bill of exchange.
(3) An order to pay out of a particular fund is not unconditional within the meaning of this section; but an unqualified order to pay, coupled with (a) an indication of a particular fund out of which the drawee is to re-imburse himself or a particular account to be debited with the amount, or (b) a statement of the transaction which gives rise to the bill is unconditional.
(4) A bill is not invalid by reason –
  (a) that it is not dated;
  (b) that it does not specify the value given, or that any value has been given therefore;
  (c) that it does not specify the place where it is drawn or the place where it is payable.

4 Inland and foreign bills

(1) An inland bill is a bill which is or on the face of it purports to be –
  (a) both drawn and payable within the British Islands; or
  (b) drawn within the British Islands upon some person resident therein. Any other bill is a foreign bill.

  For the purposes of the Act 'British Islands' mean any part of the United Kingdom of Great Britain and Ireland, the islands of Man, Guernsey, Jersey, Alderney, and Sark, and the islands adjacent to any of them being part of the dominions of Her Majesty.
(2) Unless the contrary appear on the face of the bill the holder may treat it as an inland bill.

5 Effect where different parties to bill are the same person

(1) A bill may be drawn payable to, or to the order of, the drawer; or it may be drawn payable to, or to the order of, the drawee.
(2) Where in a bill drawer and drawee are the same person, or where the drawee is a fictitious person or a person not having capacity to contract, the holder may treat the instrument, at his option, either as a bill of exchange or as a promissory note.

6 Address to drawee

(1) The drawee must be named or otherwise indicated in a bill with reasonable certainty.
(2) A bill may be addressed to two or more drawees whether they are partners or not, but an order addressed to two drawees in the alternative or to two or more drawees in succession is not a bill of exchange.

7 Certainty required as to payee

(1) Where a bill is not payable to bearer, the payee must be named or otherwise indicated therein with reasonable certainty.
(2) A bill may be made payable to two or more payees jointly, or it may be made payable in the alternative to one of two, or one or some of several payees. A bill may also be made payable to the holder of an office for the time being.
(3) Where the payee is a fictitious or non-existing person the bill may be treated as payable to bearer.

8 What bills are negotiable

(1) When a bill contains words prohibiting transfer, or indicating an intention that it should not be transferable, it is valid as between the parties thereto, but is not negotiable.
(2) A negotiable bill may be payable either to order or to bearer.
(3) A bill is payable to bearer which is expressed to be so payable or on which the only or last indorsement is an indorsement in blank.
(4) A bill is payable to order which is expressed to be so payable, or which is expressed to be payable to a particular person, and does not contain words prohibiting transfer or indicating an intention that it should not be transferable.
(5) Where a bill, either originally or by indorsement, is expressed to be payable to the order of a specified person, and not to him or his order, it is nevertheless payable to him or his order at his option.

9 Sum payable

(1) The sum payable by a bill is a sum certain within the meaning of this Act, although it was required to be paid –
    (a) with interest;
    (b) by stated instalments;
    (c) by stated instalments, with a provision that upon default in payment of any instalment the whole shall become due;
    (d) according to an indicated rate of exchange or according to a rate of exchange to be ascertained as directed by the bill.
(2) Where the sum payable is expressed in words and also in figures, and there is a discrepancy between the two, the sum denoted by the words is the amount payable.
(3) Where a bill is expressed to be payable with interest, unless the instrument otherwise provides, interest runs from the date of the bill, and if the bill is undated from the issue thereof.

10 Bill payable on demand

(1) A bill is payable on demand –
    (a) which is expressed to be payable on demand, or at sight, or on presentation; or
    (b) in which no time for payment is expressed.
(2) Where a bill is accepted or indorsed when it is overdue, it shall, as regards the acceptor who so accepts, or any indorser who so indorses it, be deemed a bill payable on demand.

11 Bill payable at a future time

A bill is payable at a determinable future time within the meaning of this Act which is expressed to be payable –

(1) At a fixed period after date or sight.
(2) On or at a fixed period after the occurrence of a specified event which is certain to happen, though the time of happening may be uncertain.
(3) An instrument expressed to be payable on a contingency is not a bill, and the happening of the event does not cure the defect.

12 Omission of date in bill payable after date

Where a bill expressed to be payable at a fixed period after date is issued undated, or where the acceptance of a bill payable at a fixed period after sight is undated, any holder may insert therein the true date of issue or acceptance, and the bill shall be payable accordingly.

Provided that – (1) where the holder in good faith and by mistake inserts a wrong date, and (2) in every case where a wrong date is inserted, if the bill subsequently comes into the hands of a holder in due course the bill shall not be avoided thereby, but shall operate and be payable as if the date so inserted had been the true date.

13 Ante-dating and post-dating

(1) Where a bill or an acceptance or any indorsement on a bill is dated, the date shall, unless the contrary be proved, be deemed to be the true date of the drawing, acceptance, or indorsement, as the case may be.
(2) A bill is not invalid by reason only that it is ante-dated or post-dated, or that it bears date on a Sunday.

14 Computation of time of payment

Where a bill is not payable on demand the day on which it falls due is determined as follows:

(1) The bill is due and payable in all cases on the last day of the time of payment as fixed by the bill or, if that is a non-business day, on the succeeding business day.
(2) Where a bill is payable at a fixed period after date, after sight, or after the happening of a specified event, the time of payment is determined by excluding the day from which the time is to begin to run and by including the day of payment.
(3) Where a bill is payable at a fixed period after sight, the time begins to run from the date of the acceptance if the bill be accepted, and from the date of noting or protest if the bill be noted or protested for non-acceptance, or for non-delivery.
(4) The term 'month' in a bill means a calendar month.

15 Case of need

The drawer of a bill and any indorser may insert therein the name of a person to whom the holder may resort in case of need, that is to say, in case the bill is dishonoured by non-acceptance or non-payment. Such person is called the referee in case of need. It is in the option of the holder to resort to the referee in case of need or not as he may think fit.

16 Optional stipulations by drawer or indorser

The drawer of a bill, and any indorser, may insert therein an express stipulation –

(1) Negativing or limiting his own liability to the holder.
(2) Waiving as regards himself some or all of the holder's duties.

17 Definition and requisites of acceptance

(1) The acceptance of a bill is the signification by the drawee of his assent to the order of the drawer.
(2) An acceptance is invalid unless it complies with the following conditions, namely –
  (a) it must be written on the bill and be signed by the drawee. The mere signature of the drawee without additional words is sufficient;
  (b) it must not express that the drawee will perform his promise by any other means than the payment of money.

18 Time for acceptance

A bill may be accepted –

(1) Before it has been signed by the drawer, or while otherwise incomplete.
(2) When it is overdue, or after it has been dishonoured by a previous refusal to accept, or by non-payment.
(3) When a bill payable after sight is dishonoured by non-acceptance, and the drawee subsequently accepts it, the holder, in the absence of any different agreement, is entitled to have the bill accepted as of the date of first presentment to the drawee for acceptance.

19 General and qualified acceptances

(1) An acceptance is either (a) general or (b) qualified.
(2) A general acceptance assents without qualification to the order of the drawer. A qualified acceptance in expressed terms varies the effect of the bill as drawn. In particular an acceptance is qualified which is –
  (a) conditional, that is to say, which makes payment by the acceptor dependent on the fulfilment of a condition therein stated;
  (b) partial, that is to say, an acceptance to pay part only of the amount for which the bill is drawn;
  (c) local, that is to say, an acceptance to pay only at a particular specified place;
  (d) an acceptance to pay at a particular place is a general acceptance, unless it expressly states that the bill is to be paid there only and not elsewhere;
  (e) qualified as to time;
  (f) the acceptance of some one or more of the drawees, but not of all.

20 Inchoate instruments

(1) Where a simple signature on a blank paper is delivered by the signer in order that it may be converted into a bill, it operates as a *prima facie* authority to fill it up as a complete bill for any amount using the signature for that of the drawer, or the acceptor, or an indorser; and, in like manner, when a bill is wanting in any material particular, the person in possession of it has a *prima facie* authority to fill up the omission in any way he thinks fit.

(2) In order that any such instrument when completed may be enforceable against any person who became a party thereto prior to its completion, it must be filled up within a reasonable time, and strictly in accordance with the authority given. Reasonable time for this purpose is a question of fact. Provided that if any such instrument after completion is negotiated to a holder in due course it shall be valid and effectual for all purposes in his hands, and he may enforce it as if it had been filled up within a reasonable time and strictly in accordance with the authority given.

21 Delivery

(1) Every contract on a bill, whether it be the drawer's, the acceptor's, or an indorser's, is incomplete and revocable, until delivery of the instrument in order to give effect thereto. Provided that where an acceptance is written on a bill, and the drawee gives notice to or according to the directions of the person entitled to the bill that he has accepted it, the acceptance then becomes complete and irrevocable.

(2) As between immediate parties, and as regards a remote party other than a holder in due course, the delivery –

   (a) in order to be effectual must be made either by or under the authority of the party drawing, accepting, or indorsing, as the case may be;

   (b) may be shown to have been conditional or for a special purpose only, and not for the purpose of transferring the property in the bill. But if the bill be in the hands of a holder in due course a valid delivery of the bill by all parties prior to him so as to make them liable to him is conclusively presumed.

(3) Where a bill is no longer in the possession of a party who has signed it as drawer, acceptor, or indorser, a valid and unconditional delivery by him is presumed until the contrary is proved.

Capacity and authority of parties

22 Capacity of parties

(1) Capacity to incur liability as a party to a bill is coextensive with capacity to contract. Provided that nothing in this section shall enable a corporation to make itself liable as drawer, acceptor, or indorser of a bill unless it is competent to it so to do under the law for the time being in force relating to corporations.

(2) Where a bill is drawn or indorsed by an infant, minor, or corporation having no capacity or power to incur liability on a bill, the drawing or indorsement entitles the holder to receive payment of the bill, and to enforce it against any other party thereto.

23 Signature essential to liability

No person is liable as drawer, indorser, or acceptor of a bill who has not signed it as such: Provided that –

(1) Where a person signs a bill in a trade or assumed name, he is liable thereon as if he had signed it in his own name.
(2) The signature of the name of the firm is equivalent to the signature by the person so signing of the names of all persons liable as partners in that firm.

24 Forged or unauthorised signature

Subject to the provisions of this Act, where a signature on a bill is forged or placed thereon without the authority of the person whose signature it purports to be, the forged or unauthorised signature is wholly inoperative, and no right to retain the bill or to give a discharge therefore or to enforce payment thereof against any party thereto can be acquired through or under that signature, unless the party against whom it is sought to retain or enforce payment of the bill is precluded from setting up the forgery or want of authority.

Provided that nothing in this section shall affect the ratification of an unauthorised signature not amounting to a forgery.

25 Procuration signatures

A signature by procuration operates as notice that the agent has but a limited authority to sign, and the principal is only bound by such signature if the agent in so signing was acting within the actual limits of his authority.

26 Person signing as agent or in representative capacity

(1) Where a person signs a bill as drawer, indorser, or acceptor, and adds words to his signature, indicating that he signs for or on behalf of a principal, or in a representative character, he is not personally liable thereon; but the mere addition to his signature of words describing him as an agent, or as filling a representative character, does not exempt him from personal liability.
(2) In determining whether a signature on a bill is that of the principal or that of the agent by whose hand it is written, the construction most favourable to the validity of the instrument shall be adopted.

The consideration for a bill

27 Value and holder for value

(1) Valuable consideration for a bill may be constituted by –
    (a) any consideration sufficient to support a simple contract;
    (b) an antecedent debt or liability. Such a debt or liability is deemed valuable consideration whether the bill is payable on demand or at a future time.
(2) Where value has at any time been given for a bill the holder is deemed to be a holder for value as regards the acceptor and all parties to the bill who became parties prior to such time.

(3) Where the holder of a bill has a lien on it arising either from contract or by implication of law, he is deemed to be a holder for value to the extent of the sum for which he has a lien.

28 Accommodation bill or party

(1) An accommodation party to a bill is a person who has signed a bill as drawer, acceptor, or indorser, without receiving value therefore, and for the purpose of lending his name to some other person.
(2) An accommodation party is liable on the bill to a holder for value; and it is immaterial whether, when such holder took the bill, he knew such party to be an accommodation party or not.

29 Holder in due course

(1) A holder in due course is a holder who has taken a bill, complete and regular on the face of it, under the following conditions, namely –
    (a) that he became the holder of it before it was overdue, and without notice that it had been previously dishonoured, if such was the fact;
    (b) that he took the bill in good faith and for value, and that at the time the bill was negotiated to him he had no notice of any defect in the title of the person who negotiated it.
(2) In particular the title of a person who negotiates a bill is defective within the meaning of this Act when he obtained the bill, or the acceptance thereof, by fraud, duress, or force and fear, or other unlawful means, or an illegal consideration, or when he negotiates it in breach of faith, or under such circumstances as amount to a fraud.
(3) A holder (whether for value or not), who derives his title to a bill through a holder in due course, and who is not himself a party to any fraud or illegality affecting it, has all the rights of that holder in due course as regards the acceptor and all parties to the bill prior to that holder.

30 Presumption of value and good faith

(1) Every party whose signature appears on a bill is *prima facie* deemed to have become a party thereto for value.
(2) Every holder of a bill is *prima facie* deemed to be a holder in due course; but if in an action on a bill it is admitted or proved that the acceptance, issue, or subsequent negotiation of the bill is affected with fraud, duress, or force and fear, or illegality, the burden of proof is shifted, unless and until the holder proves that, subsequent to the alleged fraud or illegality, value has in good faith been given for the bill.

Negotiation of bills

31 Negotiation of bill

(1) A bill is negotiated when it is transferred from one person to another in such a manner as to constitute the transferee the holder of the bill.

(2) A bill payable to bearer is negotiated by delivery.
(3) A bill payable to order is negotiated by the indorsement of the holder completed by delivery.
(4) Where the holder of a bill payable to his order transfers it for value without indorsing it, the transfer gives the transferee such title as the transferor had in the bill, and the transferee in addition acquires the right to have the indorsement of the transferor.
(5) Where any person is under obligation to indorse a bill in a representative capacity, he may indorse the bill in such terms as to negative personal liability.

32 Requisites of a valid indorsement

An indorsement in order to operate as a negotiation must comply with the following conditions, namely –

(1) It must be written on the bill itself and be signed by the indorser. The simple signature of the indorser on the bill without additional words is sufficient. An indorsement written on an *allonge*, or on a 'copy' of a bill issued or negotiated in a country where 'copies' are recognised, is deemed to be written on the bill itself.
(2) It must be an indorsement of the entire bill. A partial indorsement, that is to say, an indorsement which purports to transfer to the indorsee a part only of the amount payable, or which purports to transfer the bill to two or more indorsees severally, does not operate as a negotiation of the bill.
(3) Where a bill is payable to the order of two or more payees or indorsees who are not partners all must indorse, unless the one indorsing has authority to indorse for the others.
(4) Where, in a bill payable to order, the payee or indorsee is wrongly designated, or his name is mis-spelt, he may indorse the bill as therein described, adding, if he thinks fit, his proper signature.
(5) Where there are two or more indorsements on a bill, each indorsement is deemed to have been made in the order in which it appears on the bill, until the contrary is proved.
(6) An indorsement may be made in blank or special. It may also contain terms making it restrictive.

33 Conditional indorsement

Where a bill purports to be indorsed conditionally the condition may be disregarded by the payer, and payment to the indorsee is valid whether the condition has been fulfilled or not.

34 Indorsement in blank and special indorsement

(1) An indorsement in blank specifies no indorsee, and a bill so indorsed becomes payable to bearer.
(2) A special indorsement specifies the person to whom, or to whose order, the bill is to be payable.
(3) The provisions of this Act relating to a payee apply with the necessary modifications to an indorsee under a special indorsement.

(4) When a bill has been indorsed in blank, any holder may convert the blank indorsement into a special indorsement by writing above the indorsee's signature a direction to pay the bill to or to the order of himself or some other person.

35 Restrictive indorsement

(1) An indorsement is restrictive which prohibits the further negotiation of the bill or which expresses that it is a mere authority to deal with the bill as thereby directed and not a transfer of the ownership thereof, as, for example, if a bill be indorsed 'Pay D. only,' or 'Pay D. for the account of X.,' or 'Pay D. or order for collection.'
(2) A restrictive indorsement gives the indorsee the right to receive payment of the bill and to sue any party thereto that his indorser could have sued, but gives him no power to transfer his rights as indorsee unless it expressly authorises him to do so.
(3) Where a restrictive indorsement authorises further transfer, all subsequent indorsees take the bill with the same rights and subject to the same liabilities as the first indorsee under the restrictive indorsement.

36 Negotiation of overdue or dishonoured bill

(1) Where a bill is negotiable in its origin it continues to be negotiable until it has been –
  (a) restrictively indorsed; or
  (b) discharged by payment or otherwise.
(2) Where an overdue bill is negotiated, it can only be negotiated subject to any defect of title affecting it at its maturity, and thenceforward no person who takes it can acquire or give a better title than that which the person from whom he took it had.
(3) A bill payable on demand is deemed to be overdue within the meaning and for the purposes of this section, when it appears on the face of it to have been in circulation for an unreasonable length of time. What is an unreasonable length of time for this purpose is a question of fact.
(4) Except where an indorsement bears date after the maturity of the bill, every negotiation is *prima facie* deemed to have been effected before the bill was overdue.
(5) Where a bill which is not overdue has been dishonoured any person who takes it with notice of the dishonour takes it subject to any defect of title attaching thereto at the time of dishonour, but nothing in this sub-section shall affect the rights of a holder in due course.

37 Negotiation of bill to party already liable thereon

Where a bill is negotiated back to the drawer, or to a prior indorser or to the acceptor, such party may, subject to the provisions of this Act, re-issue and further negotiate the bill, but he is not entitled to enforce payment of the bill against any intervening party to whom he was previously liable.

38 Rights of the holder

The rights and powers of the holder of a bill are as follows –

(1) He may sue on the bill in his own name.

(2) Where he is a holder in due course, he holds the bill free from any defect of title of prior parties, as well as from mere personal defences available to prior parties among themselves, and may enforce payment against all parties liable on the bill.
(3) Where his title is defective (a) if he negotiates the bill to a holder in due course, that holder obtains a good and complete title to the bill, and (b) if he obtains payment of the bill the person who pays him in due course gets a valid discharge for the bill.

General duties of the holder

39 When presentment for acceptance is necessary

(1) Where a bill is payable after sight, presentment for acceptance is necessary in order to fix the maturity of the instrument.
(2) Where a bill expressly stipulates that it shall be presented for acceptance, or where a bill is drawn payable elsewhere than at the residence or place of business of the drawee, it must be presented for acceptance before it can be presented for payment.
(3) In no other case is presentment for acceptance necessary in order to render liable any party to the bill.
(4) Where the holder of a bill, drawn payable elsewhere than at the place of business or residence of the drawee, has not time, with the exercise of reasonable diligence, to present the bill for acceptance before presenting it for payment on the day that it falls due, the delay caused by presenting the bill for acceptance before presenting it for payment is excused, and does not discharge the drawer and indorsers.

40 Time for presenting bill payable after sight

(1) Subject to the provisions of this Act, when a bill payable after sight is negotiated, the holder must either present it for acceptance or negotiate it within a reasonable time.
(2) If he does not do so, the drawer and all indorsers prior to that holder are discharged.
(3) In determining what is a reasonable time within the meaning of this section, regard shall be had to the nature of the bill, the usage of trade with respect to similar bills, and the facts of the particular case.

41 Rules as to presentment for acceptance, and excuses for non-presentment

(1) A bill is duly presented for acceptance which is presented in accordance with the following rules –
  (a) the presentment must be made by or on behalf of the holder to the drawee or to some person authorised to accept or refuse acceptance on his behalf at a reasonable hour on a business day and before the bill is overdue;
  (b) where a bill is addressed to two or more drawees, who are not partners, presentment must be made to them all, unless one has authority to accept for all, then presentment may be made to him only;
  (c) where the drawee is dead presentment may be made to his personal representative;
  (d) where the drawee is bankrupt, presentment may be made to him or to his trustee;

(e) where authorised by agreement or usage, a presentment through a postal operator is sufficient.

(2) Presentment in accordance with these rules is excused, and a bill may be treated as dishonoured by non-acceptance –

(a) where the drawee is dead or bankrupt, or is a fictitious person or a person not having capacity to contract by bill;

(b) where, after the exercise of reasonable diligence, such presentment cannot be effected;

(c) where, although the presentment has been irregular, acceptance has been refused on some other ground.

(3) The fact that the holder has reason to believe that the bill, on presentment, will be dishonoured does not excuse presentment.

42 Non-acceptance

When a bill is duly presented for acceptance and is not accepted within the customary time, the person presenting it must treat it as dishonoured by non-acceptance. If he does not, the holder shall lose his right of recourse against the drawer and indorsers.

43 Dishonour by non-acceptance and its consequences

(1) A bill is dishonoured by non-acceptance –

(a) when it is duly presented for acceptance, and such an acceptance as is prescribed by this Act is refused or cannot be obtained; or

(b) when presentment for acceptance is excused and the bill is not accepted.

(2) Subject to the provisions of this Act when a bill is dishonoured by non-acceptance, an immediate right of recourse against the drawer and indorsers accrues to the holder, and no presentment for payment is necessary.

44 Duties as to qualified acceptances

(1) The holder of a bill may refuse to take a qualified acceptance, and if he does not obtain an unqualified acceptance may treat the bill as dishonoured by non-acceptance.

(2) Where a qualified acceptance is taken, and the drawer or an indorser has not expressly or impliedly authorised the holder to take a qualified acceptance, or does not subsequently assent thereto, such drawer or indorser is discharged from his liability on the bill. The provisions of this sub-section do not apply to a partial acceptance, whereof due notice has been given. Where a foreign bill has been accepted as to part, it must be protested as to the balance.

(3) When the drawer or indorser of a bill receives notice of a qualified acceptance, and does not within a reasonable time express his dissent to the holder he shall be deemed to have assented thereto.

45 Rules as to presentment for payment

Subject to the provisions of this Act a bill must be duly presented for payment. If it be not so presented the drawer and indorsers shall be discharged. A bill is duly presented for payment which is presented in accordance with the following rules –

(1) Where the bill is not payable on demand, presentment must be made on the day it falls due.

(2) Where the bill is payable on demand, then, subject to the provisions of this Act, presentment must be made within a reasonable time after its issue in order to render the drawer liable, and within a reasonable time after its indorsement, in order to render the indorser liable. In determining what is a reasonable time, regard shall be had to the nature of the bill, the usage of trade with regard to similar bills, and the facts of the particular case.

(3) Presentment must be made by the holder or by some person authorised to receive payment on his behalf at a reasonable hour on a business day, at the proper place as hereinafter defined, either to the person designated by the bill as payer, or to some person authorised to pay or refuse payment on his behalf if with the exercise of reasonable diligence such person can there be found.

(4) A bill is presented at the proper place –
   (a) where a place of payment is specified in the bill and the bill is there presented;
   (b) where no place of payment is specified, but the address of the drawee or acceptor is given in the bill, and the bill is there presented;
   (c) where no place of payment is specified and no address given, and the bill is presented at the drawee's or acceptor's place of business if known, and if not, at his ordinary residence if known;
   (d) in any other case if presented to the drawee or acceptor wherever he can be found, or if presented at his last known place of business or residence.

(5) Where a bill is presented at the proper place, and after the exercise of reasonable diligence no person authorised to pay or refuse payment can be found there, no further presentment to the drawee or acceptor is required.

(6) Where a bill is drawn upon, or accepted by two or more persons who are not partners, and no place of payment is specified, presentment must be made to them all.

(7) Where the drawee or acceptor of a bill is dead, and no place of payment is specified, presentment must be made to a personal representative, if such there be, and with the exercise of reasonable diligence can be found.

(8) Where authorised by agreement or usage a presentment through a postal operator is sufficient.

46 Excuses for delay or non-presentment for payment

(1) Delay in making presentment for payment is excused when the delay is caused by circumstances beyond the control of the holder, and not imputable to his default, misconduct, or negligence. When the cause of delay ceases to operate presentment must be made with reasonable diligence.

(2) Presentment for payment is dispensed with –
   (a) where, after the exercise of reasonable diligence presentment, as required by this Act, cannot be effected. The fact that the holder has reason to believe that the bill will, on presentment, be dishonoured, does not dispense with the necessity for presentment;
   (b) where the drawee is a fictitious person;
   (c) as regards the drawer where the drawee or acceptor is not bound as between himself and the drawer, to accept or pay the bill, and the drawer has no reason to believe that the bill would be paid if presented;

(d) as regards an indorser, where the bill was accepted or made for the accommodation of that indorser, and he has no reason to expect that the bill would be paid if presented;
(e) by waiver of presentment, express or implied.

47 Dishonour by non-payment

(1) A bill is dishonoured by non-payment (a) when it is duly presented for payment and payment is refused or cannot be obtained, or (b) when presentment is excused and the bill is overdue and unpaid.
(2) Subject to the provisions of this Act, when a bill is dishonoured by non-payment, an immediate right of recourse against the drawer and indorsers accrues to the holder.

48 Notice of dishonour and effect of non-notice

Subject to the provisions of this Act, when a bill has been dishonoured by non-acceptance or by non-payment, notice of dishonour must be given to the drawer and each indorser, and any drawer or indorser to whom such notice is not given is discharged. Provided that –

(1) Where a bill is dishonoured by non-acceptance, and notice of dishonour is not given, the rights of a holder in due course, subsequent to the omission, shall not be prejudiced by the omission.
(2) Where a bill is dishonoured by non-acceptance, and due notice of dishonour is given, it shall not be necessary to give notice of a subsequent dishonour by non-payment unless the bill shall in the meantime have been accepted.

49 Rules as to notice of dishonour

Notice of dishonour in order to be valid and effectual must be given in accordance with the following rules –

(1) The notice must be given by or on behalf of the holder, or by or on behalf of an indorser who, at the time of giving it, is himself liable on the bill.
(2) Notice of dishonour may be given by an agent either in his own name, or in the name of any party entitled to give notice whether that party be his principal or not.
(3) Where the notice is given by or on behalf of the holder, it enures for the benefit of all subsequent holders and all prior indorsers who have a right of recourse against the party to whom it is given.
(4) Where notice is given by or on behalf of an indorser entitled to give notice as hereinbefore provided, it enures for the benefit of the holder and all indorsers subsequent to the party to whom notice is given.
(5) The notice may be given in writing or by personal communication, and may be given in any terms which sufficiently identify the bill, and intimate that the bill has been dishonoured by non-acceptance or non-payment.
(6) The return of a dishonoured bill to the drawer or an indorser is, in point of form, deemed a sufficient notice of dishonour.

(7) A written notice need not be signed, and an insufficient written notice may be supplemented and validated by verbal communication. A misdescription of the bill shall not vitiate the notice unless the party to whom the notice is given is in fact misled thereby.

(8) Where notice of dishonour is required to be given to any person, it may be given either to the party himself, or to his agent in that behalf.

(9) Where the drawer or indorser is dead, and the party giving notice knows it, the notice must be given to a personal representative if such there be, and with the exercise of reasonable diligence he can be found.

(10) Where the drawer or indorser is bankrupt, notice may be given either to the party himself or to the trustee.

(11) Where there are two or more drawers or indorsers who are not partners, notice must be given to each of them, unless one of them has authority to receive such notice for the others.

(12) The notice may be given as soon as the bill is dishonoured and must be given within a reasonable time thereafter. In the absence of special circumstances notice is not deemed to have been given within a reasonable time, unless –

  (a) where the person giving and the person to receive notice reside in the same place, the notice is given or sent off in time to reach the latter on the day after the dishonour of the bill;

  (b) where the person giving and the person to receive notice reside in different places, the notice is sent off on the day after the dishonour of the bill, if there be a postal a convenient hour on that day, and if there be no such post on that day then by the next post thereafter.

(13) Where a bill when dishonoured is in the hands of an agent, he may either himself give notice to the parties liable on the bill or he may give notice to his principal. If he give notice to his principal, he must do so within the same time as if he were the holder, and the principal upon receipt of such notice has himself the same time for giving notice as if the agent had been an independent holder.

(14) Where a party to a bill receives due notice of dishonour, he has after the receipt of such notice the same period of time for giving notice to antecedent parties that the holder has after the dishonour.

(15) Where a notice of dishonour is duly addressed and posted, the sender is deemed to have given due notice of dishonour, notwithstanding any miscarriage by the postal operator concerned.

50 Excuses for non-notice and delay

(1) Delay in giving notice of dishonour is excused where the delay is caused by circumstances beyond the control of the party giving notice, and not imputable to his default, misconduct, or negligence. When the cause of delay ceases to operate the notice must be given with reasonable diligence.

(2) Notice of dishonour is dispensed with –

  (a) when, after the exercise of reasonable diligence, notice as required by this Act cannot be given to or does not reach the drawer or indorser sought to be charged;

  (b) by waiver express or implied. Notice of dishonour may be waived before the time of giving notice has arrived, or after the omission to give due notice;

(c) as regards the drawer in the following cases, namely, (1) where drawer and drawee are the same person, (2) where the drawee is a fictitious person or a person not having capacity to contract, (3) where the drawer is the person to whom the bill is presented for payment, (4) where the drawee or acceptor is as between himself and the drawer under no obligation to accept or pay the bill, (5) where the drawer has countermanded payment;

(d) as regards the indorser in the following cases, namely, (1) where the drawee is a fictitious person or a person not having capacity to contract, and the indorser was aware of the fact at the time he indorsed the bill, (2) where the indorser is the person to whom the bill is presented for payment, (3) where the bill was accepted or made for his accommodation.

51 Noting or protest of bill

(1) Where an inland bill has been dishonoured it may, if the holder thinks fit, be noted for non-acceptance or non-payment, as the case may be; but it shall not be necessary to note or protest any such bill in order to preserve the recourse against the drawer or indorser.

(2) Where a foreign bill, appearing on the face of it to be such, has been dishonoured by non-acceptance it must be duly protested for non-acceptance, and where such a bill, which has not been previously dishonoured by non-acceptance, is dishonoured by non-payment it must be duly protested for non-payment. If it be not so protested the drawer and indorsers are discharged. Where a bill does not appear on the face of it to be a foreign bill, protest thereof in case of dishonour is unnecessary.

(3) A bill which has been protested for non-acceptance may be subsequently protested for non-payment.

(4) Subject to the provisions of this Act, when a bill is noted or protested, it may be noted on the day of its dishonour and must be noted not later than the next succeeding business day. When a bill has been duly noted, the protest may be subsequently extended as of the date of the noting.

(5) Where the acceptor of a bill becomes bankrupt or insolvent or suspends payment before it matures, the holder may cause the bill to be protested for better security against the drawer and indorsers.

(6) A bill must be protested at the place where it is dishonoured: Provided that –

(a) when a bill is presented through a postal operator, and returned by post dishonoured, it may be protested at the place to which it is returned and on the day of its return if received during business hours, and if not received during business hours, then not later than the next business day;

(b) when a bill drawn payable at the place of business or residence of some person other than the drawee has been dishonoured by non-acceptance, it must be protested for non-payment at the place where it is expressed to be payable, and no further presentment for payment to, or demand on, the drawee is necessary.

(7) A protest must contain a copy of the bill, and must be signed by the notary making it, and must specify –

(a) the person at whose request the bill is protested;

(b) the place and date of protest, the cause or reason for protesting the bill, the demand made, and the answer given, if any, or the fact that the drawee or acceptor could not be found.

(7A) In subsection (7) 'notary' includes a person who, for the purposes of the Legal Services Act 2007, is an authorised person in relation to any activity with constitutes a notarial activity (within the meaning of that Act).

(8) Where a bill is lost or destroyed, or is wrongly detained from the person entitled to hold it, protest may be made on a copy or written particulars thereof.

(9) Protest is dispensed with by any circumstance which would dispense with notice of dishonour. Delay in noting or protesting is excused when the delay is caused by circumstances beyond the control of the holder, and not imputable to his default, misconduct, or negligence. When the cause of delay ceases to operate the bill must be noted or protested with reasonable diligence.

52 Duties of holder as regards drawee or acceptor

(1) When a bill is accepted generally presentment for payment is not necessary in order to render the acceptor liable.

(2) When by the terms of a qualified acceptance presentment for payment is required, the acceptor, in the absence of an express stipulation to that effect, is not discharged by the omission to present the bill for payment on the day that it matures.

(3) In order to render the acceptor of a bill liable it is not necessary to protest it, or that notice dishonour should be given to him.

(4) Where the holder of a bill presents it for payment, he shall exhibit the bill to the person from whom he demands payment, and when a bill is paid the holder shall forthwith deliver it up to the party paying it.

Liabilities of parties

53 Funds in hands of drawee

(1) A bill, of itself, does not operate as an assignment of funds in the hands of the drawee available for the payment thereof, and the drawee of a bill who does not accept as required by this Act is not liable on the instrument. This subsection shall not extend to Scotland.

(2) In Scotland, where the drawee of a bill other than a cheque has in his hands funds available for the payment thereof, the bill operates as an assignment of the sum for which it is drawn in favour of the holder, from the time when the bill is presented to the drawee.

54 Liability of acceptor

The acceptor of a bill, by accepting it –

(1) Engages that he will pay it according to the tenor of his acceptance.

(2) Is precluded from denying to a holder in due course –

  (a) the existence of the drawer, the genuineness of his signature, and his capacity and authority to draw the bill;

(b) in the case of a bill payable to drawer's order, the then capacity of the drawer to indorse, but not the genuineness or validity of his indorsement;
(c) in the case of a bill payable to the order of a third person, the existence of the payee and his then capacity to indorse, but not the genuineness or validity of his indorsement.

55 Liability of drawer or indorser

(1) The drawer of a bill by drawing it –
 (a) engages that on due presentment it shall be accepted and paid according to its tenor, and that if it be dishonoured he will compensate the holder or any indorser who is compelled to pay it, provided that the requisite proceedings on dishonour be duly taken;
 (b) is precluded from denying to a holder in due course the existence of the payee and his then capacity to indorse.
(2) The indorser of a bill by indorsing it –
 (a) engages that on due presentment it shall be accepted and paid according to its tenor, and that if it be dishonoured he will compensate the holder or a subsequent indorser who is compelled to pay it, provided that the requisite proceedings on dishonour be duly taken;
 (b) is precluded from denying to a holder in due course the genuineness and regularity in all respects of the drawer's signature and all previous endorsements;
 (c) is precluded from denying to his immediate or a subsequent indorsee that the bill was at the time of his indorsement a valid and subsisting bill, and that he had then a good title thereto.

56 Stranger signing bill liable as indorser

Where a person signs a bill otherwise than as drawer or acceptor, he thereby incurs the liabilities of an indorser to a holder in due course.

57 Measure of damages against parties to dishonoured bill

Where a bill is dishonoured, the measure of damages, which shall be deemed to be liquidated damages, shall be as follows –

(1) The holder may recover from any party liable on the bill, and the drawer who has been compelled to pay the bill may recover from the acceptor, and an indorser who has been compelled to pay the bill may recover from the acceptor or from the drawer, or from a prior indorser –
 (a) the amount of the bill;
 (b) interest thereon from the time of presentment for payment if the bill is payable on demand, and from the maturity of the bill in any other case;
 (c) the expenses of noting, or, when protest is necessary, and the protest has been extended, the expenses of protest.
(2) [Repealed].

(3) Where by this Act interest may be recovered as damages, such interest may, if justice require it, be withheld wholly or in part, and where a bill is expressed to be payable with interest at a given rate, interest as damages may or may not be given at the same rate as interest proper.

58 Transferor by delivery and transferee

(1) Where the holder of a bill payable to bearer negotiates it by delivery without indorsing it he is called a 'transferor by delivery'.
(2) A transferor by delivery is not liable on the instrument.
(3) A transferor by delivery who negotiates a bill thereby warrants to his immediate transferee being a holder for value that the bill is what it purports to be, that he has a right to transfer it, and that at the time of transfer he is not aware of any fact which renders it valueless.

Discharge of bill

59 Payment in due course

(1) A bill is discharged by payment in due course by or on behalf of the drawee or acceptor. 'Payment in due course' means payment made at or after the maturity of the bill to the holder thereof in good faith and without notice that his title to the bill is defective.
(2) Subject to the provisions herein-after contained, when a bill is paid by the drawer or an indorser it is not discharged; but –
  (a) where a bill payable to, or to the order of, a third party is paid by the drawer, the drawer may enforce payment thereof against the acceptor, but may not re-issue the bill;
  (b) where a bill is paid by an indorser, or where a bill payable to drawer's order is paid by the drawer, the party paying it is remitted to his former rights as regards the acceptor or antecedent parties, and he may, if he thinks fit, strike out his own subsequent indorsements, and again negotiate the bill.
(3) Where an accommodation bill is paid in due course by the party accommodated the bill is discharged.

60 Banker paying demand draft whereon indorsement is forged

When a bill payable to order on demand is drawn on a banker, and the banker on whom it is drawn pays the bill in good faith and in the ordinary course of business, it is not incumbent on the banker to show that the indorsement of the payee or any subsequent indorsement was made by or under the authority of the person whose indorsement it purports to be, and the banker is deemed to have paid the bill in due course, although such indorsement has been forged or made without authority.

61 Acceptor the holder at maturity

When the acceptor of a bill is or becomes the holder of it at or after its maturity, in his own right, the bill is discharged.

62 Express waiver

(1) When the holder of a bill at or after its maturity absolutely and unconditionally renounces his rights against the acceptor the bill is discharged. The renunciation must be in writing, unless the bill is delivered up to the acceptor.
(2) The liabilities of any party to a bill may in like manner be renounced by the holder before, at, or after its maturity: but nothing in this section shall affect the rights of a holder in due course without notice of the renunciation.

63 Cancellation

(1) Where a bill is intentionally cancelled by the holder or his agent, and the cancellation is apparent thereon, the bill is discharged.
(2) In like manner any party liable on a bill may be discharged by the intentional cancellation of his signature by the holder or his agent. In such case any indorser who would have had a right of recourse against the party whose signature is cancelled is also discharged.
(3) A cancellation made unintentionally, or under a mistake, or without the authority of the holder is inoperative; but where a bill or any signature thereon appears to have been cancelled the burden of proof lies on the party who alleges that the cancellation was made unintentionally, or under a mistake, or without authority.

64 Alteration of bill

(1) Where a bill or acceptance is materially altered without the assent of all parties liable on the bill, the bill is avoided except as against a party who has himself made, authorised, or assented to the alteration, and subsequent indorsers. Provided that, where a bill has been materially altered, but the alteration is not apparent, and the bill is in the hands of a holder in due course, such holder may avail himself of the bill as if it had not been altered, and may enforce payment of it according to its original tenor.
(2) In particular the following alterations are material, namely, any alteration of the date, the sum payable, the time of payment, the place of payment, and, where a bill has been accepted generally, the addition of a place of payment without the acceptor's assent.

Acceptance and payment for honour

65 Acceptance for honour supra protest

(1) Where a bill of exchange has been protested for dishonour by non-acceptance, or protested for better security, and is not overdue, any person, not being a party already liable thereon, may, with the consent of the holder, intervene and accept the bill supra protest, for the honour of any party liable thereon, or for the honour of the person for whose account the bill is drawn.
(2) A bill may be accepted for honour for part only of the sum for which it is drawn.
(3) An acceptance for honour supra protest in order to be valid must –
    (a) be written on the bill, and indicate that it is an acceptance for honour;
    (b) be signed by the acceptor for honour.

(4) Where an acceptance for honour does not expressly state for whose honour it is made, it is deemed to be an acceptance for the honour of the drawer.

(5) Where a bill payable after sight is accepted for honour, its maturity is calculated from the date of the noting for non-acceptance, and not from the date of the acceptance for honour.

66 Liability of acceptor for honour

(1) The acceptor for honour of a bill by accepting it engages that he will, on due presentment, pay the bill according to the tenor of his acceptance, if it is not paid by the drawee, provided it has been duly presented for payment, and protested for non-payment, and that he receives notice of these facts.

(2) The acceptor for honour is liable to the holder and to all parties to the bill subsequent to the party for whose honour he has accepted.

67 Presentment to acceptor for honour

(1) Where a dishonoured bill has been accepted for honour supra protest, or contains a reference in case of need, it must be protested for non-payment before it is presented for payment to the acceptor for honour, or referee in case of need.

(2) Where the address of the acceptor for honour is in the same place where the bill is protested for non-payment, the bill must be presented to him not later than the day following its maturity; and where the address of the acceptor for honour is in some place other than the place where it was protested for non-payment, the bill must be forwarded not later than the day following its maturity for presentment to him.

(3) Delay in presentment or non-presentment is excused by any circumstance which would excuse delay in presentment for payment or non-presentment for payment.

(4) When a bill of exchange is dishonoured by the acceptor for honour it must be protested for non-payment by him.

68 Payment for honour supra protest

(1) Where a bill has been protested for non-payment, any person may intervene and pay it supra protest for the honour of any party liable thereon, or for the honour of the person for whose account the bill is drawn.

(2) Where two or more persons offer to pay a bill for the honour of different parties, the person whose payment will discharge most parties to the bill shall have the preference.

(3) Payment for honour supra protest, in order to operate as such and not as a mere voluntary payment, must be attested by a notarial act of honour which may be appended to the protest or form an extension of it.

(4) The notarial act of honour must be founded on a declaration made by the payer for honour, or his agent in that behalf, declaring his intention to pay the bill for honour, and for whose honour he pays.

(5) Where a bill has been paid for honour, all parties subsequent to the party for whose honour it is paid are discharged, but the payer for honour is subrogated for, and succeeds to both the rights and duties of, the holder as regards the party for whose honour he pays, and all parties liable to that party.

(6) The payer for honour on paying to the holder the amount of the bill and the notarial expenses incidental to its dishonour is entitled to receive both the bill itself and the protest. If the holder does not on demand deliver them up he shall be liable to the payer for honour in damages.
(7) Where the holder of a bill refuses to receive payment supra protest he shall lose his right of recourse against any party who would have been discharged by such payment.

Lost instruments

69 Holder's right to duplicate of lost bill

Where a bill has been lost before it is overdue the person who was the holder of it may apply to the drawer to give him another bill of the same tenor, giving security to the drawer if required to indemnify him against all persons whatever in case the bill alleged to have been lost shall be found again. If the drawer on request as aforesaid refuses to give such duplicate bill he may be compelled to do so.

70 Action on lost bill

In any action or proceeding upon a bill, the court or a judge may order that the loss of the instrument shall not be set up, provided an indemnity be given to the satisfaction of the court or judge against the claims of any other person upon the instrument in question.

Bill in a set

71 Rules as to sets

(1) Where a bill is drawn in a set, each part of the set being numbered, and containing a reference to the other parts the whole of the parts constitute one bill.
(2) Where the holder of a set indorses two or more parts to different persons, he is liable on every such part, and every indorser subsequent to him is liable on the part he has himself indorsed as if the said parts were separate bills.
(3) Where two or more parts of a set are negotiated to different holders in due course, the holder whose title first accrues is as between such holders deemed the true owner of the bill; but nothing in this sub-section shall affect the rights of a person who in due course accepts or pays the part first presented to him.
(4) The acceptance may be written on any part, and it must be written on one part only. If the drawee accepts more than one part, and such accepted parts get into the hands of different holders in due course, he is liable on every such part as if it were a separate bill.
(5) When the acceptor of a bill drawn in a set pays it without requiring the part bearing his acceptance to be delivered up to him, and that part at maturity is outstanding in the hands of a holder in due course, he is liable to the holder thereof.
(6) Subject to the preceding rules, where any one part of a bill drawn in a set is discharged by payment or otherwise, the whole bill is discharged.

Conflict of laws

72 Rules where laws conflict

Where a bill drawn in one country is negotiated, accepted, or payable in another, the rights, duties, and liabilities of the parties thereto are determined as follows –

(1) The validity of a bill as regards requisites in form is determined by the law of the place of issue, and the validity as regards requisites in form of the supervening contracts, such as acceptance, or indorsement, or acceptance supra protest, is determined by the law of the place where such contract was made.
 Provided that –
 (a) where a bill is issued out of the United Kingdom it is not invalid by reason only that it is not stamped in accordance with the law of the place of issue;
 (b) where a bill, issued out of the United Kingdom, conforms, as regards requisites in form, to the law of the United Kingdom, it may, for the purpose of enforcing payment thereof, be treated as valid as between all persons who negotiate, hold, or become parties to it in the United Kingdom.
(2) Subject to the provisions of this Act, the interpretation of the drawing, indorsement, acceptance, or acceptance supra protest of a bill, is determined by the law of the place where such contract is made. Provided that where an inland bill is indorsed in a foreign country the indorsement shall as regards the payer be interpreted according to the law of the United Kingdom.
(3) The duties of the holder with respect to presentment for acceptance or payment and the necessity for or sufficiency of a protest or notice of dishonour, or otherwise, are determined by the law of the place where the act is done or the bill is dishonoured.
(4) [Repealed].
(5) Where a bill is drawn in one country and is payable in another, the due date thereof is determined according to the law of the place where it is payable.

Part III Cheques on a Banker

73 Cheque defined

A cheque is a bill of exchange drawn on a banker payable on demand.

Except as otherwise provided in this Part, the provisions of this Act applicable to a bill of exchange payable on demand apply to a cheque.

74 Presentment of cheque for payment

Subject to the provisions of this Act –

(1) Where a cheque is not presented for payment within a reasonable time of its issue, and the drawer or the person on whose account it is drawn had the right at the time of such presentment as between him and the banker to have the cheque paid and suffers actual damage through the delay, he is discharged to the extent of such damage, that is to say, to the extent to which such drawer or person is a creditor of such banker to a larger amount than he would have been had such cheque been paid.

(2) In determining what is a reasonable time regard shall be had to the nature of the instrument, the usage of trade and of bankers, and the facts of the particular case.
(3) The holder of such cheque as to which such drawer or person is discharged shall be a creditor, in lieu of such drawer or person, of such banker to the extent of such discharge, and entitled to recover the amount from him.

74A Presentment of cheque for payment: Alternative place of presentment

Where the banker on whom a cheque is drawn –

(a) has by notice published in the London, Edinburgh and Belfast Gazette specified an address at which cheques drawn on him may be presented; and
(b) has not by notice so published cancelled the specification of that address, the cheque is also presented at the proper place if it is presented there.

74B Presentment of cheque for payment: Alternative means of presentment by banker

(1) A banker may present a cheque for payment to the banker on whom it is drawn by notifying him of its essential features by electronic means or otherwise, instead of by presenting the cheque itself.
(2) If a cheque is presented for payment under this section, presentment need not be made at the proper place or at a reasonable hour on a business day.
(3) If, before the close of business on the next business day following presentment of a cheque under this section, the banker on whom the cheque is drawn requests the banker by whom the cheque was presented to present the cheque itself –
    (a) the presentment under this section shall be disregarded; and
    (b) this section shall not apply in relation to the subsequent presentment of the cheque.
(4) A request under subsection (3) above for the presentment of a cheque shall not constitute dishonour of the cheque by non-payment.
(5) Where presentment of a cheque is made under this section, the banker who presented the cheque and the banker on whom it is drawn shall be subject to the same duties in relation to the collection and payment of the cheque as if the cheque itself has been presented for payment.
(6) For the purposes of this section, the essential features of a cheque are –
    (a) the serial number of the cheque;
    (b) the code which identifies the banker on whom the cheque is drawn;
    (c) the account number of the drawer of the cheque; and
    (d) the amount of the cheque is entered by the drawer of the cheque.

74C Cheques presented for payment under S 74b: Disapplication of S 52(4)

Section 52(4) above –

(a) so far as relating to presenting a bill for payment, shall not apply to presenting a cheque for payment under s 74B above; and
(b) so far as relating to a bill which is paid, shall not apply to a cheque which is paid following presentment under that section.

75 Revocation of banker's authority

The duty and authority of a banker to pay a cheque drawn on him by his customer are determined by –

(1) Countermand of payment.
(2) Notice of the customer's death.

75A

[Repealed]

Crossed cheques

76 General and special crossings defined

(1) Where a cheque bears across its face an addition of –
  (a) the words 'and company' or any abbreviation thereof between two parallel transverse lines, either with or without the words 'not negotiable'; or
  (b) two parallel transverse lines simply, either with or without the words 'not negotiable', that addition constitutes a crossing, and the cheque is crossed generally.
(2) Where a cheque bears across its face an addition of the name of a banker, either with or without the words 'not negotiable,' that addition constitutes a crossing, and the cheque is crossed specially and to that banker.

77 Crossing by drawer or after issue

(1) A cheque may be crossed generally or specially by the drawer.
(2) Where a cheque is uncrossed, the holder may cross it generally or specially.
(3) Where a cheque is crossed generally the holder may cross it specially.
(4) Where a cheque is crossed generally or specially, the holder may add the words 'not negotiable'.
(5) Where a cheque is crossed specially, the banker to whom it is crossed may again cross it specially to another banker for collection.
(6) Where an uncrossed cheque, or a cheque crossed generally, is sent to a banker for collection, he may cross it specially to himself.

78 Crossing a material part of cheque

A crossing authorised by this Act is a material part of the cheque; it shall not be lawful for any person to obliterate or, except as authorised by this Act, to add to or alter the crossing.

79 Duties of banker as to crossed cheques

(1) Where a cheque is crossed specially to more than one banker except when crossed to an agent for collection being a banker, the banker on whom it is drawn shall refuse payment thereof.

(2) Where the banker on whom a cheque is drawn which is so crossed nevertheless pays the same, or pays a cheque crossed generally otherwise than to a banker, or if crossed specially otherwise than to the banker to whom it is crossed, or his agent for collection being a banker, he is liable to the true owner of the cheque for any loss he may sustain owing to the cheque having been so paid.

Provided that where a cheque is presented for payment which does not at the time of presentment appear to be crossed, or to have had a crossing which has been obliterated, or to have been added to or altered otherwise than as authorised by this Act, the banker paying the cheque in good faith and without negligence shall not be responsible or incur any liability, nor shall the payment be questioned by reason of the cheque having been crossed, or of the crossing having been obliterated or having been added to or altered otherwise than as authorised by this Act, and of payment having been made otherwise than to a banker or to the banker to whom the cheque is or was crossed, or to his agent for collection being a banker, as the case may be.

80 Protection to banker and drawer where cheque is crossed

Where the banker, on whom a crossed cheque (including a cheque which under section 81A below or otherwise is not transferable) is drawn, in good faith and without negligence pays it, if crossed generally, to a banker, and if crossed specially, to the banker to whom it is crossed, or his agent for collection being a banker, the banker paying the cheque, and, if the cheque has come into the hands of the payee, the drawer, shall respectively be entitled to the same rights and be placed in the same position as if payment of the cheque had been made to the true owner thereof.

81 Effect of crossing on holder

Where a person takes a crossed cheque which bears on it the words 'not negotiable,' he shall not have and shall not be capable of giving a better title to the cheque than that which the person from whom he took it had.

81A Non-transferable cheques

(1) Where a cheque is crossed and bears across its face the words 'account payee' or 'a/c payee' either with or without the word 'only', the cheque shall not be transferable, but shall only be valid as between the parties thereto.

(2) A banker is not to be treated for the purposes of section 80 above as having been negligent by reason only of his failure to concern himself with any purported indorsement of a cheque which under subsection (1) above or otherwise is not transferable.

82 [Repealed]

Part IV Promissory notes

83 Promissory note defined

(1) A promissory note is an unconditional promise in writing made by one person to another signed by the maker, engaging to pay, on demand or at a fixed or determinable

future time, a sum certain in money, to, or to the order of, a specified person or to bearer.

(2) An instrument in the form of a note payable to maker's order is not a note within the meaning of this section unless and until it is indorsed by the maker.

(3) A note is not invalid by reason only that it contains also a pledge of collateral security with authority to sell or dispose thereof.

(4) A note which is, or on the face of it purports to be, both made and payable within the British Islands is an inland note. Any other note is a foreign note.

84 Delivery necessary

A promissory note is inchoate and incomplete until delivery thereof to the payee or bearer.

85 Joint and several notes

(1) A promissory note may be made by two or more makers, and they may be liable thereon jointly, or jointly and severally according to its tenor.

(2) Where a note runs 'I promise to pay' and is signed by two or more persons it is deemed to be their joint and several note.

86 Note payable on demand

(1) Where a note payable on demand has been indorsed, it must be presented for payment within a reasonable time of the indorsement. If it be not so presented the indorser is discharged.

(2) In determining what is reasonable time, regard shall be had to the nature of the instrument, the usage of trade, and the facts of the particular case.

(3) Where a note payable on demand is negotiated, it is not deemed to be overdue, for the purpose of affecting the holder with defects of title of which he had no notice, by reason that it appears that a reasonable time for presenting it for payment has elapsed since its issue.

87 Presentment of note for payment

(1) Where a promissory note is in the body of it made payable at a particular place, it must be presented for payment at that place in order to render the maker liable. In any other case, presentment for payment is not necessary in order to render the maker liable.

(2) Presentment for payment is necessary in order to render the indorser of a note liable.

(3) Where a note is in the body of it made payable at a particular place, presentment at that place is necessary in order to render an indorser liable; but when a place of payment is indicated by way of memorandum only, presentment at that place is sufficient to render the indorser liable, but a presentment to the maker elsewhere, if sufficient in other respects, shall also suffice.

88 Liability of maker

The maker of a promissory note by making it –

(1) Engages that he will pay it according to its tenor.
(2) Is precluded from denying to a holder in due course the existence of the payee and his then capacity to indorse.

89 Application of Part II to notes

(1) Subject to the provisions in this part, and except as by this section provided, the provisions of this Act relating to bills of exchange apply, with the necessary modifications, to promissory notes.
(2) In applying those provisions the maker of a note shall be deemed to correspond with the acceptor of a bill, and the first indorser of a note shall be deemed to correspond with the drawer of an accepted bill payable to drawer's order.
(3) The following provisions as to bills do not apply to notes; namely, provisions relating to –
    (a) presentment for acceptance;
    (b) acceptance;
    (c) acceptance supra protest;
    (d) bills in a set.
(4) Where a foreign note is dishonoured protest thereof is unnecessary.

Part V Supplementary

90 Good Faith

A thing is deemed to be done in good faith, within the meaning of this Act, where it is in fact done honestly, whether it is done negligently or not.

91 Signature

(1) Where, by this Act, any instrument or writing is required to be signed by any person it is not necessary that he should sign it with his own hand, but it is sufficient if his signature is written thereon by some other person by or under his authority.
(2) In the case of a corporation, where, by this act, any instrument or writing is required to be signed, it is sufficient if the instrument or writing be sealed with the corporate seal. But nothing in this section shall be construed as requiring the bill or note of a corporation to be under seal.

92 Computation of time

Where, by this Act, the time limited for doing any act or thing is less than three days, in reckoning time, non-business days are excluded. Non-business days for the purposes of this Act mean –

(a) Saturday, Sunday, Good Friday, Christmas Day;
(b) a bank holiday under the Banking and Financial Dealings Act 1971;
(c) a day appointed by Royal proclamation as a public fast or thanksgiving day;
(d) a day declared by an order under section 2 of the Banking and Financial Dealings Act 1971 to be a non-business day.

Any other day is a business day.

93 When noting equivalent to protest

For the purposes of this Act, where a bill or note is required to be protested within a specified time or before some further proceeding is taken, it is sufficient that the bill has been noted for protest before the expiration of the specified time or the taking of the proceeding; and the formal protest may be extended at any time thereafter as of the date of the noting.

94 Protest when notary not accessible

(1) Where a dishonoured bill or note is authorised or required to be protested, and the services of a notary cannot be obtained at the place where the bill is dishonoured, any householder or substantial resident of the place may, in the presence of two witnesses, give a certificate, signed by them, attesting the dishonour of the bill, and the certificate shall in respects operate as if it were a formal protest of the bill. The form given in Schedule 1 to this Act may be used with necessary modifications, and if used shall be sufficient.
(2) In subsection (1), 'notary' includes a person who, for the purposes of the Legal Services Act 2007, is an authorised person in relation to any activity which constitutes a notarial activity (within the meaning of that Act).

95–100 [Omitted]

Factors Act 1889

Preliminary

1 Definitions

For the purposes of this Act –

(1) The expression "mercantile agent" shall mean a mercantile agent having in the customary course of his business as such agent authority either to sell goods, or to consign goods for the purpose of sale, or to buy goods, or to raise money on the security of goods:
(2) A person shall be deemed to be in possession of goods or of the documents of title to goods, where the goods or documents are in his actual custody or are held by any other person subject to his control or for him or on his behalf:
(3) The expression "goods" shall include wares and merchandise:
(4) The expression "document of title" shall include any bill of lading, dock warrant, warehouse-keeper's certificate, and warrant or order for the delivery of goods, and any other document used in the ordinary course of business as proof of the possession or control of goods, or authorising or purporting to authorise, either by endorsement or by delivery, the possessor of the document to transfer or receive goods thereby represented:
(5) The expression "pledge" shall include any contract pledging, or giving a lien or security on, goods, whether in consideration of an original advance or of any further or continuing advance or of any pecuniary liability:
(6) The expression "person" shall include any body of persons corporate or unincorporate.

Dispositions by mercantile agents

2 Powers of mercantile agent with respect to disposition of goods

(1) Where a mercantile agent is, with the consent of the owner, in possession of goods or of the documents of title to goods, any sale, pledge, or other disposition of the goods, made by him when acting in the ordinary course of business of a mercantile agent, shall, subject to the provisions of this Act, be as valid as if he were expressly authorised by the owner of the goods to make the same; provided that the person taking under the disposition acts in good faith, and has not at the time of the disposition notice that the person making the disposition has not authority to make the same.
(2) Where a mercantile agent has, with the consent of the owner, been in possession of goods or of the documents of title to goods, any sale, pledge, or other disposition, which would have been valid if the consent had continued, shall be valid notwithstanding the determination of the consent: provided that the person taking under the disposition has not at the time thereof notice that the consent has been determined.
(3) Where a mercantile agent has obtained possession of any documents of title to goods by reason of his being or having been, with the consent of the owner, in possession of the goods represented thereby, or of any other documents of title to the goods, his possession of the first-mentioned documents shall, for the purposes of this Act, be deemed to be with the consent of the owner.
(4) For the purposes of this Act the consent of the owner shall be presumed in the absence of evidence to the contrary.

3 Effect of pledges of documents of title

A pledge of the documents of title to goods shall be deemed to be a pledge of the goods.

4 Pledge for antecedent debt

Where a mercantile agent pledges goods as security for a debt or liability due from the pledgor to the pledgee before the time of the pledge, the pledgee shall acquire no further right to the goods than could have been enforced by the pledgor at the time of the pledge.

5 Rights acquired by exchange of goods or documents

The consideration necessary for the validity of a sale, pledge, or other disposition, of goods, in pursuance of this Act, may be either a payment in cash, or the delivery or transfer of other goods, or of a document of title to goods, or of a negotiable security, or any other valuable consideration; but where goods are pledged by a mercantile agent in consideration of the delivery or transfer of other goods, or of a document of title to goods, or of a negotiable security, the pledgee shall acquire no right or interest in the goods so pledged in excess of the value of the goods, documents, or security when so delivered or transferred in exchange.

6 Agreements through clerks, etc.

For the purposes of this Act an agreement made with a mercantile agent through a clerk or other person authorised in the ordinary course of business to make contracts of sale or pledge on his behalf shall be deemed to be an agreement with the agent.

7 Provisions as to consignors and consignees

(1) Where the owner of goods has given possession of the goods to another person for the purpose of consignment or sale, or has shipped the goods in the name of another person, and the consignee of the goods has not had notice that such person is not the owner of the goods, the consignee shall, in respect of advances made to or for the use of such person, have the same lien on the goods as if such person were the owner of the goods, and may transfer any such lien to another person.

(2) Nothing in this section shall limit or effect the validity of any sale, pledge, or disposition, by a mercantile agent.

Dispositions by sellers and buyers of goods

8 Disposition by seller remaining in possession

Where a person, having sold goods, continues, or is, in possession of the goods or of the documents of title to the goods, the delivery or transfer by that person, or by a mercantile agent acting for him, of the goods or documents of title under any sale, pledge, or other disposition thereof, or under any agreement for sale, pledge, or other disposition thereof, to any person receiving the same in good faith and without notice of the previous sale, shall have the same effect as if the person making the delivery or transfer were expressly authorised by the owner of the goods to make the same.

9 Disposition by a buyer obtaining possession

Where a person, having bought or agreed to buy goods, obtains with the consent of the seller possession of the goods or the documents of title to the goods, the delivery or transfer, by that person or by a mercantile agent acting for him, of the goods or documents of title, under any sale, pledge, or other disposition thereof, or under any agreement for sale, pledge, or other disposition thereof, to any person receiving the same in good faith and without notice of any lien or other right of the original seller in respect of the goods, shall have the same effect as if the person making the delivery or transfer were a mercantile agent in possession of the goods or documents of title with the consent of the owner. For the purposes of this section –

(i) the buyer under a conditional sale agreement shall be deemed not to be a person who has bought or agreed to buy goods, and

(ii) "conditional sale agreement" means an agreement for the sale of goods which is a consumer credit agreement within the meaning of the Consumer Credit Act 1974 under which the purchase price or part of it is payable by instalments, and the property in the goods is to remain in the seller (notwithstanding that the buyer is to be in possession of the goods) until such conditions as to the payment of instalments or otherwise as may be specified in the agreement are fulfilled.

10 Effect of transfer of documents on vendor's lien or right of stoppage in transitu

Where a document of title to goods has been lawfully transferred to a person as a buyer or owner of the goods, and that person transfers the document to a person who takes the document in good faith and for valuable consideration, the last-mentioned transfer shall have the same effect for defeating any vendor's lien or right of stoppage in transitu as the transfer of a bill of lading has for defeating the right of stoppage in transitu.

Supplemental

11 Mode of transferring documents

For the purposes of this Act, the transfer of a document may be by endorsement, or, where the document is by custom or by its express terms transferable by delivery, or makes the goods deliverable to the bearer, then by delivery.

12 Saving for rights of true owner

(1) Nothing in this Act shall authorise an agent to exceed or depart from his authority as between himself and his principal, or exempt him from any liability, civil or criminal, for so doing.

(2) Nothing in this Act shall prevent the owner of goods from recovering the goods from an agent or his trustee in bankruptcy at any time before the sale or pledge thereof, or shall prevent the owner of goods pledged by an agent from having the right to redeem the goods at any time before the sale thereof, on satisfying the claim for which the goods were pledged, and paying to the agent, if by him required, any money in respect of which the agent would by law be entitled to retain the goods or the documents of title thereto, or any of them, by way of lien as against the owner, or from recovering from any person with whom the goods have been pledged any balance of money remaining in his hands as the produce of the sale of the goods after deducting the amount of his lien.

(3) Nothing in this Act shall prevent the owner of goods sold by an agent from recovering from the buyer the price agreed to be paid for the same, or any part of that price, subject to any right of set off on the part of the buyer against the agent.

13 Saving for common law powers of agent

The provisions of this Act shall be construed in amplification and not in derogation of the powers exerciseable by an agent independently of this Act.

14 and 15 [Repealed]

16 Extent of Act

This Act shall not extend to Scotland.

17 [Omitted]

Marine Insurance Act 1906

Marine insurance

1 Marine insurance defined

A contract of marine insurance is a contract whereby the insurer undertakes to indemnify the assured, in manner and to the extent thereby agreed, against marine losses, that is to say, the losses incident to marine adventure.

2 Mixed sea and land risks

(1) A contract of marine insurance may, by its express terms, or by usage of trade, be extended so as to protect the assured against losses on inland waters or on any land risk which may be incidental to any sea voyage.
(2) Where a ship in course of building, or the launch of a ship, or any adventure analogous to a marine adventure, is covered by a policy in the form of a marine policy, the provisions of this Act, in so far as applicable, shall apply thereto; but, except as by this section provided, nothing in this Act shall alter or affect any rule of law applicable to any contract of insurance other than a contract of marine insurance as by this Act defined.

3 Marine adventure and maritime perils defined

(1) Subject to the provisions of this Act, every lawful marine adventure may be the subject of a contract of marine insurance.
(2) In particular there is a marine adventure where –
  (a) Any ship goods or other moveables are exposed to maritime perils. Such property is in this Act referred to as "insurable property";
  (b) The earning or acquisition of any freight, passage money, commission, profit, or other pecuniary benefit, or the security for any advances, loan, or disbursements, is endangered by the exposure of insurable property to maritime perils;
  (c) Any liability to a third party may be incurred by the owner of, or other person interested in or responsible for, insurable property, by reason of maritime perils.

"Maritime perils" means the perils consequent on, or incidental to, the navigation of the sea, that is to say, perils of the seas, fire, war, perils, pirates, rovers, thieves, captures, seizures, restraints, and detainment's of princes and peoples, jettisons, barratry, and any other perils, either of the like kind or which may be designated by the policy.

Insurable interest

4 Avoidance of wagering or gaming contracts

(1) Every contract of marine insurance by way of gaming or wagering is void.
(2) A contract of marine insurance is deemed to be a gaming or wagering contract –
  (a) Where the assured has not an insurable interest as defined by this Act, and the contract is entered into with no expectation of acquiring such an interest; or
  (b) Where the policy is made "interest or no interest", or "without further proof of interest than the policy itself," or "without benefit of salvage to the insurer", or subject to any other like term.

Provided that, where there is no possibility of salvage, a policy may be effected without benefit of salvage to the insurer.

5 Insurable interest defined

(1) Subject to the provisions of this Act, every person has an insurable interest who is interested in a marine adventure.

(2) In particular a person is interested in a marine adventure where he stands in any legal or equitable relation to the adventure or to any insurable property at risk therein, in consequence of which he may benefit by the safety or due arrival of insurable property, or may be prejudiced by its loss, or by damage thereto, or by the detention thereof, or may incur liability in respect thereof.

6 When interest must attach

(1) The assured must be interested in the subject-matter insured at the time of the loss though he need not be interested when the insurance is effected: Provided that where the subject-matter is insured "lost or not lost," the assured may recover although he may not have acquired his interest until after the loss, unless at the time of effecting the contract of insurance the assured was aware of the loss, and the insurer was not.

(2) Where the assured has no interest at the time of the loss, he cannot acquire interest by any act or election after he is aware of the loss.

7 Defeasible or contingent interest

(1) A defeasible interest is insurable, as also is a contingent interest.

(2) In particular, where the buyer of goods has insured them, he has an insurable interest, notwithstanding that he might, at his election, have rejected the goods, or have treated them as at the seller's risk, by reason of the latter's delay in making delivery or otherwise.

8 Partial interest

A partial interest of any nature is insurable.

9 Re-insurance

(1) The insurer under a contract of marine insurance has an insurable interest in his risk, and may re-insure in respect of it.

(2) Unless the policy otherwise provides, the original assured has no right or interest in respect of such re-insurance.

10 Bottomry

The lender of money on bottomry or respondentia has an insurable interest in respect of the loan.

11 Master's and seamen's wages

The master or any member of the crew of a ship has an insurable interest in respect of his wages.

12 Advance freight

In the case of advance freight, the person advancing the freight has an insurable interest, in so far as such freight is not repayable in case of loss.

13 Charges of insurance

The assured has an insurable interest in the charges of any insurance which he may effect.

14 Quantum of interest

(1) Where the subject-matter insured is mortgaged, the mortgagor has an insurable interest in the full value thereof, and the mortgagee has an insurable interest in respect of any sum due or to become due under the mortgage.
(2) A mortgagee, consignee, or other person having an interest in the subject-matter insured may insure on behalf and for the benefit of other persons interested as well as for his own benefit.
(3) The owner of insurable property has an insurable interest in respect of the full value thereof, notwithstanding that some third person may have agreed, or be liable, to indemnify him in case of loss.

15 Assignment of interest

Where the assured assigns or otherwise parts with his interest in the subject-matter insured, he does not thereby transfer to the assignee his rights under the contract of insurance, unless there be an express or implied agreement with the assignee to that effect.

But the provisions of this section do not affect a transmission of interest by operation of law.

Insurable value

16 Measure of insurable value

Subject to any express provision or valuation in the policy, the insurable value of the subject-matter insured must be ascertained as follows –

(1) In insurance on ship, the insurable value is the value, at the commencement of the risk, of the ship, including her outfit, provisions and stores for the officers and crew, money advanced for seamen's wages, and other disbursements (if any) incurred to make the ship fit for the voyage or adventure contemplated by the policy, plus the charges of insurance upon the whole: The insurable value, in the case of a steam-ship, includes also the machinery, boilers, and coals and engine stores if owned by the assured, and, in the case of a ship engaged in a special trade, the ordinary fittings requisite for that trade.
(2) In insurance on freight, whether paid in advance or otherwise, the insurable value is the gross amount of the freight at the risk of the assured, plus the charges of insurance.

(3) In insurance on goods or merchandise, the insurable value is the prime cost of the property insured, plus the expenses of and incidental to shipping and the charges of insurance upon the whole.
(4) In insurance on any other subject-matter, the insurable value is the amount at the risk of the assured when the policy attaches, plus the charges of insurance.

Disclosure and representations

*17 Insurance is **Uberrimae fidei***

A contract of marine insurance is a contract based upon the utmost good faith...

[Words in S. 17 omitted (12.8.2016) by virtue of Insurance Act 2015 (c. 4), ss.14(3)(a), 23(2) (with ss. 14(3)(b), 22(1)]

18 Disclosure by assured

[Now omitted by Insurance Act 2015 – see Part 7 – section 21 provision consequential on Part 2]

19 Disclosure by agent effecting insurance

[Now repealed by Insurance Act 2015 – see Part 7 – section 21 provision consequential on Part 2]

20 Representations pending negotiation of contract

[Now repealed by Insurance Act 2015 – see Part 7 – section 21 provision consequential on Part 2]

21 When contract is deemed to be concluded

A contract of marine insurance is deemed to be concluded when the proposal of the assured is accepted by the insurer, whether the policy be then issued or not; and, for the purpose of showing when the proposal was accepted, reference may be made to the slip or covering note or other customary memorandum of the contract.

The policy

22 Contract must be embodied in policy

Subject to the provisions of any statute, a contract of marine insurance is inadmissible in evidence unless it is embodied in a marine policy in accordance with this Act. The policy may be executed and issued either at the time when the contract is concluded, or afterwards.

23 What policy must specify

A marine policy must specify –

(1) The name of the assured, or of some person who effects the insurance on his behalf.
(2)–(5) [Repealed].

24 Signature of insurer

(1) A marine policy must be signed by or on behalf of the insurer, provided that in the case of a corporation the corporate seal may be sufficient, but nothing in this section shall be construed as requiring the subscription of a corporation to be under seal.
(2) Where a policy is subscribed by or on behalf of two or more insurers, each subscription, unless the contrary be expressed, constitutes a distinct contract with the assured.

25 Voyage and time policies

(1) Where the contract is to insure the subject-matter "at and from," or from one place to another or other, the policy is called a "voyage policy," and where the contract is to insure the subject-matter for a definite period of time the policy is called a "time policy." A contract for both voyage and time may be included in the same policy.
(2) [Repealed].

26 Designation of subject-matter

(1) The subject-matter insured must be designated in a marine policy with reasonable certainty.
(2) The nature and extent of the interest of the assured in the subject-matter insured need not be specified in the policy.
(3) Where the policy designates the subject-matter insured in general terms, it shall be construed to apply to the interest intended by the assured to be covered.
(4) In the application of this section regard shall be had to any usage regulating the designation of the subject-matter insured.

27 Valued policy

(1) A policy may be either valued or unvalued.
(2) A valued policy is a policy which specifies the agreed value of the subject-matter insured.
(3) Subject to the provisions of this Act, and in the absence of fraud, the value fixed by the policy is, as between the insurer and assured, conclusive of the insurable value of the subject intended to be insured, whether the loss be total or partial.
(4) Unless the policy otherwise provides, the value fixed by the policy is not conclusive for the purpose of determining whether there has been a constructive total loss.

28 Unvalued policy

An unvalued policy is a policy which does not specify the value of the subject-matter insured, but subject to the limit of the sum insured, leaves the insurable value to be subsequently ascertained, in the manner herein-before specified.

29 Floating policy by ship or ships

(1) A floating policy is a policy which describes the insurance in general terms, and leaves the name of the ship or ships and other particulars to be defined by subsequent declaration.
(2) The subsequent declaration or declarations may be made by indorsement on the policy, or in other customary manner.
(3) Unless the policy otherwise provides, the declarations must be made in the order of dispatch or shipment. They must, in the case of goods, comprise all consignments within the terms of the policy, and the value of the goods or other property must be honestly stated, but an omission or erroneous declaration may be rectified even after loss or arrival, provided the omission or declaration was made in good faith.
(4) Unless the policy otherwise provides, where a declaration of value is not made until after notice of loss or arrival, the policy must be treated as an unvalued policy as regards the subject-matter of that declaration.

30 Construction of terms in policy

(1) A policy may be in the form in the First Schedule to this Act.
(2) Subject to the provisions of this Act, and unless the context of the policy otherwise requires, the terms and expressions mentioned in the First Schedule to this Act shall be construed as having the scope and meaning in that schedule assigned to them.

31 Premium to be arranged

(1) Where an insurance is effected at a premium to be arranged, and no arrangement is made, a reasonable premium is payable.
(2) Where an insurance is effected on the terms that an additional premium is to be arranged in a given event, and that event happens but no arrangement is made, then a reasonable additional premium is payable.

Double insurance

32 Double insurance

(1) Where two or more policies are effected by or on behalf of the assured on the same adventure and interest or any part thereof, and the sums insured exceed the indemnity allowed by this Act, the assured is said to be over-insured by double insurance.
(2) Where the assured is over-insured by double insurance –
    (a) The assured, unless the policy otherwise provides, may claim payment from the insurers in such order as he may think fit, provided that he is not entitled to receive any sum in excess of the indemnity allowed by this Act;
    (b) Where the policy under which the assured claims is a valued policy, the assured must give credit as against the valuation for any sum received by him under any other policy without regard to the actual value of the subject-matter insured;
    (c) Where the policy under which the assured claims is an unvalued policy he must give credit, as against the full insurable value, for any sum received by him under any other policy;

(d) where the assured receives any sum in excess of the indemnity allowed by this Act, he is deemed to hold such sum in trust for the insurers, according to their right of contribution among themselves.

Warranties, etc.

33 Nature of warranty

(1) A warranty, in the following sections relating to warranties, means a promissory warranty, that is to say, a warranty by which the assured undertakes that some particular thing shall or shall not be done, or that some condition shall be fulfilled, or whereby he affirms or negatives the existence of a particular state of facts.
(2) A warranty may be express or implied.
(3) A warranty, as above defined, is a condition which must be exactly complied with, whether it be material to the risk or not.

[Words in s. 33(3) omitted (12.8.2016) by virtue of Insurance Act 2015 (c. 4), ss. 10(7)(a), 23(2) (with s. 22(2)]

34 When breach of warranty excused

[S. 34 repealed (12.8.2016) by virtue of Insurance Act 2015 (c. 4), ss. 10(7)(b), 23(2) (with s. 22(2)]

35 Express warranties

(1) An express warranty may be in any form of words from which the intention to warrant is to be inferred.
(2) An express warranty must be included in, or written upon, the policy, or must be contained in some document incorporated by reference into the policy.
(3) An express warranty does not exclude an implied warranty, unless it be inconsistent therewith.

36 Warranty of neutrality

(1) Where insurable property, whether ship or goods, is expressly warranted neutral, there is an implied condition that the property shall have a neutral character at the commencement of the risk, and that, so far as the assured can control the matter, its neutral character shall be preserved during the risk.
(2) Where a ship is expressly warranted "neutral" there is also an implied condition that, so far as the assured can control the matter she shall be properly documented, that is to say, that she shall carry the necessary papers to establish her neutrality, and that she shall not falsify or suppress her papers, or use simulated papers. If any loss occurs through breach of this condition, the insurer may avoid the contract.

37 No implied warranty of nationality

There is no implied warranty as to the nationality of a ship, or that her nationality shall not be changed during the risk.

38 Warranty of good safety

Where the subject-matter insured is warranted "well" or "in good safety" on a particular day, it is sufficient if it be safe at any time during that day.

39 Warranty of seaworthiness of ship

(1) In a voyage policy there is an implied warranty that at the commencement of the voyage the ship shall be seaworthy for the purpose of the particular adventure insured.
(2) Where the policy attaches while the ship is in port, there is also an implied warranty that she shall, at the commencement of the risk, be reasonably fit to encounter the ordinary perils of the port.
(3) Where the policy relates to a voyage which is performed in different stages, during which the ship requires different kinds of or further preparation or equipment, there is an implied warranty that at the commencement of each stage the ship is seaworthy in respect of such preparation or equipment for the purposes of that stage.
(4) A ship is deemed to be seaworthy when she is reasonably fit in all respects to encounter the ordinary perils of the seas of the adventure insured.
(5) In a time policy there is no implied warranty that the ship shall be seaworthy at any stage of the adventure, but where, with the privity of the assured, the ship is sent to sea in an unseaworthy state, the insurer is not liable for any loss attributable to unseaworthiness.

40 No implied warranty that goods are seaworthy

(1) In a policy on goods or other moveables there is no implied warranty that the goods or moveables are seaworthy.
(2) In a voyage policy on goods or other moveables there is an implied warranty that at the commencement of the voyage the ship is not only seaworthy as a ship, but also that she is reasonably fit to carry the goods or other moveables to the destination contemplated by the policy.

41 Warranty of legality

There is an implied warranty that the adventure insured is a lawful one, and that, so far as the assured can control the matter, the adventure shall be carried out in a lawful manner.

The voyage

42 Implied condition as to commencement of risk

(1) Where the subject-matter is insured by a voyage policy "at and from" or "from" a particular place, it is not necessary that the ship should be at that place when the contract is concluded, but there is an implied condition that the adventure shall be commenced within a reasonable time, and that if the adventure be not so commenced the insurer may avoid the contract.

(2) The implied condition may be negatived by showing that the delay was caused by circumstances known to the insurer before the contract was concluded, or by showing that he waived the condition.

43 Alteration of port of departure

Where the place of departure is specified by the policy, and the ship instead of sailing from that place sails from any other place, the risk does not attach.

44 Sailing for different destination

Where the destination is specified in the policy, and the ship, instead of sailing for that destination, sails for any other destination, the risk does not attach.

45 Change of voyage

(1) Where, after the commencement of the risk, the destination of the ship is voluntarily changed from the destination contemplated by the policy, there is said to be a change of voyage.
(2) Unless the policy otherwise provides, where there is a change of voyage, the insurer is discharged from liability as from the time of change, that is to say, as from the time when the determination to change it is manifested; and it is immaterial that the ship may not in fact have left the course of voyage contemplated by the policy when the loss occurs.

46 Deviation

(1) Where a ship, without lawful excuse, deviates from the voyage contemplated by the policy, the insurer is discharged from liability as from the time of deviation, and it is immaterial that the ship may have regained her route before any loss occurs.
(2) There is a deviation from the voyage contemplated by the policy –
  (a) Where the course of the voyage is specifically designated by the policy, and that course is departed from; or
  (b) Where the course of the voyage is not specifically designated by the policy, but the usual and customary course is departed from.
(3) The intention to deviate is immaterial; there must be a deviation in fact to discharge the insurer from his liability under the contract.

47 Several ports of discharge

(1) Where several ports of discharge are specified by the policy, the ship may proceed to all or any of them, but, in the absence of any usage or sufficient cause to the contrary, she must proceed to them, or such of them as she goes to, in the order designated by the policy. If she does not there is a deviation.
(2) Where the policy is to "ports of discharge," within a given area, which are not named, the ship must, in the absence of any usage or sufficient cause to the contrary, proceed to them, or such of them as she goes to, in their geographical order. If she does not there is a deviation.

48 Delay in voyage

In the case of a voyage policy, the adventure insured must be prosecuted throughout its course with reasonable dispatch, and, if without lawful excuse it is not so prosecuted, the insurer is discharged from liability as from the time when the delay became unreasonable.

49 Excuses for deviation or delay

(1) Deviation or delay in prosecuting the voyage contemplated by the policy is excused –
  (a) Where authorised by any special term in the policy; or
  (b) Where caused by circumstances beyond the control of the master and his employer; or
  (c) Where reasonably necessary in order to comply with an express or implied warranty; or
  (d) Where reasonably necessary for the safety of the ship or subject-matter insured; or
  (e) For the purpose of saving human life, or aiding a ship in distress where human life may be in danger; or
  (f) Where reasonably necessary for the purpose of obtaining medical or surgical aid for any person on board the ship; or
  (g) Where caused by the barratrous conduct of the master or crew, if barratry be one of the perils insured against.

(2) When the cause excusing the deviation or delay ceases to operate, the ship must resume her course, and prosecute her voyage, with reasonable dispatch.

Assignment of policy

50 When and how policy is assignable

(1) A marine policy is assignable unless it contains terms expressly prohibiting assignment. It may be assigned either before or after loss.

(2) Where a marine policy has been assigned so as to pass the beneficial interest in such policy, the assignee of the policy is entitled to sue thereon in his own name; and the defendant is entitled to make any defence arising out of the contract which he would have been entitled to make if the action had been brought in the name of the person by or on behalf of whom the policy was effected.

(3) A marine policy may be assigned by indorsement thereon or in other customary manner.

51 Assured who has no interest cannot assign

Where the assured has parted with or lost his interest in the subject-matter insured, and has not, before or at the time of so doing, expressly or impliedly agreed to assign the policy, any subsequent assignment of the policy is inoperative:

Provided that nothing in this section affects the assignment of a policy after loss.

The premium

52 When premium payable

Unless otherwise agreed, the duty of the assured or his agent to pay the premium, and the duty of the insurer to issue the policy to the assured or his agent, are concurrent conditions, and the insurer is not bound to issue the policy until payment or tender of the premium.

53 Policy effected through broker

(1) Unless otherwise agreed, where a marine policy is effected on behalf of the assured by a broker, the broker is directly responsible to the insurer for the premium, and the insurer is directly responsible to the assured for the amount which may be payable in respect of losses, or in respect of returnable premium.

(2) Unless otherwise agreed, the broker has, as against the assured, a lien upon the policy for the amount of the premium and his charges in respect of effecting the policy; and, where he has dealt with the person who employs him as a principal, he has also a lien on the policy in respect of any balance on any insurance account which may be due to him from such person, unless when the debt was incurred he had reason to believe that such person was only an agent.

54 Effect of receipt on policy

Where a marine policy effected on behalf of the assured by a broker acknowledges the receipt of the premium, such acknowledgement is, in the absence of fraud, conclusive as between the insurer and the assured, but not as between the insurer and broker.

Loss and abandonment

55 Included and excluded losses

(1) Subject to the provisions of this Act, and unless the policy otherwise provides, the insurer is liable for any loss proximately caused by a peril insured against, but, subject as aforesaid, he is not liable for any loss which is not proximately caused by a peril insured against.

(2) In particular –

  (a) The insurer is not liable for any loss attributable to the wilful misconduct of the assured, but, unless the policy otherwise provides, he is liable for any loss proximately caused by a peril insured against, even though the loss would not have happened but for the misconduct or negligence of the master or crew;

  (b) Unless the policy otherwise provides, the insurer on ship or goods is not liable for any loss proximately caused by delay, although the delay be caused by a peril insured against;

  (c) Unless the policy otherwise provides, the insurer is not liable for ordinary wear and tear, ordinary leakage and breakage, inherent vice or nature of the subject-matter insured, or for any loss proximately caused by rats or vermin, or for any injury to machinery not proximately caused by maritime perils.

56 Partial and total loss

(1) A loss may be either total or partial. Any loss other than a total loss, as hereinafter defined, is a partial loss.

(2) A total loss may be either an actual total loss, or a constructive total loss.

(3) Unless a different intention appears from the terms of the policy, an insurance against total loss includes a constructive, as well as an actual, total loss.

(4) Where the assured brings an action for a total loss and the evidence proves only a partial loss, he may, unless the policy otherwise provides, recover for a partial loss.

(5) Where goods reach their destination in specie, but by reason of obliteration of marks, or otherwise, they are incapable of identification, the loss, if any, is partial, and not total.

57 Actual total loss

(1) Where the subject-matter insured is destroyed, or so damaged as to cease to be a thing of the kind insured, or where the assured is irretrievably deprived thereof, there is an actual total loss.

(2) In the case of an actual total loss no notice of abandonment need be given.

58 Missing ship

Where the ship concerned in the adventure is missing, and after the lapse of a reasonable time no news of her has been received, an actual total loss may be presumed.

59 Effect of transhipment, etc.

Where, by a peril insured against, the voyage is interrupted at an intermediate port or place, under such circumstances as, apart from any special stipulation in the contract of affreightment, to justify the master in landing and reshipping the goods or other moveables, or in transhipping them, and sending them on to their destination, the liability of the insurer continues, notwithstanding the landing or transhipment.

60 Constructive total loss defined

(1) Subject to any express provision in the policy, there is a constructive total loss where the subject-matter insured is reasonably abandoned on account of its actual total loss appearing to be unavoidable, or because it could not be preserved from actual total loss without an expenditure which would exceed its value when the expenditure had been incurred.

(2) In particular, there is a constructive total loss –

   (i) Where the assured is deprived of the possession of his ship or goods by a peril insured against, and (a) it is unlikely that he can recover the ship or goods, as the case may be, or (b) the cost of recovering the ship or goods, as the case may be, would exceed their value when recovered; or

   (ii) In the case of damage to a ship, where she is so damaged by a peril insured against that the cost of repairing the damage would exceed the value of the ship when repaired. In estimating the cost of repairs, no deduction is to be made in respect of general average contributions to those repairs payable by other interests, but account is to be taken of the expense of future salvage operations and of any future general average contributions to which the ship would be liable if repaired; or

   (iii) In the case of damage to goods, where the cost of repairing the damage and forwarding the goods to their destination would exceed their value on arrival.

61 Effect of constructive total loss

Where there is a constructive total loss the assured may either treat the loss as a partial loss, or abandon the subject-matter insured to the insurer and treat the loss as if it were an actual total loss.

62 Notice of abandonment

(1) Subject to the provisions of this section, where the assured elects to abandon the subject-matter insured to the insurer, he must give notice of abandonment. If he fails to do so the loss can only be treated as a partial loss.
(2) Notice of abandonment may be given in writing, or by word of mouth, or partly in writing and partly by word of mouth, and may be given in any terms which indicate the intention of the assured to abandon his insured interest in the subject-matter insured unconditionally to the insurer.
(3) Notice of abandonment must be given with reasonable diligence after the receipt of reliable information of the loss, but where the information is of a doubtful character the assured is entitled to a reasonable time to make inquiry.
(4) Where notice of abandonment is properly given, the rights of the assured are not prejudiced by the fact that the insurer refuses to accept the abandonment.
(5) The acceptance of an abandonment may be either express or implied from the conduct of the insurer. The mere silence of the insurer after notice is not acceptance.
(6) Where notice of abandonment is accepted the abandonment is irrevocable. The acceptance of the notice conclusively admits liability for the loss and the sufficiency of the notice.
(7) Notice of abandonment is unnecessary where, at the time when the assured receives information of the loss, there would be no possibility of benefit to the insurer if notice were given to him.
(8) Notice of abandonment may be waived by the insurer.
(9) Where an insurer has re-insured his risk, no notice of abandonment need be given by him.

63 Effect of abandonment

(1) Where there is a valid abandonment the insurer is entitled to take over the interest of the assured in whatever may remain of the subject-matter insured, and all proprietary rights incidental thereto.
(2) Upon the abandonment of a ship, the insurer thereof is entitled to any freight in course of being earned, and which is earned by her subsequent to the casualty causing the loss, less the expenses of earning it incurred after the casualty; and, where the ship is carrying the owner's goods, the insurer is entitled to a reasonable remuneration for the carriage of them subsequent to the casualty causing the loss.

Partial losses (including salvage and general average and particular charges)

64 Particular average loss

(1) A particular average loss is a partial loss of the subject-matter insured, caused by a peril insured against, and which is not a general average loss.

(2) Expenses incurred by or on behalf of the assured for the safety or preservation of the subject-matter insured, other than general average and salvage charges, are called particular charges. Particular charges are not included in particular average.

65 Salvage charges

(1) Subject to any express provision in the policy, salvage charges incurred in preventing a loss by perils insured against may be recovered as a loss by those perils.
(2) "Salvage charges" means the charges recoverable under maritime law by a salvor independently of contract. They do not include the expenses of services in the nature of salvage rendered by the assured or his agents, or any person employed for hire by them, for the purpose of averting a peril insured against. Such expenses, where properly incurred, may be recovered as particular charges or as a general average loss, according to the circumstances under which they were incurred.

66 General average loss

(1) A general average loss is a loss caused by or directly consequential on a general average act. It includes a general average expenditure as well as a general average sacrifice.
(2) There is a general average act where any extraordinary sacrifice or expenditure is voluntarily and reasonably made or incurred in time of peril for the purpose of preserving the property imperilled in the common adventure.
(3) Where there is a general average loss, the party on whom it falls is entitled, subject to the conditions imposed by maritime law, to a rateable contribution from the other parties interested, and such contribution is called a general average contribution.
(4) Subject to any express provision in the policy, where the assured has incurred a general average expenditure, he may recover from the insurer in respect of the proportion of the loss which falls upon him; and, in the case of a general average sacrifice, he may recover from the insurer in respect of the whole loss without having enforced his right of contribution from the other parties liable to contribute.
(5) Subject to any express provision in the policy, where the assured has paid, or is liable to pay, a general average contribution in respect of the subject insured, he may recover therefore from the insurer.
(6) In the absence of express stipulation, the insurer is not liable for any general average loss or contribution where the loss was not incurred for the purpose of avoiding, or in connection with the avoidance of, a peril insured against.
(7) Where ship, freight, and cargo, or any two of those interests, are owned by the same assured, the liability of the insurer in respect of general average losses or contributions is to be determined as if those subjects were owned by different persons.

Measure of indemnity

67 Extent of liability of insurer for loss

(1) The sum which the assured can recover in respect of a loss on a policy by which he is insured, in the case of an unvalued policy to the full extent of the insurable value, or, in

the case of a valued policy to the full extent of the value fixed by the policy is called the measure of indemnity.

(2) Where there is a loss recoverable under the policy, the insurer, or each insurer if there be more than one, is liable for such proportion of the measure of indemnity as the amount of his subscription bears to the value fixed by the policy in the case of a valued policy, or to the insurable value in the case of an unvalued policy.

68 Total loss

Subject to the provisions of this Act and to any express provision in the policy, where there is a total loss of the subject-matter insured –

(1) If the policy be a valued policy, the measure of indemnity is the sum fixed by the policy.
(2) If the policy be an unvalued policy, the measure of indemnity is the insurable value of the subject-matter insured.

69 Partial loss of ship

Where a ship is damaged, but is not totally lost, the measure of indemnity, subject to any express provision in the policy, is as follows –

(1) Where the ship has been repaired, the assured is entitled to the reasonable cost of the repairs, less the customary deductions, but not exceeding the sum insured in respect of any one casualty.
(2) Where the ship has been only partially repaired, the assured is entitled to the reasonable cost of such repairs, computed as above, and also to be indemnified for the reasonable depreciation, if any, arising from the unrepaired damage, provided that the aggregate amount shall not exceed the cost of repairing the whole damage, computed as above.
(3) Where the ship has not been repaired, and has not been sold in her damaged state during the risk, the assured is entitled to be indemnified for the reasonable depreciation arising from the unrepaired damage, but not exceeding the reasonable cost of repairing such damage, computed as above.

70 Partial loss of freight

Subject to any express provision in the policy, where there is a partial loss of freight, the measure of indemnity is such proportion of the sum fixed by the policy in the case of a valued policy, or of the insurable value in the case of an unvalued policy, as the proportion of freight lost by the assured bears to the whole freight at the risk of the assured under the policy.

71 Partial loss of goods, merchandise, etc.

Where there is a partial loss of goods, merchandise or other moveables, the measure of indemnity, subject to any express provision in the policy, is as follows –

(1) Where part of the goods, merchandise or other moveables insured by a valued policy is totally lost, the measure of indemnity is such proportion of the sum fixed by the policy

as the insurable value of the part lost bears to the insurable value of the whole, ascertained as in the case of an unvalued policy.

(2) Where part of the goods, merchandise, or other moveables insured by an unvalued policy is totally lost, the measure of indemnity is the insurable value of the part lost, ascertained as in case of total loss.

(3) Where the whole or any part of the goods or merchandise insured has been delivered damaged at its destination, the measure of indemnity is such proportion of the sum fixed by the policy in the case of a valued policy, or of the insurable value in the case of an unvalued policy, as the difference between the gross sound and damaged valued at the place of arrival bears to the gross sound value.

(4) "Gross value" means the wholesale price, or, if there be no such price, the estimated value, with, in either case, freight, landing charges, and duty paid beforehand; provided that, in the case of goods or merchandise customarily sold in bond, the bonded price is deemed to be the gross value. "Gross proceeds" means the actual price obtained at a sale where all charges on sale are paid by the sellers.

72 Apportionment of valuation

(1) Where different species of property are insured under a single valuation, the valuation must be apportioned over the different species in proportion to their respective insurable values, as in the case of an unvalued policy. The insured value of any part of a species is such proportion of the total insured value of the same as the insurable value of the part bears to the insurable value of the whole, ascertained in both cases as provided by this Act.

(2) Where a valuation has to be apportioned, and particulars of the prime cost of each separate species, quality, or description of goods cannot be ascertained, the division of the valuation may be made over the net arrived sound values of the different species, qualities, or descriptions of goods.

73 General average contributions and salvage charges

(1) Subject to any express provision in the policy, where the assured has paid, or is liable for, any general average contribution, the measure of indemnity is the full amount of such contribution, if the subject-matter liable to contribution is insured for its full contributory value, or if only part of it be insured, the indemnity payable by the insurer must be reduced in proportion to the under insurance, and where there has been a particular average loss which constitutes a deduction from the contributory value, and for which the insurer is liable, that amount must be deducted from the insured value in order to ascertain what the insurer is liable to contribute.

(2) Where the insurer is liable for salvage charges the extent of his liability must be determined on the like principle.

74 Liabilities to third parties

Where the assured has effected an insurance in express terms against any liability to a third party, the measure of indemnity, subject to any express provision in the policy, is the amount paid or payable by him to such third party in respect of such liability.

75 General provisions as to measure of indemnity

(1) Where there has been a loss in respect of any subject-matter not expressly provided for in the foregoing provisions of this Act, the measure of indemnity shall be ascertained, as nearly as may be, in accordance with those provisions, in so far as applicable to the particular case.
(2) Nothing in the provisions of this Act relating to the measure of indemnity shall affect the rules relating to double insurance, or prohibit the insurer from disproving interest wholly or in part, or from showing that at the time of the loss the whole or any part of the subject-matter insured was not at risk under the policy.

76 Particular average warranties

(1) Where the subject-matter insured is warranted free from particular average, the assured cannot recover for a loss of part, other than a loss incurred by a general average sacrifice, unless the contract contained in the policy be apportionable; but, if the contract be apportionable, the assured may recover for a total loss of any apportionable part.
(2) Where the subject-matter insured is warranted free from particular average, either wholly or under a certain percentage, the insurer is nevertheless liable for salvage charges, and for particular charges and other expenses properly incurred pursuant to the provisions of the suing and labouring clause in order to avert a loss insured against.
(3) Unless the policy otherwise provides, where the subject-matter insured is warranted free from particular average under a specified percentage, a general average loss cannot be added to a particular average loss to make up the specified percentage.
(4) For the purpose of ascertaining whether the specified percentage has been reached, regard shall be had only to the actual loss suffered by the subject-matter insured. Particular charges and the expenses of and incidental to ascertaining and proving the loss must be excluded.

77 Successive losses

(1) Unless the policy otherwise provides, and subject to the provisions of this Act, the insurer is liable for successive losses, even though the total amount of such losses may exceed the sum insured.
(2) Where, under the same policy, a partial loss, which has not been repaired or otherwise made good, is followed by a total loss, the assured can only recover in respect of the total loss: Provided that nothing in this section shall affect the liability of the insurer under the suing and labouring clause.

78 Suing and labouring clause

(1) Where the policy contains a suing and labouring clause, the engagement thereby entered into is deemed to be supplementary to the contract of insurance, and the assured may recover from the insurer any expenses properly incurred pursuant to the clause, notwithstanding that the insurer may have paid for a total loss, or that the subject-matter may have been warranted free from particular average, either wholly or under a certain percentage.

(2) General average losses and contributions and salvage charges, as defined by this Act, are not recoverable under the suing and labouring clause.
(3) Expenses incurred for the purpose of averting or diminishing any loss not covered by the policy are not recoverable under the suing and labouring clause.
(4) It is the duty of the assured and his agents, in all cases, to take such measures as may be reasonable for the purpose of averting or minimising a loss.

Rights of insurer on payment

79 Right of subrogation

(1) Where the insurer pays for a total loss, either of the whole, or in the case of goods of any apportionable part, of the subject-matter insured, he thereupon becomes entitled to take over the interest of the assured in whatever may remain of the subject-matter so paid for, and he is thereby subrogated to all the rights and remedies of the assured in and in respect of that subject-matter as from the time of the casualty causing the loss.
(2) Subject to the foregoing provisions, where the insurer pays for a partial loss, he acquires no title to the subject-matter insured, or such part of it as may remain, but he is thereupon subrogated to all rights and remedies of the assured in and in respect of the subject-matter insured as from the time of the casualty causing the loss, in so far as the assured has been indemnified, according to this Act, by such payment for the loss.

80 Right of contribution

(1) Where the assured is over-insured by double insurance, each insurer is bound, as between himself and the other insurers, to contribute rateably to the loss in proportion to the amount for which he is liable under his contract.
(2) If any insurer pays more than his proportion of the loss, he is entitled to maintain an action for contribution against the other insurers, and is entitled to the like remedies as a surety who has paid more than his proportion of the debt.

81 Effect of under insurance

Where the assured is insured for an amount less than the insurable value or, in the case of a valued policy, for an amount less than the policy valuation, he is deemed to be his own insurer in respect of the uninsured balance.

Return of premium

82 Enforcement of return

Where the premium or a proportionate part thereof is, by this Act, declared to be returnable –

(a) If already paid, it may be recovered by the assured from the insurer; and
(b) If unpaid, it may be retained by the assured or his agent.

83 Return by agreement

Where the policy contains a stipulation for the return of the premium, or a proportionate part thereof, on the happening of a certain event, and that event happens, the premium, or, as the case may be, the proportionate part thereof, is thereupon returnable to the assured.

84 Return for failure of consideration

(1) Where the consideration for the payment of the premium totally fails, and there has been no fraud or illegality on the part of the assured or his agents, the premium is thereupon returnable to the assured.

(2) Where the consideration for the payment of the premium is apportionable and there is a total failure of any apportionable part of the consideration, a proportionate part of the premium is, under the like conditions, thereupon returnable to the assured.

(3) In particular –

(a) Where the policy is void, or is avoided by the insurer as from the commencement of the risk, the premium is returnable, provided that there has been no fraud or illegality on the part of the assured; but if the risk is not apportionable, and has once attached, the premium is not returnable;

(b) Where the subject-matter insured, or part thereof, has never been imperilled, the premium, or, as the case may be, a proportionate part thereof, is returnable; Provided that where the subject-matter has been insured lost or not lost' and has arrived in safety at the time when the contract is concluded, the premium is returnable unless, at such time, the insurer knew of the safe arrival;

(c) Where the assured has no insurable interest throughout the currency of the risk, the premium is returnable, provided that this rule does not apply to a policy effected by way of gaming or wagering;

(d) Where the assured has a defeasible interest which is terminated during the currency of the risk, the premium is not returnable;

(e) Where the assured has over-insured under an unvalued policy, a proportionate part of the several premiums is returnable;

(f) Subject to the foregoing provisions, where the assured has over-insured by double insurance, a proportionate part of the several premiums is returnable;

Provided that, if the policies are effected at different times, and any earlier policy has at any time borne the entire risk, or if a claim has been paid on the policy in respect of the full sum insured thereby, no premium is returnable in respect of that policy, and when the double insurance is effected knowingly by the assured no premium is returnable.

Mutual insurance

85 Modification of Act in case of mutual insurance

(1) Where two or more persons mutually agree to insure each other against marine losses there is said to be a mutual insurance.

(2) The provisions of this Act relating to the premium do not apply to mutual insurance, but a guarantee, or such other arrangement as may be agreed upon, may be substituted for the premium.

(3) The provisions of this Act, in so far as they may be modified by the agreement of the parties, may in the case of mutual insurance be modified by the terms of the policies issued by the association, or by the rules and regulations of the association.
(4) Subject to the exceptions mentioned in this section, the provisions of this Act apply to a mutual insurance.

Supplemental

86 Ratification by assured

Where a contract of marine insurance is in good faith effected by one person on behalf of another, the person on whose behalf it is effected may ratify the contract even after he is aware of a loss.

87 Implied obligations varied by agreement or usage

(1) Where any right, duty, or liability would arise under a contract of marine insurance by implication of law, it may be negatived or varied by express agreement, or by usage, if the usage be such as to bind both parties to the contract.
(2) The provisions of this section extend to any right, duty, or liability declared by this Act which may be lawfully modified by agreement.

88 Reasonable time, etc. a question of fact

Where by this Act any reference is made to reasonable time, reasonable premium, or reasonable diligence, the question what is reasonable is a question of fact.

89 Slip as evidence

Where there is a duly stamped policy, reference may be made, as heretofore, to the slip or covering note, in any legal proceeding.

90 Interpretation of terms

In this Act, unless the context or subject-matter otherwise requires –

"Action" includes counter-claim and set off.

"Freight" includes the profit derivable by a shipowner from the employment of his ship to carry his own goods or moveables, as well as freight payable by a third party, but does not include passage money.

"Moveables" means any moveable tangible property, other than the ship, and includes money, valuable securities, and other documents.

"Policy" means a marine policy.

91 Savings

(1) Nothing in this Act, or in any repeal effected thereby, shall affect –

(a) The provisions of the Stamp Act 1891, or any enactment for the time being in force relating to the revenue;
(b) The provisions of the Companies Act 1862, or any enactment amending or substituted for the same;
(c) The provisions of any statute not expressly repealed by this Act.

(2) The rules of the common law including the law merchant, save in so far as they are inconsistent with the express provisions of this Act, shall continue to apply to contracts of marine insurance.

92–93 [Omitted]

94 Short title

This Act may be cited as the Marine Insurance Act 1906.

First Schedule

Form of policy

Be it known that as well in own name as for and in the name and names of all and every other person or persons to whom the same doth, may, or shall appertain, in part or in all doth make assurance and cause

and them, and every of them, to be insured lost or not lost, at and from

Upon any kind of goods and merchandises, and also upon the body, tackle, apparel, ordnance, munition, artillery, boat, and other furniture, of and in the good ship or vessel called the

whereof is master under God, for this present voyage,

or whosoever else shall go for master in the said ship, or by whatsoever other name or names the said ship, or the master thereof, is or shall be named or called; beginning the adventure upon the said goods and merchandised from the loading thereof aboard the said ship.

upon the said ship, etc.

and so shall continue and endure, during her abode there, upon the said ship, etc. And further, until the said ship, with all her ordnance, tackle, apparel, etc., and goods and merchandises whatsoever shall be arrived at

upon the said ship, etc. until she hath moored at anchor twenty-four hours in good safety; and upon the goods and merchandises, until the same be there discharged and safely landed. And it shall be lawful for the said ship, etc., in this voyage, to proceed and sail to and touch and stay at any ports or places whatsoever

without prejudice to this insurance. The said ship, etc., goods and merchandises, etc., for so much as concerns the assured by agreement between the assured and assurers in this policy, are and shall be valued at

Touching the adventures and perils which we the assurers are contented to bear and do take upon us in this voyage: they are of the seas, men of war, fire, enemies, pirates, rovers, thieves, jettisons, letters of mart and countermart, surprisals, takings at sea, arrests, restraints, and detainments of all kings, princes, and people, of what nation, condition, or quality soever, barratry of the master and mariners, and of all other perils, losses, and misfortunes, that have or shall come to the hurt, detriment, or damage of the said goods and merchandises, and ship, etc., or any part thereof. And in case of any loss or misfortune it shall be lawful to the assured, their factors, servants and assigns, to sue, labour, and travel for, in and about the defence, safeguards, and recovery of the said goods and merchandises, and ship, etc., or any part thereof, without prejudice to this insurance; to the charges whereof we, the assurers, will contribute each one according to the rate and quantity of his sum herein assured. And it is especially declared and agreed that no acts of the insurer or insured in recovering, saving, or preserving the property insured shall be considered as a waiver, or acceptance of abandonment. And it is agreed by us, the insurers, that this writing or policy of assurance shall be of as much force and effect as the surest writing or policy of assurance heretofore made in Lombard Street, or in the Royal Exchange, or elsewhere in London. And so we, the assurers, are contented, and do hereby promise and bind ourselves, each one for his own part, our heirs, executors, and goods to the assured, their executors, administrators, and assigns, for the true performance of the premises, confessing ourselves paid the consideration due unto us for this assurance by the assured, at and after the rate of

In Witness whereof we, the assurers, have subscribed our names and sums assured in London.

N.B. – Corn, fish, salt, fruit, flour, and seed are warranted free from average, unless general, or the ship be stranded-sugar, tobacco, hemp, flax, hides and skins are warranted free from average, under five pounds per cent, and all other goods, also the ship and freight, are warranted free from average, under three pounds per cent, unless general, or the ship be stranded.

Rules for construction of policy

The following are the rules referred to by this Act for the construction of a policy in the above or other like form, where the context does not otherwise require –

(1) Where the subject-matter is insured "lost or not lost", and the loss has occurred before the contract is concluded, the risk attaches unless, at such time the assured was aware of the loss, and the insurer was not.
(2) Where the subject-matter is insured "from" a particular place, the risk does not attach until the ship starts on the voyage insured.
(3)
   (a) Where a ship is insured "at and from" a particular place, and she is at that place in good safety when the contract is concluded, the risk attaches immediately.
   (b) If she be not at that place when the contract is concluded, the risk attaches as soon as she arrives there in good safety, and, unless the policy otherwise provides, it is immaterial that she is covered by another policy for a specified time after arrival.
   (c) Where chartered freight is insured "at and from" a particular place, and the ship is at that place in good safety when the contract is concluded the risk attaches immediately. If she be not there when the contract is concluded, the risk attaches as soon as she arrives there in good safety.
   (d) Where freight, other than chartered freight, is payable without special conditions and is insured "at and from" a particular place, the risk attaches pro rata as the goods or merchandise are shipped; provided that if there be cargo in readiness which belongs to the shipowner, or which some other person has contracted with him to ship, the risk attaches as soon as the ship is ready to receive such cargo.
(4) Where goods or other moveables are insured "from the loading thereof," the risk does not attach until such goods or moveables are actually on board, and the insurer is not liable for them while in transit from the shore to the ship.

(5) Where the risk on goods or other moveables continues until they are "safely landed, they must be landed in the customary manner and within a reasonable time after arrival" at the port of discharge, and if they are not so landed the risk ceases.
(6) In the absence of any further licence or usage, the liberty to touch and stay "at any port or place whatsoever" does not authorise the ship to depart from the course of her voyage from the port of departure to the port of destination.
(7) The term "perils of the seas" refers only to fortuitous accidents or casualties of the seas. It does not include the ordinary action of the winds and waves.
(8) The term "pirates" includes passengers who mutiny and rioters who attack the ship from the shore.
(9) The term "thieves" does not cover clandestine theft or a theft committed by any one of the ship's company, whether crew or passengers.
(10) The term "arrests, etc., of kings, princes, and people" refers to a political or executive acts, and does not include a loss caused by riot or by ordinary judicial process.
(11) The term "barratry" includes every wrongful act wilfully committed by the master or crew to the prejudice of the owner, or, as the case may be, the charterer.
(12) The term "all other perils" includes only perils similar in kind to the perils specifically mentioned in the policy.
(13) The term "average unless general" means a partial loss of subject-matter insured other than a general average loss, and does not include "particular charges".
(14) Where the ship has stranded, the insurer is liable for the excepted losses, although the loss is not attributable to the stranding, provided that when the stranding takes place the risk has attached and, if the policy be on goods, that the damaged goods are on board.
(15) The term "ship" includes the hull, materials and outfit, stores and provisions for the officers and crew, and, in the case of vessels engaged in a special trade, the ordinary fittings requisite for the trade, and also, in the case of a steamship, the machinery, boilers, and coals and engine stores, if owned by the assured.
(16) The term "freight" includes the profit derivable by a shipowner from the employment of his ship to carry his own goods or moveables, as well as freight payable by a third party, but does not include passage money.
(17) The term "goods" means goods in the nature of merchandise, and does not include personal effects or provisions and stores for use on board. In the absence of any usage to the contrary, deck cargo and living animals must be insured specifically, and not under the general denomination of goods. [Note: by virtue of the Public Order Act 1986 the words "rioters" in rule 8 and "riot" in rule 10 shall be construed in accordance with section 1 of that Act.]

Administration of Justice Act 1920

Part II Reciprocal enforcement of judgments in the United Kingdom and in other parts of His Majesty's dominions

9 Enforcement in the United Kingdom of judgments obtained in superior courts in other British dominions

(1) Where a judgment has been obtained in a superior court in any part of His Majesty's dominions outside the United Kingdom to which this Part of this Act extends, the judgment creditor may apply to the High Court in England or Northern Ireland or to the Court of Session in Scotland, at any time within twelve months after the date of

the judgment, or such longer period as may be allowed by the court, to have the judgment registered in the court, and on any such application the court may, if in all the circumstances of the case they think it just and convenient that the judgment should be enforced in the United Kingdom, and subject to the provisions of this section, order the judgment to be registered accordingly.

(2) No judgment shall be ordered to be registered under this section if –
  (a) the original court acted without jurisdiction; or
  (b) the judgment debtor, being a person who was neither carrying on business nor ordinarily resident within the jurisdiction of the original court, did not voluntarily appear or otherwise submit or agree to submit to the jurisdiction of that court; or
  (c) the judgment debtor, being the defendant in the proceedings, was not duly served with the process of the original court and did not appear, notwithstanding that he was ordinarily resident or was carrying on business within the jurisdiction of that court or agreed to submit to the jurisdiction of that court; or
  (d) the judgment was obtained by fraud; or
  (e) the judgment debtor satisfies the registering court either that an appeal is pending, or that he is entitled and intends to appeal, against the judgment; or
  (f) the judgment was in respect of a cause of action which for reasons of public policy or for some other similar reason could not have been entertained by the registering court.

(3) Where a judgment is registered under this section –
  (a) the judgment shall, as from the date of registration, be of the same force and effect, and proceedings may be taken thereon, as if it had been a judgment originally obtained or entered up on the date of registration in the registering court;
  (b) the registering court shall have the same control and jurisdiction over the judgment as it has over similar judgments given by itself, but in so far only as relates to execution under this section;
  (c) the reasonable costs of and incidental to the registration of the judgment (including the costs of obtaining a certified copy thereof from the original court and of the application for registration) shall be recoverable in like manner as if they were sums payable under the judgment.

(4) and (5) [Omitted].

Foreign Judgments (Reciprocal Enforcement) Act 1933

Part I Registration of foreign judgments

1 Power to extend Part I of Act to foreign countries giving reciprocal treatment

(1) If, in the case of any foreign country, Her Majesty is satisfied that, in the event of the benefits conferred by this Part of this Act being extended to, or to any particular class of, judgments given in the courts of that country or in any particular class of those courts, substantial reciprocity of treatment will be assured as regards the enforcement in that country of similar judgments given in similar courts of the United Kingdom, She may order in Council direct –
  (a) that this Part of this Act shall extend to that country;

(b) that such courts of that country as are specified in the Order shall be recognised courts of that country for the purposes of this Part of this Act; and
(c) that judgments of any such recognised court, or such judgments of any class so specified, shall, if within subsection (2) of this section, be judgments to which this Part of this Act applies.

(2) Subject to subsection (2A) of this section, a judgment of a recognised court is within this subsection if it satisfies the following conditions, namely –
(a) it is either final and conclusive as between the judgment debtor and the judgment creditor or requires the former to make an interim payment to the latter; and
(b) there is payable under it a sum of money, not being a sum payable in respect of taxes or other charges of a like nature or in respect of a fine or other penalty; and
(c) it is given after the coming into force of the Order in Council which made that court a recognised court.

(2A) The following judgments of a recognised court are not within subsection (2) of this section –
(a) a judgment given by that court on appeal from a court which is not a recognised court;
(b) a judgment or other instrument which is regarded for the purposes of its enforcement as a judgment of that court but which was given or made in another country;
(c) a judgment given by that court in proceedings founded on a judgment of a court in another country and having as their object the enforcement of that judgment.

(3) For the purposes of this section, a judgment shall be deemed to be final and conclusive notwithstanding that an appeal may be pending against it, or that it may still be subject to appeal, in the courts of the country of the original court.

(4) and (5) [Omitted].

2 Application for, and effect of, registration of foreign judgment

(1) A person, being a judgment creditor under a judgment to which this Part of this Act applies, may apply to the High Court at any time within six years after the date of the judgment, or, where there have been proceedings by way of appeal against the judgment, after the date of the last judgment given in those proceedings, to have the judgment registered in the High Court, and on any such application the court shall, subject to proof of the prescribed matters and to the other provisions of this Act, order the judgment to be registered: Provided that a judgment shall not be registered if at the date of the application –
(a) it has been wholly satisfied; or
(b) it could not be enforced by execution in the country of the original court.

(2) Subject to the provisions of this Act with respect to the setting aside of registration –
(a) a registered judgment shall, for the purposes of execution, be of the same force and effect; and
(b) proceedings may be taken on a registered judgment; and
(c) the sum for which a judgment is registered shall carry interest; and
(d) the registering court shall have the same control over the execution of a registered judgment;

as if the judgment had been a judgment originally given in the registering court and entered on the date of registration:

Provided that execution shall not issue on the judgment so long as, under this Part of this Act and the Rules of Court made thereunder, it is competent for any party to made an application to have the registration of the judgment set aside, or, where such an application is made, until after the application has been finally determined.

(3) [Repealed].

(4) If at the date of the application for registration the judgment of the original court has been partly satisfied, the judgment shall not be registered in respect of the whole sum payable under the judgment of the original court, but only in respect of the balance remaining payable at that date.

(5) If, on an application for the registration of a judgment, it appears to the registering court that the judgment is in respect of different matters and that some, but not all, of the provisions of the judgment are such that if those provisions had been contained in separate judgments those judgments could properly have been registered, the judgment may be registered in respect of the provisions aforesaid but not in respect of any other provisions contained therein.

(6) [Omitted].

3 [Omitted]

4 Cases in which registered judgments must, or may, be set aside

(1) On an application in that behalf duly made by any party against whom a registered judgment may be enforced, the registration of the judgment –

(a) shall be set aside if the registering court is satisfied –

(i) that the judgment is not a judgment to which this Part of the Act applied or was registered in contravention of the foregoing provisions of this Act; or

(ii) that the courts of the country of the original court had no jurisdiction in the circumstances of the case; or

(iii) that the judgment debtor, being the defendant in the proceedings in the original court, did not (notwithstanding that process may have been duly served on him in accordance with the law of the country of the original court) receive notice of those proceedings in sufficient time to enable him to defend the proceedings and did not appear; or

(iv) that the judgment was obtained by fraud; or

(v) that the enforcement of the judgment would be contrary to public policy in the country of the registering court; or

(vi) that the rights under the judgment are not vested in the person by whom the application for registration was made;

(b) may be set aside if the registering court is satisfied that the matter in dispute in the proceedings in the original court had previously to the date of the judgment in the original court been the subject of a final and conclusive judgment by a court having jurisdiction in the matter.

(2) For the purposes of this section the courts of the country of the original court shall, subject to the provisions of subsection (3) of this section, be deemed to have had jurisdiction –

(a) in the case of a judgment given in an action *in personam:*

(i) if the judgment debtor, being a defendant in the original court, submitted to the jurisdiction of that court by voluntarily appearing in the proceedings; or

(ii) if the judgment debtor was plaintiff in, or counter-claimed in, the proceedings in the original court; or

(iii) if the judgment debtor, being a defendant in the original court, had before the commencement of the proceedings agreed, in respect of the subject matter of the proceedings, to submit to the jurisdiction of that court or of the courts of the country of that court; or

(iv) if the judgment debtor, being a defendant in the original court, was at the time when the proceedings were instituted resident in, or being a body corporate had its principal place of business in, the country of that court; or

(v) if the judgment debtor, being a defendant in the original court, had an office or place of business in the country of that court and the proceedings in that court were in respect of a transaction effected through or at that office or place;

(b) in the case of a judgment given in an action of which the subject matter was immovable property or in an action *in rem* of which the subject matter was movable property, if the property in question was at the time of the proceedings in the original court situate in the country of that court;

(c) in the case of a judgment given in an action other than any such action as is mentioned in paragraph (a) or paragraph (b) of this subsection, if the jurisdiction of the original court is recognised by the law of the registering court.

(3) Notwithstanding anything in subsection (2) of this section, the courts of the country of the original court shall not be deemed to have had jurisdiction –

(a) if the subject matter of the proceedings was immovable property outside the country of the original court; or

(b) [repealed];

(c) if the judgment debtor, being a defendant in the original proceedings, was a person who under the rules of public international law was entitled to immunity from the jurisdiction of the courts of the country of the original court and did not submit to the jurisdiction of that court.

5 Powers of registering court on application to set aside registration

(1) If, on an application to set aside the registration of a judgment, the applicant satisfies the registering court either that an appeal is pending, or that he is entitled and intends to appeal, against the judgment, the court, if it thinks fit, may, on such terms as it may think just, either set aside the registration or adjourn the application to set aside the registration until after the expiration of such period as appears to the court to be reasonably sufficient to enable the applicant to take the necessary steps to have the appeal disposed of by the competent tribunal.

(2) Where the registration of a judgment is set aside under the last foregoing subsection, or solely for the reason that the judgment was not at the date of the application for registration enforceable by execution in the country of the original court, the setting aside of the registration shall not prejudice a further application to register the judgment when the appeal has been disposed of or if and when the judgment becomes enforceable by execution in that country, as the case may be.

(3) Where the registration of a judgment is set aside solely for the reason that the judgment, notwithstanding that it had at the date of application for registration been partly satisfied, was registered for the whole sum payable thereunder, the registering court shall, on the application of the judgment creditor, order judgment to be registered for the balance remaining payable at that date.

6 Foreign judgments which can be registered not to be enforceable otherwise

No proceedings for the recovery of a sum payable under a foreign judgment, being a judgment to which the Part of this Act applies, other than proceedings by way of registration of the judgment, shall be entertained by any court in the United Kingdom.

7 [Omitted]

Part II Miscellaneous and general

8 General effect of certain foreign judgments

(1) Subject to the provisions of this section, a judgment to which Part I of this Act applies or would have applied if a sum of money had been payable thereunder, whether it can be registered or not, and whether, if it can be registered, it is registered or not, shall be recognised in any court in the United Kingdom as conclusive between the parties thereto in all proceedings founded on the same cause of action and may be relied on by way of defence or counter-claim in any such proceedings.

(2) This section shall not apply in the case of any judgment –

(a) where the judgment has been registered and the registration thereof has been set aside on some ground other than:

(i) that a sum of money was not payable under the judgment; or

(ii) that the judgment had been wholly or partly satisfied; or

(iii) that at the date of the application the judgment could not be enforced by execution in the country of the original court; or

(b) where the judgment has not been registered, it is shown (whether it could have been registered or not) that if it had been registered the registration thereof would have been set aside on an application for that purpose on some ground other than one of the grounds specified in paragraph (a) of this subsection.

(3) Nothing in this section shall be taken to prevent any court in the United Kingdom recognising any judgment as conclusive of any matter of law or fact decided therein if that judgment would have been so recognised before the passing of this Act.

9–14 [Omitted]

Law Reform (Frustrated Contracts) Act 1943

1 Adjustment of rights and liabilities of parties to frustrated contracts

(1) Where a contract governed by English law has become impossible of performance or been otherwise frustrated, and the parties thereto have for that reason been discharged from the further performance of the contract, the following provisions of this section shall, subject to the provisions of section two of this Act, have effect in relation thereto.

(2) All sums paid or payable to any party in pursuance of the contract before the time when the parties were so discharged (in this Act referred to as 'the time of discharge') shall, in the case of sums so paid, be recoverable from him as money received by him for the use of the party by whom the sums were paid, and, in the case of sums so payable, cease to be so payable: Provided that, if the party to whom the sums were so paid or payable incurred expenses before the time of discharge in, or for the purpose of, the performance of the contract, the court may, if it considers it just to do so having regard to all the circumstances of the case, allow him to retain or, as the case may be, recover the whole or any part of the sums so paid or payable, not being an amount in excess of the expenses so incurred.

(3) Where any party to the contract has, by reason of anything done by any other party thereto in, or for the purpose of, the performance of the contract, obtained a valuable benefit (other than a payment of money to which the last foregoing subsection applies) before the time of discharge, there shall be recoverable from him by the said other party such sum (if any), not exceeding the value of the said benefit to the party obtaining it, as the court considers just, having regard to all the circumstances of the case and, in particular –

   (a) the amount of any expenses incurred before the time of discharge by the benefited party in, or for the purpose of, the performance of the contract, including any sums paid or payable by him to any other party in pursuance of the contract and retained or recoverable by that party under the last foregoing subsection; and

   (b) the effect, in relation to the said benefit, of the circumstances giving rise to the frustration of the contract.

(4) In estimating, for the purposes of the foregoing provisions of this section, the amount of any expenses incurred by any party to the contract, the court may, without prejudice to the generality of the said provisions, include such sum as appears to be reasonable in respect of overhead expenses and in respect of any work or services performed personally by the said party.

(5) In considering whether any sum ought to be recovered or retained under the foregoing provisions of this section by any party to the contract, the court shall not take into account any sums which have, by reason of the circumstances giving rise to the frustration of the contract, become payable to that party under any contract of insurance unless there was an obligation to insure imposed by an express term of the frustrated contract or by or under any enactment.

(6) Where any person has assumed obligations under the contract in consideration of the conferring of a benefit by any other party to the contract upon any other person, whether a party to the contract or not, the court may, if in all the circumstances of the

case it considers it just to do so, treat for the purposes of subsection (3) of this section any benefit so conferred as a benefit obtained by the person who has assumed the obligations as aforesaid.

2 Provision as in application of this Act

(1) This Act shall apply to contracts, whether made before or after the commencement of this Act, as respects which the time of discharge is on or after the first day of July, nineteen hundred and forty-three, but not to contracts as respect which the time of discharge is before the said date.

(2) This Act shall apply to contracts to which the Crown is a party in like manner as to contracts between subjects.

(3) Where any contract to which this Act applies contains any provisions which, upon the true construction of the contract, is intended to have effect in the event of circumstances arising which operate, or would but for the said provision operate, to frustrate the contract, or is intended to have effect whether such circumstances arise or not, the court shall give effect to the said provision and shall only give effect to the foregoing section of this Act to such extent, if any, as appears to the court to be consistent with the said provision.

(4) Where it appears to the court that a part of any contract to which this Act applies can properly be severed from the remainder of the contract, being a part wholly performed before the time of discharge, or so performed except for the payment in respect of that part of the contract of sums which are or can be ascertained under the contract, the court shall treat that part of the contract as if it were a separate contract and had not been frustrated and shall treat the foregoing section of this Act as only applicable to the remainder of that contract.

(5) This Act shall not apply –

  (a) to any charterparty, except a time charterparty or a charterparty by way of demise, or to any contract (other than a charterparty) for the carriage of goods by sea; or

  (b) to any contract of insurance, save as is provided by subsection (5) of the foregoing section; or

  (c) to any contract to which section seven of the Sale of Goods Act 1979 (which avoids contracts for the sale of specific goods which perish before the risk has passed to the buyer) applies, or to any other contract for the sale, or for the sale and delivery, of specific goods, where the contract is frustrated by reason of the fact that the goods have perished.

3 [Omitted]

Arbitration Act 1950

Part II Enforcement of certain foreign awards

35 Awards to which Part II applies

(1) This Part of this Act applies to any award made after the twenty-eighth day of July, nineteen hundred and twenty-four –

(a) in pursuance of an agreement for arbitration to which the protocol set out in the First Schedule to this Act applies; and

(b) between persons of whom one is subject to the jurisdiction of some one of such Powers as His Majesty, being satisfied that reciprocal provisions have been made, may by Order in Council declare to be parties to the convention set out in the Second Schedule to this Act, and of whom the other is subject to the jurisdiction of some other of the Powers aforesaid; and

(c) in one of such territories as His Majesty, being satisfied that reciprocal provisions have been made; may by Order in Council declare to be territories to which the said convention applies;

(d) and an award to which this Part of this Act applies is in this Part of this Act referred to as 'a foreign award'.

(2) and (3) [Omitted].

36 Effect of foreign awards

(1) A foreign award shall, subject to the provisions of this Part of this Act, be enforceable in England either by action or in the same manner as the award of an arbitrator is enforceable by virtue of section sixty-six of the Arbitration Act 1996.

(2) Any foreign award which would be enforceable under this Part of this Act shall be treated as binding for all purposes on the persons as between whom it was made, and may accordingly be relied on by any of those persons by way of defence, set off or otherwise in any legal proceedings in England, and any references in this Part of this Act to enforcing a foreign award shall be construed as including references to relying on an award.

37 Conditions for enforcement of foreign awards

(1) In order that a foreign award may be enforceable under this Part of this Act it must have –

(a) been made in pursuance of an agreement for arbitration which was valid under the law by which it was governed;

(b) been made by the tribunal provided for in the agreement or constituted in a manner agreed upon by the parties;

(c) been made in conformity with the law governing the arbitration procedure;

(d) become final in the country in which it was made;

(e) been in respect of a matter which may lawfully be referred to arbitration under the law of England;

(f) and the enforcement thereof must not be contrary to the public policy or the law of England.

(2) Subject to the provisions of this subsection, a foreign award shall not be enforceable under this Part of this Act if the court dealing with the case is satisfied that –

(a) the award has been annulled in the country in which it was made; or

(b) the party against whom it is sought to enforce the award was not given notice of the arbitration proceedings in sufficient time to enable him to present his case or was under some legal incapacity and was not properly represented; or

(c) the award does not deal with all the questions referred or contains decisions on matters beyond the scope of the agreement for arbitration.

Provided that, if the award does not deal with all the questions referred, the court may, if it thinks fit, either postpone the enforcement of the award or order its enforcement subject to the giving of such security by the person seeking to enforce it as the court may think fit.

(3) If a party seeking to resist the enforcement of a foreign award proves that there is any ground other than the non-existence of the conditions specified in paragraphs (a), (b) and (c) of subsection (1) of this section, or the existence of the conditions specified in paragraphs (b) and (c) of subsection (2) of this section, entitling him to contest the validity of the award, the court may, if it thinks fit, either refuse to enforce the award or adjourn the hearing until after the expiration of such period as appears to the court to be reasonably sufficient to enable that party to take the necessary steps to have the award annulled by the competent tribunal.

38 [Omitted]

39 Meaning of 'final award'

For the purposes of this Part of this Act, an award shall not be deemed final if any proceedings for the purpose of contesting the validity of the award are pending in the country in which it was made.

40–44 [Omitted]

First Schedule

Protocol on Arbitration Clauses Signed on Behalf of His Majesty at a Meeting of the Assembly of the League of Nations Held on the Twenty-Fourth Day of September, Nineteen Hundred and Twenty-Three

The undersigned, being duly authorised, declare that they accept, on behalf of the countries which they represent, the following provisions: –

(1) Each of the Contracting States recognises the validity of an agreement whether relating to existing or future differences between parties, subject respectively to the jurisdiction of different Contracting States by which the parties to a contract agree to submit to arbitration all or any differences that may arise in connection with such contract relating to commercial matters or to any other matter capable of settlement by arbitration, whether or not the arbitration is to take place in a country to whose jurisdiction none of the parties is subject.

Each Contracting State reserves the right to limit the obligation mentioned above to contracts which are considered as commercial under its national law. Any Contracting State which avails itself of this right will notify the secretary-general of the League of Nations, in order that the other Contracting States may be so informed.

(2) The arbitral procedure, including the constitution of the arbitral tribunal, shall be governed by the will of the parties and by the law of the country in whose territory the

arbitration takes place. The Contracting States agree to facilitate all steps in the procedure which require to be taken in their own territories, in accordance with the provisions of their law governing arbitral procedure applicable to existing differences.

(3) Each Contracting State undertakes to ensure the execution by its authorities and in accordance with the provisions of its national laws of arbitral awards made in its own territory under the preceding Articles.

(4) The tribunals of the Contracting Parties, on being seized of a dispute regarding a contract made between persons to whom Article 1 applies and including an arbitration agreement whether referring to present or future differences which is valid in virtue of the said Article and capable of being carried into effect, shall refer the parties on the application of either of them to the decision of the arbitrators. Such reference shall not prejudice the competence of the judicial tribunals in case the agreement or the arbitration cannot proceed or become inoperative.

Articles 5–8 [Omitted].

Second Schedule

Convention on the Execution of Foreign Arbitral Awards Signed at Geneva on Behalf of His Majesty on the Twenty-Sixth Day of September, Nineteen Hundred and Twenty-Seven

Article 1

In the territories of any High Contracting Party to which the present Convention applies, an arbitral award made in pursuance of an agreement, whether relating to existing or future differences (hereinafter called 'a submission to arbitration') covered by the Protocol on Arbitration Clauses, opened at Geneva on September 24, 1923, shall be recognised as binding and shall be enforced in accordance with the rules of the procedure of the territory where the award is relied upon, provided that the said award has been made in a territory of one of the High Contracting Parties to which the present Convention applies and between persons who are subject to the jurisdiction of one of the High Contracting Parties.

To obtain such recognition or enforcement, it shall, further, be necessary –

(a) that the award has been made in pursuance of a submission to arbitration which is valid under the law applicable thereto;

(b) that the subject-matter of the award is capable of settlement by arbitration under the law of the country in which the award is sought to be relied upon;

(c) that the award has been made by the Arbitral Tribunal provided for in the submission to arbitration or constituted in the manner agreed upon by the parties and in conformity with the law governing the arbitration procedure;

(d) that the award has become final in the country in which it has been made, in the sense that it will not be considered as such if it is open to opposition, *appel* or *pourvoi en cassation* (in the countries where such forms of procedure exist) or if it is proved that any proceedings for the purpose of contesting the validity of the award are pending;

(e) that the recognition or enforcement of the award is not contrary to the public policy or to the principles of the law of the country in which it is sought to be relied upon.

Article 2

Even if the conditions laid down in Article 1 hereof are fulfilled, recognition and enforcement of the award shall be refused if the Court is satisfied –

(a) that the award has been annulled in the country in which it was made;
(b) that the party against whom it is sought to use the award was not given notice of the arbitration proceedings in sufficient time to enable him to present his case; or that, being under a legal incapacity, he was not properly represented;
(c) that the award does not deal with the differences contemplated by or falling within the terms of the submission to arbitration or that it contains decisions on matters beyond the scope of the submission to arbitration.

If the award has not covered all the questions submitted to the arbitral tribunal, the competent authority of the country where recognition or enforcement of the award is sought can, if it thinks fit, postpone such recognition or enforcement or grant it subject to such guarantee as that authority may decide.

Article 3

If the party against whom the award has been made proves that, under the law governing the arbitration procedure, there is a ground, other than the grounds referred to in Article 1 (a) and (c), and Article 2 (b) and (c), entitling him to contest the validity of the award in a Court of Law, the Court may, if it thinks fit, either refuse recognition or enforcement of the award or adjourn the consideration thereof, giving such party a reasonable time within which to have the award annulled by the competent tribunal.

Article 4

The party relying upon an award or claiming its enforcement must supply in particular –

(1) The original award or a copy thereof duly authenticated, according to the requirements of the law of the country in which it was made.
(2) Documentary or other evidence to prove that the award has become final, in the sense defined in Article 1 (d), in the country in which it was made.
(3) When necessary, documentary or other evidence to prove that the conditions laid down in Article 1, paragraph 1 and paragraph 2 (a) and (c), have been fulfilled.

A translation of the award and of the other documents mentioned in this Article into the official language of the country where the award is sought to be relied upon may be demanded. Such translation must be certified correct by a diplomatic or consular agent of the country to which the party who seeks to rely upon the award belongs or by a sworn translator of the country where the award is sought to be relied upon.

Article 5

The provisions of the above Articles shall not deprive any interested party of the right of availing himself of an arbitral award in the manner and to the extent allowed by the law or the treaties of the country where such award is sought to be relied upon.

Articles 6–11 [Omitted].

Cheques Act 1957

1 Protection of bankers paying unindorsed or irregularly indorsed cheques, etc.

(1) Where a banker in good faith and in the ordinary course of business pays a cheque drawn on him which is not indorsed or is irregularly indorsed, he does not, in doing so, incur any liability by reason only of the absence of, or irregularity in, indorsement, and he is deemed to have paid it in due course.

(2) Where a banker in good faith and in the ordinary course of business pays any such instrument as the following, namely –

- (a) a document issued by a customer of his which, though not a bill of exchange, is intended to enable a person to obtain payment from him of the sum mentioned in the document;
- (b) a draft payable on demand drawn by him upon himself, whether payable at the head office or some other office of his bank;

he does not, in doing so, incur any liability by reason only of the absence of, or irregularity in, indorsement, and the payment discharges the instrument.

2 Rights of bankers collecting cheques not indorsed by holders

A banker who gives value for, or has a lien on, a cheque payable to order which the holder delivers to him for collection without indorsing it, has such (if any) rights as he would have had if, upon delivery the holder had indorsed it in blank.

3 Unindorsed cheques as evidence of payment

(1) An unindorsed cheque which appears to have been paid by the banker on whom it is drawn is evidence of the receipt by the payee of the sum payable by the cheque.

(2) For the purposes of subsection (1) above, a copy of a cheque to which that subsection applies is evidence of the cheque if –

- (a) the copy is made by the banker in whose possession the cheque is after presentment; and
- (b) it is certified by him to be a true copy of the original.

4 Protection of bankers collecting payment of cheques, etc.

(1) Where a banker, in good faith and without negligence –

- (a) receives payment for a customer of an instrument to which this section applies; or
- (b) having credited a customer's account with the amount of such an instrument, receives payment thereof for himself,
- (c) and the customer has no title, or a defective title, to the instrument, the banker does not incur any liability to the true owner of the instrument by reason only of having received payment thereof.

(2) This section applies to the following instruments, namely –

(a) cheques (including cheques which under section 81A(1) of the Bills of Exchange Act 1882 or otherwise are not transferable);
(b) any document issued by a customer of a banker which, though not a bill of exchange, is intended to enable a person to obtain payment from that banker of the sum mentioned in the document;
(c) any document issued by a public officer which is intended to enable a person to obtain payment from the Paymaster General or the Queen's and Lord Treasurer's Remembrancer of the sum mentioned in the document but is not a bill of exchange;
(d) any draft payable on demand drawn by a banker upon himself, whether payable at the head office or some other office of his bank.

(3) A banker is not to be treated for the purposes of this section as having been negligent by reason only of his failure to concern himself with absence of, or irregularity in, indorsement of an instrument.

5 Application of certain provisions of Bills of Exchange Act 1882, to instruments not being Bills of Exchange

The provisions of the Bills of Exchange Act 1882 relating to crossed cheques shall, so far as applicable, have effect in relation to instruments (other than cheques) to which the last foregoing section applies as they have effect in relation to cheques.

6 Construction, saving and repeal

1 This Act shall be construed as one with the Bills of Exchange Act 1882.
2 The foregoing provisions of this Act do not make negotiable any instrument which, apart from them, is not negotiable.

Carriage by Air Act 1961

1 Convention to have force of law

(1) The applicable provisions of the Carriage by Air Conventions have the force of law in the United Kingdom in relation to any carriage by air to which they apply, irrespective of the nationality of the aircraft performing that carriage.
(2) Subsection (1) does not apply in relation to Community air carriers to the extent that the provisions of the Council Regulation have the force of law in the United Kingdom.
(3) Subsection (1) is subject to the other provisions of this Act.
(4) If more than one of the Carriage by Air Conventions applies to a carriage by air, the applicable provisions that have the force of law in the United Kingdom are those of whichever is the most recent applicable Convention in force.
(5) The Carriage by Air Conventions are –
(a) the Convention known as 'the Warsaw Convention as amended at The Hague, 1955' ('the Convention');
(b) that Convention as further amended by Protocol No. 4 of Montreal, 1975 ('the Convention as amended'); and

(c) the Convention known as 'the Montreal Convention 1999' ('the Montreal Convention').

(6) 'The applicable provisions' means –

(a) the provisions of the Convention set out in Schedule 1;

(b) the provisions of the Convention as amended set out in Schedule 1A; and

(c) the provisions of the Montreal Convention set out in Schedule 1B;

(d) so far as they relate to the rights and liabilities of carriers, carriers' servants and agents, passengers, consignors, consignees and other persons.

(7) In this Act a reference to an Article of, or Protocol to, any of the Carriage by Air Conventions is a reference to that Article or Protocol as it appears in the Schedule in which it is set out.

(8) If there is any inconsistency between the text in English in Part I of Schedule 1 or 1A and the text in French in Part II of that Schedule, the French text shall prevail.

2 and 3 [Omitted]

4 Limitation of liability

(1) It is hereby declared that the limitations on liability in the applicable provisions mentioned in subsection (1A) apply whatever the nature of the proceedings by which liability may be enforced.

(1A) The provisions are –

(a) Article 22 of the Convention;

(b) Article 22 of the Convention as amended; and

(c) Articles 21 and 22 of the Montreal Convention.

(1B) The limitation for each passenger in –

(a) paragraph (1) of Article 22 of the Convention or of the Convention as amended; and

(b) Article 21 and paragraph (1) of Article 22 of the Montreal Convention, applies to the aggregate liability of the carrier in all proceedings which may be brought against him under the law of any part of the United Kingdom, together with any proceedings brought against him outside the United Kingdom.

(2) A court before which proceedings are brought to enforce a liability which is limited by a provision mentioned in subsection 3A may at any stage of the proceedings make any such order as appears to the court to be just and equitable in view of that provision, and of any other proceedings which have been, or are likely to be, commenced in the United Kingdom or elsewhere to enforce the liability in whole or in part.

(3) Without prejudice to the last foregoing subsection, a court before which proceedings are brought to enforce a liability which is limited by a provision mentioned in subsection 3A shall, where the liability is, or may be, partly enforceable in other proceedings in the United Kingdom or elsewhere, have jurisdiction to award an amount less than the court would have awarded if the limitation applied solely to the proceedings before the court, or to make any part of its award conditional on the result of any other proceedings.

(3A) The provisions are –
  a Article 22 of the Convention;
  b Article 22 of the Convention as amended; and
  c Articles 21, 22 and 44 of the Montreal Convention.
(4) and (5) [Omitted].

4A Notice of partial loss

(1) References to damage in the provisions mentioned in subsection (2) shall be construed as including loss of part of the baggage or cargo in question and the reference to the receipt of baggage or cargo shall, in relation to loss of part of it, be construed as receipt of the remainder of it.
(2) The provisions are –
  (a) Article 26(2) of the Convention;
  (b) Article 26(2) of the Convention as amended; and
  (c) Article 31(2) of the Montreal Convention.

5 Time for bringing proceedings

(1) No action against a carrier's servant or agent which arises out of damage to which any of the Carriage by Air Conventions applies relates shall, if he was acting within the scope of his employment, be brought after more than two years, reckoned from the date of arrival at the destination or from the date on which the aircraft ought to have arrived, or from the date on which the carriage stopped.
(2) The provisions mentioned in subsection (4) shall not be read as applying to any proceedings for contribution between persons liable for any damage to which any of the Carriage by Air Conventions relates, but no action shall be brought by a tortfeasor to obtain a contribution from a carrier in respect of a tort to which the said Article 29 applies after the expiration of two years from the time when judgment is obtained against the person seeking to obtain the contribution.
(3) Subsections (1) and (2) and the provisions mentioned in subsection (4) shall have effect as if references in those provisions to an action included references to arbitral proceedings; and the provisions of section 14 of the Arbitration Act 1996 apply to determine when such proceedings are commenced.
(4) The provisions are –
  (a) Article 29 of the Convention;
  (b) Article 29 of the Convention as amended; and
  (c) Article 35 of the Montreal Convention.
(5) If the Montreal Convention applies, 'carrier' in this section includes an actual carrier as defined by Article 39 of that Convention.

6 Contributory negligence

(1) It is hereby declared that for the purposes of the provisions mentioned in subsection (2) the Law Reform (Contributory Negligence) Act 1945 (including that Act as applied to Scotland), and section two of the Law Reform (Miscellaneous Provisions) Act

(Northern Ireland) 1948, are provisions of the law of the United Kingdom under which a court may exonerate the carrier wholly or partly from his liability.

(2) The provisions are –
   (a) Article 21 of the Convention;
   (b) Article 21 of the Convention as amended; and
   (c) Article 20 of the Montreal Convention.

7–14 [Omitted]

Schedule 1 [Omitted]

Schedule 1A

The Warsaw Convention with the Amendment Made to it by the Hague Protocol and Protocol No. 4 Signed at Montreal, 1975

Part I The English Text

Convention for the Unification of Certain Rules Relating to International Carriage by Air

Chapter I Scope-Definitions

Article 1

(1) This Convention applies to all international carriage of persons, baggage or cargo performed by aircraft for reward. It applies equally to gratuitous carriage by aircraft performed by an air transport undertaking.

(2) For the purposes of this Convention, the expression international carriage means any carriage in which, according to the agreement between the parties, the place of departure and the place of destination, whether or not there be a break in the carriage or a trans-shipment, are situated either within the territories of two High Contracting Parties or within the territory of a single High Contracting Party if there is an agreed stopping place within the territory of another State, even if that State is not a High Contracting Party. Carriage between two points within the territory of a single High Contracting Party without an agreed stopping place within the territory of another State is not international carriage for the purposes of this Convention.

(3) Carriage to be performed by several successive air carriers is deemed, for the purposes of this Convention, to be one undivided carriage if it has been regarded by the parties as a single operation, whether it had been agreed upon under the form of a single contract or a series of contracts, and it does not lose its international character merely because one contract or a series of contracts is to be performed entirely within the territory of the same State.

Article 2

(1) This Convention applies to carriage performed by the State or by legally constituted public bodies provided it falls within the conditions laid down in Article 1.
(2) In the carriage of postal items the carrier shall be liable only to the relevant postal administration in accordance with the rules applicable to the relationship between the carriers and the postal administrations.
(3) Except as provided in paragraph (2) of this Article, the provisions of this Convention shall not apply to the carriage of postal items.

Chapter II Documents of Carriage

Section 1 – Passenger Ticket

Article 3

(1) In respect of the carriage of passengers an individual or collective document of carriage shall be delivered containing –
    (a) an indication of the places of departure and destination;
    (b) if the places of departure and destination are within the territory of a single High Contracting Party, one or more agreed stopping places being within the territory of another State, an indication of at least one such stopping place;
    (c) a notice to the effect that, if the passenger's journey involves an ultimate destination or stop in a country other than the country of departure, the Warsaw Convention may be applicable and that the Convention governs and in most cases limits the liability of carriers for death or personal injury and in respect of loss of or damage to baggage.
(2) The passenger ticket shall constitute *prima facie* evidence of the conclusion and conditions of the contract of carriage. The absence, irregularity or loss of the passenger ticket does not affect the existence or the validity of the contract of carriage which shall, none the less, be subject to the rules of this Convention. Nevertheless, if, with the consent of the carrier, the passenger embarks without a passenger ticket having been delivered, or if the ticket does not include the notice required by paragraph (1)(c) of this Article, the carrier shall not be entitled to avail himself of the provisions of Article 22.

Section 2 – Baggage Check

Article 4

(1) In respect of the carriage of checked baggage, a baggage check shall be delivered, which, unless combined with or incorporated in a document of carriage which complies with the provisions of Article 3, paragraph (1), shall contain –
    (a) an indication of the places of departure and destination;
    (b) if the places of departure and destination are within the territory of a single High Contracting Party, one or more agreed stopping places being within the territory of another State, an indication of at least one such stopping place;
    (c) a notice to the effect that, if the carriage involves an ultimate destination or stop in a country other than the country of departure, the Warsaw Convention may be

applicable and that the Convention governs and in most cases limits the liability of carriers in respect of loss or damage to baggage.

(2) The passenger ticket shall constitute *prima facie* evidence of the registration of the baggage and of the conditions of the contract of carriage. The absence, irregularity or loss of the baggage check does not affect the existence or the validity of the contract of carriage which shall, none the less, be subject to the rules of this Convention. Nevertheless, if the carrier takes charge of the baggage without a baggage check (unless combined with or incorporated in the passenger ticket which complies with the provisions of Article 3, paragraph (1)(c)) does not include the notice required by paragraph (1)(c) of this Article, he shall not be entitled to avail himself of the provisions of Article 22, paragraph (2).

Section 3 – Documentation Relating to Cargo

Article 5

(1) In respect of the carriage of cargo an air waybill shall be delivered.

(2) Any other means which would preserve a record of the carriage to be performed may, with the consent of the consignor, be substituted for the delivery of an air waybill. If such other means are used, the carrier shall, if so requested by the consignor, deliver to the consignor a receipt for the cargo permitting identification of the consignment and access to the information contained in the record preserved by such other means.

(3) The impossibility of using, at points of transit and destination, the other means which would preserve the record of the carriage referred to in paragraph (2) of this Article does not entitle the carrier to refuse to accept the cargo for carriage.

Article 6

(1) The air waybill shall be made out by the consignor in three original parts.

(2) The first part shall be marked 'for the carrier'; it shall be signed by the consignor. The second part shall be marked 'for the consignee'; it shall be signed by the consignor and by the carrier. The third part shall be signed by the carrier and handed by him to the consignor after the cargo has been accepted.

(3) The signature of the carrier and that of the consignor may be printed or stamped.

(4) If, at the request of the consignor, the carrier makes out the air waybill, he shall be deemed, subject to proof to the contrary, to have done so on behalf of the consignor.

Article 7

When there is more than one package –

(a) the carrier of cargo has the right to require the consignor to make out separate air waybills;

(b) the consignor has the right to require the carrier to deliver separate receipts when the other means referred to in paragraph (2) of Article 5 are used.

Article 8

The air waybill and the receipt for the cargo shall contain –

(a) an indication of the places of departure and destination;
(b) if the places of departure and destination are within the territory of a single High Contracting Party, one or more agreed stopping places being within the territory of another State, an indication of at least one such stopping place; and
(c) an indication of the weight of the consignment.

Article 9

Non-compliance with the provisions of Articles 5 to 8 shall not affect the existence or the validity of the contract of carriage, which shall, none the less, be subject to the rules of this Convention including those relating to limitation of liability.

Article 10

(1) The consignor is responsible for the correctness of the particulars and statements relating to the cargo inserted by him or on his behalf in the air waybill or furnished by him or on his behalf to the carrier for insertion in the receipt for the cargo or for insertion in the record preserved by the other means referred to in paragraph (2) of Articles.
(2) The consignor shall indemnify the carrier against all damage suffered by him, or by any other person to whom the carrier is liable, by reason of the irregularity, incorrectness or incompleteness of the particulars and statements furnished by the consignor or on his behalf.
(3) Subject to the provisions of paragraphs (1) and (2) of this Article, the carrier shall indemnify the consignor against all damage suffered by him, or by any other person to whom the consignor is liable, by reason of the irregularity, incorrectness or incompleteness of the particulars and statements inserted by the carrier or on his behalf in the receipt for the cargo or in the record preserved by the other means referred to in paragraph (2) of Article 5.

Article 11

(1) The air waybill or the receipt for the cargo is *prima facie* evidence of the conclusion of the contract, of the acceptance of the cargo and of the conditions of carriage mentioned therein.
(2) Any statements in the air waybill or the receipt for the cargo relating to the weight, dimensions and packing of the cargo, as well as those relating to the number of packages, are *prima facie* evidence of the facts stated; those relating to the quantity, volume and condition of the cargo do not constitute evidence against the carrier except so far as they both have been, and are stated in the air waybill to have been, checked by him in the presence of the consignor, or relate to the apparent condition of the cargo.

Article 12

(1) Subject to his liability to carry out all his obligations under the contract of carriage, the consignor has the right to dispose of the cargo by withdrawing it at the airport of departure or destination, or by stopping it in the course of the journey on any landing, or by calling for it to be delivered at the place of destination or in the course of the journey to a person other than the consignee originally designated, or by requiring it to be returned to the airport of departure. He must not exercise this right of disposition in such a way as to prejudice the carrier or other consignors and he must repay any expenses occasioned by the exercise of this right.

(2) If it is impossible to carry out the orders of the consignor the carrier must so inform him forthwith.

(3) If the carrier obeys the orders of the consignor for the disposition of the cargo without requiring the production of the part of the air waybill or the receipt for the cargo delivered to the latter, he will be liable, without prejudice to his right of recovery from the consignor, for any damage which may be caused thereby to any person who is lawfully in possession of that part of the air waybill or the receipt for the cargo.

(4) The right conferred on the consignor ceases at the moment when that of the consignee begins in accordance with Article 13. Nevertheless, if the consignee declines to accept the cargo, or if he cannot be communicated with, the consignor resumes his right of disposition.

Article 13

(1) Except when the consignor has exercised his right under Article 12, the consignee is entitled, on arrival of the cargo at the place of destination, to require the carrier to deliver the cargo to him, on payment of the charges due and on complying with the conditions of carriage.

(2) Unless it is otherwise agreed, it is the duty of the carrier to give notice to the consignee as soon as the cargo arrives.

(3) If the carrier admits the loss of the cargo, or if the cargo has not arrived at the expiration of seven days after the date on which it ought to have arrived, the consignee is entitled to enforce against the carrier the rights which flow from the contract of carriage.

Article 14

The consignor and the consignee can respectively enforce all the rights given them by Articles 12 and 13, each in his own name, whether he is acting in his own interest or in the interest of another, provided that he carries out the obligations imposed by the contract of carriage.

Article 15

(1) Articles 12, 13, and 14 do not affect either the relations of the consignor and the consignee with each other or the mutual relations of third parties whose rights are derived either from the consignor or from the consignee.

(2) The provisions of Articles 12, 13 and 14 can only be varied by express provision in the air waybill or the receipt for the cargo.

Article 16

(1) The consignor must furnish such information and such documents as are necessary to meet the formalities of customs, octroi or police before the cargo can be delivered to the consignee. The consignor is liable to the carrier for any damage occasioned by the absence, insufficiency or irregularity of any such information or documents, unless the damage is due to the fault of the carrier, his servants or agents.

(2) The carrier is under no obligation to enquire into the correctness or sufficiency of such information or documents.

Chapter III Liability of the carrier

Article 17

The carrier is liable for damage sustained in event of the death or personal wounding of a passenger or any other bodily injury suffered by a passenger, if the accident which caused the damage so sustained took place on board the aircraft or in the course of any of the operations of embarking or disembarking.

Article 18

(1) The carrier is liable for damage sustained in the event of the destruction or loss of, or damage to, any registered baggage, if the occurrence which caused the damage so sustained took place during the carriage by air.

(2) The carrier is liable for damage sustained in the event of the destruction or loss of, or damage to, cargo upon condition only that the occurrence which caused the damage so sustained took place during the carriage by air.

(3) However, the carrier is not liable if he proves that the destruction, loss of, or damage to, the cargo resulted solely from one or more of the following –
   (a) inherent defect, quality or vice of that cargo;
   (b) defective packing of that cargo performed by a person other than the carrier or his servants or agents;
   (c) an act of war or an armed conflict;
   (d) an act of public authority carried out in connection with the entry, exit or transit of the cargo.

(4) The carriage by air within the meaning of the preceding paragraphs of this Article comprises the period during which the cargo is in the charge of the carrier, whether in an airport or on board an aircraft, or, in the case of a landing outside an airport, in any place whatsoever.

(5) The period of the carriage by air does not extend to any carriage by land, by sea or by river performed outside an airport. If, however, such carriage takes place in performance of a contract for carriage by air, for the purpose of loading, delivery or transhipment, any damage is presumed, subject to proof to the contrary, to have been the result of an event which took place during the carriage by air.

Article 19

The carrier is liable for damage occasioned by delay in the carriage by air of passengers, baggage or cargo.

Article 20

In the case of passengers and baggage, and in the case of damage occasioned by delay in the carriage of cargo, the carrier shall not be liable if he proves that he and his servants and agents have taken all necessary measures to avoid the damage or that it was impossible for them to take such measures.

Article 21

(1) In the carriage of passengers and baggage, if the carrier proves that the damage was caused by or contributed to by the negligence of the person suffering the damage, the Court may, in accordance with the provisions of its own law, exonerate the carrier wholly or partly from his liability.

(2) In the carriage of cargo, if the carrier proves that the damage was caused by or contributed to by the negligence or other wrongful act or omission of the person claiming compensation, or the person from whom he derives his rights, the carrier shall be wholly or partly exonerated from his liability to the claimant to the extent that such negligence or wrongful act or omission caused or contributed to the damage.

Article 22

(1) In the carriage of persons the liability of the carrier for each passenger is limited to the sum of 16,600 Special Drawing Rights. Where, in accordance with the law of the court seised of the case, damages may be awarded in the form of periodical payments, the equivalent capital value of the said payments shall not exceed this limit. Nevertheless, by special contract, the carrier and the passenger may agree to a higher limit of liability.

(2)

(a) in the carriage of registered baggage, the liability of the carrier is limited to a sum of 17 special drawing rights per kilogramme, unless the consignor has made, at the time when the package was handed over to the carrier, a special declaration of interest in delivery at destination and has paid a supplementary sum if the case so requires. In that case the carrier will be liable to pay a sum not exceeding the declared sum, unless he proves that that sum is greater than the consignor's actual interest in delivery at destination;

(b) in the carriage of cargo, the liability of the carrier is limited to a sum of 17 Special Drawing Rights per kilogramme, unless the consignor has made, at the same time when the package was handed over to the carrier, a special declaration of interest in delivery at destination and has paid a supplementary sum if the case so requires. In that case the carrier will be liable to pay a sum not exceeding the declared sum, unless he proves that that sum is greater than the consignor's actual interest in delivery at destination;

(c) in the case of loss, damage or delay of part of registered baggage or cargo, or of any object contained therein, the weight to be taken into consideration in determining the amount to which the carrier's liability is limited shall be only the total weight of the package or packages concerned. Nevertheless, when the loss, damage or delay of a part of the registered baggage or cargo, or of an object contained therein, affects the value of other packages covered by the same baggage check or the same air waybill, the total weight of such package or packages shall also be taken into consideration in determining the limit of liability.

(3) As regards objects of which the passenger takes charge himself the liability of the carrier is limited to 332 Special Drawing Rights per passenger.

(4) The limits prescribed in this Article shall not prevent the court in an action relating to the carriage of cargo from awarding in accordance with its own law, in addition, the whole or part of the court costs and of the other expenses of the litigation incurred by the plaintiff. The foregoing provision shall not apply if the amount of the damages awarded, excluding court costs and other expenses of the litigation, does not exceed the sum which the carrier has offered in writing to the plaintiff within a period of six months from the date of the occurrence causing the damage, or before the commencement of the action, if that is later.

(5) The sums mentioned in terms of special drawing right in this Article shall be deemed to refer to the special drawing right as defined by the International Monetary Fund. Conversion of the sums into national currencies shall, in case of judicial proceedings, be made according to the value of such currencies in terms of the special drawing right at the date of the judgment.

(6) The value of a national currency, in terms of the Special Drawing Right, of a High Contracting Party which is a Member of the International Monetary Fund, shall be calculated in accordance with the method of valuation applied by the International Monetary Fund, in effect at the date of the judgment for its operations and transactions. The value of a national currency, in terms of the Special Drawing Right, of a High Contracting Party which is not a Member of the International Monetary Fund, shall be calculated in a manner determined by that High Contracting Party. Nevertheless, those States which are not Members of the International Monetary Fund and whose law does not permit the application of the provisions of paragraph (2)(b) of Article 22 may, at the time of ratification or accession or at any time thereafter, declare that the limit of liability of the carrier in judicial proceedings in their territories is fixed at a sum of two hundred and fifty monetary units per kilogramme. This monetary unit corresponds to sixty-five and a half milligrammes of gold of millesimal fineness nine hundred. This sum may be converted into the national currency concerned in round figures. The conversion of this sum into national currency shall be made according to the law of the State concerned.

Article 23

(1) Any provision tending to relieve the carrier of liability or to fix a lower limit than that which is laid down in this Convention shall be null and void, but the nullity of any such provision does not involve the nullity of the whole contract, which shall remain subject to the provisions of this Convention.

(2) Paragraph (1) of this Article shall not apply to provisions governing loss or damage resulting from the inherent defect, quality or vice of the cargo carried.

Article 24

(1) In the carriage of passengers, baggage and cargo, any action for damages, however founded, can only be brought subject to the conditions and limits of liability set out in this Convention without prejudice to the question as to who are the persons who have the right to bring suit and what are their respective rights.
(2) In the carriage of cargo, any action for damages, however founded, whether under this Convention or in contract or in tort or otherwise, can only be brought subject to the conditions and limits of liability set out in this Convention without prejudice to the question as to who are the persons who have the right to bring suit and what are their respective rights. Such limits of liability constitute maximum limits and may not be exceeded whatever the circumstances which give rise to the liability.

Article 25

In the carriage of passengers and baggage, the limits of liability specified in Article 22 shall not apply if it is proved that the damage resulted from an act or omission of the carrier, his servants or agents, done with intent to cause damage or recklessly and with knowledge that damage would probably result; provided that, in the case of such act or omission of a servant or agent, it is also proved that he was acting within the scope of his employment.

Article 25A

(1) If an action is brought against a servant or agent of the carrier arising out of damage to which the Convention relates, such servant or agent, if he proves that he acted within the scope of his employment, shall be entitled to avail himself of the limits of liability which that carrier himself is entitled to invoke under Article 22.
(2) The aggregate of the amounts recoverable from the carrier, his servants and agents, in that case, shall not exceed the said limits.
(3) In the carriage of passengers and baggage, the provisions of paragraphs (1) and (2) of this Article shall not apply if it is proved that the damage resulted from an act or omission of the servant or agent done with intent to cause damage or recklessly and with knowledge that damage would probably result.

Article 26

(1) Receipt by the person entitled to delivery of baggage or cargo without complaint is *prima facie* evidence that the same have been delivered in good condition and in accordance with the document of carriage.
(2) In the case of damage, the person entitled to delivery must complain to the carrier forthwith after the discovery of the damage, and at the latest, within seven days from the date of receipt in the case of baggage and fourteen days from the date of receipt in the case of

cargo. In the case of delay the complaint must be made at the latest within twenty-one days from the date on which the baggage or cargo has been placed at his disposal.

(3) Every complaint must be made in writing upon the document of carriage or by separate notice in writing despatched within the times aforesaid.

(4) Failing complaint within the times aforesaid, no action shall lie against the carrier, save in the case of fraud on his part.

Article 27

In the case of the death of the person liable, an action for damages lies in accordance with the terms of this Convention against those legally representing his estate.

Article 28

(1) An action for damages must be brought, at the option of the plaintiff, in the territory of one of the High Contracting Parties, either before the court having jurisdiction where the carrier is ordinarily resident, or has his principal place of business, or has an establishment by which the contract has been made or before the court having jurisdiction at the place of destination.

(2) Questions of procedure shall be governed by the law of the court seised of the case.

Article 29

(1) The right to damages shall be extinguished if an action is not brought within two years, reckoned from the date of arrival at the destination, or from the date on which the aircraft ought to have arrived, or from the date on which the carriage stopped.

(2) The method of calculating the period of limitation shall be determined by the law of the court seised of the case.

Article 30

(1) In the case of carriage to be performed by various successive carriers and falling within the definition set out in the third paragraph of Article 1, each carrier who accepts passengers, baggage or cargo is subjected to the rules set out in this Convention, and is deemed to be one of the contracting parties to the contract of carriage in so far as the contract deals with that part of the carriage which is performed under his supervision.

(2) In the case of carriage of this nature, the passenger or his representative can take action only against the carrier who performed the carriage during which the accident or the delay occurred, save in the case where, by express agreement, the first carrier assumed liability for the whole journey.

(3) As regards baggage or cargo, the passenger or consignor will have a right of action against the first carrier, and the passenger or consignee who is entitled to delivery will have a right of action against the last carrier, and further, each may take action against the carrier who performed the carriage during which the destruction, loss, damage or delay took place. These carriers will be jointly and severally liable to the passenger or to the consignor or consignee.

Article 30A

Nothing in this Convention shall prejudice the question whether a person liable for damage in accordance with its provisions has a right of recourse against any other person.

Chapter IV Provisions relating to combined carriage

Article 31

(1) In the case of combined carriage performed partly by air and partly by any other mode of carriage, the provisions of this Convention apply only to the carriage by air, provided that the carriage by air falls within the terms of Article 1.
(2) Nothing in this Convention shall prevent the parties in the case of combined carriage from inserting in the documents of air carriage conditions relating to other modes of carriage, provided that the provisions of this Convention are observed as regards the carriage by air.

Chapter V General and final provisions

Article 32

Any clause contained in the contract and all special agreements entered into before the damage occurred by which the parties purport to infringe the rules laid down by this Convention, whether by deciding the law to be applied, or by altering the rules as to jurisdiction, shall be null and void. Nevertheless for the carriage of cargo arbitration clauses are allowed, subject to this Convention, if the arbitration is to take place within one of the jurisdictions referred to in the first paragraph of Article 28.

Article 33

Except as provided in paragraph (3) of Article 5, nothing in this Convention shall prevent the carrier either from refusing to enter into any contract of carriage or from making regulations which do not conflict with the provisions of this Convention.

Article 34

The provisions of Articles 3 to 8 inclusive relating to documents of carriage shall not apply in the case of carriage performed in extraordinary circumstances outside the normal scope of an air carrier's business.

Article 35

The expression 'days' when used in this Convention means current days not working days.

Article 40A

(1) [Omitted].

(2) For the purposes of the Convention the word territory means not only the metropolitan territory of a State but also all other territories for the foreign relations of which that State is responsible.

Articles 36–42 [Omitted]. 7676

Schedule 1B

[The Montreal Convention 1999]

Convention for the Unification of Certain Rules for International Carriage by Air

Chapter I General provisions

Article 1 Scope of application

(1) This Convention applies to all international carriage of persons, baggage or cargo performed by aircraft for reward. It applies equally to gratuitous carriage by aircraft performed by an air transport undertaking.

(2) For the purposes of this Convention, the expression *international carriage* means any carriage in which, according to the agreement between the parties, the place of departure and the place of destination, whether or not there be a break in the carriage or a transhipment, are situated either within the territories of two States Parties, or within the territory of a single State Party if there is an agreed stopping place within the territory of another State, even if that State is not a State Party. Carriage between two points within the territory of a single State Party without an agreed stopping place within the territory of another State is not international carriage for the purposes of this Convention.

(3) Carriage to be performed by several successive carriers is deemed, for the purposes of this Convention, to be one undivided carriage if it has been regarded by the parties as a single operation, whether it had been agreed upon under the form of a single contract or of a series of contracts, and it does not lose its international character merely because one contract or a series of contracts is to be performed entirely within the territory of the same State.

(4) This Convention applies also to carriage as set out in Chapter V, subject to the terms contained therein.

Article 2 Carriage performed by state and carriage of postal items

(1) This Convention applies to carriage performed by the State or by legally constituted public bodies provided it falls within the conditions laid down in Article 1.

(2) In the carriage of postal items, the carrier shall be liable only to the relevant postal administration in accordance with the rules applicable to the relationship between the carriers and the postal administrations.

(3) Except as provided in paragraph 2 of this Article, the provisions of this Convention shall not apply to the carriage of postal items.

Chapter II Documentation and duties of the parties relating to the carriage of passengers, baggage and cargo

Article 3 Passengers and baggage

(1) In respect of carriage of passengers, an individual or collective document of carriage shall be delivered containing:
   (a) an indication of the places of departure and destination;
   (b) if the places of departure and destination are within the territory of a single State Party, one or more agreed stopping places being within the territory of another State, an indication of at least one such stopping place.

(2) Any other means which preserves the information indicated in paragraph 1 may be substituted for the delivery of the document referred to in that paragraph. If any such other means is used, the carrier shall offer to deliver to the passenger a written statement of the information so preserved.

(3) The carrier shall deliver to the passenger a baggage identification tag for each piece of checked baggage.

(4) The passenger shall be given written notice to the effect that where this Convention is applicable it governs and may limit the liability of carriers in respect of death or injury and for destruction or loss of, or damage to, baggage, and for delay.

(5) Non-compliance with the provisions of the foregoing paragraphs shall not affect the existence or the validity of the contract of carriage, which shall, nonetheless, be subject to the rules of this Convention including those relating to limitation of liability.

Article 4 Cargo

(1) In respect of the carriage of cargo, an air waybill shall be delivered.

(2) Any other means which preserves a record of the carriage to be performed may be substituted for the delivery of an air waybill. If such other means are used, the carrier shall, if so requested by the consignor, deliver to the consignor a cargo receipt permitting identification of the consignment and access to the information contained in the record preserved by such other means.

Article 5 Contents of air waybill or cargo receipt

The air waybill or the cargo receipt shall include:

(a) an indication of the places of departure and destination;
(b) if the places of departure and destination are within the territory of a single State Party, one or more agreed stopping places being within the territory of another State, an indication of at least one such stopping place; and
(c) an indication of the weight of the consignment.

Article 6 Document relating to the nature of the cargo

The consignor may be required, if necessary to meet the formalities of customs, police and similar public authorities, to deliver a document indicating the nature of the cargo. This provision creates for the carrier no duty, obligation or liability resulting therefrom.

Article 7 Description of air waybill

(1) The air waybill shall be made out by the consignor in three original parts.
(2) The first part shall be marked 'for the carrier'; it shall be signed by the consignor. The second part shall be marked 'for the consignee'; it shall be signed by the consignor and by the carrier. The third part shall be signed by the carrier who shall hand it to the consignor after the cargo has been accepted.
(3) The signature of the carrier and that of the consignor may be printed or stamped.
(4) If, at the request of the consignor, the carrier makes out the air waybill, the carrier shall be deemed, subject to proof to the contrary, to have done so on behalf of the consignor.

Article 8 Documentation for multiple packages

When there is more than one package:

(a) the carrier of cargo has the right to require the consignor to make out separate air waybills;
(b) the consignor has the right to require the carrier to deliver separate cargo receipts when the other means referred to in paragraph 2 of Article 4 are used.

Article 9 Non-compliance with documentary requirements

Non-compliance with the provisions of Articles 4 to 8 shall not affect the existence or the validity of the contract of carriage, which shall, nonetheless, be subject to the rules of this Convention including those relating to limitation of liability.

Article 10 Responsibility for particulars of documentation

(1) The consignor is responsible for the correctness of the particulars and statements relating to the cargo inserted by it or on its behalf in the air waybill or furnished by it or on its behalf to the carrier for insertion in the cargo receipt or for insertion in the record preserved by the other means referred to in paragraph 2 of Article 4. The foregoing shall also apply where the person acting on behalf of the consignor is also the agent of the carrier.
(2) The consignor shall indemnify the carrier against all damage suffered by it, or by any other person to whom the carrier is liable, by reason of the irregularity, incorrectness or incompleteness of the particulars and statements furnished by the consignor or on its behalf.
(3) Subject to the provisions of paragraphs 1 and 2 of this Article, the carrier shall indemnify the consignor against all damage suffered by it, or by any other person to whom the consignor is liable, by reason of the irregularity, incorrectness or incompleteness of the particulars and statements inserted by the carrier or on its behalf in the cargo receipt or in the record preserved by the other means referred to in paragraph 2 of Article 4.

Article 11 Evidentiary value of documentation

(1) The air waybill or the cargo receipt is *prima facie* evidence of the conclusion of the contract, of the acceptance of the cargo and of the conditions of carriage mentioned therein.

(2) Any statements in the air waybill or the cargo receipt relating to the weight, dimensions and packing of the cargo, as well as those relating to the number of packages, are *prima facie* evidence of the facts stated; those relating to the quantity, volume and condition of the cargo do not constitute evidence against the carrier except so far as they both have been, and are stated in the air waybill or the cargo receipt to have been, checked by it in the presence of the consignor, or relate to the apparent condition of the cargo.

Article 12 Right of disposition of cargo

(1) Subject to its liability to carry out all its obligations under the contract of carriage, the consignor has the right to dispose of the cargo by withdrawing it at the airport of departure or destination, or by stopping it in the course of the journey on any landing, or by calling for it to be delivered at the place of destination or in the course of the journey to a person other than the consignee originally designated, or by requiring it to be returned to the airport of departure. The consignor must not exercise this right of disposition in such a way as to prejudice the carrier or other consignors and must reimburse any expenses occasioned by the exercise of this right.
(2) If it is impossible to carry out the instructions of the consignor, the carrier must so inform the consignor forthwith.
(3) If the carrier carries out the instructions of the consignor for the disposition of the cargo without requiring the production of the part of the air waybill or the cargo receipt delivered to the latter, the carrier will be liable, without prejudice to its right of recovery from the consignor, for any damage which may be caused thereby to any person who is lawfully in possession of that part of the air waybill or the cargo receipt.
(4) The right conferred on the consignor ceases at the moment when that of the consignee begins in accordance with Article 13. Nevertheless, if the consignee declines to accept the cargo, or cannot be communicated with, the consignor resumes its right of disposition.

Article 13 Delivery of the cargo

(1) Except when the consignor has exercised its right under Article 12, the consignee is entitled, on arrival of the cargo at the place of destination, to require the carrier to deliver the cargo to it, on payment of the charges due and on complying with the conditions of carriage.
(2) Unless it is otherwise agreed, it is the duty of the carrier to give notice to the consignee as soon as the cargo arrives.
(3) If the carrier admits the loss of the cargo, or if the cargo has not arrived at the expiration of seven days after the date on which it ought to have arrived, the consignee is entitled to enforce against the carrier the rights which flow from the contract of carriage.

Article 14 Enforcement of the rights of consignor and consignee

The consignor and the consignee can respectively enforce all the rights given to them by Articles 12 and 13, each in its own name, whether it is acting in its own interest or in the interest of another, provided that it carries out the obligations imposed by the contract of carriage.

Article 15 Relations of consignor and consignee or mutual relations of third parties

(1) Articles 12, 13 and 14 do not affect either the relations of the consignor and the consignee with each other or the mutual relations of third parties whose rights are derived either from the consignor or from the consignee.
(2) The provisions of Articles 12, 13 and 14 can only be varied by express provision in the air waybill or the cargo receipt.

Article 16 Formalities of customs, police or other public authorities

(1) The consignor must furnish such information and such documents as are necessary to meet the formalities of customs, police and any other public authorities before the cargo can be delivered to the consignee. The consignor is liable to the carrier for any damage occasioned by the absence, insufficiency or irregularity of any such information or documents, unless the damage is due to the fault of the carrier, its servants or agents.
(2) The carrier is under no obligation to enquire into the correctness or sufficiency of such information or documents.

Chapter III Liability of the carrier and extent of compensation for damage

Article 17 Death and injury of passengers – damage to baggage

(1) The carrier is liable for damage sustained in case of death or bodily injury of a passenger upon condition only that the accident which caused the death or injury took place on board the aircraft or in the course of any of the operations of embarking or disembarking.
(2) The carrier is liable for damage sustained in case of destruction or loss of, or of damage to, checked baggage upon condition only that the event which caused the destruction, loss or damage took place on board the aircraft or during any period within which the checked baggage was in the charge of the carrier. However, the carrier is not liable if and to the extent that the damage resulted from the inherent defect, quality or vice of the baggage. In the case of unchecked baggage, including personal items, the carrier is liable if the damage resulted from its fault or that of its servants or agents.
(3) If the carrier admits the loss of the checked baggage, or if the checked baggage has not arrived at the expiration of twenty-one days after the date on which it ought to have arrived, the passenger is entitled to enforce against the carrier the rights which flow from the contract of carriage.
(4) Unless otherwise specified, in this Convention the term 'baggage' means both checked baggage and unchecked baggage.

Article 18 Damage to cargo

(1) The carrier is liable for damage sustained in the event of the destruction or loss of, or damage to, cargo upon condition only that the event which caused the damage so sustained took place during the carriage by air.

(2) However, the carrier is not liable if and to the extent it proves that the destruction, or loss of, or damage to, the cargo resulted from one or more of the following:
   (a) inherent defect, quality or vice of that cargo;
   (b) defective packing of that cargo performed by a person other than the carrier or its servants or agents;
   (c) an act of war or an armed conflict;
   (d) an act of public authority carried out in connection with the entry, exit or transit of the cargo.

(3) The carriage by air within the meaning of paragraph 1 of this Article comprises the period during which the cargo is in the charge of the carrier.

(4) The period of the carriage by air does not extend to any carriage by land, by sea or by inland waterway performed outside an airport. If, however, such carriage takes place in the performance of a contract for carriage by air, for the purpose of loading, delivery or transhipment, any damage is presumed, subject to proof to the contrary, to have been the result of an event which took place during the carriage by air. If a carrier, without the consent of the consignor, substitutes carriage by another mode of transport for the whole or part of a carriage intended by the agreement between the parties to be carriage by air, such carriage by another mode of transport is deemed to be within the period of carriage by air.

Article 19 Delay

The carrier is liable for damage occasioned by delay in the carriage by air of passengers, baggage or cargo. Nevertheless, the carrier shall not be liable for damage occasioned by delay if it proves that it and its servants and agents took all measures that could reasonably be required to avoid the damage or that it was impossible for it or them to take such measures.

Article 20 Exoneration

If the carrier proves that the damage was caused or contributed to by the negligence or other wrongful act or omission of the person claiming compensation, or the person from whom he or she derives his or her rights, the carrier shall be wholly or partly exonerated from its liability to the claimant to the extent that such negligence or wrongful act or omission caused or contributed to the damage. When by reason of death or injury of a passenger compensation is claimed by a person other than the passenger, the carrier shall likewise be wholly or partly exonerated from its liability to the extent that it proves that the damage was caused or contributed to by the negligence or other wrongful act or omission of that passenger. This Article applies to all the liability provisions in this Convention, including paragraph 1 of Article 21.

Article 21 Compensation in case of death or injury of passengers

(1) For damages arising under paragraph 1 of Article 17 not exceeding 100,000 Special Drawing Rights for each passenger, the carrier shall not be able to exclude or limit its liability.

(2) The carrier shall not be liable for damages arising under paragraph 1 of Article 17 to the extent that they exceed for each passenger 100,000 Special Drawing Rights if the carrier proves that:

(a) such damage was not due to the negligence or other wrongful act or omission of the carrier or its servants or agents; or
(b) such damage was solely due to the negligence or other wrongful act or omission of a third party.

Article 22 Limits of liability in relation to delay, baggage and cargo

(1) In the case of damage caused by delay as specified in Article 19 in the carriage of persons, the liability of the carrier for each passenger is limited to 4,150 Special Drawing Rights.
(2) In the carriage of baggage, the liability of the carrier in the case of destruction, loss, damage or delay is limited to 1,000 Special Drawing Rights for each passenger unless the passenger has made, at the time when the checked baggage was handed over to the carrier, a special declaration of interest in delivery at destination and has paid a supplementary sum if the case so requires. In that case the carrier will be liable to pay a sum not exceeding the declared sum, unless it proves that the sum is greater than the passenger's actual interest in delivery at destination.
(3) In the carriage of cargo, the liability of the carrier in the case of destruction, loss, damage or delay is limited to a sum of 17 Special Drawing Rights per kilogramme, unless the consignor has made, at the time when the package was handed over to the carrier, a special declaration of interest in delivery at destination and has paid a supplementary sum if the case so requires. In that case the carrier will be liable to pay a sum not exceeding the declared sum, unless it proves that the sum is greater than the consignor's actual interest in delivery at destination.
(4) In the case of destruction, loss, damage or delay of part of the cargo, or of any object contained therein, the weight to be taken into consideration in determining the amount to which the carrier's liability is limited shall be only the total weight of the package or packages concerned. Nevertheless, when the destruction, loss, damage or delay of a part of the cargo, or of an object contained therein, affects the value of other packages covered by the same air waybill, or the same receipt or, if they were not issued, by the same record preserved by the other means referred to in paragraph 2 of Article 4, the total weight of such package or packages shall also be taken into consideration in determining the limit of liability.
(5) The foregoing provisions of paragraphs 1 and 2 of this Article shall not apply if it is proved that the damage resulted from an act or omission of the carrier, its servants or agents, done with intent to cause damage or recklessly and with knowledge that damage would probably result; provided that, in the case of such act or omission of a servant or agent, it is also proved that such servant or agent was acting within the scope of its employment.
(6) The limits prescribed in Article 21 and in this Article shall not prevent the court from awarding, in accordance with its own law, in addition, the whole or part of the court costs and of the other expenses of the litigation incurred by the plaintiff, including interest. The foregoing provision shall not apply if the amount of the damages awarded, excluding court costs and other expenses of the litigation, does not exceed the sum which the carrier has offered in writing to the plaintiff within a period of six months from the date of the occurrence causing the damage, or before the commencement of the action, if that is later.

Articles 23 and 24 [Omitted].

Article 25 Stipulation on limits

A carrier may stipulate that the contract of carriage shall be subject to higher limits of liability than those provided for in this Convention or to no limits of liability whatsoever.

Article 26 Invalidity of contractual provisions

Any provision tending to relieve the carrier of liability or to fix a lower limit than that which is laid down in this Convention shall be null and void, but the nullity of any such provision does not involve the nullity of the whole contract, which shall remain subject to the provisions of this Convention.

Article 27 Freedom to contract

Nothing contained in this Convention shall prevent the carrier from refusing to enter into any contract of carriage, from waiving any defences available under the Convention, or from laying down conditions which do not conflict with the provisions of this Convention.

Article 28 Advance payments

In the case of aircraft accidents resulting in death or injury of passengers, the carrier shall, if required by its national law, make advance payments without delay to a natural person or persons who are entitled to claim compensation in order to meet the immediate economic needs of such persons. Such advance payments shall not constitute a recognition of liability and may be offset against any amounts subsequently paid as damages by the carrier.

Article 29 Basis of claims

In the carriage of passengers, baggage and cargo, any action for damages, however founded, whether under this Convention or in contract or in tort or otherwise, can only be brought subject to the conditions and such limits of liability as are set out in this Convention without prejudice to the question as to who are the persons who have the right to bring suit and what are their respective rights. In any such action, punitive, exemplary or any other non-compensatory damages shall not be recoverable.

Article 30 Servants, agents – aggregation of claims

(1) If an action is brought against a servant or agent of the carrier arising out of damage to which the Convention relates, such servant or agent, if they prove that they acted within the scope of their employment, shall be entitled to avail themselves of the conditions and limits of liability which the carrier itself is entitled to invoke under this Convention.

(2) The aggregate of the amounts recoverable from the carrier, its servants and agents, in that case, shall not exceed the said limits.

(3) Save in respect of the carriage of cargo, the provisions of paragraphs 1 and 2 of this Article shall not apply if it is proved that the damage resulted from an act or omission of the servant or agent done with intent to cause damage or recklessly and with knowledge that damage would probably result.

Article 31 Timely notice of complaints

(1) Receipt by the person entitled to delivery of checked baggage or cargo without complaint is *prima facie* evidence that the same has been delivered in good condition and in accordance with the document of carriage or with the record preserved by the other means referred to in paragraph 2 of Article 3 and paragraph 2 of Article 4.
(2) In the case of damage, the person entitled to delivery must complain to the carrier forthwith after the discovery of the damage, and, at the latest, within seven days from the date of receipt in the case of checked baggage and fourteen days from the date of receipt in the case of cargo. In the case of delay, the complaint must be made at the latest within twenty-one days from the date on which the baggage or cargo have been placed at his or her disposal.
(3) Every complaint must be made in writing and given or dispatched within the times aforesaid.
(4) If no complaint is made within the times aforesaid, no action shall lie against the carrier, save in the case of fraud on its part.

Article 32 Death of person liable

In the case of the death of the person liable, an action for damages lies in accordance with the terms of this Convention against those legally representing his or her estate.

Article 33 Jurisdiction

(1) An action for damages must be brought, at the option of the plaintiff, in the territory of one of the States Parties, either before the court of the domicile of the carrier or of its principal place of business, or where it has a place of business through which the contract has been made or before the court at the place of destination.
(2) In respect of damage resulting from the death or injury of a passenger, an action may be brought before one of the courts mentioned in paragraph 1 of this Article, or in the territory of a State Party in which at the time of the accident the passenger has his or her principal and permanent residence and to or from which the carrier operates services for the carriage of passengers by air, either on its own aircraft, or on another carrier's aircraft pursuant to a commercial agreement, and in which that carrier conducts its business of carriage of passengers by air from premises leased or owned by the carrier itself or by another carrier with which it has a commercial agreement.
(3) For the purposes of paragraph 2:
    (a) 'commercial agreement' means an agreement, other than an agency agreement, made between carriers and relating to the provision of their joint services for carriage of passengers by air;

(b) 'principal and permanent residence' means the one fixed and permanent abode of the passenger at the time of the accident. The nationality of the passenger shall not be the determining factor in this regard.

(4) Questions of procedure shall be governed by the law of the court seised of the case.

Article 34 Arbitration

(1) Subject to the provisions of this Article, the parties to the contract of carriage for cargo may stipulate that any dispute relating to the liability of the carrier under this Convention shall be settled by arbitration. Such agreement shall be in writing.
(2) The arbitration proceedings shall, at the option of the claimant, take place within one of the jurisdictions referred to in Article 33.
(3) The arbitrator or arbitration tribunal shall apply the provisions of this Convention.
(4) The provisions of paragraphs 2 and 3 of this Article shall be deemed to be part of every arbitration clause or agreement, and any term of such clause or agreement which is inconsistent therewith shall be null and void.

Article 35 Limitation of actions

(1) The right to damages shall be extinguished if an action is not brought within a period of two years, reckoned from the date of arrival at the destination, or from the date on which the aircraft ought to have arrived, or from the date on which the carriage stopped.
(2) The method of calculating that period shall be determined by the law of the court seised of the case.

Article 36 Successive carriage

(1) In the case of carriage to be performed by various successive carriers and falling within the definition set out in paragraph 3 of Article 1, each carrier which accepts passengers, baggage or cargo is subject to the rules set out in this Convention and is deemed to be one of the parties to the contract of carriage in so far as the contract deals with that part of the carriage which is performed under its supervision.
(2) In the case of carriage of this nature, the passenger or any person entitled to compensation in respect of him or her can take action only against the carrier which performed the carriage during which the accident or the delay occurred, save in the case where, by express agreement, the first carrier has assumed liability for the whole journey.
(3) As regards baggage or cargo, the passenger or consignor will have a right of action against the first carrier, and the passenger or consignee who is entitled to delivery will have a right of action against the last carrier, and further, each may take action against the carrier which performed the carriage during which the destruction, loss, damage or delay took place. These carriers will be jointly and severally liable to the passenger or to the consignor or consignee.

Article 37 Right of recourse against third parties

Nothing in this Convention shall prejudice the question whether a person liable for damage in accordance with its provisions has a right of recourse against any other person.

Chapter IV Combined carriage

Article 38 Combined carriage

(1) In the case of combined carriage performed partly by air and partly by any other mode of carriage, the provisions of this Convention shall, subject to paragraph 4 of Article 18, apply only to the carriage by air, provided that the carriage by air falls within the terms of Article 1.
(2) Nothing in this Convention shall prevent the parties in the case of combined carriage from inserting in the document of air carriage conditions relating to other modes of carriage, provided that the provisions of this Convention are observed as regards the carriage by air.

Chapter V Carriage by air performed by a person other than the contracting carrier

Article 39 Contracting carrier – actual carrier

The provisions of this Chapter apply when a person (hereinafter referred to as 'the contracting carrier') as a principal makes a contract governed by this Convention with a passenger or consignor or with a person acting on behalf of the passenger or consignor, and another person (hereinafter referred to as 'the actual carrier') performs, by virtue of authority from the contracting carrier, the whole or part of the carriage, but is not with respect to such part a successive carrier within the meaning of this Convention. Such authority shall be presumed in the absence of proof to the contrary.

Article 40 Respective liability of contracting and actual carriers

If an actual carrier performs the whole or part of carriage which, according to the contract referred to in Article 39, is governed by this Convention, both the contracting carrier and the actual carrier shall, except as otherwise provided in this Chapter, be subject to the rules of this Convention, the former for the whole of the carriage contemplated in the contract, the latter solely for the carriage which it performs.

Article 41 Mutual liability

(1) The acts and omissions of the actual carrier and of its servants and agents acting within the scope of their employment shall, in relation to the carriage performed by the actual carrier, be deemed to be also those of the contracting carrier.
(2) The acts and omissions of the contracting carrier and of its servants and agents acting within the scope of their employment shall, in relation to the carriage performed by the actual carrier, be deemed to be also those of the actual carrier. Nevertheless, no such act or omission shall subject the actual carrier to liability exceeding the amounts referred to in Articles 21, 22, 23 and 24. Any special agreement under which the contracting carrier assumes obligations not imposed by this Convention or any waiver of rights or defences conferred by this Convention or any special declaration of interest in delivery at destination contemplated in Article 22 shall not affect the actual carrier unless agreed to by it.

Article 42 Addressee of complaints and instructions

Any complaint to be made or instruction to be given under this Convention to the carrier shall have the same effect whether addressed to the contracting carrier or to the actual carrier. Nevertheless, instructions referred to in Article 12 shall only be effective if addressed to the contracting carrier.

Article 43 Servants and agents

In relation to the carriage performed by the actual carrier, any servant or agent of that carrier or of the contracting carrier shall, if they prove that they acted within the scope of their employment, be entitled to avail themselves of the conditions and limits of liability which are applicable under this Convention to the carrier whose servant or agent they are, unless it is proved that they acted in a manner that prevents the limits of liability from being invoked in accordance with this Convention.

Article 44 Aggregation of damages

In relation to the carriage performed by the actual carrier, the aggregate of the amounts recoverable from that carrier and the contracting carrier, and from their servants and agents acting within the scope of their employment, shall not exceed the highest amount which could be awarded against either the contracting carrier or the actual carrier under this Convention, but none of the persons mentioned shall be liable for a sum in excess of the limit applicable to that person.

Article 45 Addressee of claims

In relation to the carriage performed by the actual carrier, an action for damages may be brought, at the option of the plaintiff, against that carrier or the contracting carrier, or against both together or separately. If the action is brought against only one of those carriers, that carrier shall have the right to require the other carrier to be joined in the proceedings, the procedure and effects being governed by the law of the court seised of the case.

Article 46 Additional jurisdiction

Any action for damages contemplated in Article 45 must be brought, at the option of the plaintiff, in the territory of one of the States Parties, either before a court in which an action may be brought against the contracting carrier, as provided in Article 33, or before the court having jurisdiction at the place where the actual carrier has its domicile or its principal place of business.

Article 47 Invalidity of contractual provisions

Any contractual provision tending to relieve the contracting carrier or the actual carrier of liability under this Chapter or to fix a lower limit than that which is applicable according to this Chapter shall be null and void, but the nullity of any such provision does not involve the nullity of the whole contract, which shall remain subject to the provisions of this Chapter.

Article 48 Mutual relations of contracting and actual carriers

Except as provided in Article 45, nothing in this Chapter shall affect the rights and obligations of the carriers between themselves, including any right of recourse or indemnification.

Chapter VI Other provisions

Article 49 Mandatory application

Any clause contained in the contract of carriage and all special agreements entered into before the damage occurred by which the parties purport to infringe the rules laid down by this Convention, whether by deciding the law to be applied, or by altering the rules as to jurisdiction, shall be null and void.

Article 50 Insurance

States Parties shall require their carriers to maintain adequate insurance covering their liability under this Convention. A carrier may be required by the State Party into which it operates to furnish evidence that it maintains adequate insurance covering its liability under this Convention.

Article 51 Carriage performed in extraordinary circumstances

The provisions of Articles 3 to 5, 7 and 8 relating to the documentation of carriage shall not apply in the case of carriage performed in extraordinary circumstances outside the normal scope of a carrier's business.

Article 52 Definition of days

The expression 'days' when used in this Convention means calendar days, not working days.

Carriage by Air (Supplementary Provisions) Act 1962

1 Supplementary Convention to have force of law

(1) The provisions of the Convention, supplementary to the Warsaw Convention, for the unification of certain rules relating to international carriage by air performed by a person other than the contracting carrier, as set out in the Schedule to this Act, shall, so far as they relate to the rights and liabilities of carriers, carriers' servants and agents, passengers, consignors, consignees, and other persons, and subject to the provisions of this Act, have the force of law in the United Kingdom in relation to any carriage by air to which the Convention applies, irrespective of the nationality of the aircraft performing that carriage.

(2) If there is any inconsistency between the text in English in Part I of the Schedule to this Act and the text in French in Part II of that Schedule, the text in French shall prevail.

2–7 [Omitted]

Schedule

Part 1 The English Text

Convention Supplementary to the Warsaw Convention, for the Unification of Certain Rules Relating to International Carriage by Air Performed by a Person Other than the Contracting Carrier

Article I

In this Convention –

(a) [Omitted];
(b) 'contracting carrier' means a person who as a principal makes an agreement for carriage governed by the Warsaw Convention with a passenger or consignor or with a person acting on behalf of the passenger or consignor;
(c) 'actual carrier' means a person, other than the contracting carrier, who, by virtue of authority from the contracting carrier, performs the whole or part of the carriage contemplated in paragraph (b), but who is not with respect to such part a successive carrier within the meaning of the Warsaw Convention. Such authority is presumed in the absence of proof to the contrary.

Article II

If an actual carrier performs the whole or part of carriage which, according to the agreement referred to in Article I, paragraph (b), is governed by the Warsaw Convention, both the contracting carrier and the actual carrier shall, except as otherwise provided in this Convention, be subject to the rules of the Warsaw Convention, the former for the whole of the carriage contemplated in the agreement, the latter solely for the carriage which he performs.

Article III

1. The acts and omissions of the actual carrier and of his servants and agents acting within the scope of their employment shall, in relation to the carriage performed by the actual carrier, be deemed to be also those of the contracting carrier.
2. The acts and omissions of the contracting carrier and of his servants and agents acting within the scope of their employment shall, in relation to the carriage performed by the actual carrier, be deemed to be also those of the actual carrier. Nevertheless, no such act or omission shall subject the actual carrier to liability exceeding the limits specified in Article 22 or Article 22A of the Warsaw Convention. Any special agreement under which the contracting carrier assumes obligations not imposed by the Warsaw Convention or any waiver of rights conferred by that Convention or any special declaration of interest in delivery at destination contemplated in Article 22 of the said Convention, shall not affect the actual carrier unless agreed to by him.

Article IV

Any complaint to be made or order to be given under the Warsaw Convention to the carrier shall have the same effect whether addressed to the contracting carrier or to the actual carrier. Nevertheless, orders referred to in Article 12 of the Warsaw Convention shall only be effective if addressed to the contracting carrier.

Article V

In relation to the carriage performed by the actual carrier, any servant or agent of that carrier or of the contracting carrier shall, if he proves that he acted within the scope of his employment, be entitled to avail himself of the limits of liability which are applicable under this Convention to the carrier whose servant or agent he is unless it is proved that he acted in a manner which, under the Warsaw Convention, prevents the limits of liability from being invoked.

Article VI

In relation to the carriage performed by the actual carrier, the aggregate of the amounts recoverable from that carrier and the contracting carrier, and from their servants and agents acting within the scope of their employment, shall not exceed the highest amount which could be awarded against either the contracting carrier or the actual carrier under this Convention, but none of the persons mentioned shall be liable for a sum in excess of the limit applicable to him.

Article VII

In relation to the carriage performed by the actual carrier, an action for damages may be brought, at the option of the plaintiff, against that carrier or the contracting carrier, or against both together or separately. If the action is brought against only one of those carriers, that carrier shall have the right to require the other carrier to be joined in the proceedings, the procedure and effects being governed by the law of the court seised of the case.

Article VIII

Any action for damages contemplated in Article VII of this Convention must be brought, at the option of the plaintiff, either before a court in which an action may be brought against the contracting carrier, as provided in Article 28 of the Warsaw Convention, or before the court having jurisdiction at the place where the actual carrier is ordinarily resident or has his principal place of business.

Article IX

1. Any contractual provision tending to relieve the contracting carrier or the actual carrier of liability under this Convention or to fix a lower limit than that which is applicable according to this Convention shall be null and void, but the nullity of any such

provision does not involve the nullity of the whole agreement, which shall remain subject to the provisions of this Convention.

2. In respect of the carriage performed by the actual carrier, the preceding paragraph shall not apply to contractual provisions governing loss or damage resulting from the inherent defect, quality or vice of the cargo carried.
3. Any clause contained in an agreement for carriage and all special agreements entered into before the damage occurred by which the parties purport to infringe the rules laid down by this Convention, whether by deciding the law to be applied, or by altering the rules as to jurisdiction, shall be null and void. Nevertheless, for the carriage of cargo arbitration clauses are allowed, subject to this Convention, if the arbitration is to take place in one of the jurisdictions referred to in Article VIII.

Article X

Except as provided in Article VII, nothing in this Convention shall affect the rights and obligations of the two carriers between themselves.

Articles XI to XVIII [Omitted].

Carriage of Goods by Road Act 1965

1 Convention to have force of law

Subject to the following provisions of this Act, the provisions of the Convention on the Contract for the International Carriage of Goods by Road (in this Act referred to as 'the Convention'), as set out in the Schedule to this Act, shall have the force of law in the United Kingdom so far as they relate to the rights and liabilities of persons concerned in the carriage of goods by road under a contract to which the Convention applies.

2–13 [Omitted]

14 Short title interpretation and commencement

(1) [Omitted].

(2) The persons who, for the purposes of this Act, are persons concerned in the carriage of goods by road under a contract to which the Convention applies are –

- (a) the sender;
- (b) the consignee;
- (c) any carrier who, in accordance with Article 34 in the Schedule to this Act or otherwise, is a party to the contract of carriage;
- (d) any person for whom such a carrier is responsible by virtue of Article 3 in the Schedule to this Act;
- (e) any person to whom the rights and liabilities of any of the persons referred to in paragraphs (a) to (d) of this subsection have passed (whether by assignment or assignation or by operation of law).

(3) and (4) [Omitted].

Schedule

Convention on the Contract for the International Carriage of Goods by Road

Chapter I Scope of application

Article 1

1. This Convention shall apply to every contract for the carriage of goods by road in vehicles for reward, when the place of taking over of the goods and the place designated for delivery, as specified in the contract, are situated in two different countries, of which at least one is a Contracting country, irrespective of the place of residence and the nationality of the parties.
2. For the purposes of this Convention, 'vehicles' means motor vehicles, articulated vehicles, trailers and semi-trailers as defined in Article 4 of the Convention on Road Traffic dated 19th September 1949.
3. This Convention shall apply also where carriage coming within its scope is carried out by States or by governmental institutions or organisations.
4. This Convention shall not apply –
   (a) to carriage performed under the terms of any international postal convention;
   (b) to funeral consignments;
   (c) to furniture removal.
5. The Contracting Parties agree not to vary any of the provisions of this Convention by special agreements between two or more of them, except to make it inapplicable to their frontier traffic or to authorise the use in transport operations entirely confined to their territory of consignment notes representing a title to the goods.

Article 2

1. Where the vehicle containing the goods is carried over part of the journey by sea, rail, inland waterways or air, and, except where the provisions of Article 14 are applicable, the goods are not unloaded from the vehicle, this Convention shall nevertheless apply to the whole of the carriage. Provided that to the extent that it is proved that any loss, damage or delay in delivery of the goods which occurs during the carriage by the other means of transport was not caused by an act or omission of the carrier by road, but by some event which could only have occurred in the course of and by reason of the carriage by that other means of transport, the liability of the carrier by road shall be determined not by this Convention, but in the manner in which the liability of the carrier by the other means of transport would have been determined if a contract for the carriage of the goods alone had been made by the sender with the carrier by the other means of transport in accordance with the conditions prescribed by law for the carriage of goods by that means of transport. If, however, there are no such prescribed conditions, the liability of the carrier by road shall be determined by this Convention.
2. If the carrier by road is also himself the carrier by the other means of transport, his liability shall also be determined in accordance with the provisions of paragraph 1 of this Article, but as if, in his capacities as carrier by road and as carrier by the other means of transport, he were two separate persons.

Chapter II Persons for whom the carrier is responsible

Article 3

For the purposes of this Convention the carrier shall be responsible for the acts and omissions of his agents and servants and of any other persons of whose services he makes use for the performance of the carriage, when such agents, servants or other persons are acting within the scope of their employment, as if such acts or omissions were his own.

Chapter III Conclusion and performance of the contract of carriage

Article 4

The contract of carriage shall be confirmed by the making out of a consignment note. The absence, irregularity or loss of the consignment note shall not affect the existence or the validity of the contract of carriage which shall remain subject to the provisions of this Convention.

Article 5

1. The consignment note shall be made out in three original copies signed by the sender and by the carrier. These signatures may be printed or replaced by the stamps of the sender and the carrier if the law of the country in which the consignment note has been made out so permits. The first copy shall be handed to the sender, the second shall accompany the goods and the third shall be retained by the carrier.
2. When the goods which are to be carried have to be loaded in different vehicles, or are of different kinds or are divided into different lots, the sender or the carrier shall have the right to require a separate consignment note to be made out for each vehicle used, or for each kind or lot of goods.

Article 6

1. The consignment note shall contain the following particulars –
   (a) the date of the consignment note and the place at which it is made out;
   (b) the name and address of the sender;
   (c) the name and address of the carrier;
   (d) the place and the date of taking over the goods and the place designated for delivery;
   (e) the name and address of the consignee;
   (f) the description in common use of the nature of the goods and the method of packing, and, in the case of dangerous goods, their generally recognised description;
   (g) the number of packages and their special marks and numbers;
   (h) the gross weight of the goods or their quantity otherwise expressed;
   (i) charges relating to the carriage (carriage charges, supplementary charges, customs duties and other charges incurred from the making of the contract to the time of delivery);
   (j) the requisite instructions for Customs and other formalities;

   (k) a statement that the carriage is subject, notwithstanding any clause to the contrary, to the provisions of this Convention.
2. Where applicable, the consignment note shall also contain the following particulars –
   (a) a statement that transhipment is not allowed;
   (b) the charges which the sender undertakes to pay;
   (c) the amount of 'cash on delivery' charges;
   (d) a declaration of the value of the goods and the amount representing special interest in delivery;
   (e) the sender's instructions to the carrier regarding insurance of the goods;
   (f) the agreed time-limit within which the carriage is to be carried out;
   (g) a list of the documents handed to the carrier.
3. The parties may enter in the consignment note any other particulars which they may deem useful.

Article 7

1. The sender shall be responsible for all expenses, loss and damage sustained by the carrier by reason of the inaccuracy or inadequacy of –
   (a) the particulars specified in Article 6, paragraph 1, (b), (d), (e), (f), (g), (h) and (j);
   (b) the particulars specified in Article 6, paragraph 2;
   (c) any other particulars or instructions given by him to enable the consignment note to be made out or for the purpose of their being entered therein.
2. If, at the request of the sender, the carrier enters in the consignment note the particulars referred to in paragraph 1 of this Article, he shall be deemed, unless the contrary is proved, to have done so on behalf of the sender.
3. If the consignment note does not contain the statement specified in Article 6, paragraph 1 (k), the carrier shall be liable for all expenses, loss and damage sustained through such omission by the person entitled to dispose of the goods.

Article 8

1. On taking over the goods, the carrier shall check –
   (a) the accuracy of the statements in the consignment note as to the number of packages and their marks and numbers, and
   (b) the apparent condition of the goods and their packaging.
2. Where the carrier has no reasonable means of checking the accuracy of the statements referred to in paragraph 1(a) of this Article, he shall enter his reservations in the consignment note together with the grounds on which they are based. He shall likewise specify the grounds for any reservations which he makes with regard to the apparent condition of the goods and their packaging. Such reservations shall not bind the sender unless he has expressly agreed to be bound by them in the consignment note.
3. The sender shall be entitled to require the carrier to check the gross weight of the goods or their quantity otherwise expressed. He may also require the contents of the packages to be checked. The carrier shall be entitled to claim the cost of such checking. The result of the checks shall be entered in the consignment note.

Article 9

1. The consignment note shall be *prima facie* evidence of the making of the contract of carriage, the conditions of the contract and the receipt of the goods by the carrier.
2. If the consignment note contains no specific reservations by the carrier, it shall be presumed, unless the contrary is proved, that the goods and their packaging appeared to be in good condition when the carrier took them over and that the number of packages, their marks and numbers corresponded with the statements in the consignment note.

Article 10

The sender shall be liable to the carrier for damage to persons, equipment or other goods, and for any expenses due to defective packing of the goods, unless the defect was apparent or known to the carrier at the time when he took over the goods and he made no reservations concerning it.

Article 11

1. For the purposes of the Customs or other formalities which have to be completed before delivery of the goods, the sender shall attach the necessary documents to the consignment note or place them at the disposal of the carrier and shall furnish him with all the information which he requires.
2. The carrier shall not be under any duty to enquire into either the accuracy or the adequacy of such documents and information. The sender shall be liable to the carrier for any damage caused by the absence, inadequacy or irregularity of such documents and information, except in the case of some wrongful act or neglect on the part of the carrier.
3. The liability of the carrier for the consequences arising from the loss or incorrect use of the documents specified in and accompanying the consignment note or deposited with the carrier shall be that of an agent, provided that the compensation payable by the carrier shall not exceed that payable in the event of loss of the goods.

Article 12

1. The sender has the right to dispose of the goods, in particular by asking the carrier to stop the goods in transit, to change the place at which delivery is to take place or to deliver the goods to a consignee other than the consignee indicated in the consignment notice.
2. The right shall cease to exist when the second copy of the consignment note is handed to the consignee or when the consignee exercises his right under Article 13, paragraph 1; from that time onwards the carrier shall obey the orders of the consignee.
3. The consignee shall, however, have the right of disposal from the time when the consignment note is drawn up, if the sender makes an entry to that effect in the consignment note.
4. If in exercising his right of disposal the consignee has ordered the delivery of the goods to another person, that other person shall not be entitled to name other consignees.
5. The exercise of the right of disposal shall be subject to the following conditions –
   (a) that the sender or, in the case referred to in paragraph 3 of this Article, the consignee who wishes to exercise the right produces the first copy of the consignment

note on which the new instructions to the carrier have been entered and indemnifies the carrier against all expenses, loss and damage involved in carrying out such instruction;

(b) that the carrying out of such instructions is possible at the time when the instructions reach the person who is to carry them out and does not either interfere with the normal working of the carrier's undertaking or prejudice the senders or consignees of other consignments;

(c) that the instructions do not result in a division of the consignment.

6. When, by reason of the provisions of paragraph 5(b) of this Article, the carrier cannot carry out the instructions which he receives, he shall immediately notify the person who give him such instructions.
7. A carrier who has not carried out the instructions given under the conditions provided for in this Article, or who has carried them out without requiring the first copy of the consignment note to be produced, shall be liable to the person entitled to make a claim for any loss or damage caused thereby.

Article 13

1. After arrival of the goods at the place designated for delivery, the consignee shall be entitled to require the carrier to deliver to him, against a receipt, the second copy of the consignment note and the goods. If the loss of the goods is established or if the goods have not arrived after the expiry of the period provided for in Article 19, the consignee shall be entitled to enforce in his own name against the carrier any rights arising from the contract of carriage.
2. The consignee who avails himself of the rights granted to him under paragraph 1 of this Article shall pay the charges shown to be due on the consignment note, but in the event of dispute on this matter the carrier shall not be required to deliver the goods unless security has been furnished by the consignee.

Article 14

1. If for any reason it is or becomes impossible to carry out the contract in accordance with the terms laid down in the consignment note before the goods reach the place designated for delivery, the carrier shall ask for instructions from the person entitled to dispose of the goods in accordance with the provisions of Article 12.
2. Nevertheless, if circumstances are such as to allow the carriage to be carried out under conditions differing from those laid down in the consignment note and if the carrier has been unable to obtain instructions in reasonable time from the person entitled to dispose of the goods in accordance with the provisions of Article 12, he shall take such steps as seem to him to be in the best interests of the person entitled to dispose of the goods.

Article 15

1. Where circumstances prevent delivery of the goods after their arrival at the place designated for delivery, the carrier shall ask the sender for his instructions. If the consignee

refuses the goods the sender shall be entitled to dispose of them without being obliged to produce the first copy of the consignment note.

2. Even if he has refused the goods, the consignee may nevertheless require delivery so long as the carrier has not received instruction to the contrary from the sender.
3. When circumstances preventing delivery of the goods arise after the consignee, in exercise of his rights under Article 12, paragraph 3, has given an order for the goods to be delivered to another person, paragraphs 1 and 2 of this Article shall apply as if the consignee were the sender and that other person were the consignee.

Article 16

1. The carrier shall be entitled to recover the cost of his request for instructions and any expenses entailed in carrying out such instructions, unless such expenses were caused by the wrongful act or neglect of the carrier.
2. In the cases referred to in Article 14, paragraph 1, and in Article 15, the carrier may immediately unload the goods for account of the person entitled to dispose of them and thereupon the carriage shall be deemed to be at an end. The carrier shall then hold the goods on behalf of the person so entitled. He may however entrust them to a third party, and in that case he shall not be under any liability except for the exercise of reasonable care in the choice of such third party. The charges due under the consignment note and all other expenses shall remain chargeable against the goods.
3. The carrier may sell the goods, without awaiting instructions from the person entitled to dispose of them, if the goods are perishable or their condition warrants such a course, or when the storage expenses would be out of proportion to the value of the goods. He may also proceed to the sale of the goods in other cases if after the expiry of a reasonable period he has not received from the person entitled to dispose of the goods instructions to the contrary which he may reasonably be required to carry out.
4. If the goods have been sold pursuant to this Article, the proceeds of sale, after deduction of the expenses chargeable against the goods, shall be placed at the disposal of the person entitled to dispose of the goods. If these charges exceed the proceeds of sale, the carrier shall be entitled to the difference.
5. The procedure in the case of sale shall be determined by the law or custom of the place where the goods are situated.

Chapter IV Liability of the carrier

Article 17

1. The carrier shall be liable for the total or partial loss of the goods and for damage thereto occurring between the time when he takes over the goods and time of delivery, as well as for any delay in delivery.
2. The carrier shall however be relieved of liability if the loss, damage or delay was caused by the wrongful act or neglect of the claimant, by the instructions of the claimant given otherwise than as the result of a wrongful act or neglect on the part of the carrier, by inherent vice of the goods or through circumstances which the carrier could not avoid and the consequences of which he was unable to prevent.

3. The carrier shall not be relieved of liability by reason of the defective condition of the vehicle used by him in order to perform the carriage, or by reason of the wrongful act or neglect of the person from whom he may have hired the vehicle or of the agents or servants of the latter.
4. Subject to Article 18, paragraphs 2 to 5, the carrier shall be relieved of liability when the loss or damage arises from the special risks inherent in one or more of the following circumstances –
   (a) use of open unsheeted vehicles, when their use has been expressly agreed and specified in the consignment note;
   (b) the lack of, or defective condition of packing in the case of goods which, by their nature, are liable to wastage or to be damaged when not packed or when not properly packed;
   (c) handling, loading, stowage or unloading of the goods by sender, the consignee or persons acting on behalf of the sender or the consignee;
   (d) the nature of certain kinds of goods which particularly exposes them to total or partial loss or to damage, especially through breakage, rust, decay, dessiccation, leakage, normal wastage, or the action of moths or vermin;
   (e) insufficiency or inadequacy of marks or numbers on the packages;
   (f) the carriage of livestock.
5. Where under this Article the carrier is not under any liability in respect of some of the factors causing the loss, damage or delay, he shall only be liable to the extent that those factors for which he is liable under this Article have contributed to the loss, damage or delay, he shall only be liable to the extent that those factors for which he is liable under this Article have contributed to the loss, damage or delay.

Article 18

1. The burden of proving that loss, damage or delay was due to one of the causes specified in Article 17, paragraph 2, shall rest upon the carrier.
2. When the carrier established that in the circumstances of the case, the loss or damage could be attributed to one or more of the special risks referred to in Article 17, paragraph 4, it shall be presumed that it was so caused. The claimant shall however be entitled to prove that the loss or damage was not, in fact, attributable either wholly or partly to one of these risks.
3. This presumption shall not apply in the circumstances set out in Article 17, paragraph 4 (a), if there has been an abnormal shortage, or a loss of any package.
4. If the carriage is performed in vehicles specially equipped to protect the goods from the effects of heat, cold, variations in temperature or the humidity of the air, the carrier shall not be entitled to claim the benefit of Article 17, paragraph 4(d), unless he proves that all steps incumbent on him in the circumstances with respect to the choice, maintenance and use of such equipment were taken and that he complied with any special instructions issued to him.
5. The carrier shall not be entitled to claim the benefit of Article 17, paragraph 4(f), unless he proves that all steps normally incumbent on him in the circumstances were taken and that he complied with any special instructions issued to him.

Article 19

Delay in delivery shall be said to occur when the goods have not been delivered within the agreed time-limit or when, failing an agreed time-limit, the actual duration of the carriage having regard to the circumstances of the case, and in particular, in the case of partial loads, the time required for making up a complete load in the normal way, exceeds the time it would be reasonable to allow a diligent carrier.

Article 20

1. The fact that goods have not been delivered within thirty days following the expiry of the agreed time-limit, or, if there is no agreed time-limit, within sixty days from the time when the carrier took over the goods, shall be conclusive evidence of the loss of the goods, and the person entitled to make a claim may thereupon treat them as lost.
2. The person so entitled may, on receipt of compensation for the missing goods, request in writing that he shall be notified immediately should the goods be recovered in the course of the year following the payment of compensation. He shall be given a written acknowledgement of such request.
3. Within the thirty days following receipt of such notification, the person entitled as aforesaid may require the goods to be delivered to him against payment of the charges shown to be due on the consignment note and also against refund of the compensation he received less any charges included therein but without prejudice to any claims to compensation for delay in delivery under Article 23 and, where applicable, Article 26.
4. In the absence of the request mentioned in paragraph 2 or of any instructions given within the period of thirty days specified in paragraph 3, or if the goods are not recovered until more than one year after the payment of compensation, the carrier shall be entitled to deal with them in accordance with the law of the place where the goods are situated.

Article 21

Should the goods have been delivered to the consignee without collection of the 'cash on delivery' charge which should have been collected by the carrier under the terms of the contract of carriage, the carrier shall be liable to the sender for compensation not exceeding the amount of such charge without prejudice to his right of action against the consignee.

Article 22

1. When the sender hands goods of a dangerous nature to the carrier, he shall inform the carrier of the exact nature of the danger and indicate, if necessary, the precautions to be taken. If this information has not been entered in the consignment note, the burden of proving, by some other means, that the carrier knew the exact nature of the danger constituted by the carriage of the said goods shall rest upon the sender or the consignee.
2. Goods of a dangerous nature which, in the circumstances referred to in paragraph 1 of this Article, the carrier did not know were dangerous, may, at any time or place, be unloaded, destroyed or rendered harmless by the carrier without compensation; further,

the sender shall be liable for all expenses, loss or damage arising out of their handing over for carriage or of their carriage.

Article 23

1. When, under the provisions of this Convention, a carrier is liable for compensation in respect of total or partial loss of goods, such compensation shall be calculated by reference to the value of the goods at the place and time at which they were accepted for carriage.
2. The value of the goods shall be fixed accordingly to the commodity exchange price or, if there is no such price, according to the current market price or, if there is no commodity exchange price or current market price, by reference to the normal value of goods of the same kind and quality.
3. Compensation shall not, however, exceed 8.33 units of account per kilogram of gross weight short.
4. In addition, the carriage charges, Customs duties and other charges incurred in respect of the carriage of the goods shall be refunded in full in case of total loss and in proportion to the loss sustained in case of partial loss, but no further damages shall be payable.
5. In the case of delay, if the claimant proves that damage has resulted therefrom the carrier shall pay compensation for such damage not exceeding the carriage charges.
6. Higher compensation may only be claimed where the value of the goods or a special interest in delivery has been declared in accordance with Articles 24 and 26.
7. The unit of account mentioned in this Convention is the Special Drawing Right as defined by the International Monetary Fund. The amount mentioned in paragraph 3 of this Article shall be converted into the national currency of the State of the Court seised of the case on the basis of the value of that currency on the date of the judgment or the date agreed upon by the Parties.

Article 24

The sender may, against payment of a surcharge to be agreed upon, declare in the consignment note a value for the goods exceeding the limit laid down in Article 23, paragraph 3, and in that case the amount of the declared value shall be substituted for that limit.

Article 25

1. In case of damage, the carrier shall be liable for the amount by which the goods have diminished in value, calculated by reference to the value of the goods fixed in accordance with Article 23, paragraphs 1, 2 and 4.
2. The compensation may not, however, exceed –
   (a) if the whole consignment has been damaged the amount payable in the case of total loss;
   (b) if part only of the consignment has been damaged, the amount payable in the case of loss of the part affected.

Article 26

1. The sender may, against payment of a surcharge to be agreed upon, fix the amount of a special interest in delivery in the case of loss or damage or of the agreed time-limit being exceeded, by entering such amount in the consignment note.
2. If a declaration of a special interest in delivery has been made, compensation for the additional loss or damage proved may be claimed, up to the total amount of the interest declared, independently of the compensation provided for in Articles 23, 24 and 25.

Article 27

1. The claimant shall be entitled to claim interest on compensation payable. Such interest, calculated at five per centum per annum, shall accrue from the date on which the claim was sent in writing to the carrier or, if no such claim has been made, from the date on which legal proceedings were instituted.
2. When the amounts on which the calculation of the compensation is based are not expressed in the currency of the country in which payment is claimed, conversion shall be at the rate of exchange applicable on the day and at the place of payment of compensation.

Article 28

1. In cases where, under the law applicable, loss, damage or delay arising out of carriage under this Convention gives rise to an extra-contractual claim, the carrier may avail himself of the provisions of this Convention which exclude his liability or which fix or limit the compensation due.
2. In cases where the extra-contractual liability for loss, damage or delay of one of the persons for whom the carrier is responsible under the terms of Article 3 is in issue, such person may also avail himself of the provisions of this Convention which exclude the liability of the carrier or which fix or limit the compensation due.

Article 29

1. The carrier shall not be entitled to avail himself of the provisions of this chapter which exclude or limit his liability or which shift the burden of proof if the damage was caused by his wilful misconduct or by such default on his part as, in accordance with the law of the court or tribunal seised of the case, is considered as equivalent to wilful misconduct.
2. The same provision shall apply if the wilful misconduct or default is committed by the agents or servants of the carrier or by any other persons of whose services he makes use for the performance of the carriage, when such agents, servants or other persons are acting within the scope of their employment. Furthermore, in such a case such agents, servants or other persons shall not be entitled to avail themselves, with regard to their personal liability, of the provisions of this chapter referred to in paragraph 1.

Chapter V Claims and actions

Article 30

1. If the consignee takes delivery of the goods without duly checking their condition with the carrier or without sending him reservations giving a general indication of the loss or damage, not later than the time of delivery in the case of apparent loss or damage and within seven days of delivery, Sundays and public holidays excepted, in the case of loss or damage which is not apparent, the fact of his taking delivery shall be *prima facie* evidence that he has received the goods in the condition described in the consignment note. In the case of loss or damage which is not apparent the reservations referred to shall be made in writing.
2. When the condition of the goods has been duly checked by the consignee and the carrier, evidence contradicting the result of this checking shall only be admissible in the case of loss or damage which is not apparent and provided that the consignee has duly sent reservations in writing to the carrier within seven days, Sundays and public holidays excepted, from the date of checking.
3. No compensation shall be payable for delay in delivery unless a reservation has been sent in writing to the carrier, within twenty-one days from the time that the goods were placed at the disposal of the consignee.
4. In calculating the time-limits provided for in this Article the date of delivery, or the date of checking, or the date when the goods were placed at the disposal of the consignee, as the case may be, shall not be included.
5. The carrier and the consignee shall give each other every reasonable facility for making the requisite investigations and checks.

Article 31

1. In legal proceedings arising out of carriage under this Convention, the plaintiff may bring an action in any court or tribunal of a contracting country designated by agreement between the parties and, in addition, in the courts or tribunals of a country within whose territory –
    (a) the defendant is ordinarily resident, or has his principal place of business, or the branch or agency through which the contract of carriage was made; or
    (b) the place where the goods were taken over by the carrier or the place designated for delivery is situated, and in no other courts or tribunals.
2. Where in respect of a claim referred to in paragraph 1 of this Article an action is pending before a court or tribunal competent under that paragraph, or where in respect of such a claim a judgment has been entered by such a court or tribunal no new action shall be started between the same parties on the same grounds unless the judgment of the court or tribunal before which the first action was brought is not enforceable in the country in which the fresh proceedings are brought.
3. When a judgment entered by a court or tribunal of a contracting country in any such action as is referred to in paragraph 1 of this Article has become enforceable in that country, it shall also become enforceable in each of the other contracting States, as soon as the formalities required in the country concerned have been complied with. The formalities shall not permit the merits of the case to be reopened.

4. The provisions of paragraph 3 of this Article shall apply to judgments after trial, judgments by default and settlements confirmed by an order of the court, but shall not apply to interim judgments or to awards of damages, in addition to costs against a plaintiff who wholly or partly fails in his action.
5. Security for costs shall not be required in proceedings arising out of carriage under the Convention from nationals of contracting countries resident or having their place of business in one of those countries.

Article 32

1. The period of limitation for an action arising out of carriage under this Convention shall be one year. Nevertheless, in the case of wilful misconduct, or such default as in accordance with the law of the court or tribunal seised of the case, is considered as equivalent to wilful misconduct, the period of limitation shall be three years. The period of limitation shall begin to run –
   (a) in the case of partial loss, damage or delay in delivery, from the date of delivery;
   (b) in the case of total loss, from the thirtieth day after the expiry of the agreed time-limit or where there is no agreed time-limit from the sixtieth day from the date on which the goods were taken over by the carrier;
   (c) in all other cases, on the expiry of a period of three months after the making of the contract of carriage.
   (d) The day on which the period of limitation begins to run shall not be included in the period.
2. A written claim shall suspend the period of limitation until such date as the carrier rejects the claim by notification in writing and returns the documents attached thereto. If a part of the claim is admitted the period of limitation shall start to run again only in respect of that part of the claim still in dispute. The burden of proof of the receipt of the claim, or of the reply and of the return of the documents, shall rest with the party relying upon these facts. The running of the period of limitation shall not be suspended by further claims having the same object.
3. Subject to the provisions of paragraph 2 above, the extension of the period of limitation shall be governed by the law of the court or tribunal seised of the case. That law shall also govern the fresh accrual of rights of action.
4. A right of action which has become barred by lapse of time may not be exercised by way of counter-claim or set-off.

Article 33

The contract of carriage may contain a clause conferring competence on an arbitration tribunal if the clause conferring competence on the tribunal provides that the tribunal shall apply this Convention.

Chapter VI Provisions relating to carriage performed by successive carriers

Article 34

If carriage governed by a single contract is performed by successive road carriers, each of them shall be responsible for the performance of the whole operation, the second carrier and each succeeding carrier becoming a party to the contract of carriage, under the terms of the consignment note, by reason of his acceptance of the goods and the consignment note.

Article 35

1. A carrier accepting the goods from a previous carrier shall give the latter a dated and signed receipt. He shall enter his name and address on the second copy of the consignment note. Where applicable, he shall enter on the second copy of the consignment note and on the receipt reservations of the kind provided for in Article 8, paragraph 2.
2. The provisions of Article 9 shall apply to the relations between successive carriers.

Article 36

Except in the case of a counter-claim or a set-off raised in an action concerning a claim based on the same contract of carriage, legal proceedings in respect of liability for loss, damage or delay may only be brought against the first carrier, the last carrier or the carrier who was performing that portion of the carriage during which the event causing the loss, damage or delay occurred; an action may be brought at the same time against several of these carriers.

Article 37

A carrier who has paid compensation in compliance with the provisions of this Convention, shall be entitled to recover such compensation, together with interest thereon and all costs and expenses incurred by reason of the claim, from the other carriers who have taken part in the carriage, subject to the following provisions –

(a) the carrier responsible for the loss or damage shall be solely liable for the compensation whether paid by himself or by another carrier;
(b) when the loss or damage has been caused by the action of two or more carriers, each of them shall pay an amount proportionate to his share of liability; should it be impossible to apportion the liability, each carrier shall be liable in proportion to the share of the payment for the carriage which is due to him;
(c) if it cannot be ascertained to which carriers liability is attributable for the loss or damage, the amount of the compensation shall be apportioned between all the carriers as laid down in (b) above.

Article 38

If one of the carriers is insolvent, the share of the compensation due from him and unpaid by him shall be divided among the other carriers in proportion to the share of the payment for the carriage due to them.

Article 39

1. No carrier against whom a claim is made under Articles 37 and 38 shall be entitled to dispute the validity of the payment made by the carrier making the claim if the amount

of the compensation was determined by judicial authority after the first mentioned carrier had been given due notice of the proceedings and afforded an opportunity of entering an appearance.

2. A carrier wishing to take proceedings to enforce his right of recovery may make his claim before the competent court or tribunal of the country in which one of the carriers concerned is ordinarily resident, or has his principal place of business or the branch or agency through which the contract of carriage was made. All the carriers concerned may be made defendants in the same action.
3. The provisions of Article 31, paragraphs 3 and 4, shall apply to judgments entered in the proceedings referred to in Articles 37 and 38.
4. The provisions of Article 32 shall apply to claims between carriers. The period of limitation shall, however, begin to run either on the date of the final judicial decision fixing the amount of compensation payable under the provisions of this Convention, or, if there is no such judicial decision, from the actual date of payment.

Article 40

Carriers shall be free to agree among themselves on provisions other than those laid down in Articles 37 and 38.

Chapter VII Nullity of stipulations contrary to the Convention

Article 41

1. Subject to the provisions of Article 40, any stipulation which would directly or indirectly derogate from the provisions of this Convention shall be null and void. The nullity of such a stipulation shall not involve the nullity of the other provisions of the contract.
2. In particular, a benefit of insurance in favour of the carrier or any other similar clause, or any clause shifting the burden of proof shall be null and void.

Protocol of Signature

1. This Convention shall not apply to traffic between the United Kingdom of Great Britain and Northern Ireland and the Republic of Ireland.

Uniform Laws on International Sales Act 1967

1 Application of Uniform Law on the International Sale of Goods

(1) In this Act 'the Uniform Law on Sales' means the Uniform Law on the International Sale of Goods forming the Annex to the First Convention and set out, with the modification provided for by Article III of that Convention, in Schedule 1 to this Act; and 'the First Convention' means the Convention relating to a Uniform Law on the International Sale of Goods done at The Hague on 1st July 1964.

(2) The Uniform Law on Sales shall, subject to the following provisions of this section, have the force of the law in the United Kingdom.

(3) While an Order of Her Majesty in Council is in force declaring that a declaration by the United Kingdom under Article V of the First Convention (application only by choice of parties) has been made and not withdrawn the Uniform Law on Sales shall apply to a contract of sale only if it has been chosen by the parties to the contract as the law of the contract.

(4) In determining the extent of the application of the Uniform Law on Sales by virtue of Article 4 thereof (choice of parties) –

(a) and (b) [Omitted];

(c) in relation to a contract made on or after 1 February 1978, no provision of that law shall be so regarded except sections 12 to 15B of the Sale of Goods Act 1979.

(5) to (8) [Omitted].

2 Application of Uniform Law on the Formation of Contracts for the International Sale of Goods

(1) In this Act 'the Uniform Law on Formation' means the Law forming Annex I to the Second Convention as set out, with the modifications provided for by paragraph 3 of Article I of that Convention, in Schedule 2 to this Act; and 'the Second Convention' means the Convention relating to a Uniform Law on the Formation of Contracts for the International Sale of Goods done at The Hague on 1st July 1964.

(2) Subject to subsection (3) of this section the Uniform Law on Formation shall have the force of law in the United Kingdom.

(3) The Uniform Law on Formation shall not apply to offers, replies and acceptances made before such date as Her Majesty may by Order in Council declare to be the date on which the Second Convention comes into force in respect of the United Kingdom.

(4) [Omitted].

3–5 [Omitted]

Schedules

Schedule 1 The Uniform Law on the International Sale of Goods

Chapter I Sphere of application of the Law

Article 1

1. The present Law shall apply to contracts of sale of goods entered into by parties whose places of business are in the territories of different Contracting States, in each of the following cases –
   (a) where the contract involves the sale of goods which are at the time of the conclusion of the contract in the course of carriage or will be carried from the territory of one State to the territory of another;
   (b) where the acts constituting the offer and the acceptance have been effected in the territories of different States;

   (c) where delivery of the goods is to be made in the territory of a State other than that within whose territory the acts constituting the offer and the acceptance have been effected.
2. Where a party to the contract does not have a place of business, reference shall be made to his habitual residence.
3. The application of the present Law shall not depend on the nationality of the parties.
4. In the case of contracts by correspondence, offer and acceptance shall be considered to have been effected in the territory of the same State only if the letters, telegrams or other documentary communications which contain them have been sent and received in the territory of that State.
5. For the purpose of determining whether the parties have their places of business or habitual residences in 'different States', any two or more States shall not be considered to be 'different State' if a valid declaration to that effect made under Article II of the Convention dated the 1st day of July 1964 relating to a Uniform Law on the International Sale of Goods is in force in respect of them.

Article 2

Rules of private international law shall be excluded for the purposes of the application of the present Law, subject to any provision to the contrary in the said Law.

Article 3

The parties to a contract of sale shall be free to exclude the application thereto of the present Law either entirely or partially. Such exclusion may be express or implied.

Article 4

The present Law shall also apply where it has been chosen as the law of the contract by the parties, whether or not their places of business or their habitual residences are in different States and whether or not such States are Parties to the Convention dated the 1st day of July 1964 relating to the Uniform Law on the International Sale of Goods, to the extent that it does not affect the application of any mandatory provisions of law which would have been applicable if the parties had not chosen the Uniform Law.

Article 5

1. The present Law shall not apply to sales –
   (a) of stocks, shares, investment securities, negotiable instruments or money;
   (b) of any ship, vessel or aircraft, which is or will be subject to registration;
   (c) of electricity;
   (d) by authority of law or on execution or distress.
2. The present Law shall not affect the application of any mandatory provision of national law for the protection of a party to a contract which contemplates the purchase of goods by that party by payment of the price by instalments.

Article 6

Contracts for the supply of goods to be manufactured or produced shall be considered to be sales within the meaning of the present Law, unless the party who orders the goods undertakes to supply an essential and substantial part of the materials necessary for such manufacture or production.

Article 7

The present Law shall apply to sales regardless of the commercial or civil character of the parties or of the contracts.

Article 8

The present Law shall govern only the obligations of the seller and the buyer arising from a contract of sale. In particular, the present Law shall not, except as otherwise expressly provided there, be concerned with the formation of the contract, nor with the effect which the contract may have on the property in the goods sold, nor with the validity of the contract or of any of its provisions or of any usage.

Chapter II General provisions

Article 9

1. The parties shall be bound by any usage which they have expressly or impliedly made applicable to their contract and by any practices which they have established between themselves.
2. They shall also be bound by usages which reasonable persons in the same situation as the parties usually consider to be applicable to their contract. In the event of conflict with the present Law, the usages shall prevail unless otherwise agreed by the parties.
3. Where expressions, provisions or forms of contract commonly used in commercial practice are employed, they shall be interpreted according to the meaning usually given to them in the trade concerned.

Article 10

For the purposes of the present Law, a breach of contract shall be regarded as fundamental wherever the party in breach knew, or ought to have known, at the time of the conclusion of the contract, that a reasonable person in the same situation as the other party would not have entered into the contract if he had foreseen the breach and its effects.

Article 11

Where under the present Law an act is required to be performed 'promptly', it shall be performed within as short a period as possible, in the circumstances, from the moment when the act could reasonably be performed.

Article 12

For the purposes of the present Law, the expression 'current price' means a price based upon an official market quotation, or, in the absence of such a quotation, upon those factors which, according to the usage of the market, serve to determine the price.

Article 13

For the purposes of the present Law, the expression 'a party knew or ought to have known', or any similar expression, refers to what should have been known to a reasonable person in the same situation.

Article 14

Communications provided for by the present Law shall be made by the means usual in the circumstances.

Article 15

A contract of sale need not be evidenced by writing and shall not be subject to any other requirements as to form. In particular, it may be proved by means of witnesses.

Article 16

Where under the provisions of the present Law one party to a contract of sale is entitled to require performance of any obligation by the other party, a court shall not be bound to enter or enforce a judgment providing for specific performance except in accordance with the provisions of Article VII of the Convention dated the 1st day of July 1964 relating to a Uniform Law on the International Sale of Goods.

Article 17

Questions concerning matters governed by the present Law which are not expressly settled therein shall be settled in conformity with the general principals on which the present Law is based.

Chapter III Obligations of the seller

Article 18

The seller shall effect delivery of the goods, hand over any documents relating thereto and transfer the property in the goods, as required by the contract and the present Law.

Section I – Delivery of the goods

Article 19

1. Delivery consists in the handing over of goods which conform with the contract.

2. Where the contract of sale involves carriage of the goods and no other place for delivery has been agreed upon, delivery shall be effected by handing over the goods to the carrier for transmission to the buyer.
3. Where the goods handed over to the carrier are not clearly appropriated to performance of the contract by being marked with an address or by some other means, the seller shall, in addition to handing over the goods, sent to the buyer notice of the consignment and, if necessary, some document specifying the goods.

Sub-Section 1. Obligations of the seller as regards the date and place of delivery

A – Date of Delivery

Article 20

Where the parties have agreed upon a date for delivery or where such date is fixed by usage, the seller shall, without the need for any other formality, be bound to deliver the goods at that date, provided that the date thus fixed is determined or determinable by the calendar or is fixed in relation to a definite event, the date of which can be ascertained by the parties.

Article 21

Where by agreement of the parties or by usage delivery shall be effected within a certain period (such as a particular month or season), the seller may fix the precise date of delivery, unless the circumstances indicate that the fixing of the date was reserved to the buyer.

Article 22

Where the date of delivery has not been determined in accordance with the provisions of Articles 20 or 21, the seller shall be bound to deliver the goods within a reasonable time after the conclusion of the contract, regard being had to the nature of the goods and to the circumstances.

B – Place of delivery

Article 23

1. Where the contract of sale does not involve carriage of the goods, the seller shall deliver the goods at the place where he carried on business at the time of the conclusion of the contract, or, in the absence of a place of business, at his habitual residence.
2. If the sale relates to specific goods and the parties knew that the goods were at a certain place at the time of the conclusion of the contract, the seller shall deliver the goods at that place. The same rule shall apply if the goods sold are unascertained goods to be taken from a specified stock or if they are to be manufactured or produced at a place known to the parties at the time of the conclusion of the contract.

C – Remedies for the seller's failure to perform his obligations as regards the date and place of delivery

Article 24

1. Where the seller fails to perform his obligations as regards the date or the place of delivery, the buyer may, as provided in Articles 25 to 32 –
   (a) require performance of the contract by the seller;
   (b) declare the contract avoided.
2. The buyer may also claim damages as provided in Article 82 or in Articles 84 to 87.
3. In no case shall the seller be entitled to apply to a court or arbitral tribunal to grant him a period of grace.

Article 25

The buyer shall not be entitled to require performance of the contract by the seller, if it is in conformity with usage and reasonably possible for the buyer to purchase goods to replace those to which the contract relates. In this case the contract shall be *ipso facto* avoided as from the time when such purchases should be effected.

(a) Remedies as regards the date of delivery

Article 26

1. Where the failure to deliver the goods at the date fixed amounts to a fundamental breach of the contract, the buyer may either require performance by the seller or declare the contract avoided. He shall inform the seller of his decision within a reasonable time; otherwise the contract shall be *ipso facto* avoided.
2. If the seller requests the buyer to make known his decision under paragraph 1 of this Article and the buyer does not comply promptly, the contract shall be *ipso facto* avoided.
3. If the seller has effected delivery before the buyer has made known his decision under paragraph 1 of this Article and the buyer does not exercise promptly his right to declare the contract avoided, the contract cannot be avoided.
4. Where the buyer has chosen performance of the contract and does not obtain it within a reasonable time, he may declare the contract avoided.

Article 27

1. Where failure to deliver the goods at the date fixed does not amount to a fundamental breach of the contract, the seller shall retain the right to effect delivery and the buyer shall retain the right to require performance of the contract by the seller.
2. The buyer may however grant the seller an additional period of time of reasonable length. Failure to deliver the goods at the date fixed shall amount to a fundamental breach of the contract whenever a price for such goods is quoted on a market where the buyer can obtain them.

Article 28

Failure to deliver the goods at the date fixed shall amount to a fundamental breach of the contract whenever a price for such goods is quoted on a market where the buyer can obtain them.

Article 29

Where the seller tenders delivery of the goods before the date fixed, the buyer may accept or reject delivery; if he accepts, he may reserve the right to claim damages in accordance with Article 82.

(b) Remedies as regards the place of delivery

Article 30

1. Where failure to deliver the goods at the place fixed amounts to a fundamental breach of the contract, and failure to deliver the goods at the date fixed would also amount to a fundamental breach, the buyer may either require performance of the contract by the seller or declare the contract avoided. The buyer shall inform the seller of his decision within a reasonable time; otherwise the contract shall be *ipso facto* avoided.
2. If the seller requests the buyer to make known his decision under paragraph 1 of this Article and the buyer does not comply promptly, the contract shall be *ipso facto* avoided.
3. If the seller has transported the goods to the place fixed before the buyer has made known his decision under paragraph 1 of this Article and the buyer does not exercise promptly his right to declare the contract avoided, the contract cannot be avoided.

Article 31

1. In cases not provided for in Article 30, the seller shall retain the right to effect delivery at the place fixed and the buyer shall retain the right to require performance of the contract by the seller.
2. The buyer may however grant the seller an additional period of time of reasonable length. Failure to deliver within this period at the place fixed shall amount to a fundamental breach of the contract.

Article 32

1. If delivery is to be effected by handing over the goods to a carrier and the goods have been handed over at a place other than that fixed, the buyer may declare the contract avoided, whenever the failure to deliver the goods at the place fixed amounts to a fundamental breach of the contract. He shall lose this right if he has not promptly declared the contract avoided.
2. The buyer shall have the same right, in the circumstances and on the conditions provided in paragraph 1 of this Article, if the goods have been despatched to some place other than that fixed.
3. If despatch from a place or to a place other than that fixed does not amount to a fundamental breach of the contract, the buyer may only claim damages in accordance with Article 82.

Sub-Section 2. Obligations of the seller as regards the conformity of the goods

A – Lack of conformity

Article 33

1. The seller shall not have fulfilled his obligation to deliver the goods, where he has handed over –
   (a) part only of the goods sold or a larger or a smaller quantity of the goods than he contracted to sell;
   (b) goods which are not those to which the contract relates or goods of a different kind;
   (c) goods which lack the qualities of a sample or model which the seller has handed over or sent to the buyer, unless the seller has submitted it without any express or implied undertaking that the goods would conform therewith;
   (d) goods which do not possess the qualities necessary for their ordinary or commercial use;
   (e) goods which do not possess the qualities for some particular purpose expressly or impliedly contemplated by the contract;
   (f) in general, goods which do not possess the qualities and characteristics expressly or impliedly contemplated by the contract.
2. No difference in quantity, lack of part of the goods or absence of any quality or characteristic shall be taken into consideration where it is not material.

Article 34

In the cases to which Article 33 relates, the rights conferred on the buyer by the present Law exclude all other remedies based on lack of conformity of the goods.

Article 35

1. Whether the goods are in conformity with the contract shall be determined by their condition at the time when risk passes. However, if risk does not pass because of a declaration of avoidance of the contract or of a demand for other goods in replacement, the conformity of the goods with the contract shall be determined by their condition at the time when risk would have passed had they been in conformity with the contract.
2. The seller shall be liable for the consequences of any lack of conformity occurring after the time fixed in paragraph 1 of this Article if it was due to an act of the seller or of a person for whose conduct he is responsible.

Article 36

The seller shall not be liable for the consequences of any lack of conformity of the kind referred to in sub-paragraphs (d), (e) or (f) of paragraph 1 of Article 33, if at the time of the conclusion of the contract the buyer knew, or could not have been unaware of, such lack of conformity.

Article 37

If the seller has handed over goods before the date fixed for delivery he may, up to that date, deliver other goods which are in conformity with the contract or remedy any defects in the goods handed over, provided that the exercise of this right does not cause the buyer either unreasonable inconvenience or unreasonable expense.

B – Ascertainment and notification of lack of conformity

Article 38

1. The buyer shall examine the goods, or cause them to be examined, promptly.
2. In case of carriage of the goods the buyer shall examine them at the place of destination.
3. If the goods are redespatched by the buyer without transhipment and the seller knew or ought to have known, at the time when the contract was concluded, of the possibility of such redespatch, examination of the goods may be deferred until they arrive at the new destination.
4. The methods of examination shall be governed by the agreement of the parties or, in the absence of such agreement, by the law or usage of the place where the examination is to be effected.

Article 39

1. The buyer shall lose the right to rely on a lack of conformity of the goods if he has not given the seller notice thereof promptly after he has discovered the lack of conformity or ought to have discovered it. If a defect which could not have been revealed by the examination of the goods provided for in Article 38 is found later, the buyer may nonetheless rely on that defect, provided that he gives the seller notice thereof promptly after its discovery. In any event, the buyer shall lose the right to rely on a lack of conformity of the goods if he has not given notice thereof to the seller within a period of two years from the date on which the goods were handed over, unless the lack of conformity constituted a breach of a guarantee covering a longer period.
2. In giving notice to the seller of any lack of conformity, the buyer shall specify its nature and invite the seller to examine the goods or to cause them to be examined by his agent.
3. Where any notice referred to in paragraph 1 of this Article has been sent by letter, telegram or other appropriate means, the fact that such notice is delayed or fails to arrive at its destination shall not deprive the buyer of the right to rely thereon.

Article 40

The seller shall not be entitled to rely on the provisions of Articles 38 and 39 if the lack of conformity relates to facts of which he knew, or of which he could not have been unaware, and which he did not disclose.

C – Remedies for lack of conformity

Article 41

1. Where the buyer has given due notice to the seller of the failure of the goods to confirm with the contract, the buyer may, as provided in Articles 42 to 46 –

   (a) require performance of the contract by the seller;
   (b) declare the contract avoided;
   (c) reduce the price.
2. The buyer may also claim damages as provided in Article 82 or in Articles 84 to 87.

Article 42

1. The buyer may require the seller to perform the contract –
   (a) if the sale relates to goods to be produced or manufactured by the seller, by remedying defects in the goods, provided the seller is in a position to remedy the defects;
   (b) if the sales relates to specific goods, by delivering the goods to which the contract refers or the missing part thereof;
   (c) if the sale relates to unascertained goods, by delivering other goods which are in conformity with the contract or by delivering the missing part or quantity, except where the purchase of goods in replacement is in conformity with usage and reasonably possible.
2. If the buyer does not obtain performance of the contract by the seller within a reasonable time, he shall retain the rights provided in Articles 43 to 46.

Article 43

The buyer may declare the contract avoided if the failure of the goods to conform to the contract and also the failure to deliver on the date fixed amount to fundamental breaches of the contract. The buyer shall lose his right to declare the contract avoided if he does not exercise it promptly after giving the seller notice of the lack of conformity or, in the case to which paragraph 2 of Article 42 applies, after the expiration of the period referred to in that paragraph.

Article 44

1. In cases not provided for in Article 43, the seller shall retain, after the date fixed for the delivery of the goods, the right to deliver any missing part or quantity of the goods or to deliver other goods which are in conformity with the contract or to remedy any defect in the goods handed over, provided that the exercise of this right does not cause the buyer either unreasonable inconvenience or unreasonable expense.
2. The buyer may however fix an additional period of time of reasonable length for the further delivery or for the remedying of the defect. If at the expiration of the additional period the seller has not delivered to goods or remedied the defect, the buyer may choose between requiring the performance of the contract or reducing the price in accordance with Article 46 or, provided that he does so promptly, declare the contract avoided.

Article 45

1. Where the seller has handed over part only of the goods or an insufficient quantity or where part only of the goods handed over is in conformity with the contract, the provisions of Articles 43 and 44 shall apply in respect of the part or quantity which is missing or which does not conform with the contract.

2. The buyer may declare the contract avoided in its entirety only if the failure to effect delivery completely and in conformity with the contract amounts to a fundamental breach of the contract.

Article 46

Where the buyer has neither obtained performance of the contract by the seller nor declared the contract avoided, the buyer may reduce the price in the same proportion as the value of the goods at the time of the conclusion of the contract has been diminished because of their lack of conformity with the contract.

Article 47

Where the seller has proffered to the buyer a quantity of unascertained goods greater than that provided for in the contract, the buyer may reject or accept the excess quantity. If the buyer rejects the excess quantity, the seller shall be liable only for damages in accordance with Article 82. If the buyer accepts the whole or part of the excess quantity, he shall pay for it at the contract rate.

Article 48

The buyer may exercise the rights provided in Articles 43 to 46, even before the time fixed for delivery, if it is clear that goods which would be handed over would not be in conformity with the contract.

Article 49

1. The buyer shall lose his right to reply on lack of conformity with the contract at the expiration of a period of one year after he has given notice as provided in Article 39, unless he has been prevented from exercising his right because of fraud on the part of the seller.
2. After the expiration of this period, the buyer shall not be entitled to rely on the lack of conformity, even by way of defence to an action. Nevertheless, if the buyer has not paid for the goods and provided that he has given due notice of the lack of conformity promptly, as provided in Article 39, he may advance as a defence to a claim for payment of the price a claim for a reduction in the price or for damages.

Section II – Handing over documents

Article 50

Where the seller is bound to hand over to the buyer any documents relating to the goods, he shall do so at the time and place fixed by the contract or by usage.

Article 51

If the seller fails to hand over the documents as provided in Article 50 at the time and place fixed or if he hands over documents which are not in conformity with those which he was bound to hand over, the buyer shall have the same rights as those provided under Articles 24 to 32 or under Articles 41 to 49, as the case may be.

Section III – Transfer of property

Article 52

1. Where the goods are subject to a right or claim of a third person, the buyer, unless he agreed to take the goods subject to such right or claim, shall notify the seller of such right or claim, unless the seller already knows thereof, and request that the goods should be freed therefrom within reasonable time or that other goods free from all rights and claims of third persons to be delivered to him by the seller.
2. If the seller complies with a request made under paragraph 1 of this Article and the buyer nevertheless suffers a loss, the buyer may claim damages in accordance with Article 82.
3. If the seller fails to comply with a request made under paragraph 1 of the Article and a fundamental breach of the contract results thereby, the buyer may declare the contract avoided and claim damages in accordance with Articles 84 to 87. If the buyer does not declare the contract avoided or if there is no fundamental breach of the contract, the buyer shall have the right to claim damages in accordance with Article 82.
4. The buyer shall lose his right to declare the contract avoided if he fails to act in accordance with paragraph 1 of this Article within a reasonable time from the moment when he became aware or ought to have become aware of the right or claim of the third person in respect of the goods.

Article 53

The rights conferred on the buyer by Article 52 exclude all other remedies based on the fact that the seller has failed to perform his obligation to transfer the property in the goods or that the goods are subject to a right or claim of a third person.

Section IV – Other oligations of the seller

Article 54

1. If the seller is bound to despatch the goods to the buyer, he shall make, in the usual way and on the usual terms, such contracts as are necessary for the carriage of the goods to the place fixed.
2. If the seller is not bound by the contract to effect insurance in respect of the carriage of the goods, he shall provide the buyer, at his request, with all information necessary to enable him to effect such insurance.

Article 55

1. If the seller fails to perform any obligation other than those referred to in Articles 20 to 53, the buyer may –
   (a) where such failure amounts to a fundamental breach of the contract, declare the contract avoided, provided that he does so promptly, and claim damages in accordance with Articles 84 to 87, or

(b) in any other case, claim damages in accordance with Article 82.

2. The buyer may also require performance by the seller of his obligation unless the contract is avoided.

Chapter IV Obligations of the buyer

Article 56

The buyer shall pay the price for the goods and take delivery of them, as required by the contract and the present law.

Section I – Payment of the price

A – Fixing the price

Article 57

Where a contract has been concluded but does not state a price or make provision for the determination of the price, the buyer shall be bound to pay the price generally charged by the seller at the time of the conclusion of the contract.

Article 58

Where the price is fixed according to the weight of the goods, it shall, in case of doubt, be determined by the net weight.

B – Place and date of payment

Article 59

1. The buyer shall pay the price to the seller at the seller's place of business or, if he does not have a place of business, at his habitual residence, or where the payment is to be made against the handing over of the goods or of documents, at the place where such handing over takes place.
2. Where in consequence of a change in the place of business or habitual residence of the seller subsequent to the conclusion of the contract, the expenses incidental to payment are increased, such increase shall be borne by the seller.

Article 60

Where the parties have agreed upon a date for the payment of the price or where such a date is fixed by usage, the buyer shall, without the need for any other formality, pay the price at that date.

C – Remedies for non-payment

Article 61

1. If the buyer fails to pay the price in accordance with the contract and with the present law, the seller may require the buyer to perform his obligation.

2. The seller shall not be entitled to require payment of the price by the buyer if it is in conformity with usage and reasonably possible for the seller to resell the goods. In that case the contract shall be *ipso facto* avoided as from the time when such resale should be effected.

Article 62

1. Where failure to pay the price at the date fixed amounts to a fundamental breach of the contract, the seller may either require the buyer to pay the price or declare the contract avoided. He shall inform the buyer of his decision within a reasonable time; otherwise the contract shall be *ipso facto* avoided.
2. Where the failure to pay the price at the date fixed does not amount to a fundamental breach of the contract, the seller may grant to the buyer an additional period of time of reasonable length. If the buyer has not paid the price at the expiration of the additional period, the seller may either require the payment of the price by the buyer or provided that he does so promptly, declare the contract avoided.

Article 63

1. Where the contract is avoided because of failure to pay the price, the seller shall have the right to claim damages in accordance with Articles 84 to 87.
2. Where the contract is not avoided, the seller shall have the right to claim damages in accordance with Articles 82 and 83.

Article 64

In no case shall the buyer be entitled to apply to a court or arbitral tribunal to grant him a period of grace for the payment of the price.

Section II – Taking delivery

Article 65

Taking delivery consists in the buyer's doing all such acts as are necessary in order to enable the seller to hand over the goods and actually taking them over.

Article 66

1. Where the buyer's failure to take delivery of the goods in accordance with the contract amounts to a fundamental breach of the contract or gives the seller good grounds for fearing that the buyer will not pay the price, the seller may declare the contract avoided.
2. Where the failure to take delivery of the goods does not amount to a fundamental breach of contract, the seller may grant to the buyer an additional period, the seller may declare the contract avoided, provided that he does so promptly.

Article 67

1. If the contract reserves to the buyer the right subsequently to determine the form, measurement or other features of the goods (sale by specification) and he fails to make such

specification either on the date expressly or impliedly agreed upon or within a reasonable time after receipt of a request from the seller, the seller may declare the contract avoided, provided that he does so promptly, or to make the specification himself in accordance with the requirements of the buyer in so far as these are known to him.

2. If the seller makes the specification himself, he shall inform the buyer of the details thereof and shall fix a reasonable period of time within which the buyer may submit a different specification. If the buyer fails to do so the specification made by the seller shall be binding.

Article 68

1. Where the contract is avoided because of the failure of the buyer to accept delivery of the goods or to make a specification, the seller shall have the right to claim damages in accordance with Articles 84 to 87.
2. Where the contract is not avoided, the seller shall have the right to claim damages in accordance with Article 82.

Section III – Other obligations of the buyer

Article 69

The buyer shall take the steps provided for in the contract, by usage or by laws and regulations in force, for the purpose of making provision for or guaranteeing payment of the price, such as the acceptance of a bill of exchange, the opening of a documentary credit or the giving of a banker's guarantee.

Article 70

1. If the buyer fails to perform any obligation other than those referred to in Sections I and II of this Chapter, the seller may –
   (a) where such failure amounts to a fundamental breach of the contract, declare the contract avoided, provided that he does so promptly, and claim damages in accordance with Articles 84 to 87; or
   (b) in any other case, claim damages in accordance with Article 82.
2. The seller may also require performance by the buyer of his obligation, unless the contract is avoided.

Chapter V Provisions common to the obligations of the seller and of the buyer

Section I – Concurrence between delivery of the goods and payment of the price

Article 71

Except as otherwise provided in Article 72, delivery of the goods and payment of the price shall be concurrent conditions. Nevertheless, the buyer shall not be obliged to pay the price until he has had an opportunity to examine the goods.

Article 72

1. Where the contract involves carriage of the goods and where delivery is by virtue of paragraph 2 of Article 19, effected by handing over the goods to the carrier, the seller may either postpone despatch of the goods until he receives payment or proceed to despatch them on terms that reserve to himself the right of disposal of the goods during transit. In the latter case, he may require that the goods shall not be handed over to the buyer at the place of destination except against payment of the price and the buyer shall not be bound to pay the price until he has had an opportunity to examine the goods.
2. Nevertheless, when the contract requires payment against documents, the buyer shall not be entitled to refuse payment of the price on the ground that he has not had the opportunity to examine the goods.

Article 73

1. Each party may suspend the performance of his obligations whenever, after the conclusion of the contract, the economic situation of the other party appears to have become so difficult that there is good reason to fear that he will not perform a material part of his obligations.
2. If the seller has already despatched the goods before the economic situation of the buyer described in paragraph 1 of this Article becomes evident, he may prevent the handing over of the goods to the buyer even if the latter holds a document which entitles him to obtain them.
3. Nevertheless, the seller shall not be entitled to prevent the handing over of the goods if they are claimed by a third person who is a lawful holder of a document which entitles him to obtain the goods unless the document contains a reservation concerning the effects of its transfer or unless the seller can prove that the holder of the document when he acquired it, knowingly acted to the detriment of the seller.

Section II – Exemptions

Article 74

1. Where one of the parties has not performed one of his obligations, he shall not be liable for such non-performance if he can prove that it was due to circumstances which according to the intention of the parties at the time of the conclusion of the contract, he was not bound to take into account or to avoid or to overcome; in the absence of any expression of the intention of the parties, regard shall be had to what reasonable persons in the same situation would have intended.
2. Where the circumstances which gave rise to the non-performance of the obligation constituted only a temporary impediment to performance, the party in default shall nevertheless be permanently relieved of his obligation if, by reason of the delay, performance would be so radically changed as to amount to the performance of an obligation quite different from that contemplated by the contract.
3. The relief provided by this Article for one of the parties shall not include the avoidance of the contract under some other provision of the present Law or deprive the other party of any right which he has under the present Law to reduce the price, unless the

circumstances which entitled the first party to relief were caused by the act of the other party or of some person for whose conduct he was responsible.

Section III – Supplementary rules concerning the avoidance of the contract

A – Supplementary grounds for avoidance

Article 75

1. Where, in the case of contracts for delivery of goods by instalments, by reason of any failure by one party of his obligations under the contract in respect of any instalment, the other party has good reason to fear failure of performance in respect of future instalments, he may declare the contract avoided for the future, provided that he does so promptly.
2. The buyer may also, provided that he does so promptly, declare the contract avoided in respect of future deliveries or in respect of deliveries already made or both, if by reason of their interdependence such deliveries would be worthless to him.

Article 76

Where prior to the date fixed for performance of the contract it is clear that one of the parties will commit a fundamental breach of the contract, the other party shall have the right to declare the contract avoided.

Article 77

Where the contract has been avoided under Article 75 or Article 76, the party declaring the contract avoided may claim damages in accordance with Articles 84 to 87.

B – Effects of avoidance

Article 78

1. Avoidance of the contract releases both parties from their obligations thereunder, subject to any damages which may be due.
2. If one party has performed the contract either wholly or in part, he may claim the return of whatever he has supplied or paid under the contract. If both parties are required to make restitution, they shall do so concurrently.

Article 79

1. The buyer shall lose his right to declare the contract avoided where it is impossible for him to return the goods in the condition in which he received them.
2. Nevertheless, the buyer may declare the contract avoided –
   (a) if the goods or part of the goods have perished or deteriorated as a result of the defect which justifies the avoidance;
   (b) if the goods or part of the goods have perished or deteriorated as a result of the examination prescribed in Article 38;

(c) if part of the goods have been consumed or transformed by the buyer in the course of normal use before the lack of conformity with the contract was discovered;
(d) if the impossibility of returning the goods or of returning them in the condition in which they were received is not due to the act of the buyer, or of some other person for whose conduct he is responsible;
(e) if the deterioration of transformation of the goods is unimportant.

Article 80

The buyer who has lost the right to declare the contract avoided by virtue of Article 79 shall retain all the other rights conferred on him by the present Law.

Article 81

1. Where the seller is under an obligation to refund the price, he shall also be liable for the interest thereon at the rate fixed by Article 83, as from the date of payment.
2. The buyer shall be liable to account to the seller for all benefits which he has derived from the goods or part of them, as the case may be –
   (a) where he is under an obligation to return the goods or part of them;
   (b) where it is impossible for him to return the goods or part of them, but the contract is nevertheless avoided.

Section IV – Supplementary rules concerning damages

A – Damages where the contract is not avoided

Article 82

Where the contract is not avoided, damages for a breach of contract by one party shall consist of a sum equal to the loss of profit, suffered by the other party. Such damages shall not exceed the loss which the party in breach ought to have foreseen at the time of the conclusion of the contract, in the light of the facts and matters which then were known or ought to have been known to him, as a possible consequence of the breach of the contract.

Article 83

Where the breach of contract consists of delay in the payment of the price, the seller shall in any event be entitled to interest on such sum as in arrear at a rate equal to the official discount rate in the country where he has his place of business, or if he has no place of business, his habitual residence, plus 1%.

B – Damages where the contract is avoided

Article 84

1. In the case of avoidance of the contract, where there is a current price for the goods, damages shall be equal to the difference between the price fixed by the contract and the current price on the date on which the contract is avoided.

2. In calculating the amount of damages under paragraph 1 of this Article, the current price to be taken into account shall be that prevailing in the market in which the transaction took place, if there is no such current price or if its application is inappropriate, the price in a market which serves as a reasonable substitute, making due allowance for differences in the cost of transporting goods.

Article 85

If the buyer has bought goods in replacement or the seller has resold goods in a reasonable manner, he may recover the difference between the contract price and the price paid for the goods bought in replacement or that obtained by the resale.

Article 86

The damages referred to in Articles 84 and 85 may be increased by the amount of any reasonable expenses incurred as a result of the breach or up to the amount of any loss, including loss of profit, which should have been foreseen by the party in breach, at the time of the conclusion of the contract, in the light of the facts and matters which were known or ought to have been known to him, as a possible consequence of the breach of the contract.

Article 87

If there is no current price for the goods, damages shall be calculated on the same basis as that provided in Article 82.

C – General provisions concerning damages

Article 88

The party who relies on a breach of the contract shall adopt all reasonable measures to mitigate the loss resulting from the breach. If he fails to adopt such measures, the party in breach may claim reduction in the damages.

Article 89

In case of fraud, damages shall be determined by the rules applicable in respect of contracts of sale not governed by the present law.

Section V – Expenses

Article 90

The expenses of delivery shall be borne by the seller; all expenses after delivery shall be borne by the buyer.

Section VI – Preservation of the goods

Article 91

Where the buyer is in delay in taking delivery of the goods or in paying the price, the seller shall take reasonable steps to preserve the goods; he shall have the right to retain them until he has been reimbursed his reasonable expenses by the buyer.

Article 92

1. Where the goods have been received by the buyer, he shall take reasonable steps to preserve them if he intends to reject them: he shall have the right to retain them until he has been reimbursed his reasonable expenses by the seller.
2. Where the goods despatched to the buyer have been put at his disposal at their place of destination and he exercises the right to reject them he shall be bound to take possession of them on behalf of the seller, provided that this may be done without payment of the price and without reasonable inconvenience or unreasonable expense. This provision shall not apply where the seller or a person authorised to take charge of the goods on his behalf is present at such destination.

Article 93

The party who is under an obligation to take steps to preserve the goods may deposit them in the warehouse of a third person at the expense of the other party provided that the expense incurred is not unreasonable.

Article 94

1. The party who, in the cases to which Articles 91 and 92 apply, is under an obligation to take steps to preserve the goods may sell them by any appropriate means, provided that there has been unreasonable delay by the other party in accepting them or taking them back or in paying the costs of preservation and provided that due notice has been given to the other party of the intention to sell.
2. The party selling the goods shall have the right to retain out of the proceeds of sale an amount equal to the reasonable costs of preserving the goods and of selling them and shall transmit the balance to the other party.

Article 95

Where, in the cases to which Articles 91 and 92 apply, the goods are subject to loss or rapid deterioration or their preservation would involve unreasonable expense, the party under the duty to preserve them is bound to sell them in accordance with Article 94.

Chapter VI Passing of the risk

Article 96

Where the risk has passed to the buyer, he shall pay the price notwithstanding the loss or deterioration of the goods, unless this is due to the act of the seller or of some other person for whose conduct the seller is responsible.

Article 97

1. The risk shall pass to the buyer when delivery of the goods is effected in accordance with the provision of the contract and the present Law.
2. In the case of the handing over of goods which are not in conformity with the contract, the risk shall pass to the buyer from the moment when the handing over has, apart from the lack of conformity, been effected in accordance with the provisions of the contract and of the present Law, where the buyer has neither declared the contract avoided nor required goods in replacement.

Article 98

1. Where the handing over of the goods is delayed owing to the breach of an obligation of the buyer, the risk shall pass to the buyer as from the last date when, apart from such breach, the handing over could have been made in accordance with the contract.
2. Where the contract relates to a sale of unascertained goods, delay on the part of the buyer shall cause the risk to pass only when the seller has set aside goods manifestly appropriated to the contract and has notified the buyer that this has been done.
3. Where unascertained goods are of such a kind that the seller cannot set aside a part of them until the buyer takes delivery, it shall be sufficient for the seller to do all acts necessary to enable the buyer to take delivery.

Article 99

1. Where the sale is of goods in transit by sea, the risk shall be borne by the buyer as from the time at which the goods were handed over to the carrier.
2. Here the seller, at the time of the conclusion of the contract, knew or ought to have known that the goods had been lost or had deteriorated, the risk shall remain with him until the time of the conclusion of the contract.

Article 100

If, in the case to which paragraph 3 of Article 19 applies, the seller, at the time of sending the notice or other document referred to in that paragraph knew or ought to have known that the goods had been lost or had deteriorated after they were handed over to the carrier, the risk shall remain with the seller until the time of sending such notice or document.

Article 101

The passing of the risk shall not necessarily be determined by the provisions of the contract concerning expenses.

Schedule 2

The Uniform Law on the Formation of Contracts for the International Sales of Goods

Article 1

The present law shall apply to the formation of contracts of sale of goods which, if they were concluded, would be governed by the Uniform Law on the International Sale of Goods.

Article 2

1. The provision of the following Articles shall apply except to the extent that it appears from the preliminary negotiations, the offer, the reply, the practices which the parties have established between themselves or usage, that other rules apply.
2. However, a term of the offer stipulating that silence shall amount to acceptance is invalid.

Article 3

An offer or an acceptance need not be evidenced by writing and shall not be subject to any other requirement as to form. In particular, they may be proved by means of witnesses.

Article 4

1. The communication which one person addresses to one or more specific persons with the object of concluding a contract of sale shall not constitute an offer unless it is sufficiently definite to permit the conclusion of the contract by acceptance and indicates the intention of the offeror to be bound.
2. This communication may be interpreted by reference to and supplemented by the preliminary negotiations, any practices which the parties have established between themselves, usage and the provisions of the Uniform Law on the International Sale of Goods.

Article 5

1. The offer shall not bind the offeror until it has been communicated to the offeree; it shall lapse if its withdrawal is communicated to the offeree before or at the same time as the offer.
2. After an offer has been communicated to the offeree it can be revoked unless the revocation is not made in good faith or in conformity with fair dealing or unless the offer states a fixed time for acceptance or otherwise indicates that it is firm or irrevocable.
3. An indication that the offer is firm or irrevocable may be express or implied from the circumstances, the preliminary negotiations, any practices which the parties have established between themselves or usage.
4. A revocation of an offer shall only have effect if it has been communicated to the offeree before he has despatched his acceptance or has done any act treated as acceptance under paragraph 2 of Article 6.

Article 6

1. Acceptance of an offer consists of a declaration communicated by any means whatsoever to the offeror.
2. Acceptance may also consist of the despatch of the goods or of the price or of any other act which my be considered to be equivalent to the declaration referred to in paragraph 1 of this Article either by virtue of the offer or as a result of practices which the parties have established between themselves or usage.

Article 7

1. An acceptance containing additions, limitations or other modifications shall be a rejection of the offer and shall constitute a counter-offer.
2. However, a reply to an offer which purports to be an acceptance but which contains additional or different terms which do not materially alter the terms of the offer shall constitute an acceptance unless the offeror promptly objects to the discrepancy; if he does not so object the terms of the contract shall be the terms of the offer with the modifications contained in the acceptance.

Article 8

1. A declaration of acceptance of an offer shall have effect only if it is communicated to the offeror within the time he has fixed or, if no such time is fixed, within a reasonable time, due account being taken of the circumstances of the transaction, including the rapidity of the means of communication employed by the offeror, and usage. In the case of an oral offer, the acceptance shall be immediate, if the circumstances do not show that the offeree shall have time for reflection.
2. If a time for acceptance is fixed by an offeror in a letter or in a telegram, it shall be presumed to begin to run from the day the letter was dated or the hour of the day the telegram was handed in for despatch.
3. If an acceptance consists of an act referred to in paragraph 2 of Article 6, the act shall have effect only if it is done within the period laid down in paragraph 1 of the present Article.

Article 9

1. If the acceptance is late, the offeror may nevertheless consider it to have arrived in due time on condition that he promptly so informs the acceptor orally or by despatch of a notice.
2. If however the acceptance is communicated late, it shall be considered to have been communicated in due time, if the letter or document which contains the acceptance shows that it has been sent in such circumstances that if its transmission had been normal it would have been communicated in due time; this provision shall not however apply if the offeror has promptly informed the acceptor orally or by despatch of a notice that he considers his offer as having lapsed.

Article 10

An acceptance cannot be revoked except by a revocation which is communicated to the offeror before or at the same time as the acceptance.

Article 11

The formation of the contract is not affected by the death of the parties or by his becoming incapable of contracting before acceptance unless the contrary results from the intention of the parties, usage or the nature of the transaction.

Article 12

1. For the purpose of the present law, the expression 'to be communicated' means to be delivered at the address of the person to whom the communication is directed.
2. Communications provided for by the present Law shall be made by the means usual in the circumstances.

Article 13

1. 'Usage' means any practice or method of dealing which reasonable persons in the same situation as the parties usually consider to be applicable to the formation of their contract.
2. Where expressions, provisions or forms of contract commonly used in commercial practice are employed, they shall be interpreted according to the meaning usually given to them in the trade concerned.

Carriage of Goods by Sea Act 1971

1 Application of Hague Rules as amended

(1) In this Act, 'the Rules' means the International Convention for the unification of certain rules of law relating to bills of lading signed at Brussels on 25th August 1924, as amended by the Protocol signed at Brussels on 23rd February 1968 and by the Protocol signed at Brussels on 21st December 1979.

(2) The provisions of the Rules as set out in the Schedule to this Act shall have the force of law.

(3) Without prejudice to subsection (2) above, the said provisions shall have effect (and have the force of law) in relation to and in connection with the carriage of goods by sea in ships where the port of shipment is a port in the United Kingdom, whether or not the carriage is between ports in two different states within the meaning of Article X of the Rules.

(4) Subject to subsection (6) below, nothing in this section shall be taken as applying anything in the Rules to any contract for the carriage of goods by sea, unless the contract expressly or by implication provides for the issue of a bill of lading or any similar document of title.

(5) [Repealed].

(6) Without prejudice to Article X(c) of the Rules, the Rules shall have the force of law in relation to –

 (a) any bill of lading if the contract contained in or evidenced by it expressly provides that the Rules shall govern the contract; and

 (b) any receipt which is a non-negotiable document marked as such if the contract contained in or evidenced by it is a contract for the carriage of goods by sea which expressly provides that the Rules are to govern the contract as if the receipt were a bill of lading,

but subject, where paragraph (b) applies, to any necessary modifications and in particular with the omission in Article III of the Rules of the second sentence of paragraph 4 and of paragraph 7.

(7) If and so far as the contract contained in or evidenced by a bill of lading or receipt within paragraph (a) or (b) of subsection (6) above applies to deck cargo or live animals, the Rules as given the force of law by that subsection shall have effect as if Article 1(c) did not exclude deck cargo and live animals. In this subsection 'deck cargo' means cargo which by the contract of carriage is stated as being carried on deck and is so carried.

1A Conversion of special drawing rights into sterling

(1) For the purposes of Article IV of the Rules the value on a particular day of one special drawing right shall be treated as equal to such *a* sum in sterling as the International Monetary Fund have fixed as being the equivalent of one special drawing right –
  (a) for that day; or
  (b) if no sum has been so fixed for that day, for the last day before that day for which a sum has been so fixed.

(2) A certificate given by or on behalf of the Treasury stating –
  (a) that a particular sum in sterling has been fixed as aforesaid for a particular day; or
  (b) that no sum has been so fixed for a particular day and that a particular sum in sterling has been so fixed for a day which is the last day for which a sum has been so fixed before the particular day,

shall be conclusive evidence of those matters for the purpose of subsection (1) above; and a document purporting to be such a certificate shall in any proceedings be received in evidence and, unless the contrary is proved, be deemed to be such a certificate.

(3) The Treasury may charge a reasonable fee for any certificate given in pursuance of subsection (2) above, and any fee received by the Treasury by virtue of this subsection shall be paid into the Consolidated Fund.

2 [Omitted]

3 Absolute warranty of seaworthiness not to be implied in contracts to which Rules apply

There shall not be implied in any contract for the carriage of goods by sea to which Rules apply by virtue of this Act any absolute undertaking by the carrier of the goods to provide a seaworthy ship.

4–5 [Omitted]

6 Supplemental

(1)–(3) [Omitted].

(4) It is hereby declared that for the purposes of Article VIII of the Rules section 186 of the Merchant Shipping Act 1995 (which entirely exempts shipowners and others in certain circumstances for loss of, or damage to, goods) is a provision relating to limitation of liability.

Schedule

The Hague Rules as Amended by the Brussels Protocol 1968

Article I

In these Rules the following words are employed with the meaning set out below –

(a) 'Carrier' includes the owner or the charterer who enters into a contract of carriage with a shipper.
(b) 'Contract of carriage' applies only to contracts of carriage covered by a bill of lading or any similar document of title, in so far as such document relates to the carriage of goods by sea, including any bill of lading or any similar document as aforesaid issued under or pursuant to a charter party from the moment at which such bill of lading or similar document of title regulates the relations between a carrier and a holder of the same.
(c) 'Goods' includes goods, wares, merchandise and articles of every kind whatsoever except live animals and cargo which by the contract of carriage is stated as being carried on deck and is so carried.
(d) 'Ship' means any vessel used for the carriage of goods by sea.
(e) 'Carriage of goods' covers the period from the time when the goods are loaded on to the time they are discharged from the ship.

Article II

Subject to the provisions of Article VI, under every contract of carriage of goods by sea the carrier, in relation to the loading, handling, stowage, carriage, custody, care and discharge of such goods, shall be subject to the responsibilities and liabilities, and entitled to the rights and immunities hereinafter set forth.

Article III

1. The carrier shall be bound before and at the beginning of the voyage to exercise due diligence to –
   (a) make the ship seaworthy;
   (b) properly man, equip and supply the ship;
   (c) make the holds, refrigerating and cool chambers, and all other parts of the ship in which goods are carried, fit and safe for their reception, carriage and preservation.
2. Subject to the provisions of Article IV, the carrier shall properly and carefully load, handle, stow, carry, keep, care for, and discharge the goods carried.
3. After receiving the goods into his charge the carrier or the master or agent of the carrier shall, on demand of the shipper, issue to the shipper a bill of lading showing among other things –
   (a) the leading marks necessary for identification of the goods as the same are furnished in writing by the shipper before the loading of such goods starts, provided such marks are stamped or otherwise shown clearly upon the goods if uncovered, or on the cases or coverings in which such goods are contained, in such a manner as should ordinarily remain legible until the end of the voyage;

(b) either the number of packages or pieces, or the quantity, or weight, as the case may be, as furnished in writing by the shipper;

(c) the apparent order and conditions of the goods. Provided that no carrier, master or agent of the carrier shall be bound to state or show in the bill of lading any marks, number, quantity, or weight which he has reasonable grounds for suspecting not accurately to represent the goods actually received or which he has had no reasonable means of checking.

(4) Such a bill of lading shall be *prima facie* evidence of the receipt by the carrier of the goods as therein described in accordance with paragraph 3(a), (b) and (c). However, proof to the contrary shall not be admissible when the bill of lading has been transferred to a third party acting in good faith.

(5) The shipper shall be deemed to have guaranteed to the carrier the accuracy at the time of shipment of the marks, number, quantity and weight, as furnished by him, and the shipper shall indemnify the carrier against all loss, damages and expenses arising or resulting from inaccuracies in such particulars. The right of the carrier to such indemnity shall in no way limit his responsibility and liability under the contract of carriage to any person other than the shipper.

(6) Unless notice of loss or damage and the general nature of such loss or damage be given in writing to the carrier or his agent at the port of discharge before or at the time of the removal of the goods into the custody of the person entitled to delivery thereof under the contract of carriage, or, if the loss or damage be not apparent, within three days, such removal shall be *prima facie* evidence of the delivery by the carrier of the goods as described in the bill of lading.

The notice in writing need not be given if the state of the goods has, at the time of their receipt been the subject of joint survey or inspection.

Subject to paragraph *6 bis* the carrier and the ship shall in any event be discharged from all liability whatsoever in respect of the goods, unless suit is brought within one year of their delivery or of the date when they should have been delivered. This period may, however, be extended if the parties so agree after the cause of action has arisen.

In the case of any actual or apprehended loss or damage the carrier and the receiver shall give all reasonable facilities to each other for inspecting and tallying the goods.

6.*bis*.An action for indemnity against a third person may be brought even after the expiration of the year provided for in the preceding paragraph if brought within the time allowed by the law of the Court seized of the case. However, the time allowed shall be not less than three months, commencing from the day when the person bringing such action for indemnity has settled the claim or has been served with process in the action against himself.

(7) After the goods are loaded the bill of lading to be issued by the carrier, master, or agent of the carrier to the shipper shall, if the shipper so demands, be a 'shipped' bill of lading, provided that if the shipper shall have previously taken up any document of title to such goods, he shall surrender the same as against the issue of the 'shipped' bill of lading, but at the option of the carrier such document of title may be noted at the port of shipment by the carrier, master, or agent with the name or names of the ship or ships upon which the goods have been shipped and the date or dates of shipment, and when so noted, if it shows the particulars mentioned in paragraph 3 of Article III, shall for the purpose of this Article be deemed to constitute a 'shipped' bill of lading.

(8) Any clause, covenant, or agreement in a contract of carriage relieving the carrier or the ship from liability for loss or damage to, or in connection with goods, arising from negligence, fault, or failure in the duties and obligations provided in this Article or lessening such liability otherwise than as provided in these Rules shall be null and void and of no effect. A benefit of insurance in favour of the carrier or similar clause shall be deemed to be a clause relieving the carrier from liability.

Article IV

1. Neither the carrier nor the ship shall be liable for loss or damage arising or resulting from unseaworthiness unless caused by want of due diligence on the part of the carrier to make the ship seaworthy, and to secure that the ship is properly manned, equipped and supplied, and to make the holds, refrigerating and cool chambers and all other parts of the ship in which goods are carried fit and safe for their reception, carriage and preservation in accordance with the provisions of paragraph 1 of Article III. Whenever loss or damage has resulted from unseaworthiness the burden of proving the exercise of due diligence shall be on the carrier or other person claiming exemption under this article.
2. Neither the carrier nor the ship shall be liable for loss or damage arising or resulting from –

    (a) act, neglect, or default of the master, mariner, pilot, or the servants of the carrier in the navigation or in the management of the ship;
    (b) fire, unless caused by the actual fault or privity of the carrier;
    (c) perils, dangers and accidents of the sea or other navigable waters;
    (d) act of God;
    (e) act of war;
    (f) act of public enemies;
    (g) arrest or restraint of princes, rulers or people, or seizure under legal process;
    (h) quarantine restrictions;
    (i) act or omission of the shipper or owner of the goods, his agent or representative;
    (j) strikes or lockouts or stoppage or restraint of labour from whatever cause, whether partial or general;
    (k) riots and civil commotions;
    (l) saving or attempting to save life or property at sea;
    (m) wastage in bulk or weight or any other loss or damage arising from inherent defect, quality or vice of the goods;
    (n) insufficiency of packing;
    (o) insufficiency or inadequacy of marks;
    (p) latent defects not discoverable by due diligence;
    (q) any other cause arising without the actual fault or privity of the carrier, or without the fault or neglect of the agents or servants of the carrier, but the burden of proof shall be on the person claiming the benefit of this exception to show that neither the actual fault or privity of the carrier nor the fault or neglect of the agents or servants of the carrier contributed to the loss or damage.

3. The shipper shall not be responsible for loss or damage sustained by the carrier or the ship arising or resulting from any cause without the act, fault or neglect of the shipper, his agents or his servants.

4. Any deviation in saving or attempting to save life or property at sea or any reasonable deviation shall not be deemed to be an infringement or breach of these Rules or of the contract of carriage, and the carrier shall not be liable for any loss or damage resulting therefrom.
5.
   (a) Unless the nature and value of such goods have been declared by the shipper before shipment and inserted in the bill of lading, neither the carrier nor the ship shall in any event be or become liable for any loss or damage to or in connection with the goods in an amount exceeding 666.67 units of account per package or unit or 2 units of account per kilogram of gross weight of the goods lost or damaged, whichever is the higher.
   (b) The total amount recoverable shall be calculated by reference to the value of such goods at the place and time at which the goods are discharged from the ship in accordance with the contract or should have been so discharged. The value of the goods shall be fixed according to the commodity exchange price, or, if there be no such price, according to the current market price, or if there be no commodity exchange price or current market price, by reference to the normal value of goods of the same kind and quality.
   (c) Where a container, pallet or similar article of transport is used to consolidate goods, the number of packages or units enumerated in the bill of lading as packed in such article of transport shall be deemed the number of packages or units for the purpose of this paragraph as far as these packages or units are concerned. Except as aforesaid such article of transport shall be considered the package or unit.
   (d) The unit of account mentioned in this Article is the special drawing right as defined by the International Monetary Fund. The amounts mentioned in subparagraph (a) of this paragraph shall be converted into national currency on the basis of the value of that currency on a date to be determined by the law of the Court seized of the case.
   (e) Neither the carrier nor the ship shall be entitled to the benefit of the limitation of liability provided for in this paragraph if it is proved that the damage resulted from an act or omission of the carrier done with intent to cause damage, or recklessly and with knowledge that damage would probably result.
   (f) The declaration mentioned in sub-paragraph (a) of this paragraph if embodied in the bill of lading shall be *prima facie* evidence, but shall not be binding or conclusive on the carrier.
   (g) By agreement between the carrier, master or agent of the carrier and the shipper other maximum amounts than those mentioned in sub-paragraph (a) of this paragraph may be fixed, provided that no maximum amount so fixed shall be less than the appropriate maximum mentioned in that sub-paragraph.
   (h) Neither the carrier nor the ship shall be responsible in any event for loss or damage to, or in connection with goods, if the nature or value thereof has been knowingly mis-stated by the shipper in the bill of lading.
6. Goods of an inflammable, explosive or dangerous nature to the shipment whereof the carrier, master or agent of the carrier has not consented with knowledge of their nature and character, may at any time before discharge be landed at any place, or destroyed or rendered innocuous by the carrier without compensation and the shipper of such goods

shall be liable for all damages and expenses directly or indirectly arising out of or resulting from such shipment. If any such goods shipped with such knowledge and consent shall become a danger to the ship or cargo, they may in like manner be landed at any place, or destroyed or rendered innocuous by the carrier without liability on the part of the carrier except to general average, if any.

Article IV *bis*

1. The defences and limits of liability provided for in these Rules shall apply in any action against the carrier in respect of loss or damage to goods covered by a contract of carriage whether the action be founded in contract or in tort.
2. If such an action is bought against a servant or agent of the carrier (such servant or agent not being an independent contractor), such servant or agent shall be entitled to avail himself of the defences and limits of liability which the carrier is entitled to invoke under these Rules.
3. The aggregate of the amounts recoverable from the carrier, and such servants and agents, shall in no case exceed the limit provided for in these Rules.
4. Nevertheless, a servant or agent of the carrier shall not be entitled to avail himself of the provisions of this Article, if it is proved that the damage resulted from an act or omission of the servant or agent done with intent to cause damage or recklessly and with knowledge that damage would probably result.

Article V

A carrier shall be at liberty to surrender in whole or in part all or any of his rights and immunities or to increase any of his responsibilities and obligations under these Rules, provided such surrender or increase shall be embodied in the bill of lading issued to the shipper. The provisions of these Rules shall not be applicable to charter parties, but if bills of lading are issued in the case of a ship under a charter party they shall comply with the terms of these Rules. Nothing in these Rules shall be held to prevent the insertion in a bill of lading of any lawful provision regarding general average.

Article VI

Notwithstanding the provisions of the preceding Articles, a carrier, master or agent of the carrier and a shipper shall in regard to any particular goods be at liberty to enter into any agreement in any terms as to the responsibility and liability of the carrier for such goods, and as to the rights and immunities of the carrier in respect of such goods, or his obligation as to seaworthiness, so far as this stipulation is not contrary to public policy, or the care or diligence of his servant or agents in regard to the loading, handling, stowage, carriage, custody, care and discharge of the goods carried by sea, provided that in this case no bill of lading has been or shall be issued and that the terms agreed shall be embodied in a receipt which shall be a non-negotiable document and shall be marked as such. Any agreement so entered into shall have legal effect.

Provided that this Article shall not apply to ordinary commercial shipments made in the ordinary course of trade, but only to other shipments where the character or condition of the property to be carried or the circumstances, terms and conditions under which the carriage is to be performed are such as reasonably to justify a special agreement.

Article VII

Nothing herein contained shall prevent a carrier or a shipper from entering into any agreement, stipulation, condition, reservation or exemption as to the responsibility and liability of the carrier or the ship for the loss or damage to, or in connection with, the custody and care and handling of goods prior to the loading on, and subsequent to the discharge from, the ship on which the goods are carried by sea.

Article VIII

The provisions of these Rules shall not affect the rights and obligations or the carrier under any statute for the time being in force relating to the limitation of the liability of owners of sea-going vessels.

Article IX

These rules shall not affect the provisions of any international Convention or national law governing liability for nuclear damage.

Article X

The provisions of these Rules shall apply to every bill of lading relating to the carnage of goods between ports in two different States if –

(a) the bill of lading is issued in a contracting State; or
(b) the carriage is from a port in a contracting State; or
(c) the contract contained in or evidenced by the bill of lading provides that these Rules or legislation of any State giving effect to them are to govern the contract,

whatever may be the nationality of the ship, the carrier, the shipper, the consignee, or any other interested person.

Articles XI–XVI [Omitted]

Unfair Contract Terms Act 1977

1–25 [Omitted]

Miscellaneous

26 International supply contracts

(1) The limits imposed by this Act on the extent to which a person may exclude or restrict liability by reference to a contract term do not apply to liability arising under such a contract as is described in subsection (3) below.

(2) The terms of such a contract are not subject to any requirement of reasonableness under Section 3; and nothing in Part II of this Act shall require the incorporation of the terms of such a contract to be fair and reasonable for them to have effect.

(3) Subject to subsection (4), that description of contract is one whose characteristics are the following –

(a) either it is a contract of sale or goods or it is one under or in pursuance of which the possession or ownership of goods passes; and

(b) it is made by parties whose places of business (or, if they have none, habitual residences) are in the territories of different States (the Channel Islands and the Isle of Man being treated for this purpose as different States from the United Kingdom).

[…]

(4) A contract falls within subsection (3) above only if either –

(a) the goods in question are, at the time of the conclusion of the contract, in the course of carriage, or will be carried, from the territory of one State to the territory of another; or

(b) the acts constituting the offer and acceptance have been done in territories of different states; or

(c) the contract provides for the goods to be delivered to the territory of a State other than that within those territory those acts were done.

27 Choice of law clauses

1 Where the law applicable to a contract is the law of any part of the United Kingdom only by choice of the parties (and apart from that choice would be the law of some country outside the United Kingdom) sections 2 to 7 and 16 to 21 of this Act operate as part of the law applicable to the contract.

2 This Act has effect notwithstanding any contract term which applies or purports to apply the law of some country outside the United Kingdom, where –

(a) the term appears to the court, or arbitrator or arbiter to have been imposed wholly or mainly for the purpose of enabling the party imposing it to evade the operation of this Act;

28–32 [Omitted]

Schedule 1

Scope of Sections 2 to 4 and 7

[Omitted].

State Immunity Act 1978

Part I Proceedings in United Kingdom by or against other states

Immunity from jurisdiction

1 General immunity from jurisdiction

(1) A State is immune from the jurisdiction of the courts of the United Kingdom except as provided in the following provisions of this part of the Act.

(2) A court shall give effect to the immunity conferred by this section even though the State does not appear in the proceedings in question.

Exceptions from immunity

2 Submission to jurisdiction

(1) A state is not immune as respects proceedings in respect of which it has submitted to the jurisdiction of the courts of the United Kingdom.
(2) A state may submit after the dispute giving rise to the proceedings has arisen or by a prior written agreement: but a provision in any agreement that it is to be governed by the law of the United Kingdom is not to be regarded as a submission.
(3) A state is deemed to have submitted –
 (a) if it has instituted the proceedings; or
 (b) subject to subsections (4) and (5) below, if it has intervened or taken any step in the proceedings.
(4) Subsection (3)(b) above does not apply to intervention or any step taken for the purpose only of –
 (a) claiming immunity; or
 (b) asserting an interest in property in circumstances such that the State would have been entitled to immunity if the proceedings had been brought against it.
(5) Subsection (3)(b) above does not apply to any step taken by the State in ignorance of facts entitling it to immunity if those facts could not reasonably have been ascertained and immunity is claimed as soon as reasonably practicable.
(6) A submission in respect of any proceedings extends to any appeal but not to any counter-claim unless it arises out of the same legal relationship or facts as the claim.
(7) The head of a State's diplomatic mission in the United Kingdom, or the person for the time being performing his functions, shall be deemed to have authority to submit on behalf of the State in respect of any proceedings; and any person who has entered into a contract on behalf of and with the authority of a State shall be deemed to have authority to submit on its behalf in respect of proceedings arising out of the contract.

3 Commercial transactions and contracts to be performed in the United Kingdom

(1) A state is not immune as respects proceedings relating to –
 (a) a commercial transaction entered into by the State; or
 (b) an obligation of the State which by virtue of a contract (whether a commercial transaction or not) falls to be performed wholly or partly in the United Kingdom.
(2) This section does not apply if the parties to the dispute are States or have otherwise agreed in writing; and subsection (1)(b) above does not apply if the contract (not being a commercial transaction) was made in the territory of the State concerned and the obligation in question is governed by its administrative law.
(3) In this section 'commercial transaction' means –
 (a) any contract for the supply of goods or services;

(b) any loan or other transaction for the provision of finance and any guarantee or indemnity in respect of any such transaction or of any other financial obligation; and

(c) any other transaction or activity (whether of a commercial industrial, financial, professional or other similar character) into which a state enters or in which it engages otherwise than in the exercise of sovereign authority,

but neither paragraph of subsection (1) above applies to a contract of employment between a State and an individual.

4–8 [Omitted]

9 Arbitrations

(1) Where a State has agreed in writing to submit a dispute which has arisen, or may arise, to arbitration, the State is not immune as respects proceedings in the courts of the United Kingdom which relate to the arbitration.

(2) This section has effect subject to any contrary provision in the arbitration agreement and does not apply to any arbitration agreement between states.

10 Ships used for commercial purposes

(1) This section applies to –

(a) Admiralty proceedings; and

(b) proceedings on any claim which could be made the subject of Admiralty proceedings.

(2) A State is not immune as respects –

(a) an action *in rem* against a ship belonging to that State; or

(b) an action *in personam* for enforcing a claim in connection with such a ship,

if, at the time when the cause of action arose, the ship was in use or intended for use for commercial purposes.

(3) Where an action *in rem* is brought against a ship belonging to a State for enforcing a claim in connection with another ship belonging to that State, subsection (2) (a) above does not apply as respects the first-mentioned ship unless at the time when the cause of action relating to the other ship arose, both ships were in use or intended for use for commercial purposes.

(4) A State is not immune as respects –

(a) an action *in rem* against a cargo belonging to that State if both the cargo and the ship carrying it were, at the time when the cause of action arose, in use or intended for use for commercial purposes; or

(b) an action *in personam* for enforcing a claim in connection with such a cargo if the ship carrying it was then in use or intended for use as aforesaid.

(5) In the foregoing provisions references to a ship or cargo belonging to a State include references to a ship or cargo in its possession or control or in which it claims an interest; and, subject to subsection (4) above, subsection (2) above applies to property other than a ship as it applies to a ship.

(6) Sections 3 to 5 above do not apply to proceedings of the kind described in subsection (1) above if the State in question is a party to the Brussels Convention and the claim relates to the operation of a ship owned or operated by that State, the carriage of cargo or passengers on any such ship or the carriage of cargo owned by that State on any other ship.

11–13 [Omitted]

Supplementary provisions

14 States entitled to immunities and privileges

(1) The immunities and privileges conferred by this Part of this Act apply to any foreign or commonwealth State other than the United Kingdom; and references to a State include references to –
  (a) the sovereign or other head of that State in his public capacity;
  (b) the government of that State; and
  (c) any department of that government, but not to any entity (hereafter referred to as a 'separate entity') which is distinct from the executive organs of the government of the State and capable of suing or being sued.

(2) A separate entity is immune from the jurisdiction of the courts of the United Kingdom if, and only if –
  (a) the proceedings relate to anything done by it in the exercise of sovereign authority; and
  (b) the circumstances are such that a State (or, in the case of proceedings to which Section 10 above applies, a State which is not a party to the Brussels Convention) would have been so immune.

(3) If a separate entity (not being a State's central bank or other monetary authority) submits to the jurisdiction in respect of proceedings in the case of which it is entitled to immunity by virtue of subsection (2) above, subsections (1) to (4) of section 13 above shall apply to it in respect of those proceedings as if references to a State were references to that entity.

(4) Property of a State's central bank or other monetary authority shall not be regarded for the purposes of subsection (4) of section 13 above as in use or intended for use for commercial purposes; and where any such bank or authority is a separate entity subsections (1) to (3) of that section shall apply to it as if references to a State were references to the bank or authority.

(5) Section 12 above applies to proceedings against the constituent territories of a federal State; and her Majesty may by Order in Council provide for the other provisions of this Part of this Act to apply to any such constituent territory specified in the Order as they apply to a State.

(6) Where the provisions of this Part of this Act do not apply to a constituent territory by virtue of any such Order subsections (2) and (3) above shall apply to it as if it were a separate entity.

15–16 [Omitted]

17 Interpretation of Part I

(1) In this Part of the Act 'the Brussels Convention' means the International Convention for the Unification of Certain Rules Concerning the Immunity of State-owned Ships

signed in Brussels on 10th April 1926; 'commercial purposes' means purposes of such transactions or activities as are mentioned in section 3(3) above; 'ship' includes hovercraft.

(2) In sections 2(2) and 13(3) above references to an agreement include references to a treaty, convention or other international agreement.

(3) For the purposes of sections 3 to 8 above the territory of the United Kingdom shall be deemed to include any dependent territory in respect of which the United Kingdom is a party to the European Convention on State Immunity.

(4) In sections 3(1), 4(1), 5 and 16(2) above references to the United Kingdom include references to its territorial waters and any area designated under section 1(7) of the Continental Shelf Act 1964.

(5) In relation to Scotland in this Part of this Act 'action *in rem*' means such an action only in relation to Admiralty proceedings.

18–23 [Omitted]

Sale of Goods Act 1979

Part I [Omitted]

Part II Formation of the contract

Contract of sale

2 Contract of sale

(1) A contract of sale of goods is a contract by which the seller transfers or agrees to transfer the property in goods to the buyer for a money consideration, called the price.

(2) There may be a contract of sale between one part owner and another.

(3) A contract of sale may be absolute or conditional.

(4) Where under a contract of sale the property in the goods is transferred from the seller to the buyer the contract is called a sale.

(5) Where under a contract of sale the transfer of the property in the goods is to take place at a future time or subject to some condition later to be fulfilled the contract is called an agreement to sell.

(6) An agreement to sell becomes a sale when the time elapses or the conditions are fulfilled subject to which the property in the goods is to be transferred.

3 Capacity to buy and sell

(1) Capacity to buy and sell is regulated by the general law concerning capacity to contract and to transfer and acquire property.

(2) Where necessaries are sold and delivered to a minor or a person who by reason of or drunkenness is incompetent to contract, he must pay a reasonable price for them.

(3) In subsection (2) above 'necessaries' means goods suitable to the condition in life of the minor or other person concerned and to his actual requirements at the time of the sale and delivery.

Formalities of contract

4 How contract of sale is made

(1) Subject to this and any other Act, a contract of sale may be made in writing (either with or without seal), or by word of mouth, or partly in writing and partly by word of mouth, or may be implied from the conduct of the parties.
(2) Nothing in this section affects the law relating to corporations.

Subject matter of contract

5 Existing or future goods

(1) The goods which form the subject of a contract of sale may be either existing goods, owned or possessed by the seller, or goods to be manufactured or acquired by him after the making of the contract of sale, in this Act called future goods.
(2) There may be a contract for the sale of goods the acquisition of which by the seller depends on a contingency which may or may not happen.
(3) Where by a contract of sale the seller purports to effect a present sale of future goods, the contract operates as an agreement to sell the goods.

6 Goods which have perished

Where there is a contract for the sale of specific goods, and the goods without the knowledge of the seller have perished at the time when the contract is made, the contract is void.

7 Goods perishing before sale but after agreement to sell

Where there is an agreement to sell specific goods and subsequently the goods, without any fault on the part of the seller or buyer perish before the risk passes to the buyer, the agreement is avoided.

The price

8 Ascertainment of price

(1) The price in a contract of sale may be fixed by the contract, or may be left to be fixed in a manner agreed by the contract, or may be determined by the course of dealing between the parties.
(2) Where the price is not determined as mentioned in subsection (1) above the buyer must pay a reasonable price.
(3) What is a reasonable price is a question of fact dependent on the circumstances of each particular case.

9 Agreement to sell at valuation

(1) Where there is an agreement to sell goods on the terms that the price is to be fixed by the valuation of a third party, and he cannot or does not make the valuation, the

agreement is avoided; but if the goods or any part of them have been delivered to and appropriated by the buyer he must pay a reasonable price for them.

(2) Where the third party is prevented from making the valuation by the fault of the seller or buyer, the party not at fault may maintain an action for damages against the party at fault.

Implied terms, etc.

10 Stipulations about time

(1) Unless a different intention appears from the terms of the contract, stipulations as to time of payment are not of the essence of a contract of sale.

(2) Whether any other stipulation as to time is or is not of the essence of the contract depends on the terms of the contract.

(3) In a contract of sale 'month' *prima facie* means calendar month.

11 When condition to be treated as warranty

(1) This section does not apply to Scotland.

(2) Where a contract of sale is subject to a condition to be fulfilled by the seller the buyer may waive the condition, or may elect to treat the breach of the condition as a breach of warranty and not as a ground for treating the contract as repudiated.

(3) Whether a stipulation in a contract of sale is a condition, the breach of which may give rise to a right to treat the contract as repudiated, or a warranty, the breach of which may give rise to a claim for damages but not a right to reject the goods and treat the contract as repudiated, depends in each case on the construction of the contract; and a stipulation may be a condition, although called a warranty in the contract.

(4) Subject to section 35A below, where a contract of sale is not severable and the buyer has accepted the goods or part of them, the breach of a condition to be fulfilled by the seller can only be treated as a breach of warranty, and not as a ground for rejecting the goods and treating the contract as repudiated, unless there is an express or implied term of the contract to that effect.

(4A) Subsection (4) does not apply to a contract to which Chapter 2 of Part 1 of the Consumer Rights Act 2015 applies (but see the provision made about such contracts in sections 19 to 22 of that Act).

(5) [Repealed].

(6) Nothing in this section affects a condition or warranty whose fulfilment is excused by law by reason of impossibility or otherwise.

(7) [Omitted].

12 implied terms about title, etc.

(1) In a contract of sale, other than one to which subsection (3) below applies, there is an implied term on the part of the seller that in the case of a sale he has the right to sell the goods, and in the case of an agreement to sell he will have such a right at the time when the property is to pass.

(2) In a contract of sale, other than one to which subsection (3) below applies, there is also an implied term that –
  (a) the goods are free, and will remain free until the time when the property is to pass, from any charge or encumbrance not disclosed or known to the buyer before the contract is made; and
  (b) the buyer will enjoy quiet possession of the goods except so far as it may be disturbed by the owner or other person entitled to the benefit of any charge or encumbrance so disclosed or known.

(3) This subsection applies to a contract of sale in the case of which there appears from the contract or is to be inferred from its circumstances an intention that the seller should transfer only such title as he or a third person may have.

(4) In a contract to which subsection (3) above applies there is an implied term that all charges or encumbrances known to the seller and not known to the buyer have been disclosed to the buyer before the contract is made.

(5) In a contract to which subsection (3) above applies there is also an implied term that none of the following will disturb the buyer's quiet possession of the goods, namely –
  (a) the seller;
  (b) in a case where the parties to the contract intend that the seller should transfer only such title as a third person may have, that person;
  (c) anyone claiming through or under the seller or that third person otherwise than under a charge or encumbrance disclosed or known to the buyer before the contract is made.

(5A) As regards England and Wales and Northern Ireland, the term implied by subsection (1) above is a condition and the terms implied by subsections (2), (4) and (5) above are warranties.

(6) [Omitted].

(7) This section does not apply to a contract to which Chapter 2 of Part 1 of the Consumer Rights Act 2015 applies (but see the provision made about such contracts in section 17 of that Act).

13 Sale by description

(1) Where there is a contract for the sale of goods by description, there is an implied term that the goods will correspond with the description.

(1A) As regards England and Wales and Northern Ireland, the term implied by subsection (1) above is a condition.

(2) If the sale is by sample as well as by description it is not sufficient that the bulk of the goods correspond with the sample if the goods do not also correspond with the description.

(3) A sale of goods is not prevented from being a sale by description by reason only that, being exposed for sale or hire, they are selected by the buyer.

(4) [Omitted].

(5) This section does not apply to a contract to which Chapter 2 of Part 1 of the Consumer Rights Act 2015 applies (but see the provision made about such contracts in section 11 of that Act).

14 Implied terms about quality or fitness

(1) Except as provided by this section and section 15 below and subject to any other enactment, there is no implied term about the quality or fitness for any particular purpose of goods supplied under a contract of sale.

(2) Where the seller sells goods in the course of a business, there is an implied term that the goods supplied under the contract are of satisfactory quality.

(2A) For the purposes of this Act, goods are of satisfactory quality if they meet the standard that a reasonable person would regard as satisfactory, taking account of any description of the goods, the price (if relevant) and all the other relevant circumstances.

(2B) For the purposes of this Act, the quality of the goods includes their state and condition and the following (among others) are in appropriate cases aspects of the quality of goods –

- (a) fitness for all the purposes for which goods of the kind in question are commonly supplied;
- (b) appearance and finish;
- (c) freedom from minor defects;
- (d) safety; and
- (e) durability.

(2C) The term implied by subsection (2) above does not extend to any matter making the quality of goods unsatisfactory –

- (a) which is specifically drawn to the buyer's attention before the contract is made;
- (b) where the buyer examines the goods before the contract is made, which that examination ought to reveal; or
- (c) in the case of a contract for sale by sample, which would have been apparent on a reasonable examination of the sample.

(2D) to (2F) [Omitted].

(3) Where the seller sells goods in the course of a business and the buyer, expressly or by implication, makes known –

- (a) to the seller; or
- (b) where the purchase price or part of it is payable by instalments and the goods were previously sold by a credit-broker to the seller, to that credit-broker,

any particular purpose for which the goods are being bought, there is an implied term that the goods supplied under the contract are reasonable fit for that purpose, whether or not that is a purpose for which such goods are commonly supplied, except where the circumstances show that the buyer does not rely, or that it is unreasonable for him to rely, on the skill or judgment of the seller or credit-broker.

(4) An implied term or warranty about quality or fitness for a particular purpose may be annexed to a contract of sale by usage.

(5) The preceding provisions of this section apply to a sale by a person who in the course of a business is acting as agent for another as they apply to a sale by a principal in the course of a business, except where that other is not selling in the course of a business and either the buyer knows that fact or reasonable steps are taken to bring it to the notice of the buyer before the contract is made.

(6) As regards England and Wales and Northern Ireland, the terms implied by subsections (2) and (3) above are conditions.

(7) and (8)[Omitted].
(9) This section does not apply to a contract to which Chapter 2 of Part 1 of the Consumer Rights Act 2015 applies (but see the provision made about such contracts in sections 9, 10 and 18 of that Act).

Sale by sample

15 Sale by sample

(1) A contract of sale is a contract for sale by sample where there is an express or implied term to that effect in the contract.
(2) In the case of a contract for sale by sample there is an implied term –
  (a) that the bulk will correspond with the sample in quality;
  (b) [Repealed];
  (c) that the goods will be free from any defect, making their quality unsatisfactory, which would not be apparent on reasonable examination of the sample.
(3) As regards England and Wales and Northern Ireland, the term implied by subsection (2) above is a condition.
(4) [Omitted].
(5) This section does not apply to a contract to which Chapter 2 of Part 1 of the Consumer Rights Act 2015 applies (but see the provision made about such contracts in sections 13 and 18 of that Act).

Miscellaneous

15A Modification of remedies for breach of condition in non-consumer cases

(1) Where in the case of a contract of sale –
  (a) the buyer would, apart from this subsection, have the right to reject goods by reason of a breach on the part of the seller of a term implied by section 13, 14 or 15 above, but
  (b) the breach is so slight that it would be unreasonable for him to reject them, the breach is not to be treated as a breach of condition but may be treated as a breach of warranty.
(2) This section applies unless a contrary intention appears in, or is to be implied from, the contract.
(3) It is for the seller to show that a breach fell within subsection (1)(b) above.
(4) This section does not apply to Scotland.

15B Remedies for breach of contract as respects Scotland

(1) Where in a contract of sale the seller is in breach of any term of the contract (express or implied), the buyer shall be entitled –
  (a) to claim damages, and
  (b) if the breach is material, to reject any goods delivered under the contract and treat it as repudiated.

(1A) Subsection (1) does not apply to a contract to which Chapter 2 of Part 1 of the Consumer Rights Act 2015 applies (but see the provision made about such contracts in sections 19 to 22 of that Act).

(3) This section applies to Scotland only.

Part III Effects of the contract

Transfer of property as between seller and buyer

16 Goods must be ascertained

Subject to section 20A below, where there is a contract for the sale of unascertained goods no property in the goods is transferred to the buyer unless and until the goods are ascertained.

17 Property passes when intended to pass

(1) Where there is a contract for the sale of specific or ascertained goods the property in them is transferred to the buyer at such time as the parties to the contract intend it to be transferred.

(2) For the purpose of ascertaining the intention of the parties regard shall be had to the terms of the contract, the conduct of the parties and the circumstances of the case.

18 Rules for ascertaining intention

Unless a different intention appears, the following are rules for ascertaining the intention of the parties as to the time at which the property in the goods is to pass to the buyer.

Rule 1—Where there is an unconditional contract for the sale of specific goods in a deliverable state the property in the goods passes to the buyer when the contract is made, and it is immaterial whether the time of payment or the time of delivery, or both, be postponed.

Rule 2—Where there is a contract for the sale of specific goods and the seller is bound to do something to the goods for the purpose of putting them into a deliverable state, the property does not pass until the thing is done and the buyer has notice that it has been done.

Rule 3—Where there is a contract for the sale of specific goods in a deliverable state but the seller is bound to weigh, measure, test or do some other act or thing with reference to the goods for the purpose of ascertaining the price, the property does not pass until the act or thing is done and the buyer has notice that it has been done.

Rule 4—When goods are delivered to the buyer on approval or on sale or return or other similar terms the property in the goods passes to the buyer –

(a) when he signifies his approval or acceptance to the seller or does any other act adopting the transaction;

(b) if he does not signify his approval or acceptance to the seller but retains the goods without giving notice of rejection, then, if a time has been fixed for the return of the goods on the expiration of that time, and if no time has been fixed, on the expiration of a reasonable time.

Rule 5—(1) Where there is a contract for the sale of unascertained or future goods by description, and goods of that description and in a deliverable state are unconditionally appropriated to the contract, either by the seller with the assent of the buyer or by the buyer with the assent of the seller, the property in the goods then passes to the buyer; and the assent may be express or implied, and may be given either before or after the appropriation is made.

(2) Where, in pursuance of the contract, the seller delivers the goods to the buyer or to a carrier or other bailee or custodier (whether named by the buyer or not) for the purpose of transmission to the buyer, and does not reserve the right of disposal, he is to be taken to have unconditionally appropriated the goods to the contract.

(3) Where there is a contract for the sale of a specified quantity of unascertained goods in a deliverable state forming part of a bulk which is identified either in the contract or by subsequent agreement between the parties and the bulk is reduced to (or to less than) that quantity, then, if the buyer under that contract is the only buyer to whom goods are then due out of the bulk –

(a) the remaining goods are to be taken as appropriated to that contract at the time when the bulk is so reduced; and

(b) the property in those goods then passes to that buyer.

(4) Paragraph (3) above applies also (with the necessary modifications) where a bulk is reduced to (or to less than) the aggregate of the quantities due to a single buyer under separate contracts relating to that bulk and he is the only buyer to whom goods are then due out of that bulk.

19 Reservation of right of disposal

(1) Where there is a contract for the sale of specific goods or where goods are subsequently appropriated to the contract, the seller may, by the terms of the contract or appropriation, reserve the right of disposal of the goods until certain conditions are fulfilled; and in such a case, notwithstanding the delivery of the goods to the buyer, or to the carrier or other bailee or custodier for the purpose of transmission to the buyer, the property in the goods does not pass to the buyer until the conditions imposed by the seller are fulfilled.

(2) Where goods are shipped and by the bill of lading the goods are deliverable to the order of the seller or his agent, the seller is *prima facie* to be taken to reserve the right of disposal.

(3) Where the seller of goods draws on the buyer for the price and transmits the bill of exchange and bill of lading to the buyer together to secure acceptance or payment of the bill of exchange, the buyer is bound to return the bill of lading if he does not honour the bill of exchange, and if he wrongfully retains the bill of lading the property in the goods does not pass to him.

20 Passing of Risk

(1) Unless otherwise agreed, the goods remain at the seller's risk until the property in them is transferred to the buyer, but when the property in them is transferred to the buyer the goods are at the buyer's risk whether delivery has been made or not.

(2) But where delivery has been delayed through the fault of either buyer or seller the goods are at the risk of the party at fault as regards any loss which might not have occurred but for such fault.
(3) Nothing in this section affects the duties or liabilities of either seller or buyer as a bailee or custodier of the goods of the other party.
(4) This section does not apply to a contract to which Chapter 2 of Part 1 of the Consumer Rights Act 2015 applies (but see the provision made about such contracts in section 29 of that Act)."

20A Undivided shares in goods forming part of a bulk

(1) This section applies to a contract for the sale of a specified quantity of unascertained goods if the following conditions are met –
 (a) the goods or some of them form part of a bulk which is identified either in the contract or by subsequent agreement between the parties; and
 (b) the buyer has paid the price for some or all of the goods which are the subject of the contract and which form part of the bulk.
(2) Where this section applies, then (unless the parties agree otherwise), as soon as the conditions specified in paragraphs (a) and (b) of subsection (1) above are met or at such later time as the parties may agree –
 (a) property in an undivided share in the bulk is transferred to the buyer; and
 (b) the buyer becomes an owner in common of the bulk.
(3) Subject to subsection (4) below, for the purposes of this section, the undivided share of a buyer in a bulk at any time shall be such share as the quantity of goods paid for and due to the buyer out of the bulk bears to the quantity of goods in the bulk at that time.
(4) Where the aggregate of the undivided shares of buyers in a bulk determined under subsection (3) above would at any time exceed the whole of the bulk at that time, the undivided share in the bulk of each buyer shall be reduced proportionately so that the aggregate of the undivided shares is equal to the whole bulk.
(5) Where a buyer has paid the price for only some of the goods due to him out of a bulk, any delivery to the buyer out of the bulk shall, for the purposes of this section, be ascribed in the first place to the goods in respect of which payment has been made.
(6) For the purposes of this section payment of part of the price for any goods shall be treated as payment for a corresponding part of the goods.

20B Deemed consent by co-owner to dealings in bulk goods

(1) A person who has become an owner in common of a bulk by virtue of section 20A above shall be deemed to have consented to –
 (a) any delivery of goods out of the bulk to any other owner in common of the bulk, being goods which are due to him under his contract;
 (b) any dealing with or removal, delivery or disposal of goods in the bulk by any other person who is an owner in common of the bulk in so far as the goods fall within that co-owner's undivided share in the bulk at the time of the dealing, removal, delivery or disposal.

(2) No cause of action shall accrue to anyone against a person by reason of that person having acted in accordance with paragraph (a) or (b) of subsection (1) above in reliance on any consent deemed to have been given under that subsection.

(3) Nothing in this section or section 20A above shall –
   (a) impose an obligation on a buyer of goods out of a bulk to compensate any other buyer of goods out of that bulk for any shortfall in the goods received by that other buyer;
   (b) affect any contractual arrangement between buyers of goods out of a bulk for adjustments between themselves; or
   (c) affect the rights of any buyer under his contract.

Transfer of title

21 Sale by person not the owner

(1) Subject to this Act, where goods are sold by a person who is not their owner and who does not sell them under the authority or with the consent of the owner, the buyer acquires no better title to the goods than the seller had, unless the owner of the goods is by his conduct precluded from denying the seller's authority to sell.

(2) Nothing in this Act affects –
   (a) the provisions of the Factors Acts or any enactment enabling the apparent owner of goods to dispose of them as if he were their true owner;
   (b) the validity of any contract of sale under any special common law or statutory power of sale or under the order of a court of competent jurisdiction.

22 [Repealed]

23 Sale under voidable title

When the seller of goods has a voidable title to them, but his title has not been avoided at the time of the sale, the buyer acquires a good title to the goods, provided he buys them in good faith and without notice of the seller's defect of title.

24 Seller in possession after sale

Where a person having sold goods continues or is in possession of the goods, or of the documents of title to the goods, the delivery or transfer by that person, or by a mercantile agent acting for him, of the goods or documents of title under any sale, pledge, or other disposition thereof, to any person receiving the same in good faith and without notice of the previous sale, has the same effect as if the person making the delivery or transfer were expressly authorised by the owner of the goods to make the same.

25 Buyer in possession after sale

(1) Where a person having bought or agreed to buy goods obtains, with the consent of the seller, possession of the goods or the documents of title to the goods or documents of title, under any sale, pledge, or other disposition thereof, to any person receiving the

same in good faith and without notice of any lien or other right of the original seller in respect of the goods, has the same effect as if the person making the delivery or transfer were a mercantile agent in possession of the goods or documents of title with the consent of the owner.

(2) For the purposes of subsection (1) above –
  (a) the buyer under a conditional sale agreement is to be taken not to be a person who has bought or agreed to buy goods; and
  (b) 'conditional sale agreement' means an agreement for the sale of goods which is a consumer credit agreement within the meaning of the Consumer Credit Act 1974 under which the purchase price or part of it is payable by instalments, and the property in the goods is to remain in the seller (notwithstanding that the buyer is to be in possession of the goods) until such conditions as to the payment of instalments or otherwise as may be specified in the agreement are fulfilled.

(3) and (4) [Omitted].

26 Supplementary to Sections 24 and 25

In sections 24 and 25 above 'mercantile agent' means a mercantile agent having in the customary course of his business as such agent authority either –

(a) to sell goods; or
(b) to consign goods for the purpose of sale; or
(c) to buy goods; or
(d) to raise money on the security of goods.

Part IV Performance of the contract

27 Duties of seller and buyer

It is the duty of the seller to deliver the goods, and of the buyer to accept and pay for them, in accordance with the terms of the contract of sale.

28 Payment and delivery are concurrent conditions

Unless otherwise agreed, delivery of the goods and payment of the price are concurrent conditions, that is to say, the seller must be ready and willing to give possession of the goods to the buyer in exchange for the price and the buyer must be ready and willing to pay the price in exchange for possession of the goods.

29 Rules about delivery

(1) Whether it is for the buyer to take possession of the goods or for the seller to send them to the buyer is a question depending in each case on the contract, express or implied, between the parties.

(2) Apart from any such contract, express or implied, the place of delivery is the seller's place of business if he has one, and if not, his residence; except that, if the contract is for

the sale of specific goods, which to the knowledge of the parties when the contract is made are in some other place, then that place is the place of delivery.

(3) Where under the contract of sale the seller is bound to send the goods to the buyer, but no time for sending them is fixed, the seller is bound to send them within a reasonable time.

(3A) Subsection (3) does not apply to a contract to which Chapter 2 of Part 1 of the Consumer Rights Act 2015 applies (but see the provision made about such contracts in section 28 of that Act).

(4) Where the goods at the time of sale are in the possession of a third person, there is no delivery by seller to buyer unless and until the third person acknowledges to the buyer that he holds the goods on his behalf; but nothing in this section affects the operation of the issue or transfer of any document of title to goods.

(5) Demand or tender of delivery may be treated as ineffectual unless made at a reasonable hour; and what is a reasonable hour is a question of fact.

(6) Unless otherwise agreed, the expenses of and incidental to putting the goods into a deliverable state must be borne by the seller.

30 Delivery of wrong quantity

(1) Where the seller delivers to the buyer a quantity of goods less than he contracted to sell, the buyer may reject them, but if the buyer accepts the goods so delivered he must pay for them at the contract rate.

(2) Where the seller delivers to the buyer a quantity of goods larger than he contracted to sell, the buyer may accept the goods included in the contract and reject the rest, or he may reject the whole.

(2A) A buyer may not –

(a) where the seller delivers a quantity of goods less than he contracted to sell, reject the goods under subsection (1) above; or

(b) where the seller delivers a quantity of goods larger than he contracted to sell, reject the whole under subsection (2) above,

if the shortfall or, as the case may be, excess is so slight that it would be unreasonable for him to do so.

(2B) It is for the seller to show that a shortfall or excess fell within subsection (2A) above.

(2C) Subsections (2A) and (2B) above do not apply to Scotland.

(2D) Where the seller delivers a quantity of goods –

(a) less than he contracted to sell, the buyer shall not be entitled to reject the goods under subsection (1) above,

(b) larger than he contracted to sell, the buyer shall not be entitled to reject the whole under subsection (2) above,

(c) unless the shortfall or excess is material.

(2E) Subsection (2D) above applies to Scotland only.

(3) Where the seller delivers to the buyer a quantity of goods larger than he contracted to sell and the buyer accepts the whole of the goods so delivered he must pay for them at the contract rate.

(4) [Repealed].

(5) This section is subject to any usage of trade, special agreement, or of course of dealing between the parties.
(6) This section does not apply to a contract to which Chapter 2 of Part 1 of the Consumer Rights Act 2015 applies (but see the provision made about such contracts in section 25 of that Act).

31 Instalment deliveries

(1) Unless otherwise agreed, the buyer of goods is not bound to accept delivery of them by instalments.
(2) Where there is a contract for the sale of goods to be delivered by stated instalments, which are to be separately paid for, and the seller makes defective deliveries in respect of one or more instalments or the buyer neglects or refuses to take delivery of or pay for one or more instalments, it is a question in each case depending on the terms of the contract and the circumstances of the case whether the breach of contract is a repudiation of the whole contract or whether it is a severable breach giving rise to a claim for compensation but not to a right to treat the whole contract as repudiated.
(3) This section does not apply to a contract to which Chapter 2 of Part 1 of the Consumer Contract Rights Act 2015 applies (but see the provision made about such contracts in section 26 of that Act).

32 Delivery to carrier

(1) Where, in pursuance of a contract of sale, the seller is authorised or required to send the goods to the buyer, delivery of the goods to a carrier (whether named by the buyer or not) for the purpose of transmission to the buyer is *prima facie* deemed to be a delivery of the goods to the buyer.
(2) Unless otherwise authorised by the buyer, the seller must make such contract with the carrier on behalf of the buyer as may be reasonable having regard to the nature of the goods and the other circumstances of the case; and if the seller omits to do so, and the goods are lost or damaged in course of transit, the buyer may decline to treat the delivery to the carrier as a delivery to himself or may hold the seller responsible in damages.
(3) Unless otherwise agreed, where goods are sent by the seller to the buyer by a route involving sea transit, under circumstances in which it is usual to insure, the seller must give such notice to the buyer as may enable him to insure them during their sea transit; and if the seller fails to do so, the goods are at his risk during such sea transit.
(4) [Omitted].
(5) This section does not apply to a contract to which Chapter 2 of Part 1 of the Consumer Contract Rights Act 2015 applies (but see the provision made about such contracts in section 29 of that Act).

33 Risk where goods are delivered at distant place

(1) Where the seller of goods agrees to deliver them at his own risk at a place other than that where they are when sold, the buyer must nevertheless (unless otherwise agreed) take any risk of deterioration in the goods necessarily incident to the course of transit.

(2) This section does not apply to a contract to which Chapter 2 of Part 1 of the Consumer Contract Rights Act 2015 applies (but see the provision made about such contracts in section 29 of that Act).

34 Buyer's right of examining the goods

(1) Unless otherwise agreed, when the seller tenders delivery of goods to the buyer, he is bound on request to afford the buyer a reasonable opportunity of examining the goods for the purpose of ascertaining whether they are in conformity with the contract and, in the case of a contract for sale by sample, of comparing the bulk with the sample.
(2) Nothing in this section affects the operation of section 22 (time limit for short-term right to reject) of the Consumer Rights Act 2015.

35 Acceptance

(1) The buyer is deemed to have accepted the goods subject to subsection (2) below –
   (a) when he intimates to the seller that he has accepted them; or
   (b) when the goods have been delivered to him and he does any act in relation to them which is inconsistent with the ownership of the seller.
(2) Where goods are delivered to the buyer, and he has not previously examined them, he is not deemed to have accepted them under subsection (1) above until he has had a reasonable opportunity of examining them for the purpose –
   (a) of ascertaining whether they are in conformity with the contract; and
   (b) in the case of a contract for sale by sample, of comparing the bulk with the sample.
(3) [Omitted]
(4) The buyer is also deemed to have accepted the goods when after the lapse of a reasonable time he retains the goods without intimating to the seller that he has rejected them.
(5) The questions that are material in determining for the purposes of subsection (4) above whether a reasonable time has elapsed include whether the buyer has had a reasonable opportunity of examining the goods for the purpose mentioned in subsection (2) above.
(6) The buyer is not by virtue of this section deemed to have accepted the goods merely because –
   (a) he asks for, or agrees to, their repair by or under an arrangement with the seller; or
   (b) the goods are delivered to another under a sub-sale or other disposition.
(7) Where the contract is for the sale of goods making one or more commercial units, a buyer accepting any goods included in a unit is deemed to have accepted all the goods making the unit; and in this subsection 'commercial unit' means a unit division of which would materially impair the value of the goods or the character of the unit.
(8) [Omitted].
(9) This section does not apply to a contract to which Chapter 2 of Part 1 of the Consumer Contract Rights Act 2015 applies (but see the provision made about such contracts in section 21 of that Act).

35A Right of partial rejection

(1) If the buyer –

(a) has the right to reject the goods by reason of a breach on the part of the seller that affects some or all of them; but

(b) accepts some of the goods, including, where there are any goods unaffected by the breach, all such goods, he does not by accepting them lose his right to reject the rest.

(2) In the case of a buyer having the right to reject an instalment of goods, subsection (1) above applies as if references to the goods were references to the goods comprised in the instalment.

(3) For the purposes of subsection (1) above, goods are affected by a breach if by reason of the breach they are not in conformity with the contract.

(4) This section applies unless a contrary intention appears in, or is to be implied from, the contract.

(5) This section does not apply to a contract to which Chapter 2 of Part 1 of the Consumer Contract Rights Act 2015 applies (but see the provision made about such contracts in section 21 of that Act).

36 Buyer not bound to return rejected goods

(1) Unless otherwise agreed, where goods are delivered to the buyer, and he refuses to accept them, having the right to do so, he is not bound to return them to the seller, but it is sufficient if he intimates to the seller that he refuses to accept them.

(2) This section does not apply to a contract to which Chapter 2 of Part 1 the Consumer Rights Act 2015 applies (but see the provision made about such contracts in section 20 of that Act.

37 Buyer's liability for not taking delivery of goods

(1) When the seller is ready and willing to deliver the goods, and requests the buyer to take delivery, and the buyer does not within a reasonable time after such request take delivery of the goods, he is liable to the seller for any loss occasioned by his neglect or refusal to take delivery, and also for a reasonable charge for the care and custody of the goods.

(2) Nothing in this section affects the rights of the seller where the neglect or refusal of the buyer to take delivery amounts to a repudiation of the contract.

Part V Rights of unpaid seller against the goods

Preliminary

38 Unpaid seller defined

(1) The seller of goods is an unpaid seller within the meaning of this Act –

(a) when the whole of the price has not been paid or tendered;

(b) when a bill of exchange or other negotiable instrument has been received as conditional payment, and the condition on which it was received has not been fulfilled by reason of the dishonour of the instrument or otherwise.

(2) In this Part of this Act 'seller' includes any person who is in the position of a seller, as, for instance, an agent of the seller to whom the bill of lading has been indorsed, or a consignor or agent who has himself paid (or is directly responsible for) the price.

39 Unpaid seller's rights

(1) Subject to this and any other Act, notwithstanding that the property in the goods may have passed to the buyer, the unpaid seller of goods, as such, has by implication of law –

(a) a lien on the goods or right to retain them for the price while he is in possession of them;

(b) in case of the insolvency of the buyer, a right of stopping the goods in transit after he has parted with the possession of them;

(c) a right of re-sale as limited by this Act.

(2) Where the property in goods has not passed to the buyer, the unpaid seller has (in addition to his other remedies) a right of withholding delivery similar to and co-extensive with his rights of lien or retention and stoppage in transit where the property has passed to the buyer.

40 [Repealed]

Unpaid seller's lien

41 Seller's lien

(1) Subject to this Act, the unpaid seller of goods who is in possession of them is entitled to retain possession of them until payment or tender of the price in the following cases –

(a) where the goods have been sold without any stipulation as to credit;

(b) where the goods have been sold on credit but the term of credit has expired;

(c) where the buyer becomes insolvent.

(2) The seller may exercise his lien or right of retention notwithstanding that he is in possession of the goods as agent or bailee or custodier for the buyer.

42 Part delivery

Where an unpaid seller has made part delivery of the goods, he may exercise his lien or right of retention on the remainder, unless such part delivery has been made under such circumstances as to show an agreement to waive the lien or right of retention.

43 Termination of lien

(1) The unpaid seller of goods loses his lien or right of retention in respect of them –

(a) when he delivers the goods to a carrier or other bailee or custodier for the purpose of transmission to the buyer without reserving the right of disposal of the goods;

(b) when the buyer or his agent lawfully obtains possession of the goods;

(c) by waiver of the lien or right of retention.

(2) An unpaid seller of goods who has a lien or right of retention in respect of them does not lose his lien or right of retention by reason only that he has obtained judgment or decree for the price of the goods.

Stoppage in transit

44 Right of stoppage in transit

Subject to this Act, when the buyer of goods becomes insolvent the unpaid seller who has parted with the possession of the goods has the right of stopping them in transit, that is to say, he may resume possession of the goods as long as they are in course of transit, and may retain them until payment or tender the price.

45 Duration of transit

(1) Goods are deemed to be in course of transit from the time when they are delivered to a carrier or other bailee or custodier for the purpose of transmission to the buyer, until the buyer or his agent in that behalf takes delivery of them from the carrier or other bailee or custodier.
(2) If the buyer or his agent in that behalf obtains delivery of the goods before their arrival at the appointed destination, the transit is at an end.
(3) If, after the arrival of the goods at the appointed destination, the carrier or other bailee or custodier acknowledges to the buyer or his agent that he holds the goods on his behalf and continues in possession of them as bailee or custodier for the buyer or his agent, the transit is at an end, and it is immaterial that a further destination for the goods may have been indicated by the buyer.
(4) If the goods are rejected by the buyer, and the carrier or other bailee or custodier continues in possession of them, the transit is not deemed to be at an end, even if the seller has refused to receive them back.
(5) When goods are delivered to a ship chartered by the buyer it is a question depending on the circumstances of the particular case whether they are in the possession of the master as a carrier or as agent to the buyer.
(6) Where the carrier or other bailee or custodier wrongfully refuses to deliver the goods to the buyer or his agent in that behalf, the transit is deemed to be at an end.
(7) Where part delivery of the goods has been made to the buyer or his agent in that behalf, the remainder of the goods may be stopped in transit, unless such part delivery has been made under such circumstances as to show an agreement to give up possession of the whole of the goods.

46 How stoppage in transit is effected

(1) The unpaid seller may exercise his right of stoppage in transit either by taking actual possession of the goods or by giving notice of his claim to the carrier or other bailee or custodier in whose possession the goods are.
(2) The notice may be given either to the person in actual possession of the goods or to his principal.
(3) If given to the principal, the notice is ineffective unless given at such time and under such circumstances that the principal, by the exercise of reasonable diligence, may communicate it to his servant or agent in time to prevent a delivery to the buyer.
(4) When notice of stoppage in transit is given by the seller to the carrier or other bailee or custodier in possession of the goods, he must re-deliver the goods to, or according

to the directions of, the seller; and the expenses of the redelivery must be borne by the seller.

Re-sale, etc., by buyer

47 Effect of sub-sale etc. by buyer

(1) Subject to this Act, the unpaid seller's right of lien or retention or stoppage in transit is not affected by any sale or other disposition of the goods which the buyer may have made, unless the seller has assented to it.

(2) Where a document of title to goods has been lawfully transferred to any person as buyer or owner of the goods, and that person transfers the document to a person who takes it in good faith and for valuable consideration, then –

(a) if the last-mentioned transfer was by way of sale the unpaid seller's right of lien or retention or stoppage in transit is defeated; and

(b) if the last-mentioned transfer was made by way of pledge or other disposition for value, the unpaid seller's right of lien or retention or stoppage in transit can only be exercised subject to the rights of the transferee.

Rescission and re-sale by seller

48 Rescission and re-sale by seller

(1) Subject to this section, a contract of sale is not rescinded by the mere exercise by an unpaid seller of his right of lien or retention or stoppage in transit.

(2) Where an unpaid seller who has exercised his right of lien or retention or stoppage in transit re-sells the goods, the buyer acquires a good title to them as against the original buyer.

(3) Where the goods are of a perishable nature, or where the unpaid seller gives notice to the buyer of his intention to re-sell, and the buyer does not within a reasonable time pay or tender the price, the unpaid seller may re-sell the goods and recover from the original buyer damages for any loss occasioned by his breach of contract.

(4) Where the seller expressly reserves the right of re-sale in case the buyer should make default, and on the buyer making default re-sells the goods, the original contract of sale is rescinded but without prejudice to any claim the seller may have for damages.

Part VA

48A–48F [Omitted]

Part VI Actions for breach of the contract

Seller's remedies

49 Action for price

(1) Where, under a contract of sale, the property in the goods has passed to the buyer and he wrongfully neglects or refuses to pay for the goods according to the terms of the contract, the seller may maintain an action against him for the price of the goods.

(2) Where, under a contract of sale, the price is payable on a certain day irrespective of delivery and the buyer wrongfully neglects or refuses to pay such price, the seller may maintain an action for the price, although the property in the goods has not passed and the goods have not been appropriated to the contract.
(3) Nothing in this section prejudices the right of the seller in Scotland to recover interest on the price from the date of tender of the goods, or from the date on which the price was payable, as the case may be.

50 Damages for non-acceptance

(1) Where the buyer wrongfully neglects or refuses to accept and pay for the goods, the seller may maintain an action against him for damages for non-acceptance.
(2) The measure of damages is the estimated loss directly and naturally resulting, in the ordinary course of events, from the buyer's breach of contract.
(3) Where there is an available market for the goods in question the measure of damages is *prima facie* to be ascertained by the difference between the contract price and the market or current price at the time or times when the goods ought to have been accepted or (if no time was fixed for acceptance) at the time of the refusal to accept.

Buyer's remedies

51 Damages for non-delivery

(1) Where the seller wrongfully neglects or refuses to deliver the goods to the buyer, the buyer may maintain an action against the seller for damages for non-delivery.
(2) The measure of damages is the estimated loss directly and naturally resulting, in the ordinary course of events, from the seller's breach of contract.
(3) Where there is an available market for the goods in question the measure of damages is *prima facie* to be ascertained by the difference between the contract price and the market or current price of the goods at the time or times when they ought to have been delivered or (if no time was fixed) at the time of the refusal to deliver.
(4) This section does not apply to a contract to which Chapter 2 of Part 1 of the Consumer Rights Act 2015 applies (but see the provision made about such contracts in section 19 of the Act).

52 Specific performance

(1) In any action for breach of contract to deliver specific or ascertained goods the court may, if it thinks fit, on the plaintiff's application, by its judgment or decree direct that the contract shall be performed specifically, without giving the defendant the option of retaining the goods on payment of damages.
(2) The plaintiff's application may be made at any time before judgment or decree.
(3) The judgment or decree may be unconditional, or on such terms and conditions as to damages, payment of the price and otherwise as seem just to the court.
(4) The provisions of this section shall be deemed to be supplementary to, and not in derogation of, the right of specific implement in Scotland.

(5) This section does not apply to a contract to which Chapter 2 of Part 1 of the Consumer Rights Act 2015 applies (but see the provision made about such contracts in section 19 of the Act).

53 Remedy for breach of warranty

(1) Where there is a breach of warranty by the seller, or where the buyer elects (or is compelled) to treat any breach of a condition on the part of the seller as a breach of warranty, the buyer is not by reason only of such breach of warranty entitled to reject the goods; but he may:
   (a) set up against the seller the breach of warranty in diminution or extinction of the price, or
   (b) maintain an action against the seller for damages for the breach of warranty.
(2) The measure of damages for breach of warranty is the estimated loss directly and naturally resulting, in the ordinary course of events, from the breach of warranty.
(3) In the case of breach of warranty of quality such loss is *prima facie* the difference between the value of the goods at the time of delivery to the buyer and the value they would have had if they had fulfilled the warranty.
(4) The fact that the buyer has set up the breach of warranty in diminution or extinction of the price does not prevent him from maintaining an action for the same breach of warranty if he has suffered further damage.
(4A) This section does not apply to a contract to which Chapter 2 of Part 1 of the Consumer Rights Act 2015 applies (but see the provision made about such contracts in section 19 of the Act).
(5) This section does not apply to Scotland.

53A Measure of damages as respects Scotland

(1) The measure of damages for the seller's breach of contract is the estimated loss directly and naturally resulting, in the ordinary course of events, from the breach.
(2) Where the seller's breach consists of the delivery of goods which are not of the quality required by the contract and the buyer retains the goods, such loss as aforesaid is *prima facie* the difference between the value of the goods at the time of delivery to the buyer and the value they would have had if they had fulfilled the contract.
(2A) This section does not apply to a contract to which Chapter 2 of Part 1 of the Consumer Rights Act 2015 applies (but see the provision made about such contracts in section 19 of the Act).
(3) This section applies to Scotland only.

Interest, etc.

54 Interest, etc.

(1) Nothing in this Act affects the right of the buyer or the seller to recover interest or special damages in any case where by law interest or special damages may be recoverable, or to recover money paid where the consideration for the payment of it has failed.

(2) This section does not apply to a contract to which Chapter 2 of Part 1 of the Consumer Rights Act 2015 applies (but see the provision made about such contracts in section 19 of that Act).

Part VII Supplementary

55 Exclusion of implied terms

(1) Where a right, duty or liability would arise under a contract of sale of goods by implication of law, it may (subject to the Unfair Contract Terms Act 1977) be negatived or varied by express agreement, or by the course of dealing between the parties, or by such usage as binds both parties to the contract.
(1A) Subsection (1) does not apply to a contract to which Chapter 2 of Part 1 the Consumer Rights Act 2015 applies (but see the provision made about such contracts in section 31 of that Act).
(2) An express term does not negative a term implied by this Act unless inconsistent with it.
(3) [Omitted].

56 [Omitted]

57 Auction sales

(1) Where goods are put up for sale by auction in lots, each lot is *prima facie* deemed to be the subject of a separate contract of sale.
(2) A sale by auction is complete when the auctioneer announces its completion by the fall of the hammer, or in other customary manner; and until the announcement is made any bidder may retract his bid.
(3) A sale by auction may be notified to be subject to a reserve or upset price, and a right to bid may also be reserved expressly by or on behalf of the seller.
(4) Where a sale by auction is not notified to be subject to a right to bid by or on behalf of the seller, it is not lawful for the seller to bid himself or to employ any person to bid at the sale, or for the auctioneer knowingly to take any bid from the seller or any such person.
(5) A sale contravening subsection (4) above may be treated as fraudulent by the buyer.
(6) Where, in respect of a sale by auction, a right to bid is expressly reserved (but not otherwise) the seller or any one person on his behalf may bid at the auction.

58 [Omitted]

59 Reasonable time a question of fact

Where a reference is made in this Act to a reasonable time the question what is a reasonable time is a question of fact.

60 Rights etc. enforceable by action

Where a right, duty or liability is declared by this Act, it may (unless otherwise provided by this Act) be enforced by action.

61 Interpretation

(1) In this Act, unless the context or subject matter otherwise requires –

'action' includes counterclaim and set-off, and in Scotland condescendence and claim and compensation;

'bulk' means a mass or collection of goods of the same kind which –

(a) is contained in a defined space or area; and

(b) is such that any goods in the bulk are interchangeable with any other goods therein of the same number or quantity;

'business' includes a profession and the activities of any Government department (including a Northern Ireland department) or local or public authority;

'buyer' means a person who buys or agrees to buy goods;

'contract of sale' includes an agreement to sell as well as a sale;

'credit-broker' means a person acting in the course of a business of credit brokerage carried on by him, that is a business of effecting introduction of individuals desiring to obtain credit –

(a) to persons carrying on any business so far as it relates to the provision of credit; or

(b) to other persons engaged in credit brokerage;

'defendant' includes in Scotland defender, respondent, and claimant in a multiplepoinding;

'delivery' means voluntary transfer of possession from one person to another, except that in relation to sections 20A and 20B above it includes such appropriation of goods to the contract as results in property in the goods being transferred to the buyer;

'document of title to goods' has the same meaning as it has in the Factors Acts;

'Factors Acts' means the Factors Act 1889, the Factors (Scotland) Act 1890, and any enactment amending or substituted for the same;

'fault' means wrongful act or default;

'future goods' means goods to be manufactured or acquired by the seller after the making of the contract of sale;

'goods' includes all personal chattels other than things in action and money, and in Scotland all corporeal moveables except money; and in particular 'goods' includes emblements, industrial growing crops, and things attached to or forming part of the land which are agreed to be severed before sale or under the contract of sale and includes an undivided share in goods;

'plaintiff includes pursuer, complainer, claimant in a multiplepoinding and defendant or defender counter-claiming;

'property' means the general property in goods, and not merely a special property;

'sale' includes a bargain and sale as well as a sale and delivery;

'seller' means a person who sells or agrees to sell goods;

'specific goods' means goods identified and agreed on at the time a contract of sale is made and includes an undivided share, specified as a fraction or percentage, of goods identified and agreed on as aforesaid;

'warranty' (as regards England and Wales and Northern Ireland) means an agreement with reference to goods which are the subject of a contract of sale, but collateral to the main purpose of such contract, the breach of which gives rise to a claim for damages, but not to a right to reject the goods and treat the contract as repudiated.

(2) [Repealed].
(3) A thing is deemed to be done in good faith within the meaning of this Act when it is in fact done honestly, whether it is done negligently or not.
(4) A person is deemed to be insolvent within the meaning of this Act if he has either ceased to pay his debts in the ordinary course of business or he cannot pay his debts as they become due.
(5) Goods are in a deliverable state within the meaning of this Act when they are in such a state that the buyer would under the contract be bound to take delivery of them.
(6) [Omitted].

62 Savings: Rules of law etc.

(1) [Omitted].
(2) The rules of the common law, including the law merchant, except in so far as they are inconsistent with the provisions of legislation including this Act and the Consumer Rights Act 2015, and in particular the rules relating to the law of principal and agent and the effect of fraud, misrepresentation, duress or coercion, mistake, or other invalidating cause, apply to contracts for the sale of goods.
(3) [Omitted].
(4) The provisions of this Act about contracts of sale do not apply to a transaction in the form of a contract of sale which is intended to operate by way of mortgage, pledge, charge, or other security.
(5) [Omitted].

63–64 And Schedules 1–4 [Omitted]

Civil Jurisdiction and Judgments Act 1982

Part I Implementation of the Conventions

Main implementing provisions

1 Interpretation of references to the Conventions and contracting states

(1) In this Act –

'the 1968 Convention' means the Convention on jurisdiction and the enforcement of judgments in civil and commercial matters (including the Protocol annexed to that Convention), signed at Brussels on 27th September 1968;

'the 1971 Protocol' means the Protocol on the interpretation of the 1968 Convention by the European Court, signed at Luxembourg on 3rd June 1971;

'the Accession convention' means the Convention on the accession to the 1968 convention and the 1971 Protocol of Denmark, the Republic of Ireland and the United Kingdom, signed at Luxembourg on 9th October 1978;

'the 1982 Accession Convention' means the Convention on the accession of the Hellenic Republic to the 1968 Convention and the 1971 Protocol, with the adjustments made to them by the Accession Convention, signed at Luxembourg on 25th October 1982;

'the 1989 Accession Convention' means the Convention on the accession of the Kingdom of Spain and the Portuguese Republic to the 1968 convention and the 1971 Protocol, with the adjustments made to them by the Accession convention and the 1982 Accession Convention, signed at Donostia-San Sebastian on 26th May 1989;

'the 1996 Accession Convention' means the Convention on the accession of the Republic of Austria, the Republic of Finland and the Kingdom of Sweden to the 1968 Convention and the 1971 Protocol, with the adjustments made to them by the Accession Convention, the 1982 Accession Convention and the 1989 Accession Convention, signed at Brussels on 29th November 1996;

'the 2007 Hague Convention' means the Convention on the International Recovery of Child Support and other forms of Family Maintenance done at The Hague on 23 November 2007;

'the Brussels Conventions' means the 1968 Convention, the 1971 Protocol, the Accession Convention, the 1982 Accession Convention, the 1989 Accession Convention and the 1996 Accession Convention;

'the Lugano Convention' means the Convention on jurisdiction and the recognition and enforcement of judgments in civil and commercial matters, between the European Community and the Republic of Iceland, the Kingdom of Norway, the Swiss Confederation and the Kingdom of Denmark signed on behalf of the European Community on 30th October 2007;

'the Maintenance Regulation' means Council Regulation (EC) No 4/2009 including as applied in relation to Denmark by virtue of the Agreement made on 19th October 2005 between the European Community and the Kingdom of Denmark;

'the Regulation' means Council Regulation (EC) No. 44/2001 of 22nd December 2000 on jurisdiction and the recognition and enforcement of judgments in civil and commercial matters, as amended from time to time and as applied by the Agreement made on 19th October 2005 between the European Community and the Kingdom of Denmark on jurisdiction and the recognition and enforcement of judgments in civil and commercial matters (OJ No. L 299 16.11.2005 at p 62).

(2) [Omitted].

(3) In this Act –

'2007 Hague Convention State', in any provision, in the application of that provision in relation to the 2007 Hague Convention, means a State bound by that Convention;

'Contracting State', without more, in any provision means –

(a) in the application of the provision in relation to the Brussels Conventions, a Brussels Contracting State; and

(b) in the application of the provision in relation to the Lugano Convention, a State bound by the Lugano Convention.

'Brussels Contracting State' means a state which is one of the original parties to the 1968 Convention or one of the parties acceding to that Convention under the Accession

Convention, or under the 1982 Accession Convention, or under the 1989 Accession Convention, but only with respect to any territory –

(a) to which the Brussels Conventions apply; and

(b) which is excluded from the scope of the Regulation pursuant to Articles 349 and 355 of the Treaty on the Functioning of the European Union;

'Maintenance Regulation State', in any provision, in the application of that provision in relation to the Maintenance Regulation means a Member State

'State bound by the Lugano Convention' in any provision, in the application of that provision in relation to the Lugano Convention has the same meaning as in Article 1(3) of that Convention.

'Regulation State' in any provision, in the application of that provision in relation to the Regulation, means a Member State.

(4) Any question arising as to whether it is the Regulation, any of the Brussels Conventions, or the Lugano Convention which applies in the circumstances of a particular case shall be determined as follows –

(a) in accordance with Article 64 of the Lugano Convention (which determines the relationship between the Brussels Conventions and the Lugano Convention); and

(b) in accordance with Article 68 of the Regulation (which determines the relationship between the Brussels Conventions and the Regulation).

2 The Brussels Conventions to have the force of law

(1) The Brussels Conventions shall have the force of law in the United Kingdom, and judicial notice shall be taken of them.

(2) [Omitted].

3 Interpretation of the Brussels Conventions

(1) Any question as to the meaning or effect of any provision of the Brussels Conventions shall, if not referred to the European Court in accordance with the 1971 Protocol, be determined in accordance with the principles laid down by any relevant decision of the European Court.

(2) Judicial notice shall be taken of any decision of, or expression of opinion by, the European Court on any such question.

(3) Without prejudice to the generality of subsection (1), the following reports (which are reproduced in the Official Journal of the Communities), namely –

(a) the reports by Mr P Jenard on the 1968 Convention and the 1971 Protocol;

(b) the report by Professor Peter Schlosser on the Accession Convention;

(c) the report by Professor Demetrios I Evvigenis and Professor K D Kerameus on the 1982 Accession Convention; and

(d) the report by Mr Martinho de Almeida Cruz, Mr Manuel Desantes Real and Mr P Jenard on the 1989 Accession Convention,

(e) may be considered in ascertaining the meaning or effect of any provision of the Brussels Conventions and shall be given such weight as is appropriate in the circumstances.

3A [Repealed]

3B [Repealed]

4–23 [Omitted]

Part IV Miscellaneous provisions

Provisions relating to jurisdiction

24 Interim relief and protective measures in cases of doubtful jurisdiction

(1) Any power of a court in England and Wales or Northern Ireland to grant interim relief pending trial or pending the determination of an appeal shall extend to a case where –
- (a) the issue to be tried, or which is the subject of the appeal, relates to the jurisdiction of the court to entertain the proceedings; or
- (b) the proceedings involve the reference of any matter to the European Court under the 1971 Protocol; or
- (c) the proceedings involve a reference of any matter relating to the Regulation or the Lugano Convention to the European Court under Article 267 of the Treaty on the Functioning of the European Union; or.
- (d) the proceedings involve a reference of any matter relating to the Maintenance Regulation to the European Court under Article 267 of the Treaty on the Functioning of the European Union.

(2) Any power of a court in Scotland to grant protective measures pending the decision of any hearing shall apply to a case where –
- (a) the subject of the proceedings includes a question as to the jurisdiction of the court to entertain them; or
- (b) the proceedings involve the reference of a matter to the European Court under the 1971 Protocol; or
- (c) the proceedings involve a reference of any matter relating to the Regulation or the Lugano Convention to the European Court under Article 267 of the Treaty on the Functioning of the European Union; or
- (d) the proceedings involve a reference of any matter relating to the Maintenance Regulation to the European Court under Article 267 of the Treaty on the Functioning of the European Union.

(3) Subsections (1) and (2) shall not be construed as restricting any power to grant relief of protective measures which a court may have apart from this section.

25 Interim relief in England and Wales and Northern Ireland in the absence of substantive proceedings

(1) The High Court in England and Wales or Northern Ireland shall have power to grant interim relief where –
- (a) proceedings have been or are to be commended in a Brussels Contracting State or a State bound by the Lugano Convention or a Regulation State or a Maintenance Regulation State other than the United Kingdom or in a part of the United

Kingdom other than that in which the High Court in question exercises jurisdiction; and

(b) they are or will be proceedings whose subject-matter is either within the scope of the Regulation as determined by Article 1 of the Regulation, within the scope of the Maintenance Regulation as determined by Article 1 of that Regulation or within the scope of the Lugano Convention as determined by Article 1 of the Lugano Convention (whether or not the Regulation, the Maintenance Regulation or the Lugano Convention has effect in relation to the proceedings).

(2) On an application for any interim relief under subsection (1) the court may refuse to grant that relief it, in the opinion of the court, the fact that the court has no jurisdiction apart from this section in relation to the subject-matter of the proceedings in question makes it inexpedient for the court to grant it.

(3) [Omitted]

(4) [Omitted]

(5) [Repealed]

(6) [Omitted]

(7) In this section "interim relief", in relation to the High Court in England and Wales or Northern Ireland, means interim relief of any kind which that court has power to grant in proceedings relating to matters within its jurisdiction, other than –

(a) a warrant for the arrest of property; or

(b) provision for obtaining evidence.

26 Security in Admiralty proceedings in England and Wales or Northern Ireland in case of stay, etc.

(1) Where in England and Wales or Northern Ireland a court stays or dismisses Admiralty proceedings on the ground that the dispute in question should be submitted to the determination of the courts of another part of the United Kingdom or of an overseas country, the court may, if in those proceedings property has been arrested or bail or other security has been given to prevent or obtain release from arrest –

(a) order that the property arrested be retained as security for the satisfaction of any award or judgment which –

(i) is given in respect of the dispute in the legal proceedings in favour of which those proceedings are stayed or dismissed; and

(ii) is enforceable in England and Wales or, as the case may be, in Northern Ireland; or

(b) order that the stay or dismissal of those proceedings be conditional on the provision of equivalent security for the satisfaction of any such award or judgment.

(2) Where a court makes an order under subsection (1), it may attach such conditions to the order as it thinks fit, in particular conditions with respect to the institution or prosecution of the relevant legal proceedings.

(3) Subject to any provision made by rules of court and to any necessary modifications, the same law and practice shall apply in relation to property retained in pursuance of an order made by a court under subsection (1) as would apply if it were held for the purposes of proceedings in that court.

27–30 [Omitted]

Provisions relating to recognition and enforcement of judgments

31 Overseas judgments given against states, etc.

(1) A judgment given by a court of an overseas country against a State to which that court belongs shall be recognised and enforced in the United Kingdom if, and only if –
  (a) it would be so recognised and enforced if it had not been given against a State; and
  (b) that court would have had jurisdiction in the matter if it had applied rules corresponding to those applicable to such matters in the United Kingdom in accordance with sections 2 to 11 of the State Immunity Act 1978.

(2) References in subsection (1) to a judgment given against a State include references to judgments of any of the following descriptions given in relation to a State –
  (a) judgments against the government, or a department of the government, of the State but not (except as mentioned in paragraph (c)) judgments against an entity which is distinct from the executive organs of Government;
  (b) judgments against the sovereign or head of State in his public capacity;
  (c) judgments against any such separate entity as is mentioned in paragraph (a) given in proceedings relating to anything done by it in the exercise of the sovereign authority of the State.

(3) Nothing in subsection (1) shall affect the recognition or enforcement in the United Kingdom of a judgment to which Part I of the Foreign Judgments (Reciprocal Enforcement) Act 1933 applies by virtue of section 4 of the Carriage of Goods by Road Act 1965, section 17(4) of the Nuclear Installations Act 1965, section 166(4) of the Merchant Shipping Act 1995, regulation 8 of the Railways (Convention on International Carriage by Rail) Regulations 2005.

(4) Sections 12, 13 and 14(3) and (4) of the State Immunity Act 1978 (service of process and procedural privileges) shall apply to proceedings for the recognition or enforcement in the United Kingdom of a judgment given by a court of an overseas country (whether or not that judgment is within subsection (1) of this section) as they apply to other proceedings.

(5) In this section 'state', in the case of a federal State, includes any of its constituent territories.

32 Overseas judgments given in proceedings brought in breach of agreement for settlement of disputes

(1) Subject to the following provisions of this section, a judgment given by a court of an overseas country in any proceedings shall not be recognised or enforced in the United Kingdom if –
  (a) the bringing of those proceedings in that court was contrary to an agreement under which the dispute in question was to be settled otherwise than by proceedings in the courts of that country; and
  (b) those proceedings were not brought in that court by, or with the agreement of, the person against whom the judgment was given; and

(c) that person did not counterclaim in the proceedings or otherwise submit to the jurisdiction of that court.

(2) Subsection (1) does not apply where the agreement referred to in paragraph (a) of that subsection was illegal, void or unenforceable or was incapable of being performed for reasons not attributable to the fault of the party bringing the proceedings in which the judgment was given.

(3) In determining whether a judgment given by a court of an overseas country should be recognised or enforced in the United Kingdom, a court in the United Kingdom shall not be bound by any decision of the overseas court relating to any of the matters mentioned in subsection (1) or (2).

(4) Nothing in subsection (1) shall affect the recognition or enforcement in the United Kingdom of –

(a) a judgment which is required to be recognised or enforced there under the 1968 Convention or the Lugano Convention or the Regulation or the Maintenance Regulation;

(b) a judgment to which Part I of the Foreign Judgements (Reciprocal Enforcement) Act 1933 applies by virtue of section 4 of the Carriage of Goods by Road Act 1965, section 17(4) of the Nuclear Installations Act 1965, regulation 8 of the Railways (Convention on International Carriage by Rail) Regulations 2005 or section 177(4) of the Merchant Shipping Act 1995.

33 Certain steps not to amount to submission to jurisdiction of overseas court

(1) For the purposes of determining whether a judgment given by a court of an overseas country should be recognised or enforced in England and Wales or Northern Ireland, the person against whom the judgment was given shall not be regarded as having submitted to the jurisdiction of the court by reason only of the fact that he appeared (conditionally or otherwise) in the proceedings for all or any one or more of the following purposes, namely –

(a) to contest the jurisdiction of the court;

(b) to ask the court to dismiss or start the proceedings on the ground that the dispute in question should be submitted to arbitration or to the determination of the courts of another country;

(c) to protect, or obtain the release of, property seized or threatened with seizure in the proceedings.

(2) Nothing in this section shall affect the recognition or enforcement in England and Wales or Northern Ireland of a judgment which is required to be recognised or enforced there under the 1968 Convention or the Lugano Convention or the Regulation or the Maintenance Regulation.

34 Certain judgments a bar to further proceedings on the same cause of action

No proceedings may be brought by a person in England and Wales or Northern Ireland on a cause of action in respect of which a judgment has been given in his favour in proceedings between the same parties, or their privies, in a court in another part of the United Kingdom or in a court of an overseas country, unless that judgment is not enforceable or entitled to recognition in England and Wales or, as the case may be, in Northern Ireland.

35–45 [Omitted]

Part V Supplementary and general provisions

Domicile

46 Domicile and seat of the Crown

(1) For the purposes of this Act the seat of the Crown (as determined by this section) shall be treated as its domicile.
(2) The following provisions of this section determine where the Crown has its seat –
 (a) for the purposes of the 1968 Convention and the Lugano Convention, (in each of which Article 53 equates the domicile of a legal person with its seat); and
 (b) for the purposes of this Act.
(3) Subject to the provisions of any Order in Council for the time being in force under subsection (4) –
 (a) the Crown in right of Her Majesty's government in the United Kingdom has its seat in every part of, and every place in, the United Kingdom; and
 (b) the Crown in the right of the Scottish Administration has its seat in, and in every place in, Scotland;
 (c) the Crown in right of Her Majesty's government in Northern Ireland has its seat in, and in every place in, Northern Ireland.
(4) Her Majesty may by Order in Council provide that, in the case of proceedings of any specified description against the Crown in right of Her Majesty's government in the United Kingdom, the Crown shall be treated for the purposes of the 1968 Convention, and this Act as having its seat in, and in every place in, a specified part of the United Kingdom and not in any other part of the United Kingdom.
(5) An Order in council under subsection (4) may frame a description of proceedings in any way, and in particular may do so by reference to the government department or officer of the Crown against which or against whom they fall to be instituted.
(6) [Omitted].
(7) Nothing in this section applies to the Crown otherwise than in right of Her Majesty's government in the United Kingdom or Her Majesty's government in Northern Ireland.

47–48 [Omitted]

49 Saving for powers to stay, sist, strike out or dismiss proceedings

Nothing in this Act shall prevent any court in the United Kingdom from staying, sisting, striking out or dismissing any proceedings before it, on the ground of forum non conveniens or otherwise, where to do so is not inconsistent with the 1968 Convention or, as the case may be, the Lugano Convention.

50–55 [Omitted]

Foreign Limitation Periods Act 1984

1 Application of Foreign Limitation Law

(1) Subject to the following provisions of this Act, where in any action or proceedings in a court in England and Wales the law of any other country falls (in accordance with rules of private international law applicable by any such court) to be taken into account in the determination of any matter –
  (a) the law of that country relating to limitation shall apply in respect of that matter for the purposes of the action or proceedings, subject to section 1A; and
  (b) except where that matter falls within subsection (2) below, the law of England and Wales relating to limitation shall not so apply.

(2) A matter falls within this subsection if it is a matter in the determination of which both the law of England and Wales and the law of some other country fall to be taken into account.

(3) The law of England and Wales shall determine for the purposes of any law applicable by virtue of subsection (1)(a) above whether, and the time at which, proceedings have been commenced in respect of any matter; and, accordingly, section 35 of the Limitation Act 1980 (new claims in pending proceedings) shall apply in relation to time limits applicable by virtue of subsection (1)(a) above as it applies in relation to time limits under that Act.

(4) A court in England and Wales, in exercising in pursuance of subsection (1)(a) above any discretion conferred by the law of any other country, shall so far as practicable exercise that discretion in the manner in which it is exercised in comparable cases by the courts of that other country.

(5) In this section "law", in relation to any country, shall not include rules of private international law applicable by the courts of that country or, in the case of England and Wales, this Act.

1A Extension of limitation periods because of mediation of certain cross-border disputes

(1) In this section –
  (a) "Mediation Directive" means Directive 2008/52/EC of the European Parliament and of the Council of 21 May 2008 on certain aspects of mediation in civil and commercial matters,
  (b) "mediation" has the meaning given by article 3(a) of the Mediation Directive,
  (c) "mediator" has the meaning given by article 3(b) of the Mediation Directive, and
  (d) "relevant dispute" means a dispute to which article 8(1) of the Mediation Directive applies (certain cross-border disputes).

(2) Subsection (3) applies where –
  (a) a limitation period prescribed by any law applicable by virtue of section 1(1)(a) relates to the subject of the whole or part of a relevant dispute,
  (b) a mediation in relation to the relevant dispute starts before the period expires, and

(c) if not extended by this section, the period would expire before the mediation ends or less than eight weeks after it ends.

(3) For the purposes of initiating judicial proceedings or arbitration, the limitation period expires instead at the end of eight weeks after the mediation ends (subject to subsection (4)).

(4) If a limitation period has been extended by this section, subsections (2) and (3) apply to the extended limitation period as they apply to a limitation period mentioned in subsection (2)(a).

(5) For the purposes of this section, mediation starts on the date of the agreement to mediate that is entered into by the parties and the mediator.

(6) For the purposes of this section, a mediation ends on the date of the first of these to occur –

(a) the parties reach an agreement in resolution of the relevant dispute,

(b) a party completes the notification of the other parties that it has withdrawn from the mediation,

(c) a party to whom a qualifying request is made fails to give a response reaching the other parties within 14 days of the request,

(d) after the parties are notified that the mediator's appointment has ended (by death, resignation or otherwise), they fail to agree within 14 days to seek to appoint a replacement mediator,

(e) the mediation otherwise comes to an end pursuant to the terms of the agreement to mediate.

(7) For the purpose of subsection (6), a qualifying request is a request by a party that another (A) confirm to all parties that A is continuing with the mediation.

(8) In the case of any relevant dispute, references in this section to a mediation are references to the mediation so far as it relates to that dispute, and references to a party are to be read accordingly.

(9) This section is without prejudice to any enactment which has effect for the purposes of provisions –

(a) relating to limitation or prescription periods and

(b) contained in an international agreement to which the United Kingdom is a party.

2 Exceptions to Section 1

(1) In any case in which the application of section 1 above would to any extent conflict (whether under subsection (2) below or otherwise) with public policy, that section shall not apply to the extent that its application would so conflict.

(2) The application of section 1 above in relation to any action or proceedings shall conflict with public policy to the extent that its application would cause undue hardship to a person who is, or might be made, a party to the action or proceedings.

(3) Where, under a law applicable by virtue of section 1(1)(a) above for the purposes of any action or proceedings, a limitation period is or may be extended or interrupted in respect of the absence of a party to the action or proceedings from any specified jurisdiction or country, so much of that law as provides for the extension or interruption shall be disregarded for those purposes.

(4) [Omitted].

3 Foreign judgments on limitation points

Where a court in any country outside England and Wales has determined any matter wholly or partly by reference to the law of that or any other country (including England and Wales) relating to limitation, then, for the purposes of the law relating to the effect to be given in England and Wales to that determination, that court shall, to the extent that it has so determined the matter, be deemed to have determined it on its merits.

4 Meaning of law relating to limitation

(1) Subject to subsection (3) below, references in this Act to the law of any country (including England and Wales) relating to limitation shall, in relation to any matter, be construed as references to so much of the relevant law of that country as (in any manner) makes provision with respect to a limitation period applicable to the bringing of proceedings in respect of that matter in the courts of that country and shall include –
  (a) references to so much of that law as relates to, and to the effect of, the application, extension, reduction or interruption of that period; and
  (b) a reference, where under that law there is no limitation period which is so applicable, to the rule that such proceedings may be brought within an indefinite period.

(2) In subsection (1) above 'relevant law', in relation to any country, means the procedural and substantive law applicable, apart from any rules of private international law, by the courts of that country.

(3) References in this Act to the law of England and Wales relating to limitation shall not include the rules by virtue of which a court may, in the exercise of any discretion, refuse equitable relief on the grounds of acquiescence or otherwise; but, in applying those rules to a case in relation to which the law of any country outside England and Wales is applicable by virtue of section 1(1)(a) above (not being a law that provides for a limitation period that has expired), a court in England and Wales shall have regard, in particular, to the provisions of the law that is so applicable.

5 [Repealed]; 6 and 7 [Omitted]

8 Disapplication of Sections 1, 2 and 4 where the law applicable to limitation is determined by other instruments

(1) Where in proceedings in England and Wales the law of a country other than England and Wales falls to be taken into account by virtue of any choice of law rule contained in the Rome I Regulation or the Rome II Regulation, sections 1, 2 and 4 above shall not apply in respect of that matter.

(1A) In subsection (1) the "Rome I Regulation" means Regulation (EC) No. 593/2008 of the European Parliament and of the Council on the law applicable to contractual obligations, including that Regulation as applied by regulation 5 of the Law Applicable to Contractual Obligations (England and Wales and Northern Ireland) Regulations 2009 (conflicts solely between the laws of different parts of the United Kingdom or between one or more parts of the United Kingdom and Gibraltar).

(2) In subsection (1) the "Rome II Regulation" means Regulation (EC) No. 864/2007 of the European Parliament and of the Council on the law applicable to non-contractual

obligations, including that Regulation as applied by regulation 6 of the Law Applicable to Non-Contractual Obligations (England and Wales and Northern Ireland) Regulations 2008 (conflicts solely between the laws of different parts of the United Kingdom or between one or more parts of the United Kingdom and Gibraltar).

Computer Misuse Act 1990

Computer misuse offences

1 Unauthorised access to computer material

(1) A person is guilty of an offence if –
   (a) he causes a computer to perform any function with intent to secure access to any program or data held in any computer or to enable any such access to be secured;
   (b) the access he intends to secure or to enable to be secured, is unauthorised; and
   (c) he knows at the time when he causes the computer to perform the function that that is the case.

(2) The intent a person has to have to commit an offence under this section need not be directed at –
   (a) any particular program or data;
   (b) a program or data of any particular kind; or
   (c) a program or data held in any particular computer.

(3) A person guilty of an offence under this section shall be liable –
   (a) on summary conviction in England and Wales, to imprisonment for a term not exceeding 12 months or to a fine not exceeding the statutory maximum or to both;
   (b) on summary conviction in Scotland, to imprisonment for a term not exceeding 12 months or to a fine not exceeding the statutory maximum or to both;
   (c) on conviction on indictment, to imprisonment for a term not exceeding two years or to a fine or to both.

2 Unauthorised access with intent to commit or facilitate commission of further offences

(1) A person is guilty of an offence under this section if he commits an offence under section 1 above ('the unauthorised access offence') with intent –
   (a) to commit an offence to which this section applies; or
   (b) to facilitate the commission of such an offence (whether by himself or by any other person),

   and the offence he intends to commit or facilitate is referred to below in this section as the further offence.

(2) This section applies to offences –
   (a) for which the sentence is fixed by law; or
   (b) for which a person who has attained the age of twenty-one years (eighteen in relation to England and Wales) and has no previous convictions may be sentenced to imprisonment for a term of five years (or, in England and Wales, might be so sentenced but for the restrictions imposed by section 33 of the Magistrates' Courts Act 1980).

(3) It is immaterial for the purposes of this section whether the further offence is to be committed on the same occasion as the unauthorised access offence or on any future occasion.

(4) A person may be guilty of an offence under this section even though the facts are such that the commission of the further offence is impossible.

(5) A person guilty of an offence under this section shall be liable –

(a) on summary conviction in England and Wales, to imprisonment for a term not exceeding 12 months or to a fine not exceeding the statutory maximum or to both;

(b) on summary conviction in Scotland, to imprisonment for a term not exceeding 12 months or to a fine not exceeding the statutory maximum or to both;

(c) on conviction on indictment, to imprisonment for a term not exceeding five years or to a fine or to both.

3 Unauthorised acts with intent to impair, or with recklessness as to impairing, operation of computer, etc.

(1) A person is guilty of an offence if –

(a) he does any unauthorised act in relation to a computer;

(b) at the time when he does the act he knows that it is unauthorised; and

(c) either subsection (2) or subsection (3) below applies.

(2) This subsection applies if the person intends by doing the act –

(a) to impair the operation of any computer;

(b) to prevent or hinder access to any program or data held in any computer;

(c) to impair the operation of any such program or the reliability of any such data; or

(d) to enable any of the things mentioned in paragraphs (a) to (c) above to be done.

(3) This subsection applies if the person is reckless as to whether the act will do any of the things mentioned in paragraphs (a) to (d) of subsection (2) above.

(4) The intention referred to in subsection (2) above, or the recklessness referred to in subsection (3) above, need not relate to –

(a) any particular computer;

(b) any particular program or data; or

(c) a program or data of any particular kind.

(5) In this section –

(a) a reference to doing an act includes a reference to causing an act to be done;

(b) 'act' includes a series of acts;

(c) a reference to impairing, preventing or hindering something includes a reference to doing so temporarily.

(6) A person guilty of an offence under this section shall be liable –

(a) on summary conviction in England and Wales, to imprisonment for a term not exceeding 12 months or to a fine not exceeding the statutory maximum or to both;

(b) on summary conviction in Scotland, to imprisonment for a term not exceeding 12 months or to a fine not exceeding the statutory maximum or to both;

(c) on conviction on indictment, to imprisonment for a term not exceeding ten years or to a fine or to both.

3ZA Unauthorised acts causing, or creating risk of, serious damage

(1) A person is guilty of an offence if –
   (a) the person does any unauthorised act in relation to a computer;
   (b) at the time of doing the act the person knows that it is unauthorised;
   (c) the act causes, or creates a significant risk of, serious d amage of a material kind; and
   (d) the person intends by doing the act to cause serious damage of a material kind or is reckless as to whether such damage is caused.

(2) Damage is of a "material kind" for the purposes of this section if it is –
   (a) damage to human welfare in any place;
   (b) damage to the environment of any place;
   (c) damage to the economy of any country; or
   (d) damage to the national security of any country.

(3) For the purposes of subsection (2)(a) an act causes damage to human welfare only if it causes –
   (a) loss to human life;
   (b) human illness or injury;
   (c) disruption of a supply of money, food, water, energy or fuel;
   (d) disruption of a system of communication;
   (e) disruption of facilities for transport; or
   (f) disruption of services relating to health.

(4) It is immaterial for the purposes of subsection (2) whether or not an act causing damage –
   (a) does so directly;
   (b) is the only or main cause of the damage.

(5) In this section –
   (a) a reference to doing an act includes a reference to causing an act to be done;
   (b) "act" includes a series of acts;
   (c) a reference to a country includes a reference to a territory, and to any place in, or part or region of, a country or territory.

(6) A person guilty of an offence under this section is (unless subsection (7) applies) liable, on conviction on indictment, to imprisonment for a term not exceeding 14 years, or to a fine, or to both.

(7) Where an offence under this section is committed as a result of an act causing or creating a significant risk of –
   (a) serious damage to human welfare of the kind mentioned in subsection (3)(a) or (3)(b), or
   (b) serious damage to national security,

   a person guilty of the offence is liable, on conviction on indictment, to imprisonment for life, or to a fine, or to both.

3A Making, supplying or obtaining articles for use in offence under Section 1, 3 or 3ZA

(1) A person is guilty of an offence if he makes, adapts, supplies or offers to supply any article intending it to be used to commit, or to assist in the commission of, an offence under section 1, 3 or 3ZA.

(2) A person is guilty of an offence if he supplies or offers to supply any article believing that it is likely to be used to commit, or to assist in the commission of, an offence under section 1, 3 or 3ZA.

(3) A person is guilty of an offence if he obtains any article with a view to its being supplied for use to commit, or to assist in the commission of, an offence under section 1, 3 or 3ZA.

(4) In this section 'article' includes any program or data held in electronic form.

(5) A person guilty of an offence under this section shall be liable –

(a) on summary conviction in England and Wales, to imprisonment for a term not exceeding 12 months or to a fine not exceeding the statutory maximum or to both;

(b) on summary conviction in Scotland, to imprisonment for a term not exceeding 12 months or to a fine not exceeding the statutory maximum or to both;

(c) on conviction on indictment, to imprisonment for a term not exceeding two years or to a fine or to both.

Jurisdiction

4 Territorial scope of offences under this Act

(1) Except as provided below in this section, it is immaterial for the purposes of any offence under section 1, 3 or 3ZA above –

(a) whether any act or other event proof of which is required for conviction of the offence occurred in the home country concerned; or

(b) whether the accused was in the home country concerned at the time of any such act or event.

(2) Subject to subsection (3) below, in the case of such an offence at least one significant link with domestic jurisdiction must exist in the circumstances of the case for the offence to be committed.

(3) There is no need for any such link to exist for the commission of an offence under section 1 above to be established in proof of an allegation to that effect in proceedings for an offence under section 2 above.

(4) Subject to section 8 below, where –

(a) any such link does in fact exist in the case of an offence under section 1 above; and

(b) commission of that offence is alleged in proceedings for an offence under section 2 above;

(c) section 2 above shall apply as if anything the accused intended to do or facilitate in any place outside the home country concerned which would be an offence to which section 2 applies if it took place in the home country concerned were the offence in question.

(4A) It is immaterial for the purposes of an offence under section 3A whether the accused was in the home country concerned at the time of any act or other event proof of which is required for conviction of the offence if there is a significant link with domestic jurisdiction in relation to the offence.

(5) This section is without prejudice to any jurisdiction exercisable by a court in Scotland apart from this section.

(6) References in this Act to the home country concerned are references –

(a) in the application of this Act to England and Wales, to England and Wales;
(b) in the application of this Act to Scotland, to Scotland; and
(c) in the application of this Act to Northern Ireland, to Northern Ireland.

5 Significant links with domestic jurisdiction

(1) The following provisions of this section apply for the interpretation of section 4 above.

(1A) In relation to an offence under section 1, 3, 3ZA or 3A, where the accused was in a country outside the United Kingdom at the time of the act constituting the offence there is a significant link with domestic jurisdiction if –

(a) the accused was a United Kingdom national at that time; and
(b) the act constituted an offence under the law of the country in which it occurred.

(1B) In subsection (1A)—

"country" includes territory;

"United Kingdom national" means an individual who is –

(a) a British citizen, a British overseas territories citizen, a British National (Overseas) or a British Overseas citizen;
(b) a person who under the British Nationality Act 1981 is a British subject; or
(c) a British protected person within the meaning of that Act.

(2) In relation to an offence under section 1, either of the following is a significant link with domestic jurisdiction –

(a) that the accused was in the home country concerned at the time when he did the act which caused the computer to perform the function; or
(b) that any computer containing any program or data to which the accused by doing that act secured or intended to secure unauthorised access, or enabled or intended to enable unauthorised access to be secured, was in the home country concerned at that time.

(3) In relation to an offence under section 3, either of the following is a significant link with domestic jurisdiction –

(a) that the accused was in the home country concerned at the time when he did the unauthorised act (or caused it to be done); or
(b) that the unauthorised act was done in relation to a computer in the home country concerned.

(3A) In relation to an offence under section 3ZA, any of the following is also a significant link with domestic jurisdiction –

(a) that the accused was in the home country concerned at the time when he did the unauthorised act (or caused it to be done);
(b) that the unauthorised act was done in relation to a computer in the home country concerned;
(c) that the unauthorised act caused, or created a significant risk of, serious damage of a material kind (within the meaning of that section) in the home country concerned.

6 Territorial scope of inchoate offences related to offences under this Act

(1) On a charge of conspiracy to commit an offence under this Act the following questions are immaterial to the accused's guilt –

(a) the question where any person became a party to the conspiracy; and
(b) the question whether any act, omission or other event occurred in the home country concerned.

(2) On a charge of attempting to commit an offence under this Act the following questions are immaterial to the accused's guilt –
(a) the question where the attempt was made; and
(b) the question whether it had an effect in the home country concerned.

(3) [Repealed].

(4) This section does not extend to Scotland.

7 [Omitted]

8 Relevance of external law

(1) A person is guilty of an offence triable by virtue of section 4(4) above only if what he intended to do or facilitate would involve the commission of an offence under the law in force where the whole or any part of it was intended to take place.

(2) [Repealed].

(3) A person is guilty of an offence triable by virtue of section 1(1A) of the Criminal Attempts Act 1981 only if what he had in view would involve the commission of an offence under the law in force where the whole or any part of it was intended to take place.

(4) Conduct punishable under the law in force in any place is an offence under that law for the purposes of this section, however it is described in that law.

(5) Subject to subsection (7) below, a condition specified in any of subsection (1) or (3) above shall be taken to be satisfied unless not later than rules of court may provide the defence serve on the prosecution a notice –
(a) stating that, on the facts as alleged with respect to the relevant conduct, the condition is not in their opinion satisfied;
(b) showing their grounds for that opinion; and
(c) requiring the prosecution to show that it is satisfied.

(6) In subsection (5) above 'the relevant conduct' means –
(a) where the condition in subsection (1) above is in question, what the accused intended to do or facilitate;
(b) [repealed]
(c) where the condition in subsection (3) above is in question, what the accused had in view.

(7) The court, if it thinks fit, may permit the defence to require the prosecution to show that the condition is satisfied without the prior service of a notice under subsection (5) above.

(8) If by virtue of subsection (7) above a court of solemn jurisdiction in Scotland permits the defence to require the prosecution to show that the condition is satisfied, it shall be competent for the prosecution for that purpose to examine any witness or to put in evidence any production not included in the lists lodged by it.

(9) In the Crown Court the question whether the condition is satisfied shall be decided by the judge alone.

(10) In the High Court of Justiciary and in the sheriff's court the question whether the condition is satisfied shall be decided by the judge or, as the case may be, the sheriff alone.

9 British citizenship immaterial

(1) Except as provided by section 5A in any proceedings brought in England and Wales in respect of British any offence to which this section applies it is immaterial to guilt whether or not the accused was a British citizen at the time of any act, omission or other event proof of which is required for conviction of the offence.

(2) This section applies to the following offences –

- (a) any offence under section this Act;
- (b) [repealed]
- (c) any attempt to commit an offence under this Act;
- (d) [repealed].

10–16 [Omitted]

17 Interpretation

(1) The following provisions of this section apply for the interpretation of this Act.

(2) A person secures access or to enable such access to be secured to any program or data held in a computer if by causing a computer to perform any function he –

- (a) alters or erases the program or data;
- (b) copies or moves it to any storage medium other than that in which it is held or to a different location in the storage medium in which it is held;
- (c) uses it; or
- (d) has it output from the computer in which it is held (whether by having it displayed or in any other manner);
- (e) and references to access to a program or data (and to an intent to secure such access) shall be read accordingly.

(3) For the purposes of subsection (2)(c) above a person uses a program if the function he causes the computer to perform –

- (a) causes the program to be executed; or
- (b) is itself a function of the program.

(4) For the purposes of subsection (2)(d) above –

- (a) a program is output if the instructions of which it consists are output; and
- (b) the form in which any such instructions or any other data is output (and in particular whether or not it represents a form in which, in the case of instructions, they are capable of being executed or, in the case of data, it is capable of being processed by a computer) is immaterial.

(5) Access of any kind by any person to any program or data held in a computer is unauthorised if –

- (a) he is not himself entitled to control access of the kind in question to the program or data; and
- (b) he does not have consent to access by him of the kind in question to the program or data from any person who is so entitled, but this subsection is subject to section 10.

(6) References to any program or data held in a computer include references to any program or data held in any removable storage medium which is for the time being in the computer; and a computer is to be regarded as containing any program or data held in any such medium.

(7) [Repealed].

(8) An act done in relation to a computer is unauthorised if the person doing the act (or causing it to be done) –

   (a) is not himself a person who has responsibility for the computer and is entitled to determine whether the act may be done; and

   (b) does not have consent to the act from any such person.

In this subsection 'act' includes a series of acts.

(9) References to the home country concerned shall be read in accordance with section 4(6) above.

(10) References to a program include references to part of a program.

18 [Omitted]

Contracts (Applicable Law) Act 1990

1 Meaning of 'the Conventions'

In this Act –

(a) 'the Rome Convention' means the Convention on the law applicable to contractual obligations opened for signature in Rome on 19th June 1980 and signed by the United Kingdom on 7th December 1981;

(b) 'the Luxembourg Convention' means the Convention on the accession of the Hellenic Republic to the Rome Convention signed by the United Kingdom in Luxembourg on 10th April 1984;

(c) 'the Brussels Protocol' means the first Protocol on the interpretation of the Rome Convention by the European Court signed by the United Kingdom in Brussels on 19th December 1988;

(d) 'the Funchal Convention' means the Convention on the accession of the Kingdom of Spain and the Portuguese Republic to the Rome Convention and the Brussels Protocol, with adjustments made to the Rome Convention by the Luxembourg Convention, signed by the United Kingdom in Funchal on 18th May 1992;

(e) 'the 1996 Accession Convention' means the Convention on the accession of the Republic of Austria, the Republic of Finland and the Kingdom of Sweden to the Rome Convention and the Brussels Protocol, with the adjustments made to the Rome Convention by the Luxembourg Convention and the Funchal Convention, signed by the United Kingdom in Brussels on 29th November 1996;

and these Conventions and this Protocol are together referred to as 'the Conventions'.

2 Conventions to have force of law

(1) Subject to subsections (2) and (3) below, the Conventions shall have the force of law in the United Kingdom.

(1A) The internal law for the purposes of Article 1(3) of the Rome Convention is the provisions of the regulations for the time being in force under section 424(3) of the Financial Services and Markets Act 2000.

(2) Articles 7(1) and 10(1)(e) of the Rome Convention shall not have the force of law in the United Kingdom.
(3) Notwithstanding Article 19(2) of the Rome Convention, the Conventions shall apply in the case of conflicts between the laws of different parts of the United Kingdom.
(4) [Omitted].

3 Interpretation of conventions

(1) Any question as to the meaning or effect of any provision of the Conventions shall, if not referred to the European Court in accordance with the Brussels Protocol, be determined in accordance with the principles laid down by, and any relevant decision of, the European Court.
(2) Judicial notice shall be taken of any decision of, or expression of opinion by, the European Court on any such question.
(3) Without prejudice to any practice of the courts as to the matters which may be considered apart from this subsection –
   (a) the report on the Rome Convention by Professor Mario Giuliano and Professor Paul Lagarde which is reproduced in the Official Journal of the Communities of 31st October 1980 may be considered in ascertaining the meaning or effect of any provision of that Convention; and
   (b) any report on the Brussels Protocol which is reproduced in the Official Journal of the Communities may be considered in ascertaining the meaning of effect of any provision of that Protocol.

4–9 [Omitted]

Schedule 1 The Rome Convention

Title 1 Scope of the Convention

Article 1 Scope of the convention

1. The rules of this Convention shall apply to contractual obligations in any situation involving a choice between the laws of different countries.
2. They shall not apply to –
   (a) questions involving the status or legal capacity of natural persons, without prejudice to Article 11;
   (b) contractual obligations relating to:
      — wills and succession;
      — rights in property arising out of a matrimonial relationship;
      — rights and duties arising out of a family relationship, parentage, marriage or affinity, including maintenance obligations in respect of children who are not legitimate;
   (c) obligations arising under bills of exchange, cheques and promissory notes and other negotiable instruments to the extent that the obligations under such other negotiable instruments arise out of their negotiable character;
   (d) arbitration agreements and agreements on the choice of court;

(e) questions governed by the law of companies and other bodies corporate or unincorporate such as the creation, by registration or otherwise, legal capacity, internal organisation or winding up of companies and other bodies corporate or unincorporate and the personal liability of officers and members as such for the obligations of the company or body;
(f) the question whether an agent is able to bind a principal, or an organ to bind a company or body corporate or unincorporate, to a third party;
(g) the constitution of trusts and the relationship between settlors, trustees and beneficiaries;
(h) evidence and procedure, without prejudice to Article 14.

3. The rules of this Convention do not apply to contracts of insurance which cover risks situated in the territories of the Member States of the European Economic Community. In order to determine whether a risk is situated in these territories the court shall apply its internal law.
4. The preceding paragraph does not apply to contracts of re-insurance.

Article 2 Application of law of non-contracting states

Any law specified by this Convention shall be applied whether or not it is the law of a Contracting State.

Title II Uniform rules

Article 3 Freedom of choice

1. A contract shall be governed by the law chosen by the parties. The choice must be express or demonstrated with reasonable certainty by the terms of the contract or the circumstances of the case. By their choice the parties can select the law applicable to the whole or a part only of the contract.
2. The parties may at any time agree to subject the contract to a law other than that which previously governed it, whether as a result of an earlier choice under this Article or of other provisions of this Convention. Any variation by the parties of the law to be applied made after the conclusion of the contract shall not prejudice its formal validity under Article 9 or adversely affect the rights of third parties.
3. The fact that the parties have chosen a foreign law, whether or not accompanied by the choice of a foreign tribunal, shall not, where all the other elements relevant to the situation at the time of the choice are connected with one country only, prejudice the application of rules of the law of that country which cannot be derogated from by contract, hereinafter called 'mandatory rules'.
4. The existence and validity of the consent of the parties as to the choice of the applicable law shall be determined in accordance with the provisions of Articles 8, 9 and 11.

Article 4 Applicable law in the absence of choice

1. To the extent that the law applicable to the contract has not been chosen in accordance with Article 3, the contract shall be governed by the law of the country with which it is

most closely connected. Nevertheless, a severable part of the contract which has a closer connection with another country may by way of exception be governed by the law of that other country.

2. Subject to the provisions of paragraph 5 of this Article, it shall be presumed that the contract is most closely connected with the country where the party who is to effect the performance which is characteristic of the contract has, at the time of conclusion of the contract, his habitual residence, or, in the case of a body corporate or unincorporate, its central administration. However, if the contract is entered into in the course of that party's trade or profession, that country shall be the country in which the principal place of business is situated or, where under the terms of the contract the performance is to be effected through a place of business other than the principal place of business, the country in which that other place of business is situated.
3. Notwithstanding the provisions of paragraph 2 of this Article, to the extent that the subject matter of the contract is a right in immovable property or a right to use immovable property it shall be presumed that the contract is most closely connected with the country where the immovable property is situated.
4. A contract for the carriage of goods shall not be subject to the presumption in paragraph 2. In such a contract if the country in which, at the time the contract is concluded, the carrier has his principal place of business is also the country in which the place of loading or the place of discharge or the principal place of business of the consignor is situated, it shall be presumed that the contract is most closely connected with that country. In applying this paragraph single voyage charter-parties and other contracts the main purpose of which is the carriage of goods shall be treated as contracts for the carriage of goods.
5. Paragraph 2 shall not apply if the characteristic performance cannot be determined, and the presumptions in paragraphs 2, 3 and 4 shall be disregarded if it appears from the circumstances as a whole that the contract is more closely connected with another country.

Article 5 Certain consumer contracts

1. This Article applies to a contract the object of which is the supply of goods or services to a person ('the consumer') for a purpose which can be regarded as being outside his trade or profession, or a contract for the provision of credit for that object.
2. Notwithstanding the provisions of Article 3, a choice of law made by the parties shall not have the result of depriving the consumer of the protection afforded to him by the mandatory rules of the law of the country in which he has his habitual residence:
   — if in that country the conclusion of the contract was preceded by a specific invitation addressed to him or by advertising, and he had taken in that country all the steps necessary on his part for the conclusion of the contract, or
   — if the other party or his agent received the consumer's order in that country, or
   — if the contract is for the sale of goods and the consumer travelled from that country to another country and there gave his order, provided that the consumer's journey was arranged by the seller for the purpose of inducing the consumer to buy.
3. Notwithstanding the provisions of Article 4, a contract to which this Article applies will, in the absence of choice in accordance with Article 3, be governed by the law of

the country in which the consumer has his habitual residence if it is entered into in the circumstances described in paragraph 2 of this Article.

4. This Article shall not apply to –
   (a) a contract of carriage;
   (b) a contract for the supply of services where the services are to be supplied to the consumer exclusively in a country other than that in which he has his habitual residence.
5. Notwithstanding the provisions of paragraph 4, this Article shall apply to a contract which, for an inclusive price, provides for a combination of travel and accommodation.

Article 6 Individual employment contracts

1. Notwithstanding the provisions of Article 3, in a contract of employment a choice of law made by the parties shall not have the result of depriving the employee of the protection afforded to him by the mandatory rules of the law which would be applicable under paragraph 2 in the absence of choice.
2. Notwithstanding the provisions of Article 4, a contract of employment shall, in the absence of choice in accordance with Article 3, be governed –
   (a) by the law of the country in which the employee habitually carries out his work in performance of the contract, even if he is temporarily employed in another country; or
   (b) if the employee does not habitually carry out his work in any one country, by the law of the country in which the place of business through which he was engaged is situated,
   (c) unless it appears from the circumstances as a whole that the contract is more closely connected with another country, in which case the contract shall be governed by the law of that country.

Article 7 Mandatory rules

1. When applying under this Convention the law of a country, effect may be given to the mandatory rules of the law of another country with which the situation has a close connection, if and in so far as, under the law of the latter country, those rules must be applied whatever the law applicable to the contract. In considering whether to give effect to these mandatory rules, regard shall be had to their nature and purpose and to the consequences of their application or non-application.
2. Nothing in this Convention shall restrict the application of the rules of the law of the forum in a situation where they are mandatory irrespective of the law otherwise applicable to the contract.

Article 8 Material validity

1. The existence and validity of a contract, or of any term of a contract, shall be determined by the law which would govern it under this Convention if the contract or term were valid.

2. Nevertheless a party may rely upon the law of the country in which he has his habitual residence to establish that he did not consent if it appears from the circumstances that it would not be reasonable to determine the effect of his conduct in accordance with the law specified in the preceding paragraph.

Article 9 Formal validity

1. A contract concluded between persons who are in the same country is formally valid if it satisfies the formal requirements of the law which governs it under this Convention or of the law of the country where it is concluded.
2. A contract concluded between persons who are in different countries is formally valid if it satisfies the formal requirements of the law which governs it under this Convention or of the law of one of those countries.
3. Where a contract is concluded by an agent, the country in which the agent acts is the relevant country for the purposes of paragraphs 1 and 2.
4. An act intended to have legal effect relating to an existing or contemplated contract is formally valid if it satisfies the formal requirements of the law which under this Convention governs or would govern the contract or of the law of the country where the act was done.
5. The provisions of the preceding paragraphs shall not apply to a contract to which Article 5 applies, concluded in the circumstances described in paragraph 2 of Article 5. The formal validity of such a contract is governed by the law of the country in which the consumer has his habitual residence.
6. Notwithstanding paragraphs 1 to 4 of this Article, a contract the subject matter of which is a right in immovable property or a right to use immovable property shall be subject to the mandatory requirements of form of the law of the country where the property is situated if by that law those requirements are imposed irrespective of the country where the contract is concluded and irrespective of the law governing the contract.

Article 10 Scope of the applicable law

1. The law applicable to a contract by virtue of Articles 3 to 6 and 12 of this Convention shall govern in particular –
   (a) interpretation;
   (b) performance;
   (c) within the limits of the powers conferred on the court by its procedural law, the consequences of breach, including the assessment of damages in so far as it is governed by rules of law;
   (d) the various ways of extinguishing obligations and prescription and limitation of actions;
   (e) the consequences of nullity of the contract.
2. In relation to the manner of performance and the steps to be taken in the event of defective performance regard shall be had to the law of the country in which performance takes place.

Article 11 Incapacity

In a contract concluded between persons who are in the same country, a natural person who would have capacity under the law of that country may invoke his incapacity resulting from another law only if the other party to the contract was aware of this incapacity at the time of the conclusion of the contract or was not aware thereof as a result of negligence.

Article 12 Voluntary assignment

1. The mutual obligations of assignor and assignee under a voluntary assignment of a right against another person ('the debtor') shall be governed by the law which under this Convention applies to the contract between the assignor and assignee.
2. The law governing the right to which the assignment relates shall determine its assignability, the relationship between the assignee and the debtor, the conditions under which the assignment can be invoked against the debtor and any question whether the debtor's obligations have been discharged.

Article 13 Subrogation

1. Where a person ('the creditor') has a contractual claim upon another ('the debtor'), and a third person has a duty to satisfy the creditor, or has in fact satisfied the creditor in discharge of that duty, the law which governs the third person's duty to satisfy the creditor shall determine whether the third person is entitled to exercise against the debtor the rights which the creditor had against the debtor under the law governing their relationship and, if so, whether he may do so in full or only to a limited extent.
2. The same rule applies where several persons are subject to the same contractual claim and one of them has satisfied the creditor.

Article 14 Burden of proof, etc.

1. The law governing the contract under this Convention applies to the extent that it contains, in the law of contract, rules which raise presumptions of law or determine the burden of proof.
2. A contract or an act intended to have legal effect may be proved by any mode of proof recognised by the law of the forum or by any of the laws referred to in Article 9 under which that contract or act is formally valid, provided that such mode of proof can be administered by the forum.

Article 15 Exclusion of renvoi

The application of the law of any country specified by this Convention means the application of the rules of law in force in that country other than its rules of private international law.

Article 16 'Ordre public'

The application of a rule of the law of any country specified by this Convention may be refused only if such application is manifestly incompatible with the public policy ('*ordre public*') of the forum.

Article 17 No retrospective effect

This Convention shall apply in a Contracting State to contracts made after the date on which this Convention has entered into force with respect to that State.

Article 18 Uniform interpretation

In the interpretation and application of the preceding uniform rules, regard shall be had to their international character and to the desirability of achieving uniformity in their interpretation and application.

Article 19 States with more than one legal system

1. Where a State comprises several territorial units each of which has its own rules of law in respect of contractual obligations, each territorial unit shall be considered as a country for the purposes of identifying the law applicable under this Convention.
2. A State within which different territorial units have their own rules of law in respect of contractual obligations shall not be bound to apply this Convention to conflicts solely between the laws of such units.

Article 20 Precedence of community law

This Convention shall not affect the application of provisions which, in relation to particular matters, lay down choice of law rules relating to contractual obligations and which are or will be contained in acts of the institutions of the European Communities or in national laws harmonised in implementation of such acts.

Article 21 Relationship with other conventions

This Convention shall not prejudice the application of international conventions to which a Contracting State is, or becomes, a party.

Articles 22–26 [Omitted]

Article 27 [Revoked]

Articles 28–33 [Omitted]

Schedule 3 The Brussels Protocol

Article 1

The Court of Justice of the European Communities shall have jurisdiction to give rulings on the interpretation of –

(a) the Convention on the law applicable to contractual obligations, opened for signature in Rome on 19 June 1980, hereinafter referred to as 'the Rome Convention';
(b) the Convention on accession to the Rome Convention by the States which have become Members of the European Communities since the date on which it was opened for signature;
(c) this Protocol.

Articles 2–11 [Omitted]

Schedule 4 [Omitted]

Carriage of Goods by Sea Act 1992

1 Shipping documents, etc., to which Act applies

(1) This Act applies to the following documents, that is to say –
  (a) any bill of lading;
  (b) any sea waybill; and
  (c) any ship's delivery order.
(2) References in this Act to a bill of lading –
  (a) do not include references to a document which is incapable of transfer either by endorsement or, as a bearer bill, by delivery without endorsement; but
  (b) subject to that, do include references to a received for shipment bill of lading.
(3) References in this Act to a sea waybill are references to any document which is not a bill of lading but –
  (a) is such a receipt for goods as contains or evidences a contract for the carriage of goods by sea; and
  (b) identifies the person to whom delivery of the goods is to be made by the carrier in accordance with that contract.
(4) References in this Act to a ship's delivery order are references to any document which is neither a bill of lading nor a sea waybill but contains an undertaking which –
  (a) is given under or for the purposes of a contract for the carriage by sea of the goods to which the document relates, or of goods which include those goods; and
  (b) is an undertaking by the carrier to a person identified in the document to deliver the goods to which the document relates to that person.
(5) The Secretary of State may by regulations make provision for the application of this Act to cases where an electronic communications network or any other information technology is used for effecting transactions corresponding to –
  (a) the issue of a document to which this Act applies;
  (b) the endorsement, delivery or other transfer of such a document; or
  (c) the doing of anything else in relation to such a document.
(6) [Omitted].

2 Rights under shipping documents

(1) Subject to the following provisions of this section, a person who becomes –
  (a) the lawful holder of a bill of lading;
  (b) the person who (without being an original party to the contract of carriage) is the person to whom delivery of the goods to which a sea waybill relates is to be made by the carrier in accordance with that contract; or
  (c) the person to whom delivery of the goods to which a ship's delivery order relates is to be made in accordance with the undertaking contained in the order,

shall (by virtue of becoming the holder of the bill or, as the case may be, the person to whom delivery is to be made) have transferred to and vested in him all rights of suit under the contract of carriage as if he had been a party to that contract.

(2) Where, when a person becomes the lawful holder of a bill of lading, possession of the bill no longer gives a right (as against the carrier) to possession of the goods to which the bill relates, that person shall not have any rights transferred to him by virtue of subsection (1) above unless he becomes the holder of the bill –
 (a) by virtue of a transaction effected in pursuance of any contractual or other arrangements made before the time when such a right to possession ceased to attach to possession of the bill; or
 (b) as a result of the rejection to that person by another person of goods or documents delivered to the other person in pursuance of any such arrangements.
(3) The rights vested in any person by virtue of the operation of subsection (1) above in relation to a ship's delivery order –
 (a) shall be so vested subject to the terms of the order; and
 (b) where the goods to which the order relates form a part only of the goods to which the contract of carriage relates, shall be confined to rights in respect of the goods to which the order relates.
(4) Where, in the case of any document to which this Act applies –
 (a) a person with any interest or right in or in relation to goods to which the document relates sustains loss or damage in consequence of a breach of the contract of carriage; but
 (b) subsection (1) above operates in relation to that document so that rights of suit in respect of that breach are vested in another person,

 the other person shall be entitled to exercise those rights for the benefit of the person who sustained the loss or damage to the same extent as they could have been exercised if they had been vested in the person for whose benefit they are exercised.
(5) Where rights are transferred by virtue of the operation of subsection (1) above in relation to any document, the transfer for which that subsection provides shall extinguish any entitlement to those rights which derives –
 (a) where that document is a bill of lading, from a person's having been an original party to the contract of carriage; or
 (b) in the case of any document to which this Act applies, from the previous operation of that subsection in relation to that document;
 (c) but the operation of that subsection shall be without prejudice to any rights which derive from a person's having been an original party to the contract contained in, or evidenced by, a sea waybill and, in relation to a ship's delivery order, shall be without prejudice to any rights deriving otherwise than from the previous operation of that subsection in relation to that order.

3 Liabilities under shipping documents

(1) Where subsection (1) of section 2 of this Act operates in relation to any document to which this Act applies and the person in whom rights are vested by virtue of that subsection –
 (a) takes or demands delivery from the carrier of any of the goods to which the document relates;
 (b) makes a claim under the contract of carriage against the carrier in respect of any of those goods; or

(c) is a person who, at a time before those rights were vested in him, took or demanded delivery from the carrier of any of those goods,

that person shall (by virtue of taking or demanding delivery or making the claim or, in a case falling within paragraph (c) above, of having the rights vested in him) become subject to the same liabilities under that contract as if he had been a party to that contract.

(2) Where the goods to which a ship's delivery order relates form a part only of the goods to which the contract of carriage relates, the liabilities to which any person is subject by virtue of the operation of this section in relation to that order shall exclude liabilities in respect of any goods to which the order does not relate.

(3) This section, so far as it imposes liabilities under any contract on any person, shall be without prejudice to the liabilities under the contract of any person as an original party to the contract.

4 Representations in bills of lading

A bill of lading which –

(a) represents goods to have been shipped on board a vessel or to have been received for shipment on board a vessel; and

(b) has been signed by the master of the vessel or by a person who was not the master but has the express, implied or apparent authority of the carrier to sign bills of lading,

shall, in favour of a person who has become the lawful holder of the bill, be conclusive evidence against the carrier of the shipment of the goods or, as the case may be, of their receipt for shipment.

5 Interpretation, etc.

(1) In this Act –

'bill of lading', 'sea waybill' and 'ship's delivery order' shall be construed in accordance with section 1 above;

'the contract of carriage' –

(a) in relation to a bill of lading or sea waybill, means the contract contained in or evidenced by that bill or waybill; and

(b) in relation to a ship's delivery order, means the contract under or for the purposes of which the undertaking contained in the order is given;

(c) 'holder', in relation to a bill of lading, shall be construed in accordance with subsection (2) below;

(d) 'information technology' includes any computer or other technology by means of which information or other matter may be recorded or communicated without being reduced to documentary form.

(2) References in this Act to the holder of a bill of lading are references to any of the following persons, that is to say –

(a) a person with possession of the bill who, by virtue of being the person identified in the bill, is the consignee of the goods to which the bill relates;

(b) a person with possession of the bill as a result of the completion, by delivery of the bill, of any endorsement of the bill or, in the case of a bearer bill, of any other transfer of the bill;

(c) a person with possession of the bill as a result of any transaction by virtue of which he would have become a holder falling within paragraph (a); or

(d) above had not the transaction been effected at a time when possession of the bill no longer gave a right (as against the carrier) to possession of the goods to which the bill relates; and a person shall be regarded for the purposes of this Act as having become the lawful holder of a bill of lading wherever he has become the holder of the bill in good faith.

(3) References in this Act to a person's being identified in a document include references to his being identified by a description which allows for the identity of the person in question to be varied, in accordance with the terms of the document, after its issue; and the reference in section 1(3)(b) of this Act to a document's identifying a person shall be construed accordingly.

(4) Without prejudice to sections 2(2) and 4 above, nothing in this Act shall preclude its operation in relation to a case where the goods to which a document relates –

(a) cease to exist after the issue of the document; or

(b) cannot be identified (whether because they are mixed with other goods or for any other reason);

(c) and references in this Act to the goods to which a document relates shall be construed accordingly.

(5) The preceding provisions of this Act shall have effect without prejudice to the application, in relation to any case, of the rules (the Hague-Visby Rules) which for the time being have the force of law by virtue of section 1 of the Carriage of Goods by Sea Act 1971.

6 [Omitted]

Private International Law (Miscellaneous Provisions) Act 1995

Part III Choice of Law in Tort and Delict

9 Purpose of Part III

(1) The rules in this Part apply for choosing the law (in this Part referred to as 'the applicable law') to be used for determining issues relating to tort or (for the purposes of the law of Scotland) delict.

(2) The characterisation for the purposes of private international law of issues arising in a claim as issues relating to tort or delict is a matter for the courts of the forum.

(3) The rules in this Part do not apply in relation to issues arising in any claim excluded from the operation of this Part by section 13 below.

(4) The applicable law shall be used for determining the issues arising in a claim, including in particular the question whether an actionable tort or delict has occurred.

(5) The applicable law to be used for determining the issues arising in a claim shall exclude any choice of law rules forming part of the law of the country or countries concerned.

(6) For the avoidance of doubt (and without prejudice to the operation of section 14 below) this Part applies in relation to events occurring in the forum as it applies in relation to events occurring in any other country.
(7) In this Part as it extends to any country within the United Kingdom, 'the forum' means England and Wales, Scotland or Northern Ireland, as the case may be.
(8) In this Part 'delict' includes quasi-delict.

10 Abolition of certain common law rules

The rules of the common law, in so far as they –
(a) require actionability under both the law of the forum and the law of another country for the purpose of determining whether a tort or delict is actionable; or
(b) allow (as an exception from the rules falling within paragraph (a) above) for the law of a single country to be applied for the purpose of determining the issues, or any of the issues, arising in the case in question, are hereby abolished so far as they apply to any claim in tort or delict which is not excluded from the operation of this Part by section 13 below.

11 Choice of applicable law: The general rule

(1) The general rule is that the applicable law is the law of the country in which the events constituting the tort or delict in question occur.
(2) Where elements of those events occur in different countries, the applicable law under the general rule is to be taken as being –
    (a) for a cause of action in respect of personal injury caused to an individual or death resulting from personal injury, the law of the country where the individual was when he sustained the injury;
    (b) for a cause of action in respect of damage to property, the law of the country where the property was when it was damaged; and
    (c) in any other case, the law of the country in which the most significant element or elements of those events occurred.
(3) In this section 'personal injury' includes disease or any impairment of physical or mental condition.

12 Choice of applicable law: Displacement of general rule

(1) If it appears, in all the circumstances, from a comparison of –
    (a) the significance of the factors which connect a tort or delict with the country whose law would be the applicable law under the general rule; and
    (b) the significance of any factors connecting the tort or delict with another country,

that it is substantially more appropriate for the applicable law for determining the issues arising in the case, or any of those issues, to be the law of the other country, the general rule is displaced and the applicable law for determining those issues or that issue (as the case may be) is the law of that other country.

(2) The factors that may be taken into account as connecting a tort or delict with a country for the purposes of this section include, in particular, factors relating to the parties, to any of the events which constitute the tort or delict in question or to any of the circumstances or consequences of those events.

13 Exclusion of defamation claims from Part III

(1) Nothing in this Part applies to affect the determination of issues arising in any defamation claim.

(2) For the purposes of this section 'defamation claim' means –
  - (a) any claim under the law of any part of the United Kingdom for libel or slander or for slander of title, slander of goods or other malicious falsehood and any claim under the law of Scotland for verbal injury; and
  - (b) any claim under the law of any other country corresponding to or otherwise in the nature of a claim mentioned in paragraph (a) above.

14 Transitional provision and savings

(1) Nothing in this Part applies to acts or omissions giving rise to a claim which occur before the commencement of this Part.

(2) Nothing in this Part affects any rules of law (including rules of private international law) except those abolished by section 10 above.

(3) Without prejudice to the generality of subsection (2) above, nothing in this Part –
  - (a) authorises the application of the law of a country outside the forum as the applicable law for determining issues arising in any claim in so far as to do so:
    - (i) would conflict with principles of public policy; or
    - (ii) would give effect to such a penal, revenue or other public law as would not otherwise be enforceable under the law of the forum; or
  - (b) affects any rules of evidence, pleading or practice or authorises questions of procedure in any proceedings to be determined otherwise than in accordance with the law of the forum.

(4) This Part has effect without prejudice to the operation of any rule of law which either has effect notwithstanding the rules of private international law applicable in the particular circumstances or modifies the rules of private international law that would otherwise be so applicable.

15 Crown application

(1) This Part applies in relation to claims by or against the Crown as it applies in relation to claims to which the Crown is not a party.

(2) In subsection (1) above a reference to the Crown does not include a reference to Her Majesty in Her private capacity or to Her Majesty in right of Her Duchy of Lancaster or to the Duke of Cornwall.

(3) Without prejudice to the generality of section 14(2) above, nothing in this section affects any rule of law as to whether proceedings of any description may be brought against the Crown.

15A Disapplication of Part III where the rules in the Rome II Regulation apply

(1) Nothing in this Part applies to affect the determination of issues relating to tort which fall to be determined under the Rome II Regulation.

(2) In subsection (1) the "Rome II Regulation" means Regulation (EC) No. 864/2007 of the European Parliament and of the Council on the law applicable to non-contractual obligations, including that Regulation as applied by regulation 6 of the Law Applicable to Non-Contractual Obligations (England and Wales and Northern Ireland) Regulations 2008 (conflicts solely between the laws of different parts of the United Kingdom or between one or more parts of the United Kingdom and Gibraltar).
(3) This section extends to England and Wales and Northern Ireland only.

15B Disapplication of Part III where the rules in the Rome II Regulation apply: Scotland

(1) Nothing in this Part applies to affect the determination of issues relating to delict which fall to be determined under the Rome II Regulation.
(2) In subsection (1) "the Rome II Regulation" means Regulation (EC) No. 864/2007 of the European Parliament and of the Council on the law applicable to non-contractual obligations (Rome II), including that Regulation as applied by regulation 4 of the Law Applicable to Non-Contractual Obligations (Scotland) Regulations 2008 (conflicts falling within Article 25(2) of Regulation (EC) No. 864/2007).
(3) This section extends to Scotland only.

16–19 and Schedule 1 [Omitted]

Arbitration Act 1996

Part I Arbitration pursuant to an arbitration agreement

Introductory

1 General principles

The provisions of this Part are founded on the following principles, and shall be construed accordingly –

(a) the object of arbitration is to obtain the fair resolution of disputes by an impartial tribunal without unnecessary delay or expense;
(b) the parties should be free to agree how their disputes are resolved, subject only to such safeguards as are necessary in the public interest;
(c) in matters governed by this Part the court should not intervene except as provided by this Part.

2 Scope of application of provisions

(1) The provisions of this Part apply where the seat of the arbitration is in England and Wales or Northern Ireland.
(2) The following sections apply even if the seat of the arbitration is outside England and Wales or Northern Ireland or no seat has been designated or determined –
    (a) sections 9 to 11 (stay of legal proceedings, etc.); and
    (b) section 66 (enforcement of arbitral awards).

(3) The powers conferred by the following sections apply even if the seat of the arbitration is outside England and Wales or Northern Ireland or no seat has been designated or determined –
  (a) section 43 (securing the attendance of witnesses); and
  (b) section 44 (court powers exercisable in support of arbitral proceedings), but the court may refuse to exercise any such power if, in the opinion of the court, the fact that the seat of the arbitration is outside England and Wales or Northern Ireland, or that when designated or determined the seat is likely to be outside England and Wales or Northern Ireland, makes it inappropriate to do so.

(4) The court may exercise a power conferred by any provision of this Part not mentioned in subsection (2) or (3) for the purpose of supporting the arbitral process where –
  (a) no seat of the arbitration has been designated or determined; and
  (b) by reason of a connection with England and Wales or Northern Ireland the court is satisfied that it is appropriate to do so.

(5) Section 7 (separability of arbitration agreement) and section 8 (death of a party) apply where the law applicable to the arbitration agreement is the law of England and Wales or Northern Ireland even if the seat of the arbitration is outside England and Wales or Northern Ireland or has not been designated or determined.

3 The seat of the arbitration

In this Part 'the seat of the arbitration' means the juridical seat of the arbitration designated –

(a) by the parties to the arbitration agreement; or
(b) by any arbitral or other institution or person vested by the parties with powers in that regard; or
(c) by the arbitral tribunal if so authorised by the parties,

or determined, in the absence of any such designation, having regard to the parties' agreement and all the relevant circumstances.

4 Mandatory and non-mandatory provisions

(1) The mandatory provisions of this Part are listed in Schedule 1 and have effect notwithstanding any agreement to the contrary.
(2) The other provisions of this Part (the 'non-mandatory provisions') allow the parties to make their own arrangements by agreement but provide rules which apply in the absence of such agreement.
(3) The parties may make such arrangements by agreeing to the application of institutional rules or providing any other means by which a matter may be decided.
(4) It is immaterial whether or not the law applicable to the parties' agreement is the law of England and Wales or, as the case may be, Northern Ireland.
(5) The choice of a law other than the law of England and Wales or Northern Ireland as the applicable law in respect of a matter provided for by a non-mandatory provision of this Part is equivalent to an agreement making provision about that matter.
(6) For this purpose an applicable law determined in accordance with the parties' agreement, or which is objectively determined in the absence of any express or implied choice, shall be treated as chosen by the parties.

5 Agreements to be in writing

(1) The provisions of this Part apply only where the arbitration agreement is in writing, and any other agreement between the parties as to any matter is effective for the purposes of this Part only if in writing. The expressions 'agreement', 'agree' and 'agreed' shall be construed accordingly.

(2) There is an agreement in writing –
  (a) if the agreement is made in writing (whether or not it is signed by the parties);
  (b) if the agreement is made by exchange of communications in writing; or
  (c) if the agreement is evidenced in writing.

(3) Where parties agree otherwise than in writing by reference to terms which are in writing, they make an agreement in writing.

(4) An agreement is evidenced in writing if an agreement made otherwise than in writing is recorded by one of the parties, or by a third party, with the authority of the parties to the agreement.

(5) An exchange of written submissions in arbitral or legal proceedings in which the existence of an agreement otherwise than in writing is alleged by one party against another party and not denied by the other party in his response constitutes as between those parties an agreement in writing to the effect alleged.

(6) References in this Part to anything being written or in writing include its being recorded by any means.

The arbitration agreement

6 Definition of arbitration agreement

(1) In this Part an 'arbitration agreement' means an agreement to submit to arbitration present or future disputes (whether they are contractual or not).

(2) The reference in an agreement to a written form of arbitration clause or to a document containing an arbitration clause constitutes an arbitration agreement if the reference is such as to make that clause part of the agreement.

7 Separability of arbitration agreement

Unless otherwise agreed by the parties, an arbitration agreement which forms or was intended to form part of another agreement (whether or not in writing) shall not be regarded as invalid, non-existent or ineffective because that other agreement is invalid, or did not come into existence or has become ineffective, and it shall for that purpose be treated as a distinct agreement.

8 Whether agreement discharged by death of a party

(1) Unless otherwise agreed by the parties, an arbitration agreement is not discharged by the death of a party and may be enforced by or against the personal representatives of that party.

(2) Subsection (1) does not affect the operation of any enactment or rule of law by virtue of which a substantive right or obligation is extinguished by death.

Stay of legal proceedings

9 Stay of legal proceedings

(1) A party to an arbitration agreement against whom legal proceedings are brought (whether by way of claim or counterclaim) in respect of a matter which under the agreement is to be referred to arbitration may (upon notice to the other parties to the proceedings) apply to the court in which the proceedings have been brought to stay the proceedings so far as they concern that matter.

(2) An application may be made notwithstanding that the matter is to be referred to arbitration only after the exhaustion of other dispute resolution procedures.

(3) An application may not be made by a person before taking the appropriate procedural step (if any) to acknowledge the legal proceedings against him or after he has taken any step in those proceedings to answer the substantive claim.

(4) On an application under this section the court shall grant a stay unless satisfied that the arbitration agreement is null and void, inoperative, or incapable of being performed.

(5) If the court refuses to stay the legal proceedings, any provision that an award is a condition precedent to the bringing of legal proceedings in respect of any matter is of no effect in relation to those proceedings.

10 Reference of interpleader issue to arbitration

(1) Where in legal proceedings relief by way of interpleader is granted and any issue between the claimants is one in respect of which there is an arbitration agreement between them, the court granting the relief shall direct that the issue be determined in accordance with the agreement unless the circumstances are such that proceedings brought by a claimant in respect of the matter would not be stayed.

(2) Where subsection (1) applies but the court does not direct that the issue be determined in accordance with the arbitration agreement, any provision that an award is a condition precedent to the bringing of legal proceedings in respect of any matter shall not affect the determination of that issue by the court.

11 Retention of security where Admiralty proceedings stayed

(1) Where Admiralty proceedings are stayed on the ground that the dispute in question should be submitted to arbitration, the court granting the stay may, if in those proceedings property has been arrested or bail or other security has been given to prevent or obtain release from arrest –

    (a) order that the property arrested be retained as security for the satisfaction of any award given in the arbitration in respect of that dispute; or

    (b) order that the stay of those proceedings be conditional on the provision of equivalent security for the satisfaction of any such award.

(2) Subject to any provision made by rules of court and to any necessary modifications, the same law and practice shall apply in relation to property retained in pursuance of an order as would apply if it were held for the purposes of proceedings in the court making the order.

Commencement of arbitral proceedings

12 Power of court to extend time for beginning arbitral proceedings, etc.

(1) Where an arbitration agreement to refer future disputes to arbitration provides that a claim shall be barred, or the claimant's right extinguished, unless the claimant takes within a time fixed by the agreement some step –
  (a) to begin arbitral proceedings; or
  (b) to begin other dispute resolution procedures which must be exhausted before arbitral proceedings can be begun,

the court may by order extend the time for taking that step.

(2) Any party to the arbitration agreement may apply for such an order (upon notice to the other parties), but only after a claim has arisen and after exhausting any available arbitral process for obtaining an extension of time.

(3) The court shall make an order only if satisfied –
  (a) that the circumstances are such as were outside the reasonable contemplation of the parties when they agreed the provision in question, and that it would be just to extend the time; or
  (b) that the conduct of one party makes it unjust to hold the other party to the strict terms of the provision in question.

(4) The court may extend the time for such period and on such terms as it thinks fit, and may do so whether or not the time previously fixed (by agreement or by a previous order) has expired.

(5) An order under this section does not affect the operation of the Limitation Acts (see section 13).

(6) The leave of the court is required for any appeal from a decision of the court under this section.

13 Application of Limitation Acts

(1) The Limitation Acts apply to arbitral proceedings as they apply to legal proceedings.

(2) The court may order that in computing the time prescribed by the Limitation Acts for the commencement of proceedings (including arbitral proceedings) in respect of a dispute which was the subject matter –
  (a) of an award which the court orders to be set aside or declares to be of no effect; or
  (b) of the affected part of an award which the court orders to be set aside in part, or declares to be in part of no effect,

the period between the commencement of the arbitration and the date of the order referred to in paragraph (a) or (b) shall be excluded.

(3) In determining for the purposes of the Limitation Acts when a cause of action accrued, any provision that an award is a condition precedent to the bringing of legal proceedings in respect of a matter to which an arbitration agreement applies shall be disregarded.

(4) In this Part 'the Limitation Acts' means –
  (a) in England and Wales, the Limitation Act 1980, the Foreign Limitation Periods Act 1984 and any other enactment (whenever passed) relating to the limitation of actions;

(b) in Northern Ireland, the Limitation (Northern Ireland) Order 1985 and any other enactment (whenever passed) relating to the limitation of actions.

14 Commencement of arbitral proceedings

(1) The parties are free to agree when arbitral proceedings are to be regarded as commenced for the purposes of this Part and for the purposes of the Limitation Acts.
(2) If there is no such agreement the following provisions apply.
(3) Where the arbitrator is named or designated in the arbitration agreement, arbitral proceedings are commenced in respect of a matter when one party serves on the other party or parties a notice in writing requiring him or them to submit that matter to the person so named or designated.
(4) Where the arbitrator or arbitrators are to be appointed by the parties, arbitral proceedings are commenced in respect of a matter when one party serves on the other party or parties notice in writing requiring him or them to appoint an arbitrator or to agree to the appointment of an arbitrator in respect of that matter.
(5) Where the arbitrator or arbitrators are to be appointed by a person other than a party to the proceedings, arbitral proceedings are commenced in respect of a matter when one party gives notice in writing to that person requesting him to make the appointment in respect of that matter.

The arbitral tribunal

15 The arbitral tribunal

(1) The parties are free to agree on the number of arbitrators to form the tribunal and whether there is to be a chairman or umpire.
(2) Unless otherwise agreed by the parties, an agreement that the number of arbitrators shall be two or any other even number shall be understood as requiring the appointment of an additional arbitrator as chairman of the tribunal.
(3) If there is no agreement as to the number of arbitrators, the tribunal shall consist of a sole arbitrator.

16 Procedure for appointment of arbitrators

(1) The parties are free to agree on the procedure for appointing the arbitrator or arbitrators, including the procedure for appointing any chairman or umpire.
(2) If or to the extent that there is no such agreement, the following provisions apply.
(3) If the tribunal is to consist of a sole arbitrator, the parties shall jointly appoint the arbitrator not later than 28 days after service of a request in writing by either party to do so.
(4) If the tribunal is to consist of two arbitrators, each party shall appoint one arbitrator not later than 14 days after service of a request in writing by either party to do so.
(5) If the tribunal is to consist of three arbitrators –
    (a) each party shall appoint one arbitrator not later than 14 days after service of a request in writing by either party to do so; and

(b) the two so appointed shall forthwith appoint a third arbitrator as the chairman of the tribunal.

(6) If the tribunal is to consist of two arbitrators and an umpire –
(a) each party shall appoint one arbitrator not later than 14 days after service of a request in writing by either party to do so; and
(b) the two so appointed may appoint an umpire at any time after they themselves are appointed and shall do so before any substantive hearing or forthwith if they cannot agree on a matter relating to the arbitration.

(7) In any other case (in particular, if there are more than two parties) section 18 applies as in the case of a failure of the agreed appointment procedure.

17 Power in case of default to appoint sole arbitrator

(1) Unless the parties otherwise agree, where each of two parties to an arbitration agreement is to appoint an arbitrator and one party ('the party in default') refuses to do so, or fails to do so within the time specified, the other party, having duly appointed his arbitrator, may give notice in writing to the party in default that he proposes to appoint his arbitrator to act as sole arbitrator.

(2) If the party in default does not within 7 clear days of that notice being given –
(a) make the required appointment; and
(b) notify the other party that he has done so,
the other party may appoint his arbitrator as sole arbitrator whose award shall be binding on both parties as if he had been so appointed by agreement.

(3) Where a sole arbitrator has been appointed under subsection (2), the party in default may (upon notice to the appointing party) apply to the court which may set aside the appointment.

(4) The leave of the court is required for any appeal from a decision of the court under this section.

18 Failure of appointment procedure

(1) The parties are free to agree what is to happen in the event of a failure of the procedure for the appointment of the arbitral tribunal. There is no failure if an appointment is duly made under section 17 (power in case of default to appoint sole arbitrator), unless that appointment is set aside.

(2) If or to the extent that there is no such agreement any party to the arbitration agreement may (upon notice to the other parties) apply to the court to exercise its powers under this section.

(3) Those powers are –
(a) to give directions as to the making of any necessary appointments;
(b) to direct that the tribunal shall be constituted by such appointments (or any one or more of them) as have been made;
(c) to revoke any appointments already made;
(d) to make any necessary appointments itself.

(4) An appointment made by the court under this section has effect as if made with the agreement of the parties.

(5) The leave of the court is required for any appeal from a decision of the court under this section.

19 Court to have regard to agreed qualifications

In deciding whether to exercise, and in considering how to exercise, any of its powers under section 16 (procedure for appointment of arbitrators) or section 18 (failure of appointment procedure), the court shall have due regard to any agreement of the parties as to the qualifications required of the arbitrators.

20 Chairman

(1) Where the parties have agreed that there is to be a chairman, they are free to agree what the functions of the chairman are to be in relation to the making of decisions, orders and awards.
(2) If or to the extent that there is no such agreement, the following provisions apply.
(3) Decisions, orders and awards shall be made by all or a majority of the arbitrators (including the chairman).
(4) The view of the chairman shall prevail in relation to a decision, order or award in respect of which there is neither unanimity nor a majority under subsection (3).

21 Umpire

(1) Where the parties have agreed that there is to be an umpire, they are free to agree what the functions of the umpire are to be, and in particular –
    (a) whether he is to attend the proceedings; and
    (b) when he is to replace the other arbitrators as the tribunal with power to make decisions, orders and awards.
(2) If or to the extent that there is no such agreement, the following provisions apply.
(3) The umpire shall attend the proceedings and be supplied with the same documents and other materials as are supplied to the other arbitrators.
(4) Decisions, orders and awards shall be made by the other arbitrators unless and until they cannot agree on a matter relating to the arbitration.
(5) In that event they shall forthwith give notice in writing to the parties and the umpire, whereupon the umpire shall replace them as the tribunal with power to make decisions, orders and awards as if he were sole arbitrator.
(6) If the arbitrators cannot agree but fail to give notice of that fact, or if any of them fails to join in the giving of notice, any party to the arbitral proceedings may (upon notice to the other parties and to the tribunal) apply to the court which may order that the umpire shall replace the other arbitrators as the tribunal with power to make decisions, orders and awards as if he were sole arbitrator.
(7) The leave of the court is required for any appeal from a decision of the court under this section.

22 Decision-making where no chairman or umpire

(1) Where the parties agree that there shall be two or more arbitrators with no chairman or umpire, the parties are free to agree how the tribunal is to make decisions, orders and awards.

(2) If there is no such agreement, decisions, orders and awards shall be made by all or a majority of the arbitrators.

23 Revocation of arbitrator's authority

(1) The parties are free to agree in what circumstances the authority of an arbitrator may be revoked.
(2) If or to the extent that there is no such agreement the following provisions apply.
(3) The authority of an arbitrator may not be revoked except –
  (a) by the parties acting jointly; or
  (b) by an arbitral or other institution or person vested by the parties with powers in that regard.
(4) Revocation of the authority of an arbitrator by the parties acting jointly must be agreed in writing unless the parties also agree (whether or not in writing) to terminate the arbitration agreement.
(5) Nothing in this section affects the power of the court –
  (a) to revoke an appointment under section 18 (powers exercisable in case of failure of appointment procedure); or
  (b) to remove an arbitrator on the grounds specified in section 24.

24 Power of court to remove arbitrator

(1) A party to arbitral proceedings may (upon notice to the other parties, to the arbitrator concerned and to any other arbitrator) apply to the court to remove an arbitrator on any of the following grounds –
  (a) that circumstances exist that give rise to justifiable doubts as to his impartiality;
  (b) that he does not possess the qualifications required by the arbitration agreement;
  (c) that he is physically or mentally incapable of conducting the proceedings or there are justifiable doubts as to his capacity to do so;
  (d) that he has refused or failed:
    (i) properly to conduct the proceedings; or
    (ii) to use all reasonable despatch in conducting the proceedings or making an award,

  and that substantial injustice has been or will be caused to the applicant.

(2) If there is an arbitral or other institution or person vested by the parties with power to remove an arbitrator, the court shall not exercise its power of removal unless satisfied that the applicant has first exhausted any available recourse to that institution or person.
(3) The arbitral tribunal may continue the arbitral proceedings and make an award while an application to the court under this section is pending.
(4) Where the court removes an arbitrator, it may make such order as it thinks fit with respect to his entitlement (if any) to fees or expenses, or the repayment of any fees or expenses already paid.
(5) The arbitrator concerned is entitled to appear and be heard by the court before it makes any order under this section.

(6) The leave of the court is required for any appeal from a decision of the court under this section.

25 Resignation of arbitrator

(1) The parties are free to agree with an arbitrator as to the consequences of his resignation as regards –
  (a) his entitlement (if any) to fees or expenses; and
  (b) any liability thereby incurred by him.
(2) If or to the extent that there is no such agreement the following provisions apply.
(3) An arbitrator who resigns his appointment may (upon notice to the parties) apply to the court –
  (a) to grant him relief from any liability thereby incurred by him; and
  (b) to make such order as it thinks fit with respect to his entitlement (if any) to fees or expenses or the repayment of any fees or expenses already paid.
(4) If the court is satisfied that in all the circumstances it was reasonable for the arbitrator to resign, it may grant such relief as is mentioned in subsection (3)(a) on such terms as it thinks fit.
(5) The leave of the court is required for any appeal from a decision of the court under this section.

26 Death of arbitrator or person appointing him

(1) The authority of an arbitrator is personal and ceases on his death.
(2) Unless otherwise agreed by the parties, the death of the person by whom an arbitrator was appointed does not revoke the arbitrator's authority.

27 Filling of vacancy, etc.

(1) Where an arbitrator ceases to hold office, the parties are free to agree –
  (a) whether and if so how the vacancy is to be filled;
  (b) whether and if so to what extent the previous proceedings should stand; and
  (c) what effect (if any) his ceasing to hold office has on any appointment made by him (alone or jointly).
(2) If or to the extent that there is no such agreement, the following provisions apply.
(3) The provisions of sections 16 (procedure for appointment of arbitrators) and 18 (failure of appointment procedure) apply in relation to the filling of the vacancy as in relation to an original appointment.
(4) The tribunal (when reconstituted) shall determine whether and if so to what extent the previous proceedings should stand. This does not affect any right of a party to challenge those proceedings on any ground which had arisen before the arbitrator ceased to hold office.
(5) His ceasing to hold office does not affect any appointment by him (alone or jointly) of another arbitrator, in particular any appointment of a chairman or umpire.

28 Joint and several liability of parties to arbitrators for fees and expenses

(1) The parties are jointly and severally liable to pay to the arbitrators such reasonable fees and expenses (if any) as are appropriate in the circumstances.

(2) Any party may apply to the court (upon notice to the other parties and to the arbitrators) which may order that the amount of the arbitrators' fees and expenses shall be considered and adjusted by such means and upon such terms as it may direct.

(3) If the application is made after any amount has been paid to the arbitrators by way of fees or expenses, the court may order the repayment of such amount (if any) as is shown to be excessive, but shall not do so unless it is shown that it is reasonable in the circumstances to order repayment.

(4) The above provisions have effect subject to any order of the court under sections 24(4) or 25(3)(b) (order as to entitlement to fees or expenses in case of removal or resignation of arbitrator).

(5) Nothing in this section affects any liability of a party to any other party to pay all or any of the costs of the arbitration (see sections 59 to 65) or any contractual right of an arbitrator to payment of his fees and expenses.

(6) In this section references to arbitrators include an arbitrator who has ceased to act and an umpire who has not replaced the other arbitrators.

29 Immunity of arbitrator

(1) An arbitrator is not liable for anything done or omitted in the discharge or purported discharge of his functions as arbitrator unless the act or omission is shown to have been in bad faith.

(2) Subsection (1) applies to an employee or agent of an arbitrator as it applies to the arbitrator himself.

(3) This section does not affect any liability incurred by an arbitrator by reason of his resigning (but see section 25).

Jurisdiction of the arbitral tribunal

30 Competence of tribunal to rule on its own jurisdiction

(1) Unless otherwise agreed by the parties, the arbitral tribunal may rule on its own substantive jurisdiction, that is, as to –
   (a) whether there is a valid arbitration agreement;
   (b) whether the tribunal is properly constituted; and
   (c) what matters have been submitted to arbitration in accordance with the arbitration agreement.

(2) Any such ruling may be challenged by any available arbitral process of appeal or review or in accordance with the provisions of this Part.

31 Objection to substantive jurisdiction of tribunal

(1) An objection that the arbitral tribunal lacks substantive jurisdiction at the outset of the proceedings must be raised by a party not later than the time he takes the first step in the proceedings to contest the merits of any matter in relation to which he challenges the

tribunal's jurisdiction. A party is not precluded from raising such an objection by the fact that he has appointed or participated in the appointment of an arbitrator.

(2) Any objection during the course of the arbitral proceedings that the arbitral tribunal is exceeding its substantive jurisdiction must be made as soon as possible after the matter alleged to be beyond its jurisdiction is raised.

(3) The arbitral tribunal may admit an objection later than the time specified in subsection (1) or (2) if it considers the delay justified.

(4) Where an objection is duly taken to the tribunal's substantive jurisdiction and the tribunal has power to rule on its own jurisdiction, it may –
  (a) rule on the matter in an award as to jurisdiction; or
  (b) deal with the objection in its award on the merits. If the parties agree which of these courses the tribunal should take, the tribunal shall proceed accordingly.

(5) The tribunal may in any case, and shall if the parties so agree, stay proceedings whilst an application is made to the court under section 32 (determination of preliminary point of jurisdiction).

32 Determination of preliminary point of jurisdiction

(1) The court may, on the application of a party to arbitral proceedings (upon notice to the other parties), determine any question as to the substantive jurisdiction of the tribunal. A party may lose the right to object (see section 73).

(2) An application under this section shall not be considered unless –
  (a) it is made with the agreement in writing of all the other parties to the proceedings; or
  (b) it is made with the permission of the tribunal and the court is satisfied:
    (i) that the determination of the question is likely to produce substantial savings in costs;
    (ii) that the application was made without delay; and
    (iii) that there is good reason why the matter should be decided by the court.

(3) An application under this section, unless made with the agreement of all the other parties to the proceedings, shall state the grounds on which it is said that the matter should be decided by the court.

(4) Unless otherwise agreed by the parties, the arbitral tribunal may continue the arbitral proceedings and make an award while an application to the court under this section is pending.

(5) Unless the court gives leave, no appeal lies from a decision of the court whether the conditions specified in subsection (2) are met.

(6) The decision of the court on the question of jurisdiction shall be treated as a judgment of the court for the purposes of an appeal. But no appeal lies without the leave of the court which shall not be given unless the court considers that the question involves a point of law which is one of general importance or is one which for some other special reason should be considered by the Court of Appeal.

The arbitral proceedings

33 General duty of the tribunal

(1) The tribunal shall –

(a) act fairly and impartially as between the parties, giving each party a reasonable opportunity of putting his case and dealing with that of his opponent; and
(b) adopt procedures suitable to the circumstances of the particular case, avoiding unnecessary delay or expense, so as to provide a fair means for the resolution of the matters falling to be determined.

(2) The tribunal shall comply with that general duty in conducting the arbitral proceedings, in its decisions on mátters of procedure and evidence and in the exercise of all other powers conferred on it.

34 Procedural and evidential matters

(1) It shall be for the tribunal to decide all procedural and evidential matters, subject to the right of the parties to agree any matter.

(2) Procedural and evidential matters include –
(a) when and where any part of the proceedings is to be held;
(b) the language or languages to be used in the proceedings and whether translations of any relevant documents are to be supplied;
(c) whether any and if so what form of written statements of claim and defence are to be used, when these should be supplied and the extent to which such statements can be later amended;
(d) whether any and if so which documents or classes of documents should be disclosed between and produced by the parties and at what stage;
(e) whether any and if so what questions should be put to and answered by the respective parties and when and in what form this should be done;
(f) whether to apply strict rules of evidence (or any other rules) as to the admissibility, relevance or weight of any material (oral, written or other) sought to be tendered on any matters of fact or opinion, and the time, manner and form in which such material should be exchanged and presented;
(g) whether and to what extent the tribunal should itself take the initiative in ascertaining the facts and the law;
(h) whether and to what extent there should be oral or written evidence or submissions.

(3) The tribunal may fix the time within which any directions given by it are to be complied with, and may if it thinks fit extend the time so fixed (whether or not it has expired).

35 Consolidation of proceedings and concurrent hearings

(1) The parties are free to agree –
(a) that the arbitral proceedings shall be consolidated with arbitral proceedings; or
(b) that concurrent hearings shall be held on such terms as may be agreed.

(2) Unless the parties agree to confer such power on the tribunal, the tribunal has no power to order consolidation of proceedings or concurrent hearings.

36 Legal or other representation

Unless otherwise agreed by the parties, a party to arbitral proceedings may be represented in the proceedings by a lawyer or other person chosen by him.

37 Power to appoint experts, legal advisers or assessors

(1) Unless otherwise agreed by the parties –

  (a) the tribunal may:

    (i) appoint experts or legal advisers to report to it and the parties; or

    (ii) appoint assessors to assist it on technical matters,

    and may allow any such expert, legal adviser or assessor to attend the proceedings; and

  (b) the parties shall be given a reasonable opportunity to comment on any information, opinion or advice offered by any such person.

(2) The fees and expenses of an expert, legal adviser or assessor appointed by the tribunal for which the arbitrators are liable are expenses of the arbitrators for the purposes of this Part.

38 General powers exercisable by the tribunal

(1) The parties are free to agree on the powers exercisable by the arbitral tribunal for the purposes of and in relation to the proceedings.

(2) Unless otherwise agreed by the parties the tribunal has the following powers.

(3) The tribunal may order a claimant to provide security for the costs of the arbitration. This power shall not be exercised on the ground that the claimant is –

  (a) an individual ordinarily resident outside the United Kingdom; or

  (b) a corporation or association incorporated or formed under the law of a country outside the United Kingdom, or whose central management and control is exercised outside the United Kingdom.

(4) The tribunal may give directions in relation to any property which is the subject of the proceedings or as to which any question arises in the proceedings, and which is owned by or is in the possession of a party to the proceedings –

  (a) for the inspection, photographing, preservation, custody or detention of the property by the tribunal, an expert or a party; or

  (b) ordering that samples be taken from, or any observation be made of or experiment conducted upon, the property.

(5) The tribunal may direct that a party or witness shall be examined on oath or affirmation, and may for that purpose administer any necessary oath or take any necessary affirmation.

(6) The tribunal may give directions to a party for the preservation for the purposes of the proceedings of any evidence in his custody or control.

39 Power to make provisional awards

(1) The parties are free to agree that the tribunal shall have power to order on a provisional basis any relief which it would have power to grant in a final award.

(2) This includes, for instance, making –

  (a) a provisional order for the payment of money or the disposition of property as between the parties; or

  (b) an order to make an interim payment on account of the costs of the arbitration.

(3) Any such order shall be subject to the tribunal's final adjudication; and the tribunal's final award, on the merits or as to costs, shall take account of any such order.
(4) Unless the parties agree to confer such power on the tribunal, the 'tribunal has no such power'. This does not affect its powers under section 47 (awards on different issues, etc.).

40 General duty of parties

(1) The parties shall do all things necessary for the proper and expeditious conduct of the arbitral proceedings.
(2) This includes –
 (a) complying without delay with any determination of the tribunal as to procedural or evidential matters, or with any order or directions of the tribunal; and
 (b) where appropriate, taking without delay any necessary steps to obtain a decision of the court on a preliminary question of jurisdiction or law (see sections 32 and 45).

41 Powers of tribunal in case of party's default

(1) The parties are free to agree on the powers of the tribunal in case of a party's failure to do something necessary for the proper and expeditious conduct of the arbitration.
(2) Unless otherwise agreed by the parties, the following provisions apply.
(3) If the tribunal is satisfied that there has been inordinate and inexcusable delay on the part of the claimant in pursuing his claim and that the delay –
 (a) gives rise, or is likely to give rise, to a substantial risk that it is not possible to have a fair resolution of the issues in that claim; or
 (b) has caused, or is likely to cause, serious prejudice to the respondent,

 the tribunal may make an award dismissing the claim.
(4) If without showing sufficient cause a party –
 (a) fails to attend or be represented at an oral hearing of which due notice was given; or
 (b) where matters are to be dealt with in writing, fails after due notice to submit written evidence or make written submission, the tribunal may continue the proceedings in the absence of that party or as the case may be, without any written evidence or submissions on his behalf, and may make an award on the basis of the evidence before it.
(5) If without showing sufficient cause a party fails to comply with an order or directions of the tribunal, the tribunal may make a peremptory order to the same effect, prescribing such time for compliance with it as the tribunal considers appropriate.
(6) If a claimant fails to comply with a peremptory order of the tribunal to provide security for costs, the tribunal may make an award dismissing his claim.
(7) If a party fails to comply with any other kind of peremptory order then, without prejudice to section 42 (enforcement by court of tribunal peremptory orders), the tribunal may do any of the following –
 (a) direct that the party in default shall not be entitled to rely upon any allegation or material which was the subject matter of the order;
 (b) draw such adverse inferences from the act of non-compliance as the circumstances justify;

(c) proceed to an award on the basis of such materials as have been properly provided to it;
(d) make such order as it thinks fit as to the payment of costs of the arbitration incurred in consequence of the non-compliance.

Powers of court in relation to arbitral proceedings

42 Enforcement of peremptory orders of tribunal

(1) Unless otherwise agreed by the parties the court may make an order requiring a party to comply with a peremptory order made by the tribunal.
(2) An application for an order under this section may be made –
  (a) by the tribunal (upon notice to the parties);
  (b) by a party to the arbitral proceedings with the permission of the tribunal (and upon notice to the other parties); or
  (c) where the parties have agreed that the powers of the court under this section shall be available.
(3) The court shall not act unless it is satisfied that the applicant has exhausted any available arbitral process in respect of failure to comply with the tribunal's order.
(4) No order shall be made under this section unless the court is satisfied that the person to whom the tribunal's order was directed has failed to comply with it within the time prescribed in the order or, if no time was prescribed, within a reasonable time.
(5) The leave of the court is required for any appeal from a decision of the court under this section.

43 Securing the attendance of witnesses

(1) A party to arbitral proceedings may use the same court procedures as are available in relation to legal proceedings to secure the attendance before the tribunal of a witness in order to give oral testimony or to produce documents or other material evidence.
(2) This may only be done with the permission of the tribunal or the agreement of the other parties.
(3) The court procedures may only be used if –
  (a) the witness is in the United Kingdom; and
  (b) the arbitral proceedings are being conducted in England and Wales or, as the case may be, Northern Ireland.
(4) A person shall not be compelled by virtue of this section to produce any document or other material evidence which he could not be compelled to produce in legal proceedings.

44 Court powers exercisable in support of arbitral proceedings

(1) Unless otherwise agreed by the parties, the court has for the purposes of and in relation to arbitral proceedings the same power of making orders about the matters listed below as it has for the purposes of and in relation to legal proceedings.
(2) Those matters are –

(a) the taking of the evidence of witnesses;
(b) the preservation of evidence;
(c) making orders relating to property which is the subject of the proceedings or as to which any question arises in the proceedings:
  (i) for the inspection, photographing, preservation, custody or detention of the property; or
  (ii) ordering that samples be taken from, or any observation be made of or experiment conducted upon, the property;
  (iii) and for that purpose authorising any person to enter any premises in the possession or control of a party to the arbitration;
(d) the sale of any goods the subject of the proceedings;
(e) the granting of an interim injunction or the appointment of a receiver.

(3) If the case is one of urgency, the court may, on the application of a party or proposed party to the arbitral proceedings, make such orders as it thinks necessary for the purpose of preserving evidence or assets.

(4) If the case is not one of urgency, the court shall act only on the application of a party to the arbitral proceedings (upon notice to the other parties and to the tribunal) made with the permission of the tribunal or the agreement in writing of the other parties.

(5) In any case the court shall act only if or to the extent that the arbitral tribunal, and any arbitral or other institution or person vested by the parties with power in that regard, has no power or is unable for the time being to act effectively.

(6) If the court so orders, an order made by it under this section shall cease to have effect in whole or in part on the order of the tribunal or of any such arbitral or other institution or person having power to act in relation to the subject-matter of the order.

(7) The leave of the court is required for any appeal from a decision of the court under this section.

45 Determination of preliminary point of law

(1) Unless otherwise agreed by the parties, the court may on the application of a party to arbitral proceedings (upon notice to the other parties) determine any question of law arising in the course of the proceedings which the court is satisfied substantially affects the rights of one or more of the parties. An agreement to dispense with reasons for the tribunal's award shall be considered an agreement to exclude the court's jurisdiction under this section.

(2) An application under this section shall not be considered unless –
(a) it is made with the agreement of all the other parties to the proceedings; or
(b) it is made with the permission of the tribunal and the court is satisfied:
  (i) that the determination of the question is likely to produce substantial savings in costs; and
  (ii) that the application was made without delay.

(3) The application shall identify the question of law to be determined and, unless made with the agreement of all the other parties to the proceedings, shall state the grounds on which it is said that the question should be decided by the court.

(4) Unless otherwise agreed by the parties, the arbitral tribunal may continue the arbitral proceedings and make an award while an application to the court under this section is pending.

(5) Unless the court gives leave, no appeal lies from a decision of the court whether the conditions specified in subsection (2) are met.

(6) The decision of the court on the question of law shall be treated as a judgment of the court for the purposes of an appeal. But no appeal lies without the leave of the court which shall not be given unless the court considers that the question is one of general importance, or is one which for some other special reason should be considered by the Court of Appeal.

The award

46 Rules applicable to substance of dispute

(1) The arbitral tribunal shall decide the dispute –
 (a) in accordance with the law chosen by the parties as applicable to the substance of the dispute; or
 (b) if the parties so agree, in accordance with such other considerations as are agreed by them or determined by the tribunal.

(2) For this purpose the choice of the laws of a country shall be understood to refer to the substantive laws of that country and not its conflict of laws rules.

(3) If or to the extent that there is no such choice or agreement, the tribunal shall apply the law determined by the conflict of laws rules which it considers applicable.

47 Awards on different issues, etc.

(1) Unless otherwise agreed by the parties, the tribunal may make more than one award at different times on different aspects of the matters to be determined.

(2) The tribunal may, in particular, make an award relating –
 (a) to an issue affecting the whole claim; or
 (b) to a part only of the claims or cross-claims submitted to it for decision.

(3) If the tribunal does so, it shall specify in its award the issue, or the claim or part of a claim, which is the subject matter of the award.

48 Remedies

(1) The parties are free to agree on the powers exercisable by the arbitral tribunal as regards remedies.

(2) Unless otherwise agreed by the parties, the tribunal has the following powers.

(3) The tribunal may make a declaration as to any matter to be determined in the proceedings.

(4) The tribunal may order the payment of a sum of money, in any currency.

(5) The tribunal has the same powers as the court –
 (a) to order a party to do or refrain from doing anything;
 (b) to order specific performance of a contract (other than a contract relating to land);
 (c) to order the rectification, setting aside or cancellation of a deed or other document.

49 Interest

(1) The parties are free to agree on the powers of the tribunal as regards the award of interest.

(2) Unless otherwise agreed by the parties the following provisions apply.

(3) The tribunal may award simple or compound interest from such dates, at such rates and with such rests as it considers meets the justice of the case –

(a) on the whole or part of any amount awarded by the tribunal, in respect of any period up to the date of the award;

(b) on the whole or part of any amount claimed in the arbitration and outstanding at the commencement of the arbitral proceedings but paid before the award was made, in respect of any period up to the date of payment.

(4) The tribunal may award simple or compound interest from the date of the award (or any later date) until payment, at such rates and with such rests as it considers meets the justice of the case, on the outstanding amount of any award (including any award of interest under subsection (3) and any award as to costs).

(5) References in this section to an amount awarded by the tribunal include an amount payable in consequence of a declaratory award by the tribunal.

(6) The above provisions do not affect any other power of the tribunal to award interest.

50 Extension of time for making award

(1) Where the time for making an award is limited by or in pursuance of the arbitration agreement, then, unless otherwise agreed by the parties, the court may in accordance with the following provisions by order extend that time.

(2) An application for an order under this section may be made –

(a) by the tribunal (upon notice to the parties); or

(b) by any party to the proceedings (upon notice to the tribunal and the other parties),

but only after exhausting any available arbitral process for obtaining an extension of time.

(3) The court shall only make an order if satisfied that a substantial injustice would otherwise be done.

(4) The court may extend the time for such period and on such term as it thinks fit, and may do so whether or not the time previously fixed (by or under the agreement or by a previous order) has expired.

(5) The leave of the court is required for any appeal from a decision of the court under this section.

51 Settlement

(1) If during arbitral proceedings the parties settle the dispute, the following provisions apply unless otherwise agreed by the parties.

(2) The tribunal shall terminate the substantive proceedings and, if so requested by the parties and not objected to by the tribunal, shall record the settlement in the form of an agreed award.

(3) An agreed award shall state that it is an award of the tribunal and shall have the same status and effect as any other award on the merits of the case.

(4) The following provisions of this Part relating to awards (sections 52 to 58) apply to an agreed award.

(5) Unless the parties have also settled the matter of the payment of the costs of the arbitration, the provisions of this Part relating to costs (sections 59 to 65) continue to apply.

52 Form of award

(1) The parties are free to agree on the form of an award.
(2) If or to the extent that there is no such agreement, the following provisions apply.
(3) The award shall be in writing signed by all the arbitrators or all those assenting to the award.
(4) The award shall contain the reasons for the award unless it is an agreed award or the parties have agreed to dispense with reasons.
(5) The award shall state the seat of the arbitration and the date when the award is made.

53 Place where award treated as made

Unless otherwise agreed by the parties, where the seat of the arbitration is in England and Wales or Northern Ireland, any award in the proceedings shall be treated as made there, regardless of where it was signed, despatched or delivered to any of the parties.

54 Date of award

(1) Unless otherwise agreed by the parties, the tribunal may decide what is to be taken to be the date on which the award was made.
(2) In the absence of any such decision, the date of the award shall be taken to be the date on which it is signed by the arbitrator or, where more than one arbitrator signs the award, by the last of them.

55 Notification of award

(1) The parties are free to agree on the requirements as to notification of the award to the parties.
(2) If there is no such agreement, the award shall be notified to the parties by service on them of copies of the award, which shall be done without delay after the award is made.
(3) Nothing in this section affects section 56 (power to withhold award in case of non-payment).

56 Power to withhold award in case of non-payment

(1) The tribunal may refuse to deliver an award to the parties except upon full payment of the fees and expenses of the arbitrators.
(2) If the tribunal refuses on that ground to deliver an award, a party to the arbitral proceedings may (upon notice to the other parties and the tribunal) apply to the court, which may order that –
    (a) the tribunal shall deliver the award on the payment into court by the applicant of the fees and expenses demanded, or such lesser amount as the court may specify;
    (b) the amount of the fees and expenses properly payable shall be determined by such means and upon such terms as the court may direct; and

(c) out of the money paid into court there shall be paid out such fees and expenses as may be found to be properly payable and the balance of the money (if any) shall be paid out to the applicant.

(3) For this purpose the amount of fees and expenses properly payable is the amount the applicant is liable to pay under section 28 or any agreement relating to the payment of the arbitrators.

(4) No application to the court may be made where there is any available arbitral process for appeal or review of the amount of the fees or expenses demanded.

(5) References in this section to arbitrators include an arbitrator who has ceased to act and an umpire who has not replaced the other arbitrators.

(6) The above provisions of this section also apply in relation to any arbitral or other institution or person vested by the parties with powers in relation to the delivery of the tribunal's award. As they so apply, the references to the fees and expenses of the arbitrators shall be construed as including the fees and expenses of that institution or person.

(7) The leave of the court is required for any appeal from a decision of the court under this section.

(8) Nothing in this section shall be construed as excluding an application under section 28 where payment has been made to the arbitrators in order to obtain the award.

57 Correction of award or additional award

(1) The parties are free to agree on the powers of the tribunal to correct an award or make an additional award.

(2) If or to the extent there is no such agreement, the following provisions apply.

(3) The tribunal may on its own initiative or on the application of a party –

(a) correct an award so as to remove any clerical mistake or error arising from an accidental slip or omission or clarify or remove any ambiguity in the award; or

(b) make an additional award in respect of any claim (including a claim for interest or costs) which was presented to the tribunal but was not dealt with in the award.

(c) These powers shall not be exercised without first affording the other parties a reasonable opportunity to make representations to the tribunal.

(4) Any application for the exercise of those powers must be made within 28 days of the date of the award or such longer period as the parties may agree.

(5) Any correction of an award shall be made within 28 days of the date the application was received by the tribunal or, where the correction is made by the tribunal on its own initiative, within 28 days of the date of the award or, in either case, such longer period as the parties may agree.

(6) Any additional award shall be made within 56 days of the date of the original award or such longer period as the parties may agree.

(7) Any correction of an award shall form part of the award.

58 Effect of award

(1) Unless otherwise agreed by the parties, an award made by the tribunal pursuant to an arbitration agreement is final and binding both on the parties and on any persons claiming through or under them.

(2) This does not affect the right of a person to challenge the award by any available arbitral process of appeal or review or in accordance with the provisions of this Part.

Costs of the arbitration

59 Costs of the arbitration

(1) References in this Part to the costs of the arbitration are to –
  (a) the arbitrators' fees and expenses;
  (b) the fees and expenses of any arbitral institution concerned; and
  (c) the legal or other costs of the parties.

(2) Any such reference includes the costs of or incidental to any proceedings to determine the amount of the recoverable costs of the arbitration (see section 63).

60 Agreement to pay costs in any event

An agreement which has the effect that a party is to pay the whole or part of the costs of the arbitration in any event is only valid if made after the dispute in question has arisen.

61 Award of costs

(1) The tribunal may make an award allocating the costs of the arbitration as between the parties, subject to any agreement of the parties.

(2) Unless the parties otherwise agree, the tribunal shall award costs on the general principle that costs should follow the event except where it appears to the tribunal that in the circumstances this is not appropriate in relation to the whole or part of the costs.

62 Effect of agreement or award about costs

Unless the parties otherwise agree, any obligation under an effect of agreement between them as to how the costs of the arbitration are to be borne, or under an award allocating the costs of the arbitration, extends only to such costs as are recoverable.

63 The recoverable costs of the arbitration

(1) The parties are free to agree what costs of the arbitration are recoverable.

(2) If or to the extent there is no such agreement, the following provisions apply.

(3) The tribunal may determine by award the recoverable costs of the arbitration on such basis as it thinks fit. If it does so, it shall specify –
  (a) the basis on which it has acted; and
  (b) the items of recoverable costs and the amount referable to each.

(4) If the tribunal does not determine the recoverable costs of the arbitration, any party to the arbitral proceedings may apply to the court (upon notice to the other parties) which may –
  (a) determine the recoverable costs of the arbitration on such basis as it thinks fit; or
  (b) order that they shall be determined by such means and upon such terms as it may specify.

(5) Unless the tribunal or the court determines otherwise –
    (a) the recoverable costs of the arbitration shall be determined on the basis that there shall be allowed a reasonable amount in respect of all costs reasonably incurred; and
    (b) any doubt as to whether costs were reasonably incurred or were reasonable in amount shall be resolved in favour of the paying party.

(6) The above provisions have effect subject to section 64 (recoverable fees and expenses of arbitrators).

(7) Nothing in this section affects any right of the arbitrators, any expert, legal adviser or assessor appointed by the tribunal, or any arbitral institution, to payment of their fees and expenses.

64 Recoverable fees and expenses of arbitrators

(1) Unless otherwise agreed by the parties, the recoverable costs of the arbitration shall include in respect of the fees and expenses of the arbitrators only such reasonable fees and expenses as are appropriate in the circumstances.

(2) If there is any question as to what reasonable fees and expenses are appropriate in the circumstances, and the matter is not already before the court on an application under section 63(4), the court may on the application of any party (upon notice to the other parties) –
    (a) determine the matter; or
    (b) order that it be determined by such means and upon such terms as the court may specify.

(3) Subsection (1) has effect subject to any order of the court under section 24(4) or 25(3)(b) (order as to entitlement to fees or expenses in case of removal or resignation of arbitrator).

(4) Nothing in this section affects any right of the arbitrator to payment of his fees and expenses.

65 Power to limit recoverable costs

(1) Unless otherwise agreed by the parties, the tribunal may direct that the recoverable costs of the arbitration, or of any part of the arbitral proceedings, shall be limited to a specified amount.

(2) Any direction may be made or varied at any stage, but this must be done sufficiently in advance of the incurring of costs to which it relates, or the taking of any steps in the proceedings which may be affected by it, for the limit to be taken into account.

Powers of the court in relation to award

66 Enforcement of the award

(1) An award made by the tribunal pursuant to an arbitration agreement may, by leave of the court, be enforced in the same manner as a judgment or order of the court to the same effect.

(2) Where leave is so given, judgment may be entered in terms of the award.

(3) Leave to enforce an award shall not be given where, or to the extent that, the person against whom it is sought to be enforced shows that the tribunal lacked substantive jurisdiction to make the award. The right to raise such an objection may have been lost (see section 73).
(4) Nothing in this section affects the recognition or enforcement of an award under any other enactment or rule of law, in particular under Part II of the Arbitration Act 1950 (enforcement of awards under Geneva Convention) or the provisions of Part III of this Act relating to the recognition and enforcement of awards under the New York Convention or by an action on the award.

67 Challenging the award: Substantive jurisdiction

(1) A party to arbitral proceedings may (upon notice to the other parties and to the tribunal) apply to the court –
   (a) challenging any award of the arbitral tribunal as to its substantive jurisdiction; or
   (b) for an order declaring an award made by the tribunal on the merits to be of no effect, in whole or in part, because the tribunal did not have substantive jurisdiction.
   (c) A party may lose the right to object (see section 73) and the right to apply is subject to the restrictions in section 70(2) and (3).
(2) The arbitral tribunal may continue the arbitral proceedings and make a further award while an application to the court under this section is pending in relation to an award as to jurisdiction.
(3) On an application under this section challenging an award of the arbitral tribunal as to its substantive jurisdiction, the court may by order –
   (a) confirm the award;
   (b) vary the award; or
   (c) set aside the award in whole or in part.
(4) The leave of the court is required for any appeal from a decision of the court under this section.

68 Challenging the award: Serious irregularity

(1) A party to arbitral proceedings may (upon notice to the other parties and to the tribunal) apply to the court challenging an award in the proceedings on the ground of serious irregularity affecting the tribunal, the proceedings or the award. A party may lose the right to object (see section 73) and the right to apply is subject to the restrictions in section 70(2) and (3).
(2) Serious irregularity means an irregularity of one or more of the following kinds which the court considers has caused or will cause substantial injustice to the applicant –
   (a) failure by the tribunal to comply with section 33 (general duty of tribunal);
   (b) the tribunal exceeding its powers (otherwise than by exceeding its substantive jurisdiction: see section 67);
   (c) failure by the tribunal to conduct the proceedings in accordance with the procedure agreed by the parties;
   (d) failure by the tribunal to deal with all the issues that were put to it;

(e) any arbitral or other institution or person vested by the parties with powers in relation to the proceedings or the award exceeding its powers;
(f) uncertainty or ambiguity as to the effect of the award;
(g) the award being obtained by fraud or the award or the way in which it was procured being contrary to public policy;
(h) failure to comply with the requirements as to the form of the award; or
(i) any irregularity in the conduct of the proceedings or in the award which is admitted by the tribunal or by any arbitral or other institution or person vested by the parties with powers in relation to the proceedings or the award.

(3) If there is shown to be serious irregularity affecting the tribunal, the proceedings or the award, the court may –
(a) remit the award to the tribunal, in whole or in part, for reconsideration;
(b) set the award aside in whole or in part; or
(c) declare the award to be of no effect, in whole or in part.

The court shall not exercise its power to set aside or to declare an award to be of no effect, in whole or in part, unless it is satisfied that it would be inappropriate to remit the matters in question to the tribunal for reconsideration.

The leave of the court is required for any appeal from a decision of the court under this section.

69 Appeal on point of law

(1) Unless otherwise agreed by the parties, a party to arbitral proceedings may (upon notice to the other parties and to the tribunal) appeal to the court on a question of law arising out of an award made in the proceedings. An agreement to dispense with reasons for the tribunal's award shall be considered an agreement to exclude the court's jurisdiction under this section.

(2) An appeal shall not be brought under this section except –
(a) with the agreement of all the other parties to the proceedings; or
(b) with the leave of the court.
(c) The right to appeal is also subject to the restrictions in section 70(2).

(3) Leave to appeal shall be given only if the court is satisfied –
(a) that the determination of the question will substantially affect the rights of one or more of the parties;
(b) that the question is one which the tribunal was asked to determine;
(c) that, on the basis of the findings of fact in the award:
(i) the decision of the tribunal on the question is obviously wrong; or
(ii) the question is one of general public importance and the decision of the tribunal is at least open to serious doubt; and
(d) that, despite the agreement of the parties to resolve the matter by arbitration, it is just and proper in all the circumstances for the court to determine the question.

(4) An application for leave to appeal under this section shall identify the question of law to be determined and state the grounds on which it is alleged that leave to appeal should be granted.

(5) The court shall determine an application for leave to appeal under this section without a hearing unless it appears to the court that a hearing is required.

(6) The leave of the court is required for any appeal from a decision of the court under this section to grant or refuse leave to appeal.

(7) On an appeal under this section the court may by order –

(a) confirm the award;

(b) vary the award;

(c) remit the award to the tribunal, in whole or in part, for reconsideration in the light of the court's determination; or

(d) set aside the award in whole or in part.

(e) The court shall not exercise its power to set aside an award, in whole or in part, unless it is satisfied that it would be inappropriate to remit the matters in question to the tribunal for reconsideration.

(8) The decision of the court on an appeal under this section shall be treated as a judgment of the court for the purposes of a further appeal. But no such appeal lies without the leave of the court which shall not be given unless the court considers that the question is one of general importance or is one which for some other special reason should be considered by the Court of Appeal.

70 Challenge or appeal: Supplementary provisions

(1) The following provisions apply to an application or appeal under sections 67, 68 or 69.

(2) An application or appeal may not be brought if the applicant or provisions appellant has not first exhausted –

(a) any available arbitral process of appeal or review; and

(b) any available recourse under section 57 (correction of award or additional award).

(3) Any application or appeal must be brought within 28 days of the date of the award or, if there has been any arbitral process of appeal or review, of the date when the applicant or appellant was notified of the result of that process.

(4) If on an application or appeal it appears to the court that the award –

(a) does not contain the tribunal's reasons; or

(b) does not set out the tribunal's reasons in sufficient detail to enable the court properly to consider the application or appeal,

the court may order the tribunal to state the reasons for its award in sufficient detail for that purpose.

(5) Where the court makes an order under subsection (4), it may make such further order as it thinks fit with respect to any additional costs of the arbitration resulting from its order.

(6) The court may order the applicant or appellant to provide security for the costs of the application or appeal, and may direct that the application or appeal be dismissed if the order is not complied with. The power to order security for costs shall not be exercised on the ground that the applicant or appellant is:

(a) an individual ordinarily resident outside the United Kingdom; or

(b) a corporation or association incorporated or formed under the law of a country outside the United Kingdom, or whose central management and control is exercised outside the United Kingdom.

(7) The court may order that any money payable under the award shall be brought into court or otherwise secured pending the determination of the application or appeal, and may direct that the application or appeal be dismissed if the order is not complied with.

(8) The court may grant leave to appeal subject to conditions to the same or similar effect as an order under subsection (6) or (7). This does not affect the general discretion of the court to grant leave subject to conditions.

71 Challenge or appeal: Effect of order of court

(1) The following provisions have effect where the court makes an order under sections 67, 68 or 69 with respect to an award.
(2) Where the award is varied, the variation has effect as part of the tribunal's award.
(3) Where the award is remitted to the tribunal, in whole or in part, for reconsideration, the tribunal shall make a fresh award in respect of the matters remitted within three months of the date of the order for remission or such longer or shorter period as the court may direct.
(4) Where the award is set aside or declared to be of no effect, in whole or in part, the court may also order that any provision that an award is a condition precedent to the bringing of legal proceedings in respect of a matter to which the arbitration agreement applies, is of no effect as regards the subject matter of the award or, as the case may be, the relevant part of the award.

Miscellaneous

72 Saving for rights of person who takes no part in proceedings

(1) A person alleged to be a party to arbitral proceedings but who takes no part in the proceedings may question –
   (a) whether there is a valid arbitration agreement;
   (b) whether the tribunal is properly constituted; or
   (c) what matters have been submitted to arbitration in accordance with the arbitration agreement,
   (d) by proceedings in the court for a declaration or injunction or other appropriate relief.
(2) He also has the same right as a party to the arbitral proceedings to challenge an award –
   (a) by an application under section 67 on the ground of lack of substantive jurisdiction in relation to him; or
   (b) by an application under section 68 on the ground of serious irregularity (within the meaning of that section) affecting him, and section 70(2) (duty to exhaust arbitral procedures) does not apply in his case.

73 Loss of right to object

(1) If a party to arbitral proceedings takes part, or continues to take part, in the proceedings without making, either forthwith or within such time as is allowed by the arbitration agreement or the tribunal or by any provision of this Part, any objection –
   (a) that the tribunal lacks substantive jurisdiction;
   (b) that the proceedings have been improperly conducted;
   (c) that there has been a failure to comply with the arbitration agreement or with any provision of this Part; or

(d) that there has been any other irregularity affecting the tribunal or the proceedings,
(e) he may not raise that objection later, before the tribunal or the court, unless he shows that, at the time he took part or continued to take part in the proceedings, he did not know and could not with reasonable diligence have discovered the grounds for the objection.

(2) Where the arbitral tribunal rules that it has substantive jurisdiction and a party to arbitral proceedings who could have questioned that ruling –
(a) by any available arbitral process of appeal or review; or
(b) by challenging the award,

does not do so, or does not do so within the time allowed by the arbitration agreement or any provision of this Part, he may not object later to the tribunal's substantive jurisdiction on any ground which was the subject of that ruling.

74 Immunity of arbitral institutions, etc.

(1) An arbitral or other institution or person designated or requested by the parties to appoint or nominate an arbitrator is not liable for anything done or omitted in the discharge or purported discharge of that function unless the act or omission is shown to have been in bad faith.
(2) An arbitral or other institution or person by whom an arbitrator is appointed or nominated is not liable, by reason of having appointed or nominated him, for anything done or omitted by the arbitrator (or his employees or agents) in the discharge or purported discharge of his functions as arbitrator.
(3) The above provisions apply to an employee or agent of an arbitral or other institution or person as they apply to the institution or person himself.

75 Charge to secure payment of solicitors' costs

The powers of the court to make declarations and orders under section 73 of the Solicitors Act 1974 or Article 71H of the Solicitors (Northern Ireland) Order 1976 (power to charge property recovered in the proceedings with the payment of solicitors' costs) may be exercised in relation to arbitral proceedings as if those proceedings were proceedings in the court.

Supplementary

76 Service of notices, etc.

(1) The parties are free to agree on the manner of service of any notice or other document required or authorised to be given or served in pursuance of the arbitration agreement or for the purposes of the arbitral proceedings.
(2) If or to the extent that there is no such agreement the following provisions apply.
(3) A notice or other document may be served on a person by any effective means.
(4) If a notice or other document is addressed, pre-paid and delivered by post –
(a) to the addressee's last known principal residence or, if he is or has been carrying on a trade, profession or business, his last known principal business address; or

(b) where the addressee is a body corporate, to the body's registered or principal office, it shall be treated as effectively served.

(5) This section does not apply to the service of documents for the purposes of legal proceedings, for which provision is made by rules of court.

(6) References in this Part to a notice or other document include any form of communication in writing and references to giving or serving a notice or other document shall be construed accordingly.

77 Powers of court in relation to service of documents

(1) This section applies where service of a document on a person in the manner agreed by the parties, or in accordance with provisions of section 76 having effect in default of agreement, is not reasonably practicable.

(2) Unless otherwise agreed by the parties, the court may make such order as it thinks fit –

(a) for service in such manner as the court may direct; or

(b) dispensing with service of the document.

(3) Any party to the arbitration agreement may apply for an order, but only after exhausting any available arbitral process for resolving the matter.

(4) The leave of the court is required for any appeal from a decision of the court under this section.

78 Reckoning periods of time

(1) The parties are free to agree on the method of reckoning periods of time for the purposes of any provision agreed by them or any provision of this Part having effect in default of such agreement.

(2) If or to the extent there is no such agreement, periods of time shall be reckoned in accordance with the following provisions.

(3) Where the act is required to be done within a specified period after or from a specified date, the period begins immediately after that date.

(4) Where the act is required to be done a specified number of clear days after a specified date, at least that number of days must intervene between the day on which the act is done and that date.

(5) Where the period is a period of seven days or less which would include a Saturday, Sunday or a public holiday in the place where anything which has to be done within the period falls to be done, that day shall be excluded.

(6) In relation to England and Wales or Northern Ireland, a 'public holiday' means Christmas Day, Good Friday or a day which under the Banking and Financial Dealings Act 1971 is a bank holiday.

79 Power of court to extend time limits relating to arbitral proceedings

(1) Unless the parties otherwise agree, the court may by order extend any time limit agreed by them in relation to any matter relating to the arbitral proceedings or specified in any

provision of this Part having effect in default of such agreement. This section does not apply to a time limit to which section 12 applies (power of court to extend time for beginning arbitral proceedings, etc.).

(2) An application for an order may be made –
  (a) by any party to the arbitral proceedings (upon notice to the other parties and to the tribunal); or
  (b) by the arbitral tribunal (upon notice to the parties).

(3) The court shall not exercise its power to extend a time limit unless it is satisfied –
  (a) that any available recourse to the tribunal, or to any arbitral or other institution or person vested by the parties with power in that regard, has first been exhausted; and
  (b) that a substantial injustice would otherwise be done.

(4) The court's power under this section may be exercised whether or not the time has already expired.

(5) An order under this section may be made on such terms as the court thinks fit.

(6) The leave of the court is required for any appeal from a decision of the court under this section.

80 Notice and other requirements in connection with legal proceedings

(1) References in this Part to an application, appeal or other step in relation to legal proceedings being taken 'upon notice' to the other parties to the arbitral proceedings, or to the tribunal, are to such notice of the originating process as is required by rules of court and do not impose any separate requirement.

(2) Rules of court shall be made –
  (a) requiring such notice to be given as indicated by any provision of this Part; and
  (b) as to the manner, form and content of any such notice.

(3) Subject to any provision made by rules of court, a requirement to give notice to the tribunal of legal proceedings shall be construed –
  (a) if there is more than one arbitrator, as a requirement to give notice to each of them; and
  (b) if the tribunal is not fully constituted, as a requirement to give notice to any arbitrator who has been appointed.

(4) References in this Part to making an application or appeal to the court within a specified period are to the issue within that period of the appropriate originating process in accordance with rules of court.

(5) Where any provision of this Part requires an application or appeal to be made to the court within a specified time, the rules of court relating to the reckoning of periods, the extending or abridging of periods, and the consequences of not taking a step within the period prescribed by the rules, apply in relation to that requirement.

(6) Provision may be made by rules of court amending the provisions of this Part –
  (a) with respect to the time within which any application or appeal to the court must be made;
  (b) so as to keep any provision made by this Part in relation to arbitral proceedings in step with the corresponding provision of rules of court applying in relation to proceedings in the court; or

(c) so as to keep any provision made by this Part in relation to legal proceedings in step with the corresponding provision of rules of court applying generally in relation to proceedings in the court.

(7) Nothing in this section affects the generality of the power to make rules of court.

81 Saving for certain matters governed by common law

(1) Nothing in this Part shall be construed as excluding the operation of any rule of law consistent with the provisions of this Part, in particular, any rule of law as to –
  (a) matters which are not capable of settlement by arbitration;
  (b) the effect of an oral arbitration agreement; or
  (c) the refusal of recognition or enforcement of an arbitral award on grounds of public policy.

(2) Nothing in this Act shall be construed as reviving any jurisdiction of the court to set aside or remit an award on the ground of errors of fact or law on the face of the award.

82 Minor definitions

(1) In this Part –

'arbitrator', unless the context otherwise requires, includes an umpire;

'available arbitral process', in relation to any matter, includes any process of appeal to or review by an arbitral or other institution or person vested by the parties with powers in relation to that matter;

'claimant', unless the context otherwise requires, includes a counterclaimant, and related expressions shall be construed accordingly;

'dispute' includes any difference;

'enactment' includes an enactment contained in Northern Ireland legislation;

'legal proceedings' means civil proceedings in the High Court or a county court;

'peremptory order' means an order made under section 41(5) or made in exercise of any corresponding power conferred by the parties;

'premises' includes land, buildings, moveable structures, vehicles, vessels, aircraft and hovercraft;

'question of law' means –

for a court in England and Wales, a question of the law of England and Wales, and

for a court in Northern Ireland, a question of the law of Northern Ireland;

'substantive jurisdiction', in relation to an arbitral tribunal, refers to the matters specified in section 30(1)(a) to (c), and references to the tribunal exceeding its substantive jurisdiction shall be construed accordingly.

(2) References in this Part to a party to an arbitration agreement include any person claiming under or through a party to the agreement.

83 Index of defined expressions: Part I

In this Part the expressions listed explained by the provision indicated –

agreement, agree and agreed	section 5(1)
agreement in writing	section 5(2) to (5)
arbitration agreement	sections 6 and 5(1)
arbitrator	section 82(1)
available arbitral process	section 82(1)
claimant	section 82(1)
commencement (in relation to arbitral proceedings)	section 14
costs of the arbitration	section 59
the court	section 105
dispute	section 82(1)
enactment	section 82(1)
legal proceedings	section 82(1)
Limitation Acts	section 13(4)
notice (or other document), party –	section 76(6)
– in relation to an arbitration agreement	section 82(2)
– where section 106(2) or (3) applies	section 106(4)
peremptory order	section 82(1) (and see section 41(5))
premises	section 82(1)
question of law	section 82(1)
recoverable costs	sections 63 and 64
seat of the arbitration	section 3
serve and service (of notice or other document)	section 76(6)
substantive jurisdiction (in relation to an arbitral tribunal)	section 82(1) (and see section 30(1)(a) to (c))
upon notice (to the parties or the tribunal)	section 80
written and in writing	section 5(6)

84 [Omitted]

Part II Other provisions relating to arbitration

Domestic arbitration agreements

85 Modification of Part I in relation to domestic arbitration agreement

(1) In the case of a domestic arbitration agreement the provisions of Part I are modified in accordance with the following sections.

(2) For this purpose a 'domestic arbitration agreement' means an arbitration agreement to which none of the parties is –

(a) an individual who is a national of, or habitually resident in, a state other than the United Kingdom; or

(b) a body corporate which is incorporated in, or whose central control and management is exercised in, a state other than the United Kingdom, and under which the seat of the arbitration (if the seat has been designated or determined) is in the United Kingdom.

(3) In subsection (2) 'arbitration agreement' and 'seat of the arbitration' have the same meaning as in Part I (see sections 3, 5(1) and 6).

86 Staying of legal proceedings

(1) In section 9 (stay of legal proceedings), subsection (4) (stay unless the arbitration agreement is null and void, inoperative, or incapable of being performed) does not apply to a domestic arbitration agreement.
(2) On an application under that section in relation to a domestic arbitration agreement the court shall grant a stay unless satisfied –
 (a) that the arbitration agreement is null and void, inoperative, or incapable of being performed; or
 (b) that there are other sufficient grounds for not requiring the parties to abide by the arbitration agreement.
(3) The court may treat as a sufficient ground under subsection (2)(b) the fact that the applicant is or was at any material time not ready and willing to do all things necessary for the proper conduct of the arbitration or of any other dispute resolution procedures required to be exhausted before resorting to arbitration.
(4) For the purposes of this section the question whether an arbitration agreement is a domestic arbitration agreement shall be determined by reference to the facts at the time the legal proceedings are commenced.

87 Effectiveness of agreement to exclude court's jurisdiction

(1) In the case of a domestic arbitration agreement any agreement to exclude the jurisdiction of the court under –
 (a) section 45 (determination of preliminary point of law); or
 (b) section 69 (challenging the award: appeal on point of law),

 is not effective unless entered into after the commencement of the arbitral proceedings in which the question arises or the award is made.
(2) For this purpose the commencement of the arbitral proceedings has the same meaning as in Part I (see section 14).
(3) For the purposes of this section the question whether an arbitration agreement is a domestic arbitration agreement shall be determined by reference to the facts at the time the agreement is entered into.

88–92 [Omitted]

Appointment of judges as arbitrators

93 Appointment of judges as arbitrators

(1) A judge of the Commercial Court or an official referee may, if in all the circumstances he thinks fit, accept appointment as a sole arbitrator or as umpire by or by virtue of an arbitration agreement.
(2) A judge of the Commercial Court shall not do so unless the Lord Chief Justice has informed him that, having regard to the state of business in the High Court and the Crown Court, he can be made available.

(3) An official referee shall not do so unless the Lord Chief Justice has informed him that, having regard to the state of official referees' business, he can be made available.
(4) The fees payable for the services of a judge of the Commercial Court or official referee as arbitrator or umpire shall be taken in the High Court.
(5) In this section – 'arbitration agreement' has the same meaning as in Part I; and 'official referee' means a person nominated under section 68(1)(a) of the Senior Courts Act 1981 to deal with official referees' business.
(6) The provisions of Part I of this Act apply to arbitration before a person appointed under this section with the modifications specified in Schedule 2.

Statutory arbitrations

94 Application of Part I to statutory arbitrations

(1) The provisions of Part I apply to every arbitration under an enactment (a 'statutory arbitration'), whether the enactment was passed or made before or after the commencement of this Act, subject to the adaptations and exclusions specified in sections 95 to 98.
(2) The provisions of Part I do not apply to a statutory arbitration if or to the extent that their application –
  (a) is inconsistent with the provisions of the enactment concerned, with any rules or procedure authorised or recognised by it; or
  (b) is excluded by any other enactment.
(3) In this section and the following provisions of this Part 'enactment' –
  (a) in England and Wales, includes an enactment contained in subordinate legislation within the meaning of the Interpretation Act 1978;
  (b) in Northern Ireland, means a statutory provision within the meaning of section 1(f) of the Interpretation Act (Northern Ireland) 1954.

95 General adaptation of provisions in relation to statutory arbitrations

(1) The provisions of Part I apply to a statutory arbitration –
  (a) as if the arbitration were pursuant to an arbitration agreement and as if the enactment were that agreement; and
  (b) as if the persons by and against whom a claim subject to arbitration in pursuance of the enactment may be or has been made were parties to that agreement.
(2) Every statutory arbitration shall be taken to have its seat in England and Wales or, as the case may be, in Northern Ireland.

96 Specific adaptations of provisions in relation to statutory arbitrations

(1) The following provisions of Part I apply to a statutory arbitration with the following adaptations.
(2) In section 30(1) (competence of tribunal to rule on its own relation to jurisdiction), the reference in paragraph (a) to whether there is a valid statutory arbitration agreement shall be construed as a reference to whether the arbitrations enactment applies to the dispute or difference in question.

(3) Section 35 (consolidation of proceedings and concurrent hearings) applies only so as to authorise the consolidation of proceedings, or concurrent hearings in proceedings, under the same enactment.

(4) Section 46 (rules applicable to substance of dispute) applies with the omission of subsection (1)(b) (determination in accordance with considerations agreed by parties).

97 Provisions excluded from applying to statutory arbitrations

The following provisions of Part I do not apply in relation to a statutory arbitration –

(a) section 8 (whether agreement discharged by death of a party);
(b) section 12 (power of court to extend agreed time limits);
(c) sections 9(5), –10(2) and – 71(4) (restrictions on effect of provision that award condition precedent to right to bring legal proceedings).

98 [Omitted]

Part III Recognition and enforcement of certain foreign awards

Enforcement of Geneva Convention awards

99 Continuation of Part II of the Arbitration Act 1950

Part II of the Arbitration Act 1950 (enforcement of certain foreign awards) continues to apply in relation to foreign awards within the meaning of that Part which are not also New York Convention awards.

Recognition and enforcement of New York Convention awards

100 New York Convention awards

(1) In this Part a 'New York Convention award' means an award made, in pursuance of an arbitration agreement, in the territory of a state (other than the United Kingdom) which is a party to the New York Convention.

(2) For the purposes of subsection (1) and of the provisions of this Part relating to such awards –
   (a) 'arbitration agreement' means an arbitration agreement in writing; and
   (b) an award shall be treated as made at the seat of the arbitration, regardless of where it was signed, despatched or delivered to any of the parties. In this subsection 'agreement in writing' and 'seat of the arbitration' have the same meaning as in Part I.

(3) If Her Majesty by Order in Council declares that a state specified in the Order is a party to the New York Convention, or is a party in respect of any territory so specified, the Order shall, while in force, be conclusive evidence of that fact.

(4) In this section 'the New York Convention' means the Convention on the Recognition and Enforcement of Foreign Arbitral Awards adopted by the United Nations Conference on International Commercial Arbitration on 10th June 1958.

101 Recognition and enforcement of awards

(1) A New York Convention award shall be recognised as binding on the persons as between whom it was made, and may accordingly be relied on by those persons by way of defence, set-off or otherwise in any legal proceedings in England and Wales or Northern Ireland.
(2) A New York Convention award may, by leave of the court, be enforced in the same manner as a judgment or order of the court to the same effect. As to the meaning of 'the court' see section 105.
(3) Where leave is so given, judgment may be entered in terms of the award.

102 Evidence to be produced by party seeking recognition or enforcement

(1) A party seeking the recognition or enforcement of a New York Convention award must produce –
  (a) the duly authenticated original award or a duly certified copy of it; and
  (b) the original arbitration agreement or a duly certified copy of it.
(2) If the award or agreement is in a foreign language, the party must also produce a translation of it certified by an official or sworn translator or by a diplomatic or consular agent.

103 Refusal of recognition or enforcement

(1) Recognition or enforcement of a New York Convention award shall not be refused except in the following cases.
(2) Recognition or enforcement of the award may be refused if the person against whom it is invoked proves –
  (a) that a party to the arbitration agreement was (under the law applicable to him) under some incapacity;
  (b) that the arbitration agreement was not valid under the law to which the parties subjected it or, failing any indication thereon, under the law of the country where the award was made;
  (c) that he was not given proper notice of the appointment of the arbitrator or of the arbitration proceedings or was otherwise unable to present his case;
  (d) that the award deals with a difference not contemplated by or not falling within the terms of the submission to arbitration or contains decisions on matters beyond the scope of the submission to arbitration (but see subsection (4));
  (e) that the composition of the arbitral tribunal or the arbitral procedure was not in accordance with the agreement of the parties or, failing such agreement, with the law of the country in which the arbitration took place;
  (f) that the award has not yet become binding on the parties, or has been set aside or suspended by a competent authority of the country in which, or under the law of which, it was made.
(3) Recognition or enforcement of the award may also be refused if the award is in respect of a matter which is not capable of settlement by arbitration, or if it would be contrary to public policy to recognise or enforce the award.

(4) An award which contains decisions on matters not submitted to arbitration may be recognised or enforced to the extent that it contains decisions on matters submitted to arbitration which can be separated from those on matters not so submitted.

(5) Where an application for the setting aside or suspension of the award has been made to such a competent authority as is mentioned in subsection (2)(f), the court before which the award is sought to be relied upon may, if it considers it proper, adjourn the decision on the recognition or enforcement of the award. It may also on the application of the party claiming recognition or enforcement of the award order the other party to give suitable security.

104 Saving for other bases of recognition or enforcement

Nothing in the preceding provisions of this Part affects any right to rely upon or enforce a New York Convention award at common law or under section 66.

Part IV General provisions

105 [Omitted]

106 Crown application

(1) Part I of this Act applies to any arbitration agreement to which Her Majesty, either in right of the Crown or of the Duchy of Lancaster or otherwise, or the Duke of Cornwall, is a party.

(2) Where Her Majesty is party to an arbitration agreement otherwise than in right of the Crown, Her Majesty shall be represented for the purposes of any arbitral proceedings –
   (a) where the agreement was entered into by Her Majesty in right of the Duchy of Lancaster, by the Chancellor of the Duchy or such person as he may appoint; and
   (b) in any other case, by such person as Her Majesty may appoint in writing under the Royal Sign Manual.

(3) Where the Duke of Cornwall is party to an arbitration agreement, he shall be represented for the purposes of any arbitral proceedings by such person as he may appoint.

(4) References in Part I to a party or the parties to the arbitration agreement or to arbitral proceedings shall be construed, where subsection (2) or (3) applies, as references to the person representing Her Majesty or the Duke of Cornwall.

107–110 [Omitted]

Schedule 1 Mandatory provisions of Part I

sections 9 to 11 (stay of legal proceedings);

section 12 (power of court to extend agreed time limits);

section 13 (application of Limitation Acts);

section 24 (power of court to remove arbitrator);

section 26(1) (effect of death of arbitrator);

section 28 (liability of parties for fees and expenses of arbitrators);

section 29 (immunity of arbitrator);

section 31 (objection to substantive jurisdiction of tribunal);

section 32 (determination of preliminary point of jurisdiction);

section 33 (general duty of tribunal);

section 37(2) (items to be treated as expenses of arbitrators);

section 40 (general duty of parties);

section 43 (securing the attendance of witnesses);

section 56 (power to withhold award in case of non-payment);

section 60 (effectiveness of agreement for payment of costs in any event);

section 66 (enforcement of award);

sections 67 and 68 (challenging the award: substantive jurisdiction and serious irregularity), and

sections 70 and 71 (supplementary provisions; effect of order of court) so far as relating to those sections;

section 72 (saving for rights of person who takes no part in proceedings);

section 73 (loss of right to object);

section 74 (immunity of arbitral institutions, etc.);

section 75 (charge to secure payment of solicitors' costs).

section 93(6).

Schedule 2 Modifications of Part I in relation to judge-arbitrators

Introductory

1. In this Schedule 'judge-arbitrator' means a judge of the Commercial Court or official referee appointed as arbitrator or umpire under section 93.

General

2.
   (1) Subject to the following provisions of this Schedule, references in Part I to the court shall be construed in relation to a judge-arbitrator, or in relation to the appointment of a judge-arbitrator, as references to the Court of Appeal.
   (2) The references in sections 32(6), 45(6) and 69(8) to the Court of Appeal shall in such a case be construed as references to the Supreme Court.

Arbitrator's fees

3.

   The power of the court in section 28(2) to order consideration and adjustment of the liability of a party for the fees of an arbitrator may be exercised by a judge-arbitrator.

Any such exercise of the power is subject to the powers of the Court of Appeal under sections 24(4) and 25(3)(b) (directions as to entitlement to fees or expenses in case of removal or resignation).

Exercise of court powers in support of arbitration

4.

(1) Where the arbitral tribunal consists of or includes a judge-arbitrator the powers of the court under sections 42 to 44 (enforcement of peremptory orders, summoning witnesses, and other court powers) are exercisable by the High Court and also by the judge-arbitrator himself.

(2) Anything done by a judge-arbitrator in the exercise of those powers shall be regarded as done by him in his capacity as judge of the High Court and have effect as if done by that court. Nothing in this sub-paragraph prejudices any power vested in him as arbitrator or umpire.

Extension of time for making award

5.

(1) The power conferred by section 50 (extension of time for making award) is exercisable by the judge-arbitrator himself.

(2) Any appeal from a decision of a judge-arbitrator under that section lies to the Court of Appeal with the leave of that court.

Withholding award in case of non-payment

6.

(1) The provisions of paragraph 7 apply in place of the provisions of section 56 (power to withhold award in the case of non-payment) in relation to the withholding of an award for non-payment of the fees and expenses of a judge-arbitrator.

(2) This does not affect the application of section 56 in relation to the delivery of such an award by an arbitral or other institution or person vested by the parties with powers in relation to the delivery of the award.

7.

(1) A judge-arbitrator may refuse to deliver an award except upon payment of the fees and expenses mentioned in section 56(1).

(2) The judge-arbitrator may, on an application by a party to the arbitral proceedings, order that if he pays into the High Court the fees and expenses demanded, or such lesser amount as the judge-arbitrator may specify –

(a) the award shall be delivered;

(b) the amount of the fees and expenses, properly payable shall be determined by such means and upon such terms as he may direct; and

(c) out of the money paid into court there shall be paid out such fees and expenses as may be found to be properly payable and the balance of the money (if any) shall be paid out to the applicant.

(3) For this purpose the amount of fees and expenses properly payable is the amount the applicant is liable to pay under section 28 or any agreement relating to the payment of the arbitrator.

(4) No application to the judge-arbitrator under this paragraph may be made where there is any available arbitral process for appeal or review of the amount of the fees or expenses demanded.

(5) Any appeal from a decision of a judge-arbitrator under this paragraph lies to the Court of Appeal with the leave of that court.

(6) Where a party to arbitral proceedings appeals under sub-paragraph (5), an arbitrator is entitled to appear and be heard.

Correction of award or additional award

8. Subsections (4) to (6) of section 57 (correction of award or additional award: time limit for application or exercise of power) do not apply to a judge-arbitrator.

Costs

9. Where the arbitral tribunal consists of or includes a judge-arbitrator the powers of the court under section 63(4) (determination of recoverable costs) shall be exercised by the High Court.

10.

(1) The power of the court under section 64 to determine an arbitrator's reasonable fees and expenses may be exercised by a judge-arbitrator.

(2) Any such exercise of the power is subject to the powers of the Court of Appeal under sections 24(4) and 25(3)(b) (directions as to entitlement to fees or expenses in case of removal or resignation).

Enforcement of award

11. The leave of the court required by section 66 (enforcement of award) may in the case of an award of a judge-arbitrator be given by the judge-arbitrator himself.

Solicitors' costs

12. The powers of the court to make declarations and orders under the provisions applied by section 75 (power to charge property recovered in arbitral proceedings with the payment of solicitors' costs) may be exercised by the judge-arbitrator.

Powers of court in relation to service of documents

13.

(1) The power of the court under section 77(2) (powers of court in relation to service of documents) is exercisable by the judge-arbitrator.

(2) Any appeal from a decision of a judge-arbitrator under that section lies to the Court of Appeal with the leave of that court.

Powers of court to extend time limits relating to arbitral proceedings

14.

(1) The power conferred by section 79 (power of court to extend time limits relating to arbitral proceedings) is exercisable by the judge-arbitrator himself.

(2) Any appeal from a decision of a judge-arbitrator under that section lies to the Court of Appeal with the leave of that court.

Schedules 3 and 4 [Omitted]

Contracts (Rights of Third Parties) Act 1999

1 Right of third party to enforce contractual term

(1) Subject to the provisions of this Act, a person who is not a party to a contract (a 'third party') may in his own right enforce a term of the contract if –
   (a) the contract expressly provides that he may; or
   (b) subject to subsection (2), the term purports to confer a benefit on him.

(2) Subsection (1)(b) does not apply if on a proper construction of the contract it appears that the parties did not intend the term to be enforceable by the third party.

(3) The third party must be expressly identified in the contract by name, as a member of a class or as answering a particular description but need not be in existence when the contract is entered into.

(4) This section does not confer a right on a third party to enforce a term of a contract otherwise than subject to and in accordance with any other relevant terms of the contract.

(5) For the purpose of exercising his right to enforce a term of the contract, there shall be available to the third party any remedy that would have been available to him in an action for breach of contract if he had been a party to the contract (and the rules relating to damages, injunctions, specific performance and other relief shall apply accordingly).

(6) Where a term of a contract excludes or limits liability in relation to any matter references in this Act to the third party enforcing the term shall be construed as references to his availing himself of the exclusion or limitation.

(7) In this Act, in relation to a term of a contract which is enforceable by a third party –
   'the promisor' means the party to the contract against whom the term is enforceable by the third party; and
'the promisee' means the party to the contract by whom the term is enforceable against the promisor.

2 Variation and cancellation of contract

(1) Subject to the provisions of this section, where a third party has a right under section 1 to enforce a term of the contract, the parties to the contract may not without his consent cancel the contract, or vary it in such a way as to extinguish, or alter his entitlement under, that right, if –
   (a) the third party has communicated his assent to the term to the promisor;
   (b) the promisor is aware that the third party has relied on the term; or

(c) the promisor can reasonably be expected to have foreseen that the third party would rely on the term and the third party has in fact relied on it.

(2) The assent referred to in subsection (1)(a) –

(a) may be by words or conduct; and

(b) if sent to the promisor by post or other means, shall not be regarded as communicated to the promisor until received by him.

(3) Subsection (1) is subject to any express term of the contract under which –

(a) the contract may be cancelled or varied without the consent of the third party; or

(b) the consent of the third party is required in circumstances specified in the contract instead of those set out in subsection (1)(a) to (c).

(4) Where the consent of a third party is required under subsection (1) or (3), the court may, on the application of the parties to the contract, dispense with his consent if satisfied –

(a) that his consent cannot be obtained because his whereabouts cannot reasonably be ascertained; or

(b) that he is mentally incapable of giving his consent.

(5) The court may, on the application of the parties to a contract, dispense with any consent that may be required under subsection (1)(c) if satisfied that it cannot reasonably be ascertained whether or not the third party has in fact relied on the term.

(6) If the court dispenses with a third party's consent, it may impose such conditions as it thinks fit, including a condition requiring the payment of compensation to the third party.

(7) The jurisdiction conferred by subsections (4) to (6) is exercisable by both the High Court and a county court.

3 Defences, etc., available to promisor

(1) Subsections (2) to (5) apply where, in reliance on section 1, proceedings for the enforcement of a term of a contract are brought by a third party.

(2) The promisor shall have available to him by way of defence or set-off any matter that –

(a) arises from or in connection with the contract and is relevant to the term; and

(b) would have been available to him by way of defence or set-off if the proceedings had been brought by the promisee.

(3) The promisor shall also have available to him by way of defence or set-off any matter if –

(a) an express term of the contract provides for it to be available to him in proceedings brought by the third party; and

(b) it would have been available to him by way of defence or set-off if the proceedings had been brought by the promisee.

(4) The promisor shall also have available to him –

(a) by way of defence or set-off any matter; and

(b) by way of counterclaim any matter not arising from the contract,

(c) that would have been available to him by way of defence or set-off or, as the case may be, by way of counterclaim against the third party if the third party had been a party to the contract.

(5) Subsections (2) and (4) are subject to any express term of the contract as to the matters that are not to be available to the promisor by way of defence, set-off or counterclaim.

(6) Where in any proceedings brought against him a third party seeks in reliance on section 1 to enforce a term of a contract (including, in particular, a term purporting to exclude or limit liability), he may not do so if he could not have done so (whether by reason of any particular circumstances relating to him or otherwise) had he been a party to the contract.

4 Enforcement of contract by promisee

Section 1 does not affect any right of the promisee to enforce any term of the contract.

5 Protection of promisor from double liability

Where under section 1 a term of a contract is enforceable by a third party, and the promisee has recovered from the promisor a sum in respect of –

(a) the third party's loss in respect of the term; or

(b) the expense to the promisee of making good to the third party the default of the promisor,

then, in any proceedings brought in reliance on that section by the third party, the court shall reduce any award to the third party to such extent as it thinks appropriate to take account of the sum recovered by the promisee.

6 Exceptions

(1) Section 1 confers no rights on a third party in the case of a contract on a bill of exchange, promissory note or other negotiable instrument.

(2) to (4) [Omitted].

(5) Section 1 confers no rights on a third party in the case of –

(a) a contract for the carriage of goods by sea; or

(b) a contract for the carriage of goods by rail or road, or for the carriage of cargo by air, which is subject to the rules of the appropriate international transport convention,

(c) except that a third party may in reliance on that section avail himself of an exclusion or limitation of liability in such a contract.

(6) In subsection (5) 'contract for the carriage of goods by sea' means a contract of carriage –

(a) contained in or evidenced by a bill of lading, sea waybill or a corresponding electronic transaction; or

(b) under or for the purposes of which there is given an undertaking which is contained in a ship's delivery order or a corresponding electronic transaction.

(7) For the purposes of subsection (6) –

(a) 'bill of lading', 'sea waybill' and 'ship's delivery order' have the same meaning as in the Carriage of Goods by Sea Act 1992; and

(b) a corresponding electronic transaction is a transaction within section 1(5) of that Act which corresponds to the issue, indorsement, delivery or transfer of a bill of lading, sea waybill or ship's delivery order.

(8) In subsection (5) 'the appropriate international transport convention' means –
   (a) in relation to a contract for the carriage of goods by rail, the Convention which has the force of law in the United Kingdom under regulation 3 of the Railways (Convention on International Carriage by Rail) Regulations 2005;
   (b) in relation to a contract for the carriage of goods by road, the Convention which has the force of law in the United Kingdom under section 1 of the Carriage of Goods by Road Act 1965; and
   (c) in relation to a contract for the carriage of cargo by air:
      (i) the Convention which has the force of law in the United Kingdom under section 1 of the Carriage by Air Act 1961; or
      (ii) the Convention which has the force of law under section 1 of the Carriage by Air (Supplementary Provisions) Act 1962; or
      (iii) either of the amended Conventions set out in Part B of Schedule 2 or 3 to the Carriage by Air Acts (Application of Provisions) Order 1967.

7 Supplementary provisions relating to third party

(1) Section 1 does not affect any right or remedy of a third party that exists or is available apart from this Act.
(2) Section 2(2) of the Unfair Contract Terms Act 1977 (restriction on exclusion etc. of liability for negligence) shall not apply where the negligence consists of the breach of an obligation arising from a term of a contract and the person seeking to enforce it is a third party acting in reliance on section 1.
(3) In sections 5 and 8 of the Limitation Act 1980 the references to an action founded on a simple contract and an action upon a specialty shall respectively include references to an action brought in reliance on section 1 relating to a simple contract and an action brought in reliance on that section relating to a specialty.
(4) A third party shall not, by virtue of section 1(5) or 3(4) or (6), be treated as a party to the contract for the purposes of any other Act (or any instrument made under any other Act).

8 Arbitration provisions

(1) Where –
   (a) a right under section 1 to enforce a term ('the substantive term') is subject to a term providing for the submission of disputes to arbitration ('the arbitration agreement'), and
   (b) the arbitration agreement is an agreement in writing for the purposes of Part I of the Arbitration Act 1996,

   the third party shall be treated for the purposes of that Act as a party to the arbitration agreement as regards disputes between himself and the promisor relating to the enforcement of the substantive term by the third party.
(2) Where –
   (a) a third party has a right under section 1 to enforce a term providing for one or more descriptions of dispute between the third party and the promisor to be submitted to arbitration ('the arbitration agreement'),

(b) the arbitration agreement is an agreement in writing for the purposes of Part I of the Arbitration Act 1996, and
(c) the third party does not fall to be treated under subsection (1) as a party to the arbitration agreement,

the third party shall, if he exercises the right, be treated for the purposes of that Act as a party to the arbitration agreement in relation to the matter with respect to which the right is exercised, and be treated as having been so immediately before the exercise of the right.

9 and 10 [Omitted]

Electronic Communications Act 2000

7 Electronic signatures and related certificates

(1) In any legal proceedings –
   (a) an electronic signature incorporated into or logically associated with a particular electronic communication or particular electronic data, and
   (b) the certification by any person of such a signature,
   (c) shall each be admissible in evidence in relation to any question as to the authenticity of the communication or data or as to the integrity of the communication or data.

(2) For the purposes of this section an electronic signature is so much of anything in electronic form as –
   (a) is incorporated into or otherwise logically associated with any electronic communication or electronic data; and
   (b) purports to be so incorporated or associated for the purpose of being used in establishing the authenticity of the communication or data, the integrity of the communication or data, or both.

(3) For the purposes of this section an electronic signature incorporated into or associated with a particular electronic communication or particular electronic data is certified by any person if that person (whether before or after the making of the communication) has made a statement confirming that –
   (a) the signature,
   (b) a means of producing, communicating or verifying the signature, or
   (c) a procedure applied to the signature,
   (d) is (either alone or in combination with other factors) a valid means of establishing the authenticity of the communication or data, the integrity of the communication or data, or both.

8–16 [Omitted]

Bribery Act 2010

UK ST 2010 C. 23

General bribery offences

1 Offences of bribing another person

(1) A person ("P") is guilty of an offence if either of the following cases applies.

(2) Case 1 is where –
  (a) P offers, promises or gives a financial or other advantage to another person, and
  (b) P intends the advantage –
    (i) to induce a person to perform improperly a relevant function or activity, or
    (ii) to reward a person for the improper performance of such a function or activity.
(3) Case 2 is where –
  (a) P offers, promises or gives a financial or other advantage to another person, and
  (b) P knows or believes that the acceptance of the advantage would itself constitute the improper performance of a relevant function or activity.
(4) In case 1 it does not matter whether the person to whom the advantage is offered, promised or given is the same person as the person who is to perform, or has performed, the function or activity concerned.
(5) In cases 1 and 2 it does not matter whether the advantage is offered, promised or given by P directly or through a third party.

2 Offences relating to being bribed

(1) A person ("R") is guilty of an offence if any of the following cases applies.
(2) Case 3 is where R requests, agrees to receive or accepts a financial or other advantage intending that, in consequence, a relevant function or activity should be performed improperly (whether by R or another person).
(3) Case 4 is where –
  (a) R requests, agrees to receive or accepts a financial or other advantage, and
  (b) the request, agreement or acceptance itself constitutes the improper performance by R of a relevant function or activity.
(4) Case 5 is where R requests, agrees to receive or accepts a financial or other advantage as a reward for the improper performance (whether by R or another person) of a relevant function or activity.
(5) Case 6 is where, in anticipation of or in consequence of R requesting, agreeing to receive or accepting a financial or other advantage, a relevant function or activity is performed improperly –
  (a) by R, or
  (b) by another person at R's request or with R's assent or acquiescence.
(6) In cases 3 to 6 it does not matter –
  (a) whether R requests, agrees to receive or accepts (or is to request, agree to receive or accept) the advantage directly or through a third party,
  (b) whether the advantage is (or is to be) for the benefit of R or another person.
(7) In cases 4 to 6 it does not matter whether R knows or believes that the performance of the function or activity is improper.
(8) In case 6, where a person other than R is performing the function or activity, it also does not matter whether that person knows or believes that the performance of the function or activity is improper.

3 Function or activity to which bribe relates

(1) For the purposes of this Act a function or activity is a relevant function or activity if –

(a) it falls within subsection (2), and
(b) meets one or more of conditions A to C.

(2) The following functions and activities fall within this subsection –
(a) any function of a public nature,
(b) any activity connected with a business,
(c) any activity performed in the course of a person's employment,
(d) any activity performed by or on behalf of a body of persons (whether corporate or unincorporate).

(3) Condition A is that a person performing the function or activity is expected to perform it in good faith.

(4) Condition B is that a person performing the function or activity is expected to perform it impartially.

(5) Condition C is that a person performing the function or activity is in a position of trust by virtue of performing it.

(6) A function or activity is a relevant function or activity even if it –
(a) has no connection with the United Kingdom, and
(b) is performed in a country or territory outside the United Kingdom.

(7) In this section "business" includes trade or profession.

4 Improper performance to which bribe relates

(1) For the purposes of this Act a relevant function or activity –
(a) is performed improperly if it is performed in breach of a relevant expectation, and
(b) is to be treated as being performed improperly if there is a failure to perform the function or activity and that failure is itself a breach of a relevant expectation.

(2) In subsection (1) "relevant expectation" –
(a) in relation to a function or activity which meets condition A or B, means the expectation mentioned in the condition concerned, and
(b) in relation to a function or activity which meets condition C, means any expectation as to the manner in which, or the reasons for which, the function or activity will be performed that arises from the position of trust mentioned in that condition.

(3) Anything that a person does (or omits to do) arising from or in connection with that person's past performance of a relevant function or activity is to be treated for the purposes of this Act as being done (or omitted) by that person in the performance of that function or activity.

5 Expectation test

(1) For the purposes of sections 3 and 4, the test of what is expected is a test of what a reasonable person in the United Kingdom would expect in relation to the performance of the type of function or activity concerned.

(2) In deciding what such a person would expect in relation to the performance of a function or activity where the performance is not subject to the law of any part of the United Kingdom, any local custom or practice is to be disregarded unless it is permitted or required by the written law applicable to the country or territory concerned.

(3) In subsection (2) "written law" means law contained in –

(a) any written constitution, or provision made by or under legislation, applicable to the country or territory concerned, or
(b) any judicial decision which is so applicable and is evidenced in published written sources.

Bribery of foreign public officials

6 Bribery of foreign public officials

(1) A person ("P") who bribes a foreign public official ("F") is guilty of an offence if P's intention is to influence F in F's capacity as a foreign public official.
(2) P must also intend to obtain or retain –
  (a) business, or
  (b) an advantage in the conduct of business.
(3) P bribes F if, and only if –
  (a) directly or through a third party, P offers, promises or gives any financial or other advantage –
    (i) to F, or
    (ii) to another person at F's request or with F's assent or acquiescence, and
  (b) F is neither permitted nor required by the written law applicable to F to be influenced in F's capacity as a foreign public official by the offer, promise or gift.
(4) References in this section to influencing F in F's capacity as a foreign public official mean influencing F in the performance of F's functions as such an official, which includes –
  (a) any omission to exercise those functions, and
  (b) any use of F's position as such an official, even if not within F's authority.
(5) "Foreign public official" means an individual who –
  (a) holds a legislative, administrative or judicial position of any kind, whether appointed or elected, of a country or territory outside the United Kingdom (or any subdivision of such a country or territory),
  (b) exercises a public function –
    (i) for or on behalf of a country or territory outside the United Kingdom (or any subdivision of such a country or territory), or
    (ii) for any public agency or public enterprise of that country or territory (or subdivision), or
  (c) is an official or agent of a public international organisation.
(6) "Public international organisation" means an organisation whose members are any of the following –
  (a) countries or territories,
  (b) governments of countries or territories,
  (c) other public international organisations,
  (d) a mixture of any of the above.
(7) For the purposes of subsection (3)(b), the written law applicable to F is –
  (a) where the performance of the functions of F which P intends to influence would be subject to the law of any part of the United Kingdom, the law of that part of the United Kingdom,
  (b) where paragraph (a) does not apply and F is an official or agent of a public international organisation, the applicable written rules of that organisation,

(c) where paragraphs (a) and (b) do not apply, the law of the country or territory in relation to which F is a foreign public official so far as that law is contained in –
   (i) any written constitution, or provision made by or under legislation, applicable to the country or territory concerned, or
   (ii) any judicial decision which is so applicable and is evidenced in published written sources.

(8) For the purposes of this section, a trade or profession is a business.

Failure of commercial organisations to prevent bribery

7 Failure of commercial organisations to prevent bribery

(1) A relevant commercial organisation ("C") is guilty of an offence under this section if a person ("A") associated with C bribes another person intending –
   (a) to obtain or retain business for C, or
   (b) to obtain or retain an advantage in the conduct of business for C.

(2) But it is a defence for C to prove that C had in place adequate procedures designed to prevent persons associated with C from undertaking such conduct.

(3) For the purposes of this section, A bribes another person if, and only if, A –
   (a) is, or would be, guilty of an offence under section 1 or 6 (whether or not A has been prosecuted for such an offence), or
   (b) would be guilty of such an offence if section 12(2)(c) and (4) were omitted.

(4) See section 8 for the meaning of a person associated with C and see section 9 for a duty on the Secretary of State to publish guidance.

(5) In this section –
   "partnership" means –
   (a) a partnership within the Partnership Act 1890, or
   (b) a limited partnership registered under the Limited Partnerships Act 1907,
   (c) or a firm or entity of a similar character formed under the law of a country or territory outside the United Kingdom,
   "relevant commercial organisation" means –
   (a) a body which is incorporated under the law of any part of the United Kingdom and which carries on a business (whether there or elsewhere),
   (b) any other body corporate (wherever incorporated) which carries on a business, or part of a business, in any part of the United Kingdom,
   (c) a partnership which is formed under the law of any part of the United Kingdom and which carries on a business (whether there or elsewhere), or
   (d) any other partnership (wherever formed) which carries on a business, or part of a business, in any part of the United Kingdom, and, for the purposes of this section, a trade or profession is a business.

8 Meaning of associated person

(1) For the purposes of section 7, a person ("A") is associated with C if (disregarding any bribe under consideration) A is a person who performs services for or on behalf of C.

(2) The capacity in which A performs services for or on behalf of C does not matter.

(3) Accordingly A may (for example) be C's employee, agent or subsidiary.
(4) Whether or not A is a person who performs services for or on behalf of C is to be determined by reference to all the relevant circumstances and not merely by reference to the nature of the relationship between A and C.
(5) But if A is an employee of C, it is to be presumed unless the contrary is shown that A is a person who performs services for or on behalf of C.

9 Guidance about commercial organisations preventing bribery

(1) The Secretary of State must publish guidance about procedures that relevant commercial organisations can put in place to prevent persons associated with them from bribing as mentioned in section 7(1).
(2) The Secretary of State may, from time to time, publish revisions to guidance under this section or revised guidance.
(3) The Secretary of State must consult the Scottish Ministers and the Department of Justice in Northern Ireland before publishing anything under this section.
(4) Publication under this section is to be in such manner as the Secretary of State considers appropriate.
(5) Expressions used in this section have the same meaning as in section 7.

Prosecution and penalties

10 Consent to prosecution

(1) No proceedings for an offence under this Act may be instituted in England and Wales except by or with the consent of –
  (a) the Director of Public Prosecutions,
  (b) the Director of the Serious Fraud Office, or
  (c) the Director of Revenue and Customs Prosecutions.
(2) No proceedings for an offence under this Act may be instituted in Northern Ireland except by or with the consent of –
  (a) the Director of Public Prosecutions for Northern Ireland, or
  (b) the Director of the Serious Fraud Office.
(3) No proceedings for an offence under this Act may be instituted in England and Wales or Northern Ireland by a person –
  (a) who is acting –
    (i) under the direction or instruction of the Director of Public Prosecutions, the Director of the Serious Fraud Office or the Director of Revenue and Customs Prosecutions, or
    (ii) on behalf of such a Director, or
  (b) to whom such a function has been assigned by such a Director, except with the consent of the Director concerned to the institution of the proceedings.
(4) The Director of Public Prosecutions, the Director of the Serious Fraud Office and the Director of Revenue and Customs Prosecutions must exercise personally any function under subsection (1), (2) or (3) of giving consent.
(5) The only exception is if –
  (a) the Director concerned is unavailable, and

(b) there is another person who is designated in writing by the Director acting personally as the person who is authorised to exercise any such function when the Director is unavailable.

(6) In that case, the other person may exercise the function but must do so personally.

(7) Subsections (4) to (6) apply instead of any other provisions which would otherwise have enabled any function of the Director of Public Prosecutions, the Director of the Serious Fraud Office or the Director of Revenue and Customs Prosecutions under subsection (1), (2) or (3) of giving consent to be exercised by a person other than the Director concerned.

(8) No proceedings for an offence under this Act may be instituted in Northern Ireland by virtue of section 36 of the Justice (Northern Ireland) Act 2002 (delegation of the functions of the Director of Public Prosecutions for Northern Ireland to persons other than the Deputy Director) except with the consent of the Director of Public Prosecutions for Northern Ireland to the institution of the proceedings.

(9) The Director of Public Prosecutions for Northern Ireland must exercise personally any function under subsection (2) or (8) of giving consent unless the function is exercised personally by the Deputy Director of Public Prosecutions for Northern Ireland by virtue of section 30(4) or (7) of the Act of 2002 (powers of Deputy Director to exercise functions of Director).

(10) Subsection (9) applies instead of section 36 of the Act of 2002 in relation to the functions of the Director of Public Prosecutions for Northern Ireland and the Deputy Director of Public Prosecutions for Northern Ireland under, or (as the case may be) by virtue of, subsections (2) and (8) above of giving consent.

11 Penalties

(1) An individual guilty of an offence under section 1, 2 or 6 is liable –

(a) on summary conviction, to imprisonment for a term not exceeding 12 months, or to a fine not exceeding the statutory maximum, or to both,

(b) on conviction on indictment, to imprisonment for a term not exceeding 10 years, or to a fine, or to both.

(2) Any other person guilty of an offence under section 1, 2 or 6 is liable –

(a) on summary conviction, to a fine not exceeding the statutory maximum,

(b) on conviction on indictment, to a fine.

(3) A person guilty of an offence under section 7 is liable on conviction on indictment to a fine.

(4) The reference in subsection (1)(a) to 12 months is to be read –

(a) in its application to England and Wales in relation to an offence committed before the commencement of section 154(1) of the Criminal Justice Act 2003, and

(b) in its application to Northern Ireland,

(c) as a reference to 6 months.

Other provisions about offences

12 Offences under this Act: Territorial application

(1) An offence is committed under section 1, 2 or 6 in England and Wales, Scotland or Northern Ireland if any act or omission which forms part of the offence takes place in that part of the United Kingdom.

(2) Subsection (3) applies if –
- (a) no act or omission which forms part of an offence under section 1, 2 or 6 takes place in the United Kingdom,
- (b) a person's acts or omissions done or made outside the United Kingdom would form part of such an offence if done or made in the United Kingdom, and
- (c) that person has a close connection with the United Kingdom.

(3) In such a case –
- (a) the acts or omissions form part of the offence referred to in subsection (2)(a), and
- (b) proceedings for the offence may be taken at any place in the United Kingdom.

(4) For the purposes of subsection (2)(c) a person has a close connection with the United Kingdom if, and only if, the person was one of the following at the time the acts or omissions concerned were done or made –
- (a) a British citizen,
- (b) a British overseas territories citizen,
- (c) a British National (Overseas),
- (d) a British Overseas citizen,
- (e) a person who under the British Nationality Act 1981 was a British subject,
- (f) a British protected person within the meaning of that Act,
- (g) an individual ordinarily resident in the United Kingdom,
- (h) a body incorporated under the law of any part of the United Kingdom,
- (i) a Scottish partnership.

(5) An offence is committed under section 7 irrespective of whether the acts or omissions which form part of the offence take place in the United Kingdom or elsewhere.

(6) Where no act or omission which forms part of an offence under section 7 takes place in the United Kingdom, proceedings for the offence may be taken at any place in the United Kingdom.

(7) Subsection (8) applies if, by virtue of this section, proceedings for an offence are to be taken in Scotland against a person.

(8) Such proceedings may be taken –
- (a) in any sheriff court district in which the person is apprehended or in custody, or
- (b) in such sheriff court district as the Lord Advocate may determine.

(9) In subsection (8) "sheriff court district" is to be read in accordance with section 307(1) of the Criminal Procedure (Scotland) Act 1995.

13 Defence for certain bribery offences etc.

(1) It is a defence for a person charged with a relevant bribery offence to prove that the person's conduct was necessary for –
- (a) the proper exercise of any function of an intelligence service, or
- (b) the proper exercise of any function of the armed forces when engaged on active service.

(2) The head of each intelligence service must ensure that the service has in place arrangements designed to ensure that any conduct of a member of the service which would otherwise be a relevant bribery offence is necessary for a purpose falling within subsection (1)(a).

(3) The Defence Council must ensure that the armed forces have in place arrangements designed to ensure that any conduct of –
 (a) a member of the armed forces who is engaged on active service, or
 (b) a civilian subject to service discipline when working in support of any person falling within paragraph (a),

which would otherwise be a relevant bribery offence is necessary for a purpose falling within subsection (1)(b).

(4) The arrangements which are in place by virtue of subsection (2) or (3) must be arrangements which the Secretary of State considers to be satisfactory.

(5) For the purposes of this section, the circumstances in which a person's conduct is necessary for a purpose falling within subsection (1)(a) or (b) are to be treated as including any circumstances in which the person's conduct –
 (a) would otherwise be an offence under section 2, and
 (b) involves conduct by another person which, but for subsection (1)(a) or (b), would be an offence under section 1.

(6) In this section –

"active service" means service in –
 (a) an action or operation against an enemy,
 (b) an operation outside the British Islands for the protection of life or property, or
 (c) the military occupation of a foreign country or territory,

"armed forces" means Her Majesty's forces (within the meaning of the Armed Forces Act 2006),

"civilian subject to service discipline" and "enemy" have the same meaning as in the Act of 2006,

"GCHQ" has the meaning given by section 3(3) of the Intelligence Services Act 1994,

"head" means –
 (a) in relation to the Security Service, the Director General of the Security Service,
 (b) in relation to the Secret Intelligence Service, the Chief of the Secret Intelligence Service, and
 (c) in relation to GCHQ, the Director of GCHQ,

"intelligence service" means the Security Service, the Secret Intelligence Service or GCHQ,

"relevant bribery offence" means –
 (a) an offence under section 1 which would not also be an offence under section 6,
 (b) an offence under section 2,
 (c) an offence committed by aiding, abetting, counselling or procuring the commission of an offence falling within paragraph (a) or (b),
 (d) an offence of attempting or conspiring to commit, or of inciting the commission of, an offence falling within paragraph (a) or (b), or
 (e) an offence under Part 2 of the Serious Crime Act 2007 (encouraging or assisting crime) in relation to an offence falling within paragraph (a) or (b).

14 Offences under Sections 1, 2 and 6 by bodies corporate etc.

(1) This section applies if an offence under section 1, 2 or 6 is committed by a body corporate or a Scottish partnership.

(2) If the offence is proved to have been committed with the consent or connivance of –
  (a) a senior officer of the body corporate or Scottish partnership, or
  (b) a person purporting to act in such a capacity,
  (c) the senior officer or person (as well as the body corporate or partnership) is guilty of the offence and liable to be proceeded against and punished accordingly.

(3) But subsection (2) does not apply, in the case of an offence which is committed under section 1, 2 or 6 by virtue of section 12(2) to (4), to a senior officer or person purporting to act in such a capacity unless the senior officer or person has a close connection with the United Kingdom (within the meaning given by section 12(4)).

(4) In this section –
  "director", in relation to a body corporate whose affairs are managed by its members, means a member of the body corporate,
  "senior officer" means –
    (a) in relation to a body corporate, a director, manager, secretary or other similar officer of the body corporate, and
    (b) in relation to a Scottish partnership, a partner in the partnership.

15 Offences under Section 7 by partnerships

(1) Proceedings for an offence under section 7 alleged to have been committed by a partnership must be brought in the name of the partnership (and not in that of any of the partners).

(2) For the purposes of such proceedings –
  (a) rules of court relating to the service of documents have effect as if the partnership were a body corporate, and
  (b) the following provisions apply as they apply in relation to a body corporate –
    (i) section 33 of the Criminal Justice Act 1925 and Schedule 3 to the Magistrates' Courts Act 1980,
    (ii) section 18 of the Criminal Justice Act (Northern Ireland) 1945 (c. 15 (N.I.)) and Schedule 4 to the Magistrates' Courts (Northern Ireland) Order 1981 (S.I. 1981/1675 (N.I.26)),
    (iii) section 70 of the Criminal Procedure (Scotland) Act 1995.

(3) A fine imposed on the partnership on its conviction for an offence under section 7 is to be paid out of the partnership assets.

(4) In this section "partnership" has the same meaning as in section 7.

Supplementary and final provisions

16 Application to Crown

This Act applies to individuals in the public service of the Crown as it applies to other individuals.

17–20 and Schedules 1 and 2 Omitted

Consumer Rights Act 2015

Part 1

Consumer contracts for goods, digital content and services

Chapter 1

Introduction

1 Where Part 1 applies

(1) This Part applies where there is an agreement between a trader and a consumer for the trader to supply goods, digital content or services, if the agreement is a contract.
(2) It applies whether the contract is written or oral or implied from the parties' conduct, or more than one of these combined.
(3) Any of Chapters 2, 3 and 4 may apply to a contract –
   (a) if it is a contract for the trader to supply goods, see Chapter 2;
   (b) if it is a contract for the trader to supply digital content, see Chapter 3 (also, subsection (6));
   (c) if it is a contract for the trader to supply a service, see Chapter 4 (also, subsection (6)).
(4) In each case the Chapter applies even if the contract also covers something covered by another Chapter (a mixed contract).
(5) Two or all three of those Chapters may apply to a mixed contract.
(6) For provisions about particular mixed contracts, see –
   (a) section 15 (goods and installation);
   (b) section 16 (goods and digital content).
(7) For other provision applying to contracts to which this Part applies, see Part 2 (unfair terms).

2 Key definitions

(1) These definitions apply in this Part (as well as the definitions in section 59).
(2) "Trader" means a person acting for purposes relating to that person's trade, business, craft or profession, whether acting personally or through another person acting in the trader's name or on the trader's behalf.
(3) "Consumer" means an individual acting for purposes that are wholly or mainly outside that individual's trade, business, craft or profession.
(4) A trader claiming that an individual was not acting for purposes wholly or mainly outside the individual's trade, business, craft or profession must prove it.
(5) For the purposes of Chapter 2, except to the extent mentioned in subsection (6), a person is not a consumer in relation to a sales contract if –
   (a) the goods are second hand goods sold at public auction, and
   (b) individuals have the opportunity of attending the sale in person.
(6) A person is a consumer in relation to such a contract for the purposes of –
   (a) sections 11(4) and (5), 12, 28 and 29, and

(b) the other provisions of Chapter 2 as they apply in relation to those sections.

(7) "Business" includes the activities of any government department or local or public authority.

(8) "Goods" means any tangible moveable items, but that includes water, gas and electricity if and only if they are put up for supply in a limited volume or set quantity.

(9) "Digital content" means data which are produced and supplied in digital form.

Chapter 2

Goods

What goods contracts are covered?

3 Contracts covered by this Chapter

(1) This Chapter applies to a contract for a trader to supply goods to a consumer. Consumer Rights Act 2015 (c. 15).

(2) It applies only if the contract is one of these (defined for the purposes of this Part in sections 5 to 8) –
  (a) a sales contract;
  (b) a contract for the hire of goods;
  (c) a hire-purchase agreement;
  (d) a contract for transfer of goods.

(3) It does not apply –
  (a) to a contract for a trader to supply coins or notes to a consumer for use as currency;
  (b) to a contract for goods to be sold by way of execution or otherwise by authority of law;
  (c) to a contract intended to operate as a mortgage, pledge, charge or other security;
  (d) in relation to England and Wales or Northern Ireland, to a contract made by deed and for which the only consideration is the presumed consideration imported by the deed;
  (e) in relation to Scotland, to a gratuitous contract.

(4) A contract to which this Chapter applies is referred to in this Part as a "contract to supply goods".

(5) Contracts to supply goods include –
  (a) contracts entered into between one part owner and another;
  (b) contracts for the transfer of an undivided share in goods;
  (c) contracts that are absolute and contracts that are conditional.

(6) Subsection (1) is subject to any provision of this Chapter that applies a section or part of a section to only some of the kinds of contracts listed in subsection (2).

(7) A mixed contract (see section 1(4)) may be a contract of any of those kinds.

4 Ownership of goods

(1) In this Chapter ownership of goods means the general property in goods, not merely a special property.

(2) For the time when ownership of goods is transferred, see in particular the following provisions of the Sale of Goods Act 1979 (which relate to contracts of sale) –

section 16: goods must be ascertained
section 17: property passes when intended to pass
section 18: rules for ascertaining intention
section 19: reservation of right of disposal
section 20A: undivided shares in goods forming part of a bulk
section 20B: deemed consent by co-owner to dealings in bulk goods

5 Sales contracts

(1) A contract is a sales contract if under it –
 (a) the trader transfers or agrees to transfer ownership of goods to the consumer, and
 (b) the consumer pays or agrees to pay the price.
(2) A contract is a sales contract (whether or not it would be one under subsection (1)) if under the contract –
 (a) goods are to be manufactured or produced and the trader agrees to supply them to the consumer,
 (b) on being supplied, the goods will be owned by the consumer, and
 (c) the consumer pays or agrees to pay the price.
(3) A sales contract may be conditional (see section 3(5)), but in this Part "conditional sales contract" means a sales contract under which –
 (a) the price for the goods or part of it is payable by instalments, and
 (b) the trader retains ownership of the goods until the conditions specified in the contract (for the payment of instalments or otherwise) are met; and it makes no difference whether or not the consumer possesses the goods.

Sections 6 and 8 [Omitted]

What statutory rights are there under a goods contract?

9 Goods to be of satisfactory quality

(1) Every contract to supply goods is to be treated as including a term that the quality of the goods is satisfactory.
(2) The quality of goods is satisfactory if they meet the standard that a reasonable person would consider satisfactory, taking account of –
 (a) any description of the goods,
 (b) the price or other consideration for the goods (if relevant), and
 (c) all the other relevant circumstances (see subsection (5)).
(3) The quality of goods includes their state and condition; and the following aspects (among others) are in appropriate cases aspects of the quality of goods –
 (a) fitness for all the purposes for which goods of that kind are usually supplied;
 (b) appearance and finish;
 (c) freedom from minor defects;
 (d) safety;
 (e) durability.

(4) The term mentioned in subsection (1) does not cover anything which makes the quality of the goods unsatisfactory –
  (a) which is specifically drawn to the consumer's attention before the contract is made,
  (b) where the consumer examines the goods before the contract is made, which that examination ought to reveal, or
  (c) in the case of a contract to supply goods by sample, which would have been apparent on a reasonable examination of the sample.

(5) The relevant circumstances mentioned in subsection (2)(c) include any public statement about the specific characteristics of the goods made by the trader, the producer or any representative of the trader or the producer.

(6) That includes, in particular, any public statement made in advertising or labelling.

(7) But a public statement is not a relevant circumstance for the purposes of subsection (2)(c) if the trader shows that –
  (a) when the contract was made, the trader was not, and could not reasonably have been, aware of the statement,
  (b) before the contract was made, the statement had been publicly withdrawn or, to the extent that it contained anything which was incorrect or misleading, it had been publicly corrected, or
  (c) the consumer's decision to contract for the goods could not have been influenced by the statement.

(8) In a contract to supply goods a term about the quality of the goods may be treated as included as a matter of custom.

(9) See section 19 for a consumer's rights if the trader is in breach of a term that this section requires to be treated as included in a contract.

10 Goods to be fit for particular purpose

(1) Subsection (3) applies to a contract to supply goods if before the contract is made the consumer makes known to the trader (expressly or by implication) any particular purpose for which the consumer is contracting for the goods.

(2) Subsection (3) also applies to a contract to supply goods if –
  (a) the goods were previously sold by a credit-broker to the trader,
  (b) in the case of a sales contract or contract for transfer of goods, the consideration or part of it is a sum payable by instalments, and
  (c) before the contract is made, the consumer makes known to the credit-broker (expressly or by implication) any particular purpose for which the consumer is contracting for the goods.

(3) The contract is to be treated as including a term that the goods are reasonably fit for that purpose, whether or not that is a purpose for which goods of that kind are usually supplied.

(4) Subsection (3) does not apply if the circumstances show that the consumer does not rely, or it is unreasonable for the consumer to rely, on the skill or judgment of the trader or credit-broker.

(5) In a contract to supply goods a term about the fitness of the goods for a particular purpose may be treated as included as a matter of custom.

(6) See section 19 for a consumer's rights if the trader is in breach of a term that this section requires to be treated as included in a contract.

11 Goods to be as described

(1) Every contract to supply goods by description is to be treated as including a term that the goods will match the description.
(2) If the supply is by sample as well as by description, it is not sufficient that the bulk of the goods matches the sample if the goods do not also match the description.
(3) A supply of goods is not prevented from being a supply by description just because –
   (a) the goods are exposed for supply, and
   (b) they are selected by the consumer.
(4) Any information that is provided by the trader about the goods and is information mentioned in paragraph (a) of Schedule 1 or 2 to the Consumer Contracts (Information, Cancellation and Additional Charges) Regulations 2013 (SI 2013/3134) (main characteristics of goods) is to be treated as included as a term of the contract.
(5) A change to any of that information, made before entering into the contract or later, is not effective unless expressly agreed between the consumer and the trader.
(6) See section 2(5) and (6) for the application of subsections (4) and (5) where goods are sold at public auction.
(7) See section 19 for a consumer's rights if the trader is in breach of a term that this section requires to be treated as included in a contract.

12 Other pre-contract information included in contract

(1) This section applies to any contract to supply goods.
(2) Where regulation 9, 10 or 13 of the Consumer Contracts (Information, Cancellation and Additional Charges) Regulations 2013 (SI 2013/3134) required the trader to provide information to the consumer before the contract became binding, any of that information that was provided by the trader other than information about the goods and mentioned in paragraph (a) of Schedule 1 or 2 to the Regulations (main characteristics of goods) is to be treated as included as a term of the contract.
(3) A change to any of that information, made before entering into the contract or later, is not effective unless expressly agreed between the consumer and the trader.
(4) See section 2(5) and (6) for the application of this section where goods are sold at public auction.
(5) See section 19 for a consumer's rights if the trader is in breach of a term that this section requires to be treated as included in the contract.

13 Goods to match a sample

(1) This section applies to a contract to supply goods by reference to a sample of the goods that is seen or examined by the consumer before the contract is made.
(2) Every contract to which this section applies is to be treated as including a term that –

(a) the goods will match the sample except to the extent that any differences between the sample and the goods are brought to the consumer's attention before the contract is made, and
(b) the goods will be free from any defect that makes their quality unsatisfactory and that would not be apparent on a reasonable examination of the sample.

(3) See section 19 for a consumer's rights if the trader is in breach of a term that this section requires to be treated as included in a contract.

14 Goods to match a model seen or examined

(1) This section applies to a contract to supply goods by reference to a model of the goods that is seen or examined by the consumer before entering into the contract.
(2) Every contract to which this section applies is to be treated as including a term that the goods will match the model except to the extent that any differences between the model and the goods are brought to the consumer's attention before the consumer enters into the contract.
(3) See section 19 for a consumer's rights if the trader is in breach of a term that this section requires to be treated as included in a contract.

Section 15–18 [Omitted]

What remedies are there if statutory rights under a goods contract are not met?

19 Consumer's rights to enforce terms about goods

(1) In this section and sections 22 to 24 references to goods conforming to a contract are references to –
 (a) the goods conforming to the terms described in sections 9, 10, 11, 13 and 14,
 (b) the goods not failing to conform to the contract under section 15 or 16, and
 (c) the goods conforming to requirements that are stated in the contract.
(2) But, for the purposes of this section and sections 22 to 24, a failure to conform as mentioned in subsection (1)(a) to (c) is not a failure to conform to the contract if it has its origin in materials supplied by the consumer.
(3) If the goods do not conform to the contract because of a breach of any of the terms described in sections 9, 10, 11, 13 and 14, or if they do not conform to the contract under section 16, the consumer's rights (and the provisions about them and when they are available) are –
 (a) the short-term right to reject (sections 20 and 22);
 (b) the right to repair or replacement (section 23); and
 (c) the right to a price reduction or the final right to reject (sections 20 and 24).
(4) [omitted]
(5) If the trader is in breach of a term that section 12 requires to be treated as included in the contract, the consumer has the right to recover from the trader the amount of any costs incurred by the consumer as a result of the breach, up to the amount of the price paid or the value of other consideration given for the goods.
(6) [omitted]

(7) Subsections (3) to (6) are subject to section 25 and subsections (3)(a) and (6) are subject to section 26.
(8) Section 28 makes provision about remedies for breach of a term about the time for delivery of goods.
(9) This Chapter does not prevent the consumer seeking other remedies –
  (a) for a breach of a term that this Chapter requires to be treated as included in the contract,
  (b) on the grounds that, under section 15 or 16, goods do not conform to the contract, or
  (c) for a breach of a requirement stated in the contract.
(10) Those other remedies may be ones –
  (a) in addition to a remedy referred to in subsections (3) to (6) (but not so as to recover twice for the same loss), or
  (b) instead of such a remedy, or
  (c) where no such remedy is provided for.
(11) Those other remedies include any of the following that is open to the consumer in the circumstances –
  (a) claiming damages;
  (b) seeking specific performance;
  (c) seeking an order for specific implement;
  (d) relying on the breach against a claim by the trader for the price;
  (e) for breach of an express term, exercising a right to treat the contract as at an end.
(12) It is not open to the consumer to treat the contract as at an end for breach of a term that this Chapter requires to be treated as included in the contract, or on the grounds that, under section 15 or 16, goods do not conform to the contract, except as provided by subsections (3), (4) and (6).
(13) In this Part, treating a contract as at an end means treating it as repudiated.
(14) For the purposes of subsections (3)(b) and (c) and (4), goods which do not conform to the contract at any time within the period of six months beginning with the day on which the goods were delivered to the consumer must be taken not to have conformed to it on that day.
(15) Subsection (14) does not apply if –
  (a) it is established that the goods did conform to the contract on that day, or
  (b) its application is incompatible with the nature of the goods or with how they fail to conform to the contract.

20 Right to reject

(1) The short-term right to reject is subject to section 22.
(2) The final right to reject is subject to section 24.
(3) The right to reject under section 19(6) is not limited by those sections.
(4) Each of these rights entitles the consumer to reject the goods and treat the contract as at an end, subject to subsections (20) and (21).
(5) The right is exercised if the consumer indicates to the trader that the consumer is rejecting the goods and treating the contract as at an end.

(6) The indication may be something the consumer says or does, but it must be clear enough to be understood by the trader.
(7) From the time when the right is exercised –
  (a) the trader has a duty to give the consumer a refund, subject to subsection (18), and
  (b) the consumer has a duty to make the goods available for collection by the trader or (if there is an agreement for the consumer to return rejected goods) to return them as agreed.
(8) Whether or not the consumer has a duty to return the rejected goods, the trader must bear any reasonable costs of returning them, other than any costs incurred by the consumer in returning the goods in person to the place where the consumer took physical possession of them.
(9) The consumer's entitlement to receive a refund works as follows.
(10) To the extent that the consumer paid money under the contract, the consumer is entitled to receive back the same amount of money.
(11) To the extent that the consumer transferred anything else under the contract, the consumer is entitled to receive back the same amount of what the consumer transferred, unless subsection (12) applies.
(12) To the extent that the consumer transferred under the contract something for which the same amount of the same thing cannot be substituted, the consumer is entitled to receive back in its original state whatever the consumer transferred.
(13) [Omitted]
(14) [Omitted]
(15) A refund under this section must be given without undue delay, and in any event within 14 days beginning with the day on which the trader agrees that the consumer is entitled to a refund.
(16) If the consumer paid money under the contract, the trader must give the refund using the same means of payment as the consumer used, unless the consumer expressly agrees otherwise.
(17) The trader must not impose any fee on the consumer in respect of the refund.
(18) There is no entitlement to receive a refund –
  (a) if none of subsections (10) to (12) applies,
  (b) to the extent that anything to which subsection (12) applies cannot be given back in its original state, or
  (c) where subsection (13) applies, to the extent that anything the consumer transferred under the contract cannot be divided so as to give back only the amount, or part of the amount, to which the consumer is entitled.
(19) It may be open to a consumer to claim damages where there is no entitlement to receive a refund, or because of the limits of the entitlement, or instead of a refund.
(20) Subsection (21) qualifies the application in relation to England and Wales and Northern Ireland of the rights mentioned in subsections (1) to (3) where –
  (a) the contract is a severable contract,
  (b) in relation to the final right to reject, the contract is a contract for the hire of goods, a hire-purchase agreement or a contract for transfer of goods, and
  (c) section 26(3) does not apply.
(21) The consumer is entitled, depending on the terms of the contract and the circumstances of the case –

(a) to reject the goods to which a severable obligation relates and treat that obligation as at an end (so that the entitlement to a refund relates only to what the consumer paid or transferred in relation to that obligation), or
(b) to exercise any of the rights mentioned in subsections (1) to (3) in respect of the whole contract.

21 Partial rejection of goods

(1) If the consumer has any of the rights mentioned in section 20(1) to (3), but does not reject all of the goods and treat the contract as at an end, the consumer –
(a) may reject some or all of the goods that do not conform to the contract, but
(b) may not reject any goods that do conform to the contract.

(2) If the consumer is entitled to reject the goods in an instalment, but does not reject all of those goods, the consumer –
(a) may reject some or all of the goods in the instalment that do not conform to the contract, but
(b) may not reject any goods in the instalment that do conform to the contract.

(3) If any of the goods form a commercial unit, the consumer cannot reject some of those goods without also rejecting the rest of them.

(4) A unit is a "commercial unit" if division of the unit would materially impair the value of the goods or the character of the unit.

(5) The consumer rejects goods under this section by indicating to the trader that the consumer is rejecting the goods.

(6) The indication may be something the consumer says or does, but it must be clear enough to be understood by the trader.

(7) From the time when a consumer rejects goods under this section –
(a) the trader has a duty to give the consumer a refund in respect of those goods (subject to subsection (10)), and
(b) the consumer has a duty to make those goods available for collection by the trader or (if there is an agreement for the consumer to return rejected goods) to return them as agreed.

(8) Whether or not the consumer has a duty to return the rejected goods, the trader must bear any reasonable costs of returning them, other than any costs incurred by the consumer in returning those goods in person to the place where the consumer took physical possession of them.

(9) Section 20(10) to (17) apply to a consumer's right to receive a refund under this section (and in section 20(13) and (14) references to the contract being treated as at an end are to be read as references to goods being rejected).

(10) That right does not apply –
(a) if none of section 20(10) to (12) applies,
(b) to the extent that anything to which section 20(12) applies cannot be given back in its original state, or
(c) to the extent that anything the consumer transferred under the contract cannot be divided so as to give back only the amount, or part of the amount, to which the consumer is entitled.

(11) It may be open to a consumer to claim damages where there is no right to receive a refund, or because of the limits of the right, or instead of a refund.
(12) References in this section to goods conforming to a contract are to be read in accordance with section 19(1) and (2), but they also include the goods conforming to the terms described in section 17.
(13) Where section 20(21)(a) applies the reference in subsection (1) to the consumer treating the contract as at an end is to be read as a reference to the consumer treating the severable obligation as at an end.

22 Time limit for short-term right to reject

(1) A consumer who has the short-term right to reject loses it if the time limit for exercising it passes without the consumer exercising it, unless the trader and the consumer agree that it may be exercised later.
(2) An agreement under which the short-term right to reject would be lost before the time limit passes is not binding on the consumer.
(3) The time limit for exercising the short-term right to reject (unless subsection (4) applies) is the end of 30 days beginning with the first day after these have all happened –
   (a) ownership or (in the case of a contract for the hire of goods, a hire-purchase agreement or a conditional sales contract) possession of the goods has been transferred to the consumer,
   (b) the goods have been delivered, and
   (c) where the contract requires the trader to install the goods or take other action to enable the consumer to use them, the trader has notified the consumer that the action has been taken.
(4) If any of the goods are of a kind that can reasonably be expected to perish after a shorter period, the time limit for exercising the short-term right to reject in relation to those goods is the end of that shorter period (but without affecting the time limit in relation to goods that are not of that kind).
(5) Subsections (3) and (4) do not prevent the consumer exercising the short-term right to reject before something mentioned in subsection (3)(a), (b) or (c) has happened.
(6) If the consumer requests or agrees to the repair or replacement of goods, the period mentioned in subsection (3) or (4) stops running for the length of the waiting period.
(7) If goods supplied by the trader in response to that request or agreement do not conform to the contract, the time limit for exercising the short-term right to reject is then either –
   (a) 7 days after the waiting period ends, or
   (b) if later, the original time limit for exercising that right, extended by the waiting period.
(8) The waiting period –
   (a) begins with the day the consumer requests or agrees to the repair or replacement of the goods, and
   (b) ends with the day on which the consumer receives goods supplied by the trader in response to the request or agreement.

23 Right to repair or replacement

(1) This section applies if the consumer has the right to repair or replacement (see section 19(3) and (4)).

(2) If the consumer requires the trader to repair or replace the goods, the trader must –

(a) do so within a reasonable time and without significant inconvenience to the consumer, and

(b) bear any necessary costs incurred in doing so (including in particular the cost of any labour, materials or postage).

(3) The consumer cannot require the trader to repair or replace the goods if that remedy (the repair or the replacement) –

(a) is impossible, or

(b) is disproportionate compared to the other of those remedies.

(4) Either of those remedies is disproportionate compared to the other if it imposes costs on the trader which, compared to those imposed by the other, are unreasonable, taking into account –

(a) the value which the goods would have if they conformed to the contract,

(b) the significance of the lack of conformity, and

(c) whether the other remedy could be effected without significant inconvenience to the consumer.

(5) Any question as to what is a reasonable time or significant inconvenience is to be determined taking account of –

(a) the nature of the goods, and

(b) the purpose for which the goods were acquired.

(6) A consumer who requires or agrees to the repair of goods cannot require the trader to replace them, or exercise the short-term right to reject, without giving the trader a reasonable time to repair them (unless giving the trader that time would cause significant inconvenience to the consumer).

(7) A consumer who requires or agrees to the replacement of goods cannot require the trader to repair them, or exercise the short-term right to reject, without giving the trader a reasonable time to replace them (unless giving the trader that time would cause significant inconvenience to the consumer).

(8) In this Chapter, "repair" in relation to goods that do not conform to a contract, means making them conform.

24 Right to price reduction or final right to reject

(1) The right to a price reduction is the right –

(a) to require the trader to reduce by an appropriate amount the price the consumer is required to pay under the contract, or anything else the consumer is required to transfer under the contract, and

(b) to receive a refund from the trader for anything already paid or otherwise transferred by the consumer above the reduced amount.

(2) The amount of the reduction may, where appropriate, be the full amount of the price or whatever the consumer is required to transfer.

(3) Section 20(10) to (17) applies to a consumer's right to receive a refund under subsection (1)(b).

(4) The right to a price reduction does not apply –

(a) if what the consumer is (before the reduction) required to transfer under the contract, whether or not already transferred, cannot be divided up so as to enable the trader to receive or retain only the reduced amount, or

(b) if anything to which section 20(12) applies cannot be given back in its original state.

(5) A consumer who has the right to a price reduction and the final right to reject may only exercise one (not both), and may only do so in one of these situations –

(a) after one repair or one replacement, the goods do not conform to the contract;

(b) because of section 23(3) the consumer can require neither repair nor replacement of the goods; or

(c) the consumer has required the trader to repair or replace the goods, but the trader is in breach of the requirement of section 23(2)(a) to do so within a reasonable time and without significant inconvenience to the consumer.

(6) There has been a repair or replacement for the purposes of subsection (5)(a) if –

(a) the consumer has requested or agreed to repair or replacement of the goods (whether in relation to one fault or more than one), and

(b) the trader has delivered goods to the consumer, or made goods available to the consumer, in response to the request or agreement.

(7) For the purposes of subsection (6) goods that the trader arranges to repair at the consumer's premises are made available when the trader indicates that the repairs are finished.

(8) If the consumer exercises the final right to reject, any refund to the consumer may be reduced by a deduction for use, to take account of the use the consumer has had of the goods in the period since they were delivered, but this is subject to subsections (9) and (10).

(9) No deduction may be made to take account of use in any period when the consumer had the goods only because the trader failed to collect them at an agreed time.

(10) No deduction may be made if the final right to reject is exercised in the first 6 months (see subsection (11)), unless –

(a) the goods consist of a motor vehicle, or

(b) the goods are of a description specified by order made by the Secretary of State by statutory instrument.

(11) In subsection (10) the first 6 months means 6 months beginning with the first day after these have all happened –

(a) ownership or (in the case of a contract for the hire of goods, a hirepurchase agreement or a conditional sales contract) possession of the goods has been transferred to the consumer,

(b) the goods have been delivered, and

(c) where the contract requires the trader to install the goods or take other action to enable the consumer to use them, the trader has notified the consumer that the action has been taken.

(12) In subsection (10)(a) "motor vehicle" –

(a) in relation to Great Britain, has the same meaning as in the Road Traffic Act 1988 (see sections 185 to 194 of that Act);

(b) in relation to Northern Ireland, has the same meaning as in the Road Traffic (Northern Ireland) Order 1995 (SI 1995/2994 (NI 18)) (see Parts I and V of that Order).

(13) But a vehicle is not a motor vehicle for the purposes of subsection (10)(a) if it is constructed or adapted –

(a) for the use of a person suffering from some physical defect or disability, and

(b) so that it may only be used by one such person at any one time.

(14) An order under subsection (10)(b) –

(a) may be made only if the Secretary of State is satisfied that it is appropriate to do so because of significant detriment caused to traders as a result of the application of subsection (10) in relation to goods of the description specified by the order;

(b) may contain transitional or transitory provision or savings.

(15) No order may be made under subsection (10)(b) unless a draft of the statutory instrument containing it has been laid before, and approved by a resolution of, each House of Parliament.

Other rules about remedies under goods contracts

25 Delivery of wrong quantity

(1) Where the trader delivers to the consumer a quantity of goods less than the trader contracted to supply, the consumer may reject them, but if the consumer accepts them the consumer must pay for them at the contract rate.

(2) Where the trader delivers to the consumer a quantity of goods larger than the trader contracted to supply, the consumer may accept the goods included in the contract and reject the rest, or may reject all of the goods.

(3) Where the trader delivers to the consumer a quantity of goods larger than the trader contracted to supply and the consumer accepts all of the goods delivered, the consumer must pay for them at the contract rate.

(4) Where the consumer is entitled to reject goods under this section, any entitlement for the consumer to treat the contract as at an end depends on the terms of the contract and the circumstances of the case.

(5) The consumer rejects goods under this section by indicating to the trader that the consumer is rejecting the goods.

(6) The indication may be something the consumer says or does, but it must be clear enough to be understood by the trader.

(7) Subsections (1) to (3) do not prevent the consumer claiming damages, where it is open to the consumer to do so.

(8) This section is subject to any usage of trade, special agreement, or course of dealing between the parties.

Sections 26–27 [Omitted]

28 Delivery of goods

(1) This section applies to any sales contract.

(2) Unless the trader and the consumer have agreed otherwise, the contract is to be treated as including a term that the trader must deliver the goods to the consumer.
(3) Unless there is an agreed time or period, the contract is to be treated as including a term that the trader must deliver the goods –
  (a) without undue delay, and
  (b) in any event, not more than 30 days after the day on which the contract is entered into.
(4) In this section –
  (a) an "agreed" time or period means a time or period agreed by the trader and the consumer for delivery of the goods;
  (b) if there is an obligation to deliver the goods at the time the contract is entered into, that time counts as the "agreed" time.
(5) Subsections (6) and (7) apply if the trader does not deliver the goods in accordance with subsection (3) or at the agreed time or within the agreed period.
(6) If the circumstances are that –
  (a) the trader has refused to deliver the goods,
  (b) delivery of the goods at the agreed time or within the agreed period is essential taking into account all the relevant circumstances at the time the contract was entered into, or
  (c) the consumer told the trader before the contract was entered into that delivery in accordance with subsection (3), or at the agreed time or within the agreed period, was essential, then the consumer may treat the contract as at an end.
(7) In any other circumstances, the consumer may specify a period that is appropriate in the circumstances and require the trader to deliver the goods before the end of that period.
(8) If the consumer specifies a period under subsection (7) but the goods are not delivered within that period, then the consumer may treat the contract as at an end.
(9) If the consumer treats the contract as at an end under subsection (6) or (8), the trader must without undue delay reimburse all payments made under the contract.
(10) If subsection (6) or (8) applies but the consumer does not treat the contract as at an end –
  (a) that does not prevent the consumer from cancelling the order for any of the goods or rejecting goods that have been delivered, and
  (b) the trader must without undue delay reimburse all payments made under the contract in respect of any goods for which the consumer cancels the order or which the consumer rejects.
(11) If any of the goods form a commercial unit, the consumer cannot reject or cancel the order for some of those goods without also rejecting or cancelling the order for the rest of them.
(12) A unit is a "commercial unit" if division of the unit would materially impair the value of the goods or the character of the unit.
(13) This section does not prevent the consumer seeking other remedies where it is open to the consumer to do so.
(14) See section 2(5) and (6) for the application of this section where goods are sold at public auction.

29 Passing of risk

(1) A sales contract is to be treated as including the following provisions as terms.
(2) The goods remain at the trader's risk until they come into the physical possession of –
  (a) the consumer, or
  (b) a person identified by the consumer to take possession of the goods.
(3) Subsection (2) does not apply if the goods are delivered to a carrier who –
  (a) is commissioned by the consumer to deliver the goods, and
  (b) is not a carrier the trader named as an option for the consumer.
(4) In that case the goods are at the consumer's risk on and after delivery to the carrier.
(5) Subsection (4) does not affect any liability of the carrier to the consumer in respect of the goods.
(6) See section 2(5) and (6) for the application of this section where goods are sold at public auction.

30 Goods under guarantee

(1) This section applies where –
  (a) there is a contract to supply goods, and
  (b) there is a guarantee in relation to the goods.
(2) "Guarantee" here means an undertaking to the consumer given without extra charge by a person acting in the course of the person's business (the "guarantor") that, if the goods do not meet the specifications set out in the guarantee statement or in any associated advertising –
  (a) the consumer will be reimbursed for the price paid for the goods, or
  (b) the goods will be repaired, replaced or handled in any way.
(3) The guarantee takes effect, at the time the goods are delivered, as a contractual obligation owed by the guarantor under the conditions set out in the guarantee statement and in any associated advertising.
(4) The guarantor must ensure that –
  (a) the guarantee sets out in plain and intelligible language the contents of the guarantee and the essential particulars for making claims under the guarantee,
  (b) the guarantee states that the consumer has statutory rights in relation to the goods and that those rights are not affected by the guarantee, and (c) where the goods are offered within the territory of the United Kingdom, the guarantee is written in English.
(5) The contents of the guarantee to be set out in it include, in particular –
  (a) the name and address of the guarantor, and
  (b) the duration and territorial scope of the guarantee.
(6) The guarantor and any other person who offers to supply to consumers the goods which are the subject of the guarantee must, on request by the consumer, make the guarantee available to the consumer within a reasonable time, in writing and in a form accessible to the consumer.
(7) What is a reasonable time is a question of fact.
(8) If a person fails to comply with a requirement of this section, the enforcement authority may apply to the court for an injunction or (in Scotland) an order of specific implement against that person requiring that person to comply.

(9) On an application the court may grant an injunction or (in Scotland) an order of specific implement on such terms as it thinks appropriate.

(10) In this section –
"court" means –
  (a) in relation to England and Wales, the High Court or the county court,
  (b) in relation to Northern Ireland, the High Court or a county court, and
  (c) in relation to Scotland, the Court of Session or the sheriff; "enforcement authority" means –
    (i) the Competition and Markets Authority,
    (ii) a local weights and measures authority in Great Britain, and
    (iii) the Department of Enterprise, Trade and Investment in Northern Ireland.

Can a trader contract out of statutory rights and remedies under a goods contract?

31 Liability that cannot be excluded or restricted

(1) A term of a contract to supply goods is not binding on the consumer to the extent that it would exclude or restrict the trader's liability arising under any of these provisions –
  (a) section 9 (goods to be of satisfactory quality);
  (b) section 10 (goods to be fit for particular purpose);
  (c) section 11 (goods to be as described);
  (d) section 12 (other pre-contract information included in contract);
  (e) section 13 (goods to match a sample);
  (f) section 14 (goods to match a model seen or examined);
  (g) section 15 (installation as part of conformity of the goods with the contract);
  (h) section 16 (goods not conforming to contract if digital content does not conform);
  (i) section 17 (trader to have right to supply the goods etc.);
  (j) section 28 (delivery of goods);
  (k) section 29 (passing of risk).

(2) That also means that a term of a contract to supply goods is not binding on the consumer to the extent that it would –
  (a) exclude or restrict a right or remedy in respect of a liability under a provision listed in subsection (1),
  (b) make such a right or remedy or its enforcement subject to a restrictive or onerous condition,
  (c) allow a trader to put a person at a disadvantage as a result of pursuing such a right or remedy, or
  (d) exclude or restrict rules of evidence or procedure.

(3) The reference in subsection (1) to excluding or restricting a liability also includes preventing an obligation or duty arising or limiting its extent.

(4) An agreement in writing to submit present or future differences to arbitration is not to be regarded as excluding or restricting any liability for the purposes of this section.

(5) Subsection (1)(i), and subsection (2) so far as it relates to liability under section 17, do not apply to a term of a contract for the hire of goods.

(6) But an express term of a contract for the hire of goods is not binding on the consumer to the extent that it would exclude or restrict a term that section 17 requires to be treated as included in the contract, unless it is inconsistent with that term (and see also section 62 (requirement for terms to be fair)).

(7) See Schedule 3 for provision about the enforcement of this section.

32 Contracts applying law of non-EEA State

(1) If–

  (a) the law of a country or territory other than an EEA State is chosen by the parties to be applicable to a sales contract, but

  (b) the sales contract has a close connection with the United Kingdom, this Chapter, except the provisions in subsection (2), applies despite that choice.

(2) The exceptions are –

  (a) sections 11(4) and (5) and 12;

  (b) sections 28 and 29;

  (c) section 31(1)(d), (j) and (k).

(3) For cases where those provisions apply, or where the law applicable has not been chosen or the law of an EEA State is chosen, see Regulation (EC) No. 593/2008 of the European Parliament and of the Council of 17 June 2008 on the law applicable to contractual obligations.

Chapters 3 and 4 [Omitted]

Chapter 5

General and supplementary provisions

Sections 58–60 [Omitted]

Part 2

Unfair terms

Sections 61–76 [Omitted]

Part 3

Miscellaneous and general

Chapter 1

Sections 77–80 [Omitted]

Chapter 2

Competition

Sections 81–82 [Omitted]

Chapter 3

Duty of letting agents to publicise fees etc.

Sections 83–88 [Omitted]

Chapter 4

Student complaints scheme

Section 89 [Omitted]

Chapter 5

Secondary ticketing

Sections 90–95 [Omitted]

Chapter 6

General

Sections 90–101 [Omitted]

Schedules 1–10 [Omitted]

Insurance Act 2015

Part 1

Insurance contracts: Main definitions

1 Insurance contracts: Main definitions

In this Act (apart from Part 6) –

> "consumer insurance contract" has the same meaning as in the Consumer Insurance (Disclosure and Representations) Act 2012;
>
> "non-consumer insurance contract" means a contract of insurance that is not a consumer insurance contract;
>
> "insured" means the party to a contract of insurance who is the insured under the contract, or would be if the contract were entered into;
>
> "insurer" means the party to a contract of insurance who is the insurer under the contract, or would be if the contract were entered into;
>
> "the duty of fair presentation" means the duty imposed by section 3(1).

Part 2

The duty of fair presentation

2 Application and interpretation

(1) This Part applies to non-consumer insurance contracts only.
(2) This Part applies in relation to variations of non-consumer insurance contracts as it applies to contracts, but –
  (a) references to the risk are to be read as references to changes in the risk relevant to the proposed variation, and
  (b) references to the contract of insurance are to the variation.

3 The duty of fair presentation

(1) Before a contract of insurance is entered into, the insured must make to the insurer a fair presentation of the risk.
(2) The duty imposed by subsection (1) is referred to in this Act as "the duty of fair presentation".
(3) A fair presentation of the risk is one –
  (a) which makes the disclosure required by subsection (4),
  (b) which makes that disclosure in a manner which would be reasonably clear and accessible to a prudent insurer, and
  (c) in which every material representation as to a matter of fact is substantially correct, and every material representation as to a matter of expectation or belief is made in good faith.
(4) The disclosure required is as follows, except as provided in subsection (5) –
  (a) disclosure of every material circumstance which the insured knows or ought to know, or
  (b) failing that, disclosure which gives the insurer sufficient information to put a prudent insurer on notice that it needs to make further enquiries for the purpose of revealing those material circumstances.
(5) In the absence of enquiry, subsection (4) does not require the insured to disclose a circumstance if –
  (a) it diminishes the risk,
  (b) the insurer knows it,
  (c) the insurer ought to know it,
  (d) the insurer is presumed to know it, or
  (e) it is something as to which the insurer waives information.
(6) Sections 4 to 6 make further provision about the knowledge of the insured and of the insurer, and section 7 contains supplementary provision.

4 Knowledge of insured

(1) This section provides for what an insured knows or ought to know for the purposes of section 3(4)(a).
(2) An insured who is an individual knows only –

(a) what is known to the individual, and
(b) what is known to one or more of the individuals who are responsible for the insured's insurance.

(3) An insured who is not an individual knows only what is known to one or more of the individuals who are –
(a) part of the insured's senior management, or
(b) responsible for the insured's insurance.

(4) An insured is not by virtue of subsection (2)(b) or (3)(b) taken to know confidential information known to an individual if –
(a) the individual is, or is an employee of, the insured's agent; and
(b) the information was acquired by the insured's agent (or by an employee of that agent) through a business relationship with a person who is not connected with the contract of insurance.

(5) For the purposes of subsection (4) the persons connected with a contract of insurance are –
(a) the insured and any other persons for whom cover is provided by the contract, and
(b) if the contract re-insures risks covered by another contract, the persons who are (by virtue of this subsection) connected with that other contract.

(6) Whether an individual or not, an insured ought to know what should reasonably have been revealed by a reasonable search of information available to the insured (whether the search is conducted by making enquiries or by any other means).

(7) In subsection (6) "information" includes information held within the insured's organisation or by any other person (such as the insured's agent or a person for whom cover is provided by the contract of insurance).

(8) For the purposes of this section –
(a) "employee", in relation to the insured's agent, includes any individual working for the agent, whatever the capacity in which the individual acts,
(b) an individual is responsible for the insured's insurance if the individual participates on behalf of the insured in the process of procuring the insured's insurance (whether the individual does so as the insured's employee or agent, as an employee of the insured's agent or in any other capacity), and
(c) "senior management" means those individuals who play significant roles in the making of decisions about how the insured's activities are to be managed or organised.

5 Knowledge of insurer

(1) For the purposes of section 3(5)(b), an insurer knows something only if it is known to one or more of the individuals who participate on behalf of the insurer in the decision whether to take the risk, and if so on what terms (whether the individual does so as the insurer's employee or agent, as an employee of the insurer's agent or in any other capacity).

(2) For the purposes of section 3(5)(c), an insurer ought to know something only if –
(a) an employee or agent of the insurer knows it, and ought reasonably to have passed on the relevant information to an individual mentioned in subsection (1), or

(b) the relevant information is held by the insurer and is readily available to an individual mentioned in subsection (1).

(3) For the purposes of section 3(5)(d), an insurer is presumed to know –

(a) things which are common knowledge, and

(b) things which an insurer offering insurance of the class in question to insureds in the field of activity in question would reasonably be expected to know in the ordinary course of business.

6 Knowledge: General

(1) For the purposes of sections 3 to 5, references to an individual's knowledge include not only actual knowledge, but also matters which the individual suspected, and of which the individual would have had knowledge but for deliberately refraining from confirming them or enquiring about them.

(2) Nothing in this Part affects the operation of any rule of law according to which knowledge of a fraud perpetrated by an individual ("F") either on the insured or on the insurer is not to be attributed to the insured or to the insurer (respectively), where –

(a) if the fraud is on the insured, F is any of the individuals mentioned in section 4(2)(b) or (3), or

(b) if the fraud is on the insurer, F is any of the individuals mentioned in section 5(1).

7 Supplementary

(1) A fair presentation need not be contained in only one document or oral presentation.

(2) The term "circumstance" includes any communication made to, or information received by, the insured.

(3) A circumstance or representation is material if it would influence the judgement of a prudent insurer in determining whether to take the risk and, if so, on what terms.

(4) Examples of things which may be material circumstances are –

(a) special or unusual facts relating to the risk,

(b) any particular concerns which led the insured to seek insurance cover for the risk,

(c) anything which those concerned with the class of insurance and field of activity in question would generally understand as being something that should be dealt with in a fair presentation of risks of the type in question.

(5) A material representation is substantially correct if a prudent insurer would not consider the difference between what is represented and what is actually correct to be material.

(6) A representation may be withdrawn or corrected before the contract of insurance is entered into.

8 Remedies for breach

The insurer has a remedy against the insured for a breach of the duty of fair presentation only if the insurer shows that, but for the breach, the insurer –

(a) would not have entered into the contract of insurance at all, or

(b) would have done so only on different terms.

(2) The remedies are set out in Schedule 1.

(3) A breach for which the insurer has a remedy against the insured is referred to in this Act as a "qualifying breach".

(4) A qualifying breach is either –

(a) deliberate or reckless, or

(b) neither deliberate nor reckless.

(5) A qualifying breach is deliberate or reckless if the insured –

(a) knew that it was in breach of the duty of fair presentation, or

(b) did not care whether or not it was in breach of that duty.

(6) It is for the insurer to show that a qualifying breach was deliberate or reckless.

Part 3

Warranties and other terms

9 Warranties and representations

(1) This section applies to representations made by the insured in connection with –

(a) a proposed non-consumer insurance contract, or

(b) a proposed variation to a non-consumer insurance contract.

(2) Such a representation is not capable of being converted into a warranty by means of any provision of the non-consumer insurance contract (or of the terms of the variation), or of any other contract (and whether by declaring the representation to form the basis of the contract or otherwise).

10 Breach of warranty

(1) Any rule of law that breach of a warranty (express or implied) in a contract of insurance results in the discharge of the insurer's liability under the contract is abolished.

(2) An insurer has no liability under a contract of insurance in respect of any loss occurring, or attributable to something happening, after a warranty (express or implied) in the contract has been breached but before the breach has been remedied.

(3) But subsection (2) does not apply if –

(a) because of a change of circumstances, the warranty ceases to be applicable to the circumstances of the contract,

(b) compliance with the warranty is rendered unlawful by any subsequent law, or

(c) the insurer waives the breach of warranty.

(4) Subsection (2) does not affect the liability of the insurer in respect of losses occurring, or attributable to something happening –

(a) before the breach of warranty, or

(b) if the breach can be remedied, after it has been remedied.

(5) For the purposes of this section, a breach of warranty is to be taken as remedied –

(a) in a case falling within subsection (6), if the risk to which the warranty relates later becomes essentially the same as that originally contemplated by the parties,

(b) in any other case, if the insured ceases to be in breach of the warranty.

(6) A case falls within this subsection if –

(a) the warranty in question requires that by an ascertainable time something is to be done (or not done), or a condition is to be fulfilled, or something is (or is not) to be the case, and

(b) that requirement is not complied with.

(7) In the Marine Insurance Act 1906 –

(a) in section 33 (nature of warranty), in subsection (3), the second sentence is omitted,

(b) section 34 (when breach of warranty excused) is omitted.

11 Terms not relevant to the actual loss

(1) This section applies to a term (express or implied) of a contract of insurance, other than a term defining the risk as a whole, if compliance with it would tend to reduce the risk of one or more of the following –

(a) loss of a particular kind,

(b) loss at a particular location,

(c) loss at a particular time.

(2) If a loss occurs, and the term has not been complied with, the insurer may not rely on the non-compliance to exclude, limit or discharge its liability under the contract for the loss if the insured satisfies subsection (3).

(3) The insured satisfies this subsection if it shows that the non-compliance with the term could not have increased the risk of the loss which actually occurred in the circumstances in which it occurred.

(4) This section may apply in addition to section 10.

Part 4

Fraudulent claims

12 Remedies for fraudulent claims

(1) If the insured makes a fraudulent claim under a contract of insurance –

(a) the insurer is not liable to pay the claim,

(b) the insurer may recover from the insured any sums paid by the insurer to the insured in respect of the claim, and

(c) in addition, the insurer may by notice to the insured treat the contract as having been terminated with effect from the time of the fraudulent act.

(2) If the insurer does treat the contract as having been terminated –

(a) it may refuse all liability to the insured under the contract in respect of a relevant event occurring after the time of the fraudulent act, and

(b) it need not return any of the premiums paid under the contract.

(3) Treating a contract as having been terminated under this section does not affect the rights and obligations of the parties to the contract with respect to a relevant event occurring before the time of the fraudulent act.

(4) In subsections (2)(a) and (3), "relevant event" refers to whatever gives rise to the insurer's liability under the contract (and includes, for example, the occurrence of a loss,

the making of a claim, or the notification of a potential claim, depending on how the contract is written).

13 Remedies for fraudulent claims: Group insurance

This section applies where –

(a) a contract of insurance is entered into with an insurer by a person ("A"),

(b) the contract provides cover for one or more other persons who are not parties to the contract ("the Cs"), whether or not it also provides cover of any kind for A or another insured party, and

(c) a fraudulent claim is made under the contract by or on behalf of one of the Cs ("CF").

(2) Section 12 applies in relation to the claim as if the cover provided for CF were provided under an individual insurance contract between the insurer and CF as the insured; and, accordingly –

(a) the insurer's rights under section 12 are exercisable only in relation to the cover provided for CF, and

(b) the exercise of any of those rights does not affect the cover provided under the contract for anyone else.

(3) In its application by virtue of subsection (2), section 12 is subject to the following particular modifications –

(a) the first reference to "the insured" in subsection (1)(b) of that section, in respect of any particular sum paid by the insurer, is to whichever of A and CF the insurer paid the sum to; but if a sum was paid to A and passed on by A to CF, the reference is to CF,

(b) the second reference to "the insured" in subsection (1)(b) is to A or CF,

(c) the reference to "the insured" in subsection (1)(c) is to both CF and A,

(d) the reference in subsection (2)(b) to the premiums paid under the contract is to premiums paid in respect of the cover for CF.

Part 5

Good faith and contracting out

Good faith

14 Good faith

(1) Any rule of law permitting a party to a contract of insurance to avoid the contract on the ground that the utmost good faith has not been observed by the other party is abolished.

(2) Any rule of law to the effect that a contract of insurance is a contract based on the utmost good faith is modified to the extent required by the provisions of this Act and the Consumer Insurance (Disclosure and Representations) Act 2012.

(3) Accordingly –

(a) in section 17 of the Marine Insurance Act 1906 (marine insurance contracts are contracts of the utmost good faith), the words from ", and" to the end are omitted, and

(b) the application of that section (as so amended) is subject to the provisions of this Act and the Consumer Insurance (Disclosure and Representations) Act 2012.

(4) In section 2 of the Consumer Insurance (Disclosure and Representations) Act 2012 (disclosure and representations before contract or variation), subsection (5) is omitted.

Contracting out

15 Contracting out: Consumer insurance contracts

(1) A term of a consumer insurance contract, or of any other contract, which would put the consumer in a worse position as respects any of the matters provided for in Part 3 or 4 of this Act than the consumer would be in by virtue of the provisions of those Parts (so far as relating to consumer insurance contracts) is to that extent of no effect.

(2) In subsection (1) references to a contract include a variation.

(3) This section does not apply in relation to a contract for the settlement of a claim arising under a consumer insurance contract.

16 Contracting out: Non-consumer insurance contracts

(1) A term of a non-consumer insurance contract, or of any other contract, which would put the insured in a worse position as respects representations to which section 9 applies than the insured would be in by virtue of that section is to that extent of no effect.

(2) A term of a non-consumer insurance contract, or of any other contract, which would put the insured in a worse position as respects any of the other matters provided for in Part 2, 3 or 4 of this Act than the insured would be in by virtue of the provisions of those Parts (so far as relating to non-consumer insurance contracts) is to that extent of no effect, unless the requirements of section 17 have been satisfied in relation to the term.

(3) In this section references to a contract include a variation.

(4) This section does not apply in relation to a contract for the settlement of a claim arising under a non-consumer insurance contract.

17 The transparency requirements

(1) In this section, "the disadvantageous term" means such a term as is mentioned in section 16(2).

(2) The insurer must take sufficient steps to draw the disadvantageous term to the insured's attention before the contract is entered into or the variation agreed.

(3) The disadvantageous term must be clear and unambiguous as to its effect.

(4) In determining whether the requirements of subsections (2) and (3) have been met, the characteristics of insured persons of the kind in question, and the circumstances of the transaction, are to be taken into account.

(5) The insured may not rely on any failure on the part of the insurer to meet the requirements of subsection (2) if the insured (or its agent) had actual knowledge of the disadvantageous term when the contract was entered into or the variation agreed.

18 Contracting out: Group insurance contracts

(1) This section applies to a contract of insurance referred to in section 13(1)(a); and in this section –

"A" and "the Cs" have the same meaning as in section 13,

"consumer C" means an individual who is one of the Cs, where the cover provided by the contract for that individual would have been a consumer insurance contract if entered into by that person rather than by A, and

"non-consumer C" means any of the Cs who is not a consumer C.

(2) A term of the contract of insurance, or any other contract, which puts a consumer C in a worse position as respects any matter dealt with in section 13 than that individual would be in by virtue of that section is to that extent of no effect.

(3) A term of the contract of insurance, or any other contract, which puts a non-consumer C in a worse position as respects any matter dealt with in section 13 than that person would be in by virtue of that section is to that extent of no effect, unless the requirements of section 17 have been met in relation to the term.

(4) Section 17 applies in relation to such a term as it applies to a term mentioned in section 16(2), with references to the insured being read as references to A rather than the non-consumer C.

(5) In this section references to a contract include a variation.

(6) This section does not apply in relation to a contract for the settlement of a claim arising under a contract of insurance to which this section applies.

Part 6

Amendment for the Third Parties (Rights Against Insurers) Act 2010
[Omitted]

Part 7

General

21 Provision consequential on Part 2

1 The provision made by this section is consequential on Part 2 of this Act.

2 In the Marine Insurance Act 1906, sections 18 (disclosure by assured), 19 (disclosure by agent effecting insurance) and 20 (representations pending negotiation of contract) are omitted.

3 Any rule of law to the same effect as any of those provisions is abolished.

4 [Omitted]

5 [Omitted]

6 [Omitted]

22 Application ETC of Parts 2 to 5

[Omitted]

23 Extent, Commencement and Short Title

[Omitted]

Schedules

Schedule 1

Section 8(2)

Insurer's remedies for qualifying breaches

Part 1

Contracts

General

1 This Part of this Schedule applies to qualifying breaches of the duty of fair presentation in relation to non-consumer insurance contracts (for variations to them, see Part 2).

Deliberate or reckless breaches

2 If a qualifying breach was deliberate or reckless, the insurer –
  (a) may avoid the contract and refuse all claims, and
  (b) need not return any of the premiums paid.

Other breaches

3 Paragraphs 4 to 6 apply if a qualifying breach was neither deliberate nor reckless.

4 If, in the absence of the qualifying breach, the insurer would not have entered into the contract on any terms, the insurer may avoid the contract and refuse all claims, but must in that event return the premiums paid.

5 If the insurer would have entered into the contract, but on different terms (other than terms relating to the premium), the contract is to be treated as if it had been entered into on those different terms if the insurer so requires.

6
  (1) In addition, if the insurer would have entered into the contract (whether the term relating to matters other than the premium would have been the same or different), but would have charged a higher premium, the insurer may reduce proportionately the amount to be paid on a claim.
  (2) In sub-paragraph (1), "reduce proportionately" means that the insurer need pay on the claim only X% of what it would otherwise have been under an obligation to pay under the terms of the contract (or, if applicable, under the different terms provided for by virtue of paragraph 5), where –

$$X = \frac{\text{Premium actually charged}}{\text{Higher premium}} \times 100$$

Part 2

Variations

General

7 This Part of this Schedule applies to qualifying breaches of the duty of fair presentation in relation to variations to non-consumer insurance contracts.

Deliberate or reckless breaches

8 If a qualifying breach was deliberate or reckless, the insurer –
- (a) may by notice to the insured treat the contract as having been terminated with effect from the time when the variation was made,

and
- (b) need not return any of the premiums paid.

Other breaches

9 (1) This paragraph applies if –
- (a) a qualifying breach was neither deliberate nor reckless, and
- (b) the total premium was increased or not changed as a result of the variation.

(2) If, in the absence of the qualifying breach, the insurer would not have agreed to the variation on any terms, the insurer may treat the contract as if the variation was never made, but must in that event return any extra premium paid.

(3) If sub-paragraph (2) does not apply –
- (a) if the insurer would have agreed to the variation on different terms (other than terms relating to the premium), the variation is to be treated as if it had been entered into on those different terms if the insurer so requires, and
- (b) paragraph 11 also applies if (in the case of an increased premium) the insurer would have increased the premium by more than it did, or (in the case of an unchanged premium) the insurer would have increased the premium.

10 (1) This paragraph applies if –
- (a) a qualifying breach was neither deliberate nor reckless, and
- (b) the total premium was reduced as a result of the variation.

(2) If, in the absence of the qualifying breach, the insurer would not have agreed to the variation on any terms, the insurer may treat the contract as if the variation was never made, and paragraph 11 also applies.

(3) If sub-paragraph (2) does not apply –
- (a) if the insurer would have agreed to the variation on different terms (other than terms relating to the premium), the variation is to be treated as if it had been entered into on those different terms if the insurer so requires, and
- (b) paragraph 11 also applies if the insurer would have increased the premium, would not have reduced the premium, or would have reduced it by less than it did.

Proportionate reduction

11 (1)If this paragraph applies, the insurer may reduce proportionately the amount to be paid on a claim arising out of events after the variation.

(2) In sub-paragraph (1), "reduce proportionately" means that the insurer need pay on the claim only Y% of what it would otherwise have been under an obligation to pay under the terms of the contract (whether on the original terms, or as varied, or under the different terms provided for by virtue of paragraph 9(3)(a) or 10(3)(a), as the case may be), where –

(3) In the formula in sub-paragraph (2), "P" –

(a) in a paragraph 9(3)(b) case, is the total premium the insurer would have charged,

(b) in a paragraph 10(2) case, is the original premium,

(c) in a paragraph 10(3)(b) case, is the original premium if the insurer would not have changed it, and otherwise the increased or (as the case may be) reduced total premium the insurer would have charged.

$$Y = \frac{\text{Total Premium actually charged}}{P} \times 100$$

Part 3

Supplementary

Relationship with Section 84 of the Marine Insurance Act 1906

12 Section 84 of the Marine Insurance Act 1906 (return of premium for failure of consideration) is to be read subject to the provisions of this Schedule in relation to contracts of marine insurance which are non-consumer insurance contracts.

Schedule 2

Section 20

Rights of third parties against insurers: Relevant insured persons
[Omitted]

Enterprise Act 2016

Part 1 to 4 [Omitted]

PART 5
LATE PAYMENT OF INSURANCE CLAIMS

28 Insurance contracts: Implied term about payment of claims

(1) After section 13 of the Insurance Act 2015 (remedies for fraudulent claims: group insurance) insert –

"PART 4A
LATE PAYMENT OF CLAIMS

13A Implied term about payment of claims

(1) It is an implied term of every contract of insurance that if the insured makes a claim under the contract, the insurer must pay any sums due in respect of the claim within a reasonable time.
(2) A reasonable time includes a reasonable time to investigate and assess the claim.
(3) What is reasonable will depend on all the relevant circumstances, but the following are examples of things which may need to be taken into account –
  (a) the type of insurance,
  (b) the size and complexity of the claim,
  (c) compliance with any relevant statutory or regulatory rules or guidance,
  (d) factors outside the insurer's control.
(4) If the insurer shows that there were reasonable grounds for disputing the claim (whether as to the amount of any sum payable, or as to whether anything at all is payable) –
  (a) the insurer does not breach the term implied by subsection (1) merely by failing to pay the claim (or the affected part of it) while the dispute is continuing, but
  (b) the conduct of the insurer in handling the claim may be a relevant factor in deciding whether that term was breached and, if so, when.
(5) Remedies (for example, damages) available for breach of the term implied by subsection (1) are in addition to and distinct from –
  (a) any right to enforce payment of the sums due, and
  (b) any right to interest on those sums (whether under the contract, under another enactment, at the court's discretion or otherwise)."

(2) In section 22 of that Act (application etc. of Parts 2 to 5), after subsection (3) insert –
"(3A) Part 4A applies only in relation to contracts of insurance entered into after that Part has come into force, and variations to such contracts."

29 Contracting out of the implied term about payment of claims

(1) After section 16 of the Insurance Act 2015 (contracting out: non-consumer contracts) insert –

"16A Contracting out of the implied term about payment of claims: consumer and non-consumer insurance contracts

(1) A term of a consumer insurance contract, or of any other contract, which would put the consumer in a worse position as respects any of the matters provided for in section 13A than the consumer would be in by virtue of the provisions of that section (so far as relating to consumer insurance contracts) is to that extent of no effect.
(2) A term of a non-consumer insurance contract, or of any other contract, which would put the insured in a worse position as respects deliberate or reckless breaches of the term implied by section 13A than the insured would be in by virtue of that section is to that extent of no effect.
(3) For the purposes of subsection (2) a breach is deliberate or reckless if the insurer –
  (a) knew that it was in breach, or
  (b) did not care whether or not it was in breach.
(4) A term of a non-consumer insurance contract, or of any other contract, which would put the insured in a worse position as respects any of the other matters

provided for in section 13A than the insured would be in by virtue of the provisions of that section (so far as relating to non-consumer insurance contracts) is to that extent of no effect, unless the requirements of section 17 have been satisfied in relation to the term.

(5) In this section references to a contract include a variation.

(6) This section does not apply in relation to a contract for the settlement of a claim arising under an insurance contract."

(2) In section 17(1) of that Act (the transparency requirements), after "16(2)" insert "or 16A(4)".

30 Additional time limit for actions for damages for late payment of insurance claims

After section 5 of the Limitation Act 1980 insert –

"5A Additional time limit for actions for damages for late payment of insurance claims

(1) An action in respect of breach of the term implied into a contract of insurance by section 13A of the Insurance Act 2015 (late payment of claims) may not be brought after the expiration of one year from the date on which the insurer has paid all the sums referred to in subsection (1) of that section.

(2) Any payment which extinguishes an insurer's liability to pay a sum referred to in section 13A of the Insurance Act 2015 is to be treated for the purposes of this section as payment of that sum."

Part 6 to 10 [Omitted]

Section II

STATUTORY INSTRUMENTS

The Commercial Agents (Council Directive) Regulations 1993

SI 1993 NO 3053

Part I General

Citation, commencement and applicable law

1. (1) These Regulations may be cited as the Commercial Agents (Council Directive) Regulations 1993 and shall come into force on 1st January 1994.
   (2) These Regulations govern the relations between commercial agents and their principals and, subject to paragraph (3), apply in relation to the activities of commercial agents in Great Britain.
   (3) A court or tribunal shall –
      (a) apply the law of the other Member State concerned in place of regulations 3 to 22 where the parties have agreed that the agency contract is to be governed by the law of that Member State;
      (b) (whether or not it is required to do so) apply these regulations where the law of another Member State corresponding to these regulations enables the parties to agree that the agency contract is to be governed by the law of a different Member State and the parties have agreed that it is to be governed by the law of England and Wales or Scotland.

Interpretation, application and extent

2. (1) In these Regulations –
   'commercial agent' means a self-employed intermediary who has continuing authority to negotiate the sale or purchase of goods on behalf of another person (the 'principal'), or to negotiate and conclude the sale or purchase of goods on

behalf of and in the name of that principal; but shall be understood as not including in particular:

(i) a person who, in his capacity as an officer of a company or association, is empowered to enter into commitments binding on that company or association;

(ii) a partner who is lawfully authorised to enter into commitments binding on his partners;

(iii) a person who acts as an insolvency practitioner (as that expression is defined in section 388 of the Insolvency Act 1986) or the equivalent in any other jurisdiction;

'commission' means any part of the remuneration of a commercial agent which varies with the number or value of business transactions;

'EEA Agreement' means the Agreement on the European Economic Area signed at Oporto on 2nd May 1992 as adjusted by the Protocol signed at Brussels on 17th March 1993;

'Member State' includes a State which is a contracting party to the EEA Agreement;

'restraint of trade clause' means an agreement restricting the business activities of a commercial agent following termination of the agency contract.

(2) These Regulations do not apply to –

(a) commercial agents whose activities are unpaid;

(b) commercial agents when they operate on commodity exchanges or in the commodity market;

(c) the Crown Agents for Overseas Governments and Administrations, as set up under the Crown Agents Act 1979 or its subsidiaries.

(3) The provisions of the Schedule to these Regulations have effect for the purpose of determining the persons whose activities as commercial agents are to be considered secondary.

(4) These Regulations shall not apply to the persons referred to in paragraph (3) above.

(5) These Regulations do not extend to Northern Ireland.

Part II Rights and obligations

Duties of a commercial agent to his principal

3. (1) In performing his activities a commercial agent must look after the interests of his principal and act dutifully and in good faith.

(2) In particular, a commercial agent must –

(a) make proper efforts to negotiate and, where appropriate, conclude the transactions he is instructed to take care of;

(b) communicate to his principal all the necessary information available to him;

(c) comply with reasonable instructions given by his principal.

Duties of a principal to his commercial agent

4. (1) In his relations with his commercial agent a principal must act dutifully and in good faith.

(2) In particular, a principal must –

(a) provide his commercial agent with the necessary documentation relating to the goods concerned;

(b) obtain for his commercial agent the information necessary for the performance of the agency contract, and in particular notify his commercial agent within a reasonable period once he anticipates that the volume of commercial transactions will be significantly lower than that which the commercial agent could normally have expected.

(3) A principal shall, in addition, inform his commercial agent within a reasonable period of his acceptance or refusal of, and of any non-execution by him of, a commercial transaction which the commercial agent has procured for him.

Prohibition on derogation from regulations 3 and 4 and consequence of breach

5. (1) The parties may not derogate from regulations 3 and 4 above.

(2) The law applicable to the contract shall govern the consequence of breach of the rights and obligations under regulations 3 and 4 above.

Part III Remuneration

Form and amount of remuneration in absence of agreement

6. (1) In the absence of any agreement as to remuneration between the parties, a commercial agent shall be entitled to the remuneration that commercial agents appointed for the goods forming the subject of his agency contract are customarily allowed in the place where he carries on his activities and, if there is no such customary practice, a commercial agent shall be entitled to reasonable remuneration taking into account all the aspects of the transaction.

(2) This regulation is without prejudice to the application of any enactment or rule of law concerning the level of remuneration.

(3) Where a commercial agent is not remunerated (wholly or in part) by commission, regulations 7 to 12 below shall not apply.

Entitlement to commission on transactions concluded during agency contract

7. (1) A commercial agent shall be entitled to commission on commercial transactions concluded during the period covered by the agency contract –

(a) where the transaction has been concluded as a result of his action; or

(b) where the transaction is concluded with a third party whom he has previously acquired as a customer for transactions of the same kind.

(2) A commercial agent shall also be entitled to commission on transactions concluded during the period covered by the agency contract where he has an exclusive right to a specific geographical area or to a specific group of customers and where the transaction has been entered into with a customer belonging to that area or group.

Entitlement to commission on transactions concluded after agency contract has terminated

8. Subject to regulation 9 below, a commercial agent shall be entitled to commission on commercial transactions concluded after the agency contract has terminated if –
   (a) the transaction is mainly attributable to his efforts during the period covered by the agency contract and if the transaction was entered into within a reasonable period after that contract terminated; or
   (b) in accordance with the conditions mentioned in regulation 7 above, the order of the third party reached the principal or the commercial agent before the agency contract terminated.

Apportionment of commission between new and previous commercial agents

9. (1) A commercial agent shall not be entitled to the commission referred to in regulation 7 above if that commission is payable, by virtue of regulation 8 above, to the previous commercial agent, unless it is equitable because of the circumstances for the commission to be shared between the commercial agents.
   (2) The principal shall be liable for any sum due under paragraph (1) above to the person entitled to it in accordance with that paragraph, and any sum which the other commercial agent receives to which he is not entitled shall be refunded to the principal.

When commission due and date for payment

10. (1) Commission shall become due as soon as, and to the extent that one of the following circumstances occurs –
   (a) the principal has executed the transaction; or
   (b) the principal should, according to his agreement with the third party, have executed the transaction; or
   (c) the third party has executed the transaction.
   (2) Commission shall become due at the latest when the third party has executed his part of the transaction or should have done so if the principal had executed his part of the transaction, as he should have.
   (3) The commission shall be paid not later than on the last day of the month following the quarter in which it became due, and, for the purposes of these Regulations, unless otherwise agreed between the parties, the first quarter period shall run from the date the agency contract takes effect, and subsequent periods shall run from that date in the third month thereafter or the beginning of the fourth month, whichever is the sooner.
   (4) Any agreement to derogate from paragraphs (2) and (3) above to the detriment of the commercial agent shall be void.

Extinction of right to commission

11. (1) The right to commission can be extinguished only if and to the extent that –
    (a) it is established that the contract between the third party and the principal will not be executed; and
    (b) that fact is due to a reason for which the principal is not to blame.
  (2) Any commission which the commercial agent has already received shall be refunded if the right to it is extinguished.
  (3) Any agreement to derogate from paragraph (1) above to the detriment of the commercial agent shall be void.

Periodic supply of information as to commission due and right of inspection of principal's books

12. (1) The principal shall supply his commercial agent with a statement of the commission due, not later than the last day of the month following the quarter in which the commission has become due, and such statement shall set out the main components used in calculating the amount of the commission.
  (2) A commercial agent shall be entitled to demand that he be provided with all the information (and in particular an extract from the books) which is available to his principal and which he needs in order to check the amount of the commission due to him.
  (3) Any agreement to derogate from paragraphs (1) and (2) above shall be void.
  (4) Nothing in this regulation shall remove or restrict the effect of, or prevent reliance upon, any enactment or rule of law which recognises the right of an agent to inspect the books of a principal.

Part IV Conclusion and termination of the agency contract

Right to signed written statement of terms of agency contract

13. (1) The commercial agent and principal shall each be entitled to receive from the other, on request, a signed written document setting out the terms of the agency contract including any terms subsequently agreed.
  (2) Any purported waiver of the right referred to in paragraph (1) above shall be void.

Conversion of agency contract after expiry of fixed period

14. An agency contract for a fixed period which continues to be performed by both parties after that period has expired shall be deemed to be converted into an agency contract for an indefinite period.

Minimum periods of notice for termination of agency contract

15. (1) Where an agency contract is concluded for an indefinite period either party may terminate it by notice.
  (2) The period of notice shall be –
    (a) 1 month for the first year of the contract;

(b) 2 months for the second year commenced;
(c) 3 months for the third year commenced and for the subsequent years, and the parties may not agree on any shorter periods of notice.

(3) If the parties agree on longer periods than those laid down in paragraph (2) above, the period of notice to be observed by the principal must not be shorter than that to be observed by the commercial agent.

(4) Unless otherwise agreed by the parties, the end of the period of notice must coincide with the end of a calendar month.

(5) The provisions of this regulation shall also apply to an agency contract for a fixed period where it is converted under regulation 14 above into an agency contract for an indefinite period subject to the proviso that the earlier fixed period must be taken into account in the calculation of the period of notice.

Savings with regard to immediate termination

16. These Regulations shall not affect the application of any enactment or rule of law which provides for the immediate termination of the agency contract –
(a) because of the failure of one party to carry out all or part of his obligations under that contract; or
(b) where exceptional circumstances arise.

Entitlement of commercial agent to indemnity or compensation on termination of agency contract

17. (1) This regulation has effect for the purpose of ensuring that the commercial agent is, after termination of the agency contract, indemnified in accordance with paragraphs (3) to (5) below or compensated for damage in accordance with paragraphs (6) and (7) below.

(2) Except where the agency contract otherwise provides, the commercial agent shall be entitled to be compensated rather than indemnified.

(3) Subject to paragraph (9) and to regulation 18 below, the commercial agent shall be entitled to an indemnity if and to the extent that –
(a) he has brought the principal new customers or has significantly increased the volume of business with existing customers and the principal continues to derive substantial benefits from the business with such customers; and
(b) the payment of this indemnity is equitable having regard to all the circumstances and, in particular, the commission lost by the commercial agent on the business transacted with such customers.

(4) The amount of the indemnity shall not exceed a figure equivalent to an indemnity for one year calculated from the commercial agent's average annual remuneration over the preceding five years and if the contract goes back less than five years the indemnity shall be calculated on the average for the period in question.

(5) The grant of an indemnity as mentioned above shall not prevent the commercial agent from seeking damages.

(6) Subject to paragraph (9) and to regulation 18 below, the commercial agent shall be entitled to compensation for the damage he suffers as a result of the termination of his relations with his principal.

(7) For the purpose of these Regulations such damage shall be deemed to occur particularly when the termination takes place in either or both of the following circumstances, namely circumstances which –
   (a) deprive the commercial agent of the commission which proper performance of the agency contract would have procured for him whilst providing his principal with substantial benefits linked to the activities of the commercial agent; or
   (b) have not enabled the commercial agent to amortize the costs and expenses that he had incurred in the performance of the agency contract on the advice of his principal.

(8) Entitlement to the indemnity or compensation for damage as provided for under paragraphs (2) to (7) above shall also arise where the agency contract is terminated as a result of the death of the commercial agent.

(9) The commercial agent shall lose his entitlement to the indemnity or compensation for damage in the instances provided for in paragraphs (2) to (8) above if within one year following termination of his agency contract he has not notified his principal that he intends pursuing his entitlement.

Grounds for excluding payment of indemnity or compensation under regulation 17

18. The indemnity or compensation referred to in regulation 17 above shall not be payable to the commercial agent where –
   (a) the principal has terminated the agency contract because of default attributable to the commercial agent which would justify immediate termination of the agency contract pursuant to regulation 16 above; or
   (b) the commercial agent has himself terminated the agency contract, unless such termination is justified:
      (i) by circumstances attributable to the principal; or
      (ii) on grounds of the age, infirmity or illness of the commercial agent in consequence of which he cannot reasonably be required to continue his activities; or
   (c) the commercial agent, with the agreement of his principal, assigns his rights and duties under the agency contract to another person.

Prohibition on derogation from regulations 17 and 18

19. The parties may not derogate from regulations 17 and 18 to the detriment of the commercial agent before the agency contract expires.

Restraint of trade clauses

20. (1) A restraint of trade clause shall be valid only if and to the extent that –
   (a) it is concluded in writing; and
   (b) it relates to the geographical area or the group of customers and the geographical area entrusted to the commercial agent and to the kind of goods covered by his agency under the contract.

(2) A restraint of trade clause shall be valid for not more than two years after termination of the agency contract.

(3) Nothing in this regulation shall affect any enactment or rule of law which imposes other restrictions on the validity or enforceability of restraint of trade clauses or which enables a court to reduce the obligations on the parties resulting from such clauses.

Part V Miscellaneous and supplemental

Disclosure of information

21. Nothing in these Regulations shall require information to be given where such disclosure would be contrary to public policy.

Service of notice, etc.

22. (1) Any notice, statement or other document to be given or supplied to a commercial agent or to be given or supplied to the principal under these Regulations may be so given or supplied –
    - (a) by delivering it to him;
    - (b) by leaving it at his proper address addressed to him by name;
    - (c) by sending it by post to him addressed either to his registered address or to the address of his registered or principal office,

    or by any other means provided for in the agency contract.

    (2) Any such notice, statement or document may –
    - (a) in the case of a body corporate, be given or served on the secretary or clerk of that body;
    - (b) in the case of a partnership, be given to or served on any partner or on any person having the control or management of the partnership business.

Transitional provisions

23. (1) Notwithstanding any provision in an agency contract made before 1st January 1994, these Regulations shall apply to that contract after that date and, accordingly any provision which is inconsistent with these Regulations shall have effect subject to them.

    (2) Nothing in these Regulations shall affect the rights and liabilities of a commercial agent or a principal which have accrued before 1st January 1994.

The schedule

Regulation 2(3)

1. The activities of a person as a commercial agent are to be considered secondary where it may reasonably be taken that the primary purpose of the arrangement with his principal is other than as set out in paragraph 2 below.
2. An arrangement falls within this paragraph if –
    - (a) the business of the principal is the sale, or as the case may be purchase, of goods of a particular kind; and

(b) the goods concerned are such that:
   (i) transactions are normally individually negotiated and concluded on a commercial basis; and
   (ii) procuring a transaction on one occasion is likely to lead to further transactions in those goods with that customer on future occasions, or to transactions in those goods with other customers in the same geographical area or among the same group of customers, and that accordingly it is in the commercial interests of the principal in developing the market in those goods to appoint a representative to such customers with a view to the representative devoting effort, skill and expenditure from his own resources to that end.

3. The following are indications that an arrangement falls within paragraph 2 above, and the absence of any of them is an indication to the contrary –
   (a) the principal is the manufacturer, importer or distributor of the goods;
   (b) the goods are specifically identified with the principal in the market in question rather than, or to a greater extent than, with any other person;
   (c) the agent devotes substantially the whole of his time to representative activities (whether for one principal or for a number of principals whose interests are not conflicting);
   (d) the goods are not normally available in the market in question other than by means of the agent;
   (e) the arrangement is described as one of commercial agency.
4. The following are indications that an arrangement does not fall within paragraph 2 above –
   (a) promotional material is supplied direct to potential customers;
   (b) persons are granted agencies without reference to existing agents in a particular area or in relation to a particular group;
   (c) customers normally select the goods for themselves and merely place their orders through the agent.
5. The activities of the following categories of persons are presumed, unless the contrary is established, not to fall within paragraph 2 above –
   Mail order catalogue agents for consumer goods.
   Consumer credit agents.

The Civil Jurisdiction and Judgments Act 1982 (Interim Relief) Order 1997

SI 1997 NO 302

2. The High Court in England and Wales or Northern Ireland shall have power to grant interim relief under section 25(1) of the Civil Jurisdiction and Judgments Act 1982 in relation to proceedings of the following descriptions, namely –
   (a) proceedings commenced or to be commenced otherwise than in a Brussels Contracting State, a State bound by the Lugano Convention or a Regulation State;
   (b) proceedings whose subject-matter is not within the scope of the Regulation as determined by Article 1 thereof.

The Electronic Commerce (EC Directive) Regulations 2002

SI 2002 NO 2013

1 [Omitted].

Interpretation

2—(1) In these Regulations and in the Schedule –

'commercial communication' means a communication, in any form, designed to promote, directly or indirectly, the goods, services or image of any person pursuing a commercial, industrial or craft activity or exercising a regulated profession, other than a communication –

(a) consisting only of information allowing direct access to the activity of that person including a geographic address, a domain name or an electronic mail address; or

(b) relating to the goods, services or image of that person provided that the communication has been prepared independently of the person making it (and for this purpose, a communication prepared without financial consideration is to be taken to have been prepared independently unless the contrary is shown);

'the Commission' means the Commission of the European Communities;

'consumer' means any natural person who is acting for purposes other than those of his trade, business or profession;

'coordinated field' means requirements applicable to information society service providers or information society services, regardless of whether they are of a general nature or specifically designed for them, and covers requirements with which the service provider has to comply in respect of –

(a) the taking up of the activity of an information society service, such as requirements concerning qualifications, authorisation or notification, and

(b) the pursuit of the activity of an information society service, such as requirements concerning the behaviour of the service provider, requirements regarding the quality or content of the service including those applicable to advertising and contracts, or requirements concerning the liability of the service provider,

but does not cover requirements such as those applicable to goods as such, to the delivery of goods or to services not provided by electronic means;

'the Directive' means Directive 2000/31/EC of the European Parliament and of the Council of 8 June 2000 on certain legal aspects of information society services, in particular electronic commerce, in the Internal Market (Directive on electronic commerce);

'EEA Agreement' means the Agreement on the European Economic Area signed at Oporto on 2 May 1992 as adjusted by the Protocol signed at Brussels on 17 March 1993;

'enactment' includes an enactment comprised in Northern Ireland legislation and comprised in, or an instrument made under, an Act of the Scottish Parliament;

'enforcement action' means any form of enforcement action including, in particular –

(a) in relation to any legal requirement imposed by or under any enactment, any action taken with a view to or in connection with imposing any sanction (whether criminal or otherwise) for failure to observe or comply with it; and
(b) in relation to a permission or authorisation, anything done with a view to removing or restricting that permission or authorisation;

'enforcement authority' does not include courts but, subject to that, means any person who is authorised, whether by or under an enactment or otherwise, to take enforcement action;

'established service provider' means a service provider who is a national of a member State or a company or firm as mentioned in Article 54 of the Treaty and who effectively pursues an economic activity by virtue of which he is a service provider using a fixed establishment in a member State for an indefinite period, but the presence and use of the technical means and technologies required to provide the information society service do not, in themselves, constitute an establishment of the provider; in cases where it cannot be determined from which of a number of places of establishment a given service is provided, that service is to be regarded as provided from the place of establishment where the provider has the centre of his activities relating to that service; references to a service provider being established or to the establishment of a service provider shall be construed accordingly;

'information society services' (which is summarised in recital 17 of the Directive as covering 'any service normally provided for remuneration, at a distance, by means of electronic equipment for the processing (including digital compression) and storage of data, and at the individual request of a recipient of a service)' has the meaning set out in Article 2(a) of the Directive, (which refers to Article 1(2) of Directive 98/34/EC of the European Parliament and of the Council of 22 June 1998 laying down a procedure for the provision of information in the field of technical standards and regulations, as amended by Directive 98/48/EC of 20 July 1998);

'member State' includes a State which is a contracting party to the EEA Agreement;

'recipient of the service' means any person who, for professional ends or otherwise, uses an information society service, in particular for the purposes of seeking information or making it accessible;

'regulated profession' means any profession within the meaning of either Article 1(d) of Council Directive 89/48/EEC of 21 December 1988 on a general system for the recognition of higher-education diplomas awarded on completion of professional education and training of at least three years' duration or of Article 1(f) of Council Directive 92/51/EEC of 18 June 1992 on a second general system for the recognition of professional education and training to supplement Directive 89/48/EEC;

'service provider' means any person providing an information society service;

'the Treaty' means the Treaty on the Functioning of the European Union.

(2) In regulation 4 and 5, 'requirement' means any legal requirement under the law of the United Kingdom, or any part of it, imposed by or under any enactment or otherwise.
(3) Terms used in the Directive other than those in paragraph (1) above shall have the same meaning as in the Directive.

Exclusions

3—(1) Nothing in these Regulations shall apply in respect of –

(a) the field of taxation;

(b) questions relating to information society services covered by the Data Protection Directive and the Telecommunications Data Protection Directive and Directive 2002/58/EC of the European Parliament and of the Council of 12th July 2002 concerning the processing of personal data and the protection of privacy in the electronic communications sector (Directive on privacy and electronic communications);

(c) questions relating to agreements or practices governed by cartel law; and

(d) the following activities of information society services –

(i) the activities of a public notary or equivalent professions to the extent that they involve a direct and specific connection with the exercise of public authority,

(ii) the representation of a client and defence of his interests before the courts, and

(iii) betting, gaming or lotteries which involve wagering a stake with monetary value.

(2) These Regulations shall not apply in relation to any Act passed on or after the date these Regulations are made or in relation to the exercise of a power to legislate after that date.

(3) In this regulation –

'cartel law' means so much of the law relating to agreements between undertakings, decisions by associations of undertakings or concerted practices as relates to agreements to divide the market or fix prices;

'Data Protection Directive' means Directive 95/46/EC of the European Parliament and of the Council of 24 October 1995 on the protection of individuals with regard to the processing of personal data and on the free movement of such data; and

'Telecommunications Data Protection Directive' means Directive 97/66/EC of the European Parliament and of the Council of 15 December 1997 concerning the processing of personal data and the protection of privacy in the telecommunications sector.

Internal market

4—(1) Subject to paragraph (4) below, any requirement which falls within the coordinated field shall apply to the provision of an information society service by a service provider established in the United Kingdom irrespective of whether that information society service is provided in the United Kingdom or another member State.

(2) Subject to paragraph (4) below, an enforcement authority with responsibility in relation to any requirement in paragraph (1) shall ensure that the provision of an information society service by a service provider established in the United Kingdom complies with that requirement irrespective of whether that service is provided in the United Kingdom or another member State and any power, remedy or procedure for taking enforcement action shall be available to secure compliance.

(3) Subject to paragraphs (4), (5) and (6) below, any requirement shall not be applied to the provision of an information society service by a service provider established in a member State other than the United Kingdom for reasons which fall within the coordinated field where its application would restrict the freedom to provide information society services to a person in the United Kingdom from that member State.

(4) Paragraphs (1), (2) and (3) shall not apply to those fields in the annex to the Directive set out in the Schedule.

(5) The reference to any requirements the application of which would restrict the freedom to provide information society services from another member State in paragraph (3) above does not include any requirement maintaining the level of protection for public health and consumer interests established by Community acts.

(6) To the extent that anything in these Regulations creates any new criminal offence, it shall not be punishable with imprisonment for more than two years or punishable on summary conviction with imprisonment for more than three months or with a fine of more than level 5 on the standard scale (if not calculated on a daily basis) or with a fine of more than £100 a day.

Derogations from regulation 4

5—(1) Notwithstanding regulation 4(3), an enforcement authority may take measures, including applying any requirement which would otherwise not apply by virtue of regulation 4(3) in respect of a given information society service, where those measures are necessary for reasons of –

(a) public policy, in particular the prevention, investigation, detection and prosecution of criminal offences, including the protection of minors and the fight against any incitement to hatred on grounds of race, sex, religion or nationality, and violations of human dignity concerning individual persons;

(b) the protection of public health;

(c) public security, including the safeguarding of national security and defence, or

(d) the protection of consumers, including investors,

and proportionate to those objectives.

(2) Notwithstanding regulation 4(3), in any case where an enforcement authority with responsibility in relation to the requirement in question is not party to the proceedings, a court may, on the application of any person or of its own motion, apply any requirement which would otherwise not apply by virtue of regulation 4(3) in respect of a given information society service, if the application of that enactment or requirement is necessary for and proportionate to any of the objectives set out in paragraph (1) above.

(3) Paragraphs (1) and (2) shall only apply where the information society service prejudices or presents a serious and grave risk of prejudice to an objective in paragraph (1)(a) to (d).

(4) Subject to paragraphs (5) and (6), an enforcement authority shall not take the measures in paragraph (1) above, unless it –

(a) asks the member State in which the service provider is established to take measures and the member State does not take such measures or they are inadequate; and

(b) notifies the Commission and the member State in which the service provider is established of its intention to take such measures.

(5) Paragraph (4) shall not apply to court proceedings, including preliminary proceedings and acts carried out in the course of a criminal investigation.

(6) If it appears to the enforcement authority that the matter is one of urgency, it may take the measures under paragraph (1) without first asking the member State in which the service provider is established to take measures and notifying the Commission and the member State in derogation from paragraph (4).

(7) In a case where a measure is taken pursuant to paragraph (6) above, the enforcement authority shall notify the measures taken to the Commission and to the member State concerned in the shortest possible time thereafter and indicate the reasons for urgency.

(8) In paragraph (2), 'court' means any court or tribunal.

General information to be provided by a person providing an information society service

6—(1) A person providing an information society service shall make available to the recipient of the service and any relevant enforcement authority, in a form and manner which is easily, directly and permanently accessible, the following information –

(a) the name of the service provider;

(b) the geographic address at which the service provider is established;

(c) the details of the service provider, including his electronic mail address, which make it possible to contact him rapidly and communicate with him in a direct and effective manner;

(d) where the service provider is registered in a trade or similar register available to the public, details of the register in which the service provider is entered and his registration number, or equivalent means of identification in that register;

(e) where the provision of the service is subject to an authorisation scheme, the particulars of the relevant supervisory authority;

(f) where the service provider exercises a regulated profession –

(i) the details of any professional body or similar institution with which the service provider is registered;

(ii) his professional title and the member State where that title has been granted;

(iii) a reference to the professional rules applicable to the service provider in the member State of establishment and the means to access them; and

(g) where the service provider undertakes an activity that is subject to value added tax, the identification number referred to in Article 22(1) of the sixth Council Directive 77/388/EEC of 17 May 1977 on the harmonisation of the laws of the member States relating to turnover taxes – Common system of value added tax: uniform basis of assessment.

(2) Where a person providing an information society service refers to prices, these shall be indicated clearly and unambiguously and, in particular, shall indicate whether they are inclusive of tax and delivery costs.

Commercial communications

7 A service provider shall ensure that any commercial communication provided by him and which constitutes or forms part of an information society service shall –

(a) be clearly identifiable as a commercial communication;

(b) clearly identify the person on whose behalf the commercial communication is made;

(c) clearly identify as such any promotional offer (including any discount, premium or gift) and ensure that any conditions which must be met to qualify for it are easily accessible, and presented clearly and unambiguously; and

(d) clearly identify as such any promotional competition or game and ensure that any conditions for participation are easily accessible and presented clearly and unambiguously.

Unsolicited commercial communications

8 A service provider shall ensure that any unsolicited commercial communication sent by him by electronic mail is clearly and unambiguously identifiable as such as soon as it is received.

Information to be provided where contracts are concluded by electronic means

9—(1) Unless parties who are not consumers have agreed otherwise, where a contract is to be concluded by electronic means a service provider shall, prior to an order being placed by the recipient of a service, provide to that recipient in a clear, comprehensible and unambiguous manner the information set out in (a) to (d) below –

(a) the different technical steps to follow to conclude the contract;

(b) whether or not the concluded contract will be filed by the service provider and whether it will be accessible;

(c) the technical means for identifying and correcting input errors prior to the placing of the order; and

(d) the languages offered for the conclusion of the contract.

(2) Unless parties who are not consumers have agreed otherwise, a service provider shall indicate which relevant codes of conduct he subscribes to and give information on how those codes can be consulted electronically.

(3) Where the service provider provides terms and conditions applicable to the contract to the recipient, the service provider shall make them available to him in a way that allows him to store and reproduce them.

(4) The requirements of paragraphs (1) and (2) above shall not apply to contracts concluded exclusively by exchange of electronic mail or by equivalent individual communications.

Other information requirements

10 Regulations 6, 7, 8 and 9(1) have effect in addition to any other information requirements in legislation giving effect to EU law.

Placing of the order

11—(1) Unless parties who are not consumers have agreed otherwise, where the recipient of the service places his order through technological means, a service provider shall –

(a) acknowledge receipt of the order to the recipient of the service without undue delay and by electronic means; and

(b) make available to the recipient of the service appropriate, effective and accessible technical means allowing him to identify and correct input errors prior to the placing of the order.

(2) For the purposes of paragraph (1)(a) above –

(a) the order and the acknowledgement of receipt will be deemed to be received when the parties to whom they are addressed are able to access them; and

(b) the acknowledgement of receipt may take the form of the provision of the service paid for where that service is an information society service.

(3) The requirements of paragraph (1) above shall not apply to contracts concluded exclusively by exchange of electronic mail or by equivalent individual communications.

Meaning of the term 'order'

12 Except in relation to regulation 9(1)(c) and regulation 11(1)(b) where 'order' shall be the contractual offer, 'order' may be but need not be the contractual offer for the purposes of regulations 9 and 11.

Liability of the service provider

13 The duties imposed by regulations 6, 7, 8, 9(1) and 11(1)(a) shall be enforceable, at the suit of any recipient of a service, by an action against the service provider for damages for breach of statutory duty.

Compliance with regulation 9(3)

14 Where on request a service provider has failed to comply with the requirement in regulation 9(3), the recipient may seek an order from any court having jurisdiction in relation to the contract requiring that service provider to comply with that requirement.

Right to rescind contract

15 Where a person –

(a) has entered into a contract to which these Regulations apply; and

(b) the service provider has not made available means of allowing him to identify and correct input errors in compliance with regulation 11(1)(b),

he shall be entitled to rescind the contract unless any court having jurisdiction in relation to the contract in question orders otherwise on the application of the service provider.

16 [Omitted]

Mere conduit

17—(1) Where an information society service is provided which consists of the transmission in a communication network of information provided by a recipient of the service or the provision of access to a communication network, the service provider (if he otherwise would) shall not be liable for damages or for any other pecuniary remedy or for any criminal sanction as a result of that transmission where the service provider –

(a) did not initiate the transmission;

(b) did not select the receiver of the transmission; and

(c) did not select or modify the information contained in the transmission.

(2) The acts of transmission and of provision of access referred to in paragraph (1) include the automatic, intermediate and transient storage of the information transmitted where:

(a) this takes place for the sole purpose of carrying out the transmission in the communication network; and

(b) the information is not stored for any period longer than is reasonably necessary for the transmission.

Caching

18 Where an information society service is provided which consists of the transmission in a communication network of information provided by a recipient of the service, the service provider (if he otherwise would) shall not be liable for damages or for any other pecuniary remedy or for any criminal sanction as a result of that transmission where –

(a) the information is the subject of automatic, intermediate and temporary storage where that storage is for the sole purpose of making more efficient onward transmission of the information to other recipients of the service upon their request; and

(b) the service provider –

(i) does not modify the information;

(ii) complies with conditions on access to the information;

(iii) complies with any rules regarding the updating of the information, specified in a manner widely recognised and used by industry;

(iv) does not interfere with the lawful use of technology, widely recognised and used by industry, to obtain data on the use of the information; and

(v) acts expeditiously to remove or to disable access to the information he has stored upon obtaining actual knowledge of the fact that the information at the initial source of the transmission has been removed from the network, or access to it has been disabled, or that a court or an administrative authority has ordered such removal or disablement.

Hosting

19 Where an information society service is provided which consists of the storage of information provided by a recipient of the service, the service provider (if he otherwise would) shall not be liable for damages or for any other pecuniary remedy or for any criminal sanction as a result of that storage where –

(a) the service provider –

(ii) does not have actual knowledge of unlawful activity or information and, where a claim for damages is made, is not aware of facts or circumstances from which it would have been apparent to the service provider that the activity or information was unlawful; or

(ii) upon obtaining such knowledge or awareness, acts expeditiously to remove or to disable access to the information, and

(b) the recipient of the service was not acting under the authority or the control of the service provider.

Protection of rights

20—(1) Nothing in regulations 17, 18 and 19 shall –

(a) prevent a person agreeing different contractual terms; or

(b) affect the rights of any party to apply to a court for relief to prevent or stop infringement of any rights.

(2) Any power of an administrative authority to prevent or stop infringement of any rights shall continue to apply notwithstanding regulations 17, 18 and 19.

Defence in criminal proceedings: burden of proof

21—(1) This regulation applies where a service provider charged with an offence in criminal proceedings arising out of any transmission, provision of access or storage falling within regulation 17, 18 or 19 relies on a defence under any of regulations 17, 18 and 19.

(2) Where evidence is adduced which is sufficient to raise an issue with respect to that defence, the court or jury shall assume that the defence is satisfied unless the prosecution proves beyond reasonable doubt that it is not.

Notice for the purposes of actual knowledge

22 In determining whether a service provider has actual knowledge for the purposes of regulations 18(b)(v) and 19(a)(i), a court shall take into account all matters which appear to it in the particular circumstances to be relevant and, among other things, shall have regard to –

(a) whether a service provider has received a notice through a means of contact made available in accordance with regulation 6(1)(c), and
(b) the extent to which any notice includes –
  (i) the full name and address of the sender of the notice;
  (ii) details of the location of the information in question; and
  (iii) details of the unlawful nature of the activity or information in question.

Schedule

Regulation 4(4)

1. Copyright, neighbouring rights, rights referred to in Directive 87/54/EEC and Directive 96/9/EC and industrial property rights.
2. The freedom of the parties to a contract to choose the applicable law.
3. Contractual obligations concerning consumer contracts.
4. Formal validity of contracts creating or transferring rights in real estate where such contracts are subject to mandatory formal requirements of the law of the member State where the real estate is situated.
5. The permissibility of unsolicited commercial communications by electronic mail.

The Financial Services and Markets Act 2000 (Law Applicable to Contracts of Insurance) Regulations 2009

SI 2009 NO 3075

1 Citation, commencement and interpretation

(1) These Regulations may be cited as the Financial Services and Markets Act 2000 (Law Applicable to Contracts of Insurance) Regulations 2009 and come into force on 17th December 2009.
(2) In these Regulations –
"the 2001 Regulations" means the Financial Services and Markets Act 2000 (Law Applicable to Contracts of Insurance) Regulations 2001;
"the Rome I Regulation" means Regulation (EC) No. 593/2008 of the European Parliament and of the Council of 17th June 2008 on the law applicable to contractual obligations (Rome I).
(3) Expressions used in regulations 4 and 5 and in the Rome I Regulation have the same meaning as in the Rome I Regulation unless the context requires otherwise.

2 [Omitted].

3 Application of the Rome I Regulation: Conflicts falling within Article 22(2)

Notwithstanding Article 22(2) of the Rome I Regulation, Article 7 of that Regulation applies in the case of conflicts between –

(a) the laws of different parts of the United Kingdom, or
(b) the laws of one or more parts of the United Kingdom and Gibraltar,
in relation to contracts of insurance described in Article 7 of the Rome I Regulation as it applies in the case of conflicts between the laws of different countries.

4 Contracts of insurance of risks other than large risks: Greater freedom of choice of law

Where, in the case of a contract of insurance to which Article 7(3) of the Rome I Regulation applies, the law referred to in sub-paragraph (a) or (b) of that Article, or one of the laws referred to in sub-paragraph (e) of that Article, is a law of any part of the United Kingdom, the parties to that contract may also choose as the law applicable to the contract –
(a) the law of another country; or
(b) the law of another part of the United Kingdom, if that choice complies with Article 3, Article 6 and Articles 9 to 22 of that Regulation.

5 Community co-insurers

Where the parties to the contract may choose the applicable law under the Rome I Regulation or under regulation 4, and where the risk to which the contract relates is covered by Community co-insurance (within the meaning of Council Directive 78/473/EEC on the coordination of laws, regulations and administrative provisions relating to Community insurance), co-insurers other than the leading insurer (within the meaning of that Directive) are not to be treated as parties to the contract.

Section III

EUROPEAN UNION MATERIALS

Council Regulation No 44/2001 on Jurisdiction and the Recognition and Enforcement of Judgments in Civil and Commercial Matters (Brussels I)

OJ 2001 L12/1 (16/1/2001)

Chapter I Scope

Article 1

(1) This Regulation shall apply in civil and commercial matters whatever the nature of the court or tribunal. It shall not extend, in particular, to revenue, customs or administrative matters.

(2) The Regulation shall not apply to –
  - (a) the status or legal capacity of natural persons, rights in property arising out of a matrimonial relationship, wills and succession;
  - (b) bankruptcy, proceedings related to the winding up of insolvent companies or other legal persons, judicial arrangements, compositions and analogous proceedings;
  - (c) social security;
  - (d) arbitration.

(3) In this Regulation the term 'Member State' shall mean Member State with the exception of Denmark.

Chapter II Jurisdiction

Section 1 General provisions

Article 2

(1) Subject to the provisions of this Regulation, persons domiciled in a Member State shall, whatever their nationality, be sued in the courts of that Member State.

(2) Persons who are not nationals of the Member State in which they are domiciled shall be governed by the rules of jurisdiction applicable to nationals of that State.

Article 3

(1) Persons domiciled in a Member State may be sued in the courts of another Member State only by virtue of the rules set out in Sections 2 to 7 of this Chapter.
(2) In particular the rules of national jurisdiction set out in Annex 1 shall not be applicable as against them.

Article 4

(1) If the defendant is not domiciled in a Member State, the jurisdiction of the courts of each Member State shall, subject to the provisions of Articles 22 and 23, be determined by the law of that Member State.
(2) As against such a defendant, any person domiciled in a Member State may, whatever his nationality, avail himself in that State of the rules of jurisdiction there in force, and in particular those specified in Annex 1, in the same way as the nationals of that State.

Section 2 Special jurisdiction

Article 5

A person domiciled in a Member State may, in another Member State, be sued –

(1) (a) in matters relating to a contract, in the courts for the place of performance of the obligation in question;
  (b) for the purpose of this provision and unless otherwise agreed, the place of performance of the obligation in question shall be:
    – in the case of the sale of goods, the place in a Member State where, under the contract, the goods were delivered or should have been delivered;
    – in the case of the provision of services, the place in a Member State where, under the contract, the services were provided or should have been provided;
  (c) if subparagraph (b) does not apply then subparagraph (a) applies.
(2) In matters relating to maintenance, in the courts for the place where the maintenance creditor is domiciled or habitually resident or, if the matter is ancillary to proceedings concerning the status of a person, in the court which, according to its own law, has jurisdiction to entertain those proceedings, unless that jurisdiction is based solely on the nationality of one of the parties.
(3) In matters relating to tort, delict or quasi-delict, in the courts for the place where the harmful event occurred.
(4) As regards a civil claim for damages or restitution which is based on an act giving rise to criminal proceedings, in the court seised of those proceedings, to the extent that that court has jurisdiction under its own law to entertain civil proceedings.
(5) As regards a dispute arising out of the operations of a branch, agency or other establishment, in the courts for the place in which the branch, agency or other establishment is situated.

(6) As settlor, trustee or beneficiary of a trust created by the operation of a statute, or by a written instrument, or created orally and evidenced in writing, in the courts of the Contracting State in which the trust is domiciled.

(7) As regards a dispute concerning the payment of remuneration claimed in respect of the salvage of cargo or freight, in the court under the authority of which the cargo and freight in question –
   (a) has been arrested to secure such payment; or
   (b) could have been so arrested, but bail or other security has been given, provided that this provision shall apply only if it is claimed that the defendant has an interest in the cargo or freight or had such an interest at the time of salvage.

Article 6

A person domiciled in a Member State may also be sued –

(1) Where he is one of a number of defendants, in the courts for the place where any one of them is domiciled, provided the claims are so closely connected that it is expedient to hear and determine them together to avoid the risk of irreconcilable judgments resulting from separate proceedings.

(2) As a third party in an action on a warranty or guarantee or in any other third party proceedings, in the court seised of the original proceedings, unless these were instituted solely with the objective of removing him from the jurisdiction of the court which would be competent in his case.

(3) On a counter-claim arising from the same contract or facts on which the original claim was based, in the court in which the original claim is pending.

(4) In matters relating to a contract, if the action may be combined with an action against the same defendant in matters relating to rights *in rem* in immovable property, in the court of the Member State in which the property is situated.

Article 7

Where by virtue of this Regulation a court of a Member State has jurisdiction in actions relating to liability from the use or operation of a ship, that court, or any other court substituted for this purpose by the internal law of that Member State, shall also have jurisdiction over claims for limitation of such liability.

Section 3 Jurisdiction in matters relating to insurance

Article 8

In matters relating to insurance, jurisdiction shall be determined by this section, without prejudice to the provisions of Articles 4 and 5(5).

Article 9

(1) An insurer domiciled in a Member State may be sued –

(a) in the courts of the Member State where he is domiciled; or
(b) in another Member State, in the case of actions brought by the policyholder, the insured or a beneficiary, in the courts for the place where the plaintiff is domiciled;
(c) if he is a co-insurer, in the courts of a Member State in which proceedings are brought against the leading insurer.

(2) An insurer who is not domiciled in a Member State but has a branch, agency or other establishment in one of the Member States shall, in disputes arising out of the operations of the branch, agency or establishment, be deemed to be domiciled in that Member State.

Article 10

In respect of liability insurance or insurance of immovable property, the insurer may in addition be sued in the courts for the place where the harmful event occurred. The same applies if moveable and immovable property are covered by the same insurance policy and both are adversely affected by the same contingency.

Article 11

(1) In respect of liability insurance, the insurer may also, if the law of the court permits it, be joined in proceedings which the injured party had brought against the insured.
(2) The provisions of Articles 8, 9 and 10 shall apply to actions brought by the insured party directly against the insurer, where such direct actions are permitted.
(3) If the law governing such direct actions provides that the policy-holder or the insured may be joined as a party to the action, the same court shall have jurisdiction over them.

Article 12

(1) Without prejudice to the provisions of Article 11(3), an insurer may bring proceedings only in the courts of the Member State in which the defendant is domiciled, irrespective of whether he is the policy-holder, the insured or a beneficiary.
(2) The provisions of this section should not affect the right to bring a counterclaim in the court in which, in accordance with this Section, the original claim is pending.

Article 13

The provisions of this Section may be departed from only by an agreement –

(1) which is entered into after the dispute has arisen; or
(2) which allows the policy-holder, the insured or a beneficiary to bring proceedings in courts other than those indicated in this Section; or
(3) which is concluded between a policy-holder and an insurer, both of whom are domiciled in the same Member State, and which has the effect of conferring jurisdiction on the courts of that State even if the harmful event were to occur abroad, provided that such an agreement is not contrary to the law of that State; or

(4) which is concluded with a policy-holder who is not domiciled in a Member State, except in so far as the insurance is compulsory or relates to immovable property in a Member State; or
(5) which relates to a contract of insurance in so far as it covers one or more of the risks set out in Article 14.

Article 14

The following are the risks referred to in Article 13(5) –

(1) Any loss or damage to –
 (a) sea-going ships, installations situated offshore or on the high seas, or aircraft, arising from perils which relate to their use for commercial purposes;
 (b) goods in transit other than passengers' baggage where the transit consists of or includes carriage by such ships or aircraft.
(2) Any liability, other than for bodily injury to passengers or loss of or damage to their baggage –
 (a) arising out of the use or operation of ships, installations or aircraft as referred to in point 1(a) above in so far as the law of the Member State in which such aircraft are registered does not prohibit agreements on jurisdiction regarding insurance of such risks;
 (b) for loss or damage caused by goods in transit as described in point 1(b) above.
(3) Any financial loss connected with the use or operation of ships, installations or aircraft as referred to in 1(a) above, in particular loss of freight or charter-hire.
(4) Any risk or interest connected with any of those referred to in points 1 to 3 above.
(5) Not with standing points 1 to 4, all 'large risks' as defined in Council Directive 73/ 239/ EEC(7), as amended by Council Directives 88/357/EEC(8) and 90/618/EEC(9), as they may be amended.

Section 4 Jurisdiction over consumer contracts

Article 15

(1) In matters relating to a contract concluded by a person, the consumer, for a purpose which can be regarded as being outside his trade or profession, jurisdiction shall be determined by this Section, without prejudice to the provisions of Article 4 and Article 5(5), if it is –
 (a) a contract for the sale of goods on instalment credit terms; or
 (b) it is a contract for a loan repayable by instalments, or for any other form of credit, made to finance the sale of goods; or
 (c) in all other cases, the contract has been concluded with a person who pursues commercial or professional activities in the Member State of the consumer's domicile or, by any means, directs such activities to that Member State or to several States including that Member State, and the contract falls within the scope of such activities.
(2) Where a consumer enters into a contract with a party who is not domiciled in the Member State but has a branch, agency or other establishment in one of the Member

States, that party shall, in disputes arising out of the operations of the branch, agency or establishment, be deemed to be domiciled in that State.

(3) This Section shall not apply to a contract of transport other than a contract which, for an inclusive price, provides for a combination of travel and accommodation.

Article 16

(1) A consumer may bring proceedings against the other party to a contract either in the courts of the Member State in which that party is domiciled or in the courts of the Member State in which he is himself domiciled.

(2) Proceedings may be brought against a consumer by the other party to the contract only in the courts of the Member State in which the consumer is domiciled.

(3) This Article shall not affect the right to bring a counter-claim in the court in which, in accordance with this section, the original claim is pending.

Article 17

The provisions of this section may be departed from only by an agreement –

(1) which is entered into after the dispute has arisen; or

(2) which allows the consumer to bring proceedings in courts other than those indicated in this Section; or

(3) which is entered into by the consumer and the other party to the contract, both of whom are at the time of conclusion of the contract domiciled or habitually resident in the same Member State, and which confers jurisdiction on the courts of that Member State, provided that such an agreement is not contrary to the law of that Member State.

Section 5 Jurisdiction over individual contracts of employment

Article 18

(1) In matters relating to individual contracts of employment, jurisdiction shall be determined by this Section, without prejudice to Article 4 and point 5 of Article 5.

(2) Where an employee enters into an individual contract of employment with an employer who is not domiciled in a Member State but has a branch, agency or other establishment in one of the Member States, the employer shall, in disputes arising out of the operations of the branch, agency or establishment, be deemed to be domiciled in that Member State.

Article 19

An employer domiciled in a Member State may be sued:

(1) in the courts of the Member State where he is domiciled; or

(2) in another Member State:

  (a) in the courts for the place where the employee habitually carries out his work or in the courts for the last place where he did so, or

(b) if the employee does not or did not habitually carry out his work in any one country, in the courts for the place where the business which engaged the employee is or was situated.

Article 20

(1) An employer may bring proceedings only in the courts of the Member State in which the employee is domiciled.
(2) The provisions of this Section shall not affect the right to bring a counter-claim in the court in which, in accordance with this Section, the original claim is pending.

Article 21

The provisions of this Section may be departed from only by an agreement on jurisdiction:

(1) which is entered into after the dispute has arisen; or
(2) which allows the employee to bring proceedings in courts other than those indicated in this Section.

Section 6 Exclusive jurisdiction

Article 22

The following courts shall have exclusive jurisdiction, regardless of domicile –

(1) In proceedings which have as their object rights *in rem* in immovable property or tenancies of immovable property, the courts of the Member State in which the property is situated. However, in proceedings which have as their object tenancies of immovable property concluded for temporary private use for a maximum period of six consecutive months, the courts of the Member State in which the defendant is domiciled shall also have jurisdiction, provided that the landlord and the tenant are natural persons and are domiciled in the same Member State.
(2) In proceedings which have as their object the validity of the constitution, the nullity or the dissolution of companies or other legal persons or associations of natural or legal persons, or the decisions of their organs, the courts of the Member State in which the company, legal person or association has its seat. In order to determine that seat, the court shall apply its rules of private international law.
(3) In proceedings which have as their object the validity of entries in public registers, the courts of the Member State in which the register is kept.
(4) In proceedings concerned with the registration or validity of patents, trademarks, designs, or other similar rights required to be deposited or registered, the courts of the Member State in which the deposit or registration has been applied for, has taken place or is under the terms of an international convention deemed to have taken place. Without prejudice to the jurisdiction of the European Patent Office under the Convention on the Grant of European Patents, signed at Munich on 5 October 1973, the courts of each Member State shall have exclusive jurisdiction, regardless of domicile, in proceedings concerned with the registration or validity of any European patent granted for that State.

(5) In proceedings concerned with the enforcement of judgments, the courts of the Member State in which the judgment has been or is to be enforced.

Section 7 Prorogation of jurisdiction

Article 23

(1) If the parties, one or more of whom is domiciled in a Member State, have agreed that a court or the courts of a Member State are to have jurisdiction to settle any disputes which have arisen or which may arise in connection with a particular legal relationship, that court or those courts shall have jurisdiction. Such jurisdiction shall be exclusive unless the parties have agreed otherwise. Such an agreement conferring jurisdiction shall be either:
   (a) in writing or evidenced in writing; or
   (b) in a form which accords with practices which the parties have established between themselves; or
   (c) in international trade or commerce, in a form which accords with a usage of which the parties are or ought to have been aware and which in such trade or commerce is widely known to, and regularly observed by, parties to contracts of the type involved in the particular trade or commerce concerned.

(2) Any communication by electronic means which provides a durable record of the agreement shall be equivalent to 'writing'.

(3) Where such an agreement is concluded by parties, none of whom is domiciled in a Member State, the courts of other Member States shall have no jurisdiction over their disputes unless the court or courts chosen have declined jurisdiction.

(4) The court or courts of a Member State on which a trust instrument has conferred jurisdiction shall have exclusive jurisdiction in any proceedings brought against a settlor, trustee or beneficiary, if relations between these persons or their rights or obligations under the trust are involved.

(5) Agreements or provisions of a trust instrument conferring jurisdiction shall have no legal force if they are contrary to Articles 13, 17 or 21, or if the courts whose jurisdiction they purport to exclude have exclusive jurisdiction by virtue of Article 22.

Article 24

Apart from jurisdiction derived from other provisions of this Regulation, a court of a Member State before whom a defendant enters an appearance shall have jurisdiction. This rule shall not apply where appearance was entered solely to contest the jurisdiction, or where another court has exclusive jurisdiction by virtue of Article 22.

Section 8 Examination as to jurisdiction and admissibility

Article 25

Where a court of a Member State is seised of a claim which is principally concerned with a matter over which the courts of another Member State have exclusive jurisdiction by virtue of Article 22, it shall declare of its own motion that it has no jurisdiction.

Article 26

(1) Where a defendant domiciled in one Member State is sued in a court of another Member State and does not enter an appearance, the court shall declare of its own motion that it has no jurisdiction unless its jurisdiction is derived from the provisions of this Regulation.
(2) The court shall stay the proceedings so long as it is not shown that the defendant has been able to receive the document instituting the proceedings or an equivalent document in sufficient time to enable him to arrange for his defence, or that all necessary steps have been taken to this end.
(3) Article 19 of Council Regulation (EC) No 1348/2000 of 29 May 2000 on the service in the Member States of judicial and extrajudicial documents in civil or commercial matters shall apply instead of the provisions of paragraph 2 if the document instituting the proceedings or an equivalent document had to be transmitted from one Member State to another pursuant to this Regulation.
(4) Where the provisions of Regulation (EC) No 1348/2000 are not applicable, Article 15 of the Hague Convention of 15 November 1965 on the Service Abroad of Judicial and Extrajudicial Documents in Civil or Commercial Matters shall apply if the document instituting the proceedings or an equivalent document had to be transmitted pursuant to that Convention.

Section 9 Lis pendens-related actions

Article 27

(1) Where proceedings involving the same cause of action and between the same parties are brought in the courts of different Member States, any court other than the court first seised shall of its own motion stay its proceedings until such time as the jurisdiction of the court first seised is established.
(2) Where the jurisdiction of the court first seised is established, any court other than the court first seised shall decline jurisdiction in favour of that court.

Article 28

(1) Where related actions are brought in the courts of different Member States, any court other than the court first seised may, while the actions are pending at first instance, stay its proceedings.
(2) Where these actions are pending at first instance, any court other than the court first seised may also, on the application of one of the parties, decline jurisdiction if the court first seised has jurisdiction over the actions in question and its law permits the consolidation thereof.
(3) For the purposes of this Article, actions are deemed to be related where they are so closely connected that it is expedient to hear and determine them together to avoid the risk of irreconcilable judgments resulting from separate proceedings.

Article 29

Where actions come within the exclusive jurisdiction of several courts, any court other than the court first seised shall decline jurisdiction in favour of that court.

Article 30

For the purposes of this Section, a court shall be deemed to be seised:

(1) at the time when the document instituting the proceedings or an equivalent document is lodged with the court, provided that the plaintiff has not subsequently failed to take the steps he was required to take to have service effected on the defendant, or
(2) if the document has to be served before being lodged with the court, at the time when it is received by the authority responsible for service, provided that the plaintiff has not subsequently failed to take the steps he was required to take to have the document lodged with the court.

Section 10 Provisional, including protective, measures

Article 31

Application may be made to the courts of a Member State for such provisional, including protective, measures as may be available under the law of that State, even if, under this Regulation, the courts of another Member State have jurisdiction as to the substance of the matter.

Chapter III Recognition and enforcement

Article 32

For the purposes of this Regulation, 'judgment' means any judgment given by a court or tribunal of a Member State, whatever the judgment may be called, including a decree, order, decision or writ of execution, as well as the determination of costs or expenses by an officer of the court.

Section 1 Recognition

Article 33

(1) A judgment given in a Member State shall be recognised in the other Member States without any special procedure being required.
(2) Any interested party who raises the recognition of a judgment as the principal issue in a dispute may, in accordance with the procedures provided for in Sections 2 and 3 of this Chapter, apply for a decision that the judgment be recognised. If the outcome of proceedings in a court of a Member State depends on the determination of an incidental question of recognition that court shall have jurisdiction over that question.

Article 34

A judgment shall not be recognised –

(1) If such recognition is manifestly contrary to public policy in the Member State in which recognition is sought.

(2) Where it was given in default of appearance, if the defendant was not duly served with the document which instituted the proceedings or with an equivalent document in sufficient time to enable him to arrange for his defence unless the defendant failed to commence proceedings to challenge the judgment when it was possible for him to do so.
(3) If it is irreconcilable with a judgment given in a dispute between the same parties in the Member State in which recognition is sought.
(4) If it is irreconcilable with an earlier judgment given in another Member State or in a third State involving the same cause of action and between the same parties, provided that the earlier judgment fulfils the conditions necessary for its recognition in the Member State addressed.

Article 35

(1) Moreover, a judgment shall not be recognised if it conflicts with the provisions of Sections 3, 4 or 5 of Chapter II, or in a case provided for in Article 72.
(2) In its examination of the grounds of jurisdiction referred to in the foregoing paragraph, the court or authority applied to shall be bound by the findings of fact on which the court of the Member State of origin based its jurisdiction.
(3) Subject to paragraph 1, the jurisdiction of the court of the Member State of origin may not be reviewed. The test of public policy referred to in Article 34 may not be applied to the rules relating to jurisdiction.

Article 36

Under no circumstances may a foreign judgment be reviewed as to its substance.

Article 37

(1) A court of a Member State in which recognition is sought of a judgment given in another Member State may stay the proceedings if an ordinary appeal against the judgment has been lodged.
(2) A court of a Member State in which recognition is sought of a judgment given in Ireland or the United Kingdom may stay the proceedings if enforcement is suspended in the State of origin, by reason of an appeal.

Section 2 Enforcement

Article 38

(1) A judgment given in a Member State and enforceable in that State shall be enforced in another Member State when, on the application of any interested party, it has been declared enforceable there.
(2) However, in the United Kingdom, such a judgment shall be enforced in England and Wales, in Scotland, or in Northern Ireland when, on the application of any interested party, it has been registered for enforcement in that part of the United Kingdom.

Articles 39–58 [Omitted].

Chapter V General provisions

Article 59

(1) In order to determine whether a party is domiciled in the Member State whose courts are seised of a matter, the Court shall apply its internal law.
(2) If a party is not domiciled in the Member State whose courts are seised of the matter, then, in order to determine whether the party is domiciled in another Member State, the court shall apply the law of that Member State.

Article 60

(1) For the purposes of this Regulation, a company or other legal person or association of natural or legal persons is domiciled at the place where it has its:
    (a) statutory seat, or
    (b) central administration, or
    (c) principal place of business.
(2) For the purposes of the United Kingdom and Ireland 'statutory seat' means the registered office or, where there is no such office anywhere, the place of incorporation or, where there is no such place anywhere, the place under the law of which the formation took place.
(3) In order to determine whether a trust is domiciled in the Member State whose courts are seised of the matter, the court shall apply its rules of private international law.

Article 61

Without prejudice to any more favourable provisions of national laws, persons domiciled in a Member State who are being prosecuted in the criminal courts of another Member State of which they are not nationals for an offence which was not intentionally committed may be defended by persons qualified to do so, even if they do not appear in person. However, the court seised of the matter may order appearance in person; in the case of failure to appear, a judgment given in the civil action without the person concerned having had the opportunity to arrange for his defence need not be recognised or enforced in the other Member States.

Articles 62–66 [Omitted].

Chapter VII Relations with other instruments

Article 67

This Regulation shall not prejudice the application of provisions governing jurisdiction and the recognition and enforcement of judgments in specific matters which are contained in Community instruments or in national legislation harmonised pursuant to such instruments.

Article 68

(1) This Regulation shall, as between the Member States, supersede the Brussels Convention, except as regards the territories of the Member States which fall within the territorial scope of that Convention and which are excluded from this Regulation pursuant to Article 299 of the Treaty.

(2) In so far as this Regulation replaces the provisions of the Brussels Convention between Member States, any reference to the Convention shall be understood as a reference to this Regulation.

Articles 69–76 [Omitted].

Regulation No 864/2007 of the European Parliament and of the Council on the Law Applicable to Non-Contractual Obligations (Rome II)

OJ 2007 L199/40 (31/7/2007)

Chapter I Scope

Article 1 Scope

1. This Regulation shall apply, in situations involving a conflict of laws, to non-contractual obligations in civil and commercial matters. It shall not apply, in particular, to revenue, customs or administrative matters or to the liability of the State for acts and omissions in the exercise of State authority (acta iure imperii).
2. The following shall be excluded from the scope of this Regulation:
   (a) non-contractual obligations arising out of family relationships and relationships deemed by the law applicable to such relationships to have comparable effects including maintenance obligations;
   (b) non-contractual obligations arising out of matrimonial property regimes, property regimes of relationships deemed by the law applicable to such relationships to have comparable effects to marriage, and wills and succession;
   (c) non-contractual obligations arising under bills of exchange, cheques and promissory notes and other negotiable instruments to the extent that the obligations under such other negotiable instruments arise out of their negotiable character;
   (d) non-contractual obligations arising out of the law of companies and other bodies corporate or unincorporated regarding matters such as the creation, by registration or otherwise, legal capacity, internal organisation or winding-up of companies and other bodies corporate or unincorporated, the personal liability of officers and members as such for the obligations of the company or body and the personal liability of auditors to a company or to its members in the statutory audits of accounting documents;
   (e) non-contractual obligations arising out of the relations between the settlors, trustees and beneficiaries of a trust created voluntarily;
   (f) non-contractual obligations arising out of nuclear damage;

   (g) non-contractual obligations arising out of violations of privacy and rights relating to personality, including defamation.
3. This Regulation shall not apply to evidence and procedure, without prejudice to Articles 21 and 22.
4. For the purposes of this Regulation, "Member State" shall mean any Member State other than Denmark.

Article 2 Non-contractual obligations

1. For the purposes of this Regulation, damage shall cover any consequence arising out of tort/delict, unjust enrichment, negotiorum gestio or culpa in contrahendo.
2. This Regulation shall apply also to non-contractual obligations that are likely to arise.
3. Any reference in this Regulation to:
   (a) an event giving rise to damage shall include events giving rise to damage that are likely to occur; and
   (b) damage shall include damage that is likely to occur.

Article 3 Universal application

Any law specified by this Regulation shall be applied whether or not it is the law of a Member State.

Chapter II Torts/delicts

Article 4 General rule

1. Unless otherwise provided for in this Regulation, the law applicable to a non-contractual obligation arising out of a tort/delict shall be the law of the country in which the damage occurs irrespective of the country in which the event giving rise to the damage occurred and irrespective of the country or countries in which the indirect consequences of that event occur.
2. However, where the person claimed to be liable and the person sustaining damage both have their habitual residence in the same country at the time when the damage occurs, the law of that country shall apply.
3. Where it is clear from all the circumstances of the case that the tort/delict is manifestly more closely connected with a country other than that indicated in paragraphs 1 or 2, the law of that other country shall apply. A manifestly closer connection with another country might be based in particular on a pre-existing relationship between the parties, such as a contract, that is closely connected with the tort/delict in question.

Article 5 Product liability

1. Without prejudice to Article 4(2), the law applicable to a non-contractual obligation arising out of damage caused by a product shall be:
   (a) the law of the country in which the person sustaining the damage had his or her habitual residence when the damage occurred, if the product was marketed in that country; or, failing that,

(b) the law of the country in which the product was acquired, if the product was marketed in that country; or, failing that,
(c) the law of the country in which the damage occurred, if the product was marketed in that country.

However, the law applicable shall be the law of the country in which the person claimed to be liable is habitually resident if he or she could not reasonably foresee the marketing of the product, or a product of the same type, in the country the law of which is applicable under (a), (b) or (c).

2. Where it is clear from all the circumstances of the case that the tort/delict is manifestly more closely connected with a country other than that indicated in paragraph 1, the law of that other country shall apply. A manifestly closer connection with another country might be based in particular on a pre-existing relationship between the parties, such as a contract, that is closely connected with the tort/delict in question.

Article 6 Unfair competition and acts restricting free competition

1. The law applicable to a non-contractual obligation arising out of an act of unfair competition shall be the law of the country where competitive relations or the collective interests of consumers are, or are likely to be, affected.
2. Where an act of unfair competition affects exclusively the interests of a specific competitor, Article 4 shall apply.
3. (a) The law applicable to a non-contractual obligation arising out of a restriction of competition shall be the law of the country where the market is, or is likely to be, affected.
   (b) When the market is, or is likely to be, affected in more than one country, the person seeking compensation for damage who sues in the court of the domicile of the defendant, may instead choose to base his or her claim on the law of the court seised, provided that the market in that Member State is amongst those directly and substantially affected by the restriction of competition out of which the non-contractual obligation on which the claim is based arises; where the claimant sues, in accordance with the applicable rules on jurisdiction, more than one defendant in that court, he or she can only choose to base his or her claim on the law of that court if the restriction of competition on which the claim against each of these defendants relies directly and substantially affects also the market in the Member State of that court.
4. The law applicable under this Article may not be derogated from by an agreement pursuant to Article 14.

Article 7 Environmental damage

The law applicable to a non-contractual obligation arising out of environmental damage or damage sustained by persons or property as a result of such damage shall be the law determined pursuant to Article 4(1), unless the person seeking compensation for damage chooses to base his or her claim on the law of the country in which the event giving rise to the damage occurred.

Article 8 Infringement of intellectual property rights

1. The law applicable to a non-contractual obligation arising from an infringement of an intellectual property right shall be the law of the country for which protection is claimed.

2. In the case of a non-contractual obligation arising from an infringement of a unitary Community intellectual property right, the law applicable shall, for any question that is not governed by the relevant Community instrument, be the law of the country in which the act of infringement was committed.
3. The law applicable under this Article may not be derogated from by an agreement pursuant to Article 14.

Article 9 Industrial action

Without prejudice to Article 4(2), the law applicable to a non-contractual obligation in respect of the liability of a person in the capacity of a worker or an employer or the organisations representing their professional interests for damages caused by an industrial action, pending or carried out, shall be the law of the country where the action is to be, or has been, taken.

Chapter III Unjust enrichment, negotiorum gestio and culpa in contrahendo

Article 10 Unjust enrichment

1. If a non-contractual obligation arising out of unjust enrichment, including payment of amounts wrongly received, concerns a relationship existing between the parties, such as one arising out of a contract or a tort/delict, that is closely connected with that unjust enrichment, it shall be governed by the law that governs that relationship.
2. Where the law applicable cannot be determined on the basis of paragraph 1 and the parties have their habitual residence in the same country when the event giving rise to unjust enrichment occurs, the law of that country shall apply.
3. Where the law applicable cannot be determined on the basis of paragraphs 1 or 2, it shall be the law of the country in which the unjust enrichment took place.
4. Where it is clear from all the circumstances of the case that the non-contractual obligation arising out of unjust enrichment is manifestly more closely connected with a country other than that indicated in paragraphs 1, 2 and 3, the law of that other country shall apply.

Article 11 Negotiorum gestio

1. If a non-contractual obligation arising out of an act performed without due authority in connection with the affairs of another person concerns a relationship existing between the parties, such as one arising out of a contract or a tort/delict, that is closely connected with that non-contractual obligation, it shall be governed by the law that governs that relationship.
2. Where the law applicable cannot be determined on the basis of paragraph 1, and the parties have their habitual residence in the same country when the event giving rise to the damage occurs, the law of that country shall apply.
3. Where the law applicable cannot be determined on the basis of paragraphs 1 or 2, it shall be the law of the country in which the act was performed.
4. Where it is clear from all the circumstances of the case that the non-contractual obligation arising out of an act performed without due authority in connection with the affairs

of another person is manifestly more closely connected with a country other than that indicated in paragraphs 1, 2 and 3, the law of that other country shall apply.

Article 12 Culpa in contrahendo

1. The law applicable to a non-contractual obligation arising out of dealings prior to the conclusion of a contract, regardless of whether the contract was actually concluded or not, shall be the law that applies to the contract or that would have been applicable to it had it been entered into.
2. Where the law applicable cannot be determined on the basis of paragraph 1, it shall be:
   (a) the law of the country in which the damage occurs, irrespective of the country in which the event giving rise to the damage occurred and irrespective of the country or countries in which the indirect consequences of that event occurred; or
   (b) where the parties have their habitual residence in the same country at the time when the event giving rise to the damage occurs, the law of that country; or
   (c) where it is clear from all the circumstances of the case that the non-contractual obligation arising out of dealings prior to the conclusion of a contract is manifestly more closely connected with a country other than that indicated in points (a) and (b), the law of that other country.

Article 13 Applicability of Article 8

For the purposes of this Chapter, Article 8 shall apply to non-contractual obligations arising from an infringement of an intellectual property right.

Chapter IV Freedom of choice

Article 14 Freedom of choice

1. The parties may agree to submit non-contractual obligations to the law of their choice:
   (a) by an agreement entered into after the event giving rise to the damage occurred; or
   (b) where all the parties are pursuing a commercial activity, also by an agreement freely negotiated before the event giving rise to the damage occurred.

   The choice shall be expressed or demonstrated with reasonable certainty by the circumstances of the case and shall not prejudice the rights of third parties.
2. Where all the elements relevant to the situation at the time when the event giving rise to the damage occurs are located in a country other than the country whose law has been chosen, the choice of the parties shall not prejudice the application of provisions of the law of that other country which cannot be derogated from by agreement.
3. Where all the elements relevant to the situation at the time when the event giving rise to the damage occurs are located in one or more of the Member States, the parties' choice of the law applicable other than that of a Member State shall not prejudice the application of provisions of Community law, where appropriate as implemented in the Member State of the forum, which cannot be derogated from by agreement.

Chapter V Common rules

Article 15 Scope of the law applicable

The law applicable to non-contractual obligations under this Regulation shall govern in particular:

(a) the basis and extent of liability, including the determination of persons who may be held liable for acts performed by them;
(b) the grounds for exemption from liability, any limitation of liability and any division of liability;
(c) the existence, the nature and the assessment of damage or the remedy claimed;
(d) within the limits of powers conferred on the court by its procedural law, the measures which a court may take to prevent or terminate injury or damage or to ensure the provision of compensation;
(e) the question whether a right to claim damages or a remedy may be transferred, including by inheritance;
(f) persons entitled to compensation for damage sustained personally;
(g) liability for the acts of another person;
(h) the manner in which an obligation may be extinguished and rules of prescription and limitation, including rules relating to the commencement, interruption and suspension of a period of prescription or limitation.

Article 16 Overriding mandatory provisions

Nothing in this Regulation shall restrict the application of the provisions of the law of the forum in a situation where they are mandatory irrespective of the law otherwise applicable to the non-contractual obligation.

Article 17 Rules of safety and conduct

In assessing the conduct of the person claimed to be liable, account shall be taken, as a matter of fact and in so far as is appropriate, of the rules of safety and conduct which were in force at the place and time of the event giving rise to the liability.

Article 18 Direct action against the insurer of the person liable

The person having suffered damage may bring his or her claim directly against the insurer of the person liable to provide compensation if the law applicable to the non-contractual obligation or the law applicable to the insurance contract so provides.

Article 19 Subrogation

Where a person (the creditor) has a non-contractual claim upon another (the debtor), and a third person has a duty to satisfy the creditor, or has in fact satisfied the creditor in discharge of that duty, the law which governs the third person's duty to satisfy the creditor shall determine whether, and the extent to which, the third person is entitled to exercise against the debtor the rights which the creditor had against the debtor under the law governing their relationship.

Article 20 Multiple liability

If a creditor has a claim against several debtors who are liable for the same claim, and one of the debtors has already satisfied the claim in whole or in part, the question of that debtor's right to demand compensation from the other debtors shall be governed by the law applicable to that debtor's non-contractual obligation towards the creditor.

Article 21 Formal validity

A unilateral act intended to have legal effect and relating to a non-contractual obligation shall be formally valid if it satisfies the formal requirements of the law governing the non-contractual obligation in question or the law of the country in which the act is performed.

Article 22 Burden of proof

1. The law governing a non-contractual obligation under this Regulation shall apply to the extent that, in matters of non-contractual obligations, it contains rules which raise presumptions of law or determine the burden of proof.
2. Acts intended to have legal effect may be proved by any mode of proof recognised by the law of the forum or by any of the laws referred to in Article 21 under which that act is formally valid, provided that such mode of proof can be administered by the forum.

Chapter VI Other provisions

Article 23 Habitual residence

1. For the purposes of this Regulation, the habitual residence of companies and other bodies, corporate or unincorporated, shall be the place of central administration.

   Where the event giving rise to the damage occurs, or the damage arises, in the course of operation of a branch, agency or any other establishment, the place where the branch, agency or any other establishment is located shall be treated as the place of habitual residence.
2. For the purposes of this Regulation, the habitual residence of a natural person acting in the course of his or her business activity shall be his or her principal place of business.

Article 24 Exclusion of renvoi

The application of the law of any country specified by this Regulation means the application of the rules of law in force in that country other than its rules of private international law.

Article 25 States with more than one legal system

1. Where a State comprises several territorial units, each of which has its own rules of law in respect of non-contractual obligations, each territorial unit shall be considered as a country for the purposes of identifying the law applicable under this Regulation.

2. A Member State within which different territorial units have their own rules of law in respect of non-contractual obligations shall not be required to apply this Regulation to conflicts solely between the laws of such units.

   [Note: regulation 8 of the The Law Applicable to Non-Contractual Obligations (England and Wales and Northern Ireland) Regulations 2008 SI 2008 No. 2986) states that 'Notwithstanding Article 25(2) of Regulation (EC) No. 864/2007 of the European Parliament and of the Council on the law applicable to non-contractual obligations ("Rome II"), that Regulation shall apply in the case of conflicts between—

   (a) the laws of different parts of the United Kingdom, or

   (b) between the laws of one or more parts of the United Kingdom and Gibraltar,

   as it applies in the case of conflicts between the laws of other countries.']

Article 26 Public policy of the forum

The application of a provision of the law of any country specified by this Regulation may be refused only if such application is manifestly incompatible with the public policy (ordre public) of the forum.

Article 27 Relationship with other provisions of Community law

This Regulation shall not prejudice the application of provisions of Community law which, in relation to particular matters, lay down conflict-of-law rules relating to non-contractual obligations.

Article 28 Relationship with existing international conventions

1. This Regulation shall not prejudice the application of international conventions to which one or more Member States are parties at the time when this Regulation is adopted and which lay down conflict-of-law rules relating to non-contractual obligations.
2. However, this Regulation shall, as between Member States, take precedence over conventions concluded exclusively between two or more of them in so far as such conventions concern matters governed by this Regulation.

Chapter VII Final provisions

Articles 29–30 [omitted]

Article 31 Application in time

This Regulation shall apply to events giving rise to damage which occur after its entry into force.

Article 32 Date of application

This Regulation shall apply from 11 January 2009, except for Article 29, which shall apply from 11 July 2008.

This Regulation shall be binding in its entirety and directly applicable in the Member States in accordance with the Treaty establishing the European Community.

Regulation No 1393/2007 of the European Parliament and of the Council of 13 November 2007 on the Service in The Member States of Judicial and Extrajudicial Documents in Civil or Commercial Matters (Service of Documents)

OJ 2007/L324/79 (10/12/2007)

Chapter I General provisions

Article 1 Scope

1. This Regulation shall apply in civil and commercial matters where a judicial or extra-judicial document has to be transmitted from one Member State to another for service there. It shall not extend in particular to revenue, customs or administrative matters or to liability of the State for actions or omissions in the exercise of state authority (acta iure imperii).
2. This Regulation shall not apply where the address of the person to be served with the document is not known.
3. In this Regulation, the term "Member State" shall mean the Member States with the exception of Denmark.

Article 2 Transmitting and receiving agencies

1. Each Member State shall designate the public officers, authorities or other persons, hereinafter referred to as "transmitting agencies", competent for the transmission of judicial or extrajudicial documents to be served in another Member State.
2. Each Member State shall designate the public officers, authorities or other persons, hereinafter referred to as "receiving agencies", competent for the receipt of judicial or extrajudicial documents from another Member State.
3. A Member State may designate one transmitting agency and one receiving agency, or one agency to perform both functions. A federal State, a State in which several legal systems apply or a State with autonomous territorial units shall be free to designate more than one such agency. The designation shall have effect for a period of five years and may be renewed at five-year intervals.
4. Each Member State shall provide the Commission with the following information:
   (a) the names and addresses of the receiving agencies referred to in paragraphs 2 and 3;
   (b) the geographical areas in which they have jurisdiction;
   (c) the means of receipt of documents available to them; and
   (d) the languages that may be used for the completion of the standard form set out in Annex I.

   Member States shall notify the Commission of any subsequent modification of such information.

Article 3 Central body

Each Member State shall designate a central body responsible for:

(a) supplying information to the transmitting agencies;
(b) seeking solutions to any difficulties which may arise during transmission of documents for service;
(c) forwarding, in exceptional cases, at the request of a transmitting agency, a request for service to the competent receiving agency.

A federal State, a State in which several legal systems apply or a State with autonomous territorial units shall be free to designate more than one central body.

Chapter II Judicial documents

Section 1 Transmission and service of judicial documents

Article 4 Transmission of documents

1. Judicial documents shall be transmitted directly and as soon as possible between the agencies designated pursuant to Article 2.
2. The transmission of documents, requests, confirmations, receipts, certificates and any other papers between transmitting agencies and receiving agencies may be carried out by any appropriate means, provided that the content of the document received is true and faithful to that of the document forwarded and that all information in it is easily legible.
3. The document to be transmitted shall be accompanied by a request drawn up using the standard form set out in Annex I. The form shall be completed in the official language of the Member State addressed or, if there are several official languages in that Member State, the official language or one of the official languages of the place where service is to be effected, or in another language which that Member State has indicated it can accept. Each Member State shall indicate the official language or languages of the institutions of the European Union other than its own which is or are acceptable to it for completion of the form.
4. The documents and all papers that are transmitted shall be exempted from legalisation or any equivalent formality.
5. When the transmitting agency wishes a copy of the document to be returned together with the certificate referred to in Article 10, it shall send the document in duplicate.

Article 5 [omitted]

Article 6 Receipt of documents by receiving agency

1. On receipt of a document, a receiving agency shall, as soon as possible and in any event within seven days of receipt, send a receipt to the transmitting agency by the swiftest possible means of transmission using the standard form set out in Annex I.

2. Where the request for service cannot be fulfilled on the basis of the information or documents transmitted, the receiving agency shall contact the transmitting agency by the swiftest possible means in order to secure the missing information or documents.
3. If the request for service is manifestly outside the scope of this Regulation or if non-compliance with the formal conditions required makes service impossible, the request and the documents transmitted shall be returned, on receipt, to the transmitting agency, together with the notice of return using the standard form set out in Annex I.
4. A receiving agency receiving a document for service but not having territorial jurisdiction to serve it shall forward it, as well as the request, to the receiving agency having territorial jurisdiction in the same Member State if the request complies with the conditions laid down in Article 4(3) and shall inform the transmitting agency accordingly using the standard form set out in Annex I. That receiving agency shall inform the transmitting agency when it receives the document, in the manner provided for in paragraph 1.

Article 7 Service of documents

1. The receiving agency shall itself serve the document or have it served, either in accordance with the law of the Member State addressed or by a particular method requested by the transmitting agency, unless that method is incompatible with the law of that Member State.
2. The receiving agency shall take all necessary steps to effect the service of the document as soon as possible, and in any event within one month of receipt. If it has not been possible to effect service within one month of receipt, the receiving agency shall:
   (a) immediately inform the transmitting agency by means of the certificate in the standard form set out in Annex I, which shall be drawn up under the conditions referred to in Article 10(2); and
   (b) continue to take all necessary steps to effect the service of the document, unless indicated otherwise by the transmitting agency, where service seems to be possible within a reasonable period of time.

Article 8 [omitted]

Article 9 Date of service

1. Without prejudice to Article 8, the date of service of a document pursuant to Article 7 shall be the date on which it is served in accordance with the law of the Member State addressed.
2. However, where according to the law of a Member State a document has to be served within a particular period, the date to be taken into account with respect to the applicant shall be that determined by the law of that Member State.
3. Paragraphs 1 and 2 shall also apply to the means of transmission and service of judicial documents provided for in Section 2.

Articles 10–11 [omitted]

Section 2 Other means of transmission and service of judicial documents

Article 12 Transmission by consular or diplomatic channels

Each Member State shall be free, in exceptional circumstances, to use consular or diplomatic channels to forward judicial documents, for the purpose of service, to those agencies of another Member State which are designated pursuant to Articles 2 or 3.

Article 13 Service by diplomatic or consular agents

1. Each Member State shall be free to effect service of judicial documents on persons residing in another Member State, without application of any compulsion, directly through its diplomatic or consular agents.
2. Any Member State may make it known, in accordance with Article 23(1), that it is opposed to such service within its territory, unless the documents are to be served on nationals of the Member State in which the documents originate.

Article 14 Service by postal services

Each Member State shall be free to effect service of judicial documents directly by postal services on persons residing in another Member State by registered letter with acknowledgement of receipt or equivalent.

Article 15 Direct service

Any person interested in a judicial proceeding may effect service of judicial documents directly through the judicial officers, officials or other competent persons of the Member State addressed, where such direct service is permitted under the law of that Member State.

Articles 16–26 [omitted]

Regulation No 593/2008 of the European Parliament and of the Council on the Law Applicable to Contractual Obligations (Rome I)

OJ 2008/L177/10 (4/7/2008)

Chapter I Scope

Article 1 Material scope

1. This Regulation shall apply, in situations involving a conflict of laws, to contractual obligations in civil and commercial matters.

   It shall not apply, in particular, to revenue, customs or administrative matters.
2. The following shall be excluded from the scope of this Regulation:
   (a) questions involving the status or legal capacity of natural persons, without prejudice to Article 13;

(b) obligations arising out of family relationships and relationships deemed by the law applicable to such relationships to have comparable effects, including maintenance obligations;
(c) obligations arising out of matrimonial property regimes, property regimes of relationships deemed by the law applicable to such relationships to have comparable effects to marriage, and wills and succession;
(d) obligations arising under bills of exchange, cheques and promissory notes and other negotiable instruments to the extent that the obligations under such other negotiable instruments arise out of their negotiable character;
(e) arbitration agreements and agreements on the choice of court;
(f) questions governed by the law of companies and other bodies, corporate or unincorporated, such as the creation, by registration or otherwise, legal capacity, internal organisation or winding-up of companies and other bodies, corporate or unincorporated, and the personal liability of officers and members as such for the obligations of the company or body;
(g) the question whether an agent is able to bind a principal, or an organ to bind a company or other body corporate or unincorporated, in relation to a third party;
(h) the constitution of trusts and the relationship between settlors, trustees and beneficiaries;
(i) obligations arising out of dealings prior to the conclusion of a contract;
(j) insurance contracts arising out of operations carried out by organisations other than undertakings referred to in Article 2 of Directive 2002/83/EC of the European Parliament and of the Council of 5 November 2002 concerning life assurance (1) the object of which is to provide benefits for employed or self-employed persons belonging to an undertaking or group of undertakings, or to a trade or group of trades, in the event of death or survival or of discontinuance or curtailment of activity, or of sickness related to work or accidents at work.

3. This Regulation shall not apply to evidence and procedure, without prejudice to Article 18.
4. In this Regulation, the term 'Member State' shall mean Member States to which this Regulation applies. However, in Article 3(4) and Article 7 the term shall mean all the Member States.

Article 2 Universal application

Any law specified by this Regulation shall be applied whether or not it is the law of a Member State.

Chapter II Uniform rules

Article 3 Freedom of choice

1. A contract shall be governed by the law chosen by the parties. The choice shall be made expressly or clearly demonstrated by the terms of the contract or the circumstances of the case. By their choice the parties can select the law applicable to the whole or to part only of the contract.

2. The parties may at any time agree to subject the contract to a law other than that which previously governed it, whether as a result of an earlier choice made under this Article or of other provisions of this Regulation. Any change in the law to be applied that is made after the conclusion of the contract shall not prejudice its formal validity under Article 11 or adversely affect the rights of third parties.
3. Where all other elements relevant to the situation at the time of the choice are located in a country other than the country whose law has been chosen, the choice of the parties shall not prejudice the application of provisions of the law of that other country which cannot be derogated from by agreement.
4. Where all other elements relevant to the situation at the time of the choice are located in one or more Member States, the parties' choice of applicable law other than that of a Member State shall not prejudice the application of provisions of Community law, where appropriate as implemented in the Member State of the forum, which cannot be derogated from by agreement.
5. The existence and validity of the consent of the parties as to the choice of the applicable law shall be determined in accordance with the provisions of Articles 10, 11 and 13.

Article 4 Applicable law in the absence of choice

1. To the extent that the law applicable to the contract has not been chosen in accordance with Article 3 and without prejudice to Articles 5 to 8, the law governing the contract shall be determined as follows:
   (a) a contract for the sale of goods shall be governed by the law of the country where the seller has his habitual residence;
   (b) a contract for the provision of services shall be governed by the law of the country where the service provider has his habitual residence;
   (c) a contract relating to a right *in rem* in immovable property or to a tenancy of immovable property shall be governed by the law of the country where the property is situated;
   (d) notwithstanding point (c), a tenancy of immovable property concluded for temporary private use for a period of no more than six consecutive months shall be governed by the law of the country where the landlord has his habitual residence, provided that the tenant is a natural person and has his habitual residence in the same country;
   (e) a franchise contract shall be governed by the law of the country where the franchisee has his habitual residence;
   (f) a distribution contract shall be governed by the law of the country where the distributor has his habitual residence;
   (g) a contract for the sale of goods by auction shall be governed by the law of the country where the auction takes place, if such a place can be determined;
   (h) a contract concluded within a multilateral system which brings together or facilitates the bringing together of multiple third-party buying and selling interests in financial instruments, as defined by Article 4(1), point (17) of Directive 2004/39/EC, in accordance with non-discretionary rules and governed by a single law, shall be governed by that law.

2. Where the contract is not covered by paragraph 1 or where the elements of the contract would be covered by more than one of points (a) to (h) of paragraph 1, the contract shall be governed by the law of the country where the party required to effect the characteristic performance of the contract has his habitual residence.
3. Where it is clear from all the circumstances of the case that the contract is manifestly more closely connected with a country other than that indicated in paragraphs 1 or 2, the law of that other country shall apply.
4. Where the law applicable cannot be determined pursuant to paragraphs 1 or 2, the contract shall be governed by the law of the country with which it is most closely connected.

Article 5 Contracts of carriage

1. To the extent that the law applicable to a contract for the carriage of goods has not been chosen in accordance with Article 3, the law applicable shall be the law of the country of habitual residence of the carrier, provided that the place of receipt or the place of delivery or the habitual residence of the consignor is also situated in that country. If those requirements are not met, the law of the country where the place of delivery as agreed by the parties is situated shall apply.
2. To the extent that the law applicable to a contract for the carriage of passengers has not been chosen by the parties in accordance with the second subparagraph, the law applicable shall be the law of the country where the passenger has his habitual residence, provided that either the place of departure or the place of destination is situated in that country. If these requirements are not met, the law of the country where the carrier has his habitual residence shall apply.

   The parties may choose as the law applicable to a contract for the carriage of passengers in accordance with Article 3 only the law of the country where:
   (a) the passenger has his habitual residence; or
   (b) the carrier has his habitual residence; or
   (c) the carrier has his place of central administration; or
   (d) the place of departure is situated; or
   (e) the place of destination is situated.
3. Where it is clear from all the circumstances of the case that the contract, in the absence of a choice of law, is manifestly more closely connected with a country other than that indicated in paragraphs 1 or 2, the law of that other country shall apply.

Article 6 Consumer contracts

1. Without prejudice to Articles 5 and 7, a contract concluded by a natural person for a purpose which can be regarded as being outside his trade or profession (the consumer) with another person acting in the exercise of his trade or profession (the professional) shall be governed by the law of the country where the consumer has his habitual residence, provided that the professional:
   (a) pursues his commercial or professional activities in the country where the consumer has his habitual residence, or

   (b) by any means, directs such activities to that country or to several countries including that country, and the contract falls within the scope of such activities.
2. Notwithstanding paragraph 1, the parties may choose the law applicable to a contract which fulfils the requirements of paragraph 1, in accordance with Article 3. Such a choice may not, however, have the result of depriving the consumer of the protection afforded to him by provisions that cannot be derogated from by agreement by virtue of the law which, in the absence of choice, would have been applicable on the basis of paragraph 1.
3. If the requirements in points (a) or (b) of paragraph 1 are not fulfilled, the law applicable to a contract between a consumer and a professional shall be determined pursuant to Articles 3 and 4.
4. Paragraphs 1 and 2 shall not apply to:
   (a) a contract for the supply of services where the services are to be supplied to the consumer exclusively in a country other than that in which he has his habitual residence;
   (b) a contract of carriage other than a contract relating to package travel within the meaning of Council Directive 90/ 314/EEC of 13 June 1990 on package travel, package holidays and package tours (1);
   (c) a contract relating to a right *in rem* in immovable property or a tenancy of immovable property other than a contract relating to the right to use immovable properties on a timeshare basis within the meaning of Directive 94/47/EC;
   (d) rights and obligations which constitute a financial instrument and rights and obligations constituting the terms and conditions governing the issuance or offer to the public and public take-over bids of transferable securities, and the subscription and redemption of units in collective investment undertakings in so far as these activities do not constitute provision of a financial service;
   (e) a contract concluded within the type of system falling within the scope of Article 4(1)(h).

Article 7 Insurance contracts

1. This Article shall apply to contracts referred to in paragraph 2, whether or not the risk covered is situated in a Member State, and to all other insurance contracts covering risks situated inside the territory of the Member States. It shall not apply to reinsurance contracts.
2. An insurance contract covering a large risk as defined in Article 5(d) of the First Council Directive 73/239/EEC of 24 July 1973 on the coordination of laws, regulations and administrative provisions relating to the taking-up and pursuit of the business of direct insurance other than life assurance (2) shall be governed by the law chosen by the parties in accordance with Article 3 of this Regulation.

   To the extent that the applicable law has not been chosen by the parties, the insurance contract shall be governed by the law of the country where the insurer has his habitual residence. Where it is clear from all the circumstances of the case that the contract is manifestly more closely connected with another country, the law of that other country shall apply.
3. In the case of an insurance contract other than a contract falling within paragraph 2, only the following laws may be chosen by the parties in accordance with Article 3:

(a) the law of any Member State where the risk is situated at the time of conclusion of the contract;
(b) the law of the country where the policy holder has his habitual residence;
(c) in the case of life assurance, the law of the Member State of which the policy holder is a national;
(d) for insurance contracts covering risks limited to events occurring in one Member State other than the Member State where the risk is situated, the law of that Member State;
(e) where the policy holder of a contract falling under this paragraph pursues a commercial or industrial activity or a liberal profession and the insurance contract covers two or more risks which relate to those activities and are situated in different Member States, the law of any of the Member States concerned or the law of the country of habitual residence of the policy holder.

Where, in the cases set out in points (a), (b) or (e), the Member States referred to grant greater freedom of choice of the law applicable to the insurance contract, the parties may take advantage of that freedom.

To the extent that the law applicable has not been chosen by the parties in accordance with this paragraph, such a contract shall be governed by the law of the Member State in which the risk is situated at the time of conclusion of the contract.

4. The following additional rules shall apply to insurance contracts covering risks for which a Member State imposes an obligation to take out insurance:
   (a) the insurance contract shall not satisfy the obligation to take out insurance unless it complies with the specific provisions relating to that insurance laid down by the Member State that imposes the obligation. Where the law of the Member State in which the risk is situated and the law of the Member State imposing the obligation to take out insurance contradict each other, the latter shall prevail;
   (b) by way of derogation from paragraphs 2 and 3, a Member State may lay down that the insurance contract shall be governed by the law of the Member State that imposes the obligation to take out insurance.
5. For the purposes of paragraph 3, third subparagraph, and paragraph 4, where the contract covers risks situated in more than one Member State, the contract shall be considered as constituting several contracts each relating to only one Member State.
6. For the purposes of this Article, the country in which the risk is situated shall be determined in accordance with Article 2(d) of the Second Council Directive 88/357/EEC of 22 June 1988 on the coordination of laws, regulations and administrative provisions relating to direct insurance other than life assurance and laying down provisions to facilitate the effective exercise of freedom to provide services (1) and, in the case of life assurance, the country in which the risk is situated shall be the country of the commitment within the meaning of Article 1(1) (g) of Directive 2002/83/EC.

Article 8 Individual employment contracts

1. An individual employment contract shall be governed by the law chosen by the parties in accordance with Article 3. Such a choice of law may not, however, have the result of depriving the employee of the protection afforded to him by provisions that cannot be derogated from by agreement under the law that, in the absence of choice, would have been applicable pursuant to paragraphs 2, 3 and 4 of this Article.

2. To the extent that the law applicable to the individual employment contract has not been chosen by the parties, the contract shall be governed by the law of the country in which or, failing that, from which the employee habitually carries out his work in performance of the contract. The country where the work is habitually carried out shall not be deemed to have changed if he is temporarily employed in another country.
3. Where the law applicable cannot be determined pursuant to paragraph 2, the contract shall be governed by the law of the country where the place of business through which the employee was engaged is situated.
4. Where it appears from the circumstances as a whole that the contract is more closely connected with a country other than that indicated in paragraphs 2 or 3, the law of that other country shall apply.

Article 9 Overriding mandatory provisions

1. Overriding mandatory provisions are provisions the respect for which is regarded as crucial by a country for safeguarding its public interests, such as its political, social or economic organisation, to such an extent that they are applicable to any situation falling within their scope, irrespective of the law otherwise applicable to the contract under this Regulation.
2. Nothing in this Regulation shall restrict the application of the overriding mandatory provisions of the law of the forum.
3. Effect may be given to the overriding mandatory provisions of the law of the country where the obligations arising out of the contract have to be or have been performed, in so far as those overriding mandatory provisions render the performance of the contract unlawful. In considering whether to give effect to those provisions, regard shall be had to their nature and purpose and to the consequences of their application or non-application.

Article 10 Consent and material validity

1. The existence and validity of a contract, or of any term of a contract, shall be determined by the law which would govern it under this Regulation if the contract or term were valid.
2. Nevertheless, a party, in order to establish that he did not consent, may rely upon the law of the country in which he has his habitual residence if it appears from the circumstances that it would not be reasonable to determine the effect of his conduct in accordance with the law specified in paragraph 1.

Article 11 Formal validity

1. A contract concluded between persons who, or whose agents, are in the same country at the time of its conclusion is formally valid if it satisfies the formal requirements of the law which governs it in substance under this Regulation or of the law of the country where it is concluded.
2. A contract concluded between persons who, or whose agents, are in different countries at the time of its conclusion is formally valid if it satisfies the formal requirements of the

law which governs it in substance under this Regulation, or of the law of either of the countries where either of the parties or their agent is present at the time of conclusion, or of the law of the country where either of the parties had his habitual residence at that time.

3. A unilateral act intended to have legal effect relating to an existing or contemplated contract is formally valid if it satisfies the formal requirements of the law which governs or would govern the contract in substance under this Regulation, or of the law of the country where the act was done, or of the law of the country where the person by whom it was done had his habitual residence at that time.
4. Paragraphs 1, 2 and 3 of this Article shall not apply to contracts that fall within the scope of Article 6. The form of such contracts shall be governed by the law of the country where the consumer has his habitual residence.
5. Notwithstanding paragraphs 1 to 4, a contract the subject matter of which is a right *in rem* in immovable property or a tenancy of immovable property shall be subject to the requirements of form of the law of the country where the property is situated if by that law:
   (a) those requirements are imposed irrespective of the country where the contract is concluded and irrespective of the law governing the contract; and
   (b) those requirements cannot be derogated from by agreement.

Article 12 Scope of the law applicable

1. The law applicable to a contract by virtue of this Regulation shall govern in particular:
   (a) interpretation;
   (b) performance;
   (c) within the limits of the powers conferred on the court by its procedural law, the consequences of a total or partial breach of obligations, including the assessment of damages in so far as it is governed by rules of law;
   (d) the various ways of extinguishing obligations, and prescription and limitation of actions;
   (e) the consequences of nullity of the contract.
2. In relation to the manner of performance and the steps to be taken in the event of defective performance, regard shall be had to the law of the country in which performance takes place.

Article 13 Incapacity

In a contract concluded between persons who are in the same country, a natural person who would have capacity under the law of that country may invoke his incapacity resulting from the law of another country, only if the other party to the contract was aware of that incapacity at the time of the conclusion of the contract or was not aware thereof as a result of negligence.

Article 14 Voluntary assignment and contractual subrogation

1. The relationship between assignor and assignee under a voluntary assignment or contractual subrogation of a claim against another person (the debtor) shall be governed

by the law that applies to the contract between the assignor and assignee under this Regulation.

2. The law governing the assigned or subrogated claim shall determine its assignability, the relationship between the assignee and the debtor, the conditions under which the assignment or subrogation can be invoked against the debtor and whether the debtor's obligations have been discharged.
3. The concept of assignment in this Article includes outright transfers of claims, transfers of claims by way of security and pledges or other security rights over claims.

Article 15 Legal subrogation

Where a person (the creditor) has a contractual claim against another (the debtor) and a third person has a duty to satisfy the creditor, or has in fact satisfied the creditor in discharge of that duty, the law which governs the third person's duty to satisfy the creditor shall determine whether and to what extent the third person is entitled to exercise against the debtor the rights which the creditor had against the debtor under the law governing their relationship.

Article 16 Multiple liability

If a creditor has a claim against several debtors who are liable for the same claim, and one of the debtors has already satisfied the claim in whole or in part, the law governing the debtor's obligation towards the creditor also governs the debtor's right to claim recourse from the other debtors. The other debtors may rely on the defences they had against the creditor to the extent allowed by the law governing their obligations towards the creditor.

Article 17 Set-off

Where the right to set-off is not agreed by the parties, set-off shall be governed by the law applicable to the claim against which the right to set-off is asserted.

Article 18 Burden of proof

1. The law governing a contractual obligation under this Regulation shall apply to the extent that, in matters of contractual obligations, it contains rules which raise presumptions of law or determine the burden of proof.
2. A contract or an act intended to have legal effect may be proved by any mode of proof recognised by the law of the forum or by any of the laws referred to in Article 11 under which that contract or act is formally valid, provided that such mode of proof can be administered by the forum.

Chapter III Other provisions

Article 19 Habitual residence

1. For the purposes of this Regulation, the habitual residence of companies and other bodies, corporate or unincorporated, shall be the place of central administration.

The habitual residence of a natural person acting in the course of his business activity shall be his principal place of business.

2. Where the contract is concluded in the course of the operations of a branch, agency or any other establishment, or if, under the contract, performance is the responsibility of such a branch, agency or establishment, the place where the branch, agency or any other establishment is located shall be treated as the place of habitual residence.
3. For the purposes of determining the habitual residence, the relevant point in time shall be the time of the conclusion of the contract.

Article 20 Exclusion of renvoi

The application of the law of any country specified by this Regulation means the application of the rules of law in force in that country other than its rules of private international law, unless provided otherwise in this Regulation.

Article 21 Public policy of the forum

The application of a provision of the law of any country specified by this Regulation may be refused only if such application is manifestly incompatible with the public policy (*ordre public*) of the forum.

Article 22 States with more than one legal system

1. Where a State comprises several territorial units, each of which has its own rules of law in respect of contractual obligations, each territorial unit shall be considered as a country for the purposes of identifying the law applicable under this Regulation.
2. A Member State where different territorial units have their own rules of law in respect of contractual obligations shall not be required to apply this Regulation to conflicts solely between the laws of such units.

Article 23 Relationship with other provisions of Community law

With the exception of Article 7, this Regulation shall not prejudice the application of provisions of Community law which, in relation to particular matters, lay down conflict-of-law rules relating to contractual obligations.

Article 24 Relationship with the Rome Convention

1. This Regulation shall replace the Rome Convention in the Member States, except as regards the territories of the Member States which fall within the territorial scope of that Convention and to which this Regulation does not apply pursuant to Article 299 of the Treaty.
2. In so far as this Regulation replaces the provisions of the Rome Convention, any reference to that Convention shall be understood as a reference to this Regulation.

Article 25 Relationship with existing international conventions

1. This Regulation shall not prejudice the application of international conventions to which one or more Member States are parties at the time when this Regulation is adopted and which lay down conflict-of-law rules relating to contractual obligations.
2. However, this Regulation shall, as between Member States, take precedence over conventions concluded exclusively between two or more of them in so far as such conventions concern matters governed by this Regulation.

Articles 26–27 [omitted]

Article 28 Application in time

This Regulation shall apply to contracts concluded as from 17 December 2009.

Chapter IV Final provisions

Article 29 Entry into force and application

This Regulation shall enter into force on the 20th day following its publication in the *Official Journal of the European Union.*

It shall apply from 17 December 2009 except for Article 26 which shall apply from 17 June 2009.

This Regulation shall be binding in its entirety and directly applicable in the Member States in accordance with the Treaty establishing the European Community.

Regulation (EU) No 1215/2012 of the European Parliament and of the Council of 12 December 2012 on Jurisdiction and the Recognition and Enforcement of Judgments in Civil and Commercial Matters (Recast)

Chapter I Scope and definitions

Article 1

1. This Regulation shall apply in civil and commercial matters whatever the nature of the court or tribunal. It shall not extend, in particular, to revenue, customs or administrative matters or to the liability of the State for acts and omissions in the exercise of State authority (acta iure imperii).
2. This Regulation shall not apply to:
    (a) the status or legal capacity of natural persons, rights in property arising out of a matrimonial relationship or out of a relationship deemed by the law applicable to such relationship to have comparable effects to marriage;
    (b) bankruptcy, proceedings relating to the winding-up of insolvent companies or other legal persons, judicial arrangements, compositions and analogous proceedings;
    (c) social security;
    (d) arbitration;

(e) maintenance obligations arising from a family relationship, parentage, marriage or affinity;
(f) wills and succession, including maintenance obligations arising by reason of death.

Article 2

For the purposes of this Regulation:

(a) 'judgment' means any judgment given by a court or tribunal of a Member State, whatever the judgment may be called, including a decree, order, decision or writ of execution, as well as a decision on the determination of costs or expenses by an officer of the court.

For the purposes of Chapter III, 'judgment' includes provisional, including protective, measures ordered by a court or tribunal which by virtue of this Regulation has jurisdiction as to the substance of the matter. It does not include a provisional, including protective, measure which is ordered by such a court or tribunal without the defendant being summoned to appear, unless the judgment containing the measure is served on the defendant prior to enforcement;

(b) 'court settlement' means a settlement which has been approved by a court of a Member State or concluded before a court of a Member State in the course of proceedings;
(c) 'authentic instrument' means a document which has been formally drawn up or registered as an authentic instrument in the Member State of origin and the authenticity of which:
    (i) relates to the signature and the content of the instrument; and
    (ii) has been established by a public authority or other authority empowered for that purpose;
(d) 'Member State of origin' means the Member State in which, as the case may be, the judgment has been given, the court settlement has been approved or concluded, or the authentic instrument has been formally drawn up or registered;
(e) 'Member State addressed' means the Member State in which the recognition of the judgment is invoked or in which the enforcement of the judgment, the court settlement or the authentic instrument is sought;
(f) 'court of origin' means the court which has given the judgment the recognition of which is invoked or the enforcement of which is sought.

Article 3

For the purposes of this Regulation, 'court' includes the following authorities to the extent that they have jurisdiction in matters falling within the scope of this Regulation:

(a) in Hungary, in summary proceedings concerning orders to pay (fizetési meghagyásos eljárás), the notary (közjegyzo);
(b) in Sweden, in summary proceedings concerning orders to pay (betalningsföreläggande) and assistance (handräckning), the Enforcement Authority (Kronofogdemyndigheten).

Chapter II Jurisdiction

Section 1 General provisions

Article 4

1. Subject to this Regulation, persons domiciled in a Member State shall, whatever their nationality, be sued in the courts of that Member State.
2. Persons who are not nationals of the Member State in which they are domiciled shall be governed by the rules of jurisdiction applicable to nationals of that Member State.

Article 5

1. Persons domiciled in a Member State may be sued in the courts of another Member State only by virtue of the rules set out in Sections 2 to 7 of this Chapter.
2. In particular, the rules of national jurisdiction of which the Member States are to notify the Commission pursuant to point (a) of Article 76(1) shall not be applicable as against the persons referred to in paragraph 1.

Article 6

1. If the defendant is not domiciled in a Member State, the jurisdiction of the courts of each Member State shall, subject to Article 18(1), Article 21(2) and Articles 24 and 25, be determined by the law of that Member State.
2. As against such a defendant, any person domiciled in a Member State may, whatever his nationality, avail himself in that Member State of the rules of jurisdiction there in force, and in particular those of which the Member States are to notify the Commission pursuant to point (a) of Article 76(1), in the same way as nationals of that Member State.

Section 2 Special jurisdiction

Article 7

A person domiciled in a Member State may be sued in another Member State:

(1) (a) in matters relating to a contract, in the courts for the place of performance of the obligation in question;

(b) for the purpose of this provision and unless otherwise agreed, the place of performance of the obligation in question shall be:

– in the case of the sale of goods, the place in a Member State where, under the contract, the goods were delivered or should have been delivered,

– in the case of the provision of services, the place in a Member State where, under the contract, the services were provided or should have been provided;

(c) if point (b) does not apply then point (a) applies;

(2) in matters relating to tort, delict or quasi-delict, in the courts for the place where the harmful event occurred or may occur;

(3) as regards a civil claim for damages or restitution which is based on an act giving rise to criminal proceedings, in the court seised of those proceedings, to the extent that that court has jurisdiction under its own law to entertain civil proceedings;
(4) as regards a civil claim for the recovery, based on ownership, of a cultural object as defined in point 1 of Article 1 of Directive 93/7/EEC initiated by the person claiming the right to recover such an object, in the courts for the place where the cultural object is situated at the time when the court is seised;
(5) as regards a dispute arising out of the operations of a branch, agency or other establishment, in the courts for the place where the branch, agency or other establishment is situated;
(6) as regards a dispute brought against a settlor, trustee or beneficiary of a trust created by the operation of a statute, or by a written instrument, or created orally and evidenced in writing, in the courts of the Member State in which the trust is domiciled;
(7) as regards a dispute concerning the payment of remuneration claimed in respect of the salvage of a cargo or freight, in the court under the authority of which the cargo or freight in question:
    (a) has been arrested to secure such payment; or
    (b) could have been so arrested, but bail or other security has been given;

    provided that this provision shall apply only if it is claimed that the defendant has an interest in the cargo or freight or had such an interest at the time of salvage.

Article 8

A person domiciled in a Member State may also be sued:

(1) where he is one of a number of defendants, in the courts for the place where any one of them is domiciled, provided the claims are so closely connected that it is expedient to hear and determine them together to avoid the risk of irreconcilable judgments resulting from separate proceedings;
(2) as a third party in an action on a warranty or guarantee or in any other third-party proceedings, in the court seised of the original proceedings, unless these were instituted solely with the object of removing him from the jurisdiction of the court which would be competent in his case;
(3) on a counter-claim arising from the same contract or facts on which the original claim was based, in the court in which the original claim is pending;
(4) in matters relating to a contract, if the action may be combined with an action against the same defendant in matters relating to rights in rem in immovable property, in the court of the Member State in which the property is situated.

Article 9

Where by virtue of this Regulation a court of a Member State has jurisdiction in actions relating to liability from the use or operation of a ship, that court, or any other court substituted for this purpose by the internal law of that Member State, shall also have jurisdiction over claims for limitation of such liability.

Section 3 Jurisdiction in matters relating to insurance

Article 10

In matters relating to insurance, jurisdiction shall be determined by this Section, without prejudice to Article 6 and point 5 of Article 7.

Article 11

1. An insurer domiciled in a Member State may be sued:
   (a) in the courts of the Member State in which he is domiciled;
   (b) in another Member State, in the case of actions brought by the policyholder, the insured or a beneficiary, in the courts for the place where the claimant is domiciled; or
   (c) if he is a co-insurer, in the courts of a Member State in which proceedings are brought against the leading insurer.
2. An insurer who is not domiciled in a Member State but has a branch, agency or other establishment in one of the Member States shall, in disputes arising out of the operations of the branch, agency or establishment, be deemed to be domiciled in that Member State.

Article 12

In respect of liability insurance or insurance of immovable property, the insurer may in addition be sued in the courts for the place where the harmful event occurred. The same applies if movable and immovable property are covered by the same insurance policy and both are adversely affected by the same contingency.

Article 13

1. In respect of liability insurance, the insurer may also, if the law of the court permits it, be joined in proceedings which the injured party has brought against the insured.
2. Articles 10, 11 and 12 shall apply to actions brought by the injured party directly against the insurer, where such direct actions are permitted.
3. If the law governing such direct actions provides that the policyholder or the insured may be joined as a party to the action, the same court shall have jurisdiction over them.

Article 14

1. Without prejudice to Article 13(3), an insurer may bring proceedings only in the courts of the Member State in which the defendant is domiciled, irrespective of whether he is the policyholder, the insured or a beneficiary.
2. The provisions of this Section shall not affect the right to bring a counter-claim in the court in which, in accordance with this Section, the original claim is pending.

Article 15

The provisions of this Section may be departed from only by an agreement:

(1) which is entered into after the dispute has arisen;
(2) which allows the policyholder, the insured or a beneficiary to bring proceedings in courts other than those indicated in this Section;
(3) which is concluded between a policyholder and an insurer, both of whom are at the time of conclusion of the contract domiciled or habitually resident in the same Member State, and which has the effect of conferring jurisdiction on the courts of that Member State even if the harmful event were to occur abroad, provided that such an agreement is not contrary to the law of that Member State;
(4) which is concluded with a policyholder who is not domiciled in a Member State, except in so far as the insurance is compulsory or relates to immovable property in a Member State; or
(5) which relates to a contract of insurance in so far as it covers one or more of the risks set out in Article 16.

Article 16

The following are the risks referred to in point 5 of Article 15:

(1) any loss of or damage to:
    (a) sea going ships, installations situated offshore or on the high seas, or aircraft, arising from perils which relate to their use for commercial purposes;
    (b) goods in transit other than passengers' baggage where the transit consists of or includes carriage by such ships or aircraft;
(2) any liability, other than for bodily injury to passengers or loss of or damage to their baggage:
    (a) arising out of the use or operation of ships, installations or aircraft as referred to in point 1(a) in so far as, in respect of the latter, the law of the Member State in which such aircraft are registered does not prohibit agreements on jurisdiction regarding insurance of such risks;
    (b) for loss or damage caused by goods in transit as described in point 1(b);
(3) any financial loss connected with the use or operation of ships, installations or aircraft as referred to in point 1(a), in particular loss of freight or charter-hire;
(4) any risk or interest connected with any of those referred to in points 1 to 3;
(5) not with standing points 1 to 4, all 'large risks' as defined in Directive 2009/138/EC of the European Parliament and of the Council of 25 November 2009 on the taking-up and pursuit of the business of Insurance and Reinsurance (Solvency II)[1]

Section 4 Jurisdiction over consumer contracts

Article 17

1. the consumer, for a purpose which can be regarded as being outside his trade or profession, jurisdiction shall be determined by this Section, without prejudice to Article 6 and point 5 of Article 7, if:

1 OJ L 335, 17.12.2009, p. 1.

(a) it is a contract for the sale of goods on instalment credit terms;
(b) it is a contract for a loan repayable by instalments, or for any other form of credit, made to finance the sale of goods; or
(c) in all other cases, the contract has been concluded with a person who pursues commercial or professional activities in the Member State of the consumer's domicile or, by any means, directs such activities to that Member State or to several States including that Member State, and the contract falls within the scope of such activities.

2. Where a consumer enters into a contract with a party who is not domiciled in a Member State but has a branch, agency or other establishment in one of the Member States, that party shall, in disputes arising out of the operations of the branch, agency or establishment, be deemed to be domiciled in that Member State.
3. This Section shall not apply to a contract of transport other than a contract which, for an inclusive price, provides for a combination of travel and accommodation.

Article 18

1. A consumer may bring proceedings against the other party to a contract either in the courts of the Member State in which that party is domiciled or, regardless of the domicile of the other party, in the courts for the place where the consumer is domiciled.
2. Proceedings may be brought against a consumer by the other party to the contract only in the courts of the Member State in which the consumer is domiciled.
3. This Article shall not affect the right to bring a counter-claim in the court in which, in accordance with this Section, the original claim is pending.

Article 19

The provisions of this Section may be departed from only by an agreement:

(1) which is entered into after the dispute has arisen;
(2) which allows the consumer to bring proceedings in courts other than those indicated in this Section; or
(3) which is entered into by the consumer and the other party to the contract, both of whom are at the time of conclusion of the contract domiciled or habitually resident in the same Member State, and which confers jurisdiction on the courts of that Member State, provided that such an agreement is not contrary to the law of that Member State.

Section 5 Jurisdiction over individual contracts of employment

Article 20

1. In matters relating to individual contracts of employment, jurisdiction shall be determined by this Section, without prejudice to Article 6, point 5 of Article 7 and, in the case of proceedings brought against an employer, point 1 of Article 8.
2. Where an employee enters into an individual contract of employment with an employer who is not domiciled in a Member State but has a branch, agency or other establishment

in one of the Member States, the employer shall, in disputes arising out of the operations of the branch, agency or establishment, be deemed to be domiciled in that Member State.

Article 21

1. An employer domiciled in a Member State may be sued:
   (a) in the courts of the Member State in which he is domiciled; or
   (b) in another Member State:
      (i) in the courts for the place where or from where the employee habitually carries out his work or in the courts for the last place where he did so; or
      (ii) if the employee does not or did not habitually carry out his work in any one country, in the courts for the place where the business which engaged the employee is or was situated.
2. An employer not domiciled in a Member State may be sued in a court of a Member State in accordance with point (b) of paragraph 1.

Article 22

1. An employer may bring proceedings only in the courts of the Member State in which the employee is domiciled.
2. The provisions of this Section shall not affect the right to bring a counter-claim in the court in which, in accordance with this Section, the original claim is pending.

Article 23

The provisions of this Section may be departed from only by an agreement:

(1) which is entered into after the dispute has arisen; or
(2) which allows the employee to bring proceedings in courts other than those indicated in this Section.

Section 6 Exclusive jurisdiction

Article 24

The following courts of a Member State shall have exclusive jurisdiction, regardless of the domicile of the parties:

(1) in proceedings which have as their object rights in rem in immovable property or tenancies of immovable property, the courts of the Member State in which the property is situated.

However, in proceedings which have as their object tenancies of immovable property concluded for temporary private use for a maximum period of six consecutive months, the courts of the Member State in which the defendant is domiciled shall also have jurisdiction, provided that the tenant is a natural person and that the landlord and the tenant are domiciled in the same Member State;

(2) in proceedings which have as their object the validity of the constitution, the nullity or the dissolution of companies or other legal persons or associations of natural or legal persons, or the validity of the decisions of their organs, the courts of the Member State in which the company, legal person or association has its seat. In order to determine that seat, the court shall apply its rules of private international law;
(3) in proceedings which have as their object the validity of entries in public registers, the courts of the Member State in which the register is kept;
(4) in proceedings concerned with the registration or validity of patents, trade marks, designs, or other similar rights required to be deposited or registered, irrespective of whether the issue is raised by way of an action or as a defence, the courts of the Member State in which the deposit or registration has been applied for, has taken place or is under the terms of an instrument of the Union or an international convention deemed to have taken place.
Without prejudice to the jurisdiction of the European Patent Office under the Convention on the Grant of European Patents, signed at Munich on 5 October 1973, the courts of each Member State shall have exclusive jurisdiction in proceedings concerned with the registration or validity of any European patent granted for that Member State;
(5) in proceedings concerned with the enforcement of judgments, the courts of the Member State in which the judgment has been or is to be enforced.

Section 7 Prorogation of jurisdiction

Article 25

1. If the parties, regardless of their domicile, have agreed that a court or the courts of a Member State are to have jurisdiction to settle any disputes which have arisen or which may arise in connection with a particular legal relationship, that court or those courts shall have jurisdiction, unless the agreement is null and void as to its substantive validity under the law of that Member State. Such jurisdiction shall be exclusive unless the parties have agreed otherwise. The agreement conferring jurisdiction shall be either:
   (a) in writing or evidenced in writing;
   (b) in a form which accords with practices which the parties have established between themselves; or
   (c) in international trade or commerce, in a form which accords with a usage of which the parties are or ought to have been aware and which in such trade or commerce is widely known to, and regularly observed by, parties to contracts of the type involved in the particular trade or commerce concerned.
2. Any communication by electronic means which provides a durable record of the agreement shall be equivalent to 'writing'.
3. The court or courts of a Member State on which a trust instrument has conferred jurisdiction shall have exclusive jurisdiction in any proceedings brought against a settlor, trustee or beneficiary, if relations between those persons or their rights or obligations under the trust are involved.
4. Agreements or provisions of a trust instrument conferring jurisdiction shall have no legal force if they are contrary to Articles 15, 19 or 23, or if the courts whose jurisdiction they purport to exclude have exclusive jurisdiction by virtue of Article 24.

5. An agreement conferring jurisdiction which forms part of a contract shall be treated as an agreement independent of the other terms of the contract.

The validity of the agreement conferring jurisdiction cannot be contested solely on the ground that the contract is not valid.

Article 26

1. Apart from jurisdiction derived from other provisions of this Regulation, a court of a Member State before which a defendant enters an appearance shall have jurisdiction. This rule shall not apply where appearance was entered to contest the jurisdiction, or where another court has exclusive jurisdiction by virtue of Article 24.
2. If the policyholder, the insured, a beneficiary of the insurance contract, the injured party, the consumer or the employee is the defendant, the court shall, before assuming jurisdiction under paragraph 1, ensure that the defendant is informed of his right to contest the jurisdiction of the court and of the consequences of entering or not entering an appearance.

Section 8 Examination as to jurisdiction and admissibility

Article 27

Where a court of a Member State is seised of a claim which is principally concerned with a matter over which the courts of another Member State have exclusive jurisdiction by virtue of Article 24, it shall declare of its own motion that it has no jurisdiction.

Article 28

1. Where a defendant domiciled in one Member State issued in a court of another Member State and does not enter an appearance, the court shall declare of its own motion that it has no jurisdiction unless its jurisdiction is derived from the provisions of this Regulation.
2. The court shall stay the proceedings so long as it is not shown that the defendant has been able to receive the document instituting the proceedings or an equivalent document in sufficient time to enable him to arrange for his defence, or that all necessary steps have been taken to this end.
3. Article 19 of Regulation (EC) No1393/2007 of the European Parliament and of the Council of 13 November 2007 on the service in the Member States of judicial and extra-judicial documents in civil or commercial matters (service of documents) (1) shall apply instead of paragraph 2 of this Article if the document instituting the proceedings or an equivalent document had to be transmitted from one Member State to another pursuant to that Regulation.
4. Where Regulation (EC)No1393/2007 is not applicable, Article 15 of the Hague Convention of 15 November 1965 on the Service Abroad of Judicial and Extra judicial Documents in Civil or Commercial Matters shall apply if the document instituting the proceedings or an equivalent document had to be transmitted abroad pursuant to that Convention.

Section 9 Lis pendens — related actions

Article 29

1. Without prejudice to Article 31(2), where proceedings involving the same cause of action and between the same parties are brought in the courts of different Member States, any court other than the court first seised shall of its own motion stay its proceedings until such time as the jurisdiction of the court first seised is established.
2. In cases referred to in paragraph 1, upon request by a court seised of the dispute, any other court seised shall without delay inform the former court of the date when it was seised in accordance with Article 32.
3. Where the jurisdiction of the court first seised is established, any court other than the court first seised shall decline jurisdiction in favour of that court.

Article 30

1. Where related actions are pending in the courts of different Member States, any court other than the court first seised may stay its proceedings.
2. Where the action in the court first seised is pending at first instance, any other court may also, on the application of one of the parties, decline jurisdiction if the court first seised has jurisdiction over the actions in question and its law permits the consolidation thereof.
3. For the purposes of this Article, actions are deemed to be related where they are so closely connected that it is expedient to hear and determine them together to avoid the risk of irreconcilable judgments resulting from separate proceedings.

Article 31

1. Where actions come within the exclusive jurisdiction of several courts, any court other than the court first seised shall decline jurisdiction in favour of that court.
2. Without prejudice to Article 26, where a court of a Member State on which an agreement as referred to in Article 25 confers exclusive jurisdiction is seised, any court of another Member State shall stay the proceedings until such time as the court seised on the basis of the agreement declares that it has no jurisdiction under the agreement.
3. Where the court designated in the agreement has established jurisdiction in accordance with the agreement, any court of another Member State shall decline jurisdiction in favour of that court.
4. Paragraphs 2 and 3 shall not apply to matters referred to in Sections 3, 4 or 5 where the policyholder, the insured, a beneficiary of the insurance contract, the injured party, the consumer or the employee is the claimant and the agreement is not valid under a provision contained within those Sections.

Article 32

1. For the purposes of this Section, a court shall be deemed to be seised:

   (a) at the time when the document instituting the proceedings or an equivalent document is lodged with the court, provided that the claimant has not subsequently failed to take the steps he was required to take to have service effected on the defendant; or

(b) if the document has to be served before being lodged with the court, at the time when it is received by the authority responsible for service, provided that the claimant has not subsequently failed to take the steps he was required to take to have the document lodged with the court.

The authority responsible for service referred to in point (b) shall be the first authority receiving the documents to be served.

The court, or the authority responsible for service, referred to in paragraph 1, shall note, respectively, the date of the lodging of the document instituting the proceedings or the equivalent document, or the date of receipt of the documents to be served.

Article 33

1. Where jurisdiction is based on Article 4 or on Articles 7, 8 or 9 and proceedings are pending before a court of a third State at the time when a court in a Member State is seised of an action involving the same cause of action and between the same parties as the proceedings in the court of the third State, the court of the Member State may stay the proceedings if:
   (a) it is expected that the court of the third State will give a judgment capable of recognition and, where applicable, of enforcement in that Member State; and
   (b) the court of the Member State is satisfied that a stay is necessary for the proper administration of justice.
2. The court of the Member State may continue the proceedings at any time if:
   (a) the proceedings in the court of the third State are them-selves stayed or discontinued;
   (b) it appears to the court of the Member State that the proceedings in the court of the third State are unlikely to be concluded within a reasonable time; or
   (c) the continuation of the proceedings is required for the proper administration of justice.
3. The court of the Member State shall dismiss the proceedings if the proceedings in the court of the third State are concluded and have resulted in a judgment capable of recognition and, where applicable, of enforcement in that Member State.
4. The court of the Member State shall apply this Article on the application of one of the parties or, where possible under national law, of its own motion.

Article 34

1. Where jurisdiction is based on Article 4 or on Articles 7, 8 or 9 and an action is pending before a court of a third State at the time when a court in a Member State is seised of an action which is related to the action in the court of the third State, the court of the Member State may stay the proceedings if:
   (a) it is expedient to hear and determine the related actions together to avoid the risk of irreconcilable judgments resulting from separate proceedings;
   (b) it is expected that the court of the third State will give a judgment capable of recognition and, where applicable, of enforcement in that Member State; and
   (c) the court of the Member State is satisfied that a stay is necessary for the proper administration of justice.

2. The court of the Member State may continue the proceedings at any time if:
   (a) it appears to the court of the Member State that there is no longer a risk of irreconcilable judgments;
   (b) the proceedings in the court of the third State are them-selves stayed or discontinued;
   (c) it appears to the court of the Member State that the proceedings in the court of the third State are unlikely to be concluded within a reasonable time; or
   (d) the continuation of the proceedings is required for the proper administration of justice.
3. The court of the Member State may dismiss the proceedings if the proceedings in the court of the third State are concluded and have resulted in a judgment capable of recognition and, where applicable, of enforcement in that Member State.
4. The court of the Member State shall apply this Article on the application of one of the parties or, where possible under national law, of its own motion.

Section 10 Provisional, including protective, measures

Article 35

Application may be made to the courts of a Member State for such provisional, including protective, measures as may be available under the law of that Member State, even if the courts of another Member State have jurisdiction as to the substance of the matter.

Chapter III Recognition and enforcement

Section 1 Recognition

Article 36

1. A judgment given in a Member State shall be recognised in the other Member States without any special procedure being required.
2. Any interested party may, in accordance with the procedure provided for in Subsection 2 of Section 3, apply for a decision that there are no grounds for refusal of recognition as referred to in Article 45.
3. If the outcome of proceedings in a court of a Member State depends on the determination of an incidental question of refusal of recognition, that court shall have jurisdiction over that question.

Article 37

1. A party who wishes to invoke in a Member State a judgment given in another Member State shall produce:
   (a) a copy of the judgment which satisfies the conditions necessary to establish its authenticity; and
   (b) the certificate issued pursuant to Article 53.
2. The court or authority before which a judgment given in another Member State is invoked may, where necessary, require the party invoking it to provide, in accordance

with Article 57, a translation or a transliteration of the contents of the certificate referred to in point (b) of paragraph 1. The court or authority may require the party to provide a translation of the judgment instead of a translation of the contents of the certificate if it is unable to proceed without such a translation.

Article 38

The court or authority before which a judgment given in another Member State is invoked may suspend the proceedings, in whole or in part, if:

(a) the judgment is challenged in the Member State of origin; or
(b) an application has been submitted for a decision that there are no grounds for refusal of recognition as referred to in Article 45 or for a decision that the recognition is to be refused on the basis of one of those grounds.

Section 2 Enforcement

Article 39

A judgment given in a Member State which is enforceable in that Member State shall be enforceable in the other Member States without any declaration of enforceability being required.

Article 40

An enforceable judgment shall carry with it by operation of law the power to proceed to any protective measures which exist under the law of the Member State addressed.

Article 41

1. Subject to the provisions of this Section, the procedure for the enforcement of judgments given in another Member State shall be governed by the law of the Member State addressed. A judgment given in a Member State which is enforceable in the Member State addressed shall be enforced there under the same conditions as a judgment given in the Member State addressed.
2. Not with standing paragraph 1, the grounds for refusal or of suspension of enforcement under the law of the Member State addressed shall apply in so far as they are not incompatible with the grounds referred to in Article 45.
3. The party seeking the enforcement of a judgment given in another Member State shall not be required to have a postal address in the Member State addressed. Nor shall that party be required to have an authorised representative in the Member State addressed unless such a representative is mandatory irre spective of the nationality or the domicile of the parties.

Article 42

1. For the purposes of enforcement in a Member State of a judgment given in another Member State, the applicant shall provide the competent enforcement authority with:

(a) a copy of the judgment which satisfies the conditions necessary to establish its authenticity; and
(b) the certificate issued pursuant to Article 53, certifying that the judgment is enforceable and containing an extract of the judgment as well as, where appropriate, relevant information on the recoverable costs of the proceedings and the calculation of interest.

2. For the purposes of enforcement in a Member State of a judgment given in another Member State ordering a provisional, including a protective, measure, the applicant shall provide the competent enforcement authority with:
   (a) a copy of the judgment which satisfies the conditions necessary to establish its authenticity;
   (b) the certificate issued pursuant to Article 53, containing a description of the measure and certifying that:
      (i) the court has jurisdiction as to the substance of the matter;
      (ii) the judgment is enforceable in the Member State of origin; and
   (c) where the measure was ordered without the defendant being summoned to appear, proof of service of the judgment.
3. The competent enforcement authority may, where necessary, require the applicant to provide, in accordance with Article 57, a translation or a transliteration of the contents of the certificate.
4. The competent enforcement authority may require the applicant to provide a translation of the judgment only if it is unable to proceed without such a translation.

Article 43

This paragraph shall not apply if the judgment has already been served on the person against whom enforcement is sought in one of the languages referred to in the first subparagraph or is accompanied by a translation into one of those languages.

3. This Article shall not apply to the enforcement of a protective measure in a judgment or where the person seeking enforcement proceeds to protective measures in accordance with Article 40.

Article 44

1. In the event of an application for refusal of enforcement of a judgment pursuant to Subsection 2 of Section 3. the court in the Member State addressed may, on the application of the person against whom enforcement is sought:
   (a) limit the enforcement proceedings to protective measures;
   (b) make enforcement conditional on the provision of such security as it shall determine; or
   (c) suspend, either wholly or in part, the enforcement proceedings.
2. The competent authority in the Member State addressed shall, on the application of the person against whom enforcement is sought, suspend the enforcement proceedings where the enforceability of the judgment is suspended in the Member State of origin.

Section 3 Refusal of recognition and enforcement

Subsection 1 Refusal of recognition

Article 45

1. On the application of any interested party, the recognition of a judgment shall be refused:
    (a) if such recognition is manifestly contrary to public policy (ordre public) in the Member State addressed;
    (b) where the judgment was given in default of appearance, if the defendant was not served with the document which instituted the proceedings or with an equivalent document in sufficient time and in such a way as to enable him to arrange for his defence, unless the defendant failed to commence proceedings to challenge the judgment when it was possible for him to do so;
    (c) if the judgment is irreconcilable with a judgment given between the same parties in the Member State addressed;
    (d) if the judgment is irreconcilable with an earlier judgment given in another Member State or in a third State involving the same cause of action and between the same parties, provided that the earlier judgment fulfils the conditions necessary for its recognition in the Member State addressed; or
    (e) if the judgment conflicts with:
        (i) Sections 3, 4 or 5 of Chapter II where the policyholder, the insured, a beneficiary of the insurance contract, the injured party, the consumer or the employee was the defendant; or
        (ii) Section 6 of Chapter II.
2. In its examination of the grounds of jurisdiction referred to in point (e) of paragraph 1, the court to which the application was submitted shall be bound by the findings of fact on which the court of origin based its jurisdiction.
3. Without prejudice to point (e) of paragraph 1, the jurisdiction of the court of origin may not be reviewed. The test of public policy referred to in point (a) of paragraph 1 may not be applied to the rules relating to jurisdiction.
4. The application for refusal of recognition shall be made in accordance with the procedures provided for in Subsection 2 and, where appropriate, Section 4.

Subsection 2 Refusal of enforcement

Article 46

On the application of the person against whom enforcement is sought, the enforcement of a judgment shall be refused where one of the grounds referred to in Article 45 is found to exist.

Article 47

1. The application for refusal of enforcement shall be submitted to the court which the Member State concerned has communicated to the Commission pursuant to point (a) of Article 75 as the court to which the application is to be submitted.

2. The procedure for refusal of enforcement shall, in so far as it is not covered by this Regulation, be governed by the law of the Member State addressed.
3. The applicant shall provide the court with a copy of the judgment and, where necessary, a translation or transliteration of it.

   The court may dispense with the production of the documents referred to in the first subparagraph if it already possesses them or if it considers it unreasonable to require the applicant to provide them. In the latter case, the court may require the other party to provide those documents.
4. The party seeking the refusal of enforcement of a judgment given in another Member State shall not be required to have a postal address in the Member State addressed. Nor shall that party be required to have an authorised representative in the Member State addressed unless such a representative is mandatory irrespective of the nationality or the domicile of the parties.

Article 48

The court shall decide on the application for refusal of enforcement without delay.

Article 49

1. The decision on the application for refusal of enforcement may be appealed against by either party.
2. The appeal is to be lodged with the court which the Member State concerned has communicated to the Commission pursuant to point (b) of Article 75 as the court with which such an appeal is to be lodged.

Article 50

The decision given on the appeal may only be contested by an appeal where the courts with which any further appeal is to be lodged have been communicated by the Member State concerned to the Commission pursuant to point (c) of Article 75.

Article 51

1. The court to which an application for refusal of enforcement is submitted or the court which hears an appeal lodged under Article 49 or Article 50 may stay the proceedings if an ordinary appeal has been lodged against the judgment in the Member State of origin or if the time for such an appeal has not yet expired. In the latter case, the court may specify the time within which such an appeal is to be lodged.
2. Where the judgment was given in Ireland, Cyprus or the United Kingdom, any form of appeal available in the Member State of origin shall be treated as an ordinary appeal for the purposes of paragraph 1.

Section 4 Common provisions

Article 52

Under no circumstances may a judgment given in a Member State be reviewed as to its substance in the Member State addressed.

Article 53

The court of origin shall, at the request of any interested party, issue the certificate using the form set out in Annex I.

Article 54

1. If a judgment contains a measure or an order which is not known in the law of the Member State addressed, that measure or order shall, to the extent possible, be adapted to a measure or an order known in the law of that Member State which has equivalent effects attached to it and which pursues similar aims and interests.

   Such adaptation shall not result in effects going beyond those provided for in the law of the Member State of origin.
2. Any party may challenge the adaptation of the measure or order before a court.
3. If necessary, the party invoking the judgment or seeking its enforcement may be required to provide a translation or a transliteration of the judgment.

Article 55

A judgment given in a Member State which orders a payment by way of a penalty shall be enforceable in the Member State addressed only if the amount of the payment has been finally determined by the court of origin.

Article 56

No security, bond or deposit, however described, shall be required of a party who in one Member State applies for the enforcement of a judgment given in another Member State on the ground that he is a foreign national or that he is not domiciled or resident in the Member State addressed.

Article 57

1. When a translation or a transliteration is required under this Regulation, such translation or transliteration shall be into the official language of the Member State concerned or, where there are several official languages in that Member State, into the official language or one of the official languages of court proceedings of the place where a judgment given in another Member State is invoked or an application is made, in accordance with the law of that Member State.
2. For the purposes of the forms referred to in Articles 53 and 60, translations or transliterations may also be into any other official language or languages of the institutions of the Union that the Member State concerned has indicated it can accept.
3. Any translation made under this Regulation shall be done by a person qualified to do translations in one of the Member States.

Chapter IV Authentic instruments and court settlements

[Omitted]

Chapter V General provisions

[Omitted]

Chapter VI Transitional provisions

[Omitted]

Chapter VII Relationship with other instruments

Article 67

[Omitted]

Article 68

1. This Regulation shall, as between the Member States, supersede the 1968 Brussels Convention, except as regards the territories of the Member States which fall within the territorial scope of that Convention and which are excluded from this Regulation pursuant to Article 355 of the TFEU.
2. In so far as this Regulation replaces the provisions of the 1968 Brussels Convention between the Member States, any reference to that Convention shall be understood as a reference to this Regulation.

Articles 69–72

[Omitted]

Article 73

1. This Regulation shall not affect the application of the 2007 Lugano Convention.
2. This Regulation shall not affect the application of the 1958 New York Convention.
3. This Regulation shall not affect the application of bilateral conventions and agreements between a third State and a Member State concluded before the date of entry into force of Regulation (EC) No 44/2001 which concern matters governed by this Regulation.

Chapter VIII Final provisions

Articles 74–80 [Omitted]

Article 81

This Regulation shall enter into force on the twentieth day following that of its publication in the Official Journal of the European Union. It shall apply from 10 January 2015, with the exception of Articles 75 and 76, which shall apply from 10 January 2014. This Regulation shall be binding in its entirety and directly applicable in the Member States in accordance with the Treaties.

Directive 1999/93/EC of the European Parliament and of the Council of 13 December 1999 on a Community Framework for Electronic Signatures

OJ 2000/L13/12 (19/1/2000)

Article 1 Scope

The purpose of this Directive is to facilitate the use of electronic signatures and to contribute to their legal recognition. It establishes a legal framework for electronic signatures and certain certification-services in order to ensure the proper functioning of the internal market.

It does not cover aspects related to the conclusion and validity of contracts or other legal obligations where there are requirements as regards form prescribed by national or Community law nor does it affect rules and limits, contained in national or Community law, governing the use of documents.

Article 2 Definitions

For the purpose of this Directive:

1. 'electronic signature' means data in electronic form which are attached to or logically associated with other electronic data and which serve as a method of authentication;
2. 'advanced electronic signature' means an electronic signature which meets the following requirements:
   (a) it is uniquely linked to the signatory;
   (b) it is capable of identifying the signatory;
   (c) it is created using means that the signatory can maintain under his sole control; and
   (d) it is linked to the data to which it relates in such a manner that any subsequent change of the data is detectable;
3. 'signatory' means a person who holds a signature-creation device and acts either on his own behalf or on behalf of the natural or legal person or entity he represents;
4. 'signature-creation data' means unique data, such as codes or private cryptographic keys, which are used by the signatory to create an electronic signature;
5. 'signature-creation device' means configured software or hardware used to implement the signature-creation data;
6. 'secure-signature-creation device' means a signature-creation device which meets the requirements laid down in Annex III;
7. 'signature-verification-data' means data, such as codes or public cryptographic keys, which are used for the purpose of verifying an electronic signature;
8. 'signature-verification device' means configured software or hardware used to implement the signature-verification-data;
9. 'certificate' means an electronic attestation which links signature-verification data to a person and confirms the identity of that person;
10. 'qualified certificate' means a certificate which meets the requirements laid down in Annex I and is provided by a certification-service-provider who fulfils the requirements laid down in Annex II;

11. ‘certification-service-provider’ means an entity or a legal or natural person who issues certificates or provides other services related to electronic signatures;
12. ‘electronic-signature product’ means hardware or software, or relevant components thereof, which are intended to be used by a certification-service – provider for the provision of electronic-signature services or are intended to be used for the creation or verification of electronic signatures;
13. ‘voluntary accreditation’ means any permission, setting out rights and obligations specific to the provision of certification services, to be granted upon request by the certification-service-provider concerned, by the public or private body charged with the elaboration of, and supervision of compliance with, such rights and obligations, where the certification-service-provider is not entitled to exercise the rights stemming from the permission until it has received the decision by the body.

Article 3 Market access

1. Member States shall not make the provision of certification services subject to prior authorisation.
2. Without prejudice to the provisions of paragraph 1, Member States may introduce or maintain voluntary accreditation schemes aiming at enhanced levels of certification-service provision. All conditions related to such schemes must be objective, transparent, proportionate and non-discriminatory. Member States may not limit the number of accredited certification-service-providers for reasons which fall within the scope of this Directive.
3. Each Member State shall ensure the establishment of an appropriate system that allows for supervision of certification-service-providers which are established on its territory and issue qualified certificates to the public.
4. The conformity of secure signature-creation-devices with the requirements laid down in Annex III shall be determined by appropriate public or private bodies designated by Member States. The Commission shall establish criteria for Member States to determine whether a body should be so designated. That measure, designed to amend non-essential elements of this Directive by supplementing it, shall be adopted in accordance with the regulatory procedure with scrutiny referred to in Article 9(3). A determination of conformity with the requirements laid down in Annex III made by the bodies referred to in the first subparagraph shall be recognised by all Member States.
5. The Commission may, in accordance with the procedure laid down in Article 9(2), establish and publish reference numbers of generally recognised standards for electronic-signature products in the *Official Journal of the European Communities*. Member States shall presume that there is compliance with the requirements laid down in Annex II, point (f), and Annex III when an electronic signature product meets those standards.
6. Member States and the Commission shall work together to promote the development and use of signature-verification devices in the light of the recommendations for secure signature-verification laid down in Annex IV and in the interests of the consumer.
7. Member States may make the use of electronic signatures in the public sector subject to possible additional requirements. Such requirements shall be objective, transparent, proportionate and non-discriminatory and shall relate only to the specific characteristics of the application concerned. Such requirements may not constitute an obstacle to cross-border services for citizens.

Article 4 Internal market principles

1. Each Member State shall apply the national provisions which it adopts pursuant to this Directive to certification-service-providers established on its territory and to the services which they provide. Member States may not restrict the provision of certification-services originating in another Member State in the fields covered by this Directive.
2. Member States shall ensure that electronic-signature products which comply with this Directive are permitted to circulate freely in the internal market.

Article 5 Legal effects of electronic signatures

1. Member States shall ensure that advanced electronic signatures which are based on a qualified certificate and which are created by a secure-signature-creation device:
   (a) satisfy the legal requirements of a signature in relation to data in electronic form in the same manner as a hand-written signature satisfies those requirements in relation to paper-based data; and
   (b) are admissible as evidence in legal proceedings.
2. Member States shall ensure that an electronic signature is not denied legal effectiveness and admissibility as evidence in legal proceedings solely on the grounds that it is:
   - in electronic form, or
   - not based upon a qualified certificate, or
   - not based upon a qualified certificate issued by an accredited certification-service-provider, or
   - not created by a secure signature-creation device.

Article 6 Liability

1. As a minimum, Member States shall ensure that by issuing a certificate as a qualified certificate to the public or by guaranteeing such a certificate to the public a certification-service-provider is liable for damage caused to any entity or legal or natural person who reasonably relies on that certificate;
   (a) as regards the accuracy at the time of issuance of all information contained in the qualified certificate and as regards the fact that the certificate contains all the details prescribed for a qualified certificate;
   (b) for assurance that at the time of the issuance of the certificate, the signatory identified in the qualified certificate held the signature-creation data corresponding to the signature-verification data given or identified in the certificate;
   (c) for assurance that the signature-creation data and the signature-verification data can be used in a complementary manner in cases where the certification-service-provider generates them both;

   unless the certification-service-provider proves that he has not acted negligently.
2. As a minimum Member States shall ensure that a certification-service-provider who has issued a certificate as a qualified certificate to the public is liable for damage caused to any entity or legal or natural person who reasonably relies on the certificate for failure to register revocation of the certificate unless the certification-service-provider proves that he has not acted negligently.

3. Member States shall ensure that a certification-service-provider may indicate in a qualified certificate limitations on the use of that certificate, provided that the limitations are recognisable to third parties. The certification-service-provider shall not be liable for damage arising from use of a qualified certificate which exceeds the limitations placed on it.
4. Member States shall ensure that a certification-service-provider may indicate in the qualified certificate a limit on the value of transactions for which the certificate can be used, provided that the limit is recognisable to third parties. The certification-service-provider shall not be liable for damage resulting from this maximum limit being exceeded.
5. The provisions of paragraphs 1 to 4 shall be without prejudice to Council Directive 93/13/EEC of 5 April 1993 on unfair terms in consumer contracts.

Article 7 International aspects

1. Member States shall ensure that certificates which are issued as qualified certificates to the public by a certification-service-provider established in a third country are recognised as legally equivalent to certificates issued by a certification-service-provider established within the Community if:
   (a) the certification-service-provider fulfils the requirements laid down in this Directive and has been accredited under a voluntary accreditation scheme established in a Member State; or
   (b) a certification-service-provider established within the Community which fulfils the requirements laid down in this Directive guarantees the certificate; or
   (c) the certificate or the certification-service-provider is recognised under a bilateral or multilateral agreement between the Community and third countries or international organisations.
2. In order to facilitate cross-border certification services with third countries and legal recognition of advanced electronic signatures originating in third countries, the Commission shall make proposals, where appropriate, to achieve the effective implementation of standards and international agreements applicable to certification services. In particular, and where necessary, it shall submit proposals to the Council for appropriate mandates for the negotiation of bilateral and multilateral agreements with third countries and international organisations. The Council shall decide by qualified majority.
3. Whenever the Commission is informed of any difficulties encountered by Community undertakings with respect to market access in third countries, it may, if necessary, submit proposals to the Council for an appropriate mandate for the negotiation of comparable rights for Community undertakings in these third countries. The Council shall decide by qualified majority. Measures taken pursuant to this paragraph shall be without prejudice to the obligations of the Community and of the Member States under relevant international agreements.

Article 8 Data protection

1. Member States shall ensure that certification-service-providers and national bodies responsible for accreditation or supervision comply with the requirements laid down

in Directive 95/46/EC of the European Parliament and of the Council of 24 October 1995 on the protection of individuals with regard to the processing of personal data and on the free movement of such data.

2. Member States shall ensure that a certification-service-provider which issues certificates to the public may collect personal data only directly from the data subject, or after the explicit consent of the data subject, and only insofar as it is necessary for the purposes of issuing and maintaining the certificate. The data may not be collected or processed for any other purposes without the explicit consent of the data subject.
3. Without prejudice to the legal effect given to pseudonyms under national law, Member States shall not prevent certification service providers from indicating in the certificate a pseudonym instead of the signatory's name.

Articles 9–15 [Omitted].

Annex I Requirements for qualified certificates

Qualified certificates must contain:

(a) an indication that the certificate is issued as a qualified certificate;
(b) the identification of the certification-service-provider and the State in which it is established;
(c) the name of the signatory or a pseudonym, which shall be identified as such;
(d) provision for a specific attribute of the signatory to be included if relevant, depending on the purpose for which the certificate is intended;
(e) signature-verification data which correspond to signature-creation data under the control of the signatory;
(f) an indication of the beginning and end of the period of validity of the certificate;
(g) the identity code of the certificate;
(h) the advanced electronic signature of the certification-service-provider issuing it;
(i) limitations on the scope of use of the certificate, if applicable; and
(j) limits on the value of transactions for which the certificate can be used, if applicable.

Annex II Requirements for certification-service-providers issuing qualified certificates

Certification-service-providers must:

(a) demonstrate the reliability necessary for providing certification services;
(b) ensure the operation of a prompt and secure directory and a secure and immediate revocation service;
(c) ensure that the date and time when a certificate is issued or revoked can be determined precisely;
(d) verify, by appropriate means in accordance with national law, the identity and, if applicable, any specific attributes of the person to which a qualified certificate is issued;
(e) employ personnel who possess the expert knowledge, experience, and qualifications necessary for the services provided, in particular competence at managerial level,

expertise in electronic signature technology and familiarity with proper security procedures; they must also apply administrative and management procedures which are adequate and correspond to recognised standards;

(f) use trustworthy systems and products which are protected against modification and ensure the technical and cryptographic security of the process supported by them;

(g) take measures against forgery of certificates, and, in cases where the certification-service-provider generates signature-creation data, guarantee confidentiality during the process of generating such data;

(h) maintain sufficient financial resources to operate in conformity with the requirements laid down in the Directive, in particular to bear the risk of liability for damages, for example, by obtaining appropriate insurance;

(i) record all relevant information concerning a qualified certificate for an appropriate period of time, in particular for the purpose of providing evidence of certification for the purposes of legal proceedings. Such recording may be done electronically;

(j) not store or copy signature-creation data of the person to whom the certification-service-provider provided key management services;

(k) before entering into a contractual relationship with a person seeking a certificate to support his electronic signature inform that person by a durable means of communication of the precise terms and conditions regarding the use of the certificate, including any limitations on its use, the existence of a voluntary accreditation scheme and procedures for complaints and dispute settlement. Such information, which may be transmitted electronically, must be in writing and in readily understandable language. Relevant parts of this information must also be made available on request to third-parties relying on the certificate;

(l) use trustworthy systems to store certificates in a verifiable form so that:
- only authorised persons can make entries and changes,
- information can be checked for authenticity,
- certificates are publicly available for retrieval in only those cases for which the certificate-holder's consent has been obtained, and
- any technical changes compromising these security requirements are apparent to the operator.

Annex III Requirements for secure signature-creation devices

1. Secure signature-creation devices must, by appropriate technical and procedural means, ensure at the least that:
   (a) the signature-creation-data used for signature generation can practically occur only once, and that their secrecy is reasonably assured;
   (b) the signature-creation-data used for signature generation cannot, with reasonable assurance, be derived and the signature is protected against forgery using currently available technology;
   (c) the signature-creation-data used for signature generation can be reliably protected by the legitimate signatory against the use of others.
2. Secure signature-creation devices must not alter the data to be signed or prevent such data from being presented to the signatory prior to the signature process.

Annex IV Recommendations for secure signature verification

During the signature-verification process it should be ensured with reasonable certainty that:

(a) the data used for verifying the signature correspond to the data displayed to the verifier;
(b) the signature is reliably verified and the result of that verification is correctly displayed;
(c) the verifier can, as necessary, reliably establish the contents of the signed data;
(d) the authenticity and validity of the certificate required at the time of signature verification are reliably verified;
(e) the result of verification and the signatory's identity are correctly displayed;
(f) the use of a pseudonym is clearly indicated; and
(g) any security-relevant changes can be detected.

Directive 2008/52/EC of the European Parliament and of the Council of 21 May 2008 on Certain Aspects of Mediation in Civil and Commercial Matters

OJ 2008/L13/63 (24/5/2008)

Article 1 Objective and scope

1. The objective of this Directive is to facilitate access to alternative dispute resolution and to promote the amicable settlement of disputes by encouraging the use of mediation and by ensuring a balanced relationship between mediation and judicial proceedings.
2. This Directive shall apply, in cross-border disputes, to civil and commercial matters except as regards rights and obligations which are not at the parties' disposal under the relevant applicable law. It shall not extend, in particular, to revenue, customs or administrative matters or to the liability of the State for acts and omissions in the exercise of State authority (*acta iure imperii*).
3. In this Directive, the term 'Member State' shall mean Member States with the exception of Denmark.

Article 2 Cross-border disputes

1. For the purposes of this Directive a cross-border dispute shall be one in which at least one of the parties is domiciled or habitually resident in a Member State other than that of any other party on the date on which:
   (a) the parties agree to use mediation after the dispute has arisen;
   (b) mediation is ordered by a court;
   (c) an obligation to use mediation arises under national law; or
   (d) for the purposes of Article 5 an invitation is made to the parties.
2. Notwithstanding paragraph 1, for the purposes of Articles 7 and 8 a cross-border dispute shall also be one in which judicial proceedings or arbitration following mediation between the parties are initiated in a Member State other than that in which the parties were domiciled or habitually resident on the date referred to in paragraph 1(a), (b) or (c).

3. For the purposes of paragraphs 1 and 2, domicile shall be determined in accordance with Articles 59 and 60 of Regulation (EC) No 44/2001.

Article 3 Definitions

For the purposes of this Directive the following definitions shall apply:

(a) 'Mediation' means a structured process, however named or referred to, whereby two or more parties to a dispute attempt by themselves, on a voluntary basis, to reach an agreement on the settlement of their dispute with the assistance of a mediator. This process may be initiated by the parties or suggested or ordered by a court or prescribed by the law of a Member State.

It includes mediation conducted by a judge who is not responsible for any judicial proceedings concerning the dispute in question. It excludes attempts made by the court or the judge seised to settle a dispute in the course of judicial proceedings concerning the dispute in question.

(b) 'Mediator' means any third person who is asked to conduct a mediation in an effective, impartial and competent way, regardless of the denomination or profession of that third person in the Member State concerned and of the way in which the third person has been appointed or requested to conduct the mediation.

Article 4 Ensuring quality of mediation

1. Member States shall encourage, by any means which they consider appropriate, the development of, and adherence to, voluntary codes of conduct by mediators and organisations providing mediation services, as well as other effective quality control mechanisms concerning the provision of mediation services.
2. Member States shall encourage the initial and further training of mediators in order to ensure that the mediation is conducted in an effective, impartial and competent way in relation to the parties.

Article 5 Recourse to mediation

1. A court before which an action is brought may, when appropriate and having regard to all the circumstances of the case, invite the parties to use mediation in order to settle the dispute. The court may also invite the parties to attend an information session on the use of mediation if such sessions are held and are easily available.
2. This Directive is without prejudice to national legislation making the use of mediation compulsory or subject to incentives or sanctions, whether before or after judicial proceedings have started, provided that such legislation does not prevent the parties from exercising their right of access to the judicial system.

Article 6 Enforceability of agreements resulting from mediation

1. Member States shall ensure that it is possible for the parties, or for one of them with the explicit consent of the others, to request that the content of a written agreement

resulting from mediation be made enforceable. The content of such an agreement shall be made enforceable unless, in the case in question, either the content of that agreement is contrary to the law of the Member State where the request is made or the law of that Member State does not provide for its enforceability.

2. The content of the agreement may be made enforceable by a court or other competent authority in a judgment or decision or in an authentic instrument in accordance with the law of the Member State where the request is made.
3. Member States shall inform the Commission of the courts or other authorities competent to receive requests in accordance with paragraphs 1 and 2.
4. Nothing in this Article shall affect the rules applicable to the recognition and enforcement in another Member State of an agreement made enforceable in accordance with paragraph 1.

Article 7 Confidentiality of mediation

1. Given that mediation is intended to take place in a manner which respects confidentiality, Member States shall ensure that, unless the parties agree otherwise, neither mediators nor those involved in the administration of the mediation process shall be compelled to give evidence in civil and commercial judicial proceedings or arbitration regarding information arising out of or in connection with a mediation process, except:
   (a) where this is necessary for overriding considerations of public policy of the Member State concerned, in particular when required to ensure the protection of the best interests of children or to prevent harm to the physical or psychological integrity of a person; or
   (b) where disclosure of the content of the agreement resulting from mediation is necessary in order to implement or enforce that agreement.
2. Nothing in paragraph 1 shall preclude Member States from enacting stricter measures to protect the confidentiality of mediation.

Article 8 Effect of mediation on limitation and prescription periods

1. Member States shall ensure that parties who choose mediation in an attempt to settle a dispute are not subsequently prevented from initiating judicial proceedings or arbitration in relation to that dispute by the expiry of limitation or prescription periods during the mediation process.
2. Paragraph 1 shall be without prejudice to provisions on limitation or prescription periods in international agreements to which Member States are party.

Article 9 Confidentiality of mediation

Member States shall encourage, by any means which they consider appropriate, the availability to the general public, in particular on the Internet, of information on how to contact mediators and organisations providing mediation services.

Article 10 Information on competent courts and authorities

The Commission shall make publicly available, by any appropriate means, information on the competent courts or authorities communicated by the Member States pursuant to Article 6(3).

Articles 11–14 omitted.

Section IV

CONVENTIONS

Geneva Protocol on Arbitration Clauses 1923

See the First Schedule to the Arbitration Act 1950 for text of the Convention.

International Convention for the Unification of Certain Rules Relating to Bills of Lading, Brussels, 1924 (The Hague Rules)

Article 1

In this convention the following words are employed with the meanings set out below –

(a) 'carrier' includes the owner of the vessel or the charterer who enters into a contract of carriage with a shipper;
(b) 'contract of carriage' applies only to contracts of carriage covered by a bill of lading or any similar document of title, in so far as such document relates to the carriage of goods by sea; it also applies to any bill of lading or any similar document as aforesaid issued under or pursuant to a charter party from the moment at which such instrument regulates the relations between a carrier and a holder of the same;
(c) 'goods' includes goods, wares, merchandise, and articles of every kind whatsoever except live animals and cargo which by the contract of carriage is stated as being carried on deck and is so carried;
(d) 'ship' means any vessel used for the carriage of goods by sea;
(e) 'carriage of goods' covers the period from the time when the goods are loaded on to the time they are discharged from the ship.

Article 2

Subject to the provisions of Article 6, under every contract of carriage of goods by sea the carrier, in relation to the loading, handling, stowage, carriage, custody, care, and discharge of such goods shall be subject to the responsibilities and liabilities, and entitled to the rights and immunities hereinafter set forth.

Article 3

1. The carrier shall be bound before and at the beginning of the voyage to exercise due diligence to –
   (a) make the ship seaworthy;
   (b) properly man, equip, and supply the ship;
   (c) make the holds, refrigerating and cool chambers, and all other parts of the ship in which goods are carried, fit and safe for their reception, carriage, and preservation.
2. Subject to the provisions of Article 4, the carrier shall properly and carefully load, handle, stow, carry, keep, care for, and discharge the goods carried.
3. After receiving the goods into his charge, the carrier or the master or agent of the carrier shall, on demand of the shipper, issue to the shipper a bill of lading showing among other things –
   (a) the leading marks necessary for identification of the goods as the same are furnished in writing by the shipper before the loading of such goods starts, provided such marks are stamped or otherwise shown clearly upon the goods if uncovered, or on the cases or coverings in which such goods are contained, in such a manner as should ordinarily remain legible until the end of the voyage;
   (b) either the number of packages or pieces, or the quantity; or weight, as the case may be, as furnished in writing by the shipper;
   (c) the apparent order and condition of the goods.

   Provided that no carrier, master, or agent of the carrier shall be bound to state or show in the bill of lading any marks, number, quantity, or weight which he has reasonable grounds for suspecting not accurately to represent the goods actually received or which he has had no reasonable means of checking.
4. Such a bill of lading shall be *prima facie* evidence of the receipt by the carrier of the goods as therein described in accordance with paragraph 3(a), (b) and (c).
5. The shipper shall be deemed to have guaranteed to the carrier the accuracy at the time of shipment of the marks, number, quantity, and weight, as furnished by him, and the shipper shall indemnify the carrier against all loss, damages, and expenses arising or resulting from inaccuracies in such particulars. The right of the carrier to such indemnity shall in no way limit his responsibility and liability under the contract of carriage to any person other than the shipper.
6. Unless notice of loss or damage and the general nature of such loss or damage be given in writing to the carrier or his agent at the port of discharge before or at the time of the removal of the goods into the custody of the person entitled to delivery thereof under the contract of carriage, such removal shall be *prima facie* evidence of the delivery by the carrier of the goods as described in the bill of lading. If the loss or damage is not apparent, the notice must be given within three days of the delivery. The notice in writing need not be given if the state of the goods has at the time of their receipt been the subject of joint survey or inspection. In any event the carrier and the ship shall be discharged from all liability in respect of loss or damage unless suit is brought within one year after delivery of the goods or the date when the goods should have been delivered.

In the case of any actual or apprehended loss or damage the carrier and the receiver shall give all reasonable facilities to each other for inspecting and tallying the goods.

7. After the goods are loaded, the bill of lading to be issued by the carrier, master, or agent of the carrier to the shipper shall, if the shipper so demands, be a 'shipped' bill of lading, provided that if the shipper shall have previously taken up any document of title to such goods, he shall surrender the same as against the issue of the 'shipped' bill of lading. At the option of the carrier such document of title may be noted at the port of shipment by the carrier, master, or agent with the name or names of the ship or ships upon which he goods have been shipped and the date or dates of shipment, and when so noted, if it shows the particulars mentioned in paragraph 3 or Article 3, it shall for the purpose of this Article be deemed to constitute a 'shipped' bill of lading.
8. Any clause, covenant, or agreement in a contract of carriage relieving the carrier or the ship from liability for loss or damage to or in connection with goods arising from negligence, fault, or failure in the duties and obligations provided in this Article, or lessening such liability otherwise than as provided in this convention, shall be null and void and of no effect. A benefit of insurance in favour of the carrier or similar clause shall be deemed to be a clause relieving the carrier from liability.

Article 4

1. Neither the carrier nor the ship shall be liable for loss or damage arising or resulting from unseaworthiness unless caused by want of due diligence on the part of the carrier to make the ship seaworthy and to secure that the ship is properly manned, equipped, and supplied and to make the holds, refrigerating and cool chambers, and all other parts of the ship in which goods are carried fit and safe for their reception, carriage, and preservation in accordance with the provisions of paragraph 1 of Article 3. Whenever loss or damage has resulted from unseaworthiness, the burden of proving the exercise of due diligence shall be on the carrier or other person claiming exemption under this Article.
2. Neither the carrier nor the ship shall be responsible for loss or damage arising or resulting from –
   (a) act, neglect, or default of the master, mariner, pilot, or the servants of the carrier in the navigation or in the management of the ship;
   (b) fire, unless caused by the actual fault or privity of the carrier;
   (c) perils, dangers, and accidents of the sea or other navigable waters;
   (d) act of God;
   (e) act of war;
   (f) act of public enemies;
   (g) arrest or restraint of princes, rulers, or people or seizure under legal process;
   (h) quarantine restrictions;
   (i) Act or omission of the shipper or owner of the goods, his agent, or representative;
   (j) strikes or lock-outs or stoppage or restraint of labour from whatever cause, whether partial or general;
   (k) riots and civil commotions;
   (l) saving or attempting to save life or property at sea;
   (m) wastage in bulk or weight or any other loss or damage arising from inherent defect, quality, or vice of the goods;

(n) insufficiency of packing;
(o) insufficiency or inadequacy of marks;
(p) latent defects not discoverable by due diligence;
(q) any other cause arising without the actual fault or privity of the carrier, or without the fault or neglect of the agents or servants of the carrier, but the burden of proof shall be on the person claiming the benefit of this exception to show that neither the actual fault or privity of the carrier nor the fault or neglect of the agents or servants of the carrier contributed to the loss or damage.

3. The shipper shall not be responsible for loss or damage sustained by the carrier or the ship arising or resulting from any cause without the act, fault, or neglect of the shipper, his agents, or his servants.
4. Any deviation in saving or attempting to save a life or property at sea or any reasonable deviation shall not be deemed to be an infringement or breach of this convention or of the contract of carriage, and the carrier shall not be liable for any loss or damage resulting therefrom.
5. Neither the carrier nor the ship shall in any event be or become liable for any loss or damage to or in connection with goods in an amount exceeding 100 pounds sterling per package or unit or the equivalent of that sum in other currency unless the nature and value of such goods have been declared by the shipper before shipment and inserted in the bill of lading. This declaration if embodied in the bill of lading shall be *prima facie* evidence but shall not be binding or conclusive on the carrier. By agreement between the carrier, master, or agent of the carrier and the shipper another maximum amount than that mentioned in this paragraph may be fixed, provided that such maximum shall not be less than the figure above named. Neither the carrier nor the ship shall be responsible in any event for loss or damage to, or in connection with, goods if the nature or value thereof has been knowingly mis-stated by the shipper in the bill of lading.
6. Goods of an inflammable, explosive, or dangerous nature to the shipment whereof the carrier, master, or agent of the carrier has not consented with knowledge of their nature and character may at any time before discharge be landed at any place or destroyed or rendered innocuous by the carrier without compensation, and the shipper of such goods shall be liable for all damages and expenses directly or indirectly arising out of or resulting from such shipment. If any such goods shipped with such knowledge and consent shall become a danger to the ship or cargo, they may in like manner be landed at any place or destroyed or rendered innocuous by the carrier without liability on the part of the carrier except to general average, if any.

Article 5

A carrier shall be at liberty to surrender in whole or in part all or any of his rights and immunities, or to increase any of his responsibilities and liabilities under this convention provided such surrender or increase shall be embodied in the bill of lading issued to the shipper.

The provisions of this convention shall not be applicable to charter-parties, but if bills of lading are issued in the case of a ship under a charter-party they shall comply with the terms of this convention. Nothing in these rules shall be held to prevent the insertion in a bill of lading of any lawful provision regarding general average.

Article 6

Notwithstanding the provisions of the preceding Articles, a carrier, master, or agent of the carrier and a shipper shall in regard to any particular goods be at liberty to enter into any agreement in any terms as to the responsibility and liability of the carrier for such goods, and as to the rights and immunities of the carrier in respect of such goods, or concerning his obligation as to seaworthiness so far as this stipulation is not contrary to public policy, or concerning the care or diligence of his servants or agents in regard to the loading, handling, stowage, carriage, custody, care, and discharge of the goods carried by sea, provided that in this case no bill of lading has been or shall be issued and that the terms agreed shall be embodied in a receipt which shall be a non-negotiable document and shall be marked as such.

Any agreement so entered into shall have full legal effect –

> Provided that this Article shall not apply to ordinary commercial shipments made in the ordinary course of trade, but only to other shipments where the character or condition of the property to be carried or the circumstances, terms, and conditions under which the carriage is to be performed are such as reasonably to justify a special agreement.

Article 7

Nothing herein contained shall prevent a carrier or a shipper from entering into any agreement stipulation, condition, reservation, or exemption as to the responsibility and liability of the carrier or the ship for the loss or damage to, or in connection with, the custody and care and handling of goods prior to the loading on, and subsequent to the discharge from, the ship on which the goods are carried by sea.

Article 8

The provisions of this convention shall not affect the rights and obligations of the carrier under any statute for the time being in force relating to the limitation of the liability of owners of seagoing vessels.

Article 9

The monetary units mentioned in this convention are to be taken to be gold value. Those contracting states in which the pound sterling is not a monetary unit reserve to themselves the right of translating the sums indicated in this convention in terms of pound sterling into terms of their own monetary system in round figures. The national laws may reserve to the debtor the right of discharging his debt in national currency according to the rate of exchange prevailing on the day of their arrival of the ship at the port of discharge of the goods concerned.

Article 10

The provisions of this convention shall apply to all bills of lading issued in any of the Contracting States.

Articles 11–16 [Omitted]

Geneva Convention on the Execution of Foreign Arbitral Awards 1927

See the Second Schedule to the Arbitration Act 1950 for text of the Convention.

Convention for the Unification of Certain Rules Relating to International Carriage by Air, Warsaw, 1929 (Warsaw Convention)

Chapter I Scope-definitions

Article 1

1. This Convention applies to all international carriage of persons, luggage or goods performed by aircraft for reward. It applies equally to gratuitous carriage by aircraft performed by an air transport undertaking.
2. For the purpose of this Convention the expression 'international carriage' means any carriage in which, according to the contract made by the parties, the place of departure and the place of destination, whether or not there be a break in the carriage or a transhipment, are situated either within the territories of two High Contracting Parties, or within the territory of a single High Contracting party, if there is an agreed stopping place within a territory subject to the sovereignty, suzerainty, mandate or authority of another Power, even though that Power is not a party to this convention. A carriage without such an agreed stopping place between territories subject to the sovereignty, suzerainty, mandate or authority of the same High Contracting Party is not deemed to be international for the purposes of this Convention.
3. A carriage to be performed by several successive air carriers is deemed, for the purposes of this convention, to be one undivided carriage, if it has been regarded by the parties as a single operation, whether it had been agreed upon under the form of a single contract or of a series of contracts, and it does not lose its international character merely because one contract or a series of contracts is to be performed entirely within a territory subject to the sovereignty, suzerainty, mandate or authority of the same High Contracting Party.

Article 2

1. This Convention applies to carriage performed by the State or by legally constituted public bodies provided it falls within the conditions laid down in Article 1.
2. This Convention does not apply to carriage performed under the terms of any international postal Convention.

Chapter II Documents of carriage

Section 1 – Passenger ticket

Article 3 [Omitted]

Section 2 – Luggage ticket

Article 4 [Omitted]

Section 3 – Air consignment note

Article 5

1. Every carrier of goods has the right to require the consignor to make out and over to him a document called an 'air consignment note'; every consignor has the right to require the carrier to accept this document.
2. The absence, irregularity or loss of this document does not affect the existence or the validity of the contract of carriage which shall, subject to the provisions of Article 9, be none the less governed by the rules of this Convention.

Article 6

1. The air consignment note shall be made out by the consignor in three original parts and be handed over with the goods.
2. The first part shall be marked 'for the carrier', and shall be signed by the consignor. The second part shall be marked 'for the consignee', it shall be signed by the consignor and by the carrier and shall accompany the goods. The third part shall be signed by the carrier and handed by him to the consignor after the goods have been accepted.
3. The carrier shall sign on acceptance of the goods.
4. The signature of the carrier may be stamped; that of the consignor may be printed or stamped.
5. If, at the request of the consignor, the carrier makes out the air consignment note, he shall be deemed, subject to proof to the contrary, to have done so on behalf of the consignor.

Article 7

The carrier of goods has the right to require the consignor to make out separate consignment notes when there is more than one package.

Article 8

The air consignment note shall contain the following particulars –

(a) the place and date of its execution;
(b) the place of departure and of destination;
(c) the agreed stopping places, provided that the carrier may reserve the right to alter the stopping places in case of necessity, and that if he exercises that right the alteration shall not have the affect of depriving the carriage of its international character;

(d) the name and address of the consignor;
(e) the name and address of the first carrier;
(f) the name and address of the consignee, if the case so requires;
(g) the nature of the goods;
(h) the number of the packages, the method of packing and the particular marks or numbers upon them;
(i) the weight, the quantity and the volume or dimensions of the goods;
(j) the apparent condition of the goods and of the packing;
(k) the freight, if it has been agreed upon, the date and place of payment, and the person who is to pay it;
(l) if the goods are sent for payment on delivery, the price of the goods, and, if the case so requires, the amount of the expenses incurred;
(m) the amount of the value declared in accordance with Article 22(2);
(n) the number of parts of the air consignment note;
(o) the document handed to the carrier to accompany the air consignment note;
(p) the time fixed for the completion of the carriage and a brief note of the route to be followed, if these matters have been agreed upon;
(q) a statement that the carriage is subject to the rules relating to liability established by this Convention.

Article 9

If the carrier accepts goods without an air consignment note having been made out, or if the air consignment note does not contain all the particulars set out in Article 8 (a) to (i) inclusive and (q), the carrier shall not be entitled to avail himself of the provisions of this Convention which exclude or limit his liability.

Article 10

1. The consignor is responsible for the correctness of the particulars and statements relating to the goods which he inserts in the air consignment note.
2. The consignor will be liable for all damage suffered by the carrier or any other person by reason of the irregularity, incorrectness or incompleteness of the said particulars and statements.

Article 11

1. The air consignment note is *prima facie* evidence of the conclusion of the contract, of the receipt of the goods and of the conditions of carriage.
2. The statements in the air consignment note relating to the weight, dimensions and packing of the goods, as well as those relating to the number of packages, are *prima facie* evidence of the facts stated; those relating to the quantity, volume and condition of the goods do not constitute evidence against the carrier except so far as they both have been, and are stated in the air consignment note to have been, checked by him in the presence of the consignor, or relate to the apparent condition of the goods.

Article 12

1. Subject to his liability to carry out all his obligations under the contract of carriage, the consignor has the right to dispose of the goods by withdrawing them at the aerodrome of departure or destination, or by stopping them in the course of the journey on any landing, or by calling for them to be delivered at the place of destination or in the course of the journey to a person other than the consignee named in the air consignment note, or by requiring them to be returned to the aerodrome of departure. He must not exercise this right of disposition in such a way as to prejudice the carrier or other consignors and he must repay any expenses occasioned by the exercise of this right.
2. If it is impossible to carry out the orders of the consignor the carrier must so inform him forthwith.
3. If the carrier obeys the orders of the consignor for the disposition of the goods without requiring the production of the part of the air consignment note delivered to the latter, he will be liable, without prejudice to his right of recovery from the consignor, for any damage which may be caused thereby to any person who is lawfully in possession of that part of the air consignment note.
4. The right conferred on the consignor ceases at the moment when that of the consignee begins in accordance with Article 13. Nevertheless, if the consignee declines to accept the consignment note or the goods, or if he cannot be communicated with, the consignor resumes his right of disposition.

Article 13

1. Except in the circumstances set out in the preceding Article, the consignee is entitled, on arrival of the goods at the place of destination, to require the carrier to hand over to him the air consignment note and to deliver the goods to him, on payment of the charges due and on complying with the conditions of carriage set out in the air consignment note.
2. Unless it is otherwise agreed, it is the duty of the carrier to give notice to the consignee as soon as the goods arrive.
3. If the carrier admits the loss of the goods have not arrived at the expiration of seven days after date on which they ought to have arrived, the consignee is entitled to put into force against the carrier the rights which flow from the contract of carriage.

Article 14

The consignor and the consignee can respectively enforce all the rights given them by Articles 12 and 13, each in his own name, whether he is acting in his own interest or in the interest of another, provided that he carries out the obligations imposed by the contract.

Article 15

1. Articles 12, 13 and 14 do not affect either the relations of the consignor or the consignee with each other or the mutual relations of third parties whose rights are derived either from the consignor or from the consignee.

2. The provisions of Articles 12, 13 and 14 can only be varied by express provision in the air consignment note.

Article 16

1. The consignor must furnish such information and attach to the air consignment note such documents as are necessary to meet the formalities of customs, octroi or police before the goods can be delivered to the consignee. The consignor is liable to the carrier for any damage occasioned by the absence, insufficiency or irregularity of any such information or documents, unless the damage is due to the fault of the carrier or his agents.
2. The carrier is under no obligation to enquire into the correctness or sufficiency of such information or deed.

Chapter III Liability of the carrier

Article 17

The carrier is liable for damage sustained in the event of the death or wounding of a passenger or any other bodily injury suffered by a passenger, if the accident which caused the damage so sustained took place on board the aircraft or in the course of any of the operations of embarking or disembarking.

Article 18

1. The carrier is liable for damage sustained in the event of the destruction or loss of, or of damage to, any registered luggage or any goods, if the occurrence which caused the damage so sustained took place during the carriage by air.
2. The carriage by air within the meaning for the preceding paragraph comprises the period during which the luggage or goods are in charge of the carrier, whether in an aerodrome or on board an aircraft, or, in the case of a landing outside an aerodrome, in any place whatsoever.
3. The period of the carriage by air does not extend to any carriage by land, by sea or by river performed outside an aerodrome. If, however, such a carriage takes place in the performance of a contract for carriage by air, for the purpose of loading, delivery or trans-shipment, any damage is presumed, subject to proof to the contrary, to have been the result of an event which took place during the carriage by air.

Article 19

The carrier is liable for damage occasioned by delay in the carriage by air of passengers, luggage or goods.

Article 20

1. The carrier is not liable if he proves that he and his agents have taken all necessary measures to avoid the damage or that it was impossible for him or them to take such measures.

2. In the carriage of goods and luggage the carrier is not liable if he proves that the damage was occasioned by negligent pilotage or negligence in the handling of the aircraft or in navigation and that, in all other respects, he and his agents have taken all necessary measures to avoid the damage.

Article 21

If the carrier proves that the damage was caused by or contributed to by the negligence of the injured person the court may, in accordance with the provisions of its own law, exonerate the carrier wholly or partly from his liability.

Article 22

1. In the carriage of passengers the liability of the carrier for each passenger is limited to the sum of 125,000 francs. Where, in accordance with the law of the Court seised of the case, damages may be awarded in the form of periodical payments, the equivalent capital value of the said payment shall not exceed 125,000 francs. Nevertheless, by special contract, the carrier and the passenger may agree to a higher limit of liability.
2. In the carriage of registered luggage and of goods, the liability of the carrier is limited to a sum of 250 francs per kilogram, unless the consignor has made, at the time when the package was handed over to the carrier, a special declaration of the value at delivery and has paid a supplementary sum if the case so requires. In that case the carrier will be liable to pay a sum not exceeding the declared sum, unless he proves that the sum is greater than the actual value to the consignor at delivery.
3. As regards objects of which the passenger takes charge himself the liability of the carrier is limited to 5,000 francs per passenger.
4. The sums mentioned above shall be deemed to refer to the French franc consisting of 65½ milligrams gold of millesimal fineness 900. These sums may be converted into any national currency in round figures.

Article 23

Any provision tending to relieve the carrier of liability or to fix a lower limit than that which is laid down in this convention shall be null and void, but the nullity of any such provision does not involve the nullity of the whole contract, which shall remain subject to the provisions of this Convention.

Article 24

1. In the cases covered by Articles 18 and 19 any action for damages, however founded, can only be brought subject to the conditions and limits set out in this Convention.
2. In the cases covered by Article 17 the provisions of the preceding paragraph also apply, without prejudice to the questions as to who are the persons who have the right to bring suit and what are their respective rights.

Article 25

1. The carrier shall not be entitled to avail himself of the provisions of this Convention which exclude or limit his liability, if the damage is caused by his wilful misconduct or by such default on his part as, in accordance with the law of the Court seised of the case, is considered to be equivalent to wilful misconduct.
2. Similarly the carrier shall not be entitled to avail himself of the said provisions, if the damage is caused as aforesaid by any agent of the carrier acting within the scope of his employment.

Article 26

1. Receipt by the person entitled to delivery of luggage or goods without complaint is *prima facie* evidence that the same have been delivered in good condition and in accordance with the document of carriage.
2. In the case of damage, the person entitled to delivery must complain to the carrier forthwith after the discovery of the damage, and, at the latest, within three days from the date of receipt in the case of luggage and seven days from the date of receipt in the case of goods. In the case of delay the complaint must be made at the latest within fourteen days from the date on which the luggage or goods have been placed at his disposal.
3. Every complaint must be made in writing upon the document of carriage or by separate notice in writing despatched within the times aforesaid.
4. Failing complaint within the times aforesaid, no action shall lie against the carrier, save in the case of fraud on his part.

Article 27

In the case of the death of the person liable, an action for damages lies in accordance with the terms of this Convention against those legally representing his estate.

Article 28

1. An action for damages must be brought, at the option of the plaintiff, in the territory of one of the High Contracting Parties, either before the Court having jurisdiction where the carrier is ordinarily resident, or has his principal place of business, or has an establishment by which the contract has been made or before the Court having jurisdiction at the place of destination.
2. Questions of procedure shall be governed by the law of the Court seised of the case.

Article 29

1. The right to damages shall be extinguished if an action is not brought within two years, reckoned from the date of arrival at the destination, or from the date on which the aircraft ought to have arrived, or from the date on which the carriage stopped.
2. The method of calculating the period of limitation shall be determined by the law of the Court seised of the case.

Article 30

1. In the case of carriage to be performed by various successive carriers and falling within the definition set out in the third paragraph of Article I, each carrier who accepts passengers, luggage or goods is subjected to the rules set out in this Convention, and is deemed to be one of the contracting parties to the contract of carriage in so far as the contract deals with that part of the carriage which is performed under his supervision.
2. In the case of carriage of this nature, the passenger or his representative can take action only against the carrier who performed the carriage during which the accident or the delay occurred, save in the case where, by express agreement, the first carrier has assumed liability for the whole journey.
3. As regards luggage or goods, the passenger or consignor will have a right of action against the first carrier, and the passenger or consignee who is entitled to delivery will have a right of action against the last carrier, and further, each may take action against the carrier who performed the carriage during which the destruction, loss, damage or delay took place. These carriers will be jointly and severally liable to the passenger or to the consignor or consignee.

Chapter IV Provisions to combined carriage

Article 31

1. In the case of combined carriage performed partly by air and partly by any other mode of carriage, the provisions of the Convention apply only to the carriage by air, provided that the carriage by air falls within the terms of Article 1.
2. Nothing in this Convention shall prevent the parties in the case of combined carriage from inserting in the document of air carriage conditions relating to other modes of carriage, provided that the provisions of this Convention are observed as regards the carriage by air.

Chapter V General and final provisions

Article 32

Any clause contained in the contract and all special agreements entered into before the damage occurred by which the parties purport to infringe the rules laid down by this Convention, whether by deciding the law to be applied, or by altering the rules as to jurisdiction, shall be null and void. Nevertheless for the carriage of goods arbitration clauses are allowed, subject to this Convention, if the arbitration is to take place within one of the jurisdictions referred to in the first paragraph of Article 28.

Article 33

Nothing contained in this Convention shall prevent the carrier either from refusing to enter into any contract of carriage, or from making regulations which do not conflict with the provisions of this Convention.

Article 34

This Convention does not apply to international carriage by air performed by way of experimental trial by air navigation undertakings with the view to the establishment of a regular line of air navigation, nor does it apply to carriage performed in extraordinary circumstances outside the normal scope of an air carrier's business.

Article 35

The expression 'days' when used in this Convention means current days not working days.

Articles 36–41 [Omitted]

Convention Providing a Uniform Law for Bills of Exchange and Promissory Notes, Geneva, 1930

Articles I–XI [Omitted]

Annex I Uniform law on bills of exchange and promissory notes

Title I Bills of exchange

Chapter I Issue and form of a bill of exchange

Article 1

A bill of exchange contains –

1. the term 'bill of exchange' inserted in the body of the instrument and expressed in the language employed in drawing up the instrument;
2. an unconditional order to pay a determinate sum of money;
3. the name of the person who is to pay (drawee);
4. a statement of the time of payment;
5. a statement of the place where payment is to be made;
6. the name of the person to whom or to whose order payment is to be made;
7. a statement of the date and of the place where the bill is issued;
8. the signature of the person who issues the bill (drawer).

Article 2

An instrument in which any of the requirements mentioned in the preceding Article is wanting is invalid as a bill of exchange, except in the cases specified in the following paragraphs –

A bill of exchange in which the time of payment is not specified is deemed to be payable at sight.

In default of special mention, the place specified beside the name of the drawee is deemed to be the place of payment, and at the same time the place of the domicile of the drawee.

A bill of exchange which does not mention the place of its issue is deemed to have been drawn in the place mentioned beside the name of the drawer.

Article 3

A bill of exchange may be drawn payable to drawer's order.
It may be drawn on the drawer himself.
It may be drawn for account of a third person.

Article 4

A bill of exchange may be payable at the domicile of a third person either in the locality where the drawee has his domicile or in another locality.

Article 5

When a bill of exchange is payable at sight, or at a fixed period after sight, the drawer may stipulate that the sum payable shall bear interest. In the case of any other bill of exchange, this stipulation is deemed not to be written *(non écrite)*.

The rate of interest must be specified in the bill; in default of such specification, the stipulation shall be deemed not to be written *(non écrite)*.

Interest runs from the date of the bill of exchange, unless some other date is specified.

Article 6

When the sum payable by a bill of exchange is expressed in words and also in figures, and there is a discrepancy between the two, the sum denoted by the words is the amount payable. Where the sum payable by a bill of exchange is expressed more than once in words or more than once in figures, and there is a discrepancy, the smaller sum is the sum payable.

Article 7

If a bill of exchange bears signatures of persons incapable of binding themselves by a bill of exchange, or forged signatures, or signatures of fictitious persons, or signatures which for any other reason cannot bind the persons who signed the bill of exchange or on whose behalf it was signed, the obligations of the other persons who signed it are none the less valid.

Article 8

Whosoever puts his signature on a bill of exchange as representing a person for whom he had no power to act is bound himself as a party to the bill and, if he pays, has the same rights as the person for whom he purported to act. The same rule applies to a representative who has exceeded his powers.

Article 9

The drawer guarantees both acceptance and payment.

He may release himself from guaranteeing acceptance; every stipulation by which he releases himself from the guarantee of payment is deemed not to be written *(non écrite)*.

Article 10

If a bill of exchange, which was incomplete when issued, has been completed otherwise than in accordance with the agreements entered into, the non-observance of such agreements may not be set up against the holder unless he has acquired the bill of exchange in bad faith or, in acquiring it, has been guilty of gross negligence.

Chapter II Endorsement

Article 11

Every bill of exchange, even if not expressly drawn to order, may be transferred by means of endorsement.

When the drawer has inserted in a bill of exchange the words 'not to order' or an equivalent expression, the instrument can only be transferred according to the form, and with the effects of an ordinary assignment.

The bill may be endorsed even in favour of the drawee, whether he has accepted or not, or of the drawer, or of any other party to the bill. These persons may re-endorse the bill.

Article 12

An endorsement must be unconditional. Any condition to which it is made subject is deemed not to be written *(non écrite)*.

A partial endorsement is null and void.

An endorsement 'to bearer' is equivalent to an endorsement in blank.

Article 13

An endorsement must be written on the bill of exchange or on a slip affixed thereto *(allonge)*. It must be signed by the endorser.

The endorsement may leave the beneficiary unspecified or may consist simply of the signature of the endorser (endorsement in blank). In the latter case, the endorsement, to be valid, must be written on the back of the bill of exchange or on the slip attached thereto *(allonge)*.

Article 14

An endorsement transfers all the rights arising out of a bill of exchange.

If the endorsement is in blank, the holder may –

1. fill up the blank either with his own name or with the name of some other person;
2. re-endorse the bill in blank, or to some other person;
3. transfer the bill to a third person without filling up the blank, and without endorsing it.

Article 15

In the absence of any contrary stipulation, the endorser guarantees acceptance and payment. He may prohibit any further endorsement; in this case, he gives no guarantee to the persons to whom the bill is subsequently endorsed.

Article 16

The possessor of a bill of exchange is deemed to be the lawful holder if he establishes his title to the bill through an uninterrupted series of endorsements, even if the last endorsement is in blank. In this connection, cancelled endorsements are deemed not to be written *(non écrits)*. When an endorsement in blank is followed by another endorsement, the person who signed this last endorsement is deemed to have acquired the bill by the endorsement in blank.

Where a person has been dispossessed of a bill of exchange, in any manner whatsoever, the holder who establishes his right thereto in the manner mentioned in the preceding paragraph is not bound to give up the bill unless he has acquired it in bad faith, or unless in acquiring it he has been guilty of gross negligence.

Article 17

Persons sued on a bill of exchange cannot set up against the holder defences founded on their personal relations with the drawer or with previous holders, unless the holder, in acquiring the bill, has knowingly acted to the detriment of the debtor.

Article 18

When an endorsement contains the statements 'value in collection' *('valeur en recouvrement')*, 'for collection' *('pour encaissement')*, 'by procuration' *('par procuration')* or any other phrase implying a simple mandate, the holder may exercise all rights arising out of the bill of exchange, but he can only endorse it in his capacity as agent. In this case, the parties liable can only set up against the holder defences which could be set up against the endorser.

The mandate contained in an endorsement by procuration does not terminate by reason of the death of the party giving the mandate or by reason of his becoming legally incapable.

Article 19

When an endorsement contains the statements 'value in security' *('valeur en garantie')*, 'value in pledge' *('valetur en gage')*, or any other statement implying a pledge, the holder may exercise all the rights arising out of the bill of exchange, but an endorsement by him has the effects only of an endorsement by an agent.

The parties liable cannot set up against the holder defences founded on their personal relations with the endorser, unless the holder, in receiving the bill, has knowingly acted to the detriment of the debtor.

Article 20

An endorsement after maturity has the same effects as an endorsement before maturity. Nevertheless, an endorsement after protest for non-payment, or after the expiration of the limit of time fixed for drawing up the protest, operates only as an ordinary assignment.

Failing proof to the contrary, an endorsement without date is deemed to have been placed on the bill before the expiration of the limit of time fixed for drawing up the protest.

Chapter III Acceptance

Article 21

Until maturity, a bill of exchange may be presented to the drawee for acceptance at his domicile, either by the holder or by a person who is merely in possession of the bill.

Article 22

In any bill of exchange, the drawer may stipulate that it shall be presented for acceptance with or without fixing a limit of time for presentment.

Except in the case of a bill payable at the address of a third party or in a locality other than that of the domicile of the drawee, or, except in the case of a bill drawn payable at a fixed period after sight, the drawer may prohibit presentment for acceptance.

He may also stipulate that presentment for acceptance shall not take place before a named date.

Unless the drawer has prohibited acceptance, every endorser may stipulate that the bill shall be presented for acceptance, with or without fixing a limit of time for presentment.

Article 23

Bills of exchange payable at a fixed period after sight must be presented for acceptance within one year of their date. The drawer may abridge or extend this period. These periods may be abridged by the endorsers.

Article 24

The drawee may demand that a bill shall be presented to him a second time on the day after the first presentment. Parties interested are not allowed to set up that this demand has not been complied with unless this request is mentioned in the protest.

The holder is not obliged to surrender to the drawee a bill presented for acceptance.

Article 25

An acceptance is written on the bill of exchange. It is expressed by the word 'accepted' or any other equivalent term. It is signed by the drawee. The simple signature of the drawee on the face of the bill constitutes an acceptance.

When the bill is payable at a certain time after sight, or when it must be presented for acceptance within a certain limit of time in accordance with a special stipulation, the acceptance must be dated as of the day when the acceptance is given, unless the holder requires it shall be dated as of the day of presentment. If it is undated, the holder, in order to preserve his right of recourse against the endorsers and the drawer, must authenticate the omission by a protest drawn up within the proper time.

Article 26

An acceptance is unconditional, but the drawee may restrict it to part of the sum payable.

Every other modification introduced by an acceptance into the tenor of the bill of exchange operates as a refusal to accept. Nevertheless, the acceptor is bound according to the terms of his acceptance.

Article 27

When the drawer of a bill has indicated a place of payment other than the domicile of the drawee without specifying a third party at whose address payment must be made, the drawee may name such third party at the time of acceptance. In default of this indication, the acceptor is deemed to have undertaken to pay the bill himself at the place of payment.

If a bill is payable at the domicile of the drawee, the latter may in his acceptance indicate an address in the same place where payment is to be made.

Article 28

By accepting, the drawee undertakes to pay the bill of exchange at its maturity.

In default of payment, the holder, even if he is the drawer, has a direct action on the bill of exchange against the acceptor for all that can be demanded in accordance with Articles 48 and 49.

Article 29

Where the drawee who has put his acceptance on a bill has cancelled it before restoring the bill, acceptance is deemed to be refused. Failing proof to the contrary, the cancellation is deemed to have taken place before the bill was restored.

Nevertheless, if the drawee has notified his acceptance in writing to the holder or to any party who has signed the bill, he is liable to such parties according to the terms of his acceptance.

Chapter IV 'Avals'

Article 30

Payment of a bill of exchange may be guaranteed by an '*aval*' as to the whole or part of its amount.

This guarantee may be given by a third person or even by a person who has signed as a party to the bill.

Article 31

The '*aval*' is given either on the bill itself or on an '*allonge*'.

It is expressed by the words 'good as *aval*' ('*bon pour aval*') or by any other equivalent formula. It is signed by the giver of the '*aval*'.

It is deemed to be constituted by the mere signature of the giver of the '*aval*' placed on the face of the bill, except in the case of the signature of the drawee or of the drawer.

An '*aval*' must specify for whose account it is given. In default of this it is deemed to be given for the drawer.

Article 32

The giver of an '*aval*' is bound in the same manner as the person for whom he has become guarantor.

His undertaking is valid even when the liability which he has guaranteed is inoperative for any reason other than defect of form.

He has, when he pays a bill of exchange, the rights arising out of the bill of exchange against the person guaranteed and against those who are liable to the latter on the bill of exchange.

Chapter V Maturity

Article 33

A bill of exchange may be drawn payable –

at sight;
at a fixed period after sight;
at a fixed period after date;
at a fixed date.

Bills of exchange at other maturities or payable by instalments are null and void.

Article 34

A bill of exchange at sight is payable on presentment. It must be presented for payment within a year of its date. The drawer may abridge or extend this period. These periods may be abridged by the endorsers.

The drawer may prescribe that a bill of exchange payable at sight must not be presented for payment before a named date. In this case, the period for presentation begins from the said date.

Article 35

The maturity of a bill of exchange payable at a fixed period after sight is determined either by the date of the acceptance or by the date of the protest.

In the absence of the protest, an undated acceptance is deemed, so far as regards the acceptor, to have been given on the last day of the limit of time for presentment for acceptance.

Article 36

Where a bill of exchange is drawn at one or more months after date or after sight, the bill matures on the corresponding date of the month when payment must be made. If there be no corresponding date, the bill matures on the last day of this month.

When a bill of exchange is drawn at one or more months and a-half after date or sight, entire months must first be calculated.

If the maturity is fixed at the commencement, in the middle (mid-January or mid-February, etc.) or at the end of the month, the first, fifteenth or last day of the month is to be understood.

The expressions '*eight days*' or '*fifteen days*' indicate not one or two weeks, but a period of eight or fifteen actual days.

The expression '*half-month*' means a period of fifteen days.

Article 37

When a bill of exchange is payable on a fixed day in a place where the calendar is different from the calendar in the place of issue, the day of maturity is deemed to be fixed according to the calendar of the place of payment.

When a bill of exchange drawn between two places having different calendars is payable at a fixed period after date, the day of issue is referred to the corresponding day of the calendar in the place of payment, and the maturity is fixed accordingly.

The time for presenting bills of exchange is calculated in accordance with the rules of the preceding paragraph.

These rules do not apply if a stipulation in the bill or even the simple terms of the instrument indicate an intention to adopt some different rule.

Chapter VI Payment

Article 38

The holder of a bill of exchange payable on a fixed day or at a fixed period after date or after sight must present the bill for payment either on the day on which it is payable or on one of the two business days which follow.

The presentment of a bill of exchange at a clearing-house is equivalent to a presentment for payment.

Article 39

The drawee who pays a bill of exchange may require that it shall be given up to him receipted by the holder.

The holder may not refuse partial payment.

In case of partial payment the drawee may require that mention of this payment shall be made on the bill, and that a receipt therefor shall be given to him.

Article 40

The holder of a bill of exchange cannot be compelled to receive a payment thereof before maturity.

The drawee who pays before maturity does so at his own risk and peril. He who pays at maturity is validly discharged, unless he has been guilty of fraud or gross negligence. He is bound to verify the regularity of the series of endorsements, but not the signature of the endorsers.

Article 41

When a bill of exchange is drawn payable in a currency which is not that of the place of payment, the sum payable may be paid in the currency of the country, according to its value on the date of maturity. If the debtor is in default, the holder may at his option demand that the amount of the bill be paid in the currency of the country according to the rate on the day of maturity or the day of payment.

The usages of the place of payment determine the value of foreign currency. Nevertheless, the drawer may stipulate that the sum payable shall be calculated according to a rate expressed in the bill.

The foregoing rules shall not apply to the case in which the drawer has stipulated that payment must be made in a certain specified currency (stipulation for effective payment in foreign currency).

If the amount of the bill of exchange is specified in a currency having the same denomination, but a different value in the country of issue and the country of payment, reference is deemed to be made to the currency of the place of payment.

Article 42

When a bill of exchange is not presented for payment within the limit of time fixed by Article 38, every debtor is authorised to deposit the amount with the competent authority at the charge, risk and peril of the holder.

Chapter VII Recourse for non-acceptance or non-payment

Article 43

The holder may exercise his right of recourse against the endorsers, the drawer and the other parties liable –

At maturity:
If payment has not been made;
Even before maturity:

1. if there has been total or partial refusal to accept;

2. in the event of the bankruptcy (*faillite*) of the drawee, whether he has accepted or not, or in the event of a stoppage of payment on his part, even when not declared by a judgment, or where execution has been levied against his goods without result;
3. in the event of the bankruptcy (*faillite*) of the drawer of a non-acceptable bill.

Article 44

Default of acceptance or on payment must be evidenced by an authentic act (protest for non-acceptance or non-payment).

Protest for non-acceptance must be made within the limit of time fixed for presentment for acceptance. If in the case contemplated by Article 24, paragraph I, the first presentment takes place on the last day of that time, the protest may nevertheless be drawn up on the next day.

Protest for non-payment of a bill of exchange payable on a fixed day or at a fixed period after date or sight must be made on one of the two business days following the day on which the bill is payable. In the case of a bill payable at sight, the protest must be drawn up under the conditions specified in the foregoing paragraph for the drawing up of a protest for non-acceptance.

Protest for non-acceptance dispenses with presentment for payment and protest for non-payment.

If there is a stoppage of payment on the part of the drawee, whether he has accepted or not, or if execution has been levied against his goods without result, the holder cannot exercise his right of recourse until after presentment of the bill to the drawee for payment and after the protest has been drawn up.

If the drawee, whether he accepted or not, is declared bankrupt (*faillite déclarée*), or in the event of the declared bankruptcy of the drawer of a non-acceptable bill, the production of the judgment declaring the bankruptcy suffices to enable the holder to exercise his right of recourse.

Article 45

The holder must give notice of non-acceptance or non-payment to his endorser and to the drawer within the four business days which follow the day for protest or, in case of a stipulation 'retour sans *frais*', the day for presentment. Every endorser must, within the two business days following the day on which he receives notice, notify his endorser of the notice he has received, mentioning the names and addresses of those who have given the previous notices, and so on through the series until the drawer is reached. The periods mentioned above run from the receipt of the preceding notice.

When, in conformity with the preceding paragraph, notice is given to a person who has signed a bill of exchange, the same notice must be given within the same limit of time to his *avaliseur*.

Where an endorser either has not specified his address or has specified it in an illegible manner, it is sufficient that notice should be given to the preceding endorser.

A person who must give notice may give it in any form whatever, even by simply returning the bill of exchange.

He must prove that he has given notice within the time allowed, this time-limit shall be regarded as having been observed if a letter giving the notice has been posted within the prescribed time.

A person who does not give notice within the limit of time mentioned above does not forfeit his rights. He is responsible for the injury, if any, caused by his negligence, but the damages shall not exceed the amount of the bill of exchange.

Article 46

The drawer, an endorser, or a person guaranteeing payment by *aval* (*avaliseur*) may, by the stipulation '*retour sans frais*', '*sans protet*', or any other equivalent expression written on the instrument and signed, release the holder from having a protest of non-acceptance or non-payment drawn up in order to exercise his right of recourse.

This stipulation does not release the holder from presenting the bill within the prescribed time, or from the notices he has to give. The burden of proving the non-observance of the limits of time lies on the person who seeks to set it up against the holder.

If the stipulation is written by the drawer, it is operative in respect of all persons who have signed the bill; if it is written by an endorser or an *avaliseur*, it is operative only in respect of such endorser or *avaliseur*. If, in spite of the stipulation written by the drawer, the holder has the protest drawn up, he must bear the expenses thereof. When the stipulation emanates from an endorser or *avaliseur*, the costs of the protest, if one is drawn up, may be recovered from all the persons who have signed the bill.

Article 47

All drawers, acceptors, endorsers or guarantors by *aval* of a bill of exchange are jointly and severally liable to the holder.

The holder has the right of proceeding against all these persons individually or collectively without being required to observe the order in which they have become bound.

The same right is possessed by any person signing the bill who has taken it up and paid it.

Proceedings against one of the parties liable do not prevent proceedings against the others, even though they may be subsequent to the party first proceeded against.

Article 48

The holder may recover from the person against whom he exercises his right of recourse –

1. the amount of the unaccepted or unpaid bill of exchange with interest, if interest has been stipulated for;
2. interest at the rate of 6 per cent from the date of maturity;
3. the expenses of protest and of the notices given as well as other expenses

If the right of recourse is exercised before maturity, the amount of the bill shall be subject to a discount. This discount shall be calculated according to the official rate of discount (bank-rate) ruling on the date when recourse is exercised at the place of domicile of the holder.

Article 49

A party who takes up and pays a bill of exchange can recover from the parties liable to him –

1. the entire sum which he has paid;
2. interest on the said sum calculated at the rate of 6 per cent, starting from the day when he made payment;
3. any expenses which he has incurred.

Article 50

Every party liable against whom a right of recourse is or may be exercised can require against payment that the bill shall be given up to him with the protest and a receipted account.

Every endorser who has taken up and paid a bill of exchange may cancel his own endorsement and those of subsequent endorsers.

Article 51

In the case of the exercise of the right of recourse after a partial acceptance, the party who pays the sum in respect of which the bill has not been accepted can require that this payment shall be specified on the bill and that he shall be given a receipt therefor. The holder must also give him a certified copy of the bill, together with the protest, in order to enable subsequent recourse to be exercised.

Article 52

Every person having the right of recourse may, in the absence of agreement to the contrary, reimburse himself by means of a fresh bill (redraft) to be drawn at sight on one of the parties liable to him and payable at the domicile of that party.

The redraft includes, in addition to the sums mentioned in Articles 48 and 49, brokerage and the cost of stamping the redraft.

If the redraft is drawn by the holder, the sum payable is fixed according to the rate for a sight bill drawn at the place where the original bill was payable upon the party liable at the place of his domicile. If the redraft is drawn by an endorser, the sum payable is fixed according to the rate for a sight bill drawn at the place where the drawer of the redraft is domiciled upon the place of domicile of the party liable.

Article 53

After the expiration of the limits of time fixed –

for the presentment of a bill of exchange drawn at sight or at a fixed period after sight;
for drawing up the protest for non-acceptance or non-payment;
for presentment for payment in the case of a stipulation *retour sans frais*, the holder loses his rights of recourse against the endorsers, against the drawer and against the other parties liable, with the exception of the acceptor.

In default of presentment for acceptance within the limit of time stipulated by the drawer, the holder loses his right of recourse for non-payment, as well as for non-acceptance, unless it appears from the terms of the stipulation that the drawer only meant to release himself from the guarantee of acceptance.

If the stipulation for a limit of time for presentment is contained in an endorsement, the endorser alone can avail himself of it.

Article 54

Should the presentment of the bill of exchange or the drawing up of the protest within the prescribed limits of time be prevented by an insurmountable obstacle (legal prohibition (*prescription légate*) by any State or other case of vis major), these limits of time shall be extended. The holder is bound to give notice without delay of the case of vis major to his endorser and to specify this notice, which he must date and sign, on the bill or on an *allonge*; in other respects the provisions of Article 45 shall apply.

When vis major has terminated, the holder must without delay present the bill of exchange for acceptance or payment and, if need be, draw up the protest.

If vis major continues to operate beyond thirty days after maturity, recourse may be exercised, and neither presentment nor the drawing up of a protest shall be necessary.

In the case of bills of exchange drawn at sight or at a fixed period after sight, the time-limit of thirty days shall run from the date on which the holder, even before the expiration of the time for presentment, has given notice of vis major to his endorser. In the case of bill of exchange drawn at a certain time after sight, the above time-limit of thirty days shall be added to the period after sight specified in the bill of exchange.

Facts which are purely personal to the holder or to the person whom he has entrusted with the presentment of the bill or drawing up of the bill or drawing up of the protest are not deemed to constitute cases of vis major.

Chapter VIII Intervention for honour

1. General provisions

Article 55

The drawer, an endorser, or a person giving an *aval* may specify a person who is to accept or pay in case of need.

A bill of exchange may, subject as hereinafter mentioned, be accepted or paid by a person who intervenes for the honour of any debtor against whom a right of recourse exists.

The person intervening may be a third party, even the drawee, or, save the acceptor, a party already liable on the bill of exchange.

The person intervening is bound to give, within two business days, notice of his intervention to the party for whose honour he has intervened. In default, he is responsible for the injury, if any, due to his negligence, but the damages shall not exceed the amount of the bill of exchange.

2. Acceptance by intervention (for honour)

Article 56

There may be acceptance by intervention in all cases where the holder has a right of recourse before maturity on a bill which is capable of acceptance.

When the bill of exchange indicates a person who is designated to accept or pay it in case of need at the place of payment, the holder may not exercise his rights of recourse before maturity against the person naming such referee in case of need and against subsequent signatories, unless he has presented the bill of exchange to the referee in case of need and until, if acceptance is refused by the latter, this refusal has been authenticated by a protest.

In other cases of intervention the holder may refuse an acceptance by intervention. Nevertheless, if he allows it, he loses his right of recourse before maturity against the person on whose behalf such acceptance was given and against subsequent signatories.

Article 57

Acceptance by intervention is specified on the bill of exchange. It is signed by the person intervening. It mentions the person for whose honour it has been given and, in default of such mention, the acceptance is deemed to have been given for the honour of the drawer.

Article 58

The acceptor by intervention is liable to the holder and to the endorsers, subsequent to the party for whose honour he intervened, in the same manner as such party.

Notwithstanding an acceptance by intervention, the party for whose honour it has been given and the parties liable to him may require the holder, in exchange for payment of the sum mentioned in Article 48, to deliver the bill, the protest, and a receipted account, if any.

3. Payment by intervention

Article 59

Payment by intervention may take place in all cases where, either at maturity or before maturity, the holder has a right of recourse on the bill.

Payment must include the whole amount payable by the party for whose honour it is made.

It must be made at the latest on the day following the last day allowed for drawing up the protest for non-payment.

Article 60

If a bill of exchange has been accepted by persons intervening who are domiciled in the place of payment, or if persons domiciled therein have been named as referees in case of need, the holder must present the bill to all these persons and, if necessary, have a protest for non-payment drawn up at latest on the day following the last day allowed for drawing up the protest.

In default of protest within this limit of time, the party who has named the referee in case of need, or for whose account the bill has been accepted, and the subsequent endorsers are discharged.

Article 61

The holder who refuses payment by intervention loses his right of recourse against any persons who would have been discharged thereby.

Article 62

Payment by intervention must be authenticated by a receipt given on the bill of exchange mentioning the person for whose honour payment has been made. In default of such mention, payment is deemed to have been made for the honour of the drawer.

The bill of exchange and the protest, if any, must be given up to the person paying by intervention.

Article 63

The person paying by intervention acquires the rights arising out of the bill of exchange against the party for whose honour he has paid and against persons who are liable to the latter on the bill of exchange. Nevertheless, he cannot re-endorse the bill of exchange.

Endorsers subsequent to the party for whose honour payment has been made are discharged.

In case of competition for payment by intervention, the payment which effects the greater number of releases has the preference. Any person who, with a knowledge of the facts, intervenes in a manner contrary to this rule, loses his right of recourse against those who would have been discharged.

Chapter IX Parts of a set, and copies

1. Parts of a set

Article 64

A bill of exchange can be drawn in a set of two or more identical parts.

These parts must be numbered in the body of the instrument itself; in default, each part is considered as a separate bill of exchange.

Every holder of a bill which does not specify that it has been drawn as a sole bill may, at his own expense, require the delivery of two or more parts. For this purpose he must apply to his immediate endorser, who is bound to assist him in proceeding against his own endorser, and so on in the series until the drawer is reached. The endorsers are bound to reproduce their endorsements on the new parts of the set.

Article 65

Payment made on one part of a set operates as a discharge, even though there is no stipulation that this payment annuls the effect on the other parts. Nevertheless, the drawee is liable on each accepted part which he has not recovered.

An endorser who has transferred parts of a set to different persons, as well as subsequent endorsers, are liable on all the parts bearing their signature which have not been restored.

Article 66

A party who has sent one part for acceptance must indicate on the other parts the name of the person in whose hands this part is to be found. That person is bound to give it up to the lawful holder of another part.

If he refuses, the holder cannot exercise his right of recourse until he has had a protest drawn up specifying –

1. that the part sent for acceptance has not been given up to him on his demand;
2. that acceptance or payment could not be obtained on another of the parts.

2. Copies

Article 67

Every holder of a bill of exchange has the right to make copies of it. A copy must reproduce the original exactly, with the endorsements and all other statements to be found therein. It must specify where the copy ends. It may be endorsed and guaranteed by *aval* in the same manner and with the same effects as the original.

Article 68

A copy must specify the person in possession of the original instrument. The latter is bound to hand over the said instrument to the lawful holder of the copy.

If he refuses, the holder may not exercise his right of recourse against the persons who have endorsed the copy or guaranteed it by *aval* until he has had a protest drawn up specifying that the original has not been given up to him on his demand.

Where the original instrument, after the last endorsement before the making of the copy contains a clause 'commencing from here an endorsement is only valid if made on the copy' or some equivalent formula, a subsequent endorsement on the original is null and void.

Chapter X Alterations

Article 69

In case of alteration of the text of a bill of exchange, parties who have signed subsequent to the alteration are bound according to the terms of the altered text; parties who have signed before the alteration are bound according to the terms of the original text.

Chapter XI Limitation of actions

Article 70

All actions arising out of a bill of exchange against the acceptor are barred after three years, reckoned from the date of maturity.

Actions by the holder against the endorsers and against the drawer are barred after one year from the date of a protest drawn up within proper time, or from the date of maturity where there is a stipulation *retour sans frais*.

Actions by endorsers against each other and against the drawer are barred after six months, reckoned from the day when the endorser took up and paid the bill or from the day when he himself was sued.

Article 71

Interruption of the period of limitation is only effective against the person in respect of whom the period has been interrupted.

Chapter XII General provisions

Article 72

Payment of a bill of exchange which falls due on a legal holiday (jour férié legal) cannot be demanded until the next business day. So, too, all other proceedings relating to a bill of exchange, in particular presentment for acceptance and protest, can only be taken on a business day.

Where any of these proceedings must be taken within a certain limit of time the last day of which is a legal holiday (jour férié legal), the limit of time is extended until the first business day which follows the expiration of that time. Intermediate holidays (jours fériés) are included in computing limits of time.

Article 73

Legal or contractual limits of time do not include the day on which the period commences.

Article 74

No days of grace, whether legal or judicial, are permitted.

Title II Promissory notes

Article 75

A promissory note contains –

1. the term 'promissory note' inserted in the body of the instrument and expressed in the language employed in drawing up the instrument;
2. an unconditional promise to pay a determinate sum of money;
3. a statement of the time of payment;
4. a statement of the place where payment is to be made;
5. the name of the person to whom or to whose order payment is to be made;
6. a statement of the date and of the place where the promissory note is issued;
7. the signature of the person who issues the instrument (maker).

Article 76

An instrument in which any of the requirements mentioned in the preceding Article are wanting is invalid as a promissory note except in the cases specified in the following paragraphs.

A promissory note in which the time of payment is not specified is deemed to be payable at sight.

In default of special mention, the place where the instrument is made is deemed to be the place of payment and at the same time the place of the domicile of the maker.

A promissory note which does not mention the place of its issue is deemed to have been made in the place mentioned beside the name of the maker.

Article 77

The following provisions relating to bills of exchange apply to promissory notes so far as they are not inconsistent with the nature of these instruments, viz –

endorsement (Article 11 to 20);
time of payment (Articles 33 to 37);
payment (Articles 38 to 42);
recourse in case of non-payment (Articles 43 to 50, 52 to 54);
payment by intervention (Articles 55, 59 to 63);
copies (Articles 67 and 68);
alterations (Article 69);
limitation of actions (Articles 70 and 71);
holidays, computation of limits of time and prohibition of days of grace (Articles 72, 73 and 74).

The following provisions are also applicable to a promissory note: The provisions concerning a bill of exchange payable at the address of a third party or in a locality other than that of the domicile of the drawee (Articles 4 and 27): stipulation for interest (Article 5); discrepancies as regards the sum payable (Article 6); the consequences of signature under the conditions mentioned in Article 7, the consequences of signature by a person who acts without authority or who exceeds his authority (Article 8); and provisions concerning a bill of exchange in blank (Article 10).

The following provisions are also applicable to a promissory note: Provisions relating to guarantee by *aval* (Articles 30–32); in the case provided for in Article 31, last paragraph, if the *aval* does not specify on whose behalf it has been given, it is deemed to have been given on behalf of the maker of the promissory note.

Article 78

The maker of a promissory note is bound in the same manner as an acceptor of a bill of exchange.

Promissory notes payable at a certain time after sight must be presented for the visa of the maker within the limits of time fixed by Article 23. The limit of time runs from the date of which marks the commencement of the period of time after sight.

Annex II

Articles 1–23 [Omitted]

Convention on the Law Applicable to International Sales of Goods, The Hague, 1955

Article 1

This Convention shall apply to international sales of goods.

It shall not apply to sales of securities, to sales of ships and of registered boats or aircraft, or to sales upon judicial order or by way of execution. It shall apply to sales based on documents.

For the purposes of this Convention, contracts to deliver goods to be manufactured or produced shall be placed on the same footing as sales, provided the party who assumes delivery is to furnish the necessary raw materials for their manufacture or production.

The mere declaration of the parties, relative to the application of a law or the competence of a judge or arbitrator, shall not be sufficient to confer upon a sale the international character provided for in the first paragraph of this Article.

Article 2

A sale shall be governed by the domestic law of the country designated by the Contracting Parties.

Such designation must be contained in an express clause, or unambiguously result from the provisions of the contract.

Conditions affecting the consent of the parties to the law declared applicable shall be determined by such law.

Article 3

In default of a law declared applicable by the parties under the conditions provided in the preceding Article, a sale shall be governed by the domestic law of the country in which the vendor has his habitual residence at the time when he receives the order. If the order is received by an establishment of the vendor, the sale shall be governed by the domestic law of the country in which the establishment is situated.

Nevertheless, a sale shall be governed by the domestic law of the country in which the purchaser has his habitual residence, or in which he has the establishment that has given the order, if the order has been received in such country, whether by the vendor or by his representative, agent or commercial traveller.

In case of a sale at an exchange or at a public auction, the sale shall be governed by the domestic law of the country in which the exchange is situated or the auction takes place.

Article 4

In the absence of an express clause to the contrary, the domestic law of the country in which inspection of goods delivered pursuant to a sale is to take place shall apply in respect of the form in which and the periods within which the inspection must take place, the notifications concerning the inspection and the measures to be taken in case of refusal of the goods.

Article 5

This Convention shall not apply to –

1. the capacity of the parties;
2. the form of the contract;
3. the transfer of ownership, provided that the various obligations of the parties, and especially those relating to risks, shall be subject to the law applicable to the sale pursuant to this Convention;
4. the effects of the sale as regards all persons other than the parties.

Article 6

In each of the Contracting States, the application of the law determined by this convention may be excluded on a ground of public policy.

Article 7

The Contracting States have agreed to incorporate the provisions of Articles 1–6 of this Convention in the national law of their respective countries.

Articles 8–12 [Omitted].

Hague Protocol to Amend the Convention for the Unification of Certain Rules Relating to International Carriage by Air Signed at Warsaw on 12 October 1929 (The Hague Protocol) 1955

Chapter 1 Amendments to the Convention

Article 1

In Article 1 of the Convention –

(a) paragraph (2) shall be deleted and replaced by the following:
   '(2) For the purposes of this convention, the expression international carriage means any carriage in which, according to the agreement between the parties, the place of departure and the place of destination, whether or not there be a break in the carriage or a transhipment, are situated either within the territories of two High Contracting Parties or within the territory of a single High Contracting Party if there is an agreed stopping place within the territory of another State, even if that State is not a High Contracting Party. Carriage between two points within the territory of a single High Contracting Party without an agreed stopping place within the territory of another State is not international carriage for the purposes of this Convention.'

(b) paragraph (3) shall be deleted and replaced by the following:

'(3) Carriage to be performed by several successive air carriers is deemed, for the purposes of this Convention, to be one undivided carriage if it has been regarded by the parties as a single operation, whether it has been agreed upon under the form of a single contract or of a series of contracts, and it does not lose its international character merely because one contract or a series of contracts is to be performed entirely within the territory of the same State.'

Article 2

In Article 2 of the Convention –

paragraph (2) shall be deleted and replaced by the following:

'(2) This Convention shall not apply to carriage of mail and postal packages.'

Article 3

In Article 3 of the Convention –

(a) paragraph (1) shall be deleted and replaced by the following:

'(1) In respect of the carriage of passengers a ticket shall be delivered containing –

(a) an indication of the places of departure and destination;

(b) if the places of departure and destination are within the territory of a single High Contracting Party, one or more agreed stopping places being within the territory of another State, an indication of at least one such stopping place;

(c) a notice to the effect that, if the passenger's journey involves an ultimate destination or stop in a country other than the country of departure, the Warsaw Convention may be applicable and that the Convention governs and in most cases limits the liability of carriers for death or personal injury and in respect of loss of or damage to baggage.'

(b) paragraph (2) shall be deleted and replaced by the following:

'(2) The passenger ticket shall constitute *prima facie* evidence of the conclusion and conditions of the contract of carriage. The absence, irregularity or loss of the passenger ticket does not affect the existence or the validity of the contract of carriage which shall, none the less, be subject to the rules of this Convention. Nevertheless, if, with the consent of the carrier, the passenger embarks without a passenger ticket having been delivered, or if the ticket does not include the notice required by paragraph (1) (c) of this Article, the carrier shall not be entitled to avail himself of the provisions of Article 22.'

Article 4

In Article 4 of the Convention –

(a) paragraphs (1), (2) and (3) shall be deleted and replaced by the following:

'(1) In respect of the carriage of registered baggage, a baggage check shall be delivered, which, unless combined with or incorporated in a passenger ticket which complies with the provisions of Article 3, paragraph (1), shall contain:

(a) an indication of the places of departure and destination;
(b) if the places of departure and destination are within the territory of a single High Contracting Party, one or more agreed stopping places being within the territory of another State, an indication of at least one such stopping place;
(c) a notice to the effect that, if the carriage involves an ultimate destination or stop in a country other than the country of departure, the Warsaw Convention may be applicable and that the Convention governs and in most cases limits the liability of carriers in respect of loss or damage to baggage.'

(b) paragraph (4) shall be deleted and replaced by the following:

'(2) The baggage check shall constitute *prima facie* evidence of the registration of the baggage and of the conditions of the contract of carriage. The absence, irregularity or loss of the baggage check does not affect the existence or the validity of the contract of carriage which shall, none the less, be subject to the rules of this Convention. Nevertheless, if the carrier takes charge of the baggage without a baggage check having been delivered or if the baggage check (unless combined with or incorporated in the passenger ticket which complies with the provisions of Article 3, paragraph (1)(c)) does not include the notice required by paragraph (1)(c) of this Article, he shall not be entitled to avail himself of the provisions of Article 22, paragraph (2).'

Article 5

In Article 6 of the Convention –

paragraph (3) shall be deleted and replaced by the following:

'(3) The carrier shall sign prior to the loading of the cargo on board the aircraft.'

Article 6

Article 8 of the Convention shall be deleted and replaced by the following –

'The air waybill shall contain:

(a) an indication of the places of departure and destination;
(b) if the places of departure and destination are within the territory of a single High Contracting Party, one or more agreed stopping places being within the territory of another State, an indication of at least one such stopping place;
(c) a notice to the consignor to the effect that, if the carriage involves an ultimate destination or stop in a country other than the country of departure, the Warsaw Convention may be applicable and that the Convention governs and in most cases limits the liability of carriers in respect of loss of or damage to cargo.'

Article 7

Article 9 of the Convention shall be deleted and replaced by the following –

'If, with the consent of the carrier, cargo is loaded on board the aircraft without an air waybill having been made out, or if the air waybill does not include the notice required by Article 8, paragraph (c), the carrier shall not be entitled to avail himself of the provisions of Article 22, paragraph (2).'

Article 8

In Article 10 of the Convention –
paragraph (2) shall be deleted and replaced by the following:
'(2) The consignor shall indemnify the carrier against all damage suffered by him, or by any other person to whom the carrier is liable, by reason of the irregularities, incorrectness or incompleteness of the particulars and statements furnished by the consignor.'

Article 9

To Article 15 of the Convention –
the following paragraph shall be added:
'(3) Nothing in this Convention prevents the issue of a negotiable air waybill.'

Article 10

Paragraph (2) of Article 20 of the Convention shall be deleted.

Article 11

Article 22 of the Convention shall be deleted and replaced by the following –

'(1) In the carriage of persons the liability of the carrier for each passenger is limited to the sum of two hundred and fifty thousand francs. Where, in accordance with the law of the court seised of the case, damages may be awarded in the form of periodical payments, the equivalent capital value of the said payments shall not exceed two hundred and fifty thousand francs. Nevertheless, by special contract, the carrier and the passenger may agree to a higher limit of liability.

(2) (a) In the carriage of registered baggage and of cargo, the liability of the carrier is limited to a sum of two hundred and fifty francs per kilogramme, unless the passenger or consignor has made, at the time when the package was handed over to the carrier, a special declaration of interest in delivery at destination and has paid a supplementary sum if the case so requires. In that case the carrier will be liable to pay a sum not exceeding the declared sum, unless he proves that that sum is greater than the passenger's or consignor's actual interest in delivery at destination.

(b) In the case of loss, damage or delay of part of registered baggage or cargo, or of any object contained therein, the weight to be taken into consideration in determining the amount to which the carrier's liability is limited shall be only the total weight of the package or packages concerned. Nevertheless, when the loss, damage or delay of a part of the registered baggage or cargo, or of an object contained therein, affects the value of other packages covered by the same baggage check or the same air waybill, the total weight of such package or packages shall also be taken into consideration in determining the limit of liability.

(3) As regards objects of which the passenger takes charge himself the liability of the carrier is limited to five thousand francs per passenger.
(4) The limits prescribed in this article shall not prevent the court from awarding, in accordance with its own law, in addition, the whole or part of the court costs and of the other expenses of the litigation incurred by the plaintiff. The foregoing provision shall not apply if the amount of the damages awarded, excluding court costs and other expenses of the litigation, does not exceed the sum which the carrier has offered in writing to the plaintiff within a period of six months from the date of the occurrence causing the damage, or before the commencement of the action, if that is later.
(5) The sums mentioned in francs in this Article shall be deemed to refer to a currency unit consisting of sixty-five and a half milligrammes of gold of millesimal fineness nine hundred. These sums may be converted into national currencies in round figures. Conversion of the sums into national currencies other than gold shall, in case of judicial proceedings, be made according to the gold value of such currencies at the date of the judgment.'

Article 12

In Article 23 of the Convention, the existing provision shall be renumbered as paragraph

(1) and another paragraph shall be added as follows –
'(2) Paragraph (1) of this Article shall not apply to provisions governing loss or damage resulting from the inherent defect, quality or vice of the cargo carried.'

Article 13

In Article 25 of the Convention –
paragraphs (1) and (2) shall be deleted and replaced by the following –

'The limits of liability specified in Article 22 shall not apply if it is proved that the damage resulted from an act or omission of the carrier, his servants or agents, done with intent to cause damage or recklessly and with knowledge that damage would probably result; provided that, in the case of such act or omission of a servant or agent, it is also proved that he was acting within the scope of his employment.'

Article 14

After Article 25 of the Convention, the following article shall be inserted –
'Article 25A

(1) If an action is brought against a servant or agent of the carrier arising out of damage to which this Convention relates, such servant or agent, if he proves that he acted within the scope of his employment, shall be entitled to avail himself of the limits of liability which that carrier himself is entitled to invoke under Article 22.
(2) The aggregate of the amounts recoverable from the carrier, his servants and agents, in that case, shall not exceed the said limits.
(3) The provisions of paragraphs (1) and (2) of this article shall not apply if it is proved that the damage resulted from an act or omission of the servant or agent done with intent to cause damage or recklessly and with knowledge that damage would probably result.'

Article 15

In Article 26 of the Convention –

paragraph (2) shall be deleted and replaced by the following:

'(2) In the case of damage, the person entitled to delivery must complain to the carrier forthwith after the discovery of the damage, and, at the latest, within seven days from the date of receipt in the case of baggage and fourteen days from the date of receipt in the case of cargo. In the case of delay the complaint must be made at the latest within twenty-one days from the date on which the baggage or cargo have been placed at his disposal.'

Article 16

Article 34 of the Convention shall be deleted and replaced by the following –

> 'The provisions of Articles 3 to 9 inclusive relating to documents of carriage shall not apply in the case of carriage performed in extraordinary circumstances outside the normal scope of an air carrier's business.'

Article 17

After Article 40 of the Convention the following Article shall be inserted –
'Article 40A

(1) In Article 37, paragraph (2) and Article 40, paragraph (1), the expression High Contracting Party shall mean State. In all other cases, the expression High Contracting Party shall mean a State whose ratification of or adherence to the Convention has become effective and whose denunciation thereof has not become effective.

(2) For the purposes of the Convention the word territory means not only the metropolitan territory of a State but also all other territories for the foreign relations of which that State is responsible.'

Chapter II Scope of application of the Convention as amended

Article 18

The Convention as amended by this Protocol shall apply to international carriage as defined in Article 1 of the Convention, provided that the places of departure and destination referred to in that Article are situated either in the territories of two parties to this Protocol or within the territory of a single party to this Protocol with an agreed stopping place within the territory of another State.

Chapter III Final clause

Articles 19–27 [Omitted]

Convention on the Contract for the International Carriage of Goods by Road, Geneva, 1956
See the Schedule to the Carriage of Goods by Road Act 1965 for text of the Convention.

Convention on the Recognition and Enforcement of Foreign Arbitral Awards, New York, 1958

Article I

1. This Convention shall apply to the recognition and enforcement of arbitral awards made in the territory of a State other than the State where the recognition and enforcement of such awards are sought, and arising out of differences between persons, whether physical or legal. It shall also apply to arbitral awards not considered as domestic awards in the State where their recognition and enforcement are sought.
2. The term 'arbitral awards' shall include not only awards made by arbitrators appointed for each case but also those made by permanent arbitral bodies to which the parties have submitted.
3. When signing, ratifying or acceding to this Convention, or notifying extension under Article X hereof, any State may on the basis of reciprocity declare that it will apply the Convention to the recognition and enforcement of awards made only in the territory of another Contracting State. It may also declare that it will apply the Convention only to differences arising out of legal relationships, whether contractual or not, which are considered as commercial under the national law of the State making such declaration.

Article II

1. Each Contracting State shall recognize an agreement in writing under which the parties undertake to submit to arbitration all or any differences which have arisen or which may arise between them in respect of a defined legal relationship, whether contractual or not, concerning a subject matter capable of settlement by arbitration.
2. The term 'agreement in writing' shall include an arbitral clause in a contract or an arbitration agreement, signed by the parties or contained in an exchange of letters or telegrams.
3. The court of a Contracting State, when seised of an action in a matter in respect of which the parties have made an agreement within the meaning of this Article, at the request of one of the parties, refer the parties to arbitration, unless it finds that the said agreement is null and void, inoperative or incapable of being performed.

Article III

Each Contracting State shall recognize arbitral awards as binding and enforce them in accordance with the rules of procedure of the territory where the award is relied upon, under the conditions laid down in the following Articles. There shall not be imposed substantially more onerous conditions or higher fees or charges on the recognition or enforcement of arbitral awards to which this Convention applies than are imposed on the recognition or enforcement of domestic arbitral awards.

Article IV

1. To obtain the recognition and enforcement mentioned in the preceding Article, the party applying for recognition and enforcement shall, at the time of the application, supply –

(a) the duly authenticated original award or a duly certified copy thereof;
(b) the original agreement referred to in Article II or a duly certified copy thereof.

2. If the said award or agreement is not made in an official language of the country in which the award is relied upon, the party applying for recognition and enforcement of the award shall produce a translation of these documents into such language. The translation shall be certified by an official or sworn translator or by a diplomatic or consular agent.

Article V

1. Recognition and enforcement of the award may be refused, at the request of the party against whom it is invoked, only if that party furnishes to the competent authority where the recognition and enforcement is sought, proof that –
   (a) the parties to the agreement referred to in Article II were, under the law applicable to them, under some incapacity, or the said agreement is not valid under the law to which the parties have subjected it or, failing any indication thereon, under the law of the country where the award was made; or
   (b) the party against whom the award is invoked was not given proper notice of the appointment of the arbitrator or of the arbitration proceedings or was otherwise unable to present his case; or
   (c) the award deals with a difference not contemplated by or not falling within the terms of the submission to arbitration, or it contains decisions on matters beyond the scope of the submission to arbitration, provided that, if the decisions on matters submitted to arbitration can be separated from those not so submitted, that part of the award which contains decisions on matters submitted to arbitration may be recognized and enforced; or
   (d) the composition of the arbitral authority or the arbitral procedure was not in accordance with the agreement of the parties, or, failing such agreement, was not in accordance with the law of the country where the arbitration took place; or
   (e) the award has not yet become binding on the parties, or has been set aside or suspended by a competent authority of the country in which, or under the law of which, that award was made.
2. Recognition and enforcement of an arbitral award may also be refused if the competent authority in the country where recognition and enforcement is sought finds that –
   (a) the subject matter of the difference is not capable of settlement by arbitration under the law of that country; or
   (b) the recognition or enforcement of the award would be contrary to the public policy of that country.

Articles VI–XVI [Omitted]

Convention Supplementary to the Warsaw Convention for the Unification of Certain Rules Relating to International Carriage by Air Performed by a Person Other Than the Contracting Carrier (Guadalajara) 1961

See the Schedule to the Carriage by Air (Supplementary Provisions) Act 1962.

European Convention on International Commercial Arbitration, Geneva, 1961

Article I Scope of the Convention

1. This Convention shall apply –
   (a) to arbitration agreements concluded for the purpose of settling disputes arising from international trade between physical or legal persons having, when concluding the agreement, their habitual place of residence or their seat in different contracting states;
   (b) to arbitral procedures and awards based on agreements referred to in paragraph 1(a) above.
2. For the purpose of this Convention –
   (a) the term 'arbitration agreement' shall mean either an arbitral clause in a contract or an arbitration agreement, the contract or arbitration agreement being signed by the parties, or contained in an exchange of letters, telegrams, or in a communication by teleprinter and, in relations between States whose laws do not require that an arbitration agreement be made in writing, any arbitration agreement concluded in the form authorized by these laws;
   (b) the term 'arbitration' shall mean not only settlement by arbitrators appointed for each case (ad hoc arbitration) but also by permanent arbitral institutions;
   (c) the term 'seat' shall mean the place of the situation of the establishment that has made the arbitration agreement.

Article II Right of legal persons of public law to resort to arbitration

1. In the cases referred to in Article I, paragraph 1, of this Convention, legal persons considered by the law which is applicable to them as 'legal persons of public law' have the right to conclude valid arbitration agreements.
2. On signing, ratifying or acceding to this convention any State shall be entitled to declare that it limits the above faculty to such conditions as may be stated in its declaration.

Article III Right of foreign nationals to be designated as arbitrators

In arbitration covered by this Convention, foreign nationals may be designated as arbitrators.

Article IV Organization of the arbitration

1. The parties to an arbitration agreement shall be free to submit their disputes –
   (a) to a permanent arbitral institution; in this case, the arbitration proceedings shall be held in conformity with the rules of the said institution;
   (b) to an *ad hoc* arbitral procedure; in this case, they shall be free *inter alia:*
      (i) to appoint arbitrators or to establish means for their appointment in the event of an actual dispute;
      (ii) to determine the place of arbitration; and
      (iii) to lay down the procedure to be followed by the arbitrators.

2. Where the parties have agreed to submit any disputes to an ad hoc arbitration, and where within thirty days of the notification of the request for arbitration to the respondent one of the parties fails to appoint his arbitrator, the latter shall, unless otherwise provided, be appointed at the request of the other party by the President of the competent Chamber of Commerce of the country of the defaulting party's habitual place of residence or seat at the time of the introduction of the request for arbitration. This paragraph shall also apply to the replacement of the arbitrator(s) appointed by one of the parties or by the President of the Chamber of Commerce above referred to.
3. Where the parties have agreed to submit any disputes to an ad hoc arbitration by one or more arbitrators and the arbitration agreement contains no indication regarding the organization of the arbitration, as mentioned in paragraph 1 of this Article, the necessary steps shall be taken by the arbitrator(s) already appointed, unless the parties are able to agree thereon and without prejudice to the case referred to in paragraph 2 above. Where the parties cannot agree on the appointment of the sole arbitrator or where the arbitrators appointed cannot agree on the measures to be taken, the claimant shall apply for the necessary action, where the place of arbitration has been agreed upon by the parties, at his option to the President of the Chamber of Commerce of the place of arbitration agreed upon or to the President of the competent Chamber of Commerce of the respondent's habitual place of residence or seat at the time of the introduction of the request for arbitration. Where such a place has not been agreed upon, the claimant shall be entitled at his option to apply for the necessary action either to the President of the competent Chamber of Commerce of the country of the respondent's habitual place of residence or seat at the time of the introduction of the request for arbitration, or to the Special Committee whose composition and procedure are specified in the Annex to this Convention. Where the claimant fails to exercise the rights given to him under this paragraph the respondent or the arbitrator(s) shall be entitled to do so.
4. When seised of a request the President or the Special Committee shall be entitled as need be –
   (a) to appoint the sole arbitrator, presiding arbitrator, umpire, or referee;
   (b) to replace the arbitrator(s) appointed under any procedure other than that referred to in paragraph 2 above;
   (c) to determine the place of arbitration, provided that the arbitrator(s) may fix another place of arbitration;
   (d) to establish directly or by reference to the rules and statutes of a permanent arbitral institution the rules of procedure to be followed by the arbitrator(s), provided that the arbitrators have not established these rules themselves in the absence of any agreement thereon between the parties.
5. Where the parties have agreed to submit their disputes to a permanent arbitral institution without determining the institution in question and cannot agree thereon, the claimant may request the determination of such institution in conformity with the procedure referred to in paragraph 3 above.
6. Where the arbitration agreement does not specify the mode of arbitration (arbitration by a permanent arbitral institution or an ad hoc arbitration) to which the parties have agreed to submit their dispute, and where the parties cannot agree thereon, the claimant shall be entitled to have recourse in this case to the procedure referred to in paragraph 3 above to determine the question. The President of the competent Chamber

of Commerce or the Special Committee, shall be entitled either to refer the parties to a permanent arbitral institution or to request the parties to appoint their arbitrators within such time-limits as the President of the competent Chamber of Commerce or the Special Committee may have fixed and to agree within such time-limits on the necessary measures for the functioning of the arbitration. In the latter case, the provisions of paragraphs 2, 3 and 4 of this Article shall apply.

7. Where within a period of sixty days from the moment when he was requested to fulfil one of the functions set out in paragraphs 2, 3, 4, 5 and 6 of this Article, the President of the Chamber of Commerce designated by virtue of these paragraphs has not fulfilled one of these functions, the party requesting shall be entitled to ask the Special Committee to do so.

Article V Plea as to arbitral jurisdiction

1. The party which intends to raise a plea as to the arbitrator's jurisdiction based on the fact that the arbitration agreement was either non-existent or null and void or had lapsed shall do so during the arbitration proceedings, not later than the delivery of its statement of claim or defence relating to the substance of the dispute; those based on the fact that an arbitrator has exceeded his terms of reference shall be raised during the arbitration proceedings as soon as the question on which the arbitrator is alleged to have no jurisdiction is raised during the arbitral procedure. Where the delay in raising the plea is due to a cause which the arbitrator deems justified, the arbitrator shall declare the plea admissible.
2. Pleas to the jurisdiction referred to in paragraph 1 above that have not been raised during the time-limits there referred to, may not be entered either during a subsequent stage of the arbitral proceedings where they are pleas left to the sole discretion of the parties under the law applicable by the arbitrator, or during subsequent court proceedings concerning the substance or the enforcement of the award where such pleas are left to the discretion of the parties under the rule of conflict of the court seised of the substance of the dispute or the enforcement of the award. The arbitrator's decision on the delay in raising the plea, will, however, be subject to judicial control.
3. Subject to any subsequent judicial control provided for under the *lex fori*, the arbitrator whose jurisdiction is called in question shall be entitled to proceed with the arbitration, to rule on his own jurisdiction and to decide upon the existence or the validity of the arbitration agreement or of the contract of which the agreement forms part.

Article VI Jurisdiction of courts of law

1. A plea as to the jurisdiction of the court made before the court seised by either party to the arbitration agreement, on the basis of the fact that an arbitration agreement exists shall, under penalty of estoppel, be presented by the respondent before or at the same time as the presentation of his substantial defence, depending upon whether the law of the court seised regards this plea as one of procedure or of substance.
2. In taking a decision concerning the existing or the validity of an arbitration agreement, courts of Contracting States shall examine the validity of such agreement with reference to the capacity of the parties, under the law applicable to them, and with reference to other questions –

(a) under the law to which the parties have subjected their arbitration agreement;
(b) failing any indication thereon, under the law of the country in which the award is to be made;
(c) failing any indication as to the law to which the parties have subjected the agreement, and where at the time when the question is raised in court the country in which the award is to be made cannot be determined, under the competent law by virtue of the rules of conflict of the court seised of the dispute.

The court may also refuse recognition of the arbitration agreement if under the law of their country the dispute is not capable of settlement by arbitration.

3. Where either party to an arbitration agreement has initiated arbitration proceedings before any resort is had to a court, courts of Contracting States subsequently asked to deal with the same subject-matter between the same parties or with the question whether the arbitration agreement was non-existent or null and void or had lapsed, shall stay their ruling on the arbitrator's jurisdiction until the arbitral award is made, unless they have good and substantial reasons to the contrary.
4. A request for interim measures or measures of conservation addressed to a judicial authority shall not be deemed incompatible with the arbitration agreement, or regarded as a submission of the substance of the case to the court.

Article VII Applicable law

1. The parties shall be free to determine, by agreement, the law to be applied by the arbitrators to the substance of the dispute. Failing any indication by the parties as to the applicable law, the arbitrators shall apply the proper law under the rule of conflict that the arbitrators deem applicable. In both cases the arbitrators shall take account of the terms of the contract and trade usages.
2. The arbitrators shall act as *amiables compositeurs* if the parties so decide and if they may do so under the law applicable to the arbitration.

Article VIII Reasons for the award

The parties shall be presumed to have agreed that reasons shall be given for the award unless they –

(a) either expressly declare that reasons shall not be given; or
(b) have assented to an arbitral procedure under which it is not customary to give reasons for awards, provided that in this case neither party requests before the end of the hearing, or if there has not been a hearing then before the making of the award, that reasons be given.

Article IX Setting aside of the arbitral award

1. The setting aside in a Contracting State of an arbitral award covered by this convention shall only constitute a ground for the refusal or recognition or enforcement in another Contracting State where such setting aside took place in a State in which, or under the law of which, the award has been made and for one of the following reasons –

(a) the parties to the arbitration agreement were under the law applicable to them, under some incapacity or the said agreement is not valid under the law to which the parties have subjected it or, failing any indication thereon, under the law of the country where the award was made; or
(b) the party requesting the setting aside of the award was not given proper notice of appointment of the arbitrator or of the arbitration proceedings or was otherwise unable to present his case; or
(c) the award deals with a difference not contemplated by or not falling within the terms of the submission to arbitration, or it contains decisions on matters beyond the scope of the submission to arbitration, provided that, if the decisions on matters submitted to arbitration can be separated from those not so submitted, that part of the award which contains decisions on matters submitted to arbitration need not be set aside;
(d) the composition of the arbitral authority or the arbitral procedure was not in accordance with the agreement of the parties, or failing such agreement, with the provisions of Article IV of this Convention.

2. In relations between Contracting States that are also parties to the New York Convention on the Recognition and Enforcement of Foreign Arbitral Awards of 10th June 1958, paragraph 1 of this Article limits the application of Article V (1)(e) of the New York Convention solely to the cases of setting aside set out under paragraph 1 above.

Article X [Omitted].

Agreement Relating to Application of the European Convention on International Commercial Arbitration, Paris, 1962

Article 1

In relations between physical or legal persons whose habitual residence or seat is in States Parties to the present Agreement paragraphs 2 to 7 of Article IV of the European convention on International Commercial Arbitration, opened for signature at Geneva on 21st April 1961, are replaced by the following provision:

> 'If the arbitral Agreement contains no indication regarding the measures referred to in paragraph 1 of Article IV of the European Convention on International Commercial Arbitration as a whole, or some of these measures, any difficulties arising with regard to the constitution or functioning of the arbitral tribunal shall be submitted to the decision of the competent authority at the request of the party instituting proceedings.'

Articles 2–6 [Omitted]

Convention Relating to a Uniform Law on the International Sale of Goods, The Hague, 1964

See Schedule 1 to the Uniform Law on International Sales Act 1967 for the text of the Convention.

Convention Relating to a Uniform Law on the Formation of Contracts for the International Sale of Goods, 1964

See Schedule 2 to the Uniform Laws on International Sales Act 1967 for text of the Convention.

Brussels Protocol Amending The Hague Rules Relating to Bills of Lading 1968 (Hague-Visby Rules)

See the Schedule to the Carriage of Goods by Sea Act 1972 for text of the Convention.

Guatemala Protocol 1971 Protocol to Amend the Convention for the Unification of Certain Rules Relating to International Carriage by Air Signed at Warsaw on 12th October 1929 as Amended by the Protocol Done at The Hague on 28th September 1955, Guatemala City, 8th March 1971

Chapter I Amendment to the Convention

Article I

The Convention which the provisions of the present Chapter modify is the Warsaw Convention as amended at The Hague in 1955.

Article V

In Article 18 of the Convention, paragraphs 1 and 2 shall be deleted and replaced by the following –

'1. The carrier is liable for damage sustained in the event of the destruction or loss of, or of damage to, any cargo, if the occurrence which caused the damage so sustained took place during the carriage by air.
2. The carriage by air within the meaning of the preceding paragraph comprises the period during which the cargo is in charge of the carrier, whether in an airport or on board an aircraft, or, in the case of a landing outside an airport, in any place whatsoever.'

Article VII

Article 21 of the Convention shall be deleted and replaced by the following –

'Article 21

If the carrier proves that the damage was caused or contributed to by the negligence or other wrongful act or omission of the person claiming compensation, the carrier shall be wholly or partly exonerated from his liability to such person to the extent that such negligence or wrongful act or omission caused or contributed to the damage. When by reason of the death or injury of a passenger compensation is claimed by a person other than the passenger, the carrier shall likewise be wholly or partly exonerated from his liability to the extent that he proves that the damage was caused or contributed to by the negligence or other wrongful act or omission of that passenger.'

Article VIII

Article 22 of the Convention shall be deleted and replaced by the following Article 22.

1. '[Omitted].
2. (a) In the carriage of cargo, the liability of the carrier is limited to a sum of two hundred and fifty francs per kilogramme, unless the consignor has made, at the time when the package was handed over to the carrier, a special declaration of interest in delivery at destination and has paid a supplementary sum if the case so requires. In that case the carrier will be liable to pay a sum not exceeding the declared sum, unless he proves that that sum is greater than the consignor's actual interest in delivery at destination.
   (b) In the case of loss, damage or delay of part of the cargo, or of any object contained therein, the weight to be taken into consideration in determining the amount to which the carrier's liability is limited shall be only the total weight of the package or packages concerned. Nevertheless, when the loss, damage or delay of a part of the cargo, or of any object contained therein, affects the value of other packages covered by the same air waybill, the total weight of such package or packages shall be taken into consideration in determining the limit of liability.
3. [Omitted].
4. The sums mentioned in francs in this Article and Article 42 shall be deemed to refer to a currency unit consisting of sixty-five and a half milligrammes of gold of millesimal fineness nine hundred. These sums may be converted into national currencies in round figures. Conversion of the sums into national currencies other than gold shall, in case of judicial proceedings, be made according to the gold value of such currencies at the date of the judgment.'

Article IX

Article 24 of the Convention shall be deleted and replaced by the following –

'Article 24

1. In the carriage of cargo, any action for damages, however founded, can only be brought subject to the conditions and limits set out in this Convention.'

Article X

Article 25 of the Convention shall be deleted and replaced by the following –

'Article 25

The limit of liability specified in paragraph 2 of Article 27 shall not apply if it is proved that the damage resulted from an act or omission of the carrier, his servants or agents, done with intent to cause damage or recklessly and with knowledge that damage would probably result; provided that, in the case of such act or omission of a servant or agent, it is also proved that he was acting within the scope of his employment.'

Article XI

In Article 25A of the Convention, paragraphs 1 and 3 shall be deleted and replaced by the following –

'1. If an action is brought against a servant or agent of the carrier arising out of damage to which the Convention relates, such servant or agent if he proves that he acted within the scope of his employment, shall be entitled to avail himself of the limits of liability which that carrier himself is entitled to invoke under this Convention.

3. The provisions of paragraphs 1 and 2 of this Article shall not apply to the carriage of cargo if it is proved that the damage resulted from an act or omission of the servant or agent done with intent to cause damage or recklessly and with knowledge that damage would probably result.'

Article XIII

After Article 30 of the Convention, the following Article shall be inserted –

'Article 30A

Nothing in this Convention shall prejudice the question whether a person liable for damage in accordance with its provisions has a right of recourse against any other person.'

Article XIV

After Article 35 of the Convention, the following Article shall be inserted –

'Article 35A

No provision contained in this Convention shall prevent a State from establishing and operating within its territory a system to supplement the compensation payable to claimants under the Convention in respect of death, or personal injury, of passengers. Such a system shall fulfil the following conditions:

(a) it shall not in any circumstances impose upon the carrier, his servants or agents, any liability in addition to that provided under this Convention;
(b) it shall not impose upon the carrier any financial or administrative burden other than collecting in that State contributions from passengers if required so to do;
(c) it shall not give rise to any discrimination between carriers with regard to the passengers concerned and the benefits available to the said passengers under the system shall be extended to them regardless of the carrier whose services they have used;
(d) if a passenger has contributed to the system, any person suffering damage as a consequence of death or personal injury of such passenger shall be entitled to the benefit of the system.'

Article XV

After Article 41 of the Convention the following Article shall be inserted –

'Article 42

1. Without prejudice to the provisions of Article 41, Conferences of the Parties to the Protocol done at Guatemala City on the eighth March 1971, shall be convened during the fifth and tenth years respectively after the date of entry into force of the said Protocol for the purpose of reviewing the limit established in Article 22, paragraph 1(a) of the Convention as intended by that Protocol.
2. At each of the Conferences mentioned in paragraph 1 of this Article the limit of liability in Article 22, paragraph 1(a) in force at the respective dates of these Conferences shall not be increased by an amount exceeding one hundred and eighty-seven thousand five hundred francs.
3. Subject to paragraph 2 of this Article, unless before the thirty-first December of the fifth and tenth years after the date of entry into force of the Protocol referred to in paragraph 1 of this Article the aforesaid Conferences decide otherwise by a two-thirds majority vote of the parties present and voting the limit of liability in Article 22, paragraph 1(a) in force at the respective date of these Conferences shall on those dates be increased by one hundred and eighty-seven thousand five hundred francs.
4. The applicable limit shall be that which, in accordance with the preceding paragraphs, is in effect on the date of the event which caused the death or personal injury of the passenger.'

Chapter II Scope of application of the Convention as amended

Article XVI

The Warsaw Convention as amended at The Hague in 1955 and by this Protocol shall apply to international carriage as defined in Article 1 of the Convention provided that the places of departure and destination referred to in that Article are situated either in the territories of two Parties to this Protocol or within the territory of a single Party to this Protocol with an agreed stopping place in the territory of another State.

Chapter III Final clauses

Articles XVII–XXVI [Omitted]

United Nations Convention on the Limitation Period in the International Sale of Goods, New York, 1974

Part I Substantive provisions

Sphere of application

Article 1

1. This Convention shall determine when claims of a buyer and a seller against each other arising from a contract of international sale of goods or relating to its breach, termination

or invalidity can no longer be exercised by reason on the expiration of a period of time. Such period of time is hereinafter referred to as 'the limitation period'.

2. This Convention shall not affect a particular time-limit within which one party is required, as a condition for the acquisition or exercise of his claim to give notice to the other party or perform any act other than the institution of legal proceedings.
3. In this Convention –
   (a) 'buyer', 'seller' and 'party' mean persons who buy or sell, or agree to buy or sell, goods, and the successors to and assigns of their rights or obligations under the contract of sale;
   (b) 'creditor' means a party who asserts a claim, whether or not such a claim is for a sum of money;
   (c) 'debtor' means a party against whom a creditor asserts a claim;
   (d) 'breach of contract' means the failure of a party to perform the contract or any performance not in conformity with the contract;
   (e) 'legal proceedings' includes judicial, arbitral and administrative proceedings;
   (f) 'person' includes corporation, company, partnership, association or entity, whether private or public, which can sue or be sued;
   (g) 'writing' includes telegram and telex;
   (h) 'year' means a year according to the Gregorian calendar.

Article 2

For the purposes of this Convention –

(a) a contract of sale of goods shall be considered international if, at the time of the conclusion of the contract, the buyer and the seller have their places of business in different States;
(b) the fact that the parties have their places of business in different States shall be disregarded whenever this fact does not appear either from the contract or from any dealings between, or from information disclosed by, the parties at any time before or at the conclusion of the contract;
(c) where a party to a contract of sale of goods has places of business in more than one State, the place of business shall be that which has the closest relationship to the contract and its performance, having regard to the circumstances known to or contemplated by the parties at the time of the conclusion of the contract;
(d) his habitual residence;
(e) neither the nationality of the parties nor the civil or commercial character of the parties or of the contract shall be taken into consideration.

Article 3

1. This Convention shall apply only if, at the time of the conclusion of the contract, the places of business of the parties to a contract of international sale of goods are in Contracting States.
2. Unless this Convention provides otherwise, it shall apply irrespective of the law which would otherwise by applicable by virtue of the rules of private international law.

3. This Convention shall not apply when the parties have expressly excluded its application.

Article 4

This Convention shall not apply to sales –

(a) of goods bought for personal, family or household use;
(b) by auction;
(c) on execution or otherwise by authority of law;
(d) of stocks, shares, investment securities, negotiable instruments or money;
(e) of ships, vessels or aircraft;
(f) of electricity.

Article 5

This Convention shall not apply to claims based upon –

(a) death of, or personal injury to, any person;
(b) nuclear damage caused by the goods sold;
(c) a lien, mortgage or other security interest in property;
(d) a judgment or award made in legal proceedings;
(e) a document on which direct enforcement or execution can be obtained in accordance with the law of the place where such enforcement or execution is sought;
(f) a bill of exchange, cheque or promissory note.

Article 6

1. This Convention shall not apply to contracts in which the preponderant part of the obligations of the seller consists in the supply of labour or other services.
2. Contracts for the supply of goods to be manufactured or produced shall be considered to be sales, unless the party who orders the goods undertakes to supply a substantial part of the materials necessary for such manufacture or production.

Article 7

In the interpretation and application of the provisions of this Convention, regard shall be had to its international character and to the need to promote uniformity.

The duration and commencement of the limitation period

Article 8

The limitation period shall be four years.

Article 9

1. Subject to the provisions of Articles 10, 11 and 12 the limitation period shall commence on the date on which the claim accrues.

2. The commencement of the limitation period shall not be postponed by –
   (a) a requirement that the party be given a notice as described in paragraph 2 of Article 1; or
   (b) a provision in an arbitration agreement that no right shall arise until an arbitration award has been made.

Article 10

1. A claim arising from a breach of contract shall accrue on the date on which such breach occurs.
2. A claim arising from a defect or other lack of conformity shall accrue on the date on which the goods are actually handed over to, or their tender is refused by, the buyer.
3. A claim based on fraud committed before or at the time of the conclusion of the contract or during its performance shall accrue on the date on which the fraud was or reasonably could have been discovered.

Article 11

If the seller has given an express undertaking relating to the goods which is stated to have effect for a certain period of time, whether expressed in terms of a specific period of time or otherwise, the limitation period in respect of any claim arising from the undertaking shall commence on the date on which the buyer notifies the seller of the fact on which the claim is based, but not later than on the date of the expiration of the period of the undertaking.

Article 12

1. If, in circumstances provided for by the law applicable to the contract, one party is entitled to declare the contract terminated before the time for performance is due, and exercises this right, the limitation period in respect of a claim based on any such circumstances shall commence on the date on which the declaration is made to the other party. If the contract is not declared to be terminated before performance becomes due, the limitation period shall commence on the date on which performance is due.
2. The limitation period in respect of a claim arising out of a breach by one party of a contract for the delivery of or payment for goods by instalments shall, in relation to each separate instalment, commence on the date on which the particular breach occurs. If, under the law applicable to the contract, one party is entitled to declare the contract terminated by reason of such breach, and exercises this right, the limitation period in respect of all relevant instalments shall commence on the date on which the declaration is made to the other party.

Cessation and extension of the limitation period

Article 13

The limitation period shall cease to run when the creditor performs any act which, under the law of the court where the proceedings are instituted, is recognised as commencing judicial proceedings against the debtor or as asserting his claim in such proceedings already instituted against the debtor, for the purpose of obtaining satisfaction or recognition of his claim.

Article 14

1. Where the parties have agreed to submit to arbitration, the limitation period shall cease to run when either party commences arbitral proceedings in the manner provided for in the arbitration agreement or by the law applicable to such proceedings.
2. In the absence of any such provision, arbitral proceedings shall be deemed to commence on the date on which a request that the claim in dispute be referred to arbitration is delivered at the habitual residence or place of business of the other party or, if he has no such residence or place of business, then at his last known residence or place of business.

Article 15

If any legal proceedings other than those mentioned in Articles 13 and 14, including legal proceedings commenced upon the occurrence of –

(a) the death or incapacity of the debtor;
(b) the bankruptcy or any state of insolvency affecting the whole of the property of the debtor; or
(c) the dissolution or liquidation of a corporation, company, partnership, association or entity when it is the debtor.

The limitation period shall cease to run when the creditor asserts his claim in such proceedings for the purpose of obtaining satisfaction or recognition of the claim, subject to the law governing the proceedings.

Article 16

For the purposes of Articles 13, 14 and 15, any act performed by way of counterclaim shall be deemed to have been performed on the same date as the act performed in relation to the claim against which the counterclaim is raised, provided that both the claim and the counterclaim relate to the same contract or to several contracts concluded in the course of the same transaction.

Article 17

1. Where a claim has been asserted in legal proceedings within the limitation period in accordance with Articles 13, 14, 15 or 16, but such legal proceedings have ended without a decision binding on the merits of the claim, the limitation period shall be deemed to have continued to run.
2. If, at the time such legal proceedings ended, the limitation period has expired or has less than one year to run, the creditor shall be entitled to a period of one year from the date on which the legal proceedings ended.

Article 18

1. Where legal proceedings have been commenced against one debtor, the limitation period prescribed in this Convention shall cease to run against any other party jointly and severally liable with the debtor, provided that the creditor informs such party in writing within that period that the proceedings have been commenced.
2. Where legal proceedings have been commenced by a subpurchaser against the buyer, the limitation period prescribed in this Convention shall cease to run in relation to the buyer's claim over against the seller, if the buyer informs the seller in writing within that period that the proceedings have been commenced.
3. Where the legal proceedings referred to in paragraphs 1 and 2 of this Article have ended, the limitation period in respect of the claim of the creditor or the buyer against the party jointly and severally liable or against the seller shall be deemed not to have ceased running by virtue of paragraphs 1 and 2 of this Article, but the creditor or the buyer shall be entitled to an additional year from the date on which the legal proceedings ended, if at that time the limitation period had expired or had less than one year to run.

Article 19

Where the creditor performs, in the State in which the debtor has his place of business and before the expiration of the limitation period, any act, other than the acts described in Articles 13, 14, 15 and 16, which under the law of that State has the effect of recommencing a limitation period, a new limitation period of four years shall commence on the date prescribed by that law.

Article 20

1. Where the debtor, before the expiration of the limitation period, acknowledges in writing his obligation to the creditor, a new limitation period of four years shall commence to run from the date of such acknowledgement.
2. Payment of interest or partial performance of an obligation by the debtor shall have the same effect as an acknowledgement under paragraph 1 of this Article if it can reasonably be inferred from such payment or performance that the debtor acknowledges that obligation.

Article 21

Where, as a result of a circumstance which is beyond the control of the creditor and which he could neither avoid nor overcome, the creditor has been prevented from causing the limitation period to cease to run, the limitation period shall be extended so as not to expire before the expiration of one year from the date on which the relevant circumstance ceased to exist.

Modification of the limitation period by the parties

Article 22

1. The limitation period cannot be modified or affected by any declaration or agreement between the parties, except in the cases provided for in paragraph 2 of this Article.

2. The debtor may at any time during the running of the limitation period extend the period by a declaration in writing to the creditor. This declaration may be renewed.
3. The provisions of this Article shall not affect the validity of a clause in the contract of sale which stipulates that arbitral proceedings shall be commenced within a shorter period of limitation than that prescribed by this Convention, provided that such clause is valid under the law applicable to the contract of sale.

General limit of the limitation period

Article 23

Notwithstanding the provisions of this Convention, a limitation period shall in any event expire not later than 10 years from the date on which it commenced to run under Articles 9, 10, 11 and 12 of this Convention.

Consequences of expiration of the limitation period

Article 24

Expiration of the limitation period shall be taken into consideration in any legal proceedings only if invoked by a party to such proceedings.

Article 25

1. Subject to the provisions of paragraph 2 of this Article and of Article 24, no claim shall be recognised or enforced in any legal proceedings commenced after the expiration of the limitation period.
2. Notwithstanding the expiration of the limitation period, one party may rely on his claim as a defence or for the purpose of set-off against a claim asserted by the other party, provided that in the latter case this may only be done –
   (a) if both claims relate to the same contract or to several contracts concluded in the course of the same transaction; or
   (b) if the claims could have been set-off at any time before the expiration of the limitation period.

Article 26

Where the debtor performs his obligation after the expiration of the limitation period, he shall not on that ground be entitled in any way to claim restitution even if he did not know at the time when he performed his obligation that the limitation period had expired.

Article 27

The expiration of the limitation period with respect to a principal debt shall have the same effect with respect to an obligation to pay interest on that debt.

Calculation of the period

Article 28

1. The limitation period shall be calculated in such a way that it shall expire at the end of the day which corresponds to the date on which the period commenced to run. If there is no such corresponding date, the period shall expire at the end of the last day of the last month of the limitation period.
2. The limitation period shall be calculated by reference to the date of the place where the legal proceedings are instituted.

Article 29

Where the last day of the limitation period falls on an official holiday or other dies non juridicus precluding the appropriate legal action in the jurisdiction where the creditor institutes legal proceedings or asserts a claim as envisaged in Articles 13, 14, or 15, the limitation period shall be extended so as not to expire until the end of the first day following that official holiday or dies non juridicus on which such proceedings could be instituted or on which such a claim could be asserted in that jurisdiction.

International effect

Article 30

The acts and circumstances referred to in Articles 13 through 19 which have taken place in one Contracting State shall have effect for the purposes of this Convention in another Contracting State, provided that the creditor has taken all reasonable steps to ensure that the debtor is informed of the relevant act or circumstances as soon as possible.

Montreal Additional Protocol No 1, 1975 Additional Protocol No 1 to Amend the Convention for the Unification of Certain Rules Relating to International Carriage by Air Signed at Warsaw on 12th October 1929

Chapter I Amendments to the Convention

Article I

The Convention which the provisions of the present Chapter modify is the Warsaw Convention, 1929.

Article II

Article 22 of the Convention shall be deleted and replaced by the following –

'Article 22

...

2. In the carriage of registered baggage and of cargo, the liability of the carrier is limited to a sum of 17 Special Drawing Rights per kilogramme unless the consignor has made, at the time when the package as handed over to the carrier, a special declaration of interest in delivery at destination and has paid a supplementary sum if the case so requires. In that case

the carrier will be liable to pay a sum not exceeding the declared sum, unless he proves that that sum is greater than the consignor's actual interest in delivery at destination.

...

4. The sums mentioned in terms of the Special Drawing Right in this Article shall be deemed to refer to the Special Drawing Right as defined by the International Monetary Fund. Conversion of the sums into national currencies shall, in case of judicial proceedings, be made according to the value of such currencies in terms of the Special Drawing Right at the date of the judgment.

   The value of a national currency, in terms of the Special Drawing Right, of a High Contracting Party which is a Member of the International Monetary Fund, shall be calculated in accordance with the method of valuation applied by the International Monetary Fund, in effect at the date of the judgment, for its operations and transactions. The value of a national currency, in terms of the Special Drawing Right, of a High Contracting Party which is not a Member of the International Monetary Fund, shall be calculated in a manner determined by that High Contracting Party. Nevertheless those States which are not Members of the International Monetary Fund and whose law does not permit the application of the provisions of paragraphs 1, 2 and 3 of Article 22 may at the time of ratification or accession or at any time thereafter declare that the limit of liability of the carrier in judicial proceedings in their territories is fixed at a sum of 125,000 monetary units per passenger with respect to paragraph 1 of Article 22; 250 monetary units per kilogramme with respect to paragraph 2 of Article 22; and 5,000 monetary units per passenger with respect to paragraph 3 of Article 22. This monetary unit corresponds to sixty-five and a half milligrammes of gold of millesimal fineness nine hundred. These sums may be converted into the national currency concerned in round figures. The conversion of these sums into national currency shall be made according to the law of the State concerned.'

Chapter II Scope of application of Convention as amended

Article III

The Warsaw Convention as amended by this Protocol shall apply to international carriage as detailed in Article I of the Convention provided that the place of departure and destination referred to in that Article are situated either in the territories of two Parties to this Protocol or within the territory of a single Party to this Protocol with an agreed stopping place in the territory of another State.

Chapter III Final clauses

Articles IV–XIII [Omitted]

Montreal Additional Protocol No 2, 1975 Additional Protocol No 2 to Amend the Convention for the Unification of Certain Rules Relating to International Carriage by Air Signed at Warsaw on 12th October 1929 as Amended by the Protocol Done at The Hague on 28th September 1955

Chapter I Amendments to the Convention

Article I

The Convention which the provisions of the present Chapter modify is the Warsaw Convention as amended at The Hague in 1955.

Article II

Article 22 of the Convention shall be deleted and replaced by the following –

'Article 22

. . .

2. (a) In the carriage of registered baggage and of cargo, the liability of the carrier is limited to a sum of 17 Special Drawing Rights per kilogramme, unless the passenger or consignor has made, at the time when the package was handed over to the carrier, a special declaration of interest in delivery at destination and has paid a supplementary sum if the case so requires. In that case the carrier will be liable to pay a sum not exceeding the declared sum, unless he proves that that sum is greater than the passenger's or consignor's actual interest in delivery at destination.
   (b) In the case of loss, damage or delay of part of registered baggage or cargo, or of any object contained therein, the weight to be taken into consideration in determining the amount to which the carrier's liability is limited shall be only the total weight of the package or packages concerned. Nevertheless, when the loss, damage or delay of a part of the registered baggage or cargo, or of an object contained therein, affects the value of other packages covered by the same baggage check or the same air waybill, the total weight of such package or packages shall also be taken into consideration in determining the limit of liability.

. . .

4. The limits prescribed in this Article shall not prevent the court from awarding, in accordance with its own law, in addition, the whole or part of the court costs and of the other expenses of the litigation incurred by the plaintiff. The foregoing provision shall not apply if the amount of the damages awarded, excluding court costs and other expenses of the litigation, does not exceed the sum which the carrier has offered in writing to the plaintiff within a period of six months from the date of the occurrence causing the damage, or before the commencement of the action, if that is later.
5. The sums mentioned in terms of the Special Drawing Right in this Article shall be deemed to refer to the Special Drawing Right as defined by the International Monetary Fund. Conversion of the sums into national currencies shall, in case of judicial proceedings, be made according to the value of such currencies in terms of the Special Drawing Right at the date of the judgment. The value of a national currency, in terms of the Special Drawing Right, of a High Contracting Party which is a Member of the International Monetary Fund, shall be calculated in accordance with the method of

valuation applied by the International Monetary Fund, in effect at the date of the judgment, for its operations and transactions. The value of a national currency, in terms of the Special Drawing Right, of a High Contracting Party which is not a Member of the International Monetary Fund, shall be calculated in a manner determined by that High Contracting Party.

Nevertheless, those States which are not Members of the International Monetary Fund and whose law does not permit the application of the provisions of paragraphs 1, 2(a) and 3 of Article 22 may at the time of ratification or accession or at any time thereafter, declare that the limit of liability of the carrier in judicial proceedings in their territories is fixed at a sum of 250,000 monetary units per passenger with respect to paragraph 1 of Article 22; 250 monetary units per kilogramme with respect to paragraph 2(a) of Article 22; and 5,000 monetary units per passenger with respect to paragraph 3 of Article 22. This monetary unit corresponds to sixty-five and a half milligrammes of gold of millesimal fineness nine hundred. These sums may be converted into the national currency concerned in round figures. The conversion of these sums into national currency shall be made according to the law of the State concerned.'

Chapter II Scope of application of the Convention as amended

Article III

The Warsaw Convention as amended at The Hague in 1955 and by this Protocol shall apply to international carriage as defined in Article I of the Convention, provided that the places of departure and destination referred to in that Article are situated either in the territories of two Parties to this Protocol or within the territory of a single Party to this Protocol with an agreed stopping place in the territory of another State.

Chapter III Final clauses

Articles IV–XIII [Omitted]

Montreal Additional Protocol No 3, 1975 Additional Protocol No 3 to Amend the Convention for the Unification of Certain Rules Relating to International Carriage by Air Signed at Warsaw on 12th October 1929 as Amended by the Protocols Done at The Hague on 28th September 1955 and at Guatemala City on 8th March 1971

Chapter I Amendments to the Convention

Article I

The Convention which the provisions of the present Chapter modify is the Warsaw Convention as amended at The Hague in 1955 and at Guatemala City in 1971.

Article II

Article 22 of the Convention shall be deleted and replaced by the following –

'Article 22

. . .

2. (a) In the carriage of cargo, the liability of the carrier is limited to a sum of 17 Special Drawing Rights per kilogramme, unless the consignor has made, at the time when the package was handed over to the carrier, a special declaration of interest in delivery at destination and has paid a supplementary sum if the case so requires. In that case the carrier will be liable to pay a sum not exceeding the declared sum, unless he proves that that sum is greater than the consignor's actual interest in delivery at destination.
   (b) In the case of loss, damage or delay of part of the cargo, or of any object contained therein, the weight to be taken into consideration in determining the amount to which the carrier's liability is limited shall be only the total weight of the package or packages concerned. Nevertheless, when the loss, damage or delay of a part of the cargo, or of an object contained therein, affects the value of other packages covered by the same air waybill, the total weight of such package or packages shall also be taken into consideration in determining the limit of liability.

. . .

4. The sums mentioned in terms of Special Drawing Right in this Article shall be deemed to refer to the Special Drawing Right as defined by the International Monetary Fund. Conversion of the sums into national currencies shall, in case of judicial proceedings, be made according to the value of such currencies in terms of the Special Drawing Right at the date of the judgment. The value of a national currency, in terms of the Special Drawing Right, of a High Contracting Party which is a Member of the International Monetary Fund, shall be calculated in accordance with the method of valuation applied by the International Monetary Fund, in effect at the date of the judgment, for its operations and transactions. The value of a national currency, in terms of the Special Drawing Right, of a High Contracting Party which is not a Member of the International Monetary Fund, shall be calculated in a manner determined by that High Contracting Party.

   Nevertheless, those States which are not Members of the International Monetary Fund and whose law does not permit the application of the provisions of paragraphs 1 and 2(a) of Article 22 may, at the time of ratification or accession or at any time thereafter declare that the limit of liability of the carrier in judicial proceedings in their territories is fixed at a sum of 150,000 monetary units per passenger with respect to paragraph 1(a) of Article 22; 62,500 monetary units per passenger with respect to paragraph 1(b) of Article 22; 15,000 monetary units per passenger with respect to paragraph 1(c) of Article 22; and 250 monetary units per kilogramme with respect to paragraph 2(a) of Article 22. A State applying the provisions of this paragraph may also declare that the sum referred to in paragraphs 2 and 3 of Article 42 shall be the sum of 187,500 monetary units. This monetary unit corresponds to sixty-five and a half milligrammes of gold of millesimal fineness nine hundred. These sums may be converted into the national currency concerned in round figures. The conversion of these sums into national currency shall be made according to the law of the State concerned.'

Article III

In Article 42 of the Convention –

paragraphs 2 and 3 shall be deleted and replaced by the following:

'2. At each of the Conferences mentioned in paragraph 1 of this Article the limit of liability in Article 22, paragraph 1(a) in force at the respective date of these Conferences shall be increased by an amount not exceeding 12,500 Special Drawing Rights.
3. Subject to paragraph 2 of this article, unless before the thirty-first December of the fifth and tenth year after the date of entry into force of the Protocol referred to in paragraph 1 of this Article the aforesaid Conferences decide otherwise by a two-thirds majority vote of the Parties present and voting, the limit of liability in Article 22 paragraph 1(a) in force at the respective dates of these Conferences shall on those dates be increased by 12,500 Special Drawing Rights.'

Chapter II Scope of application of the Convention as amended

Article IV

The Warsaw Convention as amended at The Hague in 1955 and at Guatemala City in 1971 and by this Protocol shall apply to international carriage as defined in Article I of the Convention, provided that the place of departure and destination referred to in that Article are situated either in the territories of two Parties to this Protocol or within the territory of a single Party to this Protocol with an agreed stopping place in the territory of another State.

Chapter III Final clauses

Articles V–XIV [Omitted]

Montreal Additional Protocol No 4, 1975 Additional Protocol No 4 to Amend the Convention for the Unification of Certain Rules Relating to International Carriage by Air Signed at Warsaw on 12th October 1929 as Amended by the Protocol Done at The Hague on 28th September 1955

Chapter I Amendments to the Convention

Article I

The Convention which the provisions of the present Chapter modify is the Warsaw Convention as amended at The Hague in 1955.

Article III

In Chapter II of the Convention –

Section III (Articles 5 to 16) shall be deleted and replaced by the following:

'Section III – Documentation relating to cargo

Article 5

1. In respect of the carriage or cargo an air waybill shall be delivered.
2. Any other means which would preserve a record of the carriage to be performed may, with the consent of the consignor, be substituted for the delivery of an air waybill. If such other means are used, the carrier shall if so requested by the consignor deliver to the consignor a receipt for the cargo permitting identification of the consignment and access to the information contained in the record preserved by such other means.
3. The impossibility of using, at points of transit and destination, the other means which would preserve the record of the carriage referred to in paragraph 2 of this Article does not entitle the carrier to refuse to accept the cargo for carriage.

Article 6

1. The air waybill shall be made out by the consignor in three original parts.
2. The first part shall be marked 'for the carrier'; it shall be signed by the consignor. The second part shall be marked 'for the consignee'; it shall be signed by the consignor and by the carrier. The third part shall be signed by the carrier and handed by him to the consignor after the cargo has been accepted.
3. The signature of the carrier and that of the consignor may be printed or stamped.
4. If, at the request of the consignor, the carrier makes out the air waybill, he shall be deemed, subject to proof to the contrary, to have done so on behalf of the consignor.

Article 7

When there is more than one package –

(a) the carrier of cargo has the right to require the consignor to make out separate air waybills;
(b) the consignor has the right to require the carrier to deliver separate receipts when the other means referred to in paragraph 2 of Article 5 are used.

Articles

The air waybill and receipt for the cargo shall contain –

(a) an indication of the places of departure and destination;
(b) if the places of departure and destination are within the territory of a single High Contracting Party, one or more agreed stopping places being within the territory of another State, an indication of at least one such stopping place; and
(c) an indication of the weight of the consignment.

Article 9

Non-compliance with the provisions of Articles 5 to 8 shall not affect the existence or the validity of the contract of carriage, which shall, none the less, be subject to the rules of this Convention including those relating to limitation of liability.

Article 10

1. The consignor is responsible for the correctness of the particulars and statements relating to the cargo inserted by him or on his behalf in the air waybill or furnished by him or on his behalf to the carrier for insertion in the receipt for the cargo or for insertion in the record preserved by the other means referred to in paragraph 2 of Article 5.
2. The consignor shall indemnify the carrier against all damage suffered by him, or by any other person to whom the carrier is liable, by reason of the irregularity, incorrectness or incompleteness of the particulars and statements furnished by the consignor or on his behalf.
3. Subject to the provisions of paragraphs 1 and 2 of this Article, the carrier shall indemnify the consignor against all damage suffered by him, or by any other person to whom the consignor is liable, by reason of the irregularity, incorrectness or incompleteness of the particulars and statements inserted by the carrier or on his behalf in the receipt for the cargo or in the record preserved by the other means referred to in paragraph 2 of Article 5.

Article 11

1. The air waybill or the receipt for the cargo is prima facie evidence of the conclusion of the contract, of the acceptance of the cargo and of the conditions of carriage mentioned therein.
2. Any statements in the air waybill or the receipt for the cargo relating to the weight, dimensions and packing of the cargo, as well as those relating to the number of packages, are prima facie evidence of the facts stated; those relating to the quantity, volume and condition of the cargo do not constitute evidence against the carrier except so far as they both have been, and are stated in the air waybill to have been, checked by him in the presence of the consignor or relate to the apparent condition of the cargo.

Article 12

1. Subject to his liability to carry out all his obligations under the contract of carriage, the consignor has the right to dispose of the cargo by withdrawing it at the airport of departure or destination, or by stopping it in the course of the journey on any landing, or by calling for it to be delivered at the place of destination or in the course of the journey to a person other than the consignee originally designated, or by requiring it to be returned to the airport of departure. He must not exercise this right of disposition in such a way as to prejudice the carrier or other consignor and he must repay any expenses occasioned by the exercise of this right.
2. If it is impossible to carry out the orders of the consignor, the carrier has to inform him forthwith.
3. If the carrier obeys the orders of the consignor for the disposition of the cargo without requiring the production of the part of the air waybill or the receipt for the cargo delivered to the latter, he will be liable, without prejudice to his right of recovery from the consignor, for any damage which may be caused thereby to any person who is lawfully in possession of that part of the air waybill or the receipt for the cargo.

4. The right conferred on the consignor ceases at the moment when that of the consignee begins in accordance with Article 13. Nevertheless, if the consignee declines to accept the cargo, or if he cannot be communicated with, the consignor resumes his right of disposition.

Article 13

1. Except when the consignor has exercised his right under Article 12, the consignee is entitled, on arrival of the cargo at the place of destination, to require the carrier to deliver the cargo to him, on payment of the charges due and on complying with the conditions of carriage.
2. Unless it is otherwise agreed, it is the duty of the carrier to give notice to the consignee as soon as the cargo arrives.
3. If the carrier admits the loss of the cargo or if the cargo has not arrived at the expiration of seven days after the date on which it ought to have arrived, the consignee is entitled to enforce against the carrier the rights which flow from the contract of carriage.

Article 14

The consignor and the consignee can respectively enforce all the rights given them by Articles 12 and 13, each in his own name, whether he is acting in his own interest or in the interest of another, provided that he carries out the obligations imposed by the contract of carriage.

Article 15

1. Articles 12, 13 and 14 do not affect the relations of the consignor and the consignee with each other or the mutual relations of third parties whose rights are derived either from the consignor or from the consignee.
2. The provisions of Articles 12, 13 and 14 can only be varied by express provision in the air waybill or the receipt for the cargo.

Article 16

1. The consignor must furnish such information and such documents as are necessary to meet the formalities of customs, octroi or police before the cargo can be delivered to the consignee. The consignor is liable to the carrier for any damage occasioned by the absence, insufficiency or irregularity of any such information or documents unless the damage is due to the fault of the carrier, his servants or agents.
2. The carrier is under no obligation to enquire into the correctness or sufficiency of the information or documents.'

Article IV

Article 18 of the Convention shall be deleted and replaced by the following –

'Article 18

1. The carrier is liable for damage sustained in the event of the destruction or loss of, or damage to any registered baggage, if the occurrence which caused the damage so sustained took place during the carriage by air.
2. The carrier is liable for damage sustained in the event of the destruction or loss of, or damage to, cargo upon condition only that the occurrence which caused the damage so sustained took place during the carriage by air.
3. However, the carrier is not liable if he proves that the destruction, loss of, or damage to, the cargo resulted from one or more of the following –
   (a) inherent defect, quality or vice of that cargo;
   (b) defective packing of that cargo performed by a person other than the carrier or his servants or agents;
   (c) an act of war or an armed conflict;
   (d) an act of public authority carried out in connexion with the entry, exit or transit of the cargo.
4. The carriage by air within the meaning of the preceding paragraphs of this Article comprises the period during which the baggage or cargo is in the charge of the carrier, whether in an airport or on board an aircraft, or, in the case of a landing outside an airport, in any place whatsoever.
5. The period of the carriage by air does not extend to any carriage by land, by sea or by river performed outside an airport. If, however, such carriage takes place in the performance of a contract for carriage by air, for the purpose of loading, delivery or transhipment, any damage is presumed, subject to proof to the contrary, to have been the result of an event which took place during the carriage by air.'

Article V

Article 20 of the Convention shall be deleted and replaced by the following:

'Article 20

In the case of passengers and baggage, and in the case of damage occasioned by delay in the carriage of cargo, the carrier shall not be liable if he proves that he and his servants and agents have taken all necessary measures to avoid the damage or that it was impossible for them to take such measures.'

Article VI

Article 21 of the Convention shall be deleted and replaced by the following:

'Article 21

. . .

2. In the carriage of cargo, if the carrier proves that the damage was caused by or contributed to by the negligence or other wrongful act or omission of the person claiming compensation, or the person from whom he derives his rights, the carrier shall be

wholly or partly exonerated from his liability to the claimant to the extent that such negligence or wrongful act or omission caused or contributed to the damage.'

Article VII

In Article 22 of the Convention –

(a) in paragraph 2(a) the words 'and of cargo' shall be deleted.
(b) after paragraph 2(a) the following paragraph shall be inserted:
'(b) In the carriage of cargo, the liability of the carrier is limited to a sum of 17 Special Drawing Rights per kilogramme, unless the consignor has made, at the time when the package was handed over to the carrier, a special declaration of interest in delivery at destination and has paid a supplementary sum if the case so requires. In that case the carrier will be liable to pay a sum not exceeding the declared sum, unless he proves that the sum is greater than the consignor's actual interest in delivery at destination.'
(c) paragraph 2(b) shall be designated as paragraph 2(c).
(d) after paragraph 5 the following paragraph shall be inserted
'6. The sums mentioned in terms of the Special Drawing Right in this Article shall be deemed to refer to the Special Drawing Right as defined by the International Monetary Fund. Conversion of the sums into national currencies shall, in case of judicial proceedings, be made according to the value of such currencies in terms of the Special Drawing Right at the date of the judgment. The value of a national currency, in terms of the Special Drawing Right, of a High Contracting Party which is a Member of the International Monetary Fund, shall be calculated in accordance with the method of valuation applied by the International Monetary Fund, in effect at the date of the judgment for its operations and transactions. The value of a national currency, in terms of the Special Drawing Right, of a High Contracting Party which is not a Member of the International Monetary Fund, shall be calculated in a manner determined, 'by that High Contracting Party.

Nevertheless, those States which are not Members of the International Monetary Fund and whose law does not permit the application of the provisions of paragraph 2(b) of Article 22 may, at the time of ratification or accession or at any time thereafter, declare that the limit of liability of the carrier in judicial proceedings in their territories is fixed at a sum of two hundred and fifty monetary units per kilogramme This monetary unit corresponds to sixty-five and a half milligrammes of gold of millesimal fineness nine hundred. This sum may be converted into the national currency concerned in round figures. The conversion of this sum into the national currency shall be made according to the laws of the State concerned.'

Article VIII

Article 24 of the Convention shall be deleted and replaced by the following –

'Article 24

...

2. In the carriage of cargo, any action for damages, however founded, whether under this Convention or in contract or in tort or otherwise, can only be brought subject to the

conditions and limits of liability set out in this Convention, without prejudice to the question as to who are the persons who have the right to bring suit and what are their respective rights. Such limit of liability constitute maximum limits and may not be exceeded whatever the circumstances which gave rise to the liability.'

Article XIII

Article 34 of the Convention shall be deleted and replaced by the following –

'Article 34

The provisions of Articles 3 to 8 inclusive relating to documents of carriage shall not apply in the case of carriage performed in extraordinary circumstances outside the normal scope of an air carrier's business.'

Chapter II Scope of application of the Convention as amended

Article XIV

The Warsaw Convention as amended at The Hague in 1955 and by this Protocol shall apply to international carriage as defined in Article I of the Convention, provided that the places of departure and destination referred to in that Article are situated either in the territories of two Parties to this Protocol or within the territory of a single Party to this Protocol with an agreed stopping place in the territory of another State.

Chapter III Final clauses

Articles XV–XXV [Omitted]

United Nations Convention on the Carriage of Goods by Sea, Hamburg, 1978 (Hamburg Rules)

Part I General provisions

Article 1 Definitions

In this Convention –

1. 'Carrier' means any person by whom or in whose name a contract of carriage of goods by sea has been concluded with a shipper.
2. 'Actual carrier' means any person to whom the performance of the carriage of the goods, or of part of the carriage, has been entrusted by the carrier, and includes any other person to whom such performance has been entrusted.
3. 'Shipper' means any person by whom or in whose name or on whose behalf a contract of carriage of goods by sea has been concluded with a carrier, or any person by whom or in whose name or on whose behalf the goods are actually delivered to the carrier in relation to the contract of carriage by sea.
4. 'Consignee' means the person entitled to take delivery of the goods.
5. 'Goods' includes live animals; where the goods are consolidated in a container, pallet or similar article of transport or where they are packed, 'goods' includes such article of transport or packaging if supplied by the shipper.

6. 'Contract of carriage by sea' means any contract whereby the carrier undertakes against payment of freight to carry goods by sea from one port to another; however, a contract which involves carriage by sea and also carriage by some other means is deemed to be a contract of carriage by sea for the purposes of this Convention only in so far as it relates to the carriage by sea.
7. 'Bill of lading' means a document which evidences a contract of carriage by sea and the taking over or loading of the goods by the carrier, and by which the carrier undertakes to deliver the goods against surrender of the document. A provision in the document that the goods are to be delivered to the order of a named person, or to order, or to bearer, constitutes such an undertaking.
8. 'Writing' includes, *inter alia*, telegram and telex.

Article 2 Scope of application

1. The provisions of this Convention are applicable to all contracts of carriage by sea between two different States, if –
   - (a) the port of loading as provided for in the contract of carriage by sea is located in a Contracting State; or
   - (b) the port of discharge as provided for in the contract of carriage by sea is located in a Contracting State; or
   - (c) one of the optional ports of discharge provided for in the contract of carriage by sea is the actual port of discharge and such port is located in a Contracting State; or
   - (d) the bill of lading or other document evidencing the contract of carriage by sea is issued in a Contracting State; or
   - (e) the bill of lading or other document evidencing the contract of carriage by sea provides that the provisions of this Convention or the legislation of any State giving effect to them are to govern the contract.
2. The provisions of this Convention are applicable without regard to the nationality of the ship, the carrier, the actual carrier, the shipper, the consignee or any other interested person.
3. The provisions of this Convention are not applicable to charter-parties. However, where a bill of lading is issued pursuant to a charter-party, the provisions of the Convention apply to such a bill of lading if it governs the relation between the carrier and the holder of the bill of lading, not being the charterer.
4. If a contract provides for future carriage of goods in a series of shipments during an agreed period, the provisions of this Convention apply to each shipment. However, where a shipment is made under a charter-party, the provisions of paragraph 3 of this Article apply.

Article 3 Interpretation of the convention

In the interpretation and application of the provisions of this Convention regard shall be had to its international character and to the need to promote uniformity.

Part II Liability of the carrier

Article 4 Period of responsibility

1. The responsibility of the carrier for the goods under this Convention covers the period during which the carrier is in charge of the goods at the port of loading, during the carriage and at the port of discharge.
2. For the purpose of paragraph 1 of this Article, the carrier is deemed to be in charge of the goods –
   (a) from the time he has taken over the goods from;
      (i) the shipper, or a person acting on his behalf; or
      (ii) an authority or other third party to whom, pursuant to law or regulations applicable at the port of loading, the goods must be handed over for shipment;
   (b) until the time he has delivered the goods:
      (i) by handing over the goods to the consignee; or
      (ii) in cases where the consignee does not receive the goods from the carrier, by placing them at the disposal of the consignee in accordance with the contract or with the law or with the usage of the particular trade, applicable at the port of discharge; or
      (iii) by handing over the goods to an authority or other third party to whom, pursuant to law or regulations applicable at the port of discharge, the goods must be handed over.
3. In paragraphs 1 and 2 of this Article, reference to the carrier or to the consignee means, in addition to the carrier or the consignee, the servants or agents, respectively of the carrier or the consignee.

Article 5 Basis of liability

1. The carrier is liable for loss resulting from loss of or damage to the goods, as well as from delay in delivery, if the occurrence which caused the loss, damage or delay took place while the goods were in his charge as defined in Article 4, unless the carrier proves that he, his servants or agents took all measures that could reasonably be required to avoid the occurrence and its consequences.
2. Delay in delivery occurs when the goods have not been delivered at the port of discharge provided for in the contract of carriage by sea within the time expressly agreed upon or, in the absence of such agreement, within the time which it would be reasonable to require of a diligent carrier, having regard to the circumstances of the case.
3. The person entitled to make a claim for the loss of goods may treat the goods as lost if they have not been delivered as required by Article 4 within 60 consecutive days following the expiry of the time for delivery according to paragraph 2 of this Article.
4. (a) The carrier is liable:
      (i) for loss of or damage to the goods or delay in delivery caused by fire, if the claimant proves that the fire arose from fault or neglect on the part of the carrier, his servants or agents;
      (ii) for such loss, damage or delay in delivery which is proved by the claimant to have resulted from the fault or neglect of the carrier, his servants or agents, in

taking all measures that could reasonably be required to put out the fire and avoid or mitigate its consequences.

(b) In case of fire on board the ship affecting the goods, if the claimant or the carrier so desires, a survey in accordance with shipping practices must be held into the cause and circumstances of the fire, and a copy of the surveyor's report shall be made available on demand to the carrier and the claimant.

5. With respect to live animals, the carrier is not liable for loss, damage or delay in delivery resulting from any special risks inherent in that kind of carriage. If the carrier proves that he has complied with any special instructions given to him by the shipper respecting the animals and that, in the circumstances of the case, the loss, damage or delay in delivery could be attributed to such risks, it is presumed that the loss, damage or delay in delivery was so caused, unless there is proof that all or a part of the loss, damage or delay in delivery resulted from fault or neglect on the part of the carrier, his servants or agents.
6. The carrier is not liable, except in general average, where loss, damage or delay in delivery resulted from measures to save life or from reasonable measures to save property at sea.
7. Where fault or neglect on the part of the carrier, his servants or agents combines with another cause to produce loss, damage or delay in delivery the carrier is liable only to the extent that the loss, damage or delay in delivery is attributable to such fault or neglect, provided that the carrier proves the amount of the loss, damage or delay in delivery not attributable thereto.

Article 6 Limits of liability

1. (a) The liability of the carrier for loss resulting from loss of or damage to goods according to the provisions of Article 5 is limited to an amount equivalent to 835 units of account per package or other shipping unit or 2.5 units of account per kilogram of gross weight of the goods lost or damaged, whichever is the higher.

   (b) The liability of the carrier for delay in delivery according to the provisions of Article 5 is limited to an amount equivalent to two and a half times the freight payable for the goods delayed, but not exceeding the total freight payable under the contract of carriage of goods by sea.

   (c) In no case shall the aggregate liability of the carrier, under both subparagraphs (a) and (b) of this paragraph, exceed the limitation which would be established under subparagraph (a) of this paragraph for total loss of the goods with respect to which such liability was incurred.
2. For the purpose of calculating which amount is the higher in accordance with paragraph 1(a) of this Article, the following rules apply –

   (a) where a container, pallet or similar article of transport is used to consolidate goods, the package or other shipping units enumerated in the bill of lading, if issued, or otherwise in any other document evidencing the contract of carriage by sea, as packed in such article of transport are deemed packages or shipping units. Except as aforesaid the goods in such article of transport are deemed one shipping unit;

   (b) in cases where the article of transport itself has been lost or damaged, that article of transport, if not owned or otherwise supplied by the carrier, is considered one separate shipping unit.
3. Unit of account means the unit of account mentioned in Article 26.

4. By agreement between the carrier and the shipper, limits of liability exceeding those provided for in paragraph 1 may be fixed.

Article 7 Application to non-contractual claims

1. The defences and limits of liability provided for in this Convention apply in any action against the carrier in respect of loss or damage to the goods covered by the contract of carriage by sea, as well as of delay in delivery whether the action is founded in contract, in tort or otherwise.
2. If such an action is brought against a servant or agent of the carrier, such servant or agent, if he proves that he acted within the scope of his employment, is entitled to avail himself of the defences and limits of liability which the carrier is entitled to invoke under this Convention.
3. Except as provided in Article 8, the aggregate of the amounts recoverable from the carrier and from any persons referred to in paragraph 2 of this Article shall not exceed the limits of liability provided for in this convention.

Article 8 Loss of right to limit responsibility

1. The carrier is not entitled to the benefit of the limitation of liability provided for in Article 6 if it is proved that the loss, damage or delay in delivery resulted from an act or omission of the carrier done with the intent to cause such loss, damage or delay, or recklessly and with knowledge that such loss, damage or delay would probably result.
2. Notwithstanding the provisions of paragraph 2 of Article 7, a servant or agent of the carrier is not entitled to the benefit of the limitation of liability provided for in Article 6 if it is proved that the loss, damage or delay in delivery resulted from an act or omission of such servant or agent, done with the intent to cause such loss, damage or delay, or recklessly and with knowledge that such loss, damage or delay would probably result.

Article 9 Deck cargo

1. The carrier is entitled to carry the goods on deck only is such carriage is in accordance with an agreement with the shipper or with the usage of the particular trade or is required by statutory rules or regulations.
2. If the carrier and the shipper have agreed that the goods shall or may be carried on deck, the carrier must insert in the bill of lading or other document evidencing the contract of carriage by sea a statement to that effect. In the absence of such a statement the carrier has the burden of proving that an agreement for carriage on deck has been entered into; however, the carrier is not entitled to invoke such an agreement against a third party, including a consignee, who has acquired the bill of lading in good faith.
3. Where the goods have been carried on deck contrary to the provisions of paragraph 1 of this Article or where the carrier may not under paragraph 2 of this Article invoke an agreement for carriage on deck, the carrier, notwithstanding the provisions of paragraph 1 of Article 5, is liable for loss of or damage to the goods, as well as for delay in delivery, resulting solely from the carriage on deck, and the extent of his liability

is to be determined in accordance with the provisions of Article 6 or Article 8 of this Convention, as the case may be.

4. Carriage of goods on deck contrary to express agreement for carriage under deck is deemed to be an act or omission of the carrier within the meaning of Article 8.

Article 10 Liability of the carrier and actual carrier

1. Where the performance of the carriage or part thereof has been entrusted to an actual carrier, whether or not in pursuance of a liberty under the contract of carriage by sea to do so, the carrier nevertheless remains responsible for the entire carriage according to the provisions of this Convention. The carrier is responsible, in relation to the carriage performed by the actual carrier, for the acts and omissions of the actual carrier and of his servants and agents acting within the scope of their employment.
2. All the provisions of this Convention governing the responsibility of the carrier also apply to the responsibility of the actual carrier for the carriage performed by him. The provisions of paragraphs 2 and 3 of Article 7 and of paragraph 2 of Article 8 apply if an action is brought against a servant or agent of the actual carrier.
3. Any special agreement under which the carrier assumes obligations not imposed by this Convention or waives rights conferred by this Convention affects the actual carrier only if agreed to by him expressly and in writing. Whether or not the actual carrier has so agreed, the carrier nevertheless remains bound by the obligations or waivers resulting from such special agreement.
4. Where and to the extent that both the carrier and the actual carrier are liable, their liability is joint and several.
5. The aggregate of the amounts recoverable from the carrier; the actual carrier and their servants and agents shall not exceed the limits of liability provided for in this Convention.
6. Nothing in this Article shall prejudice any right of recourse as between the carrier and the actual carrier.

Article 11 Through carriage

1. Notwithstanding the provisions of paragraph 1 of Article 10, where a contract of carriage by sea provides explicitly that a specified part of the carriage covered by the said contract is to be performed by a named person other than the carrier, the contract may also provide that the carrier is not liable for loss, damage or delay in delivery caused by an occurrence which takes place while the goods are in the charge of the actual carrier during such part of the carriage. Nevertheless, any stipulation limiting or excluding such liability is without effect if no judicial proceedings can be instituted against the actual carrier in a court competent under paragraph 1 or 2 of Article 21. The burden of proving that any loss, damage or delay in delivery has been caused by such an occurrence rests upon the carrier.
2. The actual carrier is responsible in accordance with the provisions of paragraph 2 of Article 10 for loss, damage or delay in delivery caused by an occurrence which takes place while the goods are in his charge.

Part III Liability of the shipper

Article 12 General rule

The shipper is not liable for loss sustained by the carrier or the actual carrier, or for damage sustained by the ship, unless such loss or damage was caused by the fault or neglect of the shipper, his servants or agents. Nor is any servant or agent of the shipper liable for such loss or damage unless the loss or damage was caused by fault or neglect on his part.

Article 13 Special rules on dangerous goods

1. The shipper must mark or label in a suitable manner dangerous goods as dangerous.
2. Where the shipper hands over dangerous goods to the carrier or an actual carrier, as the case may be, the shipper must inform him of the dangerous character of the goods and, if necessary, of the precautions to be taken. If the shipper fails to do so and such carrier or actual carrier does not otherwise have knowledge of their dangerous character –
   (a) the shipper is liable to the carrier and any actual carrier for the loss resulting from the shipment of such goods; and
   (b) the goods may at any time be unloaded, destroyed or rendered innocuous, as the circumstances may require, without payment of compensation.
3. The provisions of paragraph 2 of this Article may not be invoked by any person if during the carriage he has taken the goods in his charge with knowledge of their dangerous character.
4. If, in cases where the provisions of paragraph 2, subparagraph b, of this Article do not apply or may not be invoked, dangerous goods become an actual danger to life or property, they may unloaded, destroyed or rendered innocuous, as the circumstances may require, without payment of compensation except where there is an obligation to contribute in general average or where the carrier is liable in accordance with the provisions of Article 5.

Part IV Transport documents

Article 14 Issue of bill of lading

1. When the carrier or the actual carrier takes the goods in his charge, the carrier must, on demand of the shipper, issue to the shipper a bill of lading.
2. The bill of lading may be signed by a person having authority from the carrier. A bill of lading signed by the master of the ship carrying the goods is deemed to have been signed on behalf of the carrier.
3. The signature on the bill of lading may be in handwriting, printed in facsimile, perforated, stamped, in symbols, or made by any other mechanical or electronic means, if not inconsistent with the law of the country where the bill of lading is issued.

Article 15 Contents of bill of lading

1. The bill of lading must include, *inter alia*, the following particulars –
   (a) the general nature of the goods, the leading marks necessary for identification of the goods, an express statement, if applicable, as to the dangerous character of the

goods, the number of packages or pieces, and the weight of the goods or their quantity otherwise expressed, all such particulars as furnished by the shipper;
(b) the apparent condition of the goods;
(c) the name and principal place of business of the carrier;
(d) the name of the shipper;
(e) the consignee if named by the shipper;
(f) the port of loading under the contract of carriage by sea and the date on which the goods were taken over by the carrier at the port of loading;
(g) the port of discharge under the contract of carriage by sea;
(h) the number of originals of the bill of lading, if more than one;
(i) the place of issuance of the bill of lading;
(j) the signature of the carrier or a person acting on his behalf;
(k) the freight to the extent payable by the consignee or other indication that freight is payable by him;
(l) the statement referred to in paragraph 3 of Article 23;
(m) the statement, if applicable, that the goods shall or may be carried on deck;
(n) the date or the period of delivery of the goods at the port of discharge if expressly agreed upon between the parties; and
(o) any increased limit or limits of liability where agreed in accordance with paragraph 4 of Article 6.

2. After the goods have been loaded on board, if the shipper so demands, the carrier must issue to the shipper a 'shipped' bill of lading which, in addition to the particulars required under paragraph 1 of this Article, must state that the goods are on board a named ship or ships, and the date or dates of loading. If the carrier has previously issued to the shipper a bill of lading or other document of title with respect to any of such goods, on request of the carrier, the shipper must surrender such document in exchange for a 'shipped' bill of lading. The carrier may amend any previously issued document in order to meet the shipper/s demand for a 'shipped' bill of lading if, as amended, such document includes all the information required to be contained in a 'shipped' bill of lading.
3. The absence in the bill of lading of one or more particulars referred to in this Article does not affect the legal character of the document as a bill of lading provided that it nevertheless meets the requirements set out in paragraph 7 of Article 1.

Article 16 Bills of lading: reservations and evidentiary effect

1. If the bill of lading contains particulars concerning the general nature, leading marks, number of packages or pieces, weight or quantity of the goods which the carrier or other person issuing the bill of lading on his behalf knows or has reasonable grounds to suspect do not accurately represent the goods actually taken over or, where a 'shipped' bill of lading is issued, loaded, or if he had no reasonable means of checking such particulars, the carrier or such other person must insert in the bill of lading a reservation specifying these inaccuracies, grounds of suspicion or the absence of reasonable means of checking.
2. If the carrier or other person issuing the bill of lading on his behalf fails to note on the bill of lading the apparent condition of the goods, he is deemed to have noted on the bill of lading that the goods were in apparent good condition.

3. Except for particulars in respect of which and to the extent to which a reservation permitted under paragraph 1 of this Article has been entered –
   (a) the bill of lading is *prima facie* evidence of the taking over or, where a 'shipped' bill of lading is issued, loading, by the carrier of the goods as described in the bill of lading; and
   (b) proof to the contrary by the carrier is not admissible if the bill of lading has been transferred to a third party, including a consignee, who in good faith has acted in reliance on the description of the goods therein.
4. A bill of lading which does not, as provided in paragraph 1 subparagraph h of Article 15, set forth the freight or otherwise indicate that freight is payable by the consignee or does not set forth demurrage incurred at the port of loading payable by the consignee, is *prima facie* evidence that no freight or such demurrage is payable by him. However, proof to the contrary by the carrier is not admissible when the bill of lading has been transferred to a third party, including a consignee, who in good faith has acted in reliance on the absence in the bill of lading of any such indication.

Article 17 Guarantees by the shipper

1. The shipper is deemed to have guaranteed to the carrier the accuracy of particulars relating to the general nature of the goods, their marks, number, weight and quantity as furnished by him for insertion in the bill of lading. The shipper must indemnify the carrier against the loss resulting from inaccuracies in such particulars. The shipper remains liable even if the bill of lading has been transferred by him. The right of the carrier to such indemnity in no way limits his liability under the contract of carriage by sea to any person other than the shipper.
2. Any letter of guarantee or agreement by which the shipper undertakes to indemnify the carrier against loss resulting from the issuance of the bill of lading by the carrier, or by a person acting on his behalf, without entering a reservation relating to particulars furnished by the shipper for insertion in the bill of lading, or to the apparent condition of the goods, is void and of no effect as against any third party, including a consignee, to whom the bill of lading has been transferred.
3. Such letter of guarantee or agreement is valid as against the shipper unless the carrier or the person acting on his behalf, by omitting the reservation referred to in paragraph 2 of this Article, intends to defraud a third party, including a consignee, who acts in reliance on the description of the goods in the bill of lading. In the latter case, if the reservation omitted relates to particulars furnished by the shipper for insertion in the bill of lading the carrier has no right of indemnity from the shipper pursuant to paragraph 1 of this Article.
4. In the case of intended fraud referred to in paragraph 3 of this Article the carrier is liable, without the benefit of the limitation of liability provided for in this Convention, for the loss incurred by a third party, including a consignee, because he has acted in reliance on the description of the goods in the bill of lading.

Article 18 Documents other than bills of lading

Where a carrier issues a document other than a bill of lading to evidence the receipt of the goods to be carried, such a document is *prima facie* evidence of the conclusion of the contract of carriage by sea and the taking over by the carrier of the goods as therein described.

Part V Claims and actions

Article 19 Notice of loss, damage or delay

1. Unless notice of loss or damage, specifying the general nature of such loss or damage, is given in writing by the consignee to the carrier not later than the working day after the day when the goods were handed over to the consignee, such handing over is *prima facie* evidence of the delivery by the carrier of the goods as described in the document of transport or, if no such document has been issued, in good condition.
2. Where the loss or damage is not apparent, the provisions of paragraph 1 of this Article apply correspondingly if notice in writing is not given within 15 consecutive days after the day when the goods were handed over to the consignee.
3. If the state of the goods at the time they were handed over to the consignee has been the subject of a joint survey or inspection by the parties, notice in writing need not be given of loss or damage ascertained during such survey or inspection.
4. In the case of any actual or apprehended loss or damage the carrier and the consignee must give all reasonable facilities to each other for inspecting and tallying the goods.
5. No compensation shall be payable for loss resulting from delay in delivery unless a notice has been given in writing to the carrier within 60 consecutive days after the day when the goods were handed over to the consignee.
6. If the goods have been delivered by an actual carrier, any notice given under this Article to him shall have the same effect as if it had been given to the carrier and any notice given to the carrier shall have effect as if given to such actual carrier.
7. Unless notice of loss or damage, specifying the general nature of the loss or damage, is given in writing by the carrier or actual carrier to the shipper not later than 90 consecutive days after the occurrence of such loss or damage or after the delivery of the goods in accordance with paragraph 2 of Article 4, whichever is later, the failure to give such notice is *prima facie* evidence that the carrier or the actual carrier has sustained no loss or damage due to the fault or neglect of the shipper, his servants or agents.
8. For the purpose of this Article, notice given to a person acting on the carrier's or the actual carrier's behalf, including the master or the officer in charge of the ship, or to a person acting on the shipper's behalf is deemed to have been given to the carrier, to the actual carrier or to the shipper, respectively.

Article 20 Limitation of actions

1. Any action relating to carriage of goods under this convention is time-barred if judicial or arbitral proceedings have not been instituted within a period of two years.
2. The limitation period commences on the day on which the carrier has delivered the goods or part thereof or, in cases where no goods have been delivered, on the last day on which the goods should have been delivered.
3. The day on which the limitation period commences is not included in the period.
4. The person against whom a claim is made may at any time during the running of the limitation period extend that period by a declaration in writing to the claimant. This period may be further extended by another declaration or declarations.
5. An action for indemnity by a person held liable may be instituted even after the expiration of the limitation period provided for in the preceding paragraphs if instituted within

the time allowed by the law of the state where proceedings are instituted. However, the time allowed shall not be less than 90 days commencing from the day when the person instituting such action for indemnity has settled the claim or has been served with process in the action against himself.

Article 21 Jurisdiction

1. In judicial proceedings relating to carriage of goods under this convention the plaintiff, at his option, may institute an action in a court which, according to the law of the State where the court is situated, is competent and within the jurisdiction of which is situated one of the following places –
   (a) the principal place of business or, in the absence thereof, the habitual residence of the defendant; or
   (b) the place where the contract was made provided that the defendant has there a place of business, branch of agency through which the contract was made; or
   (c) the port of loading or the port of discharge; or
   (d) any additional place designated for that purpose in the contract of carriage by sea.
2. (a) Notwithstanding the preceding provisions of this Article, an action may be instituted in the courts of any port or place in a Contracting State at which the carrying vessel or any other vessel of the same ownership may have been arrested in accordance with applicable rules of the law of that State and of international law. However, in such a case, at the petition of the defendant, the claimant must remove the action, at his choice, to one of the jurisdictions referred to in paragraph 1 of this Article for the determination of the claim, but before such removal the defendant must furnish security sufficient to ensure payment of any judgment that may subsequently be awarded to the claimant in the action.
   (b) All questions relating to the sufficiency or otherwise of the security shall be determined by the court of the port or place of the arrest.
3. No judicial proceedings relating to carriage of goods under this convention may be instituted in a place not specified in paragraph 1 or 2 of this Article. The provisions of this paragraph do not constitute an obstacle to the jurisdiction of the Contracting States for provisional or protective measures.
4. (a) Where an action has been instituted in a court competent under paragraph 1 or 2 of this Article or where judgment has been delivered by such a court, no new action may be started between the same parties on the same grounds unless the judgment of the court before which the first action was instituted is not enforceable in the country in which the new proceedings are instituted.
   (b) For the purpose of this Article the institution of measures with a view to obtaining enforcement of a judgment is not to be considered as the starting of a new action.
   (c) For the purpose of this Article, the removal of an action to a different court within the same country, or to a court in another country, in accordance with paragraph 2(a) of this Article, is not to be considered as the starting of a new action.
5. Notwithstanding the provisions of the preceding paragraphs, an agreement made by the parties, after a claim under the contract of carriage by sea has arisen, which designates the place where the claimant may institute an action, is effective.

Article 22 Arbitration

1. Subject to the provisions of this Article, parties may provide by agreement evidenced in writing that any dispute that may arise relating to carriage of goods under this Convention shall be referred to arbitration.
2. Where a charter-party contains a provision that disputes arising thereunder shall be referred to arbitration and a bill of lading issued pursuant to the charter-party does not contain a special annotation providing that such provision shall be binding upon the holder of the bill of lading, the carrier may not invoke such provision as against a holder having acquired the bill of lading in good faith.
3. The arbitration proceedings shall, at the option of the claimant, be instituted at one of the following places –
   (a) a place in a state within whose territory is situated:
      (i) the principal place of business of the defendant or, in the absence thereof, the habitual residence of the defendant; or
      (ii) the place where the contract was made, provided that the defendant has there a place of business, branch or agency through which the contract was made; or
      (iii) the port of loading or the port of discharge; or
   (b) any place designated for that purpose in the arbitration clause or agreement.
4. The arbitrator or arbitration tribunal shall apply the rules of this Convention.
5. The provisions of paragraphs 3 and 4 of this Article are deemed to be part of every arbitration clause or agreement, and any term, of such clause or agreement which is inconsistent therewith is null and void.
6. Nothing in this Article affects the validity of an agreement relating to arbitration made by the parties after the claim under the contract of carriage by sea has arisen.

Part VI Supplement provision

Article 23 Contractual stipulations

1. Any stipulation in a contract of carriage by sea, in a bill of lading, or in any other document evidencing the contract of carriage by sea is null and void to the extent that it derogates, directly or indirectly, from the provisions of this Convention. The nullity of such a stipulation does not affect the validity of the other provisions of the contract or document of which it forms a part. A clause assigning benefit of insurance of the goods in favour of the carrier, or any similar clause, is null and void.
2. Notwithstanding the provisions of paragraph 1 of this Article, a carrier may increase his responsibilities and obligations under this Convention.
3. Where a bill of lading or any other document evidencing the contract of carriage by sea is issued, it must contain a statement that the carriage is subject to the provisions of this Convention which nullify any stipulation derogating therefrom to the detriment of the shipper or the consignee.
4. Where the claimant in respect of the goods has incurred loss as a result of a stipulation which is null and void by virtue of the present Article, or as a result of the omission of the statement referred to in paragraph 3 of this Article, the carrier must pay compensation to the extent required in order to give the claimant compensation in accordance with the provisions of this Convention for any loss of or damage to the goods as well as

for delay in delivery. The carrier must, in addition, pay compensation for costs incurred by the claimant for the purpose of exercising his right, provided that costs incurred in the action where the foregoing provision is invoked are to be determined in accordance with the law of the State where proceedings are instituted.

Article 24 General average

1. Nothing in this Convention shall prevent the application of provisions in the contract of carriage by sea or national law regarding the adjustment of general average.
2. With the exception of Article 20, the provisions of this Convention relating to the liability of the carrier for loss of or damage to the goods also determine whether the consignee may refuse contribution in general average and the liability of the carrier to indemnify the consignee in respect of any such contribution made or any salvage paid.

Article 25 Other conventions

1. This Convention does not modify the rights or duties of the carrier, the actual carrier and their servants and agents, provided for in international conventions or national law relating to the limitation of liability of owners of seagoing ships.

2.–4. [Omitted].

5. Nothing contained in this Convention prevents a Contracting State from applying any other international convention which is already in force at the date of this Convention and which applies mandatorily to contracts of carriage of goods primarily by a mode of transport other than transport by sea. This provision also applies to any subsequent revision or amendment of such international convention.

Article 26 Unit of account

1. The unit of account referred to in Article 6 of this Convention is the Special Drawing Right as defined by the International Monetary Fund. The amounts mentioned in Article 6 are to be converted into the national currency of a State according to the value of such currency at the date of judgment or the date agreed upon by the parties. The value of a national currency, in terms of the Special Drawing Right, of a Contracting State which is a member of the International Monetary Fund is to be calculated in accordance with the method of valuation applied by the International Monetary Fund in effect at the date in question for its operations and transactions. The value of a national currency in terms of the Special Drawing Right of a Contracting State which is not a member of the International Monetary Fund is to be calculated in a manner determined by that State.
2. Nevertheless, those States which are not members of the International Monetary Fund and whose law does not permit the application of the provisions of paragraph 1 of this Article may, at the time of signature, or at the time of ratification, acceptance, approval or accession or at any time thereafter, declare that the limits of liability provided for in this Convention to be applied in their territories shall be fixed as – 12,500 monetary units per package or other shipping unit or 37.5 monetary units per kilogram of gross weight of the goods.

3. The monetary unit referred to in paragraph 2 of this Article corresponds to sixty-five and a half milligrams of gold of millesimal fineness nine hundred, the conversion of the amounts referred to in paragraph 2 into the national currency is to be made according to the law of the state concerned.
4. The calculation mentioned in the last sentence of paragraph 1 and the conversion mentioned in paragraph 3 of this Article is to be made in such a manner as to express in the national currency of the Contracting State as far as possible the same real value for the amounts in Article 6 as is expressed there in units of account. Contracting States must communicate to the depository the manner of calculation pursuant to paragraph 1 of this Article, or the result of the conversion mentioned in paragraph 3 of this Article, as the case may be, at the time of signature or when depositing their instruments of ratification, acceptance, approval or accession, or when availing themselves of the option provided for in paragraph 2 of this Article and whenever there is a change in the manner of such calculation or in the result of such conversion.

Part VII

Articles 27–34 [Omitted]

EEC Convention on Law Applicable to Contractual Obligations, Rome, 1980

See Schedule I to the Contracts (Applicable Law) Act 1990 for text of the Convention.

Protocol Amending the Convention on the Limitation Period in the International Sale of Goods, Vienna, 1980

Article I

1. Paragraph 1 of Article 3 is replaced by the following provisions –

   '1. This Convention shall apply only –
      (a) if, at the time of the conclusion of the contract, the places of business of the parties to a contract of international sale of goods are in Contracting States; or
      (b) if the rules of private international law make the law of a Contracting State applicable to the contract of sale.'

   2. Paragraph 2 of Article 3 is deleted.

   3. Paragraph 3 of Article 3 is renumbered as paragraph 2.

Article II

1. Subparagraph (a) of Article 4 is deleted and replaced by the following provision –

   '(a) of goods bought for personal, family or household use, unless the seller, at any time before or at the conclusion of the contract, neither knew nor ought to have known that the goods were bought for any such use;'

2. Subparagraph (e) of Article 4 is deleted and is replaced by the following provision:
   '(e) of ships, vessels, hovercraft or aircraft;'

Articles III–XIV [Omitted]

United Nations Convention on Contracts for the International Sale of Goods, Vienna, 1980

Part I Sphere of application and general provisions

Chapter I Sphere and application

Article 1

1. This Convention applies to contracts of sale of goods between parties whose places of business are in different States –
   (a) when the States are Contracting States; or
   (b) when the rules of private international law lead to the application of the law of a Contracting State.
2. The fact that the parties have their places of business in different States is to be disregarded whenever this fact does not appear either from the contract or from any dealings between, or from information disclosed by, the parties at any time before or at the conclusion of the contract.
3. Neither the nationality of the parties nor the civil or commercial character of the parties or of the contract is to be taken into consideration in determining the application of this Convention.

Article 2

This Convention does not apply to sales –

(a) of goods bought for personal, family or household use, unless the seller, at any time before or at the conclusion of the contract, neither knew nor ought to have known that the goods were bought for any such use;
(b) by auction;
(c) on execution or otherwise by authority of law;
(d) of stocks, shares, investment securities, negotiable instruments or money;
(e) of ships, vessels, hovercraft or aircraft;
(f) of electricity.

Article 3

1. Contracts for the supply of goods to be manufactured or produced are to be considered sales unless the party who orders the goods undertakes to supply a substantial part of the materials necessary for such manufacture or production.
2. This Convention does not apply to contracts in which the preponderant part of the obligation of the party who furnishes the goods consists in the supply of labour or other services.

Article 4

This Convention governs only the formation of the contract of sale and the rights and obligations of the seller and the buyer arising from such a contract. In particular, except as otherwise expressly provided in this Convention, it is not concerned with –

(a) the validity of the contract or of any of its provisions or of any usage;
(b) the effect which the contract may have on the property in the goods sold.

Article 5

This Convention does not apply to the liability of the seller for death or personal injury caused by the goods to any person.

Article 6

The parties may exclude the application of this Convention or, subject to Article 12, derogate from or vary the effect of any of its provisions.

Chapter II General provisions

Article 7

1. In the interpretation of this Convention, regard is to be had to its international character and to the need to promote uniformity in its application and the observance of good faith in international trade.
2. Questions concerning matters governed by this Convention which are not expressly settled in it are to be settled in conformity with the general principles on which it is based or, in the absence of such principles, in conformity with the law applicable by virtue of the rules of private international law.

Article 8

1. For the purposes of this Convention statements made by and other conduct of a party are to be interpreted according to his intent where the other party knew or could not have been unaware what that intent was.
2. If the preceding paragraph is not applicable, statements made by and other conduct of a party are to be interpreted according to the understanding that a reasonable person of the same kind as the other party would have had in the same circumstances.
3. In determining the intent of a party or the understanding a reasonable person would have had, due consideration is to be given to all relevant circumstances of the case including the negotiations, any practices which the parties have established between themselves, usages and any subsequent conduct of the parties.

Article 9

1. The parties are bound by any usage to which they have agreed and by any practices which they have established between themselves.

2. The parties are considered, unless otherwise agreed, to have impliedly made applicable to their contract or its formation a usage of which the parties knew or ought to have known and which in international trade is widely known to, and regularly observed by, parties to contracts of the type involved in the particular trade concerned.

Article 10

For the purposes of this Convention –

(a) if a party has more than one place of business, the place of business is that which has the closest relationship to the contract and its performance, having regard to the circumstances known to or contemplated by the parties at any time before or at the conclusion of the contract;
(b) if a party does not have a place of business, reference is to be made to his habitual residence.

Article 11

A contract of sale need not be concluded in or evidenced by writing and is not subject to any other requirement as to form. It may be proved by any means, including witnesses.

Article 12

Any provision of Article II, Article 29 or Part II of this Convention that allows a contract of sale or its modification or termination by agreement or any offer, acceptance or other indication of intention to be made in any form other than in writing does not apply where any party has his place of business in a Contracting State which has made a declaration under Article 96 of this Convention. The parties may not derogate from or vary the effect of this Article.

Article 13

For the purposes of this Convention 'writing' includes telegram and telex.

Part II Formation of the contract

Article 14

1. A proposal for concluding a contract addressed to one or more specific persons constitutes an offer if it is sufficiently definite and indicates the intention of the offeror to be bound in case of acceptance. A proposal is sufficiently definite if it indicates the goods and expressly or implicitly fixes or makes provision for determining the quantity and the price.
2. A proposal other than one addressed to one or more specific persons is to be considered merely as an invitation to make offers, unless the contrary is clearly indicated by the person making the proposal.

Article 15

1. An offer becomes effective when it reaches the offeree.
2. An offer, even if it is irrevocable, may be withdrawn if the withdrawal reaches the offeree before or at the same time as the offer.

Article 16

1. Until a contract is concluded an offer may be revoked if the revocation reaches the offeree before he has dispatched an acceptance.
2. However, an offer cannot be revoked –
   (a) if it indicates, whether by stating a fixed time for acceptance or otherwise, that it is irrevocable; or
   (b) if it was reasonable for the offeree to rely on the offer as being irrevocable and the offeree has acted in reliance on the offer.

Article 17

An offer, even if it is irrevocable, is terminated when a rejection reaches the offeror.

Article 18

1. A statement made by or other conduct of the offeree indicating assent to an offer is an acceptance. Silence or inactivity does not in itself amount to acceptance.
2. An acceptance of an offer becomes effective at the moment the indication of assent reaches the offeror. An acceptance is not effective if the indication of assent does not reach the offeror within the time he has fixed or, if no time is fixed, within a reasonable time, due account being taken of the circumstances of the transaction, including the rapidity of the means of communication employed by the offeror. An oral offer must be accepted immediately unless the circumstances indicate otherwise.
3. However, if, by virtue of the offer or as a result of practices which the parties have established between themselves or of usage, the offeree may indicate assent by performing an act, such as one relating to the dispatch of the goods or payment of the price, without notice to the offeror, the acceptance is effective at the moment the act is performed, provided that the act is performed within the period of time laid down in the preceding paragraph.

Article 19

1. A reply to an offer which purports to be an acceptance but contains additions, limitations or other modifications is a rejection of the offer and constitutes a counter-offer.
2. However, a reply to an offer which purports to be an acceptance but contains additional or different terms which do not materially alter the terms of the offer constitutes an acceptance, unless the offeror, without undue delay, objects orally to the discrepancy or dispatches a notice to that effect. If he does not so object, the terms of the contract are the terms of the offer with the modifications contained in the acceptance.

3. Additional or different terms relating, among other things, to the price, payment, quality and quantity of the goods, place and time of delivery, extent of one party's liability to the other or the settlement of disputes are considered to alter the terms of the offer materially.

Article 20

1. A period of time for acceptance fixed by the offeror in a telegram or a letter begins to run from the moment the telegram is handed in for dispatch or from the date shown on the letter or, if no such date is shown, from the date shown on the envelope. A period of time for acceptance fixed by the offeror by telephone, telex or other means of instantaneous communication, begins to run from the moment that the offer reaches the offeree.
2. Official holidays or non-business days occurring during the period for acceptance are included in calculating the period. However, if a notice of acceptance cannot be delivered at the address of the offeror on the last day of the period because that day falls on an official holiday or a non-business day at the place of business of the offeror, the period is extended until the first business day which follows.

Article 21

1. A late acceptance is nevertheless effective as an acceptance if without delay the offeror orally so informs the offeree or dispatches a notice to that effect.
2. If a letter or other writing containing a late acceptance shows that it has been sent in such circumstances that if its transmission had been normal it would have reached the offeror in due time, the late acceptance is effective as an acceptance unless, without delay, the offeror orally informs the offeree that he considers his offer as having lapsed or dispatches a notice to that effect.

Article 22

An acceptance may be withdrawn if the withdrawal reaches the offeror before or at the same time as the acceptance would have become effective.

Article 23

A contract is concluded at the moment when an acceptance of an offer becomes effective in accordance with the provisions of this Convention.

Article 24

For the purposes of this Part of the Convention, an offer, declaration of acceptance or any other indication of intention 'reaches' the addressee when it is made orally to him or delivered by any other means to him personally, to his place of business or mailing address or, if he does not have a place of business or mailing address, to his habitual residence.

Part III Sale of goods

Chapter I General provisions

Article 25

A breach of contract committed by one of the parties is fundamental if it results in such detriment to the other party as substantially to deprive him of what he is entitled to expect under the contract, unless the party in breach did not foresee and a reasonable person of the same kind in the same circumstances would not have foreseen such a result.

Article 26

A declaration of avoidance of the contract is effective only if made by notice to the other party.

Article 27

Unless otherwise expressly provided in this Part of the Convention, if any notice, request or other communication is given or made by a party in accordance with this Part and by means appropriate in the circumstances, a delay or error in the transmission of the communication or its failure to arrive does not deprive that party of the right to rely on the communication.

Article 28

If, in accordance with the provisions of this Convention, one party is entitled to require performance of any obligation by the other party, a court is not bound to enter a judgment for specific performance unless the court would do so under its own law in respect of similar contracts of sale not governed by this Convention.

Article 29

1. A contract may be modified or terminated by the mere agreement of the parties.
2. A contract in writing which contains a provision requiring any modification or termination by agreement to be in writing may not be otherwise modified or terminated by agreement. However, a party may be precluded by his conduct from asserting such a provision to the extent that the other party has relied on that conduct.

Chapter II Obligations of the seller

Article 30

The seller must deliver the goods, hand over any documents relating to them and transfer the property in the goods, as required by the contract and this Convention.

Section I – Delivery of the goods and handing over of documents

Article 31

If the seller is not bound to deliver the goods at any other particular place, his obligation to deliver consists –

(a) if the contract of sale involves carriage of the goods – in handing the goods over to the first carrier for transmission to the buyer;
(b) if, in cases not within the preceding subpara, the contract relates to specific goods, or unidentified goods to be drawn from a specific stock or to be manufactured or produced, and at the time of the conclusion of the contract the parties knew that the goods were at, or were to be manufactured or produced at, a particular place – in placing the goods at the buyer's disposal at that place;
(c) in other cases – in placing the goods at the buyer's disposal at the place where the seller had his place of business at the time of the conclusion of the contract.

Article 32

1. If the seller, in accordance with the contract or this Convention, hands the goods over to a carrier and if the goods are not clearly identified to the contract by markings on the goods, by shipping documents or otherwise, the seller must give the buyer notice of the consignment specifying the goods.
2. If the seller is bound to arrange for carriage of the goods, he must make such contracts as are necessary for carriage to the place fixed by means of transportation appropriate in the circumstances and according to the usual terms for such transportation.
3. If the seller is not bound to effect insurance in respect of the carriage of the goods, he must, at the buyer's request, provide him with all available information necessary to enable him to effect such insurance.

Article 33

The seller must deliver the goods –

(a) if a date is fixed by or determinable from the contract, on that date;
(b) if a period of time is fixed by or determinable from the contract, at any time within that period unless circumstances indicate that the buyer is to choose a date; or
(c) in any other case, within a reasonable time after the conclusion of the contract.

Article 34

If the seller is bound to hand over documents relating to the goods, he must hand them over at the time and place and in the form required by the contract. If the seller has handed over documents before that time, he may, up to that time, cure any lack of conformity in the documents, if the exercise of this right does not cause the buyer unreasonable inconvenience or unreasonable expense. However, the buyer retains any right to claim damages as provided for in this Convention.

Section II – Conformity of the goods and third party claims

Article 35

1. The seller must deliver goods which are of the quantity, quality and description required by the contract and which are contained or packaged in the manner required by the contract.
2. Except where the parties have agreed otherwise, the goods do not conform with the contract unless they –
   (a) are fit for the purposes for which goods of the same description would ordinarily be used;
   (b) are fit for any particular purpose expressly or impliedly made known to the seller at the time of the conclusion of the contract, except where the circumstances show that the buyer did not rely, or that it was unreasonable for him to rely, on the seller's skill and judgment;
   (c) possess the qualities of goods which the seller has held out to the buyer as a sample or model;
   (d) are contained or packaged in the manner usual for such goods or, where there is no such manner, in a manner adequate to preserve and protect the goods.
3. The seller is not liable under subparagraphs (a) to (d) of the preceding paragraph for any lack of conformity of the goods if at the time of the conclusion of the contract the buyer knew or could not have been unaware of such lack of conformity.

Article 36

1. The seller is liable in accordance with the contract and this Convention for any lack of conformity which exists at the time when the risk passes to the buyer, even though the lack of conformity becomes apparent only after that time.
2. The seller is also liable for any lack of conformity which occurs after the time indicated in the preceding paragraph and which is due to a breach of any of his obligations, including a breach of any guarantee that for a period of time the goods will remain fit for their ordinary purpose or for some particular purpose or will retain specified qualities or characteristics.

Article 37

If the seller has delivered goods before the date for delivery, he may, up to that date, deliver any missing part or make up any deficiency in the quantity of the goods delivered, or deliver goods in replacement of any non-conforming goods delivered or remedy any lack of conformity in the goods delivered, provided that the exercise of this right does not cause the buyer unreasonable inconvenience or unreasonable expense. However, the buyer retains any right to claim damages as provided for in this Convention.

Article 38

1. The buyer must examine the goods, or cause them to be examined, within a short a period as is practicable in the circumstances.

2. If the contract involves carriage of the goods, examination may be deferred until after the goods have arrived at their destination.
3. If the goods are redirected in transit or redispatched by the buyer without a reasonable opportunity for examination by him and at the time of the conclusion of the contract the seller knew or ought to have known of the possibility of such redirection or redispatch, examination may be deferred until after the goods have arrived at the new destination.

Article 39

1. The buyer loses the right to rely on a lack of conformity of the goods if he does not give notice to the seller specifying the nature of the lack of conformity within a reasonable time after he has discovered it or ought to have discovered it.
2. In any event, the buyer loses the right to rely on a lack of conformity of the goods if he does not give the seller notice thereof at the latest within a period of two years from the date on which the goods were actually handed over to the buyer, unless this time-limit is inconsistent with a contractual period of guarantee.

Article 40

The seller is not entitled to rely on the provisions of Articles 38 and 39 if the lack of conformity relates to facts of which he knew or could not have been unaware and which he did not disclose to the buyer.

Article 41

The seller must deliver goods which are free from any right or claim of a third party, unless the buyer agreed to take the goods subject to that right or claim. However, if such right or claim is based on industrial property or other intellectual property, the seller's obligation is governed by Article 42.

Article 42

1. The seller must deliver goods which are free from any right or claim of a third party based on industrial property or other intellectual property, of which at the time of the conclusion of the contract the seller knew or could not have been unaware, provided that the right or claim is based on industrial property or other intellectual property –
   (a) under the law of the State where the goods will be resold or otherwise used, if it was contemplated by the parties at the time of the conclusion of the contract that the goods would be resold or otherwise used in that State; or
   (b) in any other case, under the law of the State where the buyer has his place of business.
2. The obligation of the seller under the preceding paragraph does not extend to cases where –
   (a) at the time of the conclusion of the contract the buyer knew or could not have been unaware of the right or claim; or
   (b) the right or claim results from the seller's compliance with technical drawings, designs, formulae or other such specifications furnished by the buyer.

Article 43

1. The buyer loses the right to rely on the provisions of Article 41 or Article 42 if he does not give notice to the seller specifying the nature of the right or claim of the third party within a reasonable time after he has become aware or ought to have become aware of the right or claim.
2. The seller is not entitled to rely on the provisions of the preceding paragraph if he knew of the right or claim of the third party and the nature of it.

Article 44

Notwithstanding the provisions of paragraph 1 of Article 39 and paragraph 1 of Article 43, the buyer may reduce the price in accordance with Article 50 or claim damages, except for loss of profit, if he has a reasonable excuse for his failure to give the required notice.

Section III – Remedies for breach of contract by the seller

Article 45

1. If the seller fails to perform any of his obligations under the contract or this Convention, the buyer may –
   (a) exercise the rights provided in Articles 46 to 52;
   (b) claim damages as provided in Articles 74 to 77.
2. The buyer is not deprived of any right he may have to claim damages by exercising his right to other remedies.
3. No period of grace may be granted to the seller by a court or arbitral tribunal when the buyer resorts to a remedy for breach of contract.

Article 46

1. The buyer may require performance by the seller of his obligations unless the buyer has resorted to a remedy which is inconsistent with this requirement.
2. If the goods do not conform with the contract, the buyer may require delivery of substitute goods only if the lack of conformity constitutes a fundamental breach of contract and a request for substitute goods is made either in conjunction with notice given under Article 39 or within a reasonable time thereafter.
3. If the goods do not conform with the contract, the buyer may require the seller to remedy the lack of conformity by repair, unless this is unreasonable having regard to all the circumstances. A request for repair must be made either in conjunction with notice given under Article 39 or within a reasonable time thereafter.

Article 47

1. The buyer may fix an additional period of time of reasonable length for performance by the seller of his obligations.
2. Unless the buyer has received notice from the seller that he will not perform within the period so fixed, the buyer may not, during that period, resort to any remedy for breach

of contract. However, the buyer is not deprived thereby of any right he may have to claim damages for delay in performance.

Article 48

1. Subject to Article 49, the seller may, even after the date for delivery, remedy at his own expense any failure to perform his obligations, if he can do so without unreasonable delay and without causing the buyer unreasonable inconvenience or uncertainty of reimbursement by the seller of expenses advanced by the buyer. However, the buyer retains any right to claim damages as provided for in this Convention.
2. If the seller requests the buyer to make known whether he will accept performance and the buyer does not comply with the request within a reasonable time, the seller may perform within the time indicated in his request. The buyer may not, during that period of time, resort to any remedy which is inconsistent with performance by the seller.
3. A notice by the seller that he will perform within a specified period of time is assumed to include a request, under the preceding paragraph, that the buyer make known his decision.
4. A request or notice by the seller under paragraph 2 or 3 of this Article is not effective unless received by the buyer.

Article 49

1. The buyer may declare the contract avoided –
   (a) if the failure by the seller to perform any of his obligations under the contract or this Convention amounts to a fundamental breach of contract; or
   (b) in case of non-delivery, if the seller does not deliver the goods within the additional period of time fixed by the buyer in accordance with paragraph 1 of Article 47 or declares that he will not deliver within the period so fixed.
2. However, in cases where the seller has delivered the goods, the buyer loses the right to declare the contract avoided unless he does so –
   (a) in respect of late delivery, within a reasonable time after he has become aware that delivery has been made;
   (b) in respect of any breach other than late delivery, within a reasonable time:
      (i) after he knew or ought to have known of the breach;
      (ii) after the expiration of any additional period of time fixed by the buyer in accordance with paragraph 1 of Article 47, or after the seller has declared that he will not perform his obligations within such an additional period; or
      (iii) after the expiration of any additional period of time indicated by the seller in accordance with paragraph 2 of Article 48 or after the buyer has declared that he will not accept performance.

Article 50

If the goods do not conform with the contract and whether or not the price has already been paid, the buyer may reduce the price in the same proportion as the value that the goods actually delivered had at the time of the delivery bears to the value that conforming goods would have had at that time. However, if the seller remedies any failure to perform his obligations in accordance with Article 37 or Article 48 or if the buyer refuses to accept performance by the seller in accordance with those Articles, the buyer may not reduce the price.

Article 51

1. If the seller delivers only a part of the goods or if only a part of the goods delivered is in conformity with the contract, Articles 46 to 50 apply in respect of the part which is missing or which does not conform.
2. The buyer may declare the contract avoided in its entirety only if the failure to make delivery completely or in conformity with the contract amounts to a fundamental breach of the contract.

Article 52

1. If the seller delivers the goods before the date fixed, the buyer may take delivery or refuse to take delivery.
2. If the seller delivers a quantity of goods greater than that provided for in the contract, the buyer may take delivery or refuse to take delivery of the excess quantity. If the buyer takes delivery of all or part of the excess quantity, he must pay for it at the contract rate.

Chapter III Obligations of the buyer

Article 53

The buyer must pay the price for the goods and take delivery of them as required by the contract and this Convention.

Section I – Payment of the price

Article 54

The buyer's obligation to pay the price includes taking such steps and complying with such formalities as may be required under the contract or any laws and regulations to enable payment to be made.

Article 55

Where a contract has been validly concluded but does not expressly or implicitly fix or make provision for determining the price, the parties are considered, in the absence of any indication to the contrary, to have impliedly made reference to the price generally charged at the time of the conclusion of the contract for such goods sold under comparable circumstances in the trade concerned.

Article 56

If the price is fixed according to the weight of the goods, in case of doubt it is to be determined by the net weight.

Article 57

1. If the buyer is not bound to pay the price at any other particular place, he must pay it to the seller –
   (a) at the seller's place of business; or
   (b) if the payment is to be made against the handing over of the goods or of documents, at the place where the handing over takes place.
2. The seller must bear any increase in the expenses incidental to payment which is caused by a change in his place of business subsequent to the conclusion of the contract.

Article 58

1. If the buyer is not bound to pay the price at any other specific time, he must pay it when the seller places either the goods or documents controlling their disposition at the buyer's disposal in accordance with the contract and this Convention. The seller may make such payment a condition for handing over the goods or documents.
2. If the contract involves carriage of the goods, the seller may dispatch the goods on terms whereby the goods, or documents controlling their disposition, will not be handed over to the buyer except against payment of the price.
3. The buyer is not bound to pay the price until he has had an opportunity to examine the goods, unless the procedures for delivery or payment agreed upon by the parties are inconsistent with his having such an opportunity.

Article 59

The buyer must pay the price on the date fixed by or determinable from the contract and this convention without the need for any request or compliance with any formality on the part of the seller.

Section II – Taking delivery

Article 60

The buyer's obligation to take delivery consists –

(a) in doing all the acts which could reasonably be expected of him in order to enable the seller to make delivery; and
(b) in taking over the goods.

Section III – Remedies for breach of contract by the buyer

Article 61

1. If the buyer fails to perform any of his obligations under the contract or this Convention, the seller may –
   (a) exercise the rights provided in Articles 62 to 65;
   (b) claim damages as provided in Articles 74 to 77.

2. The seller is not deprived of any right he may have to claim damages by exercising his right to other remedies.
3. No period of grace may be granted to the buyer by a court or arbitral tribunal when the seller resorts to a remedy for breach of contract.

Article 62

The seller may require the buyer to pay the price, take delivery or perform his other obligations, unless the seller has resorted to a remedy which is inconsistent with this requirement.

Article 63

1. The seller may fix an additional period of time of reasonable length for performance by the buyer of his obligations.
2. Unless the seller has received notice from the buyer that he will not perform within the period so fixed, the seller may not, during that period, resort to any remedy for breach of contract. However, the seller is not deprived thereby of any right he may have to claim damages for delay in performance.

Article 64

1. The seller may declare the contract avoided –
   (a) if the failure by the buyer to perform any of his obligations under the contract or this Convention amounts to a fundamental breach of contract; or
   (b) if the buyer does not, within the additional period of time fixed by the seller in accordance with paragraph 1 or Article 63, perform his obligation to pay the price or take delivery of the goods, or if he declares that he will not do so within the period so fixed.
2. However, in cases where the buyer has paid the price, the seller loses the right to declare the contract avoided unless he does so –
   (a) in respect of late performance by the buyer, before the seller has become aware that performance has been rendered; or
   (b) in respect of any breach other than late performance by the buyer, within a reasonable time:
      (i) after the seller knew or ought to have known of the breach; or
      (ii) after the expiration of any additional period of time fixed by the seller in accordance with paragraph 1 or Article 63, or after the buyer has declared that he will not perform his obligations within such an additional period.

Article 65

1. If under the contract the buyer is to specify the form, measurement or other features of the goods and he fails to make such specification either on the date agreed upon within a reasonable time after receipt of a request from the seller, the seller may, without prejudice to any other rights he may have, make the specification himself in accordance with the requirements of the buyer that may be known to him.

2. If the seller makes the specification himself, he must inform the buyer of the details thereof and must fix a reasonable time within which the buyer may make a different specification. If, after receipt of such a communication, the buyer fails to do so within the time so fixed, the specification made by the seller is binding.

Chapter IV Passing of risk

Article 66

Loss of or damage to the goods after the risk has passed to the buyer does not discharge him from his obligation to pay the price, unless the loss or damage is due to an act or omission of the seller.

Article 67

1. If the contract of sale involves carriage of the goods and the seller is not bound to hand them over at a particular place, the risk passes to the buyer when the goods are handed over to the first carrier for transmission to the buyer in accordance with the contract of sale. If the seller is bound to hand the goods over to a carrier at a particular place, the risk does not pass to the buyer until the goods are handed over to the carrier at that place. The fact that the seller is authorised to retain documents controlling the disposition of the goods does not affect the passage of the risk.
2. Nevertheless, the risk does not pass to the buyer until the goods are clearly identified to the contract, whether by markings on the goods, by shipping documents, by notice given to the buyer or otherwise.

Article 68

The risk in respect of goods sold in transit passes to the buyer from the time of the conclusion of the contract. However, if the circumstances so indicate, the risk is assumed by the buyer from the time the goods were handed over to the carrier who issued the documents embodying the contract of carriage. Nevertheless, if at the time or the conclusion of the contract of sale the seller knew or ought to have known that the goods had been lost or damaged and did not disclose this to the buyer, the loss or damage is at the risk of the seller.

Article 69

1. In cases not within Articles 67 and 68, the risk passes to the buyer when he takes over the goods or, if he does not do so in due time, from the time when the goods are placed at his disposal and he commits a breach of contract by failing to take delivery.
2. However, if the buyer is bound to take over the goods at a place other than a place of business of the seller, the risk passes when delivery is due and the buyer is aware of the fact that the goods are placed at his disposal at that place.
3. If the contract relates to goods not then identified, the goods are considered not to be placed at the disposal of the buyer until they are clearly identified to the contract.

Article 70

If the seller has committed a fundamental breach of contract, Articles 67, 68 and 69 do not impair the remedies available to the buyer on account of the breach.

Chapter V Provisions common to the obligations of the seller and of the buyer

Section I – Anticipatory breach and instalment contracts

Article 71

1. A party may suspend the performance of his obligations if, after the conclusion of the contract, it becomes apparent that the other party will not perform a substantial part of his obligations as a result of:
   (a) a serious deficiency in his ability to perform or in his credit worthiness; or
   (b) his conduct in preparing to perform or in performing the contract.
2. If the seller has already dispatched the goods before the grounds described in the preceding paragraph become evident, he may prevent the handing over of the goods to the buyer even though the buyer holds a document which entitles him to obtain them. The present paragraph relates only to the rights in the goods as between the buyer and the seller.
3. A party suspending performance, whether before or after dispatch of the goods, must immediately give notice of the suspension to the other party and must continue with performance if the other party provides adequate assurance of his performance.

Article 72

1. If prior to the date for performance of the contract it is clear that one of the parties will commit a fundamental breach of contract, the other party may declare the contract avoided.
2. If time allows, the party intending to declare the contract avoided must give reasonable notice to the other party in order to permit him to provide adequate assurance of his performance.
3. The requirements of the preceding paragraph do not apply if the other party has declared that he will not perform his obligations.

Article 73

1. In the case of a contract for delivery of goods by instalments, if the failure of one party to perform any of his obligations in respect of any instalment constitutes a fundamental breach of contract with respect to that instalment, the other party may declare the contract avoided with respect to that instalment.
2. If one party's failure to perform any of his obligations in respect of any instalment gives the other party good grounds to conclude that a fundamental breach of contract will occur with respect to future instalments, he may declare the contract avoided for the future, provided that he does so within a reasonable time.

3. A buyer who declares the contract avoided in respect of any delivery may, at the same time, declare it avoided in respect of deliveries already made or of future deliveries if, by reason of their interdependence, those deliveries could not be used for the purpose contemplated by the parties at the time of the conclusion of the contract.

Section II – Damages

Article 74

Damages for breach of contract by one party consist of a sum equal to the loss, including loss of profit, suffered by the other party as a consequence of the breach. Such damages may not exceed the loss which the party in breach foresaw or ought to have foreseen at the time of the conclusion of the contract, in the light of the facts and matters of which he then knew or ought to have known, as a possible consequence of the breach of contract.

Article 75

If the contract is avoided and if, in a reasonable manner and within a reasonable time after avoidance, the buyer has bought goods in replacement or the seller has resold the goods, the party claiming damages may recover the difference between the contract price and the price in the substitute transaction as well as any further damages recoverable under Article 74.

Article 76

1. If the contract is avoided and there is a current price for the goods, the party claiming damages may, if he has not made a purchase or resale under Article 75, recover the difference between the price fixed by the contract and the current price at the time of avoidance as well as any further damages recoverable under Article 74. If, however, the party claiming damages has avoided the contract after taking over the goods, the current price at the time of such taking over shall be applied instead of the current price at the time of avoidance.
2. For the purposes of the preceding paragraph, the current price is the price prevailing at the place where delivery of the goods should have been made or, if there is no current price at that place, the price at such other place as serves as a reasonable substitute, making due allowance for differences in the cost of transporting the goods.

Article 77

A party who relies on a breach of contract must take such measures as are reasonable in the circumstances to mitigate the loss, including loss of profit, resulting from the breach. If he fails to take such measures, the party in breach may claim a reduction in the damages in the amount by which the loss should have been mitigated.

Section III – Interest

Article 78

If a party fails to pay the price or any other sum that is in arrears, the other party is entitled to interest on it, without prejudice to any claim for damages recoverable under Article 74.

Section IV – Exemptions

Article 79

1. A party is not liable for a failure to perform any of his obligations if he proves that the failure was due to an impediment beyond his control and that he could not reasonably be expected to have taken the impediment into account at the time of the conclusion of the contract or to have avoided or overcome it or its consequences.
2. If the party's failure is due to the failure by a third person whom he has engaged to perform the whole or a part of the contract, that party is exempt from liability only if –
   (a) he is exempt under the preceding paragraph; and
   (b) the person whom he has so engaged would be so exempt if the provisions of that paragraph were applied to him.
3. The exemption provided by this Article has effect for the period during which the impediment exists.
4. The party who fails to perform must give notice to the other party of the impediment and its effect on his ability to perform. If the notice is not received by the other party within a reasonable time after the party who fails to perform knew or ought to have known of the impediment, he is liable for damages resulting from such non-receipt.
5. Nothing in this Article prevents either party from exercising any right other than to claim damages under this Convention.

Article 80

A party may not rely on a failure of the other party to perform, to the extent that such failure was caused by the first party's act or omission.

Section V – Effects of avoidance

Article 81

1. Avoidance of the contract releases both parties from their obligations under it, subject to any damages which may be due. Avoidance does not affect any provision of the contract for the settlement of disputes or any other provision of the contract governing the rights and obligations of the parties consequent upon the avoidance of the contract.
2. A party who has performed the contract either wholly or in part may claim restitution from the other party of whatever the first party has supplied or paid under the contract. If both parties are bound to make restitution, they must do so concurrently.

Article 82

1. The buyer loses the right to declare the contract avoided or to require the seller to deliver substitute goods if it is impossible for him to make restitution of the goods substantially in the condition in which he received them.
2. The preceding paragraph does not apply –
   (a) if the impossibility of making restitution of the goods or of making restitution of the goods substantially in the condition in which the buyer received them is not due to his act or omission;

(b) if the goods or part of the goods have perished or deteriorated as a result of the examination provided for in Article 38; or
(c) if the goods or part of the goods have been sold in the normal course of business or have been consumed or transformed by the buyer in the course of normal use before he discovered or ought to have discovered the lack of conformity.

Article 83

A buyer who has lost the right to declare the contract avoided or to require the seller to deliver substitute goods in accordance with Article 82 retains all other remedies under the contract and this Convention.

Article 84

1. If the seller is bound to refund the price, he must also pay interest on it, from the date on which the price was paid.
2. The buyer must account to the seller for all benefits which he has derived from the goods or part of them –
   (a) if he must make restitution of the goods or part of them; or
   (b) if it is impossible for him to make restitution of all or part of the goods or to make restitution of all or part of the goods substantially in the condition in which he received them, but he has nevertheless declared the contract avoided or required the seller to deliver substitute goods.

Section VI – Preservation of the goods

Article 85

If the buyer is in delay in taking delivery of the goods or, where payment of the price and delivery of the goods are to be made concurrently, if he fails to pay the price, and the seller is either in possession of the goods or otherwise able to control their disposition, the seller must take such steps as are reasonable in the circumstances to preserve them. He is entitled to retain them until he has been reimbursed his reasonable expenses by the buyer.

Article 86

1. If the buyer has received the goods and intends to exercise any right under the contract or this Convention to reject them, he must take such steps to preserve them as are reasonable in the circumstances. He is entitled to retain them until he has been reimbursed his reasonable expenses by the seller.
2. If goods dispatched to the buyer have been placed at his disposal at their destination and he exercises the right to reject them, he must take possession of them on behalf of the seller, provided that this can be done without payment of the price and without unreasonable inconvenience or unreasonable expense. This provision does not apply if the seller or a person authorised to take charge of the goods on his behalf is present at the destination. If the buyer takes possession of the goods under this paragraph, his rights and obligations are governed by the preceding paragraph.

Article 87

A party who is bound to take steps to preserve the goods may deposit them in a warehouse of a third person at the expense of the other party provided that the expense incurred is not unreasonable.

Article 88

1. A party who is bound to preserve the goods in accordance with Article 85 or 86 may sell them by any appropriate means if there has been an unreasonable delay by the other party in taking possession of the goods or in taking them back or in paying the price or the cost of preservation, provided that reasonable notice of the intention to sell has been given to the other party.
2. If the goods are subject to rapid deterioration or their preservation would involve unreasonable expense, a party who is bound to preserve the goods in accordance with Article 85 or 86 must take reasonable measures to sell them, to the extent possible he must give notice to the other party of his intention to sell.
3. A party selling the goods has the right to retain out of the proceeds of sale an amount equal to the reasonable expenses of preserving the goods and of selling them. He must account to the other party for the balance.

Part IV

Articles 89–91 [Omitted]

Article 92

1. A Contracting State may declare at the time of the signature, ratification, acceptance, approval or accession that it will not be bound by Part II of this Convention or that it will not be bound by Part III of this Convention.
2. A Contracting State which makes a declaration in accordance with the preceding paragraph in respect of Part II or Part III of this Convention is not to be considered a contracting State within paragraph 1 or Article 1 of this Convention in respect of matters governed by the Part to which the declaration applies.

Article 93 [Omitted]

Article 94

1. Two or more Contracting States which have the same or closely related legal rules on matters governed by this convention may at any time declare that the Convention is not to apply to contracts of sale or to their formation where the parties have their places of business in those States. Such declarations may be made jointly or by reciprocal unilateral declarations.
2. A Contracting State which has the same or closely related legal rules on matters governed by this Convention as one or more non-Contracting States may at any time

declare that the Convention is not to apply to contracts of sale or to their formation where the parties have their places of business in those States.

3. [Omitted].

Article 95

Any State may declare at the time of the deposit of its instrument of ratification acceptance, approval or accession that it will not be bound by subparagraph 1(b) of Article 1 of this Convention.

Article 96

A Contracting State whose legislation requires contracts of sale to be concluded in or evidenced by writing may at any time make a declaration in accordance with Article 12 that any provision of Article 11, Article 29, or Part II of this Convention, that allows a contract of sale or its modification or termination by agreement or any offer, acceptance, or other indication or intention to be made in any form other than in writing, does not apply where any party has his place of business in that State.

Articles 97–101 [Omitted]

United Nations Convention on International Multimodal Transport of Goods, Geneva, 1980

Part I General provisions

Article 1 Definitions

For the purposes of this Convention –

1. 'International multimodal transport' means the carriage of goods by at least two different modes of transport on the basis of a multimodal transport contract from a place in one country at which the goods are taken in charge by the multimodal transport operator to a place designated for delivery situated in a different country. The operation of pick-up and delivery of goods carried out in the performance of a unimodal transport contract, as defined in such contract, shall not be considered as international multimodal transport.
2. 'Multimodal transport operator' means any person who on his own behalf or through another person acting on his behalf concludes a multimodal transport contract and who acts as a principal, not as an agent or on behalf of the consignor or of the carriers participating in the multimodal transport operations, and who assumes responsibility for the performance of the contract.
3. 'Multimodal transport contract' means a contract whereby a multimodal transport operator undertakes, against payment of freight, to perform or to procure the performance of international multimodal transport.
4. 'Multimodal transport document' means a document which evidences a multimodal transport contract, the taking in charge of the goods by the multimodal transport

operator, and an undertaking by him to deliver the goods in accordance with the terms of that contract.

5. 'Consignor' means any person by whom or in whose name or on whose behalf a multimodal transport contract has been concluded with the multimodal transport operator, or any person by whom or in whose name or on whose behalf the goods are actually delivered to the multimodal transport operator in relation to the multimodal transport contract.
6. 'Consignee' means the person entitled to take delivery of the goods.
7. 'Goods' includes any container, pallet or similar article of transport or packaging, if supplied by the consignor.
8. 'International convention' means an international agreement concluded among States in written form and governed by international law.
9. 'Mandatory national law' means any statutory law concerning carriage of goods the provision of which cannot be departed from by contractual stipulation to the detriment of the consignor.
10. 'Writing' means, *inter alia*, telegram or telex.

Article 2 Scope of application

The provisions of this Convention shall apply to all contracts of multimodal transport between places in two States, if –

(a) The place for the taking in charge of the goods by the multimodal transport operator as provided for in the multimodal transport contract is located in a Contracting State; or
(b) The place for delivery of the goods by the multimodal transport operator as provided for in the multimodal transport contract is located in a Contracting State.

Article 3 Mandatory application

1. When a multimodal transport contract has been concluded which according to Article 2 shall be governed by this Convention, the provisions of this Convention shall be mandatorily applicable to such contract.
2. Nothing in this Convention shall affect the right of the consignor to choose between multimodal transport and segmented transport.

Article 4 Regulation and control of multimodal transport

1. This Convention shall not affect, or be incompatible with, the application of any international convention or national law relating to the regulation and control of transport operations.
2. This Convention shall not affect the right of each State to regulate and control at the national level multimodal transport operations and multimodal transport operators, including the right to take measures relating to consultations, especially before the introduction of new technologies and services, between multimodal transport operators, shippers, shippers' organisations and appropriate national authorities on terms and

conditions of service; licensing of multimodal transport operators; participation in transport; and all other steps in the national economic and commercial interest.

3. The multimodal transport operator shall comply with the applicable law of the country in which he operates and with the provisions of this Convention.

Part II Documentation

Article 5 Issue of multimodal transport document

1. When the goods are taken charge by the multimodal transport operator, he shall issue a multimodal transport document which, at the option of the consignor, shall be in either negotiable or non-negotiable form.
2. The multimodal transport document shall be signed by the multimodal transport operator or by a person having authority from him. The signature on the multimodal transport document may be in hand-writing, printed in facsimile, perforated, stamped, in symbols, or made by any other mechanical or electronic means, if not inconsistent with the law of the country where the multimodal transport document is issued.
3. If the consignor so agrees, a non-negotiable multimodal transport document may be issued by making use of any mechanical or other means preserving a record of the particulars stated in Article 8 to be contained in the multimodal transport document. In such a case the multimodal transport operator, after having taken the goods in charge, shall deliver to the consignor a readable document containing all the particulars so recorded, and such document shall for the purposes of the provisions of this Convention be deemed to be a multimodal transport document.

Article 6 Negotiable multimodal transport document

1. Where a multimodal transport document is issued in negotiable form –
   (a) It shall be made out to order or to bearer;
   (b) If made out to order it shall be transferable by endorsement;
   (c) If made out to bearer it shall be transferable without endorsement;
   (d) If issued in a set of more than one original it shall indicate the number of originals in the set;
   (e) If any copies are issued each copy shall be marked 'non-negotiable copy'. Delivery of the goods may be demanded from the multimodal transport operator or a person acting on his behalf only against surrender of the negotiable multimodal transport document duly endorsed where necessary.
2. The multimodal transport operator shall be discharged from his obligation to deliver the goods if, where a negotiable multimodal transport document has been issued in a set of more than one original, he or a person acting on his behalf has in good faith delivered the goods against surrender of one of such originals.

Article 7 Non-negotiable multimodal transport

1. Where a multimodal transport document is issued in non-negotiable form it shall indicate a named consignee.

2. The muitimodal transport operator shall be discharged from his obligation to deliver the goods if he makes delivery thereof to the consignee named in such non-negotiable multimodal transport document or to such other person as he may be duly instructed, as a rule, in writing.

Article 8 Contents of the multimodal transport document

1. The multimodal transport document shall contain the following particulars–
   (a) the general nature of the goods, the leading marks necessary for identification of the goods, an express statement, if applicable, as to the dangerous character of the goods, the number of packages or pieces, and the gross weight of the goods or their quantity otherwise expressed, all such particulars as furnished by the consignor;
   (b) the apparent condition of the goods;
   (c) the name and principal place of business of the multimodal transport operator;
   (d) the name of the consignor;
   (e) the consignee, if named by the consignor;
   (f) the place and date of taking in charge of the goods by the multimodal transport operator;
   (g) the place of delivery of the goods;
   (h) the date or the period of delivery of the goods at the place of delivery, if expressly agreed upon between the parties;
   (i) a statement indicating whether the multimodal transport document is negotiable or non-negotiable;
   (j) the place and date of issue of the multimodal transport document;
   (k) the signature of the multimodal transport operator or of a person having authority from him;
   (l) the freight for each mode of transport, if expressly agreed between the parties, or the freight including its currency, to the extent payable by the consignee or other indication that freight is payable by him;
   (m) the intended journey route, modes of transport and places of transhipment, if known at the time of issuance of the multimodal transport document;
   (n) the statement referred to in paragraph 3 of Article 28;
   (o) any other particulars which the parties may agree to insert in the multimodal transport document, if not inconsistent with the law of the country where the multimodal transport document is issued.
2. The absence from the multimodal transport document of one or more of the particulars referred to in paragraph 1 of this Article shall not affect the legal character of the document as a multimodal transport document provided that it nevertheless meets the requirements set out in paragraph 4 of Article 1.

Article 9 Reservations in the multimodal transport document

1. If the multimodal transport document contains particulars concerning the general nature, leading marks, number of packets or pieces, weight or quantity of the goods which the multimodal transport operator or a person acting on his behalf knows, or has reasonable grounds to suspect, do not accurately represent the goods actually taken in

charge, or if he has no reasonable means of checking such particulars, the multimodal transport operator or a person acting on his behalf shall insert in the multimodal transport document a reservation specifying these inaccuracies, grounds of suspicion or the absence of reasonable means of checking.

2. If the multimodal transport operator or a person acting on his behalf fails to note on the multimodal transport document the apparent condition of the goods, he is deemed to have noted on the multimodal transport document that the goods were in apparent good condition.

Article 10 Evidentiary effect of the multimodal transport document

Except for particulars in respect of which and to the extent to which a reservation permitted under Article 9 has been entered –

(a) the multimodal transport document shall be *prima facie* evidence of the taking in charge by the multimodal transport operator of the goods as described therein; and
(b) proof to the contrary by the multimodal transport operator shall not be admissible if the multimodal transport document is issued in negotiable form and has been transferred to a third party, including a consignee, who has acted in good faith in reliance on the description of the goods therein.

Article 11 Liability for intentional misstatements or omissions

When the multimodal transport operator, with intent to defraud, gives in the multimodal transport document false information concerning the goods or omits any information required to be included under paragraph 1(a) or (b) of Article 8 or under Article 9, he shall be liable, without the benefit of the limitation of liability provided for in this Convention, for any loss, damage or expenses incurred by a third party, including a consignee, who acted in reliance on the description of the goods in the multimodal transport document issued.

Article 12 Guarantee by the consignor

1. The consignor shall be deemed to have guaranteed to the multimodal transport operator the accuracy, at the time the goods were taken in charge by the multimodal transport operator, of particulars relating to the general nature of the goods, their marks, number, weight and quantity and, if applicable, to the dangerous character of the goods, as furnished by him for insertion in the multimodal transport document.
2. The consignor shall indemnify the multimodal transport operator against loss resulting from inaccuracies in or inadequacies of the particulars referred to in paragraph 1 of this Article. The consignor shall remain liable even if the multimodal transport document has been transferred to him. The right of the multimodal transport operator to such indemnity shall in no way limit his liability under the multimodal transport contract to any person other than the consignor.

Article 13 Other documents

The issue of the multimodal transport document does not preclude the issue, if necessary, of other documents relating to transport or other services involved in international multimodal transport, in accordance with applicable international conventions or national law. However, the issue of such other documents shall not affect the legal character of the multimodal transport document.

Part III Liability of the multimodal transport operator

Article 14 Period of responsibility

1. The responsibility of the multimodal transport operator for the goods under this Convention covers the period from the time he takes the goods in his charge to the time of their delivery.
2. For the purpose of this Article, the multimodal transport operator is deemed to be in charge of the goods –
   (a) from the time he has taken over the goods from:
      (i) the consignor or a person acting on his behalf; or
      (ii) an authority or other third party to whom, pursuant to law or regulations applicable at the place of taking in charge, the goods must be handed over for transport;
   (b) until the time he has delivered the goods:
      (i) by handing over the goods to the consignee; or
      (ii) in cases where the consignee does not receive the goods from the multimodal transport operator, by placing them at the disposal of the consignee in accordance with the multimodal transport contract or with the law or with the usage of the particular trade applicable at the place of delivery; or
      (iii) by handing over the goods to an authority or other third party to whom, pursuant to law or regulations applicable at the place of delivery, the goods must be handed over.
3. In paragraphs 1 and 2 of this Article, reference to the multimodal transport operator shall include his servants or agents or any other person of whose services he makes use for the performance of the multimodal transport contract, and reference to the consignor or consignee shall include their servants or agents.

Article 15 The liability of the multimodal transport operator for his servants, agents and other persons

Subject to Article 21, the multimodal transport operator shall be liable for the acts and omissions of his servants or agents, when any such servant or agent is acting within the scope of his employment, or of any other person of whose services he makes use for the performance of the multimodal transport contract, when such person is acting in the performance of the contract, as if such acts and omissions were his own.

Article 16 Basis of liability

1. The multimodal transport operator shall be liable for loss resulting from loss or damage to the goods, as well as from delay in delivery, if the occurrence which caused the loss, damage or delay in delivery took place while the goods were in his charge as defined

in Article 14, unless the multimodal transport operator proves that he, his servants or agents or any other person referred to in Article 15 took all measures that could reasonably be required to avoid the occurrence and its consequences.

2. Delay in delivery occurs when the goods have not been delivered within the time expressly agreed upon or, in the absence of such agreement, within the time which it would be reasonable to require of a diligent multimodal transport operator, having regard to the circumstances of the case.
3. If the goods have not been delivered within 90 consecutive days following the date of delivery determined according to paragraph 2 of this Article, the claimant may treat the goods as lost.

Article 17 Concurrent causes

Where fault or neglect on the part of the multimodal transport operator, his servants or agents or any other person referred to in Article 15 combines with another cause to produce loss, damage or delay in delivery, the multimodal transport operator shall be liable only to the extent that the loss, damage or delay in delivery is attributable to such fault or neglect, provided that the multimodal transport operator proves the part of the loss, damage or delay in delivery not attributable thereto.

Article 18 Limitation of liability

1. When the multimodal transport operator is liable for loss resulting from loss of or damage to the goods according to Article 16, his liability shall be limited to an amount not exceeding 920 units of account per package of other shipping unit or 2.75 units of account per kilogram of gross weight of the goods lost or damaged, whichever is the higher.
2. For the purpose of calculating which amount is the higher in accordance with paragraph 1 of this Article, the following rules apply –
   (a) where a container, pallet or similar article of transport is used to consolidate goods, the packages or other shipping units enumerated in the multimodal transport document as packed in such article of transport are deemed packages or shipping units. Except as aforesaid, the goods in such article of transport are deemed one shipping unit;
   (b) in cases where the article of transport itself has been lost or damaged, that article of transport, if not owned or otherwise supplied by the multimodal transport operator, is considered one separate shipping unit.
3. Notwithstanding the provisions of paragraphs 1 and 2 of this Article, if the international multimodal transport does not, according to the contract, include carriage of goods by sea or by inland waterways, the liability of the multimodal transport operator shall be limited to an amount not exceeding 8.33 units of account per kilogram of gross weight of the goods lost or damaged.
4. The liability of the multimodal transport operator for loss resulting from delay in delivery according to the provisions of Article 16 shall be limited to an amount equivalent to two and a half times the freight payable for the goods delayed, but not exceeding the total freight payable under the multimodal transport contract.

5. The aggregate liability of the multimodal transport operator, under paragraphs 1 and 4 or paragraphs 3 and 4 of this Article, shall not exceed the limit of liability for total loss of the goods as determined by paragraphs 1 or 3 of this Article.
6. By agreement between the multimodal transport operator and the consignor, limits of liability exceeding those provided for in paragraphs 1, 3 and 4 or this Article may be fixed in the multimodal transport document.
7. 'Unit of account' means the unit of account mentioned in Article 31.

Article 19 Localised damage

When the loss of or damage to the goods occurred during one particular of the multimodal transport, in respect of which an applicable international convention or mandatory national law provides a higher limit of liability than the limit that would follow from application of paragraphs 1 to 3 of Article 18, then the limit of the multimodal transport operator's liability for such loss or damage shall be determined by reference to the provisions of such convention or mandatory national law.

Article 20 Non-contractual liability

1. The defences and limits of liability provided for in this Convention shall apply in any action against the multimodal transport operator in respect of loss resulting from loss of or damage to the goods, as well as from delay in delivery, whether the action be founded in contract, in tort or otherwise.
2. If an action in respect of loss resulting from loss of or damage to the goods or from delay in delivery is brought against the servant or agent of the multimodal transport operator, if such servant or agent proves that he acted within the scope of his employment, or against any other person of whose services he makes use for the performance of the multimodal transport contract, if such other person proves that he acted within the performance of the contract, the servant or agent of such other person shall be entitled to avail himself of the defences and limits of liability which the multimodal transport operator is entitled to invoke under this Convention.
3. Except as provided in Article 21, the aggregate of the amounts recoverable from the multimodal transport operator and from a servant or agent or any other person of whose services he makes use for the performance of the multimodal transport contract shall not exceed the limits of liability provided for in this Convention.

Article 21 Loss of the right to limit liability

1. The multimodal transport operator is not entitled to the benefit of the limitation of liability provided for in this Convention if it is proved that the loss, damage or delay in delivery resulted from an act or omission of the multimodal transport operator done with the intent to cause such loss, damage or delay or recklessly and with knowledge that such loss, damage or delay would probably result.
2. Notwithstanding paragraph 2 of Article 20, a servant or agent of the multimodal transport operator or other person of whose services he makes use for the performance of the multimodal transport contract is not entitled to the benefit of the limitation of liability

provided for in this Convention if it is proved that the loss, damage or delay in delivery resulted from an act or omission of such servant, agent or other person, done with the intent to cause such loss, damage or delay or recklessly and with knowledge that such loss, damage or delay would probably result.

Part IV Liability of the consignor

Article 22 General rule

The consignor shall be liable for loss sustained by the multimodal transport operator if such loss is caused by the fault or neglect of the consignor, or his servants or agents when such servants or agents are acting within the scope of their employment. Any servant or agent of the consignor shall be liable for such loss if the loss is caused by fault or neglect on his part.

Article 23 Special rules on dangerous goods

1. The consignor shall mark or label in a suitable manner dangerous goods as dangerous.
2. Where the consignor hands over dangerous goods to the multimodal transport operator or any person acting on his behalf, the consignor shall inform him of the dangerous character of the goods and, if necessary, the precautions to be taken. If the consignor fails to do so and the multimodal transport operator does not otherwise have knowledge of their dangerous character
   (a) the consignor shall be liable to the multimodal transport operator for all loss resulting from the shipment of such goods; and
   (b) the goods may at any time be unloaded, destroyed or rendered innocuous, as the circumstances may require, without payment of compensation.
3. The provisions of paragraph 2 of this Article may not be invoked by any person if during the multimodal transport he has taken the goods in his charge with knowledge of their dangerous character.
4. If, in cases where the provisions of paragraph 2(b) of this Article do not apply or may not be invoked, dangerous goods become an actual danger to life or property, they may be unloaded, destroyed or rendered innocuous, as the circumstances may require, without payment of compensation except where there is an obligation to contribute in general average or where the multimodal transport operator is liable in accordance with the provisions of Article 16.

Part V Claims and actions

Article 24 Notice of loss, damage or delay

1. Unless notice of loss or damage, specifying the general nature of such loss or damage, is given in writing by the consignee to the multimodal transport operator not later than the working day after the day when the goods were handed over to the consignee, such handing over is *prima facie* evidence of the delivery by the multimodal transport operator of the goods as described in the multimodal transport document.
2. Where the loss or damage is not apparent, the provisions of paragraph 1 of this Article apply correspondingly if notice in writing is not given within six consecutive days after the day when the goods were handed over to the consignee.

3. If the state of the goods at the time they were handed over to the consignee has been the subject of a joint survey or inspection by the parties or their authorised representatives at the place of delivery, notice in writing need not be given of loss or damage ascertained during such survey or inspection.
4. In the case of any actual or apprehended loss or damage the multimodal transport operator and the consignee shall give all reasonable facilities to each other for inspecting and tallying the goods.
5. No compensation shall be payable for loss resulting from delay in delivery unless notice has been given in writing to the multimodal transport operator within 60 consecutive days after the day when the goods were delivered by handing over to the consignee or when the consignee has been notified that the goods have been delivered in accordance with paragraph 2(b)(ii) or (iii) of Article 14.
6. Unless notice of loss or damage, specifying the general nature of the loss or damage, is given in writing by the multimodal transport operator to the consignor not later than 90 consecutive days after the occurrence of such loss of damage or after the delivery of the goods in accordance with paragraph 2(b) of Article 14, whichever is later, the failure to give such notice is *prima facie* evidence that the multimodal transport operator has sustained no loss or damage due to the fault or neglect of the consignor, his servants or agents.
7. If any of the notice periods provided for in paragraphs 2, 5 and 6 of this Article terminates on a day which is not a working day at the place of delivery, such period shall be extended until the next working day.
8. For the purpose of this Article, notice given to a person acting on the multimodal transport operator's behalf, including any person of whose services he makes use at the place of delivery, or to a person acting on the consignor's behalf, shall be deemed to have been given to the muitimodal transport operator, or to the consignor, respectively.

Article 25 Limitation of actions

1. Any action relating to international multimodal transport under this convention shall be time-barred if judicial or arbitral proceedings have not been instituted within a period of two years. However, if notification in writing, stating the nature and main particulars of the claim, has not been given within six months after the day when the goods were delivered or, where the goods have not been delivered, after the day on which they should have been delivered, the action shall be time-barred at the expiry of this period.
2. The limitation period commences on the day after the day on which the multimodal transport operator has delivered the goods or part thereof or, where the goods have not been delivered, on the day after the last day on which the goods should have been delivered.
3. The person against whom a claim is made may at any time during the running of the limitation period extend that period by a declaration in writing to the claimant. This period may be further extended by another declaration or declarations.
4. Provided that the provisions of another applicable international convention are not to the contrary, a recourse action for indemnity by a person held liable under this Convention may be instituted even after the expiration of the limitation period provided for in the preceding paragraphs if instituted within the time allowed by the law

of the State where proceedings are instituted; however, the time allowed shall not be less than 90 days commencing from the day when the person instituting such action for indemnity has settled the claim or has been served with process in the action against himself.

Article 26 Jurisdiction

1. In judicial proceedings relating to international multimodal transport under this Convention, the plaintiff, at his option, may institute an action in a court which, according to the law of the State where the court is situated, is competent and within the jurisdiction of which is situated one of the following places –
   (a) the principal place of business or, in the absence thereof, the habitual residence of the defendant; or
   (b) the place where the multimodal transport contract was made, provided that the defendant has there a place of business, branch or agency through which the contract was made; or
   (c) the place of taking the goods in charge for international multimodal transport or the place of delivery; or
   (d) any other place designated for that purpose in the multimodal transport contract and evidenced in the multimodal transport document.
2. No judicial proceedings relating to international multimodal transport under this Convention may be instituted in a place not specified in paragraph I of this Article. The provisions of this Article do not constitute an obstacle to the jurisdiction of the Contracting States for provisional or protective measures.
3. Notwithstanding the preceding provisions of this Article, an agreement made by the parties after a claim has arisen, which designates the place where the plaintiff may institute an action, shall be effective.
4. (a) Where an action has been instituted in accordance with the provisions of this Article or where judgment in such an action has been delivered, no new action shall be instituted between the same parties on the same grounds unless the judgment in the first action is not enforceable in the country in which the new proceedings are instituted;
   (b) For the purposes of this Article neither the institution of measures to obtain enforcement of a judgment nor the removal of an action to a different court within the same country shall be considered as the starting of a new action.

Article 27 Arbitration

1. Subject to the provisions of this Article, parties may provide by agreement evidenced in writing that any dispute that may arise relating to international multimodal transport under this Convention shall be referred to arbitration.
2. The arbitration proceedings shall, at the option of the claimant, be instituted at one of the following places –
   (a) a place in a State within whose territory is situated:
      (i) the principal place of business of the defendant or, in the absence thereof, the habitual residence of the defendant; or

(ii) the place where the multimodal transport contract was made, provided that the defendant has there a place of business, branch or agency through which the contract was made; or

(iii) the place of taking the goods in charge for international multimodal transport or the place of delivery; or

(b) any other place designated for that purpose in the arbitration clause or agreement.

3. The arbitrator or arbitration tribunal shall apply the provisions of this Convention.
4. The provisions of paragraphs 2 and 3 of this Article shall be deemed to be part of every arbitration clause or agreement and any term of such clause or agreement which is inconsistent therewith shall be null and void.
5. Nothing in this Article shall affect the validity of an agreement on arbitration made by the parties after the claim relating to the international multimodal transport has arisen.

Part VI Supplementary provisions

Article 28 Contractual stipulations

1. Any stipulation in a multimodal transport contract or multimodal transport document shall be null and void to the extent that it derogates, directly or indirectly, from the provisions of this Convention. The nullity of such a stipulation shall not affect the validity of other provisions of the contract or document of which it forms a part. A clause assigning benefit of insurance of the goods in favour of the multimodal transport operator or any similar clause shall be null and void.
2. Notwithstanding the provisions of paragraph 1 of this Article, the multimodal transport operator may, with the agreement of the consignor, increase his responsibilities and obligations under this Convention.
3. The multimodal transport document shall contain a statement that the international multimodal transport is subject to the provisions of this Convention which nullify any stipulation derogating therefrom to the detriment of the consignor or the consignee.
4. Where the claimant in respect of the goods has incurred loss as a result of a stipulation which is null and void by virtue of the present Article, or as a result of the omission of the statement referred to in paragraph 3 of this Article, the multimodal transport operator must pay compensation to the extent required in order to give the claimant compensation in accordance with the provisions of this Convention for any loss of or damage to the goods as well as for delay in delivery. The multimodal transport operator must, in addition, pay compensation for costs incurred by the claimant for the purpose of exercising his right, provided that costs incurred in the action where the foregoing provision is invoked are to be determined in accordance with the law of the State where proceedings are instituted.

Article 29 General average

1. Nothing in this Convention shall prevent the application of provisions in the multimodal transport contract or national law regarding the adjustment of general average, if and to the extent applicable.

2. With the exception of Article 25, the provisions of this Convention relating to the liability of the multimodal transport operator for loss of or damage to the goods shall also determine whether the consignee may refuse contribution in general average and the liability of the multimodal transport operator to indemnify the consignee in respect of any such contribution made or any salvage paid.

Article 30 Other conventions

1. This Convention does not modify the rights or duties provided for in the Brussels International Convention for the unification of certain rules relating to the limitation of the liability of owners of sea-going vessels of 25 August 1924; in the Brussels International Convention relating to the limitation of the liability of owners of sea-going ships of 10 October 1957; in the London Convention on limitation of liability for maritime claims of 19 November 1976; and in the Geneva Convention relating to the limitation of the liability of owners of inland navigation vessels (CLN) of 1 March 1973, including amendments to these Conventions, or national law relating to the limitation of liability of owners of sea-going ships and inland navigation vessels.
2. The provisions of Articles 26 and 27 of this Convention do not prevent the application of the mandatory provisions of any other international convention relating to matters dealt with in the said Articles, provided that the dispute arises exclusively between parties having their principal place of business in States parties to such other Convention. However, this paragraph does not affect the application of paragraph 3 of Article 27 of this Convention. [Omitted].
3. Carriage of goods such as carriage of goods in accordance with the Geneva Convention of 19 May 1956 on the Contract for the International Carriage of Goods by Road in Article 2, or the Berne Convention of 7 February 1970 concerning the Carriage of Goods by Rail, Article 2, shall not for States Parties to Conventions governing such carriage be considered as international multimodal transport within the meaning of Article 1, paragraph 1 of this Convention, in so far as such States are bound to apply the provisions of such Conventions to such carriage of goods.

Article 31 Unit of account of monetary unit and conversion

1. The unit of account referred to in Article 18 of this Convention is the Special Drawing Right as defined by the International Monetary Fund. The amounts referred to in Article 18 shall be converted into the national currency of a State according to the value of such currency on the date of the judgment or award or the date agreed upon by the parties. The value of a national currency, in terms of Special Drawing Right, of a Contracting State which is a member of the International Monetary Fund, shall be calculated in accordance with the method of valuation applied by the International Monetary Fund, in effect on the date in question, for its operations and transactions. The value of a national currency in terms of the Special Drawing Right of a Contracting State which is not a member of the International Monetary Fund shall be calculated in a manner determined by that State.
2. Nevertheless, a State which is not a member of the International Monetary Fund and whose law does not permit the application of the provisions of paragraph 1 of

this Article may, at the time of signature, ratification, acceptance, approval or accession, or at any time thereafter, declare that the limits of liability provided for in this Convention to be applied in its territory shall be fixed as follows: with regard to the limits provided for in paragraph 1 of Article 18, to 13,750 monetary units per package or other shipping unit or 41.25 monetary units per kilogram of gross weight of the goods, and with regard to the limit provided for in paragraph 3 of Article 18, to 124 monetary units.

3. The monetary unit referred to in paragraph 2 of this Article corresponds to sixty-five and a half milligrams of gold of millesimal fineness nine hundred. The conversion of the amount referred to in paragraph 2 of this Article into national currency shall be made according to the law of the State concerned.
4. The calculation mentioned in the last sentence of paragraph 1 of this Article and the conversion referred to in paragraph 3 of this Article shall be made in such a manner as to express in the national currency of the Contracting State as far as possible the same real value for the amounts in Article 18 as is expressed there in units of account.
5. Contracting States shall communicate to the depositary the manner of calculation pursuant to the last sentence of paragraph 1 of this Article, or the result of the conversion pursuant to paragraph 3 of this Article, as the case may be, at the time of signature or when depositing their instruments of ratification, acceptance, approval or accession, or when availing themselves of the option provided for in paragraph 2 of this Article and whenever there is a change in the manner of such calculation or in the result of such conversion.

Part VII

Article 32 [Omitted]

Part VIII

Articles 33–40 [Omitted]

Annex Provisions on Customs Matters Relating to International Multimodal Transport of Goods [Omitted].

Unidroit Convention on Agency in the International Sale of Goods, Geneva, 1983

Chapter I Sphere of application and general provisions

Article 1

1. This Convention applies where one person, the agent, has authority or purports to have authority on behalf of another person, the principal, to conclude a contract of sale of goods with a third party.
2. It governs not only the conclusion of such a contract by the agent but also any act undertaken by him for the purpose of concluding that contract or in relation to its performance.
3. It is concerned only with relations between the principal or the agent on the one hand, and the third party on the other.

4. It applies irrespective of whether the agent acts in his own name or in that of the principal.

Article 2

1. This Convention applies only where the principal and the third party have their places of business in different States and –
   (a) the agent has his place of business in a Contracting State; or
   (b) the rules of private international law to the application of the law of a Contracting State.
2. Where, at the time of contracting, the third party neither knew nor ought to have known that the agent was acting as an agent, the Convention only applies if the agent and the third party had their places of business in different States and if the requirements of paragraph 1 are satisfied.
3. Neither the nationality of the parties nor the civil or commercial character of the parties or of the contract of sale is to be taken into consideration in determining the application of this Convention.

Article 3

1. This Convention does not apply to –
   (a) the agency of a dealer on a stock, commodity or other exchange;
   (b) the agency of an auctioneer;
   (c) agency by operation of law in family law, in the law of matrimonial property, or in the law of succession;
   (d) agency arising from statutory or judicial authorisation to act for a person without capacity to act;
   (e) agency by virtue of a decision of a judicial or quasi-judicial authority or subject to the direct control of such an authority.
2. Nothing in this Convention affects any rule of law for the protection of consumers.

Article 4

For the purposes of this Convention –

(a) an organ, officer, or partner of a corporation, association, partnership or other entity, whether or not possessing legal personality, shall not be regarded as the agent of that entity in so far as, in the exercise of his functions as such, he acts by virtue of an authority conferred by law or by the constitutive documents of that entity;
(b) a trustee shall not be regarded as an agent of the trust, of the person who has created the trust, or of the beneficiaries.

Article 5

The principal, or an agent acting in accordance with the express or implied instructions of the principal, may agree with the third party to exclude the application of this Convention or, subject to Article II, to derogate from or vary the effect of any of its provisions.

Article 6

1. In the interpretation of this Convention, regard is to be had to its international character and to the need to promote uniformity in its application and the observance of good faith in international trade.
2. Questions concerning matters governed by this Convention which are not expressly settled in it are to be settled in conformity with the general principles on which it is based or, in the absence of such principles, in conformity with the law applicable by virtue of the rules of private international law.

Article 7

1. The principal or the agent on the one hand and the third party on the other are bound by any usage to which they have agreed and by any practices which they have established between themselves.
2. They are considered, unless otherwise agreed, to have impliedly made applicable to their relations any usage of which they knew or ought to have known and which in international trade is widely known to, and regularly observed by, parties to agency relations of the type involved in the particular trade concerned.

Article 8

For the purposes of this Convention –

(a) if a party has more than one place of business, the place of business is that which has the closest relationship to the contract of sale, having regard to the circumstances known to or contemplated by the parties at the time of contracting;
(b) if a party does not have a place of business, reference is to be made to his habitual residence.

Chapter II Establishment and scope of the authority of the agent

Article 9

1. The authorisation of the agent by the principal may be express or implied.
2. The agent has authority to perform all acts necessary in the circumstances to achieve the purposes for which the authorisation was given.

Article 10

The authorisation need not be given in or evidenced by writing and is not subject to any other requirement as to form. It may be proved by any means, including witnesses.

Article 11

Any provision of Article 10, Article 15 or Chapter IV which allows an authorisation, a ratification or a termination of authority to be made in any form other than in writing does not apply where the principal or the agent has his place of business in a Contracting State which has made a declaration under Article 27. The parties may not derogate from or vary the effect of this paragraph.

Chapter III Legal effects of acts carried out by the agent

Article 12

Where an agent acts on behalf of a principal within the scope of his authority and the third party knew or ought to have known that the agent was acting as an agent, the acts of the agent shall directly bind the principal and the third party to each other, unless it follows from the circumstances of the case, for example by a reference to a contract of commission, that the agent undertakes to bind himself only.

Article 13

1. Where the agent acts on behalf of a principal within the scope of this authority, his acts shall bind only the agent and the third party if –
   (a) the third party neither knew nor ought to have known that the agent was acting as an agent; or
   (b) it follows from the circumstances of the case, for example by a reference to a contract of commission, that the agent undertakes to bind himself only.
2. Nevertheless –
   (a) where the agent, whether by reason of the third party's failure of performance or for any other reason, fails to fulfil or is not in a position to fulfil his obligations to the principal, the principal may exercise against the third party the rights acquired on the principal's behalf by the agent, subject to any defences which the third party may set up against the agent;
   (b) where the agent fails to fulfil or is not in a position to fulfil his obligations to the third party, the third party may exercise against the principal the rights which the third party has against the agent, subject to any defences which the agent may set up against the third party and which the principal may set up against the agent.
3. The rights under paragraph 2 may be exercised only if notice of intention to exercise them is given to the agent and the third party or principal, as the case may be. As soon as the third party or principal has received such notice, he may no longer free himself from his obligations by dealing with the agent.
4. Where the agent fails to fulfil or is not in a position to fulfil his obligations to the third party because of the principal's failure of performance, the agent shall communicate the name of the principal to the third party.
5. Where the third party fails to fulfil his obligations under the contract to the agent, the agent shall communicate the name of the third party to the principal.
6. The principal may not exercise against the third party the rights acquired on his behalf by the agent if it appears from the circumstances of the case that the third party, had he known the principal's identity, would not have entered into the contract.
7. An agent may, in accordance with the express or implied instructions of the principal, agree with the third party to derogate from or vary the effect of paragraph 2.

Article 14

1. Where an agent acts without authority or acts outside the scope of his authority, his acts do not bind the principal and the third party to each other.
2. Nevertheless, where the conduct of the principal causes the third party reasonably and in good faith to believe that the agent has authority to act on behalf of the principal and that the agent is acting within the scope of that authority, the principal may not invoke against the third party the lack of authority of the agent.

Article 15

1. An act by an agent who acts without authority or who acts outside the scope of his authority may be ratified by the principal. On ratification the act produces the same effects as if it had initially been carried out with authority.
2. Where, at the time of the agent's act, the third party neither knew nor ought to have known of the lack of authority, he shall not be liable to the principal, if, at any time before ratification, he gives notice of his refusal to become bound by a ratification. Where the principal ratifies but does not do so within a reasonable time, the third party may refuse to be bound by the ratification if he promptly notifies the principal.
3. Where, however, the third party knew or ought to have known of the lack of authority of the agent, the third party may not refuse to become bound by a ratification before the expiration of any time agreed for ratification, or failing agreement, such reasonable time as the third party may specify.
4. The third party may refuse to accept a partial ratification.
5. Ratification shall take effect when notice of it reaches the third party or the ratification otherwise comes to his attention. Once effective, it may not be revoked.
6. Ratification is effective notwithstanding that the act itself could not have been effectively carried out at the time of ratification.
7. Where the act has been carried out on behalf of a corporation or other legal person before its creation, ratification is effective only if allowed by the law of the State governing its creation.
8. Ratification is subject to no requirements as to form. It may be express or may be inferred from the conduct of the principal.

Article 16

1. An agent who acts without authority or who acts outside the scope of his authority shall, failing ratification, be liable to pay the third party such compensation as will place the third party in the same position as he would have been in if the agent had acted with authority and within the scope of his authority.
2. The agent shall not be liable, however, if the third party knew or ought to have known that the agent had no authority or was acting outside the scope of his authority.

Chapter IV Termination of the authority of the agent

Article 17

The authority of the agent is terminated –

(a) when this follows from any agreement between the principal and the agent;
(b) on completion of the transaction or transactions for which the authority was created;
(c) on revocation by the principal or renunciation by the agent, whether or not this is consistent with the terms of the agreement.

Article 18

The authority of the agent is also terminated when the applicable law so provides.

Article 19

The termination of the authority shall not affect the third party unless he knew or ought to have known of the termination or the facts which caused it.

Article 20

Notwithstanding the termination of his authority, the agent remains authorised to perform on behalf of the principal or his successors the acts which are necessary to prevent damage to their interests.

Articles 21–28 [Omitted]

Article 29

A Contracting State, the whole or specific parts of the foreign trade of which are carried on exclusively by specially authorised organisations, may at any time declare that, in cases where such organisations act either as buyers or sellers in foreign trade, all these organisations or the organisations specified in the declaration shall not be considered for the purposes of Article 13, paragraphs 2(b) and 4, as agents in their relations with other organisations having their place of business in the same State.

Article 30

1. A Contracting State may at any time declare that it will apply the provisions of this Convention to specified cases falling outside its sphere of application.
2. Such declaration may, for example, provide that the Convention shall apply to –
   (a) contracts other than contracts of sale of goods;
   (b) cases where the place of business mentioned in Article 2, paragraph 1, are not situated in Contracting States.

Articles 31–35 [Omitted]

Convention on the Law Applicable to Contracts for the International Sale of Goods, The Hague, 1985

Chapter I Scope of the Convention

Article 1

This Convention determines the law applicable to contracts of sale of goods –

(a) between parties having their places of business in different States;
(b) in all other cases involving a choice between the laws of different States, unless such a choice arises solely from a stipulation by the parties as to the applicable law, even if accompanied by a choice of court or arbitration.

Article 2

The Convention does not apply to –

(a) sales by way of execution or otherwise by authority of law;
(b) sales of stocks, shares, investment securities, negotiable instruments or money, it does, however, apply to the sale of goods based on documents;
(c) sales of goods bought for personal, family or household use; it does, however, apply if the seller at the time of the conclusion of the contract neither knew nor ought to have known that the goods were bought for any such use.

Article 3

For the purposes of the Convention, 'goods' includes –

(a) ships, vessels, boats, hovercraft and aircraft;
(b) electricity.

Article 4

1. Contracts for the supply of goods to be manufactured or produced are to be considered contracts of sale unless the party who orders the goods undertakes to supply a substantial part of the materials necessary for such manufacture or production.
2. Contracts in which the preponderant part of the obligations of the party who furnishes goods consists of the supply of labour or other services are not to be considered contracts of sale.

Article 5

The Convention does not determine the law applicable to –

(a) the capacity of the parties or the consequences of nullity or invalidity of the contract resulting from the incapacity of a party;
(b) the question whether an agent is able to bind a principal, or an organ to bind a company or body corporate or unincorporate;
(c) the transfer of ownership; nevertheless, the issues specifically mentioned in Article 12 are governed by the law applicable to the contract under the Convention;
(d) the effect of the sale in respect of any person other than the parties;
(e) agreements on arbitration or on choice of court, even if such an agreement is embodied in the contract of sale.

Article 6

The law determined under the Convention applies whether or not it is the law of a Contracting State.

Chapter II Applicable law

Section 1 Determination of the applicable law

Article 7

1. A contract of sale is governed by the law chosen by the parties. The parties' agreement on this choice must be express or be clearly demonstrated by the terms of the contract and the conduct of the parties, viewed in their entirety. Such a choice may be limited to a part of the contract.
2. The parties may at any time agree to subject the contract in whole or in part to a law other than that which previously governed it, whether or not the law previously governing the contract was chosen by the parties. Any change by the parties of the applicable law made after the conclusion of the contract does not prejudice its formal validity or the rights of third parties.

Article 8

1. To the extent that the law applicable to a contract of sale has not been chosen by the parties in accordance with Article 7, the contract is governed by the law of the State where the seller has his place of business at the time of conclusion of the contract.
2. However, the contract is governed by the law of the State where the buyer has his place of business at the time of conclusion of the contract, if –
   (a) negotiations were conducted, and the contract concluded by and in the presence of the parties, in that State; or
   (b) the contract provides expressly that the seller must perform his obligation to deliver the goods in that State; or
   (c) the contract was concluded on terms determined mainly by the buyer and in response to an invitation directed by the buyer to persons invited to bid (a call for tenders).
3. By way of exception, where, in the light of the circumstances as a whole, for instance any business relations between the parties, the contract is manifestly more closely connected with a law which is not the law which would otherwise be applicable to the contract under paragraphs 1 or 2 of this Article, the contract is governed by that other law.
4. Paragraph 3 does not apply if, at the time of the conclusion of the contract, the seller and the buyer have their places of business in States having made the reservation under Article 21 paragraph 1 sub-paragraph b.
5. Paragraph 3 does not apply in respect of issues regulated in the United Nations Convention on Contracts for the International Sale of Goods (Vienna, 11 April 1980)

where, at the time for the conclusion of the contract, the seller and the buyer have their places of business in different States both of which are Parties to that Convention.

Article 9

A sale by auction or on a commodity or other exchange is governed by the law chosen by the parties in accordance with Article 7 to the extent to which the law of the State where the auction takes place or the exchange is located does not prohibit such choice. Failing a choice by the parties, or to the extent where the aution takes place or the exchange is located shall apply.

Article 10

1. Issues concerning the existence and material validity of the consent of the parties as to the choice of the applicable law are determined, where the choice of the applicable law are determined, where the choice satisfies the requirements of Article 7, by the law chosen. If under that law the choice is invalid, the law governing the contract is determined under Article 8.
2. The existence and material validity of a contract of sale, or of any term thereof, are determined by the law which under the Convention would govern the contract or term if it were valid.
3. Nevertheless, to establish that he did not consent to the choice of law, to the contract itself, or to any term thereof, a party may rely on the law of the State where he has his place of business, if in the circumstances it is not reasonable to determine that issue under the law specified in the preceding paragraphs.

Article 11

1. A contract of sale concluded between persons who are in the same State is formally valid if it satisfies the requirements either of the law which governs it under the Convention or of the law of the State where it is concluded.
2. A contract of sale concluded between persons who are in different States is formally valid if it satifies the requirements either of the law which governs it under the Convention or of the law of one of those States.
3. Where the contract is concluded by an agent, the State in which the agent acts is the relevant State for the purpose of the preceding paragraphs.
4. An act intended to have legal effect relating to an existing or contemplated contract of sale is formally valid if it satisfies the requirements either of the law which under the Convention governs or would govern the contract, or to the law of the State where the act was done.
5. The Convention does not apply to the formal validity of a contract of sale where one of the parties to the contract has, at the time of its conclusion, his place of business in State which has made the reservation provided for in Article 1 paragraph 1 sub-paragraph c.

Section 2 Scope of the applicable law

Article 12

The law applicable to a contract of sale by virtue of Articles 7, 8 or 9 governs in particular –

(a) interpretation of the contract;
(b) the rights and obligations of the parties and performance of the contracts;
(c) the at which the buyer becomes entitled to the products, fruits and income deriving from the goods;
(d) the time from which the buyer bears the risk with respect to the goods;
(e) the validity and effects as between the parties of clauses reserving title to the goods;
(f) the consequences of non performance of the contract, including the categories of loss for which compensation may be recovered, but without prejudice to the procedural law of the forum;
(g) the various ways of extinguishing obligations, as well as prescription and limitation of actions;
(h) the consequences of nullity or invalidity of the contract.

Article 13

In the absence of an express clauses to the contract, the law of the State where inspection of the goods takes place applies to the modalities and procedural requirements for such inspection.

Chapter III General provisions

Article 14

1. If a party has more than one place of business, the relevant place of business is that which has the closest relationship to the contract and its performance, having regard to the circumstance known to or contemplated by the parties at any time before or at the conclusion of the contract.
2. If a party does not have a place of business, reference is to be made to his hatitual residence.

Article 15

In the Convention 'law' means the law in force in a State other than its choice of law rules.

Article 16

In the interpretation of the Convention, regard is to be had to its international character and to the need to promote uniformity in its application.

Article 17

The Convention does not prevent the application of those provisions of the law of the forum that must be applied irrespective of the law that otherwise governs the contract.

Article 18

The application of a law determined by the Convention may be refused only where such application would be manifestly incompatible with public policy *(order public)*.

Articles 19–20 [Omitted]

Article 21

1. Any State may, at the time of signature, retification, acceptance, approval or accession, make any of the following reservations –
   (a) that it will not apply the Convention in cases covered by subparagraph (b) of Article 1;
   (b) that it will not apply paragraph 3 of Article 8 except where neither party to the contract has his place of business in a State which has made a reservation provided for under this subparagraph;
   (c) that for cases where its legislation requires contracts of sale to be concluded in or evidenced by writing, it will not apply the Convention to the formal validity of the contract, where any party has his place of business in its territory at the time of conclusion of the contract.
2. [Omitted].
3. [Omitted].

Articles 22–31 [Omitted]

Unidroit Convention on International Factoring, Ottawa, 1988

Chapter I Sphere of application and general provisions

Article 1

1. This Convention governs factoring contracts and assignments of receivables as described in this Chapter.
2. For the purposes of this convention 'factoring contract' means a contract concluded between the party (the supplier) and another party (the factor) pursuant to which –
   (a) the supplier may or will assign to the factor receivables arising from contracts of sale of goods made between the supplier and its customers (debtors) other than those for the sale of goods bought primarily for their personal, family or household use;
   (b) the factor is to perform at least two of the following functions:
      - finance for the supplier, including loans and advance payments;
      - maintenance of accounts (ledgering) relating to the receivables;
      - collection of receivables;
      - protection against default in payment by debtors;
   (c) notice of the assignment of the receivables is to be given to debtors.
3. In this Convention references to 'goods' and 'sale of goods' shall include services and the supply of services.
4. For the purposes of this Convention –
   (a) a notice in writing need not be signed but must identify the person by whom or in whose name it is given;
   (b) 'notice in writing' includes, but is not limited to, telegrams, telex and any other telecommunication capable of being reproduced in tangible form;
   (c) a notice in writing is given when it is received by the addressee.

Article 2

1. This Convention applies whenever the receivables assigned pursuant to a factoring contract arise from a contract of sale of goods between a supplier and a debtor whose places of business are in different States and –
   (a) those States and the State in which the factor has its place of business are Contracting States; or
   (b) both the contract of sale of goods and the factoring contract are governed by the law of a Contracting State.
2. A reference in this Convention to a party's place of business shall, if it has more than one place of business, mean the place of business which has the closest relationship to the relevant contract and its performance, having regard to the circumstances known to or contemplated by the parties at any time before or at the conclusion of that contract.

Article 3

1. The application of this Convention may be excluded –
   (a) by the parties to the factoring contract; or
   (b) by the parties to the contract of sale of goods, as regards receivables arising at or after the time when the factor has been given notice in writing of such exclusion.
2. Where the application of this Convention is excluded in accordance with the previous paragraph, such exclusion may be made only as regards the Convention as a whole.

Article 4

1. In the interpretation of this Convention, regard is to be had to its object and purpose as set forth in the preamble, to its international character and to the need to promote uniformity in its application and the observance of good faith in international trade.
2. Questions concerning matters governed by this convention which are not expressly settled in it are to be settled in conformity with the general principles on which it is based or, in the absence of such principles, in conformity with the law applicable by virtue of the rules of private international law.

Chapter II Rights and duties of the parties

Article 5

As between the parties to the factoring contract –

(a) a provision in the factoring contract for the assignment of existing or future receivables shall not be rendered invalid by the fact that contract does not specify them individually, if at the time of conclusion of the contract or when they come into existence they can be identified to the contract;

(b) a provision in the factoring contract by which future receivables are assigned operates to transfer the receivables to the factor when they come into existence without the need for any new act of transfer.

Article 6

1. The assignment of a receivable by the supplier to the factor shall be effective notwithstanding any agreement between the supplier and the debtor prohibiting such assignment.
2. However, such assignment shall not be effective against the debtor when, at the time of conclusion of the contract of sale of goods, it has its place of business in a Contracting State which has made a declaration under Article 18 of this Convention.
3. Nothing in paragraph 1 shall affect any obligation of good faith owed by the supplier to the debtor or any liability of the supplier to the debtor in respect of an assignment made in breach of the terms of the contract of sale of goods.

Article 7

A factoring contract may validly provide as between the parties thereto for the transfer, with or without a new act of transfer, of all or any of the supplier's rights deriving from the contract of sale of goods, including the benefit of any provision in the contract of sale of goods reserving to the supplier title to the goods or creating any security interest.

Article 8

1. The debtor is under a duty to pay the factor if, and only if, the debtor does not have knowledge of any other person's superior right to payment and notice in writing of the assignment –
   (a) is given to the debtor by the supplier or by the factor with the supplier's authority;
   (b) reasonably identifies the receivables which have been assigned and the factor to whom or for whose account the debtor is required to make payment; and
   (c) relates to receivables arising under a contract of sale of goods made at or before the time the notice is given.
2. Irrespective of any other ground on which payment by the debtor to the factor discharges the debtor from liability, payment shall be effective for this purpose if made in accordance with the previous paragraph.

Article 9

1. In a claim by the factor against the debtor for payment of a receivable arising under a contract of sale of goods the debtor may set up against the factor all defences arising under that contract of which the debtor could have availed itself if such claim had been made by the supplier.
2. The debtor may also assert against the factor any right of set-off in respect of claims existing against the supplier in whose favour the receivable arose and available to the debtor at the time a notice in writing of assignment conforming to Article 8(1) was given to the debtor.

Article 10

1. Without prejudice to the debtor's rights under Article 9, non-performance or defective or late performance of the contract of sale of goods shall not by itself entitle the debtor

to recover a sum paid by the debtor to the factor if the debtor has a right to recover that sum from the supplier.

2. The debtor who has such a right to recover from the supplier a sum paid to the factor in respect of a receivable shall nevertheless be entitled to recover that sum from the factor to the extent that –
   (a) the factor has not discharged an obligation to make payment to the supplier in respect of that receivable; or
   (b) the factor made such payment at a time when it knew of the supplier's non-performance or defective or late performance as regards the goods to which the debtor's payment relates.

Chapter III Subsequent assignments

Article 11

1. Where a receivable is assigned by a supplier to a factor pursuant to a factoring contract governed by this Convention –
   (a) the rules set out in Articles 5 to 10 shall, subject to sub-paragraph b of this paragraph, apply to any subsequent assignment of the receivable by the factor or by a subsequent assignee;
   (b) the provisions of Articles 8 to 10 shall apply as if the subsequent assignee were the factor.
2. For the purposes of this Convention, notice to the debtor of the subsequent assignment also constitutes notice of the assignment to the factor.

Article 12

This Convention shall not apply to a subsequent assignment which is prohibited by the terms of the factoring contract.

Chapter IV Final provisions

Articles 13–23 [omitted].

United Nations Convention on International Bills of Exchange and International Promissory Notes, 1988

Chapter I Sphere of application and form of the instrument

Article 1

1. This Convention applies to an international bill of exchange when it contains the heading 'International bill of exchange (UNCITAL Convention)' and also contains in its text the words 'International bill of exchange (UNCITAL Convention)'.
2. This Convention applies to an international promissory note when it contains the heading 'International promissory note (UNCITAL Convention)' and also contains in its text the words 'International promissory note (UNCITAL Convention)'.
3. This Convention does not apply to cheques.

Article 2

1. An international bill exchange is a bill of exchange which specifies at least two of the following places and indicates that any two so specified are situated in different States –
   (a) the place where the bill is drawn;
   (b) the place indicated next to the signatute of the drawer;
   (c) the place indicated next to the name of the drawer;
   (d) the place indicated next to the name of the payee;
   (e) the place of payment,

   provided that either the place where the bill is drawn or the place of payment is specified on the bill and that such place is situated in a Contracting State.
2. An international promissory note is a promissory note which specifies at least two of the following places and indicates that any two so specified are situated in a different States –
   (a) the place where the note is made;
   (b) the place indicated next to the signature of the maker;
   (c) the place indicated next to the name of the payee;
   (d) the place of payment; provided that the place of payment is specified on the note and that such place is situated in a Contracting State.
3. This Convention does not deal with the question of sanctions that may be imposed under national law in cases where an incorrect or false statement has been made on an instrument in respect of a place referred to in paragraph 1 or 2 of this Article. However, any such sanctions shall not affect the validity of the instrument or the application of this Convention.

Article 3

1. A bill of exchange is a written instrument which –
   (a) contains an unconditional order whereby the drawer directs the drawee to pay a definite sum of money to the payee or to his order;
   (b) is payable on demand or at a definite time;
   (c) is dated;
   (d) is signed by the drawer.
2. A promissory note is a written instrument which –
   (a) contains an unconditional promise whereby the maker undertakes to pay a definite sum of money to the payee or to his order;
   (b) is payable on demand or at a definite time;
   (c) is dated;
   (d) is signed by the maker.

Chapter II Interpretation

Section 1 General provisions

Article 4

In the interpretation of this Convention, regard is to be had to its international Character and to the need to promote uniformity in its application and the observance of good faith in international transactions.

Article 5

In this Convention –

(a) 'Bill' means an international bill of exchange governed by this Convention;
(b) 'Note' means an international promissory note governed by this Convention;
(c) 'Instrument' means a bill or a note;
(d) 'Drawee' means a person on whom a bill is drawn and who has not accepted it;
(e) 'Payee' means a person in whose favour the drawer directs payment to be made or to whom the maker promises to pay;
(f) 'Holder' means a person in possession of an instrument in accordance with Article 15;
(g) 'Protected Holder' means a holder who meets the requirements of Article 29;
(h) 'Guarantor' means any person any person who undertakes an obligation of gurantee under Article 46, whether governed by subparagraph b ('guranteed') or subparagraph c ('*aval*') of paragraph 4 of Article 47;
(i) 'Party' means the a person who has signed an instrument as drawer, maker, acceptor, endorser or gurantor;
(j) 'Maturity' means the time of payment referred to in paragraphs 4, 5, 6 and 7 of Article 9;
(k) 'Signature' means a handwritten signature, its facsmile or an equivalent authentication effected by any other means; 'forged signature' includes a signature by the wrongful use of such means;
(l) 'Money' or 'currency' includes a monetary unit of account which is established by an intergovernmental institution or by agreement between two or more States, provided that this Convention shall apply without prejudice to the rules of the intergovernmental institution or to stipulations of the agreements.

Article 6

For the purposes of this Convention, a person is considered to have knowledge of a fact if he has actual knowledge of that fact or could not have been unaware of its existence.

Section 2 Interpretation of formal requirements

Article 7

The sum payable by an instrument is deemed to be a definite sum although the instrument states that it is to be paid –

(a) with interest;
(b) by instalments at successive dates;
(c) by instalments at successive dates with a stipulation in the instrument that upon default in payment of any instalment the unpaid balance becomes due;
(d) according to a rate of exchange indicated in the instrument or to be determined as directed by the instrument; or
(e) in a currency other than the currency in which the sum is expressed in the instrument.

Article 8

1. If there is a discrepancy between the sum expressed in words and the sum expressed in figures, the sum payable by the instrument is the sum expressed in words.
2. If the sum is expressed more than once in words, and there is a discrepancy, the sum payable is the smaller sum. The same rule applies if the sum is expressed more than once in figures only, and there is a discrepancy.
3. If the sum is expressed in a currency having the same description as that of at least one other State than the State where payment is to be made, as indicated in the instrument, and the specified currency is not identified as the currency of any particular State, the currency is to be considered as the currency of the State where payment is to be made.
4. If an instrument states that the sum is to paid with interest, without specifying the date from which interest is to run, interest runs from the date of the instrument.
5. A stipulation stating that the sum is to be paid with interest is deemed not to have been written on the instrument unless it indicates the rate at which interest is to be paid.
6. A rate at which interest is to be paid may be expressed either as a definite rate or as a variable rate. For a variable rate to qualify for this purpose, it must vary in relation to one or more reference rates of interest in accordance with provisions stipulated in the instrument and each such reference rate must be published or otherwise available to the public and not be subject, directly or indirectly, to unilateral determination by a person who is named in the instrument at the time the bill is drawn or the note is made, unless the person is named only in the reference rate provisions.
7. If the rate at which interest is to be paid is expressed as a variable rate, it may be stipulated expressly in the instrument that such rate shall not be less than or exceed a specified rate of interest, or that the variations are otherwise limited.
8. If a variable rate does not qualify under paragraph 6 of this Article or for any reason it is not possible to determine the numerical value of the variable rate for any period, interest shall be payable for the relevant period at the rate calculated in accordance with paragraph 2 of Article 70.

Article 9

1. An instrument is deemed to be payable on demand –
   (a) if it states that it is payable at sight or on demand or on presentment or if it contains words of similar import; or
   (b) if no time of payment is expressed.
2. An instrument payable at a definite time which is accepted or endorsed or guaranteed after maturity is an instrument payable on demand as regards the acceptor, the endorser or the guarantor.
3. An instrument is deemed to be payable at a definite time if it states that it is payable –
   (a) on a stated date or at a fixed period after a stated date or at a fixed period after the date of the instrument; or
   (b) at a fixed period after sight; or
   (c) by instalments at successive dates; or
   (d) by instalments at successive dates with the stipulation in the instrument that upon default in payment of any instalment the unpaid balance becomes due.

4. The time of payment of an instrument payable at a fixed period after date is determined by reference to the date of the instrument.
5. The time of payment of a bill payable at a fixed period after sight is determined by the date of acceptance or, if the bill is dishonoured by non-acceptance, by the date of protest or, if protest is dispensed with, by the date of dishonour.
6. The time of payment of an instrument payable on demand is the date on which the instrument is presented for payment.
7. The time of payment of a note payableat a fixed period after sight is determined by the date of the visa signed by the maker on the note or, if his visa is refused, by the date of presentment.
8. If an instrument is drawn, or made, payable one or more months after a stated date or after a date of the instrument or after sight, the instrument is payable on the corresponding date of the month when payment must be made. If there is no corresponding date, the instrument is payable on the last day of that month.

Article 10

1. A bill may be drawn –
   (a) by two or more drawers;
   (b) payable to two or more payees.
2. A note may be made –
   (a) by two or more makers;
   (b) payable to two or more payees.
3. If an instrument is payable to two or more payees in the alternative, it is payable to any one of them and any one of them in possession of the instrument may exercise the rights of a holder. In any other case the instrument is payable to all of them and the rights of a holder may be exercised only by all of them.

Article 11

A bill may be drawn by the drawer –

(a) on himself;
(b) payable to his order.

Section 3 Completion of an incomplete instrument

Article 12

1. An incomplete instrument which satisfies the requirements set out in paragraph 1 of Article 1 and bears the signature of the drawer of the acceptance of the drawee, or which satisfies the requirements set out in paragraph 2 of Article 1 and subparagraph (d) of paragraph 2 of Article 3, but which lacks other elements pertaining to one or more of the requirements set out in Articles 2 and 3, may be completed, and the instrument so completed is effective as a bill or a note.
2. If such an instrument is completed without authority or otherwise than in accordance with the authority given –

(a) a party who signed the instrument before the completion may invoke such lack of authority as a defence against a holder who had knowledge of such lack of authority when he became a holder;

(b) a party who signed the instrument after the completion is liable according to the terms of the instrument so completed.

Chapter III Transfer

Article 13

An instrument is transferred –

(a) by endorsement and delivery of the instrument by the endorser to the endorsee; or
(b) by mere delivery of the instrument if the last endorsement is in blank.

Article 14

1. An endorsement must be written on the instrument or on a slip affixed thereto ('*allonge*'). It must be signed.
2. An endorsement may be –
   (a) in blank, that is, by a signature alone or by a signature accompanied by a statement to the effect that the instrument is payable to a person in possession of it;
   (b) special, that is, by a signature accompanied by an indication of the person to whom the instrument is payable.
3. A signature alone, other than that of the drawee, is an endorsement only if placed on the back of the instrument.

Article 15

1. A person is a holder if he is –
   (a) the payee in possession of the instrument; or
   (b) in possession of an instrument which has been endorsed to him, or on which the last endorsement is in blank, and on which there appears an uninterrupted series of endorsements, even if any endorsement was forged or was signed by an agent without authority.
2. If an endorsement in blank is followed by another endorsement, the person who signed this last endorsement is deemed to be an endorsee by the endorsement in blank.
3. A person is not prevented from being a holder by the fact that the instrument was obtained by him or any previous holder under circumstances, including incapacity or fraud, duress or mistake of any kind, that would give rise to a claim to, or a defence against liability on, the instrument.

Article 16

The holder of an instrument on which the last endorsement is in blank may –

(a) further endorse it either by an endorsement in blank or by a special endorsement; or

(b) convert the blank endorsement into a special endorsement by indicating in the endorsement that the instrument is payable to himself or to some other specified person; or
(c) transfer the instrument in accordance with subparagraph b of Article 13.

Article 17

1. If the drawer or the maker has inserted in the instrument such words as 'not acceptable', 'not transferable', 'not to order', 'pay (x) only', or words of similar import, the instrument may not be transferred except for purposes of collection, and any endorsement, even if it does not contain words authorising the endorsee to collect the instrument, is deemed to be an endorsement for collection.
2. If an endorsement contains the words 'not negotiable', 'not transferable', 'not to order', 'pay (x) only', or words of similar import, the instrument may not be transferred further except for purposes of collection, and any subsequent endorsement, even if it does not contain words authorising the endorsee to collect the instrument, is deemed to be an endorsement for collection.

Article 18

1. An endorsement must be unconditional.
2. A conditional endorsement transfers the instrument whether or not the condition is fulfilled. The condition is ineffective as to those parties and transferees who are subsequent to the endorsee.

Article 19

An endorsement in respect of a part of the sum due under the instrument is ineffective as an endorsement.

Article 20

If there are two or more endorsements, it is presumed, unless the contrary is proved, that each endorsement was made in the order in which it appears on the instrument.

Article 21

1. If an endorsement contains the words 'for collection', 'for deposit', 'value in collection', 'by procuration', 'pay any bank', or words of similar import authorising the endorsee to collect the instrument, the endorsee is a holder who –
   (a) may exercise all rights arising out of the instrument;
   (b) may endorse the instrument only for purposes of collection;
   (c) is subject only to the claims and defences which may be set up against the endorser.
2. The endorser for collection is not liable on the instrument to any subsequent holder.

Article 22

1. If an endorsement contains the words 'value in security', 'value in pledge', or any other words indicating a pledge, the endorsee is a holder who –

(a) may exercise all rights arising out of the instrument;
(b) may endorse the instrument only for purposes of collection;
(c) is subject only to the claims and defences specified in Articles 28 or 30.

2. If such an endorsee endorses for collection, he is not liable on the instrument to any subsequent holder.

Article 23

The holder of an instrument may transfer it to a prior party or to the drawee in accordance with Article 13; however, if the transferee has previously been a holder of the instrument, no endorsement is required, and any endorsement which would prevent him from qualifying as a holder may be struck out.

Article 24

An instrument may be transferred in accordance with Article 13 after maturity, except by the drawee, the acceptor or the maker.

Article 25

1. If an endorsement is forged, the person whose endorsement is forged, or a party who signed the instrument before the forgery, has the right to recover compensation for any damage that he may have suffered because of the forgery against –
   (a) the forger;
   (b) the person to whom the instrument was directly transferred by the forger;
   (c) a party or the drawee who paid the instrument to the forger directly or through one or more endorsees for collection.
2. However, an endorsee for collection is not liable under paragraph 1 of this Article if he is without knowledge of the forgery –
   (a) at the time he pays the principal or advises him of the receipt of payment; or
   (b) at the time he receives payment, if this is later, unless his lack of knowledge is due to his failure to act in good faith or to exercise reasonable care.
3. Furthermore, a party or the drawee who pays an instrument is not liable under paragraph 1 of this Article if, at the time he pays the instrument, he is without knowledge of the forgery, unless his lack of knowledge is due to his failure to act in good faith or to exercise reasonable care.
4. Except as against the forger, the damages recoverable under paragraph 1 of this Article may not exceed the amount referred to in Article 70 or 71.

Article 26

1. If an endorsement is made by an agent without authority or power to bind his principal in the matter, the principal, or a party who signed the instrument before such endorsement, has the right to recover compensation for any damage that he may have suffered because of such endorsement against –
   (a) the agent;

   (b) the person to whom the instrument was directly transferred by the agent;
   (c) a party or the drawee who paid the instrument to the agent directly or through one or more endorsees for collection.
2. However, an endorsee for collection is not liable under paragraph 1 of this Article if he is without knowledge that the endorsement does not bind the principal –
   (a) at the time he pays the principal or advises him of the receipt of payment; or
   (b) at the time he receives payment, if this is later, unless his lack of knowledge is due to his failure to act in good faith or to exercise reasonable care.
3. Furthermore, a party or the drawee who pays an instrument is not liable under paragraph 1 of this Article if, at the time he pays the instrument, he is without knowledge that the endorsement does not bind the principal, unless his lack of knowledge is due to his failure to act in good faith or to exercise reasonable care.
4. Except as against the agent, the damages recoverable under paragraph 1 of this Article may not exceed the amount referred to in Article 70 or 71.

Chapter IV Rights and liabilities

Section 1 The rights of a holder and a protected holder

Article 27

1. The holder of an instrument has all the rights conferred on him by this Convention against the parties to the instrument.
2. The holder may transfer the instrument in accordance with Article 13.

Article 28

1. A party may set up against a holder who is not a protected holder –
   (a) any defence that may be set up against a protected holder in accordance with paragraph 1 of Article 30;
   (b) any defence based on the underlying transaction between himself and the drawer or between himself and his transferee, but only if the holder took the instrument with knowledge of such defence or if he obtained the instrument by fraud or theft or participated at any time in a fraud or theft concerning it;
   (c) any defence arising from the circumstances as a result of which he became a party, but only if the holder took the instrument with knowledge of such defence or if he obtained the instrument by fraud or theft or participated at any time in a fraud or theft concerning it;
   (d) any defence which may be raised against an action in contract between himself and the holder;
   (e) any other defence available under this Convention.
2. The rights to an instrument of a holder who is not a protected holder are subject to any valid claim to the instrument on the part of any person, but only if he took the instrument with knowledge of such claim or if he obtained the instrument by fraud or theft or participated at any time in a fraud or theft concerning it.

3. A holder who takes an instrument after the expiration of the time-limit for presentment for payment is subject to any claim to, or defence against liability on, the instrument to which his transferor is subject.
4. A party may not raise as a defence against a holder who is not a protected holder the fact that a third person has a claim to the instrument unless –
   (a) the third person asserted a valid claim to the instrument; or
   (b) the holder acquired the instrument by theft or forged the signature of the payee or an endorsee, or participated in the theft or the forgery.

Article 29

'Protected holder' means the holder of an instrument which was complete when he took it or which was incomplete within the meaning of paragraph 1 of Article 12 and was completed in accordance with authority given, provided that when he became a holder –

(a) he was without knowledge of a defence against liability on the instrument referred to in subparagraphs (a), (b), (c) and (e) of paragraph 1 of Article 28;
(b) he was without knowledge of a valid claim to the instrument of any person;
(c) he was without knowledge of the fact that it had been dishonoured by non-acceptance or by non-payment;
(d) the time-limit provided by Article 55 for presentment of that instrument for payment had not expired; and
(e) he did not obtain the instrument by fraud or theft or participate in a fraud or theft concerning it.

Article 30

1. A party may not set up against a protected holder any defence except –
   (a) defences under Articles 33 §1, 34, 35 §1, 36 §3, 53 §1, 57 §1, 63 §1 and 84 of this Convention;
   (b) defences based on the underlying transaction between himself and such holder or arising from any fraudulent act on the part of such holder in obtaining the signature on the instrument of that party;
   (c) defences based on his incapacity to incur liability on the instrument or on the fact that he signed without knowledge that his signature made him a party to the instrument, provided that his lack of knowledge was not due to his negligence and provided that he was fraudulently induced so to sign.
2. The rights to an instrument of a protected holder are not subject to any claim to the instrument on the part of any person, except a valid claim arising from the underlying transaction between himself and the person by whom the claim is raised.

Article 31

1. The transfer of an instrument by a protected holder vests in any subsequent holder the rights to and on the instrument which the protected holder had.
2. Those rights are not vested in a subsequent holder if –

(a) he participated in a transaction which gives rise to a claim to, or a defence against liability on, the instrument;
(b) he has previously been a holder, but not a protected holder.

Article 32

Every holder is presumed to be a protected holder unless the contrary is proved.

Section 2 Liabilities of the parties

A General provisions

Article 33

1. Subject to the provisions of Articles 34 and 36, a person is not liable on an instrument unless he signs it.
2. A person who signs an instrument in a name which is not his own is liable as if he had signed it in his own name.

Article 34

A forged signature on an instrument does not impose any liability on the person whose signature was forged. However, if he consents to be bound by the forged signature or represents that it is his own, he is liable as if he had signed the instrument himself.

Article 35

1. If an instrument is materially altered –
   (a) a party who signs it after the material alteration is liable according to the terms of the altered text;
   (b) a party who signs it before the material alteration is liable according to the terms of the original text. However, if a party makes, authorises or assents to a material alteration, he is liable according to the terms of the altered text.
2. A signature is presumed to have been placed on the instrument after the material alteration unless the contrary is proved.
3. Any alteration is material which modifies the written undertaking on the instrument of any party in any respect.

Article 36

1. An instrument may be signed by an agent.
2. The signature of an agent placed by him on an instrument with the authority of his principal and showing on the instrument that he is signing in a representative capacity for that named principal, or the signature of a principal placed on the instrument by an agent with his authority, imposes liability on the principal and not on the agent.

3. A signature placed on an instrument by a person as agent but who lacks authority to sign or exceeds his authority, or by an agent who has authority to sign but who does not show on the instrument that he is signing in a representative capacity for a named person, or who shows on the instrument that he is signing in a representative capacity but does not name the person whom he represents, imposes liability on the person signing and not on the person whom he purports to represent.
4. The question whether a signature was placed on the instrument in a representative capacity may be determined only by reference to what appears on the instrument.
5. A person who is liable pursuant to paragraph 3 of this Article and who pays the instrument has the same rights as the person for whom he purported to act would have had if that person had paid the instrument.

Article 37

The order to pay contained in a bill does not of itself operate as an assignment to the payee of funds made available for payment by the drawer with the drawee.

B The drawer

Article 38

1. The drawee engages that upon dishonour of the bill by non-acceptance or by non-payment, and upon any necessary protest, he will pay the bill to the holder, or to any endorser or any endorser's guarantor who takes up and pays the bill.
2. The drawer may exclude or limit his own liability for acceptance or for payment by an express stipulation in the bill. Such a stipulation is effective only with respect to the drawer. A stipulation excluding or limiting liability for payment is effective only if another party is or becomes liable on the bill.

C The maker

Article 39

1. The maker engages that he will pay the note in accordance with its terms to the holder, or to any party who takes up and pays the note.
2. The maker may not exclude or limit his own liability by a stipulation in the note. Any such stipulation is ineffective.

D The drawee and the acceptor

Article 40

1. The drawee is not liable on a bill until he accepts it.
2. The acceptor engages that he will pay the bill in accordance with the terms of his acceptance to the holder, or to any party who takes up and pays the bill.

Article 41

1. An acceptance must be written on the bill and may be affected –

   (a) by the signature of the drawee accompanied by the word 'accepted' or by words of similar import; or
   (b) by the signature alone of the drawee.
2. An acceptance may be written on the front or on the back of the bill.

Article 42

1. An incomplete bill which satisfies the requirements set out in paragraph 1 of Article 1 may be accepted by the drawee before it has been signed by the drawer, or while otherwise incomplete.
2. A bill may be accepted before, at or after maturity, or after it has been dishonoured by non-acceptance or by non-payment.
3. If a bill drawn payable at a fixed period after sight, or a bill which must be presented for acceptance before a specified date, is accepted, the acceptor must indicate the date of his acceptance; failing such indication by the acceptor, the drawer or the holder may insert the date of acceptance.
4. If a bill drawn payable at a fixed period after sight is dishonoured by nonacceptance and the drawee subsequently accepts it, the holder is entitled to have the acceptance dated as of the date on which the bill was dishonoured.

Article 43

1. An acceptance must be unqualified. An acceptance is qualified if it is conditional or varies the terms of the bill.
2. If the drawee stipulates in the bill that his acceptance is subject to qualification –
   (a) he is nevertheless bound according to the terms of his qualified acceptance;
   (b) the bill is dishonoured by non-acceptance.
3. An acceptance relating to only a part of the sum payable is a qualified acceptance. If the holder takes such an acceptance, the bill is dishonoured by non-acceptance only as to the remaining part.
4. An acceptance indicating that payment will be made at a particular address or by a particular address or by a particular agent is not a qualified acceptance, provided that –
   (a) the place in which payment is to be made is not changed;
   (b) the bill is not drawn payable by another agent.

E The endorser

Article 44

1. The endorser engages that upon dishonour of the instrument by non-acceptance or by non-payment, and upon any necessary protest, he will pay the instrument to the holder, or to any subsequent endorser or any endorser's guarantor who takes up and pays the instrument.
2. An endorser may exclude or limit his own liability by an express stipulation in the instrument. Such a stipulation is effective only with respect to that endorser.

F The transferor by endorsement or by mere delivery

Article 45

1. Unless otherwise agreed, a person who transfers an instrument, by endorsement and delivery or by mere delivery represents to the holder to whom he transfers the instrument that –
   (a) the instrument does not bear any forged or unauthorised signature;
   (b) the instrument has not been materially altered;
   (c) at the time of transfer, he has no knowledge of any fact which would impair the right of the transferee to payment of the instrument against the acceptor of a bill or, in the case of an unaccepted bill, the drawer, or against the maker of a note.
2. Liability of the transferor under paragraph 1 of this Article is incurred only if the transferee took the instrument without knowledge of the matter giving rise to such liability.
3. If the transferor is liable under paragraph 1 of this Article, the transferee may recover, even before maturity, the amount paid by him to the transferor, with interest calculated in accordance with Article 70 against return on the instrument.

G The guarantor

Article 46

1. Payment of an instrument, whether or not it has been accepted, may be guaranteed, as to the whole or part of its amount, for the account of a party or the drawee. A guarantee may be given by any person, who may or may not already be a party.
2. A guarantee must be written on the instrument or on a slip affixed thereto ('*allonge*').
3. A guarantee is expressed by the words 'guaranteed', '*aval*', 'good as *aval*' or words of similar import, accompanied by the signature of the guarantor. For the purposes of this Convention, the words 'prior endorsements guaranteed' or words of similar import do not constitute a guarantee.
4. A guarantee may be effected by a signature alone on the front of the instrument. A signature alone on the front of the instrument, other than that of the maker, the drawer or the drawee, is a guarantee.
5. A guarantor may specify the person for whom he has become guarantor. In the absence of such specification, the person for whom he has become guarantor is the acceptor or the drawee in the case of a bill, and the maker in the case of a note.
6. A guarantor may not raise as a defence to his liability the fact that he signed the instrument before it was signed by the person for whom he is a guarantor, or while the instrument was incomplete.

Article 47

1. The liability of a guarantor on the instrument is of the same nature as that of the party for whom he has become guarantor.
2. If the person for whom he has become guarantor is the drawee, the guarantor engages –
   (a) to pay the bill at maturity to the holder, or to any party who takes up and pays the bill;
   (b) if the bill is payable at a definite time, upon dishonour by non-acceptance and upon any necessary protest, to pay it to the holder, or to any party who takes up and pays the bill.

3. In respect of defences that are personal to himself, a guarantor may set up –
   (a) against a holder who is not a protected holder only those defences which he may set up under paragraphs 1, 3 and 4 of Article 28;
   (b) against a protected holder only those defences which he may set up under paragraph 1 of Article 30.
4. In respect of defences that may be raised by the person for whom he has become a guarantor –
   (a) a guarantor may set up against a holder who is not a protected holder only those defences which the person for whom he has become a guarantor may set up against such holder under paragraphs 1, 3 and 4 of Article 28;
   (b) a guarantor who expresses his guarantee by the words 'guaranteed', 'payment guaranteed' or collection guaranteed', or words of similar import, may set up against a protected holder only those defences which the person for whom he has become a guarantor may set up against a protected holder under paragraph 1 of Article 30;
   (c) a guarantor who expresses his guarantee by the words *'aval'* or 'good as *aval*' may set up against a protected holder only:
      (i) the defence, under subparagraph (b) of paragraph 1 of Article 30, that the protected holder obtained the signature on the instrument of the person for whom he has become a guarantor by a fraudulent act;
      (ii) the defence, under Article 53 or 57, that the instrument was not presented for acceptance or for payment;
      (iii) the defence, under Article 63, that the instrument was not duly protested for non-acceptance or for non-payment;
      (iv) the defence, under Article 84, that a right of action may no longer be exercised against the person for whom he has become guarantor;
   (d) a guarantor who is not a bank or other financial institution and who expresses his guarantee by a signature alone may set up against a protected holder only the defences referred to in subparagraph b of this paragraph;
   (e) a guarantor which is a bank or other financial institution and which expresses its guarantee by a signature alone may set up against a protected holder only the defences referred to in subparagraph c of this paragraph.

Article 48

1. Payment of an instrument by the guarantor in accordance with Article 72 discharges the party for whom he became guarantor of his liability on the instrument to the extent of the amount paid.
2. The guarantor who pays the instrument may recover from the party for whom he has become guarantor and from the parties who are liable on it to that party the amount paid and any interest.

Chapter V Presentment, dishonour by non-acceptance or non-payment, and recourse

Section 1 Presentment for acceptance and dishonour by non-acceptance

Article 49

1. A bill may be presented for acceptance.
2. A bill must be presented for acceptance –
   (a) if the drawer has stipulated in the bill that it must be presented for acceptance;
   (b) if the bill is payable at a fixed period after sight; or
   (c) if the bill is payable elsewhere than at the residency or place of business of the drawee, unless it is payable on demand.

Article 50

1. The drawer may stipulate in the bill that it must not be presented for acceptance before a specified date or before the occurrence of a specified event. Except where a bill must be presented for acceptance under subparagraph b or c of paragraph 2 of Article 49, the drawer may stipulate that it must not be presented for acceptance.
2. If a bill is presented for acceptance notwithstanding a stipulation permitted under paragraph 1 of this Article and acceptance is refused, the bill is not thereby dishonoured.
3. If the drawee accepts a bill notwithstanding a stipulation that it must not be presented for acceptance, the acceptance is effective.

Article 51

A bill is duly presented for acceptance if it is presented in accordance with the following rules –

(a) the holder must present the bill to the drawee on a business day at a reasonable hour;
(b) presentment for acceptance may be made to a person or authority other than the drawee if that person or authority is entitled under the applicable law to accept the bill;
(c) if a bill is payable on a fixed date, presentment for acceptance must be made before or on that date;
(d) a bill payable on demand or at a fixed period after sight must be presented for acceptance within one year of its date;
(e) a bill in which the drawer has stated a date or time limit for presentment for acceptance must be presented on the stated date or within the stated time-limit.

Article 52

1. A necessary or optional presentment for acceptance is dispensed with if –
   (a) the drawee is dead, or no longer has the power freely to deal with his assets by reason of his insolvency, or is a fictitious person, or is a person not having capacity to incur liability on the instrument as an acceptor; or
   (b) the drawee is a corporation, partnership, association or other legal entity which has ceased to exist.
2. A necessary presentment for acceptance is dispensed with if –
   (a) a bill is payable on a fixed date, and presentment for acceptance cannot be effected before or on that date due to circumstances which are beyond the control of the holder and which he could neither avoid nor overcome; or

   (b) a bill is payable at a fixed period after sight, and presentment for acceptance cannot be effected within one year of its date due to circumstances which are beyond the control of the holder and which he could neither avoid nor overcome.
3. Subject to paragraphs 1 and 2 of this Article, delay in a necessary presentment for acceptance is excused, but presentment for acceptance is not dispensed with, if the bill is drawn with a stipulation that it must be presented for acceptance within a stated time-limit, and the delay in presentment for acceptance is caused by circumstances which are beyond the control of the holder and which he could neither avoid nor overcome. When the cause of the delay ceases to operate, presentment must be made with reasonable diligence.

Article 53

1. If a bill which must be presented for acceptance is not so presented, the drawer, the endorsers and their guarantors are not liable on the bill.
2. Failure to present a bill for acceptance does not discharge the guarantor of the drawee of liability on the bill.

Article 54

1. A bill is considered to be dishonoured by non-acceptance –
   (a) if the drawee, upon due presentment, expressly refuses to accept the bill or acceptance cannot be obtained with reasonable diligence or if the holder cannot obtain the acceptance to which he is entitled under this Convention;
   (b) if presentment for acceptance is dispensed with pursuant to Article 52, unless the bill is in fact accepted.
2. (a) If a bill is dishonoured by non-acceptance in accordance with subparagraph a of paragraph 1 of this Article, the holder may exercise an immediate right of recourse against the drawer, the endorsers and their guarantors, subject to the provisions of Article 59.
   (b) If a bill is dishonoured by non-acceptance in accordance with subparagraph (b) of paragraph 1 of this Article, the holder may exercise an immediate right of recourse against the drawer, the endorsers and their guarantors.
   (c) If a bill is dishonoured by non-acceptance in accordance with paragraph 1 of this Article, the holder may claim payment from the guarantor of the drawee upon any necessary protest.
3. If a bill payable on demand is presented for acceptance, but acceptance is refused, it is not considered to be dishonoured by non-acceptance.

Section 2 Presentment for payment and dishonour by non-payment

Article 55

An instrument is duly presented for payment if it is presented in accordance with the following rules –

(a) the holder must present the instrument to the drawee or to the acceptor or to the maker on a business day at a reasonable hour;
(b) a note signed by two or more makers may be presented to any one of them, unless the note clearly indicates otherwise;
(c) if the drawee or the acceptor or the maker is dead, presentment must be made to the persons who under the applicable law are his heirs or the persons entitled to administer his estate;
(d) presentment for payment may be made to a person or authority other than the drawee, the acceptor or the maker if that person or authority is entitled under the applicable law to pay the instrument;
(e) an instrument which is not payable on demand must be presented for payment on the date of maturity or on one of the two business days which follow;
(f) an instrument which is payable on demand must be presented for payment within one year of its date;
(g) an instrument must be presented for payment:
  (i) at the place of payment specified on the instrument; or
  (ii) if no place of payment is specified, at the address of the drawee or the acceptor or the maker indicated in the instrument; or
  (iii) if no place of payment is specified and the address of the drawee or the acceptor or the maker is not indicated, at the principal place of business or habitual residence of the drawee or the acceptor or the maker;
(h) an instrument which is presented at a clearing-house is duly presented for payment if the law of the place where the clearing-house is located or the rules or customs of that clearing-house so provide.

Article 56

1. Delay in making presentment for payment is excused if the delay is caused by circumstances which are beyond the control of the holder and which he could neither avoid nor overcome. When the cause of the delay ceases to operate, presentment must be made with reasonable diligence.
2. Presentment for payment is dispensed with –
   (a) if the drawer, an endorser or a guarantor has expressly waived presentment; such waiver:
      (i) if made on the instrument by the drawer, binds any subsequent party and benefits any holder;
      (ii) if made on the instrument by a party other than the drawer, binds only that party but benefits any holder;
      (iii) if made outside the instrument, binds only the party making it and benefits only a holder in whose favour it was made;
   (b) if an instrument is not payable on demand, and the cause of delay in making presentment referred to in paragraph 1 of this Article continues to operate beyond 30 days after maturity;
   (c) if an instrument is payable on demand, and the cause of delay in making presentment referred to in paragraph 1 of this Article continues to operate beyond 30 days after the expiration of the time-limit for presentment for payment;

(d) if the drawee, the maker or the acceptor has no longer the power freely to deal with his assets by reason of his insolvency, or is a fictitious person or a person not having capacity to make payment, or if the drawee, the maker or the acceptor is a corporation, partnership, association or other legal entity which has ceased to exist;

(e) if there is no place at which the instrument must be presented in accordance with subparagraph (g) of Article 55.

3. Presentment for payment is also dispensed with as regards a bill, if the bill has been protested for dishonour by non-acceptance.

Article 57

1. If an instrument is not duly presented for payment, the drawer, the endorsers and their guarantors are not liable on it.
2. Failure to present an instrument for payment does not discharge the acceptor, the maker and their guarantors or the guarantor of the drawee of liability on it.

Article 58

1. An instrument is considered to be dishonoured by non-payment –
   (a) if payment is refused upon due presentment or if the holder cannot obtain the payment to which he is entitled under this Convention;
   (b) if presentment for payment is dispensed with pursuant to paragraph 2 of Article 56 and the instrument is unpaid at maturity.
2. If a bill is dishonoured by non-payment, the holder may, subject to the provisions of Article 59, exercise a right of recourse against the drawer, the endorsers and their guarantors.
3. If a note is dishonoured by non-payment, the holder may, subject to the provisions of Article 59, exercise a right of recourse against the endorsers and their guarantors.

Sections – Recourse

Article 59

If an instrument is dishonoured by non-acceptance or by non-payment, the holder may exercise a right of recourse only after the instrument has been duly protested for dishonour in accordance with the provisions of Articles 60 to 62.

A Protest

Article 60

1. A protest is a statement of dishonour drawn up at the place where the instrument has been dishonoured and signed and dated by a person authorised in that respect by the law of that place. The statement must specify –
   (a) the person at whose request the instrument is protested;
   (b) the place of protest; and

   (c) the demand made and the answer given, if any, or the fact that the drawee or the acceptor or the maker could not be found.
2. A protest may be made –
   (a) on the instrument or on a slip affixed thereto ('*allonge*'); or
   (b) as a separate document, in which case it must clearly identify the instrument that has been dishonoured.
3. Unless the instrument stipulates that protest must be made, a protest may be replaced by a declaration written on the instrument and signed and dated by the drawee or the acceptor or the maker, or, in the case of an instrument domiciled with a named person for payment, by that named person; the declaration must be to the effect that acceptance or payment is refused.
4. A declaration made in accordance with paragraph 3 of this Article is a protest for the purpose of this Convention.

Article 61

Protest for dishonour of an instrument by non-acceptance or by non-payment must be made on the day on which the instrument is dishonoured or on one of the four business days which follow.

Article 62

1. Delay in protesting an instrument for dishonour is excused if the delay is caused by circumstances which are beyond the control of the holder and which he could neither avoid nor overcome. When the cause of the delay ceases to operate, protest must be made with reasonable diligence.
2. Protest for dishonour by non-acceptance or by non-payment is dispensed with –
   (a) if the drawer, an endorser or a guarantor has expressly waived protest; such waiver:
      (i) if made on the instrument by the drawer, binds any subsequent party and benefits any holder;
      (ii) if made on the instrument by a party other than the drawer, binds only that party but benefits any holder;
      (iii) if made outside the instrument, binds only the party making it and benefits only a holder in whose favour it was made;
   (b) if the cause of the delay in making protest referred to in paragraph 1 of this Article continues to operate beyond 30 days after the date of dishonour;
   (c) as regards the drawer of a bill, if the drawer and the drawee or the acceptor are the same person;
   (d) if presentment for acceptance or for payment is dispensed with in accordance with Article 52 or paragraph 2 of Article 56.

Article 63

1. If an instrument which must be protested for non-acceptance or for non-payment is not duly protested, the drawer, the endorsers and their guarantors are not liable on it.
2. Failure to protest an instrument does not discharge the acceptor, the maker and their guarantors or the guarantor of the drawee of liability on it.

B Notice of dishonour

Article 64

1. The holder, upon dishonour of an instrument by non-acceptance or by nonpayment, must give notice of such dishonour –
   (a) to the drawer and the last endorser; and
   (b) to all other endorsers and guarantors whose addresses the holder can ascertain on the basis of information contained in the instrument.
2. An endorser or a guarantor who receives notice must give notice of dishonour to the last party preceding him and liable on the instrument.
3. Notice of dishonour operates for the benefit of any party who has a right of recourse on the instrument against the party notified.

Article 65

1. Notice of dishonour may be given in any form whatever and in any terms which identify the instrument and State that it has been dishonoured. The return of the dishonoured instrument is sufficient notice, provided it is accompanied by a statement indicating that it has been dishonoured.
2. Notice of dishonour is duly given if it is communicated or sent to the party to be notified by means appropriate in the circumstances, whether or not it is received by that party.
3. The burden of proving that notice has been duly given rests upon the person who is required to give such notice.

Article 66

Notice of dishonour must be given within the two business days which follow –

(a) the day of protest or, if protest is dispensed with, the day of dishonour; or
(b) the day of receipt of notice of dishonour.

Article 67

1. Delay in giving notice of dishonour is excused if the delay is caused by circumstances which are beyond the control of the person required to give notice, and which he could neither avoid nor overcome. When the cause of the delay ceases to operate, notice must be given with reasonable diligence.
2. Notice of dishonour is dispensed with –
   (a) if, after the exercise of reasonable diligence, notice cannot be given;
   (b) if the drawer, an endorser or a guarantor has expressly waived notice of dishonour; such waiver:
      (i) if made on the instrument by the drawer, binds any subsequent party and benefits any holder;
      (ii) if made on the instrument by a party other than the drawer, binds only that party but benefits any holder;
      (iii) if made outside the instrument, binds only the party making it and benefits only a holder in whose favour it was made;

(c) as regards the drawer of the bill, if the drawer and the drawee or the acceptor are the same person.

Article 68

If a person who is required to give notice of dishonour fails to give it to a party who is entitled to receive it, he is liable for any damages which that party may suffer from such failure, provided that such damages do not exceed the amount referred to in Article 70 or 71.

Section 4 Amount payable

Article 69

1. The holder may exercise his rights on the instrument against any one party, or several or all parties, liable on it and is not obliged to observe the order in which the parties have become bound. Any party who takes up and pays the instrument may exercise his rights in the same manner against parties liable to him.
2. Proceedings against a party do not preclude proceedings against any other party, whether or not subsequent to the party originally proceeded against.

Article 70

1. The holder may recover from any party liable –
   - (a) at maturity: the amount of the instrument with interest, if interest has been stipulated for;
   - (b) after maturity:
     - (i) the amount of the instrument with interest, if interest has been stipulated for, to the date of maturity;
     - (ii) if interest has been stipulated to be paid after maturity, interest at the rate stipulated, or, in the absence of such stipulation, interest at the rate specified in paragraph 2 of this Article, calculated from the date of presentment on the sum specified in subparagraph (b)(i) of this paragraph;
     - (iii) any expenses of protest and of the notices given by him;
   - (c) before maturity:
     - (i) the amount of the instrument with interest, if interest has been stipulated for, to the date of payment; or, if no interest has been stipulated for, subject to a discount from the date of payment to the date of maturity, calculated in accordance with paragraph 4 of this Article;
     - (ii) any expenses of protest and of the notices given by him.
2. The rate of interest shall be the rate that would be recoverable in legal proceedings taken in the jurisdiction where the instrument is payable.
3. Nothing in paragraph 2 of this Article prevents a court from awarding damages or compensation for additional loss caused to the holder by reason of delay in payment.
4. The discount shall be at the official rate (discount rate) or other similar appropriate rate effective on the date when recourse is exercised at the place where the holder has his principal place of business, or, if he does not have a place of business his habitual residence, or, if there is no such rate, then at such rate as is reasonable in the circumstances.

Article 71

A party who pays an instrument and is thereby discharged in whole or in part of his liability on the instrument may recover from the parties liable to him –

(a) the entire sum which he has paid;
(b) interest on that sum at the rate specified in paragraph 2 of Article 70, from the date on which he made payment;
(c) any expenses of the notices given by him.

Chapter VI Discharge

Section 1 Discharge by payment

Article 72

1. A party is discharged of liability on the instrument when he pays the holder, or a party subsequent to himself who has paid the instrument and is in possession of it, the amount due pursuant to Article 70 or 71 –
   (a) at or after maturity; or
   (b) before maturity, upon dishonour by non-acceptance.
2. Payment before maturity other than under subparagraph (b) of paragraph 1 of this Article does not discharge the party making the payment of his liability on the instrument except in respect of the person to whom payment was made.
3. A party is not discharged of liability if he pays a holder who is not a protected holder, or a party who has taken up and paid the instrument, and knows at the time of payment that the holder or that party acquired the instrument by theft or forged the signature of the payee or an endorsee, or participated in the theft or the forgery.
4. (a) A person receiving payment of an instrument must, unless agreed otherwise, deliver:
      (i) to the drawee making such payment, the instrument;
      (ii) to any other person making such payment, the instrument, a receipted account, and any protest.
   (b) In the case of an instrument payable by instalments at successive dates, the drawee or a party making a payment of the last instalment, may require that mention of such payment be made on the instrument or on a slip affixed thereto *('allonge')* and that a receipt therefore be given to him.
   (c) If an instrument payable by instalments at successive dates is dishonoured by non-acceptance or by non-payment as to any of its instalments and a party, upon dishonour, pays the instalment, the holder who receives such payment must give the party a certified copy of the instrument and any necessary authenticated protest in order to enable such party to exercise a right on the instrument.
   (d) The person from whom payment is demanded may withhold payment if the person demanding payment does not deliver the instrument to him. Withholding payment in these circumstances does not constitute dishonour by non-payment under Article 58.
   (e) If payment is made but the person paying, other than the drawee, fails to obtain the instrument, such person is discharged but the discharge cannot be set up as a defence against a protected holder to whom the instrument has been subsequently transferred.

Article 73

1. The holder is not obliged to take partial payment.
2. If the holder who is offered partial payment does not take it, the instrument is dishonoured by non-payment.
3. If the holder takes partial payment from the drawee, the guarantor of the drawee, or the acceptor or the maker –
   (a) the guarantor of the drawee, or the acceptor or the maker is discharged of his liability on the instrument to the extent of the amount paid; and
   (b) the instrument is to be considered as dishonoured by non-payment as to the amount unpaid.
4. If the holder takes partial payment from a party to the instrument other than the acceptor, the maker or the guarantor of the drawee –
   (a) the party making payment is discharged of his liability on the instrument to the extent of the amount paid; and
   (b) the holder must give such party a certified copy of the instrument and any necessary authenticated protest in order to enable such party to exercise a right on the instrument.
5. The drawee or a party making partial payment may require that mention of such payment be made on the instrument and that a receipt therefor be given to him.
6. If the balance is paid, the person who receives it and who is in possession of the instrument must deliver to the payor the receipted instrument and any authenticated protest.

Article 74

1. The holder may refuse to take payment at a place other than the place where the instrument was presented for payment in accordance with Article 55.
2. In such case if payment is not made at the place where the instrument was presented for payment in accordance with Article 55, the instrument is considered to be dishonoured by non-payment.

Article 75

1. An instrument must be paid in the currency in which the sum payable is expressed.
2. If the sum payable is expressed in a monetary unit of account within the meaning of subparagraph 1 of Article 5 and the monetary unit of account is transferable between the person making payment and the person receiving it, then, unless the instrument specifies a currency of payment, payment shall be made by transfer of monetary units of account. If the monetary unit of account is not transferable between those persons, payment shall be made in the currency specified in the instrument or, if no such currency is specified, in the currency of the place of payment.
3. The drawer or the maker may indicate in the instrument that it must be paid in a specified currency other than the currency in which the sum payable is expressed. In that case –
   (a) the instrument must be paid in the currency so specified;
   (b) the amount payable is to be calculated according to the rate of exchange indicated in the instrument. Failing such indication, the amount payable is to be calculated

according to the rate of exchange for sight drafts (or, if there is no such rate, according to the appropriate established rate of exchange) on the date of maturity:
   (i) ruling at the place where the instrument must be presented for payment in accordance with subparagraph (g) of Article 55, if the specified currency is that of that place (local currency); or
   (ii) if the specified currency is not that of that place, according to the usages of the place where the instrument must be presented for payment in accordance with subparagraph (g) of Article 55;
(c) if such an instrument is dishonoured by non-acceptance, the amount payable is to be calculated:
   (i) if the rate of exchange is indicated in the instrument, according to that rate;
   (ii) if no rate of exchange is indicated in the instrument, at the option of the holder, according to the rate of exchange ruling on the date of dishonour or on the date of actual payment;
(d) if such an instrument is dishonoured by non-payment, the amount payable is to be calculated according to that rate:
   (i) if the rate of exchange is indicated in the instrument, according to that rate;
   (ii) if no rate of exchange is indicated in the instrument, at the option of the holder, according to the rate of exchange ruling on the date of maturity or on the date of actual payment.

4. Nothing in this Article prevents a court from awarding damages for loss caused to the holder by reason of fluctuations in rates of exchange if such loss is caused by dishonour for non-acceptance or by non-payment.
5. The rate of exchange ruling at a certain date is the rate of exchange ruling, at the option of the holder, at the place where the instrument must be presented for payment in accordance with subparagraph (g) of Article 55 or at the place of actual payment.

Article 76

1. Nothing in this Convention prevents a Contracting State from enforcing exchange control regulations applicable in its territory and its provisions relating to the protection of its currency, including regulations which it is bound to apply virtue of international agreements to which it is a party.
2. (a) If, by virtue of the application of paragraph 1 of this Article, an instrument drawn in a currency which is not that of the place of payment must be paid in local currency, the amount payable is to be calculated according to the rate of exchange for sight drafts (or, if there is no such rate, according to the appropriate established rate of exchange) on the date of presentment ruling at the place where the instrument must be presented for payment in accordance with subparagraph (g) of Article 55.
   (b) (i) if such an instrument is dishonoured by non-acceptance, the amount payable is to be calculated, at the option of the holder, at the rate of exchange ruling on the date of dishonour or on the date of actual payment;
   (ii) if such an instrument is dishonest by non-payment, the amount is to be calculated, at the option of the holder, according to the rate of exchange ruling on the date of presentment or on the date of actual payment;
   (iii) paragraphs 4 and 5 of Article 75 are applicable where appropriate.

Section 2 Discharge of other parties

Article 77

1. If a party is discharged in whole or in part of his liability on the instrument, any party who has a right on the instrument against him is discharged to the same extent.
2. Payment by the drawee of the whole or a part of the amount of a bill to the holder, or to any party who takes up and pays the bill, discharges all parties of their liability to the same extent, except where the drawee pays a holder who is not a protected holder, or a party who has taken up and paid the bill, and knows at the time of payment that the holder or that party acquired the bill by theft or forged the signature of the payee or an endorsee, or participated in the theft or the forgery.

Chapter VII Lost instruments

Article 78

1. If an instrument is lost, whether by destruction, theft or otherwise, the person who lost the instrument has, subject to the provisions of paragraph 2 of this Article, the same right to payment which he would have had if he had been in possession of the instrument. The party from whom payment is claimed cannot set up as a defence against liability on the instrument the fact that the person claiming payment is not in possession of the instrument.
2. (a) The person claiming payment of a lost instrument must state in writing to the party from whom he claims payment:
   - (i) the elements of the lost instrument pertaining to the requirements set forth in paragraph 1 or 2 of Articles 1, 2 and 3; for this purpose the person claiming payment of the lost instrument may present to that party a copy of that instrument;
   - (ii) the facts showing that, if he had been in possession of the instrument, he would have had a right to payment from the party from whom payment is claimed;
   - (iii) the facts which prevent production of the instrument.

   (b) The party from whom payment of a lost instrument is claimed may require the person claiming payment to give security in order to indemnify him for any loss which he may suffer by reason of the subsequent payment of the lost instrument.

   (c) The nature of the security and its terms are to be determined by agreement between the person claiming payment and the party from whom payment is claimed. Failing such an agreement, the court may determine whether security is called for and, if so, the nature of the security and its terms.

   (d) If the security cannot be given, the court may order the party from whom payment is claimed to deposit the sum of the lost instrument, and any interest and expenses which may be claimed under Article 70 or 71, with the court or any other competent authority or institution, and may determine the duration of such deposit. Such deposit is to be considered as payment to the person claiming payment.

Article 79

1. A party who has paid a lost instrument and to whom the instrument is subsequently presented for payment by another person must give notice of such presentment to the person whom he paid.

2. Such notice must be given on the day the instrument is presented or on one of the two business days which follow and must state the name of the person presenting the instrument and the date and place of presentment.
3. Failure to give notice renders the party who has paid the lost instrument liable for any damages which the person whom he paid may suffer from such failure, provided that the damages do not exceed the amount referred to in Article 70 or 71.
4. Delay in giving notice is excused when the delay is caused by circumstances which are beyond the control of the person who has paid the lost instrument and which he could neither avoid nor overcome. When the cause of the delay ceases to operate, notice must be given with reasonable diligence.
5. Notice is dispensed with when the cause of delay in giving notice continues to operate beyond 30 days after the last day on which it should have been given.

Article 80

1. A party who has paid a lost instrument in accordance with the provisions of Article 78 and who is subsequently required to, and does, pay the instrument, or who, by reason of the loss of the instrument, then loses his right to recover from any party liable to him, has the right –
   (a) if security was given, to realise the security; or
   (b) if an amount was deposited with the court or other competent authority or institution, to reclaim the amount so deposited.
2. The person who has given security in accordance with the provisions of subparagraph (b) of paragraph 2 of Article 78 is entitled to obtain release of the security when the party for whose benefit the security was given is no longer at risk to suffer loss because of the fact that the instrument is lost.

Article 81

For the purpose of making protest for dishonour by non-payment, a person claiming payment of a lost instrument may use a written statement that satisfies the requirements of subparagraph (a) of paragraph 2 of Article 78.

Article 82

A person receiving payment of a lost instrument in accordance with Article 78 must deliver to the party paying the written statement required under subparagraph (a) of paragraph 2 of Article 78, receipted by him, and any protest and a receipted account.

Article 83

1. A party who pays a lost instrument in accordance with Article 78 has the same rights which he would have had if he had been in possession of the instrument.
2. Such party may exercise his rights only if he is in possession of the receipted written statement referred to in Article 82.

Chapter VIII Limitation (prescription)

Article 84

1. A right of action arising on an instrument may no longer be exercised after four years have elapsed –
   (a) against the maker, or his guarantor, of a note payable on demand, from the date of the note;
   (b) against the acceptor or the maker or their guarantor of an instrument payable at a definite time, from the date of maturity;
   (c) against the guarantor of the drawee of a bill payable at a definite time, from the date of maturity or, if the bill is dishonoured by non-acceptance, from the date of protest for dishonour or, where protest is dispensed with, from the date of dishonour;
   (d) against the acceptor of a bill payable on demand or his guarantor, from the date on which it was accepted or, if no such date is shown, from the date of the bill;
   (e) against the guarantor of the drawee of a bill payable on demand, from the date on which he signed the bill or, if no such date is shown, from the date of the bill;
   (f) against the drawer or an endorser or their guarantor, from the date of protest for dishonour by non-acceptance or by non-payment or, where protest is dispensed with, from the date of dishonour.
2. A party who pays the instrument in accordance with Article 70 or 71 may exercise his right of action against a party liable to him within one year from the date on which he paid the instrument.

Chapter IX

Articles 85–90 [Omitted].

United Nations Convention on the Liability of Operators of Transport Terminals in International Trade, Vienna, 1991

Article 1 Definitions

In this Convention:

(a) 'Operator of a transport terminal' (hereinafter referred to as 'operator') means a person who, in the course of his business, undertakes to take in charge goods involved in international carriage in order to perform or to procure the performance of transport-related services with respect to the goods in an area under his control or in respect of which he has a right of access or use. However, a person is not considered an operator whenever he is a carrier under applicable rules of law governing carriage;

(b) Where goods are consolidated in a container, pallet or similar Article of transport or where they are packed, 'goods' includes such Article of transport or packaging if it was not supplied by the operator;

(c) 'International carriage' means any carriage in which the place of departure and the place of destination are identified as being located in two different States when the goods are taken in charge by the operator;

(d) Transport-related services' includes such services as storage, warehousing, loading, unloading, stowage, trimming, dunnaging and lashing;
(e) 'Notice' means a notice given in a form which provides a record of the information contained therein;
(f) 'Request' means a request made in a form which provides a record of the information contained therein.

Article 2 Scope of application

(1) This Convention applies to transport-related services performed in relation to goods which are involved in international carriage:
  (a) When the transport-related services are performed by an operator whose place of business is located in a State Party, or
  (b) When the transport-related services are performed in a State Party, or
  (c) When, according to the rules of private international law, the transport-related services are governed by the law of a State Party.
(2) If the operator has more than one place of business, the place of business is that which has the closest relationship to the transport-related services as a whole.
(3) If the operator does not have a place of business, reference is to be made to the operator's habitual residence.

Article 3 Period of responsibility

The operator is responsible for the goods from the time he has taken them in charge until the time he has handed them over to or has placed them at the disposal of the person entitled to take delivery of them.

Article 4 Issuance of document

(1) The operator may, and at the customer's request shall, within a reasonable period of time, at the option of the operator, either:
  (a) Acknowledge his receipt of the goods by signing and dating a document presented by the customer that identifies the goods, or
  (b) Issue a signed document identifying the goods, acknowledging his receipt of the goods and the date thereof, and stating their condition and quantity in so far as they can be ascertained by reasonable means of checking.
(2) If the operator does not act in accordance with either subparagraph (a) or (b) of paragraph (1), he is presumed to have received the goods in apparent good condition, unless he proves otherwise. No such presumption applies when the services performed by the operator are limited to the immediate transfer of the goods between means of transport.
(3) A document referred to in paragraph (1) may be issued in any form which preserves a record of the information contained therein. When the customer and the operator have agreed to communicate electronically, a document referred to in paragraph (1) may be replaced by an equivalent electronic data interchange message.
(4) The signature referred to in paragraph (1) means a handwritten signature, its facsimile or an equivalent authentication effected by any other means.

Article 5 Basis of liability

(1) The operator is liable for loss resulting from loss of or damage to the goods, as well as from delay in handing over the goods, if the occurrence which caused the loss, damage or delay took place during the period of the operator's responsibility for the goods as defined in Article 3, unless he proves that he, his servants or agents or other persons of whose services the operator makes use for the performance of the transport-related services took all measures that could reasonably be required to avoid the occurrence and its consequences.

(2) Where a failure on the part of the operator, his servants or agents or other persons of whose services the operator makes use for the performance of the transport-related services to take the measures referred to in paragraph (1) combines with another cause to produce loss, damage or delay, the operator is liable only to the extent that the loss resulting from such loss, damage or delay is attributable to that failure, provided that the operator proves the amount of the loss not attributable thereto.

(3) Delay in handing over the goods occurs when the operator fails to hand them over to or place them at the disposal of a person entitled to take delivery of them within the time expressly agreed upon or, in the absence of such agreement, within a reasonable time after receiving a request for the goods by such person.

(4) If the operator fails to hand over the goods to or place them at the disposal of a person entitled to take delivery of them within a period of 30 consecutive days after the date expressly agreed upon or, in the absence of such agreement, within a period of 30 consecutive days after receiving a request for the goods by such person, a person entitled to make a claim for the loss of the goods may treat them as lost.

Article 6 Limits of liability

(1) (a) The liability of the operator for loss resulting from loss of or damage to goods according to the provisions of Article 5 is limited to an amount not exceeding 8.33 units of account per kilogram of gross weight of the goods lost or damaged.

(b) However, if the goods are handed over to the operator immediately after carriage by sea or by inland waterways, or if the goods are handed over, or are to be handed over, by him for such carriage, the liability of the operator for loss resulting from loss of or damage to goods according to the provisions of Article 5 is limited to an amount not exceeding 2.75 units of account per kilogram of gross weight of the goods lost or damaged. For the purposes of this paragraph, carriage by sea or by inland waterways includes pick-up and delivery within a port.

(c) When the loss of or damage to a part of the goods affects the value of another part of the goods, the total weight of the lost or damaged goods and of the goods whose value is affected shall be taken into consideration in determining the limit of liability.

(2) The liability of the operator for delay in handing over the goods according to the provisions of Article 5 is limited to an amount equivalent to two and a half times the charges payable to the operator for his services in respect of the goods delayed, but not exceeding the total of such charges in respect of the consignment of which the goods were a part.

(3) In no case shall the aggregate liability of the operator under both paragraphs (1) and (2) exceed the limitation which would be established under paragraph (1) for total loss of the goods in respect of which such liability was incurred.

(4) The operator may agree to limits of liability exceeding those provided for in paragraphs (1), (2) and (3).

Article 7 Application to non-contractual claims

(1) The defences and limits of liability provided for in this Convention apply in any action against the operator in respect of loss of or damage to the goods, as well as delay in handing over the goods, whether the action is founded in contract, in tort or otherwise.
(2) If such an action is brought against a servant or agent of the operator, or against another person of whose services the operator makes use for the performance of the transport-related services, such servant, agent or person, if he proves that he acted within the scope of his employment or engagement by the operator, is entitled to avail himself of the defences and limits of liability which the operator is entitled to invoke under this Convention.
(3) Except as provided in Article 8, the aggregate of the amounts recoverable from the operator and from any servant, agent or person referred to in the preceding paragraph shall not exceed the limits of liability provided for in this Convention.

Article 8 Loss of right to limit liability

(1) The operator is not entitled to the benefit of the limitation of liability provided for in Article 6 if it is proved that the loss, damage or delay resulted from an act or omission of the operator himself or his servants or agents done with the intent to cause such loss, damage or delay, or recklessly and with knowledge that such loss, damage or delay would probably result.
(2) Notwithstanding the provision of paragraph (2) of Article 7, a servant or agent of the operator or another person of whose services the operator makes use for the performance of the transport-related services is not entitled to the benefit of the limitation of liability provided for in Article 6 if it is proved that the loss, damage or delay resulted from an act or omission of such servant, agent or person done with the intent to cause such loss, damage or delay, or recklessly and with knowledge that such loss, damage or delay would probably result.

Article 9 Special rules on dangerous goods

If dangerous goods are handed over to the operator without being marked, labelled, packaged or documented in accordance with any law or regulation relating to dangerous goods applicable in the country where the goods are handed over and if, at the time the goods are taken in charge by him, the operator does not otherwise know of their dangerous character, he is entitled:

(a) To take all precautions the circumstances may require, including, when the goods pose an imminent danger to any person or property, destroying the goods, rendering them innocuous, or disposing of them by any other lawful means, without payment of compensation for damage to or destruction of the goods resulting from such precautions, and
(b) To receive reimbursement for all costs incurred by him in taking the measures referred to in subparagraph (a) from the person who failed to meet any obligation under such applicable law or regulation to inform him of the dangerous character of the goods.

Article 10 Rights of security in goods

(1) The operator has a right of retention over the goods for costs and claims which are due in connection with the transport-related services performed by him in respect of the goods both during the period of his responsibility for them and thereafter. However, nothing in this Convention affects the validity under the applicable law of any contractual arrangements extending the operator's security in the goods.

(2) The operator is not entitled to retain the goods if a sufficient guarantee for the sum claimed is provided or if an equivalent sum is deposited with a mutually accepted third party or with an official institution in the State where the operator has his place of business.

(3) In order to obtain the amount necessary to satisfy his claim, the operator is entitled, to the extent permitted by the law of the State where the goods are located, to sell all or part of the goods over which he has exercised the right of retention provided for in this Article. This right to sell does not apply to containers, pallets or similar articles of transport or packaging which are owned by a party other than the carrier or the shipper and which are clearly marked as regards ownership except in respect of claims by the operator for the cost of repairs of or improvements to the containers, pallets or similar articles of transport or packaging.

(4) Before exercising any right to sell the goods, the operator shall make reasonable efforts to give notice of the intended sale to the owner of the goods, the person from whom the operator received them and the person entitled to take delivery of them from the operator. The operator shall account appropriately for the balance of the proceeds of the sale in excess of the sums due to the operator plus the reasonable costs of the sale. The right of sale shall in all other respects be exercised in accordance with the law of the State where the goods are located.

Article 11 Notice of loss, damage or delay

(1) Unless notice of loss or damage, specifying the general nature of the loss or damage, is given to the operator not later than the third working day after the day when the goods were handed over by the operator to the person entitled to take delivery of them, the handing over is *prima facie* evidence of the handing over by the operator of the goods as described in the document issued by the operator pursuant to paragraph (1)(b) of Article 4 or, if no such document was issued, in good condition.

(2) Where the loss or damage is not apparent, the provisions of paragraph (1) apply correspondingly if notice is not given to the operator within 15 consecutive days after the day when the goods reached the final recipient, but in no case later than 60 consecutive days after the day when the goods were handed over to the person entitled to take delivery of them.

(3) If the operator participated in a survey or inspection of the goods at the time when they were handed over to the person entitled to take delivery of them, notice need not be given to the operator of loss or damage ascertained during that survey or inspection.

(4) In the case of any actual or apprehended loss of or damage to the goods, the operator, the carrier and the person entitled to take delivery of the goods shall give all reasonable facilities to each other for inspecting and tallying the goods.

(5) No compensation is payable for loss resulting from delay in handing over the goods unless notice has been given to the operator within 21 consecutive days after the day when the goods were handed over to the person entitled to take delivery of them.

Article 12 Limitation of actions

(1) Any action under this Convention is time-barred if judicial or arbitral proceedings have not been instituted within a period of two years.
(2) The limitation period commences:
    (a) On the day the operator hands over the goods or part thereof to, or places them at the disposal of, a person entitled to take delivery of them, or
    (b) In cases of total loss of the goods, on the day the person entitled to make a claim receives notice from the operator that the goods are lost, or on the day that person may treat the goods as lost in accordance with paragraph (4) of Article 5, whichever is earlier.
(3) The day on which the limitation period commences is not included in the period.
(4) The operator may at any time during the running of the limitation period extend the period by a notice to the claimant. The period may be further extended by another notice or notices.
(5) A recourse action by a carrier or another person against the operator may be instituted even after the expiration of the limitation period provided for in the preceding paragraphs if it is instituted within 90 days after the carrier or other person has been held liable in an action against himself or has settled the claim upon which such action was based and if, within a reasonable period of time after the filing of a claim against a carrier or other person that may result in a recourse action against the operator, notice of the filing of such a claim has been given to the operator.

Article 13 Contractual stipulations

(1) Unless otherwise provided in this Convention, any stipulation in a contract concluded by an operator or in any document signed or issued by the operator pursuant to Article 4 is null and void to the extent that it derogates, directly or indirectly, from the provisions of this Convention. The nullity of such a stipulation does not affect the validity of the other provisions of the contract or document of which it forms a part.
(2) Notwithstanding the provisions of the preceding paragraph, the operator may agree to increase his responsibilities and obligations under this Convention.

Article 14 Interpretation of the Convention

In the interpretation of this Convention, regard is to be had to its international character and to the need to promote uniformity in its application.

Article 15 International transport conventions

This Convention does not modify any rights or duties which may arise under an international convention relating to the international carriage of goods which is binding on a State which is a party to this Convention or under any law of such State giving effect to a convention relating to the international carriage of goods.

Article 16 Unit of account

(1) The unit of account referred to in Article 6 is the Special Drawing Right as defined by the International Monetary Fund. The amounts mentioned in Article 6 are to be expressed in the national currency of a State according to the value of such currency at the date of judgment or the date agreed upon by the parties. The equivalence between the national currency of a State Party which is a member of the International Monetary Fund and the Special Drawing Right is to be calculated in accordance with the method of valuation applied by the International Monetary Fund in effect at the date in question for its operations and transactions. The equivalence between the national currency of a State Party which is not a member of the International Monetary Fund and the Special Drawing Right is to be calculated in a manner determined by that State.

(2) The calculation mentioned in the last sentence of the preceding paragraph is to be made in such a manner as to express in the national currency of the State Party as far as possible the same real value for amounts in Article 6 as is expressed there in units of account. States Parties must communicate to the depositary the manner of calculation at the time of signature or when depositing their instrument of ratification, acceptance, approval or accession and whenever there is a change in the manner of such calculation.

Final clause

Articles 17–25 [Omitted]

United Nations Convention on Independent Guarantees and Stand-By Letters of Credit, 1996

Chapter I Scope of application

Article 1 Scope of application

(1) This Convention applies to an international undertaking referred to in article 2 –
  (a) if the place of business of the guarantor/issuer at which the undertaking is issued is in a Contracting State; or
  (b) if the rules of private international law to the application of the law of a Contracting State, unless the undertaking excludes the application of the Convention.

(2) This Convention applies also to an international letter of credit not falling within article 2 if it expressly states that it is subject to this Convention.

(3) The provisions of articles 21 and 22 apply to international undertakings referred to in article 2 independently of paragraph (1) of this article.

Article 2 Undertaking

(1) For the purposes of this Convention, an undertaking is an independent commitment, known in international practice as an independent guarantee or as a stand-by letter of

credit, given by a bank or other institution or person ('guarantor/issuer') to pay to the beneficiary a certain or determinable amount upon simple demand or upon demand accompanied by other documents, in conformity with the terms and any documentary conditions of the undertaking, indicating, or from which it is to be inferred, that payment is due because of a default in the performance of an obligation, or because of another contingency, or for money borrowed or advanced, or on account of any mature indebtedness undertaken by the principal/applicant or another person.

(2) The undertaking may be given –
 (a) at the request or on the instruction of the customer ('principal/applicant') of the guarantor/issuer;
 (b) on the instruction of another bank, institution or person ('instructing party') that acts at the request of the customer ('principal/applicant') of that instructing party; or
 (c) on behalf of the guarantor/issuer itself.

(3) Payment may be stipulated in the undertaking to be made in any form, including –
 (a) payment in a specified currency or unit of account;
 (b) acceptance of a bill of exchange (draft);
 (c) payment on a deferred basis;
 (d) supply of a specified item of value.

(4) The undertaking may stipulate that the guarantor/issuer itself is the beneficiary when acting in favour of another person.

Article 3 Independence of undertaking

For the purposes of this Convention, an undertaking is independent where the guarantor/issuer's obligation to the beneficiary is not –

(a) dependent upon the existence or validity of any underlying transaction, or upon any other undertaking (including stand-by letters of credit or independent guarantees to which confirmations or counter-guarantees relate); or
(b) subject to any term or condition not appearing in the undertaking, or to any future, uncertain act or event except presentation of documents or another such act or event within a guarantor/issuer's sphere of operations.

Article 4 Internationality of undertaking

(1) An undertaking is international if the places of business, as specified in the undertaking, of any two of the following persons are in different States: guarantor/issuer, beneficiary, principal/applicant, instructing party, confirmer.

(2) For the purposes of the preceding paragraph –
 (a) if the undertaking lists more than one place of business for a given person, the relevant place of business is that which has the closest relationship to the undertaking;
 (b) if the undertaking does not specify a place of business for a given person but specifies its habitual residence, that residence is relevant for determining the international character of the undertaking.

Chapter II Interpretation

Article 5 Principles of interpretation

In the interpretation of this Convention, regard is to be had to its international character and to the need to promote uniformity in its application and the observance of good faith in the international practice of independent guarantees and stand-by letters of credit.

Article 6 Definitions

For the purposes of this Convention and unless otherwise indicated in a provision of this Convention or required by the context –

(a) 'Undertaking' includes 'counter-guarantee' and 'confirmation of an undertaking';
(b) 'Guarantor/issuer' includes 'counter-guarantor' and 'confirmer';
(c) 'Counter-guarantee' means an undertaking given to the guarantor/issuer of another undertaking by its instructing party and providing for payment upon simple demand or upon demand accompanied by other documents, in conformity with the terms and any documentary conditions of the undertaking, indicating, or from which it is to be inferred, that payment under that other undertaking has been demanded from, or made by, the person issuing that other undertaking;
(d) 'Counter-guarantor' means the person issuing a counter-guarantee;
(e) 'Confirmation' of an undertaking means an undertaking added to that of the guarantor/issuer, and authorized by the guarantor/issuer, providing the beneficiary with the option of demanding payment from the confirmer instead of from the guarantor/issuer, upon simple demand or upon demand accompanied by other documents, in conformity with the terms and any documentary conditions of the confirmed undertaking, without prejudice to the beneficiary's right to demand payment from the guarantor/issuer;
(f) 'Confirmer' means the person adding a confirmation to an undertaking;
(g) 'Document' means a communication made in a form that provides a complete record thereof.

Chapter III Form and content of undertaking

Article 7 Issuance, form and irrevocability of undertaking

(1) Issuance of an undertaking occurs when and where the undertaking leaves the sphere of control of the guarantor/issuer concerned.
(2) An undertaking may be issued in any form which preserves a complete record of the text of the undertaking and provides authentication of its source by generally accepted means or by a procedure agreed upon by the guarantor/issuer and the beneficiary.
(3) From the time of issuance of an undertaking, a demand for payment may be made in accordance with the terms and conditions of the undertaking, unless the undertaking stipulates a different time.
(4) An undertaking is irrevocable upon issuance, unless it stipulates that it is revocable.

Article 8 Amendment

(1) An undertaking may not be amended except in the form stipulated in the undertaking or, failing such stipulation, in a form referred to in paragraph (2) of article 7.
(2) Unless otherwise stipulated in the undertaking or elsewhere agreed by the guarantor/issuer and the beneficiary, an undertaking is amended upon issuance of the amendment if the amendment has previously been authorized by the beneficiary.
(3) Unless otherwise stipulated in the undertaking or elsewhere agreed by the guarantor/issuer and the beneficiary, where any amendment has not previously been authorized by the beneficiary, the undertaking is amended only when the guarantor/issuer receives a notice of acceptance of the amendment by the beneficiary in a form referred to in paragraph (2) of article 7.
(4) An amendment of an undertaking has no effect on the rights and obligations of the principal/applicant (or an instructing party) or of a confirmer of the undertaking unless such person consents to the amendment.

Article 9 Transfer of beneficiary's right to demand payment

(1) The beneficiary's right to demand payment may be transferred only if authorized in the undertaking, and only to the extent and in the manner authorized in the undertaking.
(2) If an undertaking is designated as transferable without specifying whether or not the consent of the guarantor/issuer or another authorized person is required for the actual transfer, neither the guarantor/issuer nor any other authorized person is obliged to effect the transfer except to the extent and in the manner expressly consented to by it.

Article 10 Assignment of proceeds

(1) Unless otherwise stipulated in the undertaking or elsewhere agreed by the guarantor/issuer and the beneficiary, the beneficiary may assign to another person any proceeds to which it may be, or may become, entitled under the undertaking.
(2) If the guarantor/issuer or another person obliged to effect payment has received a notice originating from the beneficiary, in a form referred to in paragraph (2) of article 7, of the beneficiary's irrevocable assignment, payment to the assignee discharges the obligor, to the extent of its payment, from its liability under the undertaking.

Article 11 Cessation of right to demand payment

(1) The right of the beneficiary to demand payment under the undertaking ceases when –
  (a) the guarantor/issuer has received a statement by the beneficiary of release from liability in a form referred to in paragraph (2) of article 7;
  (b) the beneficiary and the guarantor/issuer have agreed on the termination of the undertaking in the form stipulated in the undertaking or, failing such stipulation, in a form referred to in paragraph (2) of article 7;

(c) the amount available under the undertaking has been paid, unless the undertaking provides for the automatic renewal or for an automatic increase of the amount available or otherwise provides for continuation of the undertaking;

(d) the validity period of the undertaking expires in accordance with the provisions of article 12.

(2) The undertaking may stipulate, or the guarantor/issuer and the beneficiary may agree elsewhere, that return of the document embodying the undertaking to the guarantor/ issuer, or a procedure functionally equivalent to the return of the document in the case of the issuance of the undertaking in non-paper form, is required for the cessation of the right to demand payment, either alone or in conjunction with one of the events referred to in subparagraphs (a) and (b) of paragraph (1) of this article. However, in no case shall retention of any such document by the beneficiary after the right to demand payment ceases in accordance with subparagraph (c) or (d) of paragraph (1) of this article preserve any rights of the beneficiary under the undertaking.

Article 12 Expiry

The validity period of the undertaking expires –

(a) at the expiry date, which may be a specified calendar date or the last day of a fixed period of time stipulated in the undertaking, provided that, if the expiry date is not a business day at the place of business of the guarantor/issuer at which the undertaking is issued, or of another person or at another place stipulated in the undertaking for presentation of the demand for payment, expiry occurs on the first business day which follows;

(b) if expiry depends according to the undertaking on the occurrence of an act or event not within the guarantor/issuer's sphere of operations, when the guarantor/issuer is advised that the act or event has occurred by presentation of the document specified for that purpose in the undertaking or, if no such document is specified, of a certification by the beneficiary of the occurrence of the act or event;

(c) if the undertaking does not state an expiry date, or if the act or event on which expiry is stated to depend has not yet been established by presentation of the required document and an expiry date has not been stated in addition, when six years have elapsed from the date of issuance of the undertaking.

Chapter IV Rights, obligations and defences

Article 13 Determination of rights and obligations

(1) The rights and obligations of the guarantor/issuer and the beneficiary arising from the undertaking are determined by the terms and conditions set forth in the undertaking, including any rules, general conditions or usages specifically referred to therein, and by the provisions of this Convention.

(2) In interpreting terms and conditions of the undertaking and in settling questions that are not addressed by the terms and conditions of the undertaking or by the provisions of this Convention, regard shall be had to generally accepted international rules and usages of independent guarantee or stand-by letter of credit practice.

Article 14 Standard of conduct and liability of guarantor/issuer

(1) In discharging its obligations under the undertaking and this Convention, the guarantor/issuer shall act in good faith and exercise reasonable care having due regard to generally accepted standards of international practice of independent guarantees or stand-by letters of credit.
(2) A guarantor/issuer may not be exempted from liability for its failure to act in good faith or for any grossly negligent conduct.

Article 15 Demand

(1) Any demand for payment under the undertaking shall be made in a form referred to in paragraph (2) of article 7 and in conformity with the terms and conditions of the undertaking.
(2) Unless otherwise stipulated in the undertaking, the demand and any certification or other document required by the undertaking shall be presented, within the time that a demand for payment may be made, to the guarantor/issuer at the place where the undertaking was issued.
(3) The beneficiary, when demanding payment, is deemed to certify that the demand is not in bad faith and that none of the elements referred to in subparagraphs (a), (b) and (c) of paragraph (1) of article 19 are present.

Article 16 Examination of demand and accompanying documents

(1) The guarantor/issuer shall examine the demand and any accompanying documents in accordance with the standard of conduct referred to in paragraph (1) of article 14. In determining whether documents are in facial conformity with the terms and conditions of the undertaking, and are consistent with one another, the guarantor/issuer shall have due regard to the applicable international standard of independent guarantee or stand-by letter of credit practice.
(2) Unless otherwise stipulated in the undertaking or elsewhere agreed by the guarantor/issuer and the beneficiary, the guarantor/issuer shall have reasonable time, but not more than seven business days following the day of receipt of the demand and any accompanying documents, in which to –
    (a) examine the demand and any accompanying documents;
    (b) decide whether or not to pay;
    (c) if the decision is not to pay, issue notice thereof to the beneficiary.

    The notice referred to in subparagraph (c) above shall, unless otherwise stipulated in the undertaking or elsewhere agreed by the guarantor/issuer and the beneficiary, be made by teletransmission or, if that is not possible, by other expeditious means and indicate the reason for the decision not to pay.

Article 17 Payment

(1) Subject to article 19, the guarantor/issuer shall pay against a demand made in accordance with the provisions of article 15. Following a determination that a demand for

payment so conforms, payment shall be made promptly, unless the undertaking stipulates payment on a deferred basis, in which case payment shall be made at the stipulated time.

(2) Any payment against a demand that is not in accordance with the provisions of article 15 does not prejudice the rights of the principal/applicant.

Article 18 Set-off

Unless otherwise stipulated in the undertaking or elsewhere agreed by the guarantor/issuer and the beneficiary, the guarantor/issuer may discharge the payment obligation under the undertaking by availing itself of a right of set-off, except with any claim assigned to it by the principal/applicant or the instructing party.

Article 19 Exception to payment obligation

(1) If it is manifest and clear that –
  (a) any document is not genuine or has been falsified;
  (b) no payment is due on the basis asserted in the demand and the supporting documents; or
  (c) judging by the type and purpose of the undertaking, the demand has no conceivable basis, the guarantor/issuer, acting in good faith, has a right, as against the beneficiary, to withhold payment.

(2) For the purposes of subparagraph (c) of paragraph (1) of this article, the following are types of situations in which a demand has no conceivable basis –
  (a) the contingency or risk against which the undertaking was designed to secure the beneficiary has undoubtedly not materialized;
  (b) the underlying obligation of the principal/applicant has been declared invalid by a court or arbitral tribunal, unless the undertaking indicates that such contingency falls within the risk to be covered by the undertaking;
  (c) the underlying obligation has undoubtedly been fulfilled to the satisfaction of the beneficiary;
  (d) fulfilment of the underlying obligation has clearly been prevented by wilful misconduct of the beneficiary;
  (e) in the case of a demand under a counter-guarantee, the beneficiary of the counter-guarantee has made payment in bad faith as guarantor/issuer of the undertaking to which the counter-guarantee relates.

(3) In the circumstances set out in subparagraphs (a), (b) and (c) of paragraph (1) of this article, the principal/applicant is entitled to provisional court measures in accordance with article 20.

Chapter V Provisional court measures

Article 20 Provisional court measures

(1) Where, on an application by the principal/applicant or the instructing party, it is shown that there is a high probability that, with regard to a demand made, or expected to be

made, by the beneficiary, one of the circumstances referred to in subparagraphs (a), (b) and (c) of paragraph (1) of article 19 is present, the court, on the basis of immediately available strong evidence, may –

(a) issue a provisional order to the effect that the beneficiary does not receive payment, including an order that the guarantor/issuer hold the amount of the undertaking; or
(b) issue a provisional order to the effect that the proceeds of the undertaking paid to the beneficiary are blocked, taking into account whether in the absence of such an order the principal/applicant would be likely to suffer serious harm.

(2) The court, when issuing a provisional order referred to in paragraph (1) of this article, may require the person applying therefor to furnish such form of security as the court deems appropriate.
(3) The court may not issue a provisional order of the kind referred to in paragraph (1) of this article based on any objection to payment other than those referred to in subparagraphs (a), (b) and (c) of paragraph (1) of article 19, or use of the undertaking for a criminal purpose.

Chapter VI Conflict of laws

Article 21 Choice of applicable law

The undertaking is governed by the law the choice of which is –

(a) stipulated in the undertaking or demonstrated by the terms and conditions of the undertaking; or
(b) agreed elsewhere by the guarantor/issuer and the beneficiary.

Article 22 Determination of applicable law

Failing a choice of law in accordance with article 21, the undertaking is governed by the law of the State where the guarantor/issuer has that place of business at which the undertaking was issued.

Chapter VII Final clauses

Articles 23–29 [Omitted].

Convention on Combating Bribery of Foreign Public Officials in International Business Transactions, 1997

Preamble

The Parties,

Considering that bribery is a widespread phenomenon in international business transactions, including trade and investment, which raises serious moral and political concerns, undermines good governance and economic development, and distorts international competitive conditions;

Considering that all countries share a responsibility to combat bribery in international business transactions;

Having regard to the Revised Recommendation on Combating Bribery in International Business Transactions, adopted by the Council of the Organisation for Economic Co-operation and Development (OECD) on 23 May 1997, C(97)123/FINAL, which, *inter alia*, called for effective measures to deter, prevent and combat the bribery of foreign public officials in connection with international business transactions, in particular the prompt criminalisation of such bribery in an effective and co-ordinated manner and in conformity with the agreed common elements set out in that Recommendation and with the jurisdictional and other basic legal principles of each country;

Welcoming other recent developments which further advance international understanding and co-operation in combating bribery of public officials, including actions of the United Nations, the World Bank, the International Monetary Fund, the World Trade Organisation, the Organisation of American States, the Council of Europe and the European Union;

Welcoming the efforts of companies, business organisations and trade unions as well as other non-governmental organisations to combat bribery;

Recognising the role of governments in the prevention of solicitation of bribes from individuals and enterprises in international business transactions;

Recognising that achieving progress in this field requires not only efforts on a national level but also multilateral co-operation, monitoring and follow-up;

Recognising that achieving equivalence among the measures to be taken by the Parties is an essential object and purpose of the Convention, which requires that the Convention be ratified without derogations affecting this equivalence;

Have agreed as follows:

Article 1 The offence of bribery of foreign public officials

1. Each Party shall take such measures as may be necessary to establish that it is a criminal offence under its law for any person intentionally to offer, promise or give any undue pecuniary or other advantage, whether directly or through intermediaries, to a foreign public official, for that official or for a third party, in order that the official act or refrain from acting in relation to the performance of official duties, in order to obtain or retain business or other improper advantage in the conduct of international business.
2. Each Party shall take any measures necessary to establish that complicity in, including incitement, aiding and abetting, or authorisation of an act of bribery of a foreign public official shall be a criminal offence. Attempt and conspiracy to bribe a foreign public official shall be criminal offences to the same extent as attempt and conspiracy to bribe a public official of that Party.
3. The offences set out in paragraphs 1 and 2 above are hereinafter referred to as "bribery of a foreign public official".
4. For the purpose of this Convention:
   a. "foreign public official" means any person holding a legislative, administrative or judicial office of a foreign country, whether appointed or elected; any

person exercising a public function for a foreign country, including for a public agency or public enterprise; and any official or agent of a public international organisation;

b. "foreign country" includes all levels and subdivisions of government, from national to local;

c. "act or refrain from acting in relation to the performance of official duties" includes any use of the public official's position, whether or not within the official's authorised competence.

Article 2 Responsibility of legal persons

Each Party shall take such measures as may be necessary, in accordance with its legal principles, to establish the liability of legal persons for the bribery of a foreign public official.

Article 3 Sanctions

1. The bribery of a foreign public official shall be punishable by effective, proportionate and dissuasive criminal penalties. The range of penalties shall be comparable to that applicable to the bribery of the Party's own public officials and shall, in the case of natural persons, include deprivation of liberty sufficient to enable effective mutual legal assistance and extradition.
2. In the event that, under the legal system of a Party, criminal responsibility is not applicable to legal persons, that Party shall ensure that legal persons shall be subject to effective, proportionate and dissuasive non-criminal sanctions, including monetary sanctions, for bribery of foreign public officials.
3. Each Party shall take such measures as may be necessary to provide that the bribe and the proceeds of the bribery of a foreign public official, or property the value of which corresponds to that of such proceeds, are subject to seizure and confiscation or that monetary sanctions of comparable effect are applicable.
4. Each Party shall consider the imposition of additional civil or administrative sanctions upon a person subject to sanctions for the bribery of a foreign public official.

Article 4 Jurisdiction

1. Each Party shall take such measures as may be necessary to establish its jurisdiction over the bribery of a foreign public official when the offence is committed in whole or in part in its territory.
2. Each Party which has jurisdiction to prosecute its nationals for offences committed abroad shall take such measures as may be necessary to establish its jurisdiction to do so in respect of the bribery of a foreign public official, according to the same principles.
3. When more than one Party has jurisdiction over an alleged offence described in this Convention, the Parties involved shall, at the request of one of them, consult with a view to determining the most appropriate jurisdiction for prosecution.
4. Each Party shall review whether its current basis for jurisdiction is effective in the fight against the bribery of foreign public officials and, if it is not, shall take remedial steps.

Article 5 Enforcement

Investigation and prosecution of the bribery of a foreign public official shall be subject to the applicable rules and principles of each Party. They shall not be influenced by considerations of national economic interest, the potential effect upon relations with another State or the identity of the natural or legal persons involved.

Article 6 Statute of limitations

Any statute of limitations applicable to the offence of bribery of a foreign public official shall allow an adequate period of time for the investigation and prosecution of this offence.

Article 7 Money laundering

Each Party which has made bribery of its own public official a predicate offence for the purpose of the application of its money laundering legislation shall do so on the same terms for the bribery of a foreign public official, without regard to the place where the bribery occurred.

Article 8 Accounting

1. In order to combat bribery of foreign public officials effectively, each Party shall take such measures as may be necessary, within the framework of its laws and regulations regarding the maintenance of books and records, financial statement disclosures, and accounting and auditing standards, to prohibit the establishment of off-the-books accounts, the making of off-the-books or inadequately identified transactions, the recording of non-existent expenditures, the entry of liabilities with incorrect identification of their object, as well as the use of false documents, by companies subject to those laws and regulations, for the purpose of bribing foreign public officials or of hiding such bribery.
2. Each Party shall provide effective, proportionate and dissuasive civil, administrative or criminal penalties for such omissions and falsifications in respect of the books, records, accounts and financial statements of such companies.

Article 9 Mutual legal assistance

1. Each Party shall, to the fullest extent possible under its laws and relevant treaties and arrangements, provide prompt and effective legal assistance to another Party for the purpose of criminal investigations and proceedings brought by a Party concerning offences within the scope of this Convention and for non-criminal proceedings within the scope of this Convention brought by a Party against a legal person. The requested Party shall inform the requesting Party, without delay, of any additional information or documents needed to support the request for assistance and, where requested, of the status and outcome of the request for assistance.
2. Where a Party makes mutual legal assistance conditional upon the existence of dual criminality, dual criminality shall be deemed to exist if the offence for which the assistance is sought is within the scope of this Convention.

3. A Party shall not decline to render mutual legal assistance for criminal matters within the scope of this Convention on the ground of bank secrecy.

Article 10 Extradition

1. Bribery of a foreign public official shall be deemed to be included as an extraditable offence under the laws of the Parties and the extradition treaties between them.
2. If a Party which makes extradition conditional on the existence of an extradition treaty receives a request for extradition from another Party with which it has no extradition treaty, it may consider this Convention to be the legal basis for extradition in respect of the offence of bribery of a foreign public official.
3. Each Party shall take any measures necessary to assure either that it can extradite its nationals or that it can prosecute its nationals for the offence of bribery of a foreign public official. A Party which declines a request to extradite a person for bribery of a foreign public official solely on the ground that the person is its national shall submit the case to its competent authorities for the purpose of prosecution.
4. Extradition for bribery of a foreign public official is subject to the conditions set out in the domestic law and applicable treaties and arrangements of each Party. Where a Party makes extradition conditional upon the existence of dual criminality, that condition shall be deemed to be fulfilled if the offence for which extradition is sought is within the scope of Article 1 of this Convention.

Article 11 Responsible authorities

For the purposes of Article 4, paragraph 3, on consultation, Article 9, on mutual legal assistance and Article 10, on extradition, each Party shall notify to the Secretary-General of the OECD an authority or authorities responsible for making and receiving requests, which shall serve as channel of communication for these matters for that Party, without prejudice to other arrangements between Parties.

Article 12 Monitoring and follow-up

The Parties shall co-operate in carrying out a programme of systematic follow-up to monitor and promote the full implementation of this Convention. Unless otherwise decided by consensus of the Parties, this shall be done in the framework of the OECD Working Group on Bribery in International Business Transactions and according to its terms of reference, or within the framework and terms of reference of any successor to its functions, and Parties shall bear the costs of the programme in accordance with the rules applicable to that body.

Articles 13–14 [Omitted]

Convention for the Unification of Certain Rules for International Carriage by Air, Montreal, 1999

See Schedule 1B to the Carriage by Air Act 1961.

Uniform Rules Concerning the Contract of International Carriage of Goods by Rail (CIM) 1999

The editors and publisher thank OTIF (Intergovernmental Organisation for International Carriage by Rail) for their permission to reproduce CIM 1999.

Title I General provisions

Article 1 Scope

§1 These Uniform Rules shall apply to every contract of carriage of goods by rail for reward when the place of taking over of the goods and the place designated for delivery are situated in two different Member States, irrespective of the place of business and the nationality of the parties to the contract of carriage.

§2 These Uniform Rules shall apply also to contracts of carriage of goods by rail for reward, when the place of taking over of the goods and the place designated for delivery are situated in two different States, of which at least one is a Member State and the parties to the contract agree that the contract is subject to these Uniform Rules.

§3 When international carriage being the subject of a single contract includes carriage by road or inland waterway in internal traffic of a Member State as a supplement to transfrontier carriage by rail, these Uniform Rules shall apply.

§4 When international carriage being the subject of a single contract of carriage includes carriage by sea or transfrontier carriage by inland waterway as a supplement to carriage by rail, these Uniform Rules shall apply if the carriage by sea or inland waterway is performed on services included in the list of services provided for in Article 24 §1 of the Convention.

§5 These Uniform Rules shall not apply to carriage performed between stations situated on the territory of neighbouring States, when the infrastructure of these stations is managed by one or more infrastructure managers subject to only one of those States.

§6 Any State which is a party to a convention concerning international through carriage of goods by rail comparable with these Uniform Rules may, when it makes an application for accession to the Convention, declare that it will apply these Uniform Rules only to carriage performed on part of the railway infrastructure situated on its territory. This part of the railway infrastructure must be precisely defined and connected to the railway infrastructure of a Member State. When a State has made the above-mentioned declaration, these Uniform Rules shall apply only on the condition –

(a) that the place of taking over of the goods or the place designated for delivery as well as the route designated in the contract of carriage, is situated on the specified infrastructure; or

(b) that the specified infrastructure connects the infrastructure of two Member States and that it has been designated in the contract of carriage as a route for transit carriage.

§7 A State which has made a reservation in accordance with § 6 may withdraw it at any time by notification to the Depositary. This withdrawal shall take effect one month after the day on which the Depositary notifies it to the Member States. The declaration shall cease to have effect when the Convention referred to in § 6, first sentence, ceases to be in force for that State.

Article 2 Prescriptions of public law

Carriage to which these Uniform Rules apply shall remain subject to the prescriptions of public law, in particular the prescriptions relating to the carriage of dangerous goods as well as the prescriptions of customs law and those relating to the protection of animals.

Article 3 Definitions

For purposes of these Uniform Rules the term –

(a) 'carrier' means the contractual carrier with whom the consignor has concluded the contract of carriage pursuant to these Uniform Rules, or a successive carrier who is liable on the basis of this contract;
(b) 'substitute carrier' means a carrier, who has not concluded the contract of carriage with the consignor, but to whom the carrier referred to in letter (a) has entrusted, in whole or in part, the performance of the carriage by rail;
(c) 'General Conditions of Carriage' means the conditions of the carrier in the form of general conditions or tariffs legally in force in each Member State and which have become, by the conclusion of the contract of carriage, an integral part of it;
(d) 'intermodal transport unit' means a container, swap body, semi-trailer or other comparable loading unit used in intermodal transport.

Article 4 Derogations

§1 Member States may conclude agreements which provide for derogations from these Uniform Rules for carriage performed exclusively between two stations on either side of the frontier, when there is no other station between them.

§2 For carriage performed between two Member States, passing through a State which is not a Member State, the States concerned may conclude agreements which derogate from these Uniform Rules.

§3 Agreements referred to in §§ 1 and 2 as well as their coming into force shall be notified to the Intergovernmental Organisation for International Carriage by Rail. The Secretary General of the Organisation shall inform the Member States and interested undertakings of these notifications.

Article 5 Mandatory law

Unless provided otherwise in these Uniform Rules, any stipulation which, directly or indirectly, would derogate from these Uniform Rules shall be null and void. The nullity of such a stipulation shall not involve the nullity of the other provisions of the contract of carriage. Nevertheless, a carrier may assume a liability greater and obligations more burdensome than those provided for in these Uniform Rules.

Title II Conclusion and performance of the contract of carriage

Article 6 Contract of carriage

§1 By the contract of carriage, the carrier shall undertake to carry the goods for reward to the place of destination and to deliver them there to the consignee.

§2 The contract of carriage must be confirmed by a consignment note which accords with a uniform model. However, the absence, irregularity or loss of the consignment note shall not affect the existence or validity of the contract which shall remain subject to these Uniform Rules.

§3 The consignment note shall be signed by the consignor and the carrier. The signature can be replaced by a stamp, by an accounting machine entry or in any other appropriate manner.

§4 The carrier must certify the taking over of the goods on the duplicate of the consignment note in an appropriate manner and return the duplicate to the consignor.

§5 The consignment note shall not have effect as a bill of lading.

§6 A consignment note must be made out for each consignment. In the absence of a contrary agreement between the consignor and the carrier, a consignment note may not relate to more than one wagon load.

§7 In the case of carriage which takes place on the customs territory of the European Community or the territory on which the common transit procedure is applied, each consignment must be accompanied by a consignment note satisfying the requirements of Article 7.

§8 The international associations of carriers shall establish uniform model consignment notes in agreement with the customers' international associations and the bodies having competence for customs matters in the Member States as well as any intergovernmental regional economic integration organisation having competence to adopt its own customs legislation.

§9 The consignment note and its duplicate may be established in the form of electronic data registration which can be transformed into legible written symbols. The procedure used for the registration and treatment of data must be equivalent from the functional point of view, particularly so far as concerns the evidential value of the consignment note represented by those data.

Article 7 Wording of the consignment note

§1 The consignment note must contain the following particulars:

- (a) the place at which and the day on which it is made out;
- (b) the name and address of the consignor;
- (c) the name and address of the carrier who has concluded the contract of carriage;
- (d) the name and address of the person to whom the goods have effectively been handed over if he is not the carrier referred to in letter (c);
- (e) the place and the day of taking over of the goods;
- (f) the place of delivery;
- (g) the name and address of the consignee;
- (h) the description of the nature of the goods and the method of packing, and, in case of dangerous goods, the description provided for in the Regulation concerning the International Carriage of Dangerous Goods by Rail (RID);
- (i) the number of packages and the special marks and numbers necessary for the identification of consignments in less than full wagon loads;
- (j) the number of the wagon in the case of carriage of full wagon loads;
- (k) the number of the railway vehicle running on its own wheels, if it is handed over for carriage as goods;

(l) in addition, in the case of intermodal transport units, the category, the number or other characteristics necessary for their identification;
(m) the gross mass or the quantity of the goods expressed in other ways;
(n) a detailed list of the documents which are required by customs or other administrative authorities and are attached to the consignment note or held at the disposal of the carrier at the offices of a duly designated authority or a body designated in the contract;
(o) the costs relating to carriage (the carriage charge, incidental costs, customs duties and other costs incurred from the conclusion of the contract until delivery) in so far as they must be paid by the consignee or any other statement that the costs are payable by the consignee;
(p) a statement that the carriage is subject, notwithstanding any clause to the contrary, to these Uniform Rules.

§2 Where applicable the consignment note must also contain the following particulars:
(a) in the case of carriage by successive carriers, the carrier who must deliver the goods when he has consented to this entry in the consignment note;
(b) the costs which the consignor undertakes to pay;
(c) the amount of the cash on delivery charge;
(d) the declaration of the value of the goods and the amount representing the special interest in delivery;
(e) the agreed transit period;
(f) the agreed route;
(g) a list of the documents not mentioned in §1, letter (n) handed over to the carrier;
(h) the entries made by the consignor concerning the number and description of seals he has affixed to the wagon.

§3 The parties to the contract may enter on the consignment note any other particulars they consider useful.

Article 8 Responsibility for particulars entered on the consignment note

§1 The consignor shall be responsible for all costs, loss or damage sustained by the carrier by reason of –
(a) the entries made by the consignor in the consignment note being irregular, incorrect, incomplete or made elsewhere than in the allotted space; or
(b) the consignor omitting to make the entries prescribed by RID.

§2 If, at the request of the consignor, the carrier makes entries on the consignment note, he shall be deemed, unless the contrary is proved, to have done so on behalf of the consignor.

§3 If the consignment note does not contain the statement provided for in Article 7 §1, letter (p), the carrier shall be liable for all costs, loss or damage sustained through such omission by the person entitled.

Article 9 Dangerous goods

If the consignor has failed to make the entries prescribed by RID, the carrier may at any time unload or destroy the goods or render them innocuous, as the circumstances may require, without payment of compensation, save when he was aware of their dangerous nature on taking them over.

Article 10 Payment of costs

§1 Unless otherwise agreed between the consignor and the carrier, the costs (the carriage charge, incidental costs, customs duties and other costs incurred from the time of the conclusion of the contract to the time of delivery) shall be paid by the consignor.

§2 When by virtue of an agreement between the consignor and the carrier, the costs are payable by the consignee and the consignee has not taken possession of the consignment note nor asserted his rights in accordance with Article 17 §3, nor modified the contract of carriage in accordance with Article 18, the consignor shall remain liable to pay the costs.

Article 11 Examination

§1 The carrier shall have the right to examine at any time whether the conditions of carriage have been complied with and whether the consignment corresponds with the entries in the consignment note made by the consignor. If the examination concerns the contents of the consignment, this shall be carried out as far as possible in the presence of the person entitled; where this is not possible, the carrier shall require the presence of two independent witnesses, unless the laws and prescriptions of the State where the examination takes place provide otherwise.

§2 If the consignment does not correspond with the entries in the consignment note or if the provisions relating to the carriage of goods accepted subject to conditions have not been complied with, the result of the examination must be entered in the copy of the consignment note which accompanies the goods, and also in the duplicate of the consignment note, if it is still held by the carrier. In this case the costs of the examination shall be charged against the goods, if they have not been paid immediately.

§3 When the consignor loads the goods, he shall be entitled to require the carrier to examine the condition of the goods and their packaging as well as the accuracy of statements on the consignment note as to the number of packages, their marks and numbers as well as the gross mass of the goods or their quantity otherwise expressed. The carrier shall be obliged to proceed with the examination only if he has appropriate means of carrying it out. The carrier may demand the payment of the costs of the examination. The result of the examination shall be entered on the consignment note.

Article 12 Evidential value of the consignment note

§1 The consignment note shall be *prima facie* evidence of the conclusion and the conditions of the contract of carriage and the taking over of the goods by the carrier.

§2 If the carrier has loaded the goods, the consignment note shall be *prima facie* evidence of the condition of the goods and their packaging indicated on the consignment note or, in the absence of such indications, of their apparently good condition at the moment they were taken over by the carrier and of the accuracy of the statements in the consignment note concerning the number of packages, their marks and numbers as well as the gross mass of the goods or their quantity otherwise expressed.

§3 If the consignor has loaded the goods, the consignment note shall be *prima facie* evidence of the condition of the goods and of their packaging indicated in the consignment note or, in the absence of such indication, of their apparently good condition and of the accuracy of the statements referred to in § 2 solely in the case where the carrier has examined them and recorded on the consignment note a result of his examination which tallies.

§4 However, the consignment note will not be *prima facie* evidence in a case where it bears a reasoned reservation. A reason for a reservation could be that the carrier does not have the appropriate means to examine whether the consignment corresponds to the entries in the consignment note.

Article 13 Loading and unloading of the goods

§1 The consignor and the carrier shall agree who is responsible for the loading and unloading of the goods. In the absence of such an agreement, for packages the loading and unloading shall be the responsibility of the carrier whereas for full wagon loads loading shall be the responsibility of the consignor and unloading, after delivery, the responsibility of the consignee.

§2 The consignor shall be liable for all the consequences of defective loading carried out by him and must in particular compensate the carrier for the loss or damage sustained in consequence by him. The burden of proof of defective loading shall lie on the carrier.

Article 14 Packing

The consignor shall be liable to the carrier for any loss or damage and costs due to the absence of, or defects in, the packing of goods, unless the defectiveness was apparent or known to the carrier at the time when he took over the goods and he made no reservations concerning it.

Article 15 Completion of administrative formalities

§1 With a view to the completion of the formalities required by customs and other administrative authorities, to be completed before delivery of the goods, the consignor must attach the necessary documents to the consignment note or make them available to the carrier and furnish him with all the requisite information.

§2 The carrier shall not be obliged to check whether these documents and this information are correct and sufficient. The consignor shall be liable to the carrier for any loss or damage resulting from the absence or insufficiency of, or any irregularity in, such documents and information, save in the case of fault of the carrier.

§3 The carrier shall be liable for any consequences arising from the loss or misuse of the documents referred to in the consignment note and accompanying it or deposited with the carrier, unless the loss of the documents or the loss or damage caused by the misuse of the documents has been caused by circumstances which the carrier could not avoid and the consequences of which he was unable to prevent. Nevertheless any compensation payable shall not exceed that provided for in the event of loss of the goods.

§4 The consignor, by so indicating in the consignment note, or the consignee by giving orders as provided for in Article 18 §3 may ask –

(a) to be present himself or to be represented by an agent when the customs or other administrative formalities are carried out, for the purpose of furnishing any information or explanation required;

(b) to complete the customs or other administrative formalities himself or to have them completed by an agent, in so far as the laws and prescriptions of the State in which they are to be carried out so permit;

(c) to pay customs duties and other charges, when he or his agent is present at or completes the customs or other administrative formalities, in so far as the laws and prescriptions of the State in which they are carried out permit such payment.

In such circumstances neither the consignor, nor the consignee who has the right of disposal, nor the agent of either may take possession of the goods.

§5 If, for the completion of the customs or other administrative formalities, the consignor has designated a place where the prescriptions in force do not permit their completion, or if he has stipulated for the purpose any other procedure which cannot be followed, the carrier shall act in the manner which appears to him to be the most favourable to the interests of the person entitled and shall inform the consignor of the measures taken.

§6 If the consignor has undertaken to pay customs duties, the carrier shall have the choice of completing customs formalities either in transit or at the destination place.

§7 However, the carrier may proceed in accordance with §5 if the consignee has not taken possession of the consignment note within the period fixed by the prescriptions in force at the destination place.

§8 The consignor must comply with the prescriptions of customs or other administrative authorities with respect to the packing and sheeting of the goods. If the consignor has not packed or sheeted the goods in accordance with those prescriptions the carrier shall be entitled to do so; the resulting cost shall be charged against the goods.

Article 16 Transit periods

§1 The consignor and the carrier shall agree the transit period. In the absence of an agreement, the transit period must not exceed that which would result from the application of §§2 to 4.

§2 Subject to §§3 and 4, the maximum transit periods shall be as follows:

(a) for wagon-load consignments

- period for consignment 12 hours,
- period for carriage, for each 400 km or fraction thereof 24 hours;

(b) for less than wagon-load consignment

- period for consignments 24 hours,
- period for carriage, for each 200 km or fraction thereof 24 hours.

The distances shall relate to the agreed route or, in the absence thereof, to the shortest possible route.

§3 The carrier may fix additional transit periods of specified duration in the following cases:

(a) consignments to be carried

- by lines of a different gauge,
- by sea or inland waterway,
- by road if there is no rail link;

(b) exceptional circumstances causing an exceptional increase in traffic or exceptional operating difficulties.

The duration of the additional transit periods must appear in the General Conditions of Carriage.

§4 The transit period shall start to run after the taking over of the goods; it shall be extended by the duration of a stay caused without any fault of the carrier. The transit period shall be suspended on Sundays and statutory holidays.

Article 17 Delivery

§1 The carrier must hand over the consignment note and deliver the goods to the consignee at the place designated for delivery against receipt and payment of the amounts due according to the contract of carriage.

§2 It shall be equivalent to delivery to the consignee if, in accordance with the prescriptions in force at the place of destination,

(a) the goods have been handed over to customs or octroi authorities at their premises or warehouses, when these are not subject to the carrier's supervision;

(b) the goods have been deposited for storage with the carrier, with a forwarding agent or in a public warehouse.

§3 After the arrival of the goods at the place of destination, the consignee may ask the carrier to hand over the consignment note and deliver the goods to him. If the loss of the goods is established or if the goods have not arrived on the expiry of the period provided for in Article 29 §1, the consignee may assert, in his own name, his rights against the carrier under the contract of carriage.

§4 The person entitled may refuse to accept the goods, even when he has received the consignment note and paid the charges resulting from the contract of carriage, so long as an examination which he has demanded in order to establish alleged loss or damage has not been carried out.

§5 In other respects, delivery of the goods shall be carried out in accordance with the prescriptions in force at the place of destination.

§6 If the goods have been delivered without prior collection of a cash on delivery charge, the carrier shall be obliged to compensate the consignor up to the amount of the cash on delivery charge without prejudice to his right of recourse against the consignee.

Article 18 Right to dispose of the goods

§1 The consignor shall be entitled to dispose of the goods and to modify the contract of carriage by giving subsequent orders. He may in particular ask the carrier –

(a) to discontinue the carriage of the goods;

(b) to delay the delivery of the goods;

(c) to deliver the goods to a consignee different from the one entered on the consignment note;

(d) to deliver the goods at a place other than the place of destination entered on the consignment note.

§2 The consignor's right to modify the contract of carriage shall, notwithstanding that he is in possession of the duplicate of the consignment note, be extinguished in cases where the consignee –

(a) has taken possession of the consignment note;
(b) has accepted the goods;
(c) has asserted his rights in accordance with Article 17 §3;
(d) is entitled, in accordance with §3, to give orders; from that time onwards, the carrier shall comply with the orders and instructions of the consignee.

§3 The consignee shall have the right to modify the contract of carriage from the time when the consignment note is drawn up, unless the consignor indicates to the contrary on the consignment note.

§4 The consignee's right to modify the contract of carriage shall be extinguished in cases where he has –
(a) taken possession of the consignment note;
(b) accepted the goods;
(c) asserted his rights in accordance with Article 17 §3;
(d) given instructions for delivery of the goods to another person in accordance with §5 and when that person has asserted his rights in accordance with Article 17 §3.

§5 If the consignee has given instructions for delivery of the goods to another person, that person shall not be entitled to modify the contract of carriage.

Article 19 Exercise of the right to dispose of the goods

§1 If the consignor or, in the case referred to in Article 18 §3, the consignee wishes to modify the contract of carriage by giving subsequent orders, he must produce to the carrier the duplicate of the consignment note on which the modifications have to be entered.

§2 The consignor or, in the case referred to in Article 18 §3, the consignee must compensate the carrier for the costs and the prejudice arising from the carrying out of subsequent modifications.

§3 The carrying out of the subsequent modifications must be possible, lawful and reasonable to require at the time when the orders reach the person who is to carry them out, and must in particular neither interfere with the normal working of the carrier's undertaking nor prejudice the consignors or consignees of other consignments.

§4 The subsequent modifications must not have the effect of splitting the consignment.

§5 When, by reason of the conditions provided for in §3, the carrier cannot carry out the orders which he receives he shall immediately notify the person from whom the orders emanate.

§6 In the case of fault of the carrier he shall be liable for the consequences of failure to carry out an order or failure to carry it out properly. Nevertheless, any compensation payable shall not exceed that provided for in case of loss of the goods.

§7 If the carrier implements the consignor's subsequent modifications without requiring the production of the duplicate of the consignment note, the carrier shall be liable to the consignee for any loss or damage sustained by him if the duplicate has been passed on to the consignee. Nevertheless, any compensation payable shall not exceed that provided for in case of loss of the goods.

Article 20 Circumstances preventing carriage

§1 When circumstances prevent the carriage of goods, the carrier shall decide whether it is preferable to carry the goods as a matter of course by modifying the route or whether it is advisable, in the interest of the person entitled, to ask him for instructions while giving him any relevant information available to the carrier.

§2 If it is impossible to continue carrying the goods, the carrier shall ask for instructions from the person who has the right to dispose of the goods. If the carrier is unable to obtain instructions within a reasonable time he must take such steps as seem to him to be in the best interests of the person entitled to dispose of the goods.

Article 21 Circumstances preventing delivery

§1 When circumstances prevent delivery, the carrier must without delay inform the consignor and ask him for instructions, save where the consignor has requested, by an entry in the consignment note, that the goods be returned to him as a matter of course in the event of circumstances preventing delivery.

§2 When the circumstances preventing delivery cease to exist before arrival of instructions from the consignor to the carrier the goods shall be delivered to the consignee. The consignor must be notified without delay.

§3 If the consignee refuses the goods, the consignor shall be entitled to give instructions even if he is unable to produce the duplicate of the consignment note.

§4 When the circumstances preventing delivery arise after the consignee has modified the contract of carriage in accordance with Article 18 §§3 to 5 the carrier must notify the consignee.

Article 22 Consequences of circumstances preventing carriage and delivery

§1 The carrier shall be entitled to recover the costs occasioned by –

(a) his request for instructions,

(b) the carrying out of instructions received,

(c) the fact that instructions requested do not reach him or do not reach him in time,

(d) the fact that he has taken a decision in accordance with Article 20 §1, without having asked for instructions,

unless such costs were caused by his fault. The carrier may in particular recover the carriage charge applicable to the route followed and shall be allowed the transit periods applicable to such route.

§2 In the cases referred to in Article 20 §2 and Article 21 §1 the carrier may immediately unload the goods at the cost of the person entitled. Thereupon the carriage shall be deemed to be at an end. The carrier shall then be in charge of the goods on behalf of the person entitled. He may, however, entrust them to a third party, and shall then be responsible only for the exercise of reasonable care in the choice of such third party. The charges due under the contract of carriage and all other costs shall remain chargeable against the goods.

§3 The carrier may proceed to the sale of the goods, without awaiting instructions from the person entitled, if this is justified by the perishable nature or the condition of the goods or if the costs of storage would be out of proportion to the value of the goods. In other cases he may also proceed to the sale of the goods if within a reasonable time he has not received from the person entitled instructions to the contrary which he may reasonably be required to carry out.

§4 If the goods have been sold, the proceeds of sale, after deduction of the costs chargeable against the goods, must be placed at the disposal of the person entitled. If the proceeds of sale are less than those costs, the consignor must pay the difference.

§5 The procedure in the case of sale shall be determined by the laws and prescriptions in force at, or by the custom of, the place where the goods are situated.

§6 If the consignor, in the case of circumstances preventing carriage or delivery, fails to give instructions within a reasonable time and if the circumstances preventing carriage or delivery cannot be eliminated in accordance with §§2 and 3, the carrier may return the goods to the consignor or, if it is justified, destroy them, at the cost of the consignor.

Title III Liability

Article 23 Basis of liability

§1 The carrier shall be liable for loss or damage resulting from the total or partial loss of, or damage to, the goods between the time of taking over of the goods and the time of delivery and for the loss or damage resulting from the transit period being exceeded, whatever the railway infrastructure used.

§2 The carrier shall be relieved of this liability to the extent that the loss or damage or the exceeding of the transit period was caused by the fault of the person entitled, by an order given by the person entitled other than as a result of the fault of the carrier, by an inherent defect in the goods (decay, wastage etc.) or by circumstances which the carrier could not avoid and the consequences of which he was unable to prevent.

§3 The carrier shall be relieved of this liability to the extent that the loss or damage arises from the special risks inherent in one or more of the following circumstances:

(a) carriage in open wagons pursuant to the General Conditions of Carriage or when it has been expressly agreed and entered in the consignment note; subject to damage sustained by the goods because of atmospheric influences, goods carried in intermodal transport units and in closed road vehicles carried on wagons shall not be considered as being carried in open wagons; if for the carriage of goods in open wagons, the consignor uses sheets, the carrier shall assume the same liability as falls to him for carriage in open wagons without sheeting, even in respect of goods which, according to the General Conditions of Carriage, are not carried in open wagons;

(b) absence or inadequacy of packaging in the case of goods which by their nature are liable to loss or damage when not packed or when not packed properly;

(c) loading of the goods by the consignor or unloading by the consignee;

(d) the nature of certain goods which particularly exposes them to total or partial loss or damage, especially through breakage, rust, interior and spontaneous decay, desiccation or wastage;

(e) irregular, incorrect or incomplete description or numbering of packages;

(f) carriage of live animals;

(g) carriage which, pursuant to applicable provisions or agreements made between the consignor and the carrier and entered on the consignment note, must be accompanied by an attendant, if the loss or damage results from a risk which the attendant was intended to avert.

Article 24 Liability in case of carriage of railway vehicles as goods

§1 In case of carriage of railway vehicles running on their own wheels and consigned as goods, the carrier shall be liable for the loss or damage resulting from the loss of, or damage to, the vehicle or to its removable parts arising between the time of taking over for carriage and the time of delivery and for loss or damage resulting from exceeding the transit period, unless he proves that the loss or damage was not caused by his fault.

§2 The carrier shall not be liable for loss or damage resulting from the loss of accessories which are not mentioned on both sides of the vehicle or in the inventory which accompanies it.

Article 25 Burden of proof

§1 The burden of proving that the loss, damage or exceeding of the transit period was due to one of the causes specified in Article 23 §2 shall lie on the carrier.

§2 When the carrier establishes that, having regard to the circumstances of a particular case, the loss or damage could have arisen from one or more of the special risks referred to in Article 23 §3, it shall be presumed that it did so arise. The person entitled shall, however, have the right to prove that the loss or damage was not attributable either wholly or in part to one of those risks.

§3 The presumption according to §2 shall not apply in the case provided for in Article 23 §3, letter (a) if an abnormally large quantity has been lost or if a package has been lost.

Article 26 Successive carriers

If carriage governed by a single contract is performed by several successive carriers, each carrier, by the very act of taking over the goods with the consignment note, shall become a party to the contract of carriage in accordance with the terms of that document and shall assume the obligations arising therefrom. In such a case each carrier shall be responsible in respect of carriage over the entire route up to delivery.

Article 27 Substitute carrier

§1 Where the carrier has entrusted the performance of the carriage, in whole or in part, to a substitute carrier, whether or not in pursuance of a right under the contract of carriage to do so, the carrier shall nevertheless remain liable in respect of the entire carriage.

§2 All the provisions of these Uniform Rules governing the liability of the carrier shall also apply to the liability of the substitute carrier for the carriage performed by him. Articles 36 and 41 shall apply if an action is brought against the servants and any other persons whose services the substitute carrier makes use of for the performance of the carriage.

§3 Any special agreement under which the carrier assumes obligations not imposed by these Uniform Rules or waives rights conferred by these Uniform Rules shall be of no effect in respect of the substitute carrier who has not accepted it expressly and in writing. Whether or not the substitute carrier has accepted it, the carrier shall nevertheless remain bound by the obligations or waivers resulting from such special agreement.

§4 Where and to the extent that both the carrier and the substitute carrier are liable, their liability shall be joint and several.

§5 The aggregate amount of compensation payable by the carrier, the substitute carrier and their servants and other persons whose services they make use of for the performance of the carriage shall not exceed the limits provided for in these Uniform Rules.

§6 This article shall not prejudice rights of recourse which may exist between the carrier and the substitute carrier.

Article 28 Presumption of loss or damage in case of reconsignment

§1 When a consignment consigned in accordance with these Uniform Rules has been reconsigned subject to these same Rules and partial loss or damage has been ascertained after that reconsignment, it shall be presumed that it occurred under the latest contract of carriage if the consignment remained in the charge of the carrier and was reconsigned in the same condition as when it arrived at the place from which it was reconsigned.

§2 This presumption shall also apply when the contract of carriage prior to the reconsignment was not subject to these Uniform Rules, if these Rules would have applied in the case of a through consignment from the first place of consignment to the final place of destination.

§3 This presumption shall also apply when the contract of carriage prior to the reconsignment was subject to a convention concerning international through carriage of goods by rail comparable with these Uniform Rules, and when this convention contains the same presumption of law in favour of consignments consigned in accordance with these Uniform Rules.

Article 29 Presumption of loss of the goods

§1 The person entitled may, without being required to furnish further proof, consider the goods as lost when they have not been delivered to the consignee or placed at his disposal within thirty days after the expiry of the transit periods.

§2 The person entitled may, on receipt of the payment of compensation for the goods lost, make a written request to be notified without delay should the goods be recovered within one year after the payment of compensation. The carrier shall acknowledge such request in writing.

§3 Within thirty days after receipt of a notification referred to in §2, the person entitled may require the goods to be delivered to him against payment of the costs resulting from the contract of carriage and against refund of the compensation received, less, where appropriate, costs which may have been included therein. Nevertheless he shall retain his rights to claim compensation for exceeding the transit period provided for in Articles 33 and 35.

§4 In the absence of the request referred to in §2 or of instructions given within the period specified in §3, or if the goods are recovered more than one year after the payment of compensation, the carrier shall dispose of them in accordance with the laws and prescriptions in force at the place where the goods are situated.

Article 30 Compensation for loss

§1 In case of total or partial loss of the goods, the carrier must pay, to the exclusion of all other damages, compensation calculated according to the commodity exchange quotation or, if there is no such quotation, according to the current market price, or if there is neither such quotation nor such price, according to the usual value of goods of the same kind and quality on the day and at the place where the goods were taken over.

§2 Compensation shall not exceed 17 units of account per kilogramme of gross mass short.

§3 In case of loss of a railway vehicle running on its own wheels and consigned as goods, or of an intermodal transport unit, or of their removable parts, the compensation shall be limited, to the exclusion of all other damages, to the usual value of the vehicle or the intermodal transport unit, or their removable parts, on the day and at the place of loss. If it is impossible to ascertain the day or the place of the loss, the compensation shall be limited to the usual value on the day and at the place where the vehicle has been taken over by the carrier.

§4 The carrier must, in addition, refund the carriage charge, customs duties already paid and other sums paid in relation to the carriage of the goods lost except excise duties for goods carried under a procedure suspending those duties.

Article 31 Liability for wastage in transit

§1 In respect of goods which, by reason of their nature, are generally subject to wastage in transit by the sole fact of carriage, the carrier shall only be liable to the extent that the wastage exceeds the following allowances, whatever the length of the route:

(a) two per cent of the mass for liquid goods or goods consigned in a moist condition;

(b) one per cent of the mass for dry goods.

§2 The limitation of liability provided for in §1 may not be invoked if, having regard to the circumstances of a particular case, it is proved that the loss was not due to causes which would justify the allowance.

§3 Where several packages are carried under a single consignment note, the wastage in transit shall be calculated separately for each package if its mass on consignment is shown separately on the consignment note or can be ascertained otherwise.

§4 In case of total loss of goods or in case of loss of a package, no deduction for wastage in transit shall be made in calculating the compensation.

§5 This Article shall not derogate from Articles 23 and 25.

Article 32 Compensation for damage

§1 In case of damage to goods, the carrier must pay compensation equivalent to the loss in value of the goods, to the exclusion of all other damages. The amount shall be calculated by applying to the value of the goods defined in accordance with Article 30 the percentage of loss in value noted at the place of destination.

§2 The compensation shall not exceed:

(a) if the whole consignment has lost value through damage, the amount which would have been payable in case of total loss;

(b) if only part of the consignment has lost value through damage, the amount which would have been payable had that part been lost.

§3 In case of damage to a railway vehicle running on its own wheels and consigned as goods, or of an intermodal transport unit, or of their removable parts, the compensation shall be limited, to the exclusion of all other damages, to the cost of repair. The compensation shall not exceed the amount payable in case of loss.

§4 The carrier must also refund the costs provided for in Article 30 §4, in the proportion set out in §1.

Article 33 Compensation for exceeding the transit period

§1 If loss or damage results from the transit period being exceeded, the carrier must pay compensation not exceeding four times the carriage charge.

§2 In case of total loss of the goods, the compensation provided for in §1 shall not be payable in addition to that provided for in Article 30.

§3 In case of partial loss of the goods, the compensation provided for in §1 shall not exceed four times the carriage charge in respect of that part of the consignment which has not been lost.

§4 In case of damage to the goods, not resulting from the transit period being exceeded, the compensation provided for in §1 shall, where appropriate, be payable in addition to that provided for in Article 32.

§5 In no case shall the total of compensation provided for in §1 together with that provided for in Articles 30 and 32 exceed the compensation which would be payable in case of total loss of the goods.

§6 If, in accordance with Article 16 §1, the transit period has been established by agreement, other forms of compensation than those provided for in §1 may be so agreed. If, in this case, the transit periods provided for in Article 16 §§2 to 4 are exceeded, the person entitled may claim either the compensation provided for in the agreement mentioned above or that provided for in §§1 to 5.

Article 34 Compensation in case of declaration of value

The consignor and the carrier may agree that the consignor shall declare in the consignment note a value for the goods exceeding the limit provided for in Article 30 §2. In such a case the amount declared shall be substituted for that limit.

Article 35 Compensation in case of interest in delivery

The consignor and the carrier may agree that the consignor may declare, by entering an amount in figures in the consignment note, a special interest in delivery, in case of loss, damage or exceeding of the transit period. In case of a declaration of interest in delivery further compensation for loss or damage proved may be claimed, in addition to the compensation provided for in Articles 30, 32 and 33, up to the amount declared.

Article 36 Loss of right to invoke the limits of liability

The limits of liability provided for in Article 15 §3, Article 19 §§6 and 7, Article 30 and Articles 32 to 35 shall not apply if it is proved that the loss or damage results from an act or omission, which the carrier has committed either with intent to cause such loss or damage, or recklessly and with knowledge that such loss or damage would probably result.

Article 37 Conversion and interest

§1 Where the calculation of the compensation requires the conversion of sums expressed in foreign currency, conversion shall be at the exchange rate applicable on the day and at the place of payment of compensation.

§2 The person entitled may claim interest on compensation, calculated at five per cent per annum, from the day of the claim provided for in Article 43 or, if no such claim has been made, from the day on which legal proceedings were instituted.

§3 If the person entitled does not submit to the carrier, within a reasonable time allotted to him, the supporting documents required for the amount of the claim to be finally settled, no interest shall accrue between the expiry of the time allotted and the actual submission of such documents.

Article 38 Liability in respect of rail-sea traffic

§1 In rail-sea carriage by the services referred to in Article 24 §1 of the Convention any Member State may, by requesting that a suitable note be included in the list of services to which these Uniform Rules apply, add the following grounds for exemption from liability in their entirety to those provided for in Article 23:

- (a) fire, if the carrier proves that it was not caused by his act or default, or that of the master, a mariner, the pilot or the carrier's servants;
- (b) saving or attempting to save life or property at sea;
- (c) loading of goods on the deck of the ship, if they are so loaded with the consent of the consignor given on the consignment note and are not in wagons;
- (d) perils, dangers and accidents of the sea or other navigable waters.

§2 The carrier may only avail himself of the grounds for exemption referred to in §1 if he proves that the loss, damage or exceeding the transit period occurred in the course of the journey by sea between the time when the goods were loaded on board the ship and the time when they were unloaded from the ship.

§3 When the carrier relies on the grounds for exemption referred to in §1, he shall nevertheless remain liable if the person entitled proves that the loss, damage or exceeding the transit period is due to the fault of the carrier, the master, a mariner, the pilot or the carrier's servants.

§4 Where a sea route is served by several undertakings included in the list of services in accordance with Article 24 §1 of the Convention, the liability regime applicable to that route must be the same for all those undertakings. In addition, where those undertakings have been included in the list at the request of several Member States, the adoption of this regime must be the subject of prior agreement between those States.

§5 The measures taken in accordance with §§1 and 4 shall be notified to the Secretary General. They shall come into force at the earliest at the expiry of a period of thirty days from the day on which the Secretary General notifies them to the other Member States. Consignments already in transit shall not be affected by such measures.

Article 39 Liability in case of nuclear incidents

The carrier shall be relieved of liability pursuant to these Uniform Rules for loss or damage caused by a nuclear incident when the operator of a nuclear installation or another person who is substituted for him is liable for the loss or damage pursuant to the laws and prescriptions of a State governing liability in the field of nuclear energy.

Article 40 Persons for whom the carrier is liable

The carrier shall be liable for his servants and other persons whose services he makes use of for the performance of the carriage, when these servants and other persons are acting within the scope of their functions. The managers of the railway infrastructure on which the carriage is performed shall be considered as persons whose services the carrier makes use of for the performance of the carriage.

Article 41 Other actions

§1 In all cases where these Uniform Rules shall apply, any action in respect of liability, on whatever grounds, may be brought against the carrier only subject to the conditions and limitations laid down in these Uniform Rules.

§2 The same shall apply to any action brought against the servants or other persons for whom the carrier is liable pursuant to Article 40.

Title IV Assertion of rights

Article 42 Ascertainment of partial loss or damage

§1 When partial loss or damage is discovered or presumed by the carrier or alleged by the person entitled, the carrier must without delay, and if possible in the presence of the person entitled, draw up a report stating, according to the nature of the loss or damage, the condition of the goods, their mass and, as far as possible, the extent of the loss or damage, its cause and the time of its occurrence.

§2 A copy of the report must be supplied free of charge to the person entitled.

§3 Should the person entitled not accept the findings in the report, he may request that the condition and mass of the goods and the cause and amount of the loss or damage be ascertained by an expert appointed either by the parties to the contract of carriage or by a court or tribunal. The procedure to be followed shall be governed by the laws and prescriptions of the State in which such ascertainment takes place.

Article 43 Claims

§1 Claims relating to the contract of carriage must be addressed in writing to the carrier against whom an action may be brought.

§2 A claim may be made by persons who have the right to bring an action against the carrier.

§3 To make the claim the consignor must produce the duplicate of the consignment note. Failing this he must produce an authorisation from the consignee or furnish proof that the consignee has refused to accept the goods.

§4 To make the claim the consignee must produce the consignment note if it has been handed over to him.

§5 The consignment note, the duplicate and any other documents which the person entitled thinks fit to submit with the claim must be produced either in the original or as copies, the copies, where appropriate, duly certified if the carrier so requests.

§6 On settlement of the claim the carrier may require the production, in the original form, of the consignment note, the duplicate or the cash on delivery voucher so that they may be endorsed to the effect that settlement has been made.

Article 44 Persons who may bring an action against the carrier

§1 Subject to §§3 and 4 actions based on the contract of carriage may be brought:

(a) by the consignor, until such time as the consignee has –
   1. taken possession of the consignment note,
   2. accepted the goods, or
   3. asserted his rights pursuant to Article 17 §3 or Article 18 §3;

(b) by the consignee, from the time when he has –
   1. taken possession of the consignment note,
   2. accepted the goods, or
   3. asserted his rights pursuant to Article 17 §3 or Article 18 §3.

§2 The right of the consignee to bring an action shall be extinguished from the time when the person designated by the consignee in accordance with Article 18 §5 has taken possession of the consignment note, accepted the goods or asserted his rights pursuant to Article 17 §3.

§3 An action for the recovery of a sum paid pursuant to the contract of carriage may only be brought by the person who made the payment.

§4 An action in respect of cash on delivery payments may only be brought by the consignor.

§5 In order to bring an action the consignor must produce the duplicate of the consignment note. Failing this he must produce an authorisation from the consignee or furnish proof that the consignee has refused to accept the goods. If necessary, the consignor must prove the absence or the loss of the consignment note.

§6 In order to bring an action the consignee must produce the consignment note if it has been handed over to him.

Article 45 Carriers against whom an action may be brought

§1 Subject to §§3 and 4 actions based on the contract of carriage may be brought only against the first carrier, the last carrier or the carrier having performed the part of the carriage on which the event giving rise to the proceedings occurred.

§2 When, in the case of carriage performed by successive carriers, the carrier who must deliver the goods is entered with his consent on the consignment note, an action may be brought against him in accordance with §1 even if he has received neither the goods nor the consignment note.

§3 An action for the recovery of a sum paid pursuant to the contract of carriage may be brought against the carrier who has collected that sum or against the carrier on whose behalf it was collected.

§4 An action in respect of cash on delivery payments may be brought only against the carrier who has taken over the goods at the place of consignment.

§5 An action may be brought against a carrier other than those specified in §§1 to 4 when instituted by way of counter-claim or by way of exception in proceedings relating to a principal claim based on the same contract of carriage.

§6 To the extent that these Uniform Rules apply to the substitute carrier, an action may also be brought against him.

§7 If the plaintiff has a choice between several carriers, his right to choose shall be extinguished as soon as he brings an action against any one of them; this shall also apply if the plaintiff has a choice between one or more carriers and a substitute carrier.

Article 46 Forum

§1 Actions based on these Uniform Rules may be brought before the courts or tribunals of Member States designated by agreement between the parties or before the courts or tribunals of a State on whose territory –

(a) the defendant has his domicile or habitual residence, his principal place of business or the branch or agency which concluded the contract of carriage; or

(b) the place where the goods were taken over by the carrier or the place designated for delivery is situated.

Other courts or tribunals may not be seised.

§2 Where an action based on these Uniform Rules is pending before a court or tribunal competent pursuant to §1, or where in such litigation a judgment has been delivered by such a court or tribunal, no new action may be brought between the same parties on the same grounds unless the judgment of the court or tribunal before which the first action was brought is not enforceable in the State in which the new action is brought.

Article 47 Extinction of right of action

§1 Acceptance of the goods by the person entitled shall extinguish all rights of action against the carrier arising from the contract of carriage in case of partial loss, damage or exceeding of the transit period.

§2 Nevertheless, the right of action shall not be extinguished:

(a) in case of partial loss or damage, if –

1. the loss or damage was ascertained in accordance with Article 42 before the acceptance of the goods by the person entitled;
2. the ascertainment which should have been carried out in accordance with Article 42 was omitted solely through the fault of the carrier;

(b) in case of loss or damage which is not apparent whose existence is ascertained after acceptance of the goods by the person entitled, if he –

1. asks for ascertainment in accordance with Article 42 immediately after discovery of the loss or damage and not later than seven days after the acceptance of the goods, and
2. in addition, proves that the loss or damage occurred between the time of taking over and the time of delivery;

(c) in cases where the transit period has been exceeded, if the person entitled has, within sixty days, asserted his rights against one of the carriers referred to in Article 45 §1;

(d) if the person entitled proves that the loss or damage results from an act or omission, done with intent to cause such loss or damage, or recklessly and with knowledge that such loss or damage would probably result.

§3 If the goods have been reconsigned in accordance with Article 28 rights of action in case of partial loss or in case of damage, arising from one of the previous contracts of carriage, shall be extinguished as if there had been only a single contract of carriage.

Article 48 Limitation of actions

§1 The period of limitation for an action arising from the contract of carriage shall be one year. Nevertheless, the period of limitation shall be two years in the case of an action –

(a) to recover a cash on delivery payment collected by the carrier from the consignee;

(b) to recover the proceeds of a sale effected by the carrier;

(c) for loss or damage resulting from an act or omission done with intent to cause such loss or damage, or recklessly and with knowledge that such loss or damage would probably result;

(d) based on one of the contracts of carriage prior to the reconsignment in the case provided for in Article 28.

§2 The period of limitation shall run for actions –

(a) for compensation for total loss, from the thirtieth day after expiry of the transit period;

(b) for compensation for partial loss, damage or exceeding of the transit period, from the day when delivery took place;

(c) in all other cases, from the day when the right of action may be exercised.

The day indicated for the commencement of the period of limitation shall not be included in the period.

§3 The period of limitation shall be suspended by a claim in writing in accordance with Article 43 until the day that the carrier rejects the claim by notification in writing and returns the documents submitted with it. If part of the claim is admitted, the period of limitation shall start to run again in respect of the part of the claim still in dispute. The burden of proof of receipt of the claim or of the reply and of the return of the documents shall lie on the party who relies on those facts. The period of limitation shall not be suspended by further claims having the same object.

§4 A right of action which has become time-barred may not be exercised further, even by way of counter-claim or relied upon by way of exception.

§5 Otherwise, the suspension and interruption of periods of limitation shall be governed by national law.

Title V Relations between carriers

Article 49 Settlement of accounts

§1 Any carrier who has collected or ought to have collected, either at departure or on arrival, charges or other costs arising out of the contract of carriage must pay to the carriers concerned their respective shares. The methods of payment shall be fixed by agreement between the carriers.

§2 Article 12 shall also apply to the relations between successive carriers.

Article 50 Right of recourse

§1 A carrier who has paid compensation pursuant to these Uniform Rules shall have a right of recourse against the carriers who have taken part in the carriage in accordance with the following provisions:

(a) the carrier who has caused the loss or damage shall be solely liable for it;

(b) when the loss or damage has been caused by several carriers, each shall be liable for the loss or damage he has caused; if such distinction is impossible, the compensation shall be apportioned between them in accordance with letter (c);

(c) if it cannot be proved which of the carriers has caused the loss or damage, the compensation shall be apportioned between all the carriers who have taken part in the carriage, except those who prove that the loss or damage was not caused by them; such apportionment shall be in proportion to their respective shares of the carriage charge.

§2 In the case of insolvency of any one of these carriers, the unpaid share due from him shall be apportioned among all the other carriers who have taken part in the carriage, in proportion to their respective shares of the carriage charge.

Article 51 Procedure for recourse

§1 The validity of the payment made by the carrier exercising a right of recourse pursuant to Article 50 may not be disputed by the carrier against whom the right of recourse is exercised, when compensation has been determined by a court or tribunal and when the latter carrier, duly served with notice of the proceedings, has been afforded an opportunity to intervene in the proceedings. The court or tribunal seised of the principal action shall determine what time shall be allowed for such notification of the proceedings and for intervention in the proceedings.

§2 A carrier exercising his right of recourse must make his claim in one and the same proceedings against all the carriers with whom he has not reached a settlement, failing which he shall lose his right of recourse in the case of those against whom he has not taken proceedings.

§3 The court or tribunal must give its decision in one and the same judgment on all recourse claims brought before it.

§4 The carrier wishing to enforce his right of recourse may bring his action in the courts or tribunals of the State on the territory of which one of the carriers participating in the carriage has his principal place of business, or the branch or agency which concluded the contract of carriage.

§5 When the action must be brought against several carriers, the plaintiff carrier shall be entitled to choose the court or tribunal in which he will bring the proceedings from among those having competence pursuant to §4.

§6 Recourse proceedings may not be joined with proceedings for compensation taken by the person entitled under the contract of carriage.

Article 52 Agreements concerning recourse

The carriers may conclude agreements which derogate from Articles 49 and 50.

Council of Europe Convention on Cybercrime, Budapest, 2001

Chapter I Use of terms

Article 1 Definitions

For the purposes of this Convention:

(a) 'computer system' means any device or a group of inter-connected or related devices, one or more of which, pursuant to a program, performs automatic processing of data;
(b) 'computer data' means any representation of facts, information or concepts in a form suitable for processing in a computer system, including a program suitable to cause a computer system to perform a function;
(c) 'service provider' means:
    (i) any public or private entity that provides to users of its service the ability to communicate by means of a computer system, and
    (ii) any other entity that processes or stores computer data on behalf of such communication service or users of such service.
(d) 'traffic data' means any computer data relating to a communication by means of a computer system, generated by a computer system that formed a part in the chain of communication, indicating the communication's origin, destination, route, time, date, size, duration, or type of underlying service.

Chapter II Measures to be taken at the national level

Section 1 Substantive criminal law

Title 1 Offences against the confidentiality, integrity and availability of computer data and systems

Article 2 Illegal access

Each Party shall adopt such legislative and other measures as may be necessary to establish as criminal offences under its domestic law, when committed intentionally, the access to the whole or any part of a computer system without right. A Party may require that the offence be committed by infringing security measures, with the intent of obtaining computer data or other dishonest intent, or in relation to a computer system that is connected to another computer system.

Article 3 Illegal interception

Each Party shall adopt such legislative and other measures as may be necessary to establish as criminal offences under its domestic law, when committed intentionally, the interception without right, made by technical means, of non-public transmissions of computer data to, from or within a computer system, including electromagnetic emissions from a computer system carrying such computer data. A Party may require that the offence be committed with dishonest intent, or in relation to a computer system that is connected to another computer system.

Article 4 Data interference

1. Each Party shall adopt such legislative and other measures as may be necessary to establish as criminal offences under its domestic law, when committed intentionally, the damaging, deletion, deterioration, alteration or suppression of computer data without right.
2. A Party may reserve the right to require that the conduct described in paragraph 1 result in serious harm.

Article 5 System interference

Each Party shall adopt such legislative and other measures as may be necessary to establish as criminal offences under its domestic law, when committed intentionally, the serious hindering without right of the functioning of a computer system by inputting, transmitting, damaging, deleting, deteriorating, altering or suppressing computer data.

Article 6 Misuse of devices

1. Each Party shall adopt such legislative and other measures as may be necessary to establish as criminal offences under its domestic law, when committed intentionally and without right:
   (a) the production, sale, procurement for use, import, distribution or otherwise making available of:
      (i) a device, including a computer program, designed or adapted primarily for the purpose of committing any of the offences established in accordance with Article 2 through 5;
      (ii) a computer password, access code, or similar data by which the whole or any part of a computer system is capable of being accessed, with intent that it be used for the purpose of committing any of the offences established in Articles 2 through 5; and
   (b) the possession of an item referred to in paragraphs (a)(i) or (ii) above, with intent that it be used for the purpose of committing any of the offences established in Articles 2 through 5. A Party may require by law that a number of such items be possessed before criminal liability attaches.
2. This article shall not be interpreted as imposing criminal liability where the production, sale, procurement for use, import, distribution or otherwise making available or possession referred to in paragraph 1 of this Article is not for the purpose of committing an offence established in accordance with Articles 2 through 5 of this Convention, such as for the authorised testing or protection of a computer system.
3. Each Party may reserve the right not to apply paragraph 1 of this Article, provided that the reservation does not concern the sale, distribution or otherwise making available of the items referred to in paragraph 1 (a)(ii) of this Article.

Title 2 Computer-related offences

Article 7 Computer-related forgery

Each Party shall adopt such legislative and other measures as may be necessary to establish as criminal offences under its domestic law, when committed intentionally and without right, the input, alteration, deletion, or suppression of computer data, resulting in inauthentic data with the intent that it be considered or acted upon for legal purposes as if it were authentic, regardless whether or not the data is directly readable and intelligible. A Party may require an intent to defraud, or similar dishonest intent, before criminal liability attaches.

Article 8 Computer-related fraud

Each Party shall adopt such legislative and other measures as may be necessary to establish as criminal offences under its domestic law, when committed intentionally and without right, the causing of a loss of property to another by:

(a) any input, alteration, deletion or suppression of computer data,
(b) any interference with the functioning of a computer system,
with fraudulent or dishonest intent of procuring, without right, an economic benefit for oneself or for another.

Title 3 Content-related offences

Article 9 Offences related to child pornography [Omitted]

Title 4 Offences related to infringements of copyright and related rights

Article 10 Offences related to infringements of copyright and related rights

1. Each Party shall adopt such legislative and other measures as may be necessary to establish as criminal offences under its domestic law the infringement of copyright, as defined under the law of that Party pursuant to the obligations it has undertaken under the Paris Act of 24 July 1971 revising the Bern Convention for the Protection of Literary and Artistic Works, the Agreement on Trade-Related Aspects of Intellectual Property Rights and the WIPO Copyright Treaty, with the exception of any moral rights conferred by such Conventions, where such acts are committed wilfully, on a commercial scale and by means of a computer system.
2. Each Party shall adopt such legislative and other measures as may be necessary to establish as criminal offences under its domestic law the infringement of related rights, as defined under the law of that Party, pursuant to the obligations it has undertaken under the International Convention for the Protection of Performers, Producers of Phonograms and Broadcasting Organisations (Rome Convention), the Agreement on Trade-Related Aspects of Intellectual Property Rights and the WIPO Performances and Phonograms Treaty, with the exception of any moral rights conferred by such Conventions, where such acts are committed wilfully, on a commercial scale and by means of a computer system.

3. A Party may reserve the right not to impose criminal liability under paragraphs 1 and 2 of this article in limited circumstances, provided that other effective remedies are available and that such reservation does not derogate from the Party's international obligations set forth in the international instruments referred to in paragraphs 1 and 2 of this article.

Title 5 Ancillary liability and sanctions

Article 11 Attempt and aiding or abetting

1. Each Party shall adopt such legislative and other measures as may be necessary to establish as criminal offences under its domestic law, when committed intentionally, aiding or abetting the commission of any of the offences established in accordance with Articles 2 through 10 of the present Convention with intent that such offence be committed.
2. Each Party shall adopt such legislative and other measures as may be necessary to establish as criminal offences under its domestic law, when committed intentionally, an attempt to commit any of the offences established in accordance with Articles 3 through 5, 7, 8, 9(1)a and 9(1)c of this Convention.
3. Each Party may reserve the right not to apply, in whole or in part, paragraph 2 of this article.

Article 12 Corporate liability

1. Each Party shall adopt such legislative and other measures as may be necessary to ensure that a legal person can be held liable for a criminal offence established in accordance with this Convention, committed for its benefit by any natural person, acting either individually or as part of an organ of the legal person, who has a leading position within the legal person, based on:
   (a) a power of representation of the legal person;
   (b) an authority to take decisions on behalf of the legal person;
   (c) an authority to exercise control within the legal person.
2. Apart from the cases already provided for in paragraph 1, each Party shall take the measures necessary to ensure that a legal person can be held liable where the lack of supervision or control by a natural person referred to in paragraph 1 has made possible the commission of a criminal offence established in accordance with this Convention for the benefit of that legal person by a natural person acting under its authority.
3. Subject to the legal principles of the Party, the liability of a legal person may be criminal, civil or administrative.
4. Such liability shall be without prejudice to the criminal liability of the natural persons who have committed the offence.

Article 13 Sanctions and measures

1. Each Party shall adopt such legislative and other measures as may be necessary to ensure that the criminal offences established in accordance with Articles 2 through 11 are

punishable by effective, proportionate and dissuasive sanctions, which include deprivation of liberty.

2. Each Party shall ensure that legal persons held liable in accordance with Article 12 shall be subject to effective, proportionate and dissuasive criminal or non-criminal sanctions or measures, including monetary sanctions.

Section 2 Procedural law

Title 1 Common provisions

Article 14 Scope of procedural provisions

1. Each Party shall adopt such legislative and other measures as may be necessary to establish the powers and procedures provided for in this Section for the purpose of specific criminal investigations or proceedings.
2. Except as specifically otherwise provided in Article 21, each Party shall apply the powers and procedures referred to in paragraph 1 to:
   (a) the criminal offences established in accordance with Articles 2 through 11 of this Convention;
   (b) other criminal offences committed by means of a computer system; and
   (c) the collection of evidence in electronic form of a criminal offence.
3. (a) Each Party may reserve the right to apply the measures referred to in Article 20 only to offences or categories of offences specified in the reservation, provided that the range of such offences or categories of offences is not more restricted than the range of offences to which it applies the measures referred to in Article 21. Each Party shall consider restricting such a reservation to enable the broadest application of the measure referred to in Article 20.
   (b) Where a Party, due to limitations in its legislation in force at the time of the adoption of the present Convention, is not able to apply the measures referred to in Articles 20 and 21 to communications being transmitted within a computer system of a service provider, which system:
      (i) is being operated for the benefit of a closed group of users, and
      (ii) does not employ public communications networks and is not connected with another computer system, whether public or private,

   that Party may reserve the right not to apply these measures to such communications. Each Party shall consider restricting such a reservation to enable the broadest application of the measures referred to in Articles 20 and 21.

Article 15 Conditions and safeguards

1. Each Party shall ensure that the establishment, implementation and application of the powers and procedures provided for in this Section are subject to conditions and safeguards provided for under its domestic law, which shall provide for the adequate protection of human rights and liberties, including rights arising pursuant to obligations it has undertaken under the 1950 Council of Europe Convention for the Protection of Human Rights and Fundamental Freedoms, the 1966 United Nations International Covenant on Civil and Political Rights, and other applicable international human rights instruments, and which shall incorporate the principle of proportionality.

2. Such conditions and safeguards shall, as appropriate in view of the nature of the power or procedure concerned, *inter alia*, include judicial or other independent supervision, grounds justifying application, and limitation on the scope and the duration of such power or procedure.
3. To the extent that it is consistent with the public interest, in particular the sound administration of justice, a Party shall consider the impact of the powers and procedures in this Section upon the rights, responsibilities and legitimate interests of third parties.

Title 2 Expedited preservation of stored computer data

Article 16 Expedited preservation of stored computer data

1. Each Party shall adopt such legislative and other measures as may be necessary to enable its competent authorities to order or similarly obtain the expeditious preservation of specified computer data, including traffic data, that has been stored by means of a computer system, in particular where there are grounds to believe that the computer data is particularly vulnerable to loss or modification.
2. Where a Party gives effect to paragraph 1 above by means of an order to a person to preserve specified stored computer data in the person's possession or control, the Party shall adopt such legislative and other measures as may be necessary to oblige that person to preserve and maintain the integrity of that computer data for a period of time as long as necessary, up to a maximum of 90 days, to enable the competent authorities to seek its disclosure. A Party may provide for such an order to be subsequently renewed.
3. Each Party shall adopt such legislative or other measures as may be necessary to oblige the custodian or other person who is to preserve the computer data to keep confidential the undertaking of such procedures for the period of time provided for by its domestic law.
4. The powers and procedures referred to in this article shall be subject to Articles 14 and 15.

Article 17 Expedited preservation and partial disclosure of traffic data

1. Each Party shall adopt, in respect of traffic data that is to be preserved under Article 16, such legislative and other measures as may be necessary to:
   (a) ensure that such expeditious preservation of traffic data is available regardless of whether one or more service providers were involved in the transmission of that communication; and
   (b) ensure the expeditious disclosure to the Party's competent authority, or a person designated by that authority, of a sufficient amount of traffic data to enable the Party to identify the service providers and the path through which the communication was transmitted.
2. The powers and procedures referred to in this article shall be subject to Articles 14 and 15.

Title 3 Production order

Article 18 Production order

1. Each Party shall adopt such legislative and other measures as may be necessary to empower its competent authorities to order:
   (a) a person in its territory to submit specified computer data in that person's possession or control, which is stored in a computer system or a computer-data storage medium; and
   (b) a service provider offering its services in the territory of the Party to submit subscriber information relating to such services in that service provider's possession or control.
2. The powers and procedures referred to in this Article shall be subject to Articles 14 and 15.
3. For the purpose of this article, 'subscriber information' means any information, contained in the form of computer data or any other form, that is held by a service provider, relating to subscribers of its services, other than traffic or content data, by which can be established:
   (a) the type of the communication service used, the technical provisions taken thereto and the period of service;
   (b) the subscriber's identity, postal or geographic address, telephone and other access number, billing and payment information, available on the basis of the service agreement or arrangement;
   (c) any other information on the site of the installation of communication equipment available on the basis of the service agreement or arrangement.

Title 4 Search and seizure of stored computer data

Article 19 Search and seizure of stored computer data

1. Each Party shall adopt such legislative and other measures as may be necessary to empower its competent authorities to search or similarly access:
   (a) a computer system or part of it and computer data stored therein; and
   (b) a computer-data storage medium in which computer data may be stored in its territory.
2. Each Party shall adopt such legislative and other measures as may be necessary to ensure that where its authorities search or similarly access a specific computer system or part of it, pursuant to paragraph 1(a), and have grounds to believe that the data sought is stored in another computer system or part of it in its territory and such data is lawfully accessible from or available to the initial system, such authorities shall be able to expeditiously extend the search or similar accessing to the other system.
3. Each Party shall adopt such legislative and other measures as may be necessary to empower its competent authorities to seize or similarly secure computer data accessed according to paragraphs 1 or 2. These measures shall include the power to:
   (a) seize or similarly secure a computer system or part of it or a computer-data storage medium;
   (b) make and retain a copy of those computer data;
   (c) maintain the integrity of the relevant stored computer data; and

   (d) render inaccessible or remove those computer data in the accessed computer system.
4. Each Party shall adopt such legislative and other measures as may be necessary to empower its competent authorities to order any person who has knowledge about the functioning of the computer system or measures applied to protect the computer data therein to provide, as is reasonable, the necessary information, to enable the undertaking of the measures referred to in paragraphs 1 and 2.
5. The powers and procedures referred to in this article shall be subject to Articles 14 and 15.

Title 5 Real-time collection of computer data

Article 20 Real-time collection of traffic data

1. Each Party shall adopt such legislative and other measures as may be necessary to empower its competent authorities to:
   (a) collect or record through application of technical means on the territory of that Party; and
   (b) compel a service provider, within its existing technical capability:
      (i) to collect or record through application of technical means on the territory of that Party, or
      (ii) to co-operate and assist the competent authorities in the collection or recording of,

   traffic data, in real-time, associated with specified communications in its territory transmitted by means of a computer system.
2. Where a Party, due to the established principles of its domestic legal system, cannot adopt the measures referred to in paragraph 1(a), it may instead adopt legislative and other measures as may be necessary to ensure the real-time collection or recording of traffic data associated with specified communications in its territory through the application of technical means on that territory.
3. Each Party shall adopt such legislative and other measures as may be necessary to oblige a service provider to keep confidential the fact of the execution of any power provided for in this Article and any information relating to it.
4. The powers and procedures referred to in this article shall be subject to Articles 14 and 15.

Article 21 Interception of content data

1. Each Party shall adopt such legislative and other measures as may be necessary, in relation to a range of serious offences to be determined by domestic law, to empower its competent authorities to:
   (a) collect or record through application of technical means on the territory of that Party; and
   (b) compel a service provider, within its existing technical capability,
      (i) to collect or record through application of technical means on the territory of that Party, or

(ii) to co-operate and assist the competent authorities in the collection or recording of, content data, in real-time, of specified communications in its territory transmitted by means of a computer system.

2. Where a Party, due to the established principles of its domestic legal system, cannot adopt the measures referred to in paragraph 1(a), it may instead adopt legislative and other measures as may be necessary to ensure the real-time collection or recording of content data of specified communications in its territory through application of technical means on that territory.
3. Each Party shall adopt such legislative and other measures as may be necessary to oblige a service provider to keep confidential the fact of and any information about the execution of any power provided for in this Article.
4. The powers and procedures referred to in this Article shall be subject to Articles 14 and 15.

Section 3 Jurisdiction

Article 22 Jurisdiction

1. Each Party shall adopt such legislative and other measures as may be necessary to establish jurisdiction over any offence established in accordance with Articles 2 through 11 of this Convention, when the offence is committed:
   (a) in its territory; or
   (b) on board a ship flying the flag of that Party; or
   (c) on board an aircraft registered under the laws of that Party; or
   (d) by one of its nationals, if the offence is punishable under criminal law where it was committed or if the offence is committed outside the territorial jurisdiction of any State.
2. Each Party may reserve the right not to apply or to apply only in specific cases or conditions the jurisdiction rules laid down in paragraphs (1)b through (1)d of this Article or any part thereof.
3. Each Party shall adopt such measures as may be necessary to establish jurisdiction over the offences referred to in Article 24, paragraph (1) of this Convention, in cases where an alleged offender is present in its territory and it does not extradite him or her to another Party, solely on the basis of his or her nationality, after a request for extradition.
4. This Convention does not exclude any criminal jurisdiction exercised in accordance with domestic law.
5. When more than one Party claims jurisdiction over an alleged offence established in accordance with this Convention, the Parties involved shall, where appropriate, consult with a view to determining the most appropriate jurisdiction for prosecution.

Chapter III International co-operation

Section 1 General principles

Title 1 General principles relating to international co-operation

Article 23 General principles relating to international co-operation

The Parties shall co-operate with each other, in accordance with the provisions of this chapter, and through application of relevant international instruments on international co-operation in criminal matters, arrangements agreed on the basis of uniform or reciprocal legislation, and domestic laws, to the widest extent possible for the purposes of investigations or proceedings concerning criminal offences related to computer systems and data, or for the collection of evidence in electronic form of a criminal offence.

Title 2 Principles relating to extradition

Article 24 Extradition

1. (a) This Article applies to extradition between Parties for the criminal offences established in accordance with Articles 2 through 11 of this Convention, provided that they are punishable under the laws of both Parties concerned by deprivation of liberty for a maximum period of at least one year, or by a more severe penalty.
   (b) Where a different minimum penalty is to be applied under an arrangement agreed on the basis of uniform or reciprocal legislation or an extradition treaty, including the European Convention on Extradition (ETS No. 24), applicable between two or more parties, the minimum penalty provided for under such arrangement or treaty shall apply.
2. The criminal offences described in paragraph 1 of this Article shall be deemed to be included as extraditable offences in any extradition treaty existing between or among the Parties. The Parties undertake to include such offences as extraditable offences in any extradition treaty to be concluded between or among them.
3. If a Party that makes extradition conditional on the existence of a treaty receives a request for extradition from another Party with which it does not have an extradition treaty, it may consider this Convention as the legal basis for extradition with respect to any criminal offence referred to in paragraph 1 of this Article.
4. Parties that do not make extradition conditional on the existence of a treaty shall recognise the criminal offences referred to in paragraph 1 of this article as extraditable offences between themselves.
5. Extradition shall be subject to the conditions provided for by the law of the requested Party or by applicable extradition treaties, including the grounds on which the requested Party may refuse extradition.
6. If extradition for a criminal offence referred to in paragraph 1 of this article is refused solely on the basis of the nationality of the person sought, or because the requested Party deems that it has jurisdiction over the offence, the requested Party shall submit the case at the request of the requesting Party to its competent authorities for the purpose of prosecution and shall report the final outcome to the requesting Party in due course. Those authorities shall take their decision and conduct their investigations and proceedings in the same manner as in the case of any other offence of a comparable nature under the law of that Party.
7. (a) Each Party shall, at the time of signature or when depositing its instrument of ratification, acceptance, approval or accession, communicate to the Secretary General of the Council of Europe the name and address of each authority responsible for

making or receiving requests for extradition or provisional arrest in the absence of a treaty.

(b) The Secretary General of the Council of Europe shall set up and keep updated a register of authorities so designated by the Parties. Each Party shall ensure that the details held on the register are correct at all times.

Title 3 General principles relating to mutual assistance

Article 25 General principles relating to mutual assistance

1. The Parties shall afford one another mutual assistance to the widest extent possible for the purpose of investigations or proceedings concerning criminal offences related to computer systems and data, or for the collection of evidence in electronic form of a criminal offence.
2. Each Party shall also adopt such legislative and other measures as may be necessary to carry out the obligations set forth in Articles 27 through 35.
3. Each Party may, in urgent circumstances, make requests for mutual assistance or communications related thereto by expedited means of communication, including fax or e-mail, to the extent that such means provide appropriate levels of security and authentication (including the use of encryption, where necessary), with formal confirmation to follow, where required by the requested Party. The requested Party shall accept and respond to the request by any such expedited means of communication.
4. Except as otherwise specifically provided in articles in this chapter, mutual assistance shall be subject to the conditions provided for by the law of the requested Party or by applicable mutual assistance treaties, including the grounds on which the requested Party may refuse co-operation. The requested Party shall not exercise the right to refuse mutual assistance in relation to the offences referred to in Articles 2 to 11 solely on the ground that the request concerns an offence which it considers a fiscal offence.
5. Where, in accordance with the provisions of this chapter, the requested Party is permitted to make mutual assistance conditional upon the existence of dual criminality, that condition shall be deemed fulfilled, irrespective of whether its laws place the offence within the same category of offence or denominate the offence by the same terminology as the requesting Party, if the conduct underlying the offence for which assistance is sought is a criminal offence under its laws.

Article 26 Spontaneous information

1. A Party may, within the limits of its domestic law and without prior request, forward to another Party information obtained within the framework of its own investigations when it considers that the disclosure of such information might assist the receiving Party in initiating or carrying out investigations or proceedings concerning criminal offences established in accordance with this Convention or might to a request for co-operation by that Party under this chapter.
2. Prior to providing such information, the providing Party may request that it be kept confidential or used subject to conditions. If the receiving Party cannot comply with

such request, it shall notify the providing Party, which shall then determine whether the information should nevertheless be provided. If the receiving Party accepts the information subject to the conditions, it shall be bound by them.

Title 4 Procedures pertaining to mutual assistance requests in the absence of applicable international agreements

Article 27 Procedures pertaining to mutual assistance requests in the absence of applicable international agreements

1. Where there is no mutual assistance treaty or arrangement on the basis of uniform or reciprocal legislation in force between the requesting and requested Parties, the provisions of paragraphs 2 through 9 of this article shall apply. The provisions of this Article shall not apply where such treaty, arrangement or legislation is available, unless the Parties concerned agree to apply any or all of the remainder of this article in lieu thereof.
2. (a) Each Party shall designate a central authority or authorities that shall be responsible for sending and answering requests for mutual assistance, the execution of such requests, or the transmission of them to the authorities competent for their execution.
   (b) The central authorities shall communicate directly with each other.
   (c) Each Party shall, at the time of signature or when depositing its instrument of ratification, acceptance, approval or accession, communicate to the Secretary General of the Council of Europe the names and addresses of the authorities designated in pursuance of this paragraph.
   (d) The Secretary General of the Council of Europe shall set up and keep updated a register of central authorities so designated by the Parties. Each Party shall ensure that the details held on the register are correct at all times.
3. Mutual assistance requests under this Article shall be executed in accordance with the procedures specified by the requesting Party except where incompatible with the law of the requested Party.
4. The requested Party may, in addition to the grounds for refusal available under Article 25, paragraph (4), refuse assistance if:
   (a) the request concerns an offence which the requested Party considers a political offence or an offence connected with a political offence; or
   (b) it considers that execution of the request is likely to prejudice its sovereignty, security, ordre *public* or other essential interests.
5. The requested Party may postpone action on a request if such action would prejudice criminal investigations or proceedings conducted by its authorities.
6. Before refusing or postponing assistance, the requested Party shall, where appropriate after having consulted with the requesting Party, consider whether the request may be granted partially or subject to such conditions as it deems necessary.
7. The requested Party shall promptly inform the requesting Party of the outcome of the execution of a request for assistance. Reasons shall be given for refusal or postponement of the request. The requested Party shall also inform the requesting Party of any reasons that render impossible the execution of the request or are likely to delay it significantly.

8. The requesting Party may request that the requested Party keep confidential the fact of any request made under this chapter as well as its subject, except to the extent necessary for its execution. If the requested Party cannot comply with the request for confidentiality, it shall promptly inform the requesting Party, which shall then determine whether the request should nevertheless be executed.
9. (a) In the event of urgency, requests for mutual assistance or communications related thereto may be sent directly by judicial authorities of the requesting Party to such authorities of the requested Party. In any such cases a copy shall be sent at the same time to the central authority of the requested Party through the central authority of the requesting Party.
   (b) Any request or communication under this paragraph may be made through the International Criminal Police Organisation (Interpol).
   (c) Where a request is made pursuant to subparagraph (a) and the authority is not competent to deal with the request, it shall refer the request to the competent national authority and inform directly the requesting Party that it has done so.
   (d) Requests or communications made under this paragraph that do not involve coercive action may be directly transmitted by the competent authorities of the requesting Party to the competent authorities of the requested Party.
   (e) Each Party may, at the time of signature or when depositing its instrument of ratification, acceptance, approval or accession inform the Secretary General of the Council of Europe that, for reasons of efficiency, requests made under this paragraph are to be addressed to its central authority.

Article 28 Confidentiality and limitation on use

1. When there is no mutual assistance treaty or arrangement on the basis of uniform or reciprocal legislation in force between the requesting and the requested Parties, the provisions of this article shall apply. The provisions of this article shall not apply where such treaty, arrangement or legislation exists, unless the Parties concerned agree to apply any or all of the remainder of this article in lieu thereof.
2. The requested Party may make the furnishing of information or material in response to a request dependent on the condition that it is:
   (a) kept confidential where the request for mutual legal assistance could not be complied with in the absence of such condition, or
   (b) not used for investigations or proceedings other than those stated in the request.
3. If the requesting Party cannot comply with a condition referred to in paragraph 2, it shall promptly inform the other Party, which shall then determine whether the information is nevertheless provided. When the requesting Party accepts the condition, it shall be bound by it.
4. Any Party that furnishes information or material subject to a condition referred to in paragraph 2 may require the other Party to explain, in relation to that condition, the use made of such information or material.

Section 2 Specific provisions

Title 1 Mutual assistance regarding provisional measures

Article 29 Expedited preservation of stored computer data

1. A Party may request another Party to order or otherwise obtain the expeditious preservation of data stored by means of a computer system, which is located within the territory of that other Party and in respect of which the requesting Party intends to submit a request for mutual assistance for the search or similar access, seizure or similar securing, or disclosure of the data.
2. A request for preservation made under paragraph 1 shall specify:
   (a) the authority that is seeking the preservation;
   (b) the offence that is the subject of a criminal investigation or proceeding and a brief summary of related facts;
   (c) the stored computer data to be preserved and its relationship to the offence;
   (d) any available information to identify the custodian of the stored computer data or the location of the computer system;
   (e) the necessity of the preservation; and
   (f) that the Party intends to submit a request for mutual assistance for the search or similar access, seizure or similar securing, or disclosure of the stored computer data.
3. Upon receiving the request from another Party, the requested Party shall take all appropriate measures to preserve expeditiously the specified data in accordance with its domestic law. For the purposes of responding to a request, dual criminality shall not be required as a condition to providing such preservation.
4. A Party that requires dual criminality as a condition for responding to a request for mutual assistance for the search or similar access, seizure or similar securing, or disclosure of stored data may, in respect of offences other than those established in accordance with Articles 2 through 11 of this Convention, reserve the right to refuse the request for preservation under this article in cases where it has reason to believe that at the time of disclosure the condition of dual criminality cannot be fulfilled.
5. In addition, a request for preservation may only be refused if:
   (a) the request concerns an offence which the requested Party considers a political offence or an offence connected with a political offence; or
   (b) the requested Party considers that execution of the request is likely to prejudice its sovereignty, security, *ordre public* or other essential interests.
6. Where the requested Party believes that preservation will not ensure the future availability of the data or will threaten the confidentiality of or otherwise prejudice the requesting Party's investigation, it shall promptly so inform the requesting Party, which shall then determine whether the request should nevertheless be executed.
7. Any preservation effected in response to the request referred to in paragraph 1 shall be for a period not less than 60 days in order to enable the requesting Party to submit a request for the search or similar access, seizure or similar securing, or disclosure of the data. Following the receipt of such a request, the data shall continue to be preserved pending a decision on that request.

Article 30 Expedited disclosure of preserved traffic data

1. Where, in the course of the execution of a request made under Article 29 to preserve traffic data concerning a specific communication, the requested Party discovers that a

service provider in another State was involved in the transmission of the communication, the requested Party shall expeditiously disclose to the requesting Party a sufficient amount of traffic data in order to identify that service provider and the path through which the communication was transmitted.

2. Disclosure of traffic data under paragraph 1 may only be withheld if:
   (a) the request concerns an offence which the requested Party considers a political offence or an offence connected with a political offence; or
   (b) the requested Party considers that execution of the request is likely to prejudice its sovereignty, security, *ordre public* or other essential interests.

Title 2 Mutual assistance regarding investigative powers

Article 31 Mutual assistance regarding accessing of stored computer data

1. A Party may request another Party to search or similarly access, seize or similarly secure, and disclose data stored by means of a computer system located within the territory of the requested Party, including data that has been preserved pursuant to Article 29.
2. The requested Party shall respond to the request through application of international instruments, arrangements and laws referred to in Article 23, and in accordance with other relevant provisions of this Chapter.
3. The request shall be responded to on an expedited basis where:
   (a) there are grounds to believe that relevant data is particularly vulnerable to loss or modification; or
   (b) the instruments, arrangements and laws referred to in paragraph 2 otherwise provide for expedited co-operation.

Article 32 Trans-border access to stored computer data with consent or where publicly available

A Party may, without obtaining the authorisation of another Party:

(a) access publicly available (open source) stored computer data, regardless of where the data is located geographically; or

(b) access or receive, through a computer system in its territory, stored computer data located in another Party, if the Party obtains the lawful and voluntary consent of the person who has the lawful authority to disclose the data to the Party through that computer system.

Article 33 Mutual assistance regarding the real-time collection of traffic data

1. The Parties shall provide mutual assistance to each other in the real-time collection of traffic data associated with specified communications in their territory transmitted by means of a computer system. Subject to the provisions of paragraph 2, assistance shall be governed by the conditions and procedures provided for under domestic law.
2. Each Party shall provide such assistance at least with respect to criminal offences for which real-time collection of traffic data would be available in a similar domestic case.

Article 34 Mutual assistance regarding the interception of content data

The Parties shall provide mutual assistance to each other in the real-time collection or recording of content data of specified communications transmitted by means of a computer system to the extent permitted under their applicable treaties and domestic laws.

Title 3 24/7 Network

Article 35 24/7 Network

1. Each Party shall designate a point of contact available on a 24 hour, 7 day per week basis in order to ensure the provision of immediate assistance for the purpose of investigations or proceedings concerning criminal offences related to computer systems and data, or for the collection of evidence in electronic form of a criminal offence. Such assistance shall include facilitating, or, if permitted by its domestic law and practice, directly carrying out the following measures:
   (a) the provision of technical advice;
   (b) the preservation of data pursuant to Articles 29 and 30; and
   (c) the collection of evidence, the provision of legal information, and locating of suspects.
2. (a) A Party's point of contact shall have the capacity to carry out communications with the point of contact of another Party on an expedited basis.
   (b) If the point of contact designated by a Party is not part of that Party's authority or authorities responsible for international mutual assistance or extradition, the point of contact shall ensure that it is able to co-ordinate with such authority or authorities on an expedited basis.
3. Each Party shall ensure that trained and equipped personnel are available in order to facilitate the operation of the network.

Chapter IV Final provisions

Articles 36–48 [Omitted]

United Nations Convention against Corruption, 2003

Preamble

The States Parties to this Convention,

Concerned about the seriousness of problems and threats posed by corruption to the stability and security of societies, undermining the institutions and values of democracy, ethical values and justice and jeopardizing sustainable development and the rule of law,

Concerned also about the links between corruption and other forms of crime, in particular organized crime and economic crime, including money-laundering,

Concerned further about cases of corruption that involve vast quantities of assets, which may constitute a substantial proportion of the resources of States, and that threaten the political stability and sustainable development of those States,

Convinced that corruption is no longer a local matter but a transnational phenomenon that affects all societies and economies, making international cooperation to prevent and control it essential,

Convinced also that a comprehensive and multidisciplinary approach is required to prevent and combat corruption effectively,

Convinced further that the availability of technical assistance can play an important role in enhancing the ability of States, including by strengthening capacity and by institution-building, to prevent and combat corruption effectively,

Convinced that the illicit acquisition of personal wealth can be particularly damaging to democratic institutions, national economies and the rule of law,

Determined to prevent, detect and deter in a more effective manner international transfers of illicitly acquired assets and to strengthen international cooperation in asset recovery,

Acknowledging the fundamental principles of due process of law in criminal proceedings and in civil or administrative proceedings to adjudicate property rights,

Bearing in mind that the prevention and eradication of corruption is a responsibility of all States and that they must cooperate with one another, with the support and involvement of individuals and groups outside the public sector, such as civil society, non-governmental organizations and community-based organizations, if their efforts in this area are to be effective,

Bearing also in mind the principles of proper management of public affairs and public property, fairness, responsibility and equality before the law and the need to safeguard integrity and to foster a culture of rejection of corruption,

Commending the work of the Commission on Crime Prevention and Criminal Justice and the United Nations Office on Drugs and Crime in preventing and combating corruption,

Recalling the work carried out by other international and regional organizations in this field, including the activities of the African Union, the Council of Europe, the Customs Cooperation Council (also known as the World Customs Organization), the European Union, the League of Arab States, the Organisation for Economic Cooperation and Development and the Organization of American States,

Taking note with appreciation of multilateral instruments to prevent and combat corruption, including, inter alia, the Inter-American Convention against Corruption, adopted by the Organization of American States on 29 March 1996, the Convention on the Fight against Corruption involving Officials of the European Communities or Officials of Member States of the European Union, adopted by the Council of the European Union on 26 May 1997, the Convention on Combating Bribery of Foreign Public Officials in International Business Transactions, adopted by the Organisation for Economic Cooperation and Development on 21 November 1997, the Criminal Law Convention on Corruption, adopted by the Committee of Ministers of the Council of Europe on 27 January 1999, the Civil Law Convention on Corruption, adopted by the Committee of Ministers of the Council of Europe on 4 November 1999, and the African Union Convention on Preventing and Combating Corruption, adopted by the Heads of State and Government of the African Union on 12 July 2003,

Welcoming the entry into force on 29 September 2003 of the United Nations Convention against Transnational Organized Crime,

Have agreed as follows:

Chapter I General provisions

Article 1 Statement of purpose

The purposes of this Convention are:

(a) To promote and strengthen measures to prevent and combat corruption more efficiently and effectively;
(b) To promote, facilitate and support international cooperation and technical assistance in the prevention of and fight against corruption, including in asset recovery;
(c) To promote integrity, accountability and proper management of public affairs and public property.

Article 2 Use of terms

For the purposes of this Convention:

(a) 'Public official' shall mean: (i) any person holding a legislative, executive, administrative or judicial office of a State Party, whether appointed or elected, whether permanent or temporary, whether paid or unpaid, irrespective of that person's seniority; (ii) any other person who performs a public function, including for a public agency or public enterprise, or provides a public service, as defined in the domestic law of the State Party and as applied in the pertinent area of law of that State Party; (iii) any other person defined as a 'public official' in the domestic law of a State Party. However, for the purpose of some specific measures contained in chapter II of this Convention, 'public official' may mean any person who performs a public function or provides a public service as defined in the domestic law of the State Party and as applied in the pertinent area of law of that State Party;
(b) 'Foreign public official' shall mean any person holding a legislative, executive, administrative or judicial office of a foreign country, whether appointed or elected; and any person exercising a public function for a foreign country, including for a public agency or public enterprise;
(c) 'Official of a public international organization' shall mean an international civil servant or any person who is authorized by such an organization to act on behalf of that organization;
(d) 'Property' shall mean assets of every kind, whether corporeal or incorporeal, movable or immovable, tangible or intangible, and legal documents or instruments evidencing title to or interest in such assets;
(e) 'Proceeds of crime' shall mean any property derived from or obtained, directly or indirectly, through the commission of an offence;
(f) 'Freezing' or 'seizure' shall mean temporarily prohibiting the transfer, conversion, disposition or movement of property or temporarily assuming custody or control of property on the basis of an order issued by a court or other competent authority;
(g) 'Confiscation', which includes forfeiture where applicable, shall mean the permanent deprivation of property by order of a court or other competent authority;
(h) 'Predicate offence' shall mean any offence as a result of which proceeds have been generated that may become the subject of an offence as defined in article 23 of this Convention;

(i) 'Controlled delivery' shall mean the technique of allowing illicit or suspect consignments to pass out of, through or into the territory of one or more States, with the knowledge and under the supervision of their competent authorities, with a view to the investigation of an offence and the identification of persons involved in the commission of the offence.

Article 3 Scope of application

1. This Convention shall apply, in accordance with its terms, to the prevention, investigation and prosecution of corruption and to the freezing, seizure, confiscation and return of the proceeds of offences established in accordance with this Convention.
2. For the purposes of implementing this Convention, it shall not be necessary, except as otherwise stated herein, for the offences set forth in it to result in damage or harm to state property.

Article 4 Protection of sovereignty

1. States Parties shall carry out their obligations under this Convention in a manner consistent with the principles of sovereign equality and territorial integrity of States and that of non-intervention in the domestic affairs of other States.
2. Nothing in this Convention shall entitle a State Party to undertake in the territory of another State the exercise of jurisdiction and performance of functions that are reserved exclusively for the authorities of that other State by its domestic law.

Chapter II Preventive measures

Article 5 Preventive anti-corruption policies and practices

1. Each State Party shall, in accordance with the fundamental principles of its legal system, develop and implement or maintain effective, coordinated anticorruption policies that promote the participation of society and reflect the principles of the rule of law, proper management of public affairs and public property, integrity, transparency and accountability.
2. Each State Party shall endeavour to establish and promote effective practices aimed at the prevention of corruption.
3. Each State Party shall endeavour to periodically evaluate relevant legal instruments and administrative measures with a view to determining their adequacy to prevent and fight corruption.
4. States Parties shall, as appropriate and in accordance with the fundamental principles of their legal system, collaborate with each other and with relevant international and regional organizations in promoting and developing the measures referred to in this article. That collaboration may include participation in international programmes and projects aimed at the prevention of corruption.

Article 6 Preventive anti-corruption body or bodies

1. Each State Party shall, in accordance with the fundamental principles of its legal system, ensure the existence of a body or bodies, as appropriate, that prevent corruption by such means as:

(a) Implementing the policies referred to in article 5 of this Convention and, where appropriate, overseeing and coordinating the implementation of those policies;
(b) Increasing and disseminating knowledge about the prevention of corruption.

2. Each State Party shall grant the body or bodies referred to in paragraph 1 of this article the necessary independence, in accordance with the fundamental principles of its legal system, to enable the body or bodies to carry out its or their functions effectively and free from any undue influence. The necessary material resources and specialized staff, as well as the training that such staff may require to carry out their functions, should be provided.
3. Each State Party shall inform the Secretary-General of the United Nations of the name and address of the authority or authorities that may assist other States Parties in developing and implementing specific measures for the prevention of corruption.

Article 7 Public sector

1. Each State Party shall, where appropriate and in accordance with the fundamental principles of its legal system, endeavour to adopt, maintain and strengthen systems for the recruitment, hiring, retention, promotion and retirement of civil servants and, where appropriate, other non-elected public officials:
   (a) That are based on principles of efficiency, transparency and objective criteria such as merit, equity and aptitude;
   (b) That include adequate procedures for the selection and training of individuals for public positions considered especially vulnerable to corruption and the rotation, where appropriate, of such individuals to other positions;
   (c) That promote adequate remuneration and equitable pay scales, taking into account the level of economic development of the State Party;
   (d) That promote education and training programmes to enable them to meet the requirements for the correct, honourable and proper performance of public functions and that provide them with specialized and appropriate training to enhance their awareness of the risks of corruption inherent the performance of their functions. Such programmes may make reference to codes or standards of conduct in applicable areas.
2. Each State Party shall also consider adopting appropriate legislative and administrative measures, consistent with the objectives of this Convention and in accordance with the fundamental principles of its domestic law, to prescribe criteria concerning candidature for and election to public office.
3. Each State Party shall also consider taking appropriate legislative and administrative measures, consistent with the objectives of this Convention and in accordance with the fundamental principles of its domestic law, to enhance transparency in the funding of candidatures for elected public office and, where applicable, the funding of political parties.
4. Each State Party shall, in accordance with the fundamental principles of its domestic law, endeavour to adopt, maintain and strengthen systems that promote transparency and prevent conflicts of interest.

Article 8 Codes of conduct for public officials

1. In order to fight corruption, each State Party shall promote, inter alia, integrity, honesty and responsibility among its public officials, in accordance with the fundamental principles of its legal system.
2. In particular, each State Party shall endeavour to apply, within its own institutional and legal systems, codes or standards of conduct for the correct, honourable and proper performance of public functions.
3. For the purposes of implementing the provisions of this article, each State Party shall, where appropriate and in accordance with the fundamental principles of its legal system, take note of the relevant initiatives of regional, interregional and multilateral organizations, such as the International Code of Conduct for Public Officials contained in the annex to General Assembly resolution 51/59 of 12 December 1996.
4. Each State Party shall also consider, in accordance with the fundamental principles of its domestic law, establishing measures and systems to facilitate the reporting by public officials of acts of corruption to appropriate authorities, when such acts come to their notice in the performance of their functions.
5. Each State Party shall endeavour, where appropriate and in accordance with the fundamental principles of its domestic law, to establish measures and systems requiring public officials to make declarations to appropriate authorities regarding, inter alia, their outside activities, employment, investments, assets and substantial gifts or benefits from which a conflict of interest may result with respect to their functions as public officials.
6. Each State Party shall consider taking, in accordance with the fundamental principles of its domestic law, disciplinary or other measures against public officials who violate the codes or standards established in accordance with this article.

Article 9 Public procurement and management of public finances

1. Each State Party shall, in accordance with the fundamental principles of its legal system, take the necessary steps to establish appropriate systems of procurement, based on transparency, competition and objective criteria in decision-making, that are effective, inter alia, in preventing corruption. Such systems, which may take into account appropriate threshold values in their application, shall address, inter alia:
   (a) The public distribution of information relating to procurement procedures and contracts, including information on invitations to tender and relevant or pertinent information on the award of contracts, allowing potential tenderers sufficient time to prepare and submit their tenders;
   (b) The establishment, in advance, of conditions for participation, including selection and award criteria and tendering rules, and their publication;
   (c) The use of objective and predetermined criteria for public procurement decisions, in order to facilitate the subsequent verification of the correct application of the rules or procedures;
   (d) An effective system of domestic review, including an effective system of appeal, to ensure legal recourse and remedies in the event that the rules or procedures established pursuant to this paragraph are not followed;

   (e) Where appropriate, measures to regulate matters regarding personnel responsible for procurement, such as declaration of interest in particular public procurements, screening procedures and training requirements.
2. Each State Party shall, in accordance with the fundamental principles of its legal system, take appropriate measures to promote transparency and accountability in the management of public finances. Such measures shall encompass, inter alia:
   (a) Procedures for the adoption of the national budget;
   (b) Timely reporting on revenue and expenditure;
   (c) A system of accounting and auditing standards and related oversight;
   (d) Effective and efficient systems of risk management and internal control; and
   (e) Where appropriate, corrective action in the case of failure to comply with the requirements established in this paragraph.
3. Each State Party shall take such civil and administrative measures as may be necessary, in accordance with the fundamental principles of its domestic law, to preserve the integrity of accounting books, records, financial statements or other documents related to public expenditure and revenue and to prevent the falsification of such documents.

Article 10 Public reporting

Taking into account the need to combat corruption, each State Party shall, in accordance with the fundamental principles of its domestic law, take such measures as may be necessary to enhance transparency in its public administration, including with regard to its organization, functioning and decision-making processes, where appropriate. Such measures may include, inter alia:

(a) Adopting procedures or regulations allowing members of the general public to obtain, where appropriate, information on the organization, functioning and decision-making processes of its public administration and, with due regard for the protection of privacy and personal data, on decisions and legal acts that concern members of the public;
(b) Simplifying administrative procedures, where appropriate, in order to facilitate public access to the competent decision-making authorities; and
(c) Publishing information, which may include periodic reports on the risks of corruption in its public administration.

Article 11 Measures relating to the judiciary and prosecution services

1. Bearing in mind the independence of the judiciary and its crucial role in combating corruption, each State Party shall, in accordance with the fundamental principles of its legal system and without prejudice to judicial independence, take measures to strengthen integrity and to prevent opportunities for corruption among members of the judiciary. Such measures may include rules with respect to the conduct of members of the judiciary.
2. Measures to the same effect as those taken pursuant to paragraph 1 of this article may be introduced and applied within the prosecution service in those States Parties where it does not form part of the judiciary but enjoys independence similar to that of the judicial service.

Article 12 Private sector

1. Each State Party shall take measures, in accordance with the fundamental principles of its domestic law, to prevent corruption involving the private sector, enhance accounting and auditing standards in the private sector and, where appropriate, provide effective, proportionate and dissuasive civil, administrative or criminal penalties for failure to comply with such measures.
2. Measures to achieve these ends may include, inter alia:
   (a) Promoting cooperation between law enforcement agencies and relevant private entities;
   (b) Promoting the development of standards and procedures designed to safeguard the integrity of relevant private entities, including codes of conduct for the correct, honourable and proper performance of the activities of business and all relevant professions and the prevention of conflicts of interest, and for the promotion of the use of good commercial practices among businesses and in the contractual relations of businesses with the State;
   (c) Promoting transparency among private entities, including, where appropriate, measures regarding the identity of legal and natural persons involved in the establishment and management of corporate entities;
   (d) Preventing the misuse of procedures regulating private entities, including procedures regarding subsidies and licences granted by public authorities for commercial activities;
   (e) Preventing conflicts of interest by imposing restrictions, as appropriate and for a reasonable period of time, on the professional activities of former public officials or on the employment of public officials by the private sector after their resignation or retirement, where such activities or employment relate directly to the functions held or supervised by those public officials during their tenure;
   (f) Ensuring that private enterprises, taking into account their structure and size, have sufficient internal auditing controls to assist in preventing and detecting acts of corruption and that the accounts and required financial statements of such private enterprises are subject to appropriate auditing and certification procedures.
3. In order to prevent corruption, each State Party shall take such measures as may be necessary, in accordance with its domestic laws and regulations regarding the maintenance of books and records, financial statement disclosures and accounting and auditing standards, to prohibit the following acts carried out for the purpose of committing any of the offences established in accordance with this Convention:
   (a) The establishment of off-the-books accounts;
   (b) The making of off-the-books or inadequately identified transactions;
   (c) The recording of non-existent expenditure;
   (d) The entry of liabilities with incorrect identification of their objects;
   (e) The use of false documents; and
   (f) The intentional destruction of bookkeeping documents earlier than foreseen by the law.
4. Each State Party shall disallow the tax deductibility of expenses that constitute bribes, the latter being one of the constituent elements of the offences established in accordance with articles 15 and 16 of this Convention and, where appropriate, other expenses incurred in furtherance of corrupt conduct.

Article 13 Participation of society

1. Each State Party shall take appropriate measures, within its means and in accordance with fundamental principles of its domestic law, to promote the active participation of individuals and groups outside the public sector, such as civil society, non-governmental organizations and community-based organizations, in the prevention of and the fight against corruption and to raise public awareness regarding the existence, causes and gravity of and the threat posed by corruption. This participation should be strengthened by such measures as:
   (a) Enhancing the transparency of and promoting the contribution of the public to decision-making processes;
   (b) Ensuring that the public has effective access to information;
   (c) Undertaking public information activities that contribute to non-tolerance of corruption, as well as public education programmes, including school and university curricula;
   (d) Respecting, promoting and protecting the freedom to seek, receive, publish and disseminate information concerning corruption. That freedom may be subject to certain restrictions, but these shall only be such as are provided for by law and are necessary:
      (i) For respect of the rights or reputations of others;
      (ii) For the protection of national security or *ordre public* or of public health or morals.
2. Each State Party shall take appropriate measures to ensure that the relevant anti-corruption bodies referred to in this Convention are known to the public and shall provide access to such bodies, where appropriate, for the reporting, including anonymously, of any incidents that may be considered to constitute an offence established in accordance with this Convention.

Article 14 Measures to prevent money-laundering

1. Each State Party shall:
   (a) Institute a comprehensive domestic regulatory and supervisory regime for banks and non-bank financial institutions, including natural or legal persons that provide formal or informal services for the transmission of money or value and, where appropriate, other bodies particularly susceptible to money-laundering, within its competence, in order to deter and detect all forms of money-laundering, which regime shall emphasize requirements for customer and, where appropriate, beneficial owner identification, record-keeping and the reporting of suspicious transactions;
   (b) Without prejudice to article 46 of this Convention, ensure that administrative, regulatory, law enforcement and other authorities dedicated to combating money-laundering (including, where appropriate under domestic law, judicial authorities) have the ability to cooperate and exchange information at the national and international levels within the conditions prescribed by its domestic law and, to that end, shall consider the establishment of a financial intelligence unit to serve as a national centre for the collection, analysis and dissemination of information regarding potential money-laundering.

2. States Parties shall consider implementing feasible measures to detect and monitor the movement of cash and appropriate negotiable instruments across their borders, subject to safeguards to ensure proper use of information and without impeding in any way the movement of legitimate capital. Such measures may include a requirement that individuals and businesses report the cross-border transfer of substantial quantities of cash and appropriate negotiable instruments.
3. States Parties shall consider implementing appropriate and feasible measures to require financial institutions, including money remitters:
   (a) To include on forms for the electronic transfer of funds and related messages accurate and meaningful information on the originator;
   (b) To maintain such information throughout the payment chain; and
   (c) To apply enhanced scrutiny to transfers of funds that do not contain complete information on the originator.
4. In establishing a domestic regulatory and supervisory regime under the terms of this article, and without prejudice to any other article of this Convention, States Parties are called upon to use as a guideline the relevant initiatives of regional, interregional and multilateral organizations against money-laundering.
5. States Parties shall endeavour to develop and promote global, regional, subregional and bilateral cooperation among judicial, law enforcement and financial regulatory authorities in order to combat money-laundering.

Chapter III Criminalization and law enforcement

Article 15 Bribery of national public officials

Each State Party shall adopt such legislative and other measures as may be necessary to establish as criminal offences, when committed intentionally:

(a) The promise, offering or giving, to a public official, directly or indirectly, of an undue advantage, for the official himself or herself or another person or entity, in order that the official act or refrain from acting in the exercise of his or her official duties;
(b) The solicitation or acceptance by a public official, directly or indirectly, of an undue advantage, for the official himself or herself or another person or entity, in order that the official act or refrain from acting in the exercise of his or her official duties.

Article 16 Bribery of foreign public officials and officials of public international organizations

1. Each State Party shall adopt such legislative and other measures as may be necessary to establish as a criminal offence, when committed intentionally, the promise, offering or giving to a foreign public official or an official of a public international organization, directly or indirectly, of an undue advantage, for the official himself or herself or another person or entity, in order that the official act or refrain from acting in the exercise of his or her official duties, in order to obtain or retain business or other undue advantage in relation to the conduct of international business.
2. Each State Party shall consider adopting such legislative and other measures as may be necessary to establish as a criminal offence, when committed intentionally, the

solicitation or acceptance by a foreign public official or an official of a public international organization, directly or indirectly, of an undue advantage, for the official himself or herself or another person or entity, in order that the official act or refrain from acting in the exercise of his or her official duties.

Article 17 Embezzlement, misappropriation or other diversion of property by a public official

Each State Party shall adopt such legislative and other measures as may be necessary to establish as criminal offences, when committed intentionally, the embezzlement, misappropriation or other diversion by a public official for his or her benefit or for the benefit of another person or entity, of any property, public or private funds or securities or any other thing of value entrusted to the public official by virtue of his or her position.

Article 18 Trading in influence

Each State Party shall consider adopting such legislative and other measures as may be necessary to establish as criminal offences, when committed intentionally:

(a) The promise, offering or giving to a public official or any other person, directly or indirectly, of an undue advantage in order that the public official or the person abuse his or her real or supposed influence with a view to obtaining from an administration or public authority of the State Party an undue advantage for the original instigator of the act or for any other person;

(b) The solicitation or acceptance by a public official or any other person, directly or indirectly, of an undue advantage for himself or herself or for another person in order that the public official or the person abuse his or her real or supposed influence with a view to obtaining from an administration or public authority of the State Party an undue advantage.

Article 19 Abuse of functions

Each State Party shall consider adopting such legislative and other measures as may be necessary to establish as a criminal offence, when committed intentionally, the abuse of functions or position, that is, the performance of or failure to perform an act, in violation of laws, by a public official in the discharge of his or her functions, for the purpose of obtaining an undue advantage for himself or herself or for another person or entity.

Article 20 Illicit enrichment

Subject to its constitution and the fundamental principles of its legal system, each State Party shall consider adopting such legislative and other measures as may be necessary to establish as a criminal offence, when committed intentionally, illicit enrichment, that is, a significant increase in the assets of a public official that he or she cannot reasonably explain in relation to his or her lawful income.

Article 21 Bribery in the private sector

Each State Party shall consider adopting such legislative and other measures as may be necessary to establish as criminal offences, when committed intentionally in the course of economic, financial or commercial activities:

(a) The promise, offering or giving, directly or indirectly, of an undue advantage to any person who directs or works, in any capacity, for a private sector entity, for the person himself or herself or for another person, in order that he or she, in breach of his or her duties, act or refrain from acting;
(b) The solicitation or acceptance, directly or indirectly, of an undue advantage by any person who directs or works, in any capacity, for a private sector entity, for the person himself or herself or for another person, in order that he or she, in breach of his or her duties, act or refrain from acting.

Article 22 Embezzlement of property in the private sector

Each State Party shall consider adopting such legislative and other measures as may be necessary to establish as a criminal offence, when committed intentionally in the course of economic, financial or commercial activities, embezzlement by a person who directs or works, in any capacity, in a private sector entity of any property, private funds or securities or any other thing of value entrusted to him or her by virtue of his or her position.

Article 23 Laundering of proceeds of crime

1. Each State Party shall adopt, in accordance with fundamental principles of its domestic law, such legislative and other measures as may be necessary to establish as criminal offences, when committed intentionally:
    (a) (i) The conversion or transfer of property, knowing that such property is the proceeds of crime, for the purpose of concealing or disguising the illicit origin of the property or of helping any person who is involved in the commission of the predicate offence to evade the legal consequences of his or her action;
    (ii) The concealment or disguise of the true nature, source, location, disposition, movement or ownership of or rights with respect to property, knowing that such property is the proceeds of crime;
    (b) Subject to the basic concepts of its legal system:
        (i) The acquisition, possession or use of property, knowing, at the time of receipt, that such property is the proceeds of crime;
        (ii) Participation in, association with or conspiracy to commit, attempts to commit and aiding, abetting, facilitating and counselling the commission of any of the offences established in accordance with this article.
2. For purposes of implementing or applying paragraph 1 of this article:
    (a) Each State Party shall seek to apply paragraph 1 of this article to the widest range of predicate offences;
    (b) Each State Party shall include as predicate offences at a minimum a comprehensive range of criminal offences established in accordance with this Convention;

(c) For the purposes of subparagraph (b) above, predicate offences shall include offences committed both within and outside the jurisdiction of the State Party in question. However, offences committed outside the jurisdiction of a State Party shall constitute predicate offences only when the relevant conduct is a criminal offence under the domestic law of the State where it is committed and would be a criminal offence under the domestic law of the State Party implementing or applying this article had it been committed there;

(d) Each State Party shall furnish copies of its laws that give effect to this article and of any subsequent changes to such laws or a description thereof to the Secretary-General of the United Nations;

(e) If required by fundamental principles of the domestic law of a State Party, it may be provided that the offences set forth in paragraph 1 of this article do not apply to the persons who committed the predicate offence.

Article 24 Concealment

Without prejudice to the provisions of article 23 of this Convention, each State Party shall consider adopting such legislative and other measures as may be necessary to establish as a criminal offence, when committed intentionally after the commission of any of the offences established in accordance with this Convention without having participated in such offences, the concealment or continued retention of property when the person involved knows that such property is the result of any of the offences established in accordance with this Convention.

Article 25 Obstruction of justice

Each State Party shall adopt such legislative and other measures as may be necessary to establish as criminal offences, when committed intentionally:

(a) The use of physical force, threats or intimidation or the promise, offering or giving of an undue advantage to induce false testimony or to interfere in the giving of testimony or the production of evidence in a proceeding in relation to the commission of offences established in accordance with this Convention;

(b) The use of physical force, threats or intimidation to interfere with the exercise of official duties by a justice or law enforcement official in relation to the commission of offences established in accordance with this Convention. Nothing in this subparagraph shall prejudice the right of States Parties to have legislation that protects other categories of public official.

Article 26 Liability of legal persons

1. Each State Party shall adopt such measures as may be necessary, consistent with its legal principles, to establish the liability of legal persons for participation in the offences established in accordance with this Convention.
2. Subject to the legal principles of the State Party, the liability of legal persons may be criminal, civil or administrative.

3. Such liability shall be without prejudice to the criminal liability of the natural persons who have committed the offences.
4. Each State Party shall, in particular, ensure that legal persons held liable in accordance with this article are subject to effective, proportionate and dissuasive criminal or non-criminal sanctions, including monetary sanctions.

Article 27 Participation and attempt

1. Each State Party shall adopt such legislative and other measures as may be necessary to establish as a criminal offence, in accordance with its domestic law, participation in any capacity such as an accomplice, assistant or instigator in an offence established in accordance with this Convention.
2. Each State Party may adopt such legislative and other measures as may be necessary to establish as a criminal offence, in accordance with its domestic law, any attempt to commit an offence established in accordance with this Convention.
3. Each State Party may adopt such legislative and other measures as may be necessary to establish as a criminal offence, in accordance with its domestic law, the preparation for an offence established in accordance with this Convention.

Article 28 Knowledge, intent and purpose as elements of an offence

Knowledge, intent or purpose required as an element of an offence established in accordance with this Convention may be inferred from objective factual circumstances.

Article 29 Statute of limitations

Each State Party shall, where appropriate, establish under its domestic law a long statute of limitations period in which to commence proceedings for any offence established in accordance with this Convention and establish a longer statute of limitations period or provide for the suspension of the statute of limitations where the alleged offender has evaded the administration of justice.

Article 30 Prosecution, adjudication and sanctions

1. Each State Party shall make the commission of an offence established in accordance with this Convention liable to sanctions that take into account the gravity of that offence.
2. Each State Party shall take such measures as may be necessary to establish or maintain, in accordance with its legal system and constitutional principles, an appropriate balance between any immunities or jurisdictional privileges accorded to its public officials for the performance of their functions and the possibility, when necessary, of effectively investigating, prosecuting and adjudicating offences established in accordance with this Convention.
3. Each State Party shall endeavour to ensure that any discretionary legal powers under its domestic law relating to the prosecution of persons for offences established in accordance with this Convention are exercised to maximize the effectiveness of law enforcement measures in respect of those offences and with due regard to the need to deter the commission of such offences.

4. In the case of offences established in accordance with this Convention, each State Party shall take appropriate measures, in accordance with its domestic law and with due regard to the rights of the defence, to seek to ensure that conditions imposed in connection with decisions on release pending trial or appeal take into consideration the need to ensure the presence of the defendant at subsequent criminal proceedings.
5. Each State Party shall take into account the gravity of the offences concerned when considering the eventuality of early release or parole of persons convicted of such offences.
6. Each State Party, to the extent consistent with the fundamental principles of its legal system, shall consider establishing procedures through which a public official accused of an offence established in accordance with this Convention may, where appropriate, be removed, suspended or reassigned by the appropriate authority, bearing in mind respect for the principle of the presumption of innocence.
7. Where warranted by the gravity of the offence, each State Party, to the extent consistent with the fundamental principles of its legal system, shall consider establishing procedures for the disqualification, by court order or any other appropriate means, for a period of time determined by its domestic law, of persons convicted of offences established in accordance with this Convention from:
   (a) Holding public office; and
   (b) Holding office in an enterprise owned in whole or in part by the State.
8. Paragraph 1 of this article shall be without prejudice to the exercise of disciplinary powers by the competent authorities against civil servants.
9. Nothing contained in this Convention shall affect the principle that the description of the offences established in accordance with this Convention and of the applicable legal defences or other legal principles controlling the lawfulness of conduct is reserved to the domestic law of a State Party and that such offences shall be prosecuted and punished in accordance with that law.
10. States Parties shall endeavour to promote the reintegration into society of persons convicted of offences established in accordance with this Convention.

Article 31 Freezing, seizure and confiscation

1. Each State Party shall take, to the greatest extent possible within its domestic legal system, such measures as may be necessary to enable confiscation of:
   (a) Proceeds of crime derived from offences established in accordance with this Convention or property the value of which corresponds to that of such proceeds;
   (b) Property, equipment or other instrumentalities used in or destined for use in offences established in accordance with this Convention.
2. Each State Party shall take such measures as may be necessary to enable the identification, tracing, freezing or seizure of any item referred to in paragraph 1 of this article for the purpose of eventual confiscation.
3. Each State Party shall adopt, in accordance with its domestic law, such legislative and other measures as may be necessary to regulate the administration by the competent authorities of frozen, seized or confiscated property covered in paragraphs 1 and 2 of this article.
4. If such proceeds of crime have been transformed or converted, in part or in full, into other property, such property shall be liable to the measures referred to in this article instead of the proceeds.

5. If such proceeds of crime have been intermingled with property acquired from legitimate sources, such property shall, without prejudice to any powers relating to freezing or seizure, be liable to confiscation up to the assessed value of the intermingled proceeds.
6. Income or other benefits derived from such proceeds of crime, from property into which such proceeds of crime have been transformed or converted or from property with which such proceeds of crime have been intermingled shall also be liable to the measures referred to in this article, in the same manner and to the same extent as proceeds of crime.
7. For the purpose of this article and article 55 of this Convention, each State Party shall empower its courts or other competent authorities to order that bank, financial or commercial records be made available or seized. A State Party shall not decline to act under the provisions of this paragraph on the ground of bank secrecy.
8. States Parties may consider the possibility of requiring that an offender demonstrate the lawful origin of such alleged proceeds of crime or other property liable to confiscation, to the extent that such a requirement is consistent with the fundamental principles of their domestic law and with the nature of judicial and other proceedings.
9. The provisions of this article shall not be so construed as to prejudice the rights of bona fide third parties.
10. Nothing contained in this article shall affect the principle that the measures to which it refers shall be defined and implemented in accordance with and subject to the provisions of the domestic law of a State Party.

Article 32 Protection of witnesses, experts and victims

1. Each State Party shall take appropriate measures in accordance with its domestic legal system and within its means to provide effective protection from potential retaliation or intimidation for witnesses and experts who give testimony concerning offences established in accordance with this Convention and, as appropriate, for their relatives and other persons close to them.
2. The measures envisaged in paragraph 1 of this article may include, inter alia, without prejudice to the rights of the defendant, including the right to due process:
   (a) Establishing procedures for the physical protection of such persons, such as, to the extent necessary and feasible, relocating them and permitting, where appropriate, non-disclosure or limitations on the disclosure of information concerning the identity and whereabouts of such persons;
   (b) Providing evidentiary rules to permit witnesses and experts to give testimony in a manner that ensures the safety of such persons, such as permitting testimony to be given through the use of communications technology such as video or other adequate means.
3. States Parties shall consider entering into agreements or arrangements with other States for the relocation of persons referred to in paragraph 1 of this article.
4. The provisions of this article shall also apply to victims insofar as they are witnesses.
5. Each State Party shall, subject to its domestic law, enable the views and concerns of victims to be presented and considered at appropriate stages of criminal proceedings against offenders in a manner not prejudicial to the rights of the defence.

Article 33 Protection of reporting persons

Each State Party shall consider incorporating into its domestic legal system appropriate measures to provide protection against any unjustified treatment for any person who reports in good faith and on reasonable grounds to the competent authorities any facts concerning offences established in accordance with this Convention.

Article 34 Consequences of acts of corruption

With due regard to the rights of third parties acquired in good faith, each State Party shall take measures, in accordance with the fundamental principles of its domestic law, to address consequences of corruption. In this context, States Parties may consider corruption a relevant factor in legal proceedings to annul or rescind a contract, withdraw a concession or other similar instrument or take any other remedial action.

Article 35 Compensation for damage

Each State Party shall take such measures as may be necessary, in accordance with principles of its domestic law, to ensure that entities or persons who have suffered damage as a result of an act of corruption have the right to initiate legal proceedings against those responsible for that damage in order to obtain compensation.

Article 36 Specialized authorities

Each State Party shall, in accordance with the fundamental principles of its legal system, ensure the existence of a body or bodies or persons specialized in combating corruption through law enforcement. Such body or bodies or persons shall be granted the necessary independence, in accordance with the fundamental principles of the legal system of the State Party, to be able to carry out their functions effectively and without any undue influence. Such persons or staff of such body or bodies should have the appropriate training and resources to carry out their tasks.

Article 37 Cooperation with law enforcement authorities

1. Each State Party shall take appropriate measures to encourage persons who participate or who have participated in the commission of an offence established in accordance with this Convention to supply information useful to competent authorities for investigative and evidentiary purposes and to provide factual, specific help to competent authorities that may contribute to depriving offenders of the proceeds of crime and to recovering such proceeds.
2. Each State Party shall consider providing for the possibility, in appropriate cases, of mitigating punishment of an accused person who provides substantial cooperation in the investigation or prosecution of an offence established in accordance with this Convention.
3. Each State Party shall consider providing for the possibility, in accordance with fundamental principles of its domestic law, of granting immunity from prosecution to a

person who provides substantial cooperation in the investigation or prosecution of an offence established in accordance with this Convention.

4. Protection of such persons shall be, mutatis mutandis, as provided for in article 32 of this Convention.
5. Where a person referred to in paragraph 1 of this article located in one State Party can provide substantial cooperation to the competent authorities of another State Party, the States Parties concerned may consider entering into agreements or arrangements, in accordance with their domestic law, concerning the potential provision by the other State Party of the treatment set forth in paragraphs 2 and 3 of this article.

Article 38 Cooperation between national authorities

Each State Party shall take such measures as may be necessary to encourage, in accordance with its domestic law, cooperation between, on the one hand, its public authorities, as well as its public officials, and, on the other hand, its authorities responsible for investigating and prosecuting criminal offences. Such cooperation may include:

(a) Informing the latter authorities, on their own initiative, where there are reasonable grounds to believe that any of the offences established in accordance with articles 15, 21 and 23 of this Convention has been committed; or
(b) Providing, upon request, to the latter authorities all necessary information.

Article 39 Cooperation between national authorities and the private sector

1. Each State Party shall take such measures as may be necessary to encourage, in accordance with its domestic law, cooperation between national investigating and prosecuting authorities and entities of the private sector, in particular financial institutions, relating to matters involving the commission of offences established in accordance with this Convention.
2. Each State Party shall consider encouraging its nationals and other persons with a habitual residence in its territory to report to the national investigating and prosecuting authorities the commission of an offence established in accordance with this Convention.

Article 40 Bank secrecy

Each State Party shall ensure that, in the case of domestic criminal investigations of offences established in accordance with this Convention, there are appropriate mechanisms available within its domestic legal system to overcome obstacles that may arise out of the application of bank secrecy laws.

Article 41 Criminal record

Each State Party may adopt such legislative or other measures as may be necessary to take into consideration, under such terms as and for the purpose that it deems appropriate, any previous conviction in another State of an alleged offender for the purpose of using such information in criminal proceedings relating to an offence established in accordance with this Convention.

Article 42 Jurisdiction

1. Each State Party shall adopt such measures as may be necessary to establish its jurisdiction over the offences established in accordance with this Convention when:
   (a) The offence is committed in the territory of that State Party; or
   (b) The offence is committed on board a vessel that is flying the flag of that State Party or an aircraft that is registered under the laws of that State Party at the time that the offence is committed.
2. Subject to article 4 of this Convention, a State Party may also establish its jurisdiction over any such offence when:
   (a) The offence is committed against a national of that State Party; or
   (b) The offence is committed by a national of that State Party or a stateless person who has his or her habitual residence in its territory; or
   (c) The offence is one of those established in accordance with article 23, paragraph 1 (b) (ii), of this Convention and is committed outside its territory with a view to the commission of an offence established in accordance with article 23, paragraph 1 (a) (i) or (ii) or (b) (i), of this Convention within its territory; or
   (d) The offence is committed against the State Party.
3. For the purposes of article 44 of this Convention, each State Party shall take such measures as may be necessary to establish its jurisdiction over the offences established in accordance with this Convention when the alleged offender is present in its territory and it does not extradite such person solely on the ground that he or she is one of its nationals.
4. Each State Party may also take such measures as may be necessary to establish its jurisdiction over the offences established in accordance with this Convention when the alleged offender is present in its territory and it does not extradite him or her.
5. If a State Party exercising its jurisdiction under paragraph 1 or 2 of this article has been notified, or has otherwise learned, that any other States Parties are conducting an investigation, prosecution or judicial proceeding in respect of the same conduct, the competent authorities of those States Parties shall, as appropriate, consult one another with a view to coordinating their actions.
6. Without prejudice to norms of general international law, this Convention shall not exclude the exercise of any criminal jurisdiction established by a State Party in accordance with its domestic law.

Chapter IV International cooperation

Article 43 International cooperation

1. States Parties shall cooperate in criminal matters in accordance with articles 44 to 50 of this Convention. Where appropriate and consistent with their domestic legal system, States Parties shall consider assisting each other in investigations of and proceedings in civil and administrative matters relating to corruption.
2. In matters of international cooperation, whenever dual criminality is considered a requirement, it shall be deemed fulfilled irrespective of whether the laws of the requested State Party place the offence within the same category of offence or denominate the offence by the same terminology as the requesting State Party, if the conduct underlying the offence for which assistance is sought is a criminal offence under the laws of both States Parties.

Article 44 Extradition

1. This article shall apply to the offences established in accordance with this Convention where the person who is the subject of the request for extradition is present in the territory of the requested State Party, provided that the offence for which extradition is sought is punishable under the domestic law of both the requesting State Party and the requested State Party.
2. Notwithstanding the provisions of paragraph 1 of this article, a State Party whose law so permits may grant the extradition of a person for any of the offences covered by this Convention that are not punishable under its own domestic law.
3. If the request for extradition includes several separate offences, at least one of which is extraditable under this article and some of which are not extraditable by reason of their period of imprisonment but are related to offences established in accordance with this Convention, the requested State Party may apply this article also in respect of those offences.
4. Each of the offences to which this article applies shall be deemed to be included as an extraditable offence in any extradition treaty existing between States Parties. States Parties undertake to include such offences as extraditable offences in every extradition treaty to be concluded between them. A State Party whose law so permits, in case it uses this Convention as the basis for extradition, shall not consider any of the offences established in accordance with this Convention to be a political offence.
5. If a State Party that makes extradition conditional on the existence of a treaty receives a request for extradition from another State Party with which it has no extradition treaty, it may consider this Convention the legal basis for extradition in respect of any offence to which this article applies.
6. A State Party that makes extradition conditional on the existence of a treaty shall:
   (a) At the time of deposit of its instrument of ratification, acceptance or approval of or accession to this Convention, inform the Secretary-General of the United Nations whether it will take this Convention as the legal basis for cooperation on extradition with other States Parties to this Convention; and
   (b) If it does not take this Convention as the legal basis for cooperation on extradition, seek, where appropriate, to conclude treaties on extradition with other States Parties to this Convention in order to implement this article.
7. States Parties that do not make extradition conditional on the existence of a treaty shall recognize offences to which this article applies as extraditable offences between themselves.
8. Extradition shall be subject to the conditions provided for by the domestic law of the requested State Party or by applicable extradition treaties, including, inter alia, conditions in relation to the minimum penalty requirement for extradition and the grounds upon which the requested State Party may refuse extradition.
9. States Parties shall, subject to their domestic law, endeavour to expedite extradition procedures and to simplify evidentiary requirements relating thereto in respect of any offence to which this article applies.
10. Subject to the provisions of its domestic law and its extradition treaties, the requested State Party may, upon being satisfied that the circumstances so warrant and are urgent and at the request of the requesting State Party, take a person whose extradition is

sought and who is present in its territory into custody or take other appropriate measures to ensure his or her presence at extradition proceedings.

11. A State Party in whose territory an alleged offender is found, if it does not extradite such person in respect of an offence to which this article applies solely on the ground that he or she is one of its nationals, shall, at the request of the State Party seeking extradition, be obliged to submit the case without undue delay to its competent authorities for the purpose of prosecution. Those authorities shall take their decision and conduct their proceedings in the same manner as in the case of any other offence of a grave nature under the domestic law of that State Party. The States Parties concerned shall cooperate with each other, in particular on procedural and evidentiary aspects, to ensure the efficiency of such prosecution.
12. Whenever a State Party is permitted under its domestic law to extradite or otherwise surrender one of its nationals only upon the condition that the person will be returned to that State Party to serve the sentence imposed as a result of the trial or proceedings for which the extradition or surrender of the person was sought and that State Party and the State Party seeking the extradition of the person agree with this option and other terms that they may deem appropriate, such conditional extradition or surrender shall be sufficient to discharge the obligation set forth in paragraph 11 of this article.
13. If extradition, sought for purposes of enforcing a sentence, is refused because the person sought is a national of the requested State Party, the requested State Party shall, if its domestic law so permits and in conformity with the requirements of such law, upon application of the requesting State Party, consider the enforcement of the sentence imposed under the domestic law of the requesting State Party or the remainder thereof.
14. Any person regarding whom proceedings are being carried out in connection with any of the offences to which this article applies shall be guaranteed fair treatment at all stages of the proceedings, including enjoyment of all the rights and guarantees provided by the domestic law of the State Party in the territory of which that person is present.
15. Nothing in this Convention shall be interpreted as imposing an obligation to extradite if the requested State Party has substantial grounds for believing that the request has been made for the purpose of prosecuting or punishing a person on account of that person's sex, race, religion, nationality, ethnic origin or political opinions or that compliance with the request would cause prejudice to that person's position for any one of these reasons.
16. States Parties may not refuse a request for extradition on the sole ground that the offence is also considered to involve fiscal matters.
17. Before refusing extradition, the requested State Party shall, where appropriate, consult with the requesting State Party to provide it with ample opportunity to present its opinions and to provide information relevant to its allegation.
18. States Parties shall seek to conclude bilateral and multilateral agreements or arrangements to carry out or to enhance the effectiveness of extradition.

Article 45 Transfer of sentenced persons

States Parties may consider entering into bilateral or multilateral agreements or arrangements on the transfer to their territory of persons sentenced to imprisonment or other forms of deprivation of liberty for offences established in accordance with this Convention in order that they may complete their sentences there.

Article 46 Mutual legal assistance

1. States Parties shall afford one another the widest measure of mutual legal assistance in investigations, prosecutions and judicial proceedings in relation to the offences covered by this Convention.
2. Mutual legal assistance shall be afforded to the fullest extent possible under relevant laws, treaties, agreements and arrangements of the requested State Party with respect to investigations, prosecutions and judicial proceedings in relation to the offences for which a legal person may be held liable in accordance with article 26 of this Convention in the requesting State Party.
3. Mutual legal assistance to be afforded in accordance with this article may be requested for any of the following purposes:
   (a) Taking evidence or statements from persons;
   (b) Effecting service of judicial documents;
   (c) Executing searches and seizures, and freezing;
   (d) Examining objects and sites;
   (e) Providing information, evidentiary items and expert evaluations;
   (f) Providing originals or certified copies of relevant documents and records, including government, bank, financial, corporate or business records;
   (g) Identifying or tracing proceeds of crime, property, instrumentalities or other things for evidentiary purposes;
   (h) Facilitating the voluntary appearance of persons in the requesting State Party;
   (i) Any other type of assistance that is not contrary to the domestic law of the requested State Party;
   (j) Identifying, freezing and tracing proceeds of crime in accordance with the provisions of chapter V of this Convention;
   (k) The recovery of assets, in accordance with the provisions of chapter V of this Convention.
4. Without prejudice to domestic law, the competent authorities of a State Party may, without prior request, transmit information relating to criminal matters to a competent authority in another State Party where they believe that such information could assist the authority in undertaking or successfully concluding inquiries and criminal proceedings or could result in a request formulated by the latter State Party pursuant to this Convention.
5. The transmission of information pursuant to paragraph 4 of this article shall be without prejudice to inquiries and criminal proceedings in the State of the competent authorities providing the information. The competent authorities receiving the information shall comply with a request that said information remain confidential, even temporarily, or with restrictions on its use. However, this shall not prevent the receiving State Party from disclosing in its proceedings information that is exculpatory to an accused person. In such a case, the receiving State Party shall notify the transmitting State Party prior to the disclosure and, if so requested, consult with the transmitting State Party. If, in an exceptional case, advance notice is not possible, the receiving State Party shall inform the transmitting State Party of the disclosure without delay.
6. The provisions of this article shall not affect the obligations under any other treaty, bilateral or multilateral, that governs or will govern, in whole or in part, mutual legal assistance.

7. Paragraphs 9 to 29 of this article shall apply to requests made pursuant to this article if the States Parties in question are not bound by a treaty of mutual legal assistance. If those States Parties are bound by such a treaty, the corresponding provisions of that treaty shall apply unless the States Parties agree to apply paragraphs 9 to 29 of this article in lieu thereof. States Parties are strongly encouraged to apply those paragraphs if they facilitate cooperation.
8. States Parties shall not decline to render mutual legal assistance pursuant to this article on the ground of bank secrecy.
9. (a) A requested State Party, in responding to a request for assistance pursuant to this article in the absence of dual criminality, shall take into account the purposes of this Convention, as set forth in article 1;
   (b) States Parties may decline to render assistance pursuant to this article on the ground of absence of dual criminality. However, a requested State Party shall, where consistent with the basic concepts of its legal system, render assistance that does not involve coercive action. Such assistance may be refused when requests involve matters of a *de minimis* nature or matters for which the cooperation or assistance sought is available under other provisions of this Convention;
   (c) Each State Party may consider adopting such measures as may be necessary to enable it to provide a wider scope of assistance pursuant to this article in the absence of dual criminality.
10. A person who is being detained or is serving a sentence in the territory of one State Party whose presence in another State Party is requested for purposes of identification, testimony or otherwise providing assistance in obtaining evidence for investigations, prosecutions or judicial proceedings in relation to offences covered by this Convention may be transferred if the following conditions are met:
    (a) The person freely gives his or her informed consent;
    (b) The competent authorities of both States Parties agree, subject to such conditions as those States Parties may deem appropriate.
11. For the purposes of paragraph 10 of this article:
    (a) The State Party to which the person is transferred shall have the authority and obligation to keep the person transferred in custody, unless otherwise requested or authorized by the State Party from which the person was transferred;
    (b) The State Party to which the person is transferred shall without delay implement its obligation to return the person to the custody of the State Party from which the person was transferred as agreed beforehand, or as otherwise agreed, by the competent authorities of both States Parties;
    (c) The State Party to which the person is transferred shall not require the State Party from which the person was transferred to initiate extradition proceedings for the return of the person;
    (d) The person transferred shall receive credit for service of the sentence being served in the State from which he or she was transferred for time spent in the custody of the State Party to which he or she was transferred.
12. Unless the State Party from which a person is to be transferred in accordance with paragraphs 10 and 11 of this article so agrees, that person, whatever his or her nationality, shall not be prosecuted, detained, punished or subjected to any other restriction of his or her personal liberty in the territory of the State to which that person is transferred in

respect of acts, omissions or convictions prior to his or her departure from the territory of the State from which he or she was transferred.

13. Each State Party shall designate a central authority that shall have the responsibility and power to receive requests for mutual legal assistance and either to execute them or to transmit them to the competent authorities for execution. Where a State Party has a special region or territory with a separate system of mutual legal assistance, it may designate a distinct central authority that shall have the same function for that region or territory. Central authorities shall ensure the speedy and proper execution or transmission of the requests received. Where the central authority transmits the request to a competent authority for execution, it shall encourage the speedy and proper execution of the request by the competent authority. The Secretary-General of the United Nations shall be notified of the central authority designated for this purpose at the time each State Party deposits its instrument of ratification, acceptance or approval of or accession to this Convention. Requests for mutual legal assistance and any communication related thereto shall be transmitted to the central authorities designated by the States Parties. This requirement shall be without prejudice to the right of a State Party to require that such requests and communications be addressed to it through diplomatic channels and, in urgent circumstances, where the States Parties agree, through the International Criminal Police Organization, if possible.
14. Requests shall be made in writing or, where possible, by any means capable of producing a written record, in a language acceptable to the requested State Party, under conditions allowing that State Party to establish authenticity. The Secretary-General of the United Nations shall be notified of the language or languages acceptable to each State Party at the time it deposits its instrument of ratification, acceptance or approval of or accession to this Convention. In urgent circumstances and where agreed by the States Parties, requests may be made orally but shall be confirmed in writing forthwith.
15. A request for mutual legal assistance shall contain:
    (a) The identity of the authority making the request;
    (b) The subject matter and nature of the investigation, prosecution or judicial proceeding to which the request relates and the name and functions of the authority conducting the investigation, prosecution or judicial proceeding;
    (c) A summary of the relevant facts, except in relation to requests for the purpose of service of judicial documents;
    (d) A description of the assistance sought and details of any particular procedure that the requesting State Party wishes to be followed;
    (e) Where possible, the identity, location and nationality of any person concerned; and
    (f) The purpose for which the evidence, information or action is sought.
16. The requested State Party may request additional information when it appears necessary for the execution of the request in accordance with its domestic law or when it can facilitate such execution.
17. A request shall be executed in accordance with the domestic law of the requested State Party and, to the extent not contrary to the domestic law of the requested State Party and where possible, in accordance with the procedures specified in the request.
18. Wherever possible and consistent with fundamental principles of domestic law, when an individual is in the territory of a State Party and has to be heard as a witness or expert by the judicial authorities of another State Party, the first State Party may, at the request

of the other, permit the hearing to take place by video conference if it is not possible or desirable for the individual in question to appear in person in the territory of the requesting State Party. States Parties may agree that the hearing shall be conducted by a judicial authority of the requesting State Party and attended by a judicial authority of the requested State Party.

19. The requesting State Party shall not transmit or use information or evidence furnished by the requested State Party for investigations, prosecutions or judicial proceedings other than those stated in the request without the prior consent of the requested State Party. Nothing in this paragraph shall prevent the requesting State Party from disclosing in its proceedings information or evidence that is exculpatory to an accused person. In the latter case, the requesting State Party shall notify the requested State Party prior to the disclosure and, if so requested, consult with the requested State Party. If, in an exceptional case, advance notice is not possible, the requesting State Party shall inform the requested State Party of the disclosure without delay.
20. The requesting State Party may require that the requested State Party keep confidential the fact and substance of the request, except to the extent necessary to execute the request. If the requested State Party cannot comply with the requirement of confidentiality, it shall promptly inform the requesting State Party.
21. Mutual legal assistance may be refused:
    (a) If the request is not made in conformity with the provisions of this article;
    (b) If the requested State Party considers that execution of the request is likely to prejudice its sovereignty, security, *ordre public* or other essential interests;
    (c) If the authorities of the requested State Party would be prohibited by its domestic law from carrying out the action requested with regard to any similar offence, had it been subject to investigation, prosecution or judicial proceedings under their own jurisdiction;
    (d) If it would be contrary to the legal system of the requested State Party relating to mutual legal assistance for the request to be granted.
22. States Parties may not refuse a request for mutual legal assistance on the sole ground that the offence is also considered to involve fiscal matters.
23. Reasons shall be given for any refusal of mutual legal assistance.
24. The requested State Party shall execute the request for mutual legal assistance as soon as possible and shall take as full account as possible of any deadlines suggested by the requesting State Party and for which reasons are given, preferably in the request. The requesting State Party may make reasonable requests for information on the status and progress of measures taken by the requested State Party to satisfy its request. The requested State Party shall respond to reasonable requests by the requesting State Party on the status, and progress in its handling, of the request. The requesting State Party shall promptly inform the requested State Party when the assistance sought is no longer required.
25. Mutual legal assistance may be postponed by the requested State Party on the ground that it interferes with an ongoing investigation, prosecution or judicial proceeding.
26. Before refusing a request pursuant to paragraph 21 of this article or postponing its execution pursuant to paragraph 25 of this article, the requested State Party shall consult with the requesting State Party to consider whether assistance may be granted subject

to such terms and conditions as it deems necessary. If the requesting State Party accepts assistance subject to those conditions, it shall comply with the conditions.

27. Without prejudice to the application of paragraph 12 of this article, a witness, expert or other person who, at the request of the requesting State Party, consents to give evidence in a proceeding or to assist in an investigation, prosecution or judicial proceeding in the territory of the requesting State Party shall not be prosecuted, detained, punished or subjected to any other restriction of his or her personal liberty in that territory in respect of acts, omissions or convictions prior to his or her departure from the territory of the requested State Party. Such safe conduct shall cease when the witness, expert or other person having had, for a period of fifteen consecutive days or for any period agreed upon by the States Parties from the date on which he or she has been officially informed that his or her presence is no longer required by the judicial authorities, an opportunity of leaving, has nevertheless remained voluntarily in the territory of the requesting State Party or, having left it, has returned of his or her own free will.
28. The ordinary costs of executing a request shall be borne by the requested State Party, unless otherwise agreed by the States Parties concerned. If expenses of a substantial or extraordinary nature are or will be required to fulfil the request, the States Parties shall consult to determine the terms and conditions under which the request will be executed, as well as the manner in which the costs shall be borne.
29. The requested State Party:
    (a) Shall provide to the requesting State Party copies of government records, documents or information in its possession that under its domestic law are available to the general public;
    (b) May, at its discretion, provide to the requesting State Party in whole, in part or subject to such conditions as it deems appropriate, copies of any government records, documents or information in its possession that under its domestic law are not available to the general public.
30. States Parties shall consider, as may be necessary, the possibility of concluding bilateral or multilateral agreements or arrangements that would serve the purposes of, give practical effect to or enhance the provisions of this article.

Article 47 Transfer of criminal proceedings

States Parties shall consider the possibility of transferring to one another proceedings for the prosecution of an offence established in accordance with this Convention in cases where such transfer is considered to be in the interests of the proper administration of justice, in particular in cases where several jurisdictions are involved, with a view to concentrating the prosecution.

Article 48 Law enforcement cooperation

1. States Parties shall cooperate closely with one another, consistent with their respective domestic legal and administrative systems, to enhance the effectiveness of law enforcement action to combat the offences covered by this Convention. States Parties shall, in particular, take effective measures:
    (a) To enhance and, where necessary, to establish channels of communication between their competent authorities, agencies and services in order to facilitate the secure

and rapid exchange of information concerning all aspects of the offences covered by this Convention, including, if the States Parties concerned deem it appropriate, links with other criminal activities;

(b) To cooperate with other States Parties in conducting inquiries with respect to offences covered by this Convention concerning:
   (i) The identity, whereabouts and activities of persons suspected of involvement in such offences or the location of other persons concerned;
   (ii) The movement of proceeds of crime or property derived from the commission of such offences;
   (iii) The movement of property, equipment or other instrumentalities used or intended for use in the commission of such offences;

(c) To provide, where appropriate, necessary items or quantities of substances for analytical or investigative purposes;

(d) To exchange, where appropriate, information with other States Parties concerning specific means and methods used to commit offences covered by this Convention, including the use of false identities, forged, altered or false documents and other means of concealing activities;

(e) To facilitate effective coordination between their competent authorities, agencies and services and to promote the exchange of personnel and other experts, including, subject to bilateral agreements or arrangements between the States Parties concerned, the posting of liaison officers;

(f) To exchange information and coordinate administrative and other measures taken as appropriate for the purpose of early identification of the offences covered by this Convention.

2. With a view to giving effect to this Convention, States Parties shall consider entering into bilateral or multilateral agreements or arrangements on direct cooperation between their law enforcement agencies and, where such agreements or arrangements already exist, amending them. In the absence of such agreements or arrangements between the States Parties concerned, the States Parties may consider this Convention to be the basis for mutual law enforcement cooperation in respect of the offences covered by this Convention. Whenever appropriate, States Parties shall make full use of agreements or arrangements, including international or regional organizations, to enhance the cooperation between their law enforcement agencies.
3. States Parties shall endeavour to cooperate within their means to respond to offences covered by this Convention committed through the use of modern technology.

Article 49 Joint investigations

States Parties shall consider concluding bilateral or multilateral agreements or arrangements whereby, in relation to matters that are the subject of investigations, prosecutions or judicial proceedings in one or more States, the competent authorities concerned may establish joint investigative bodies. In the absence of such agreements or arrangements, joint investigations may be undertaken by agreement on a case-by-case basis. The States Parties involved shall ensure that the sovereignty of the State Party in whose territory such investigation is to take place is fully respected.

Article 50 Special investigative techniques

1. In order to combat corruption effectively, each State Party shall, to the extent permitted by the basic principles of its domestic legal system and in accordance with the conditions prescribed by its domestic law, take such measures as may be necessary, within its means, to allow for the appropriate use by its competent authorities of controlled delivery and, where it deems appropriate, other special investigative techniques, such as electronic or other forms of surveillance and undercover operations, within its territory, and to allow for the admissibility in court of evidence derived therefrom.
2. For the purpose of investigating the offences covered by this Convention, States Parties are encouraged to conclude, when necessary, appropriate bilateral or multilateral agreements or arrangements for using such special investigative techniques in the context of cooperation at the international level. Such agreements or arrangements shall be concluded and implemented in full compliance with the principle of sovereign equality of States and shall be carried out strictly in accordance with the terms of those agreements or arrangements.
3. In the absence of an agreement or arrangement as set forth in paragraph 2 of this article, decisions to use such special investigative techniques at the international level shall be made on a case-by-case basis and may, when necessary, take into consideration financial arrangements and understandings with respect to the exercise of jurisdiction by the States Parties concerned.
4. Decisions to use controlled delivery at the international level may, with the consent of the States Parties concerned, include methods such as intercepting and allowing the goods or funds to continue intact or be removed or replaced in whole or in part.

Chapter V Asset recovery

Article 51 General provision

The return of assets pursuant to this chapter is a fundamental principle of this Convention, and States Parties shall afford one another the widest measure of cooperation and assistance in this regard.

Article 52 Prevention and detection of transfers of proceeds of crime

1. Without prejudice to article 14 of this Convention, each State Party shall take such measures as may be necessary, in accordance with its domestic law, to require financial institutions within its jurisdiction to verify the identity of customers, to take reasonable steps to determine the identity of beneficial owners of funds deposited into high-value accounts and to conduct enhanced scrutiny of accounts sought or maintained by or on behalf of individuals who are, or have been, entrusted with prominent public functions and their family members and close associates. Such enhanced scrutiny shall be reasonably designed to detect suspicious transactions for the purpose of reporting to competent authorities and should not be so construed as to discourage or prohibit financial institutions from doing business with any legitimate customer.
2. In order to facilitate implementation of the measures provided for in paragraph 1 of this article, each State Party, in accordance with its domestic law and inspired by relevant

initiatives of regional, interregional and multilateral organizations against money-laundering, shall:

(a) Issue advisories regarding the types of natural or legal person to whose accounts financial institutions within its jurisdiction will be expected to apply enhanced scrutiny, the types of accounts and transactions to which to pay particular attention and appropriate account-opening, maintenance and record-keeping measures to take concerning such accounts; and

(b) Where appropriate, notify financial institutions within its jurisdiction, at the request of another State Party or on its own initiative, of the identity of particular natural or legal persons to whose accounts such institutions will be expected to apply enhanced scrutiny, in addition to those whom the financial institutions may otherwise identify.

3. In the context of paragraph 2 (a) of this article, each State Party shall implement measures to ensure that its financial institutions maintain adequate records, over an appropriate period of time, of accounts and transactions involving the persons mentioned in paragraph 1 of this article, which should, as a minimum, contain information relating to the identity of the customer as well as, as far as possible, of the beneficial owner.
4. With the aim of preventing and detecting transfers of proceeds of offences established in accordance with this Convention, each State Party shall implement appropriate and effective measures to prevent, with the help of its regulatory and oversight bodies, the establishment of banks that have no physical presence and that are not affiliated with a regulated financial group. Moreover, States Parties may consider requiring their financial institutions to refuse to enter into or continue a correspondent banking relationship with such institutions and to guard against establishing relations with foreign financial institutions that permit their accounts to be used by banks that have no physical presence and that are not affiliated with a regulated financial group.
5. Each State Party shall consider establishing, in accordance with its domestic law, effective financial disclosure systems for appropriate public officials and shall provide for appropriate sanctions for non-compliance. Each State Party shall also consider taking such measures as may be necessary to permit its competent authorities to share that information with the competent authorities in other States Parties when necessary to investigate, claim and recover proceeds of offences established in accordance with this Convention.
6. Each State Party shall consider taking such measures as may be necessary, in accordance with its domestic law, to require appropriate public officials having an interest in or signature or other authority over a financial account in a foreign country to report that relationship to appropriate authorities and to maintain appropriate records related to such accounts. Such measures shall also provide for appropriate sanctions for non-compliance.

Article 53 Measures for direct recovery of property

Each State Party shall, in accordance with its domestic law:

(a) Take such measures as may be necessary to permit another State Party to initiate civil action in its courts to establish title to or ownership of property acquired through the commission of an offence established in accordance with this Convention;

(b) Take such measures as may be necessary to permit its courts to order those who have committed offences established in accordance with this Convention to pay compensation or damages to another State Party that has been harmed by such offences; and
(c) Take such measures as may be necessary to permit its courts or competent authorities, when having to decide on confiscation, to recognize another State Party's claim as a legitimate owner of property acquired through the commission of an offence established in accordance with this Convention.

Article 54 Mechanisms for recovery of property through international cooperation in confiscation

1. Each State Party, in order to provide mutual legal assistance pursuant to article 55 of this Convention with respect to property acquired through or involved in the commission of an offence established in accordance with this Convention, shall, in accordance with its domestic law:
   (a) Take such measures as may be necessary to permit its competent authorities to give effect to an order of confiscation issued by a court of another State Party;
   (b) Take such measures as may be necessary to permit its competent authorities, where they have jurisdiction, to order the confiscation of such property of foreign origin by adjudication of an offence of money-laundering or such other offence as may be within its jurisdiction or by other procedures authorized under its domestic law; and
   (c) Consider taking such measures as may be necessary to allow confiscation of such property without a criminal conviction in cases in which the offender cannot be prosecuted by reason of death, flight or absence or in other appropriate cases.
2. Each State Party, in order to provide mutual legal assistance upon a request made pursuant to paragraph 2 of article 55 of this Convention, shall, in accordance with its domestic law:
   (a) Take such measures as may be necessary to permit its competent authorities to freeze or seize property upon a freezing or seizure order issued by a court or competent authority of a requesting State Party that provides a reasonable basis for the requested State Party to believe that there are sufficient grounds for taking such actions and that the property would eventually be subject to an order of confiscation for purposes of paragraph 1 (a) of this article;
   (b) Take such measures as may be necessary to permit its competent authorities to freeze or seize property upon a request that provides a reasonable basis for the requested State Party to believe that there are sufficient grounds for taking such actions and that the property would eventually be subject to an order of confiscation for purposes of paragraph 1 (a) of this article; and
   (c) Consider taking additional measures to permit its competent authorities to preserve property for confiscation, such as on the basis of a foreign arrest or criminal charge related to the acquisition of such property.

Article 55 International cooperation for purposes of confiscation

1. A State Party that has received a request from another State Party having jurisdiction over an offence established in accordance with this Convention for confiscation of

proceeds of crime, property, equipment or other instrumentalities referred to in article 31, paragraph 1, of this Convention situated in its territory shall, to the greatest extent possible within its domestic legal system:

(a) Submit the request to its competent authorities for the purpose of obtaining an order of confiscation and, if such an order is granted, give effect to it; or

(b) Submit to its competent authorities, with a view to giving effect to it to the extent requested, an order of confiscation issued by a court in the territory of the requesting State Party in accordance with articles 31, paragraph 1, and 54, paragraph 1 (a), of this Convention insofar as it relates to proceeds of crime, property, equipment or other instrumentalities referred to in article 31, paragraph 1, situated in the territory of the requested State Party.

2. Following a request made by another State Party having jurisdiction over an offence established in accordance with this Convention, the requested State Party shall take measures to identify, trace and freeze or seize proceeds of crime, property, equipment or other instrumentalities referred to in article 31, paragraph 1, of this Convention for the purpose of eventual confiscation to be ordered either by the requesting State Party or, pursuant to a request under paragraph 1 of this article, by the requested State Party.
3. The provisions of article 46 of this Convention are applicable, mutatis mutandis, to this article. In addition to the information specified in article 46, paragraph 15, requests made pursuant to this article shall contain:

   (a) In the case of a request pertaining to paragraph 1 (a) of this article, a description of the property to be confiscated, including, to the extent possible, the location and, where relevant, the estimated value of the property and a statement of the facts relied upon by the requesting State Party sufficient to enable the requested State Party to seek the order under its domestic law;

   (b) In the case of a request pertaining to paragraph 1 (b) of this article, a legally admissible copy of an order of confiscation upon which the request is based issued by the requesting State Party, a statement of the facts and information as to the extent to which execution of the order is requested, a statement specifying the measures taken by the requesting State Party to provide adequate notification to bona fide third parties and to ensure due process and a statement that the confiscation order is final;

   (c) In the case of a request pertaining to paragraph 2 of this article, a statement of the facts relied upon by the requesting State Party and a description of the actions requested and, where available, a legally admissible copy of an order on which the request is based.

4. The decisions or actions provided for in paragraphs 1 and 2 of this article shall be taken by the requested State Party in accordance with and subject to the provisions of its domestic law and its procedural rules or any bilateral or multilateral agreement or arrangement to which it may be bound in relation to the requesting State Party.
5. Each State Party shall furnish copies of its laws and regulations that give effect to this article and of any subsequent changes to such laws and regulations or a description thereof to the Secretary-General of the United Nations.
6. If a State Party elects to make the taking of the measures referred to in paragraphs 1 and 2 of this article conditional on the existence of a relevant treaty, that State Party shall consider this Convention the necessary and sufficient treaty basis.

7. Cooperation under this article may also be refused or provisional measures lifted if the requested State Party does not receive sufficient and timely evidence or if the property is of a *de minimis* value.
8. Before lifting any provisional measure taken pursuant to this article, the requested State Party shall, wherever possible, give the requesting State Party an opportunity to present its reasons in favour of continuing the measure.
9. The provisions of this article shall not be construed as prejudicing the rights of bona fide third parties.

Article 56 Special cooperation

Without prejudice to its domestic law, each State Party shall endeavour to take measures to permit it to forward, without prejudice to its own investigations, prosecutions or judicial proceedings, information on proceeds of offences established in accordance with this Convention to another State Party without prior request, when it considers that the disclosure of such information might assist the receiving State Party in initiating or carrying out investigations, prosecutions or judicial proceedings or might lead to a request by that State Party under this chapter of the Convention.

Article 57 Return and disposal of assets

1. Property confiscated by a State Party pursuant to articles 31 or 55 of this Convention shall be disposed of, including by return to its prior legitimate owners, pursuant to paragraph 3 of this article, by that State Party in accordance with the provisions of this Convention and its domestic law.
2. Each State Party shall adopt such legislative and other measures, in accordance with the fundamental principles of its domestic law, as may be necessary to enable its competent authorities to return confiscated property, when acting on the request made by another State Party, in accordance with this Convention, taking into account the rights of bona fide third parties.
3. In accordance with articles 46 and 55 of this Convention and paragraphs 1 and 2 of this article, the requested State Party shall:
   (a) In the case of embezzlement of public funds or of laundering of embezzled public funds as referred to in articles 17 and 23 of this Convention, when confiscation was executed in accordance with article 55 and on the basis of a final judgment in the requesting State Party, a requirement that can be waived by the requested State Party, return the confiscated property to the requesting State Party;
   (b) In the case of proceeds of any other offence covered by this Convention, when the confiscation was executed in accordance with article 55 of this Convention and on the basis of a final judgment in the requesting State Party, a requirement that can be waived by the requested State Party, return the confiscated property to the requesting State Party, when the requesting State Party reasonably establishes its prior ownership of such confiscated property to the requested State Party or when the requested State Party recognizes damage to the requesting State Party as a basis for returning the confiscated property;

   (c) In all other cases, give priority consideration to returning confiscated property to the requesting State Party, returning such property to its prior legitimate owners or compensating the victims of the crime.
4. Where appropriate, unless States Parties decide otherwise, the requested State Party may deduct reasonable expenses incurred in investigations, prosecutions or judicial proceedings leading to the return or disposition of confiscated property pursuant to this article.
5. Where appropriate, States Parties may also give special consideration to concluding agreements or mutually acceptable arrangements, on a case-by-case basis, for the final disposal of confiscated property.

Article 58 Financial intelligence unit

States Parties shall cooperate with one another for the purpose of preventing and combating the transfer of proceeds of offences established in accordance with this Convention and of promoting ways and means of recovering such proceeds and, to that end, shall consider establishing a financial intelligence unit to be responsible for receiving, analysing and disseminating to the competent authorities reports of suspicious financial transactions.

Article 59 Bilateral and multilateral agreements and arrangements

States Parties shall consider concluding bilateral or multilateral agreements or arrangements to enhance the effectiveness of international cooperation undertaken pursuant to this chapter of the Convention.

Chapter VI Technical assistance and information exchange

Article 60 Training and technical assistance

1. Each State Party shall, to the extent necessary, initiate, develop or improve specific training programmes for its personnel responsible for preventing and combating corruption. Such training programmes could deal, inter alia, with the following areas:
   (a) Effective measures to prevent, detect, investigate, punish and control corruption, including the use of evidence-gathering and investigative methods;
   (b) Building capacity in the development and planning of strategic anticorruption policy;
   (c) Training competent authorities in the preparation of requests for mutual legal assistance that meet the requirements of this Convention;
   (d) Evaluation and strengthening of institutions, public service management and the management of public finances, including public procurement, and the private sector;
   (e) Preventing and combating the transfer of proceeds of offences established in accordance with this Convention and recovering such proceeds;
   (f) Detecting and freezing of the transfer of proceeds of offences established in accordance with this Convention;
   (g) Surveillance of the movement of proceeds of offences established in accordance with this Convention and of the methods used to transfer, conceal or disguise such proceeds;

(h) Appropriate and efficient legal and administrative mechanisms and methods for facilitating the return of proceeds of offences established in accordance with this Convention;
(i) Methods used in protecting victims and witnesses who cooperate with judicial authorities; and
(j) Training in national and international regulations and in languages.

2. States Parties shall, according to their capacity, consider affording one another the widest measure of technical assistance, especially for the benefit of developing countries, in their respective plans and programmes to combat corruption, including material support and training in the areas referred to in paragraph 1 of this article, and training and assistance and the mutual exchange of relevant experience and specialized knowledge, which will facilitate international cooperation between States Parties in the areas of extradition and mutual legal assistance.
3. States Parties shall strengthen, to the extent necessary, efforts to maximize operational and training activities in international and regional organizations and in the framework of relevant bilateral and multilateral agreements or arrangements.
4. States Parties shall consider assisting one another, upon request, in conducting evaluations, studies and research relating to the types, causes, effects and costs of corruption in their respective countries, with a view to developing, with the participation of competent authorities and society, strategies and action plans to combat corruption.
5. In order to facilitate the recovery of proceeds of offences established in accordance with this Convention, States Parties may cooperate in providing each other with the names of experts who could assist in achieving that objective.
6. States Parties shall consider using subregional, regional and international conferences and seminars to promote cooperation and technical assistance and to stimulate discussion on problems of mutual concern, including the special problems and needs of developing countries and countries with economies in transition.
7. States Parties shall consider establishing voluntary mechanisms with a view to contributing financially to the efforts of developing countries and countries with economies in transition to apply this Convention through technical assistance programmes and projects.
8. Each State Party shall consider making voluntary contributions to the United Nations Office on Drugs and Crime for the purpose of fostering, through the Office, programmes and projects in developing countries with a view to implementing this Convention.

Article 61 Collection, exchange and analysis of information on corruption

1. Each State Party shall consider analysing, in consultation with experts, trends in corruption in its territory, as well as the circumstances in which corruption offences are committed.
2. States Parties shall consider developing and sharing with each other and through international and regional organizations statistics, analytical expertise concerning corruption and information with a view to developing, insofar as possible, common definitions, standards and methodologies, as well as information on best practices to prevent and combat corruption.
3. Each State Party shall consider monitoring its policies and actual measures to combat corruption and making assessments of their effectiveness and efficiency.

Article 62 Other measures: implementation of the Convention through economic development and technical assistance

1. States Parties shall take measures conducive to the optimal implementation of this Convention to the extent possible, through international cooperation, taking into account the negative effects of corruption on society in general, in particular on sustainable development.
2. States Parties shall make concrete efforts to the extent possible and in coordination with each other, as well as with international and regional organizations:
   (a) To enhance their cooperation at various levels with developing countries, with a view to strengthening the capacity of the latter to prevent and combat corruption;
   (b) To enhance financial and material assistance to support the efforts of developing countries to prevent and fight corruption effectively and to help them implement this Convention successfully;
   (c) To provide technical assistance to developing countries and countries with economies in transition to assist them in meeting their needs for the implementation of this Convention. To that end, States Parties shall endeavour to make adequate and regular voluntary contributions to an account specifically designated for that purpose in a United Nations funding mechanism. States Parties may also give special consideration, in accordance with their domestic law and the provisions of this Convention, to contributing to that account a percentage of the money or of the corresponding value of proceeds of crime or property confiscated in accordance with the provisions of this Convention;
   (d) To encourage and persuade other States and financial institutions as appropriate to join them in efforts in accordance with this article, in particular by providing more training programmes and modern equipment to developing countries in order to assist them in achieving the objectives of this Convention.
3. To the extent possible, these measures shall be without prejudice to existing foreign assistance commitments or to other financial cooperation arrangements at the bilateral, regional or international level.
4. States Parties may conclude bilateral or multilateral agreements or arrangements on material and logistical assistance, taking into consideration the financial arrangements necessary for the means of international cooperation provided for by this Convention to be effective and for the prevention, detection and control of corruption.

Chapter VII Mechanisms for implementation

Article 63 Conference of the States Parties to the Convention

1. A Conference of the States Parties to the Convention is hereby established to improve the capacity of and cooperation between States Parties to achieve the objectives set forth in this Convention and to promote and review its implementation.
2. The Secretary-General of the United Nations shall convene the Conference of the States Parties not later than one year following the entry into force of this Convention. Thereafter, regular meetings of the Conference of the States Parties shall be held in accordance with the rules of procedure adopted by the Conference.
3. The Conference of the States Parties shall adopt rules of procedure and rules governing the functioning of the activities set forth in this article, including rules concerning the

admission and participation of observers, and the payment of expenses incurred in carrying out those activities.

4. The Conference of the States Parties shall agree upon activities, procedures and methods of work to achieve the objectives set forth in paragraph 1 of this article, including:
   (a) Facilitating activities by States Parties under articles 60 and 62 and chapters II to V of this Convention, including by encouraging the mobilization of voluntary contributions;
   (b) Facilitating the exchange of information among States Parties on patterns and trends in corruption and on successful practices for preventing and combating it and for the return of proceeds of crime, through, inter alia, the publication of relevant information as mentioned in this article;
   (c) Cooperating with relevant international and regional organizations and mechanisms and non-governmental organizations;
   (d) Making appropriate use of relevant information produced by other international and regional mechanisms for combating and preventing corruption in order to avoid unnecessary duplication of work;
   (e) Reviewing periodically the implementation of this Convention by its States Parties;
   (f) Making recommendations to improve this Convention and its implementation;
   (g) Taking note of the technical assistance requirements of States Parties with regard to the implementation of this Convention and recommending any action it may deem necessary in that respect.
5. For the purpose of paragraph 4 of this article, the Conference of the States Parties shall acquire the necessary knowledge of the measures taken by States Parties in implementing this Convention and the difficulties encountered by them in doing so through information provided by them and through such supplemental review mechanisms as may be established by the Conference of the States Parties.
6. Each State Party shall provide the Conference of the States Parties with information on its programmes, plans and practices, as well as on legislative and administrative measures to implement this Convention, as required by the Conference of the States Parties. The Conference of the States Parties shall examine the most effective way of receiving and acting upon information, including, inter alia, information received from States Parties and from competent international organizations. Inputs received from relevant non-governmental organizations duly accredited in accordance with procedures to be decided upon by the Conference of the States Parties may also be considered.
7. Pursuant to paragraphs 4 to 6 of this article, the Conference of the States Parties shall establish, if it deems it necessary, any appropriate mechanism or body to assist in the effective implementation of the Convention.

Article 64 [Omitted]

Chapter VIII Final provisions

Article 65 Implementation of the Convention

1. Each State Party shall take the necessary measures, including legislative and administrative measures, in accordance with fundamental principles of its domestic law, to ensure the implementation of its obligations under this Convention.

2. Each State Party may adopt more strict or severe measures than those provided for by this Convention for preventing and combating corruption.

Article 66 Settlement of disputes

1. States Parties shall endeavour to settle disputes concerning the interpretation or application of this Convention through negotiation.
2. Any dispute between two or more States Parties concerning the interpretation or application of this Convention that cannot be settled through negotiation within a reasonable time shall, at the request of one of those States Parties, be submitted to arbitration. If, six months after the date of the request for arbitration, those States Parties are unable to agree on the organization of the arbitration, any one of those States Parties may refer the dispute to the International Court of Justice by request in accordance with the Statute of the Court.
3. Each State Party may, at the time of signature, ratification, acceptance or approval of or accession to this Convention, declare that it does not consider itself bound by paragraph 2 of this article. The other States Parties shall not be bound by paragraph 2 of this article with respect to any State Party that has made such a reservation.
4. Any State Party that has made a reservation in accordance with paragraph 3 of this article may at any time withdraw that reservation by notification to the Secretary-General of the United Nations.

Article 67–71 [Omitted]

United Nations Convention on the Use of Electronic Communications in International Contracts, 2005

The States Parties to this Convention,

Reaffirming their belief that international trade on the basis of equality and mutual benefit is an important element in promoting friendly relations among States,

Noting that the increased use of electronic communications improves the efficiency of commercial activities, enhances trade connections and allows new access opportunities for previously remote parties and markets, thus playing a fundamental role in promoting trade and economic development, both domestically and internationally,

Considering that problems created by uncertainty as to the legal value of the use of electronic communications in international contracts constitute an obstacle to international trade,

Convinced that the adoption of uniform rules to remove obstacles to the use of electronic communications in international contracts, including obstacles that might result from the operation of existing international trade law instruments, would enhance legal certainty and commercial predictability for international contracts and help States gain access to modern trade routes,

Being of the opinion that uniform rules should respect the freedom of parties to choose appropriate media and technologies, taking account of the principles of technological neutrality and functional equivalence, to the extent that the means chosen by the parties comply with the purpose of the relevant rules of law,

Desiring to provide a common solution to remove legal obstacles to the use of electronic communications in a manner acceptable to States with different legal, social and economic systems,

Have agreed as follows:

Chapter I Sphere of application

Article 1 Scope of application

1. This Convention applies to the use of electronic communications in connection with the formation or performance of a contract between parties whose places of business are in different States.
2. The fact that the parties have their places of business in different States is to be disregarded whenever this fact does not appear either from the contract or from any dealings between the parties or from information disclosed by the parties at any time before or at the conclusion of the contract.
3. Neither the nationality of the parties nor the civil or commercial character of the parties or of the contract is to be taken into consideration in determining the application of this Convention.

Article 2 Exclusions

1. This Convention does not apply to electronic communications relating to any of the following:
   (a) Contracts concluded for personal, family or household purposes;
   (b) (i) Transactions on a regulated exchange; (ii) foreign exchange transactions; (iii) inter-bank payment systems, inter-bank payment agreements or clearance and settlement systems relating to securities or other financial assets or instruments; (iv) the transfer of security rights in sale, loan or holding of or agreement to repurchase securities or other financial assets or instruments held with an intermediary.
2. This Convention does not apply to bills of exchange, promissory notes, consignment notes, bills of lading, warehouse receipts or any transferable document or instrument that entitles the bearer or beneficiary to claim the delivery of goods or the payment of a sum of money.

Article 3 Party autonomy

The parties may exclude the application of this Convention or derogate from or vary the effect of any of its provisions.

Chapter II General provisions

Article 4 Definitions

For the purposes of this Convention:

(a) 'Communication' means any statement, declaration, demand, notice or request, including an offer and the acceptance of an offer, that the parties are required to make or choose to make in connection with the formation or performance of a contract;

(b) 'Electronic communication' means any communication that the parties make by means of data messages;
(c) 'Data message' means information generated, sent, received or stored by electronic, magnetic, optical or similar means, including, but not limited to, electronic data interchange, electronic mail, telegram, telex or telecopy;
(d) 'Originator' of an electronic communication means a party by whom, or on whose behalf, the electronic communication has been sent or generated prior to storage, if any, but it does not include a party acting as an intermediary with respect to that electronic communication;
(e) 'Addressee' of an electronic communication means a party who is intended by the originator to receive the electronic communication, but does not include a party acting as an intermediary with respect to that electronic communication;
(f) 'Information system' means a system for generating, sending, receiving, storing or otherwise processing data messages;
(g) 'Automated message system' means a computer program or an electronic or other automated means used to initiate an action or respond to data messages or performances in whole or in part, without review or intervention by a natural person each time an action is initiated or a response is generated by the system;
(h) 'Place of business' means any place where a party maintains a non-transitory establishment to pursue an economic activity other than the temporary provision of goods or services out of a specific location.

Article 5 Interpretation

1. In the interpretation of this Convention, regard is to be had to its international character and to the need to promote uniformity in its application and the observance of good faith in international trade.
2. Questions concerning matters governed by this Convention which are not expressly settled in it are to be settled in conformity with the general principles on which it is based or, in the absence of such principles, in conformity with the law applicable by virtue of the rules of private international law.

Article 6 Location of the parties

1. For the purposes of this Convention, a party's place of business is presumed to be the location indicated by that party, unless another party demonstrates that the party making the indication does not have a place of business at that location.
2. If a party has not indicated a place of business and has more than one place of business, then the place of business for the purposes of this Convention is that which has the closest relationship to the relevant contract, having regard to the circumstances known to or contemplated by the parties at any time before or at the conclusion of the contract.
3. If a natural person does not have a place of business, reference is to be made to the person's habitual residence.
4. A location is not a place of business merely because that is:
   (a) where equipment and technology supporting an information system used by a party in connection with the formation of a contract are located; or

(b) where the information system may be accessed by other parties.

5. The sole fact that a party makes use of a domain name or electronic mail address connected to a specific country does not create a presumption that its place of business is located in that country.

Article 7 Information requirements

Nothing in this Convention affects the application of any rule of law that may require the parties to disclose their identities, places of business or other information, or relieves a party from the legal consequences of making inaccurate, incomplete or false statements in that regard.

Chapter III Use of electronic communications in international contracts

Article 8 Legal recognition of electronic communications

1. A communication or a contract shall not be denied validity or enforceability on the sole ground that it is in the form of an electronic communication.
2. Nothing in this Convention requires a party to use or accept electronic communications, but a party's agreement to do so may be inferred from the party's conduct.

Article 9 Form requirements

1. Nothing in this Convention requires a communication or a contract to be made or evidenced in any particular form.
2. Where the law requires that a communication or a contract should be in writing, or provides consequences for the absence of a writing, that requirement is met by an electronic communication if the information contained therein is accessible so as to be usable for subsequent reference.
3. Where the law requires that a communication or a contract should be signed by a party, or provides consequences for the absence of a signature, that requirement is met in relation to an electronic communication if:
   (a) A method is used to identify the party and to indicate that party's intention in respect of the information contained in the electronic communication; and
   (b) The method used is either:
      (i) As reliable as appropriate for the purpose for which the electronic communication was generated or communicated, in the light of all the circumstances, including any relevant agreement; or
      (ii) Proven in fact to have fulfilled the functions described in subparagraph (a) above, by itself or together with further evidence.
4. Where the law requires that a communication or a contract should be made available or retained in its original form, or provides consequences for the absence of an original, that requirement is met in relation to an electronic communication if:
   (a) There exists a reliable assurance as to the integrity of the information it contains from the time when it was first generated in its final form, as an electronic communication or otherwise; and

   (b) Where it is required that the information it contains be made available, that information is capable of being displayed to the person to whom it is to be made available.
5. For the purposes of paragraph 4 (a):
   (a) The criteria for assessing integrity shall be whether the information has remained complete and unaltered, apart from the addition of any endorsement and any change that arises in the normal course of communication, storage and display; and
   (b) The standard of reliability required shall be assessed in the light of the purpose for which the information was generated and in the light of all the relevant circumstances.

Article 10 Time and place of dispatch and receipt of electronic communications

1. The time of dispatch of an electronic communication is the time when it leaves an information system under the control of the originator or of the party who sent it on behalf of the originator or, if the electronic communication has not left an information system under the control of the originator or of the party who sent it on behalf of the originator, the time when the electronic communication is received.
2. The time of receipt of an electronic communication is the time when it becomes capable of being retrieved by the addressee at an electronic address designated by the addressee. The time of receipt of an electronic communication at another electronic address of the addressee is the time when it becomes capable of being retrieved by the addressee at that address and the addressee becomes aware that the electronic communication has been sent to that address. An electronic communication is presumed to be capable of being retrieved by the addressee when it reaches the addressee's electronic address.
3. An electronic communication is deemed to be dispatched at the place where the originator has its place of business and is deemed to be received at the place where the addressee has its place of business, as determined in accordance with article 6.
4. Paragraph 2 of this article applies notwithstanding that the place where the information system supporting an electronic address is located may be different from the place where the electronic communication is deemed to be received under paragraph 3 of this article.

Article 11 Invitations to make offers

A proposal to conclude a contract made through one or more electronic communications which is not addressed to one or more specific parties, but is generally accessible to parties making use of information systems, including proposals that make use of interactive applications for the placement of orders through such information systems, is to be considered as an invitation to make offers, unless it clearly indicates the intention of the party making the proposal to be bound in case of acceptance.

Article 12 Use of automated message systems for contract formation

A contract formed by the interaction of an automated message system and a natural person, or by the interaction of automated message systems, shall not be denied validity or enforceability on the sole ground that no natural person reviewed or intervened in each of the individual actions carried out by the automated message systems or the resulting contract.

Article 13 Availability of contract terms

Nothing in this Convention affects the application of any rule of law that may require a party that negotiates some or all of the terms of a contract through the exchange of electronic communications to make available to the other party those electronic communications which contain the contractual terms in a particular manner, or relieves a party from the legal consequences of its failure to do so.

Article 14 Error in electronic communications

1. Where a natural person makes an input error in an electronic communication exchanged with the automated message system of another party and the automated message system does not provide the person with an opportunity to correct the error, that person, or the party on whose behalf that person was acting, has the right to withdraw the portion of the electronic communication in which the input error was made if:
   (a) The person, or the party on whose behalf that person was acting, notifies the other party of the error as soon as possible after having learned of the error and indicates that he or she made an error in the electronic communication; and
   (b) The person, or the party on whose behalf that person was acting, has not used or received any material benefit or value from the goods or services, if any, received from the other party.
2. Nothing in this article affects the application of any rule of law that may govern the consequences of any error other than as provided for in paragraph 1.

Chapter IV Final provisions

Article 15–25 [Omitted]

Additional Protocol to the Convention on the Contract for the International Carriage of Goods by Road (CMR) Concerning the Electronic Consignment Note, 2008

Article 1 Definitions

For the purposes of this Protocol,

"Convention" means the Convention on the Contract for the International Carriage of Goods by Road (CMR);

"Electronic communication" means information generated, sent, received or stored by electronic, optical, digital or similar means with the result that the information communicated is accessible so as to be usable for subsequent reference;

"Electronic consignment note" means a consignment note issued by electronic communication by the carrier, the sender or any other party interested in the performance of a contract of carriage to which the Convention applies, including particulars logically associated with the electronic communication by attachments or otherwise linked to the electronic communication contemporaneously with or subsequent to its issue, so as to become part of the electronic consignment note;

"Electronic signature" means data in electronic form which are attached to or logically associated with other electronic data and which serve as a method of authentication.

Article 2 Scope and effect of the electronic consignment note

1. Subject to the provisions of this Protocol, the consignment note referred to in the Convention, as well as any demand, declaration, instruction, request, reservation or other communication relating to the performance of a contract of carriage to which the Convention applies, may be made out by electronic communication.
2. An electronic consignment note that complies with the provisions of this Protocol shall be considered to be equivalent to the consignment note referred to in the Convention and shall therefore have the same evidentiary value and produce the same effects as that consignment note.

Article 3 Authentication of the electronic consignment note

1. The electronic consignment note shall be authenticated by the parties to the contract of carriage by means of a reliable electronic signature that ensures its link with the electronic consignment note. The reliability of an electronic signature method is presumed, unless otherwise proved, if the electronic signature:
   (a) is uniquely linked to the signatory;
   (b) is capable of identifying the signatory;
   (c) is created using means that the signatory can maintain under his sole control; and
   (d) is linked to the data to which it relates in such a manner that any subsequent change of the data is detectable.
2. The electronic consignment note may also be authenticated by any other electronic authentication method permitted by the law of the country in which the electronic consignment note has been made out.
3. The particulars contained in the electronic consignment note shall be accessible to any party entitled thereto.

Article 4 Conditions for the establishment of the electronic consignment note

1. The electronic consignment note shall contain the same particulars as the consignment note referred to in the Convention.
2. The procedure used to issue the electronic consignment note shall ensure the integrity of the particulars contained therein from the time when it was first generated in its final form. There is integrity when the particulars have remained complete and unaltered, apart from any addition or change which arises in the normal course of communication, storage and display.
3. The particulars contained in the electronic consignment note may be supplemented or amended in the cases authorized by the Convention.

   The procedure used for supplementing or amending the electronic consignment note shall make it possible to detect as such any supplement or amendment to the electronic consignment note and shall preserve the particulars originally contained therein.

Article 5 Implementation of the electronic consignment note

1. The parties interested in the performance of the contract of carriage shall agree on the procedures and their implementation in order to comply with the requirements of this Protocol and the Convention, in particular as regards:
   (a) The method for the issuance and the delivery of the electronic consignment note to the entitled party;
   (b) An assurance that the electronic consignment note retains its integrity;
   (c) The manner in which the party entitled to the rights arising out of the electronic consignment note is able to demonstrate that entitlement;
   (d) The way in which confirmation is given that delivery to the consignee has been effected;
   (e) The procedures for supplementing or amending the electronic consignment note; and
   (f) The procedures for the possible replacement of the electronic consignment note by a consignment note issued by different means.
2. The procedures in paragraph 1 must be referred to in the electronic consignment note and shall be readily ascertainable.

Article 6 Documents supplementing the electronic consignment note

1. The carrier shall hand over to the sender, at the tatter's request, a receipt for the goods and all information necessary for identifying the shipment and for access to the electronic consignment note to which this Protocol refers.
2. The documents referred to in Article 6, paragraph 2 (g) and Article 11 of the Convention may be furnished by the sender to the carrier in the form of an electronic communication if the documents exist in this form and if the parties have agreed to procedures enabling a link to be established between these documents and the electronic consignment note to which this Protocol refers in a manner that assures their integrity.

Final provisions

Articles 7–16 [Omitted]

United Nations Convention on Contracts for the International Carriage of Goods Wholly or Partly by Sea, 2008

Chapter 1 General provisions

Article 1 Definitions

For the purposes of this Convention:

1. "Contract of carriage" means a contract in which a carrier, against the payment of freight, undertakes to carry goods from one place to another. The contract shall provide for carriage by sea and may provide for carriage by other modes of transport in addition to the sea carriage.
2. "Volume contract" means a contract of carriage that provides for the carriage of a specified quantity of goods in a series of shipments during an agreed period of time. The specification of the quantity may include a minimum, a maximum or a certain range.

3. "Liner transportation" means a transportation service that is offered to the public through publication or similar means and includes transportation by ships operating on a regular schedule between specified ports in accordance with publicly available timetables of sailing dates.
4. "Non-liner transportation" means any transportation that is not liner transportation.
5. "Carrier" means a person that enters into a contract of carriage with a shipper.
6. (a) "Performing party" means a person other than the carrier that performs or undertakes to perform any of the carrier's obligations under a contract of carriage with respect to the receipt, loading, handling, stowage, carriage, care, unloading or delivery of the goods, to the extent that such person acts, either directly or indirectly, at the carrier's request or under the carrier's supervision or control.
   (b) "Performing party" does not include any person that is retained, directly or indirectly, by a shipper, by a documentary shipper, by the controlling party or by the consignee instead of by the carrier.
7. "Maritime performing party" means a performing party to the extent that it performs or undertakes to perform any of the carrier's obligations during the period between the arrival of the goods at the port of loading of a ship and their departure from the port of discharge of a ship. An inland carrier is a maritime performing party only if it performs or undertakes to perform its services exclusively within a port area.
8. "Shipper" means a person that enters into a contract of carriage with a carrier.
9. "Documentary shipper" means a person, other than the shipper, that accepts to be named as "shipper" in the transport document or electronic transport record.
10. "Holder" means:
    (a) A person that is in possession of a negotiable transport document; and (i) if the document is an order document, is identified in it as the shipper or the consignee, or is the person to which the document is duly endorsed; or (ii) if the document is a blank endorsed order document or bearer document, is the bearer thereof; or
    (b) The person to which a negotiable electronic transport record has been issued or transferred in accordance with the procedures referred to in article 9, paragraph 1.
11. "Consignee" means a person entitled to delivery of the goods under a contract of carriage or a transport document or electronic transport record.
12. "Right of control" of the goods means the right under the contract of carriage to give the carrier instructions in respect of the goods in accordance with chapter 10.
13. "Controlling party" means the person that pursuant to article 51 is entitled to exercise the right of control.
14. "Transport document" means a document issued under a contract of carriage by the carrier that:
    (a) Evidences the carrier's or a performing party's receipt of goods under a contract of carriage; and
    (b) Evidences or contains a contract of carriage.
15. "Negotiable transport document" means a transport document that indicates, by wording such as "to order" or "negotiable" or other appropriate wording recognized as having the same effect by the law applicable to the document, that the goods have been consigned to the order of the shipper, to the order of the consignee, or to bearer, and is not explicitly stated as being "non-negotiable" or "not negotiable".

16. "Non-negotiable transport document" means a transport document that is not a negotiable transport document.
17. "Electronic communication" means information generated, sent, received or stored by electronic, optical, digital or similar means with the result that the information communicated is accessible so as to be usable for subsequent reference.
18. "Electronic transport record" means information in one or more messages issued by electronic communication under a contract of carriage by a carrier, including information logically associated with the electronic transport record by attachments or otherwise linked to the electronic transport record contemporaneously with or subsequent to its issue by the carrier, so as to become part of the electronic transport record, that:
    (a) Evidences the carrier's or a performing party's receipt of goods under a contract of carriage; and
    (b) Evidences or contains a contract of carriage.
19. "Negotiable electronic transport record" means an electronic transport record:
    (a) That indicates, by wording such as "to order", or "negotiable", or other appropriate wording recognized as having the same effect by the law applicable to the record, that the goods have been consigned to the order of the shipper or to the order of the consignee, and is not explicitly stated as being "non-negotiable" or "not negotiable"; and
    (b) The use of which meets the requirements of article 9, paragraph 1.
20. "Non-negotiable electronic transport record" means an electronic transport record that is not a negotiable electronic transport record.
21. The "issuance" of a negotiable electronic transport record means the issuance of the record in accordance with procedures that ensure that the record is subject to exclusive control from its creation until it ceases to have any effect or validity.
22. The "transfer" of a negotiable electronic transport record means the transfer of exclusive control over the record.
23. "Contract particulars" means any information relating to the contract of carriage or to the goods (including terms, notations, signatures and endorsements) that is in a transport document or an electronic transport record.
24. "Goods" means the wares, merchandise, and articles of every kind whatsoever that a carrier undertakes to carry under a contract of carriage and includes the packing and any equipment and container not supplied by or on behalf of the carrier.
25. "Ship" means any vessel used to carry goods by sea.
26. "Container" means any type of container, transportable tank or flat, swapbody, or any similar unit load used to consolidate goods, and any equipment ancillary to such unit load.
27. "Vehicle" means a road or railroad cargo vehicle.
28. "Freight" means the remuneration payable to the carrier for the carriage of goods under a contract of carriage.
29. "Domicile" means (*a*) a place where a company or other legal person or association of natural or legal persons has its (i) statutory seat or place of incorporation or central registered office, whichever is applicable, (ii) central administration or (iii) principal place of business, and (*b*) the habitual residence of a natural person.

30. "Competent court" means a court in a Contracting State that, according to the rules on the internal allocation of jurisdiction among the courts of that State, may exercise jurisdiction over the dispute.

Article 2 Interpretation of this Convention

In the interpretation of this Convention, regard is to be had to its international character and to the need to promote uniformity in its application and the observance of good faith in international trade.

Article 3 Form requirements

The notices, confirmation, consent, agreement, declaration and other communications referred to in articles 19, paragraph 2; 23, paragraphs 1 to 4; 36, subparagraphs 1 (*b*), (*c*) and (*d*); 40, subparagraph 4 (*b*); 44; 48, paragraph 3; 51, subparagraph 1 (*b*); 59, paragraph 1; 63; 66; 67, paragraph 2; 75, paragraph 4; and 80, paragraphs 2 and 5, shall be in writing. Electronic communications may be used for these purposes, provided that the use of such means is with the consent of the person by which it is communicated and of the person to which it is communicated.

Article 4 Applicability of defences and limits of liability

1. Any provision of this Convention that may provide a defence for, or limit the liability of, the carrier applies in any judicial or arbitral proceeding, whether founded in contract, in tort, or otherwise, that is instituted in respect of loss of, damage to, or delay in delivery of goods covered by a contract of carriage or for the breach of any other obligation under this Convention against:
   (a) The carrier or a maritime performing party;
   (b) The master, crew or any other person that performs services on board the ship; or
   (c) Employees of the carrier or a maritime performing party.
2. Any provision of this Convention that may provide a defence for the shipper or the documentary shipper applies in any judicial or arbitral proceeding, whether founded in contract, in tort, or otherwise, that is instituted against the shipper, the documentary shipper, or their subcontractors, agents or employees.

Chapter 2 Scope of application

Article 5 General scope of application

1. Subject to article 6, this Convention applies to contracts of carriage in which the place of receipt and the place of delivery are in different States, and the port of loading of a sea carriage and the port of discharge of the same sea carriage are in different States, if, according to the contract of carriage, any one of the following places is located in a Contracting State:
   (a) The place of receipt;
   (b) The port of loading;

   (c) The place of delivery; or
   (d) The port of discharge.
2. This Convention applies without regard to the nationality of the vessel, the carrier, the performing parties, the shipper, the consignee, or any other interested parties.

Article 6 Specific exclusions

1. This Convention does not apply to the following contracts in liner transportation:
   (a) Charter parties; and
   (b) Other contracts for the use of a ship or of any space thereon.
2. This Convention does not apply to contracts of carriage in non-liner transportation except when:
   (a) There is no charter party or other contract between the parties for the use of a ship or of any space thereon; and
   (b) A transport document or an electronic transport record is issued.

Article 7 Application to certain parties

Notwithstanding article 6, this Convention applies as between the carrier and the consignee, controlling party or holder that is not an original party to the charter party or other contract of carriage excluded from the application of this Convention. However, this Convention does not apply as between the original parties to a contract of carriage excluded pursuant to article 6.

Chapter 3 Electronic transport records

Article 8 Use and effect of electronic transport records

Subject to the requirements set out in this Convention:

(a) Anything that is to be in or on a transport document under this Convention may be recorded in an electronic transport record, provided the issuance and subsequent use of an electronic transport record is with the consent of the carrier and the shipper; and
(b) The issuance, exclusive control, or transfer of an electronic transport record has the same effect as the issuance, possession, or transfer of a transport document.

Article 9 Procedures for use of negotiable electronic transport records

1. The use of a negotiable electronic transport record shall be subject to procedures that provide for:
   (a) The method for the issuance and the transfer of that record to an intended holder;
   (b) An assurance that the negotiable electronic transport record retains its integrity;
   (c) The manner in which the holder is able to demonstrate that it is the holder; and
   (d) The manner of providing confirmation that delivery to the holder has been effected, or that, pursuant to articles 10, paragraph 2, or 47, subparagraphs 1 (*a*) (ii) and (*c*), the electronic transport record has ceased to have any effect or validity.
2. The procedures in paragraph 1 of this article shall be referred to in the contract particulars and be readily ascertainable.

Article 10 Replacement of negotiable transport document or negotiable electronic transport record

1. If a negotiable transport document has been issued and the carrier and the holder agree to replace that document by a negotiable electronic transport record:
   (a) The holder shall surrender the negotiable transport document, or all of them if more than one has been issued, to the carrier;
   (b) The carrier shall issue to the holder a negotiable electronic transport record that includes a statement that it replaces the negotiable transport document; and
   (c) The negotiable transport document ceases thereafter to have any effect or validity.
2. If a negotiable electronic transport record has been issued and the carrier and the holder agree to replace that electronic transport record by a negotiable transport document:
   (a) The carrier shall issue to the holder, in place of the electronic transport record, a negotiable transport document that includes a statement that it replaces the negotiable electronic transport record; and
   (b) The electronic transport record ceases thereafter to have any effect or validity.

Chapter 4 Obligations of the carrier

Article 11 Carriage and delivery of the goods

The carrier shall, subject to this Convention and in accordance with the terms of the contract of carriage, carry the goods to the place of destination and deliver them to the consignee.

Article 12 Period of responsibility of the carrier

1. The period of responsibility of the carrier for the goods under this Convention begins when the carrier or a performing party receives the goods for carriage and ends when the goods are delivered.
2. (a) If the law or regulations of the place of receipt require the goods to be handed over to an authority or other third party from which the carrier may collect them, the period of responsibility of the carrier begins when the carrier collects the goods from the authority or other third party.
   (b) If the law or regulations of the place of delivery require the carrier to hand over the goods to an authority or other third party from which the consignee may collect them, the period of responsibility of the carrier ends when the carrier hands the goods over to the authority or other third party.
3. For the purpose of determining the carrier's period of responsibility, the parties may agree on the time and location of receipt and delivery of the goods, but a provision in a contract of carriage is void to the extent that it provides that:
   (a) The time of receipt of the goods is subsequent to the beginning of their initial loading under the contract of carriage; or
   (b) The time of delivery of the goods is prior to the completion of their final unloading under the contract of carriage.

Article 13 Specific obligations

1. The carrier shall during the period of its responsibility as defined in article *12*, and subject to article *26*, properly and carefully receive, load, handle, stow, carry, keep, care for, unload and deliver the goods.
2. Notwithstanding paragraph 1 of this article, and without prejudice to the other provisions in chapter 4 and to chapters 5 to 7, the carrier and the shipper may agree that the loading, handling, stowing or unloading of the goods is to be performed by the shipper, the documentary shipper or the consignee. Such an agreement shall be referred to in the contract particulars.

Article 14 Specific obligations applicable to the voyage by sea

The carrier is bound before, at the beginning of, and during the voyage by sea to exercise due diligence to:

(a) Make and keep the ship seaworthy;
(b) Properly crew, equip and supply the ship and keep the ship so crewed, equipped and supplied throughout the voyage; and
(c) Make and keep the holds and all other parts of the ship in which the goods are carried, and any containers supplied by the carrier in or upon which the goods are carried, fit and safe for their reception, carriage and preservation.

Article 15 Goods that may become a danger

Notwithstanding articles 11 and 13, the carrier or a performing party may decline to receive or to load, and may take such other measures as are reasonable, including unloading, destroying, or rendering goods harmless, if the goods are, or reasonably appear likely to become during the carrier's period of responsibility, an actual danger to persons, property or the environment.

Article 16 Sacrifice of the goods during the voyage by sea

Notwithstanding articles 11, 13, and 14, the carrier or a performing party may sacrifice goods at sea when the sacrifice is reasonably made for the common safety or for the purpose of preserving from peril human life or other property involved in the common adventure.

Chapter 5 Liability of the carrier for loss, damage or delay

Article 17 Basis of liability

1. The carrier is liable for loss of or damage to the goods, as well as for delay in delivery, if the claimant proves that the loss, damage, or delay, or the event or circumstance that caused or contributed to it took place during the period of the carrier's responsibility as defined in chapter 4.

2. The carrier is relieved of all or part of its liability pursuant to paragraph 1 of this article if it proves that the cause or one of the causes of the loss, damage, or delay is not attributable to its fault or to the fault of any person referred to in article 18.
3. The carrier is also relieved of all or part of its liability pursuant to paragraph 1 of this article if, alternatively to proving the absence of fault as provided in paragraph 2 of this article, it proves that one or more of the following events or circumstances caused or contributed to the loss, damage, or delay:
   (a) Act of God;
   (b) Perils, dangers, and accidents of the sea or other navigable waters;
   (c) War, hostilities, armed conflict, piracy, terrorism, riots, and civil commotions;
   (d) Quarantine restrictions; interference by or impediments created by governments, public authorities, rulers, or people including detention, arrest, or seizure not attributable to the carrier or any person referred to in article 18;
   (e) Strikes, lockouts, stoppages, or restraints of labour;
   (f) Fire on the ship;
   (g) Latent defects not discoverable by due diligence;
   (h) Act or omission of the shipper, the documentary shipper, the controlling party, or any other person for whose acts the shipper or the documentary shipper is liable pursuant to article 33 or 34;
   (i) Loading, handling, stowing, or unloading of the goods performed pursuant to an agreement in accordance with article 13, paragraph 2, unless the carrier or a performing party performs such activity on behalf of the shipper, the documentary shipper or the consignee;
   (j) Wastage in bulk or weight or any other loss or damage arising from inherent defect, quality, or vice of the goods;
   (k) Insufficiency or defective condition of packing or marking not performed by or on behalf of the carrier;
   (l) Saving or attempting to save life at sea;
   (m) Reasonable measures to save or attempt to save property at sea;
   (n) Reasonable measures to avoid or attempt to avoid damage to the environment; or
   (o) Acts of the carrier in pursuance of the powers conferred by articles 15 and 16.
4. Notwithstanding paragraph 3 of this article, the carrier is liable for all or part of the loss, damage, or delay:
   (a) If the claimant proves that the fault of the carrier or of a person referred to in article 18 caused or contributed to the event or circumstance on which the carrier relies; or
   (b) If the claimant proves that an event or circumstance not listed in paragraph 3 of this article contributed to the loss, damage, or delay, and the carrier cannot prove that this event or circumstance is not attributable to its fault or to the fault of any person referred to in article 18.
5. The carrier is also liable, notwithstanding paragraph 3 of this article, for all or part of the loss, damage, or delay if:
   (a) The claimant proves that the loss, damage, or delay was or was probably caused by or contributed to by (i) the unseaworthiness of the ship; (ii) the improper crewing, equipping, and supplying of the ship; or (iii) the fact that the holds or other parts of the ship in which the goods are carried, or any containers supplied by the carrier in

or upon which the goods are carried, were not fit and safe for reception, carriage, and preservation of the goods; and

(b) The carrier is unable to prove either that: (i) none of the events circumstances referred to in subparagraph 5 (*a*) of this article caused the loss, damage, or delay; or (ii) it complied with its obligation to exercise due diligence pursuant to article 14.

6. When the carrier is relieved of part of its liability pursuant to this article, the carrier is liable only for that part of the loss, damage or delay that is attributable to the event or circumstance for which it is liable pursuant to this article.

Article 18 Liability of the carrier for other persons

The carrier is liable for the breach of its obligations under this Convention caused by the acts or omissions of:

(a) Any performing party;
(b) The master or crew of the ship;
(c) Employees of the carrier or a performing party; or
(d) Any other person that performs or undertakes to perform any of the carrier's obligations under the contract of carriage, to the extent that the person acts, either directly or indirectly, at the carrier's request or under the carrier's supervision or control.

Article 19 Liability of maritime performing parties

1. A maritime performing party is subject to the obligations and liabilities imposed on the carrier under this Convention and is entitled to the carrier's defences and limits of liability as provided for in this Convention if:
   (a) The maritime performing party received the goods for carriage in a Contracting State, or delivered them in a Contracting State, or performed its activities with respect to the goods in a port in a Contracting State; and
   (b) The occurrence that caused the loss, damage or delay took place: (i) during the period between the arrival of the goods at the port of loading of the ship and their departure from the port of discharge from the ship; (ii) while the maritime performing party had custody of the goods; or (iii) at any other time to the extent that it was participating in the performance of any of the activities contemplated by the contract of carriage.
2. If the carrier agrees to assume obligations other than those imposed on the carrier under this Convention, or agrees that the limits of its liability are higher than the limits specified under this Convention, a maritime performing party is not bound by this agreement unless it expressly agrees to accept such obligations or such higher limits.
3. A maritime performing party is liable for the breach of its obligations under this Convention caused by the acts or omissions of any person to which it has entrusted the performance of any of the carrier's obligations under the contract of carriage under the conditions set out in paragraph 1 of this article.
4. Nothing in this Convention imposes liability on the master or crew of the ship or on an employee of the carrier or of a maritime performing party.

Article 20 Joint and several liability

1. If the carrier and one or more maritime performing parties are liable for the loss of, damage to, or delay in delivery of the goods, their liability is joint and several but only up to the limits provided for under this Convention.
2. Without prejudice to article 61, the aggregate liability of all such persons shall not exceed the overall limits of liability under this Convention.

Article 21 Delay

Delay in delivery occurs when the goods are not delivered at the place of destination provided for in the contract of carriage within the time agreed.

Article 22 Calculation of compensation.

1. Subject to article 59, the compensation payable by the carrier for loss of or damage to the goods is calculated by reference to the value of such goods at the place and time of delivery established in accordance with article 43.
2. The value of the goods is fixed according to the commodity exchange price or, if there is no such price, according to their market price or, if there is no commodity exchange price or market price, by reference to the normal value of the goods of the same kind and quality at the place of delivery.
3. In case of loss of or damage to the goods, the carrier is not liable for payment of any compensation beyond what is provided for in paragraphs 1 and 2 of this article except when the carrier and the shipper have agreed to calculate compensation in a different manner within the limits of chapter 16.

Article 23 Notice in case of loss, damage or delay

1. The carrier is presumed, in absence of proof to the contrary, to have delivered the goods according to their description in the contract particulars unless notice of loss of or damage to the goods, indicating the general nature of such loss or damage, was given to the carrier or the performing party that delivered the goods before or at the time of the delivery, or, if the loss or damage is not apparent, within seven working days at the place of delivery after the delivery of the goods.
2. Failure to provide the notice referred to in this article to the carrier or the performing party shall not affect the right to claim compensation for loss of or damage to the goods under this Convention, nor shall it affect the allocation of the burden of proof set out in article 17.
3. The notice referred to in this article is not required in respect of loss or damage that is ascertained in a joint inspection of the goods by the person to which they have been delivered and the carrier or the maritime performing party against which liability is being asserted.
4. No compensation in respect of delay is payable unless notice of loss due to delay was given to the carrier within twenty-one consecutive days of delivery of the goods.
5. When the notice referred to in this article is given to the performing party that delivered the goods, it has the same effect as if that notice was given to the carrier, and notice given to the carrier has the same effect as a notice given to a maritime performing party.

6. In the case of any actual or apprehended loss or damage, the parties to the dispute shall give all reasonable facilities to each other for inspecting and tallying the goods and shall provide access to records and documents relevant to the carriage of the goods.

Chapter 6 Additional provisions relating to particular stages of carriage

Article 24 Deviation

When pursuant to applicable law a deviation constitutes a breach of the carrier's obligations, such deviation of itself shall not deprive the carrier or a maritime performing party of any defence or limitation of this Convention, except to the extent provided in article 61.

Article 25 Deck cargo on ships

1. Goods may be carried on the deck of a ship only if:
   (a) Such carriage is required by law;
   (b) They are carried in or on containers or vehicles that are fit for deck carriage, and the decks are specially fitted to carry such containers or vehicles; or
   (c) The carriage on deck is in accordance with the contract of carriage, or the customs, usages or practices of the trade in question.
2. The provisions of this Convention relating to the liability of the carrier apply to the loss of, damage to or delay in the delivery of goods carried on deck pursuant to paragraph 1 of this article, but the carrier is not liable for loss of or damage to such goods, or delay in their delivery, caused by the special risks involved in their carriage on deck when the goods are carried in accordance with subparagraphs 1 *(a)* or *(c)* of this article.
3. If the goods have been carried on deck in cases other than those permitted pursuant to paragraph 1 of this article, the carrier is liable for loss of or damage to the goods or delay in their delivery that is exclusively caused by their carriage on deck, and is not entitled to the defences provided for in article 17.
4. The carrier is not entitled to invoke subparagraph 1 *(c)* of this article against a third party that has acquired a negotiable transport document or a negotiable electronic transport record in good faith, unless the contract particulars state that the goods may be carried on deck.
5. If the carrier and shipper expressly agreed that the goods would be carried under deck, the carrier is not entitled to the benefit of the limitation of liability for any loss of, damage to or delay in the delivery of the goods to the extent that such loss, damage, or delay resulted from their carriage on deck.

Article 26 Carriage preceding or subsequent to sea carriage

When loss of or damage to goods, or an event or circumstance causing a delay in their delivery, occurs during the carrier's period of responsibility but solely before their loading onto the ship or solely after their discharge from the ship, the provisions of this Convention do not prevail over those provisions of another international instrument that, at the time of such loss, damage or event or circumstance causing delay:

(a) Pursuant to the provisions of such international instrument would have applied to all or any of the carrier's activities if the shipper had made a separate and direct contract with the carrier in respect of the particular stage of carriage where the loss of, or damage to goods, or an event or circumstance causing delay in their delivery occurred;

(b) Specifically provide for the carrier's liability, limitation of liability, or time for suit; and

(c) Cannot be departed from by contract either at all or to the detriment of the shipper under that instrument.

Chapter 7 Obligations of the shipper to the carrier

Article 27 Delivery for carriage

1. Unless otherwise agreed in the contract of carriage, the shipper shall deliver the goods ready for carriage. In any event, the shipper shall deliver the goods in such condition that they will withstand the intended carriage, including their loading, handling, stowing, lashing and securing, and unloading, and that they will not cause harm to persons or property.
2. The shipper shall properly and carefully perform any obligation assumed under an agreement made pursuant to article 13, paragraph 2.
3. When a container is packed or a vehicle is loaded by the shipper, the shipper shall properly and carefully stow, lash and secure the contents in or on the container or vehicle, and in such a way that they will not cause harm to persons or property.

Article 28 Cooperation of the shipper and the carrier in providing information and instructions

The carrier and the shipper shall respond to requests from each other to provide information and instructions required for the proper handling and carriage of the goods if the information is in the requested party's possession or the instructions are within the requested party's reasonable ability to provide and they are not otherwise reasonably available to the requesting party.

Article 29 Shipper's obligation to provide information, instructions and documents

1. The shipper shall provide to the carrier in a timely manner such information, instructions and documents relating to the goods that are not otherwise reasonably available to the carrier, and that are reasonably necessary:
   (a) For the proper handling and carriage of the goods, including precautions to be taken by the carrier or a performing party; and
   (b) For the carrier to comply with law, regulations or other requirements of public authorities in connection with the intended carriage, provided that the carrier notifies the shipper in a timely manner of the information, instructions and documents it requires.
2. Nothing in this article affects any specific obligation to provide certain information, instructions and documents related to the goods pursuant to law, regulations or other requirements of public authorities in connection with the intended carriage.

Article 30 Basis of shipper's liability to the carrier

1. The shipper is liable for loss or damage sustained by the carrier if the carrier proves that such loss or damage was caused by a breach of the shipper's obligations under this Convention.
2. Except in respect of loss or damage caused by a breach by the shipper of its obligations pursuant to articles 31, paragraph 2, and 32, the shipper is relieved of all or part of its liability if the cause or one of the causes of the loss or damage is not attributable to its fault or to the fault of any person referred to in article 34.
3. When the shipper is relieved of part of its liability pursuant to this article, the shipper is liable only for that part of the loss or damage that is attributable to its fault or to the fault of any person referred to in article 34.

Article 31 Information for compilation of contract particulars

1. The shipper shall provide to the carrier, in a timely manner, accurate information required for the compilation of the contract particulars and the issuance of the transport documents or electronic transport records, including the particulars referred to in article 36, paragraph 1; the name of the party to be identified as the shipper in the contract particulars; the name of the consignee, if any; and the name of the person to whose order the transport document or electronic transport record is to be issued, if any.
2. The shipper is deemed to have guaranteed the accuracy at the time of receipt by the carrier of the information that is provided according to paragraph I of this article. The shipper shall indemnify the carrier against loss or damage resulting from the inaccuracy of such information.

Article 32 Special rules on. dangerous goods

When goods by their nature or character are, or reasonably appear likely to become, a danger to persons, property or the environment:

(a) The shipper shall inform the carrier of the dangerous nature or character of the goods in a timely manner before they are delivered to the carrier or a performing party. If the shipper fails to do so and the carrier or performing party does not otherwise have knowledge of their dangerous nature or character, the shipper is liable to the carrier for loss or damage resulting from such failure to inform; and

(b) The shipper shall mark or label dangerous goods in accordance with any law, regulations or other requirements of public authorities that apply during any stage of the intended carriage of the goods. If the shipper fails to do so, it is liable to the carrier for loss or damage resulting from such failure.

Article 33 Assumption of shipper's rights and obligations by the documentary shipper

1. A documentary shipper is subject to the obligations and liabilities imposed on the shipper pursuant to this chapter and pursuant to article 55, and is entitled to the shipper's rights and defences provided by this chapter and by chapter 13.

2. Paragraph 1 of this article does not affect the obligations, liabilities, rights or defences of the shipper.

Article 34 Liability of the shipper for other persons

The shipper is liable for the breach of its obligations under this Convention caused by the acts or omissions of any person, including employees, agents and subcontractors, to which it has entrusted the performance of any of its obligations, but the shipper is not liable for acts or omissions of the carrier or a performing party acting on behalf of the carrier, to which the shipper has entrusted the performance of its obligations.

Chapter 8 Transport documents and electronic transport records

Article 35 Issuance of the transport document or the electronic transport record

Unless the shipper and the carrier have agreed not to use a transport document or an electronic transport record, or it is the custom, usage or practice of the trade not to use one, upon delivery of the goods for carriage to the carrier or performing party, the shipper or, if the shipper consents, the documentary shipper, is entitled to obtain from the carrier, at the shipper's option:

(a) A non-negotiable transport document or, subject to article 8, subparagraph (*a*), a non-negotiable electronic transport record; or
(b) An appropriate negotiable transport document or, subject to article 8, subparagraph (*a*), a negotiable electronic transport record, unless the shipper and the carrier have agreed not to use a negotiable transport document or negotiable electronic transport record, or it is the custom, usage or practice of the trade not to use one.

Article 36 Contract particulars

1. The contract particulars in the transport document or electronic transport record referred to in article 35 shall include the following information, as furnished by the shipper:
   (a) A description of the goods as appropriate for the transport;
   (b) The leading marks necessary for identification of the goods;
   (c) The number of packages or pieces, or the quantity of goods; and
   (d) The weight of the goods, if furnished by the shipper.
2. The contract particulars in the transport document or electronic transport record referred to in article 35 shall also include:
   (a) A statement of the apparent order and condition of the goods at the time the carrier or a performing party receives them for carriage;
   (b) The name and address of the carrier;
   (c) The date on which the carrier or a performing party received the goods, or on which the goods were loaded on board the ship, or on which the transport document or electronic transport record was issued; and
   (d) If the transport document is negotiable, the number of originals of the negotiable transport document, when more than one original is issued.

3. The contract particulars in the transport document or electronic transport record referred to in article 35 shall further include:
   (a) The name and address of the consignee, if named by the shipper;
   (b) The name of a ship, if specified in the contract of carriage;
   (c) The place of receipt and, if known to the carrier, the place of delivery; and
   (d) The port of loading and the port of discharge, if specified in the contract of carriage.
4. For the purposes of this article, the phrase "apparent order and condition of the goods" in subparagraph 2 (*a*) of this article refers to the order and condition of the goods based on:
   (a) A reasonable external inspection of the goods as packaged at the time the shipper delivers them to the carrier or a performing party; and
   (b) Any additional inspection that the carrier or a performing party actually performs before issuing the transport document or electronic transport record.

Article 37 Identity of the carrier

1. If a carrier is identified by name in the contract particulars, any other information in the transport document or electronic transport record relating to the identity of the carrier shall have no effect to the extent that it is inconsistent with that identification.
2. If no person is identified in the contract particulars as the carrier as required pursuant to article 36, subparagraph 2 (*b*), but the contract particulars indicate that the goods have been loaded on board a named ship, the registered owner of that ship is presumed to be the carrier, unless it proves that the ship was under a bareboat charter at the time of the carriage and it identifies this bareboat charterer and indicates its address, in which case this bareboat charterer is presumed to be the carrier. Alternatively, the registered owner may rebut the presumption of being the carrier by identifying the carrier and indicating its address. The bareboat charterer may rebut any presumption of being the carrier in the same manner.
3. Nothing in this article prevents the claimant from proving that any person other than a person identified in the contract particulars or pursuant to paragraph 2 of this article is the carrier.

Article 38 Signature

1. A transport document shall be signed by the carrier or a person acting on its behalf.
2. An electronic transport record shall include the electronic signature of the carrier or a person acting on its behalf. Such electronic signature shall identify the signatory in relation to the electronic transport record and indicate the carrier's authorization of the electronic transport record.

Article 39 Deficiencies in the contract particulars

1. The absence or inaccuracy of one or more of the contract particulars referred to in article 36, paragraphs 1, 2 or 3, does not of itself affect the legal character or validity of the transport document or of the electronic transport record.

2. If the contract particulars include the date but fail to indicate its significance, the date is deemed to be:
   (a) The date on which all of the goods indicated in the transport document or electronic transport record were loaded on board the ship, if the contract particulars indicate that the goods have been loaded on board a ship; or
   (b) The date on which the carrier or a performing party received the goods, if the contract particulars do not indicate that the goods have been loaded on board a ship.
3. If the contract particulars fail to state the apparent order and condition of the goods at the time the carrier or a performing party receives them, the contract particulars are deemed to have stated that the goods were in apparent good order and condition at the time the carrier or a performing party received them.

Article 40 Qualifying the information. relating to the goods in the contract particulars

1. The carrier shall qualify the information referred to in article 36, paragraph 1, to indicate that the carrier does not assume responsibility for the accuracy of the information furnished by the shipper if:
   (a) The carrier has actual knowledge that any material statement in the transport document or electronic transport record is false or misleading; or
   (b) The carrier has reasonable grounds to believe that a material statement in the transport document or electronic transport record is false or misleading.
2. Without prejudice to paragraph 1 of this article, the carrier may qualify the information referred to in article 36, paragraph 1, in the circumstances and in the manner set out in paragraphs 3 and 4 of this article to indicate that the carrier does not assume responsibility for the accuracy of the information furnished by the shipper.
3. When the goods are not delivered for carriage to the carrier or a performing party in a closed container or vehicle, or when they are delivered in a closed container or vehicle and the carrier or a performing party actually inspects them, the carrier may qualify the information referred to in article 36, paragraph 1, if:
   (a) The carrier had no physically practicable or commercially reasonable means of checking the information furnished by the shipper, in which case it may indicate which information it was unable to check; or
   (b) The carrier has reasonable grounds to believe the information furnished by the shipper to be inaccurate, in which case it may include a clause providing what it reasonably considers accurate information.
4. When the goods are delivered for carriage to the carrier or a performing party in a closed container or vehicle, the carrier may qualify the information referred to in:
   (a) Article 36, subparagraphs 1 (*a*), (*b*), or (*c*), if:
      (i) The goods inside the container or vehicle have not actually been inspected by the carrier or a performing party; and
      (ii) Neither the carrier nor a performing party otherwise has actual knowledge of its contents before issuing the transport document or the electronic transport record; and
   (b) Article 36, subparagraph 1 (*d*), if:

(i) Neither the carrier nor a performing party weighed the container or vehicle, and the shipper and the carrier had not agreed prior to the shipment that the container or vehicle would be weighed and the weight would be included in the contract particulars; or
(ii) There was no physically practicable or commercially reasonable means of checking the weight of the container or vehicle.

Article 41 Evidentiary effect of the contract particulars

Except to the extent that the contract particulars have been qualified in the circumstances and in the manner set out in article 40:

(a) A transport document or an electronic transport record is prima facie evidence of the carrier's receipt of the goods as stated in the contract particulars;
(b) Proof to the contrary by the carrier in respect of any contract particulars shall not be admissible, when such contract particulars are included in:
  (i) A negotiable transport document or a negotiable electronic transport record that is transferred to a third party acting in good faith; or
  (ii) A non-negotiable transport document that indicates that it must be surrendered in order to obtain delivery of the goods and is transferred to the consignee acting in good faith;
(c) Proof to the contrary by the carrier shall not be admissible against a consignee that in good faith has acted in reliance on any of the following contract particulars included in a non-negotiable transport document or a non-negotiable electronic transport record:
  (i) The contract particulars referred to in article 36, paragraph 1, when such contract particulars are furnished by the carrier;
  (ii) The number, type and identifying numbers of the containers, but not the identifying numbers of the container seals; and
  (iii) The contract particulars referred to in article 36, paragraph 2.

Article 42 "Freight prepaid"

If the contract particulars contain the statement "freight prepaid" or a statement of a similar nature, the carrier cannot assert against the holder or the consignee the fact that the freight has not been paid. This article does not apply if the holder or the consignee is also the shipper.

Chapter 9 Delivery of the goods

Article 43 Obligation to accept delivery

When the goods have arrived at their destination, the consignee that demands delivery of the goods under the contract of carriage shall accept delivery of the goods at the time or within the time period and at the location agreed in the contract of carriage or, failing such agreement, at the time and location at which, having regard to the terms of the contract, the customs, usages or practices of the trade and the circumstances of the carriage, delivery could reasonably be expected.

Article 44 Obligation to acknowledge receipt

On request of the carrier or the performing party that delivers the goods, the consignee shall acknowledge receipt of the goods from the carrier or the performing party in the manner that is customary at the place of delivery. The carrier may refuse delivery if the consignee refuses to acknowledge such receipt.

Article 45 Delivery when no negotiable transport document or negotiable electronic transport record is issued

When neither a negotiable transport document nor a negotiable electronic transport record has been issued:

(a) The carrier shall deliver the goods to the consignee at the time and location referred to in article 43. The carrier may refuse delivery if the person claiming to be the consignee does not properly identify itself as the consignee on the request of the carrier;
(b) If the name and address of the consignee are not referred to in the contract particulars, the controlling party shall prior to or upon the arrival of the goods at the place of destination advise the carrier of such name and address;
(c) Without prejudice to article 48, paragraph 1, if the goods are not deliverable because (i) the consignee, after having received a notice of arrival, does not, at the time or within the time period referred to in article 43, claim delivery of the goods from the carrier after their arrival at the place of destination, (ii) the carrier refuses delivery because the person claiming to be the consignee does not properly identify itself as the consignee, or (iii) the carrier is, after reasonable effort, unable to locate the consignee in order to request delivery instructions, the carrier may so advise the controlling party and request instructions in respect of the delivery of the goods. If, after reasonable effort, the carrier is unable to locate the controlling party, the carrier may so advise the shipper and request instructions in respect of the delivery of the goods. If, after reasonable effort, the carrier is unable to locate the shipper, the carrier may so advise the documentary shipper and request instructions in respect of the delivery of the goods;
(d) The carrier that delivers the goods upon instruction of the controlling party, the shipper or the documentary shipper pursuant to subparagraph (*c*) of this article is discharged from its obligations to deliver the goods under the contract of carriage.

Article 46 Delivery when a non-negotiable transport document that requires surrender is issued

When a non-negotiable transport document has been issued that indicates that it shall be surrendered in order to obtain delivery of the goods:

(a) The carrier shall deliver the goods at the time and location referred to in article 43 to the consignee upon the consignee properly identifying itself on the request of the carrier and surrender of the non-negotiable document. The carrier may refuse delivery if the person claiming to be the consignee fails to properly identify itself on the request of the carrier, and shall refuse delivery if the non-negotiable document is not surrendered. If more than one original of the non-negotiable document has been issued, the surrender of one original will suffice and the other originals cease to have any effect or validity;

(b) Without prejudice to article 48, paragraph 1, if the goods are not deliverable because (i) the consignee, after having received a notice of arrival, does not, at the time or within the time period referred to in article 43, claim delivery of the goods from the carrier after their arrival at the place of destination, (ii) the carrier refuses delivery because the person claiming to be the consignee does not properly identify itself as the consignee or does not surrender the document, or (iii) the carrier is, after reasonable effort, unable to locate the consignee in order to request delivery instructions, the carrier may so advise the shipper and request instructions in respect of the delivery of the goods. If, after reasonable effort, the carrier is unable to locate the shipper, the carrier may so advise the documentary shipper and request instructions in respect of the delivery of the goods;

(c) The carrier that delivers the goods upon instruction of the shipper or the documentary shipper pursuant to subparagraph *(b)* of this article is discharged from its obligation to deliver the goods under the contract of carriage, irrespective of whether the non-negotiable transport document has been surrendered to it.

Article 47 Delivery when a negotiable transport document or negotiable electronic transport record is issued

1. When a negotiable transport document or a negotiable electronic transport record has been issued:
   (a) The holder of the negotiable transport document or negotiable electronic transport record is entitled to claim delivery of the goods from the carrier after they have arrived at the place of destination, in which event the carrier shall deliver the goods at the time and location referred to in article 43 to the holder:
      (i) Upon surrender of the negotiable transport document and, if the holder is one of the persons referred to in article 1, subparagraph 10 *(a)* (i), upon the holder properly identifying itself; or
      (ii) Upon demonstration by the holder, in accordance with the procedures referred to in article 9, paragraph 1, that it is the holder of the negotiable electronic transport record;
   (b) The carrier shall refuse delivery if the requirements of subparagraph *(a)* (i) or *(a)* (ii) of this paragraph are not met;
   (c) If more than one original of the negotiable transport document has been issued, and the number of originals is stated in that document, the surrender of one original will suffice and the other originals cease to have any effect or validity. When a negotiable electronic transport record has been used, such electronic transport record ceases to have any effect or validity upon delivery to the holder in accordance with the procedures required by article 9, paragraph 1.
2. Without prejudice to article 48, paragraph 1, if the negotiable transport document or the negotiable electronic transport record expressly states that the goods may be delivered without the surrender of the transport document or the electronic transport record, the following rules apply:
   (a) If the goods are not deliverable because (i) the holder, after having received a notice of arrival, does not, at the time or within the time period referred to in

article 43, claim delivery of the goods from the carrier after their arrival at the place of destination, (ii) the carrier refuses delivery because the person claiming to be a holder does not properly identify itself as one of the persons referred to in article 1, subparagraph 10 (*a*) (i), or (iii) the carrier is, after reasonable effort, unable to locate the holder in order to request delivery instructions, the carrier may so advise the shipper and request instructions in respect of the delivery of the goods. If, after reasonable effort, the carrier is unable to locate the shipper, the carrier may so advise the documentary shipper and request instructions in respect of the delivery of the goods;

(b) The carrier that delivers the goods upon instruction of the shipper or the documentary shipper in accordance with subparagraph 2 (*a*) of this article is discharged from its obligation to deliver the goods under the contract of carriage to the holder, irrespective of whether the negotiable transport document has been surrendered to it, or the person claiming delivery under a negotiable electronic transport record has demonstrated, in accordance with the procedures referred to in article 9, paragraph 1, that it is the holder;

(c) The person giving instructions under subparagraph 2 (*a*) of this article shall indemnify the carrier against loss arising from its being held liable to the holder under subparagraph 2 (*e*) of this article. The carrier may refuse to follow those instructions if the person fails to provide adequate security as the carrier may reasonably request;

(d) *A* person that becomes a holder of the negotiable transport document or the negotiable electronic transport record after the carrier has delivered the goods pursuant to subparagraph 2 (*b*) of this article, but pursuant to contractual or other arrangements made before such delivery acquires rights against the carrier under the contract of carriage, other than the right to claim delivery of the goods;

(e) Notwithstanding subparagraphs 2 (*b*) and 2 (*d*) of this article, a holder that becomes a holder after such delivery, and that did not have and could not reasonably have had knowledge of such delivery at the time it became a holder, acquires the rights incorporated in the negotiable transport document or negotiable electronic transport record. When the contract particulars state the expected time of arrival of the goods, or indicate how to obtain information as to whether the goods have been delivered, it is presumed that the holder at the time that it became a holder had or could reasonably have had knowledge of the delivery of the goods.

Article 48 Goods remaining undelivered

1. For the purposes of this article, goods shall be deemed to have remained undelivered only if, after their arrival at the place of destination:

   (a) The consignee does not accept delivery of the goods pursuant to this chapter at the time and location referred to in article 43;

   (b) The controlling party, the holder, the shipper or the documentary shipper cannot be found or does not give the carrier adequate instructions pursuant to articles 45, 46 and 47;

   (c) The carrier is entitled or required to refuse delivery pursuant to articles 44, 45, 46 and 47;

(d) The carrier is not allowed to deliver the goods to the consignee pursuant to the law or regulations of the place at which delivery is requested; or
(e) The goods are otherwise undeliverable by the carrier.

2. Without prejudice to any other rights that the carrier may have against the shipper, controlling party or consignee, if the goods have remained undelivered, the carrier may, at the risk and expense of the person entitled to the goods, take such action in respect of the goods as circumstances may reasonably require, including:
   (a) To store the goods at any suitable place;
   (b) To unpack the goods if they are packed in containers or vehicles, or to act otherwise in respect of the goods, including by moving them; and
   (c) To cause the goods to be sold or destroyed in accordance with the practices or pursuant to the law or regulations of the place where the goods are located at the time.
3. The carrier may exercise the rights under paragraph 2 of this article only after it has given reasonable notice of the intended action under paragraph 2 of this article to the person stated in the contract particulars as the person, if any, to be notified of the arrival of the goods at the place of destination, and to one of the following persons in the order indicated, if known to the carrier: the consignee, the controlling party or the shipper.
4. If the goods are sold pursuant to subparagraph 2 (*c*) of this article, the carrier shall hold the proceeds of the sale for the benefit of the person entitled to the goods, subject to the deduction of any costs incurred by the carrier and any other amounts that are due to the carrier in connection with the carriage of those goods.
5. The carrier shall not be liable for loss of or damage to goods that occurs during the time that they remain undelivered pursuant to this article unless the claimant proves that such loss or damage resulted from the failure by the carrier to take steps that would have been reasonable in the circumstances to preserve the goods and that the carrier knew or ought to have known that the loss or damage to the goods would result from its failure to take such steps.

Article 49 Retention of goods

Nothing in this Convention affects a right of the carrier or a performing party that may exist pursuant to the contract of carriage or the applicable law to retain the goods to secure the payment of sums due.

Chapter 10 Rights of the controlling party

Article 50 Exercise and extent of right of control

1. The right of control may be exercised only by the controlling party and is limited to:
   (a) The right to give or modify instructions in respect of the goods that do not constitute a variation of the contract of carriage;
   (b) The right to obtain delivery of the goods at a scheduled port of call or, in respect of inland carriage, any place en route; and

   (c) The right to replace the consignee by any other person including the controlling party.
2. The right of control exists during the entire period of responsibility of the carrier, as provided in article 12, and ceases when that period expires.

Article 51 Identity of the controlling party and transfer of the right of control

1. Except in the cases referred to in paragraphs 2, 3 and 4 of this article:
   (a) The shipper is the controlling party unless the shipper, when the contract of carriage is concluded, designates the consignee, the documentary shipper or another person as the controlling party;
   (b) The controlling party is person. The transfer becomes notification of the transfer by controlling party; and
   (c) The controlling party right of control.
2. When a non-negotiable transport document has been issued that indicates that it shall be surrendered in order to obtain delivery of the goods:
   (a) The shipper is the controlling party and may transfer the right of control to the consignee named in the transport document by transferring the document to that person without endorsement. If more than one original of the document was issued, all originals shall be transferred in order to effect a transfer of the right of control; and
   (b) In order to exercise its right of control, the controlling party shall produce the document and properly identify itself. If more than one original of the document was issued, all originals shall be produced, failing which the right of control cannot be exercised.
3. When a negotiable transport document is issued:
   (a) The holder or, if more than one original of the negotiable transport document is issued, the holder of all originals is the controlling party;
   (b) The holder may transfer the right of control by transferring the negotiable transport document to another person in accordance with article 57. If more than one original of that document was issued, all originals shall be transferred to that person in order to effect a transfer of the right of control; and
   (c) In order to exercise the right of control, the holder shall produce the negotiable transport document to the carrier, and if the holder is one of the persons referred to in article 1, subparagraph 10 (*a*) (i), the holder shall properly identify itself. If more than one original of the document was issued, all originals shall be produced, failing which the right of control cannot be exercised.
4. When a negotiable electronic transport record is issued:
   (a) The holder is the controlling party;
   (b) The holder may transfer the right of control to another person by transferring the negotiable electronic transport record in accordance with the procedures referred to in article 9, paragraph 1; and
   (c) In order to exercise the right of control, the holder shall demonstrate, in accordance with the procedures referred to in article 9, paragraph I, that it is the holder.

Article 52 Carrier's execution of instructions

1. Subject to paragraphs 2 and 3 of this article, the carrier shall execute the instructions referred to in article 50 if:
   (a) The person giving such instructions is entitled to exercise the right of control;
   (b) The instructions can reasonably be executed according to their terms at the moment that they reach the carrier; and
   (c) The instructions will not interfere with the normal operations of the carrier, including its delivery practices.
2. In any event, the controlling party shall reimburse the carrier for any reasonable additional expense that the carrier may incur and shall indemnify the carrier against loss or damage that the carrier may suffer as a result of diligently executing any instruction pursuant to this article, including compensation that the carrier may become liable to pay for loss of or damage to other goods being carried.
3. The carrier is entitled to obtain security from the controlling party for the amount of additional expense, loss or damage that the carrier reasonably expects will arise in connection with the execution of an instruction pursuant to this article. The carrier may refuse to carry out the instructions if no such security is provided.
4. The carrier's liability for loss of or damage to the goods or for delay in delivery resulting from its failure to comply with the instructions of the controlling party in breach of its obligation pursuant to paragraph 1 of this article shall be subject to articles 17 to 23, and the amount of the compensation payable by the carrier shall be subject to articles 59 to 61.

Article 53 Deemed delivery

Goods that are delivered pursuant to an instruction in accordance with article 52, paragraph 1, are deemed to be delivered at the place of destination, and the provisions of chapter 9 relating to such delivery apply to such goods.

Article 54 Variations to the contract of carriage

1. The controlling party is the only person that may agree with the carrier to variations to the contract of carriage other than those referred to in article 50, subparagraphs I (*b*) and (*c*).
2. Variations to the contract of carriage, including those referred to in article 50, subparagraphs 1 (*b*) and (*c*), shall be stated in a negotiable transport document or in a non-negotiable transport document that requires surrender, or incorporated in a negotiable electronic transport record, or, upon the request of the controlling party, shall be stated in a non-negotiable transport document or incorporated in a nonnegotiable electronic transport record. If so stated or incorporated, such variations shall be signed in accordance with article 38.

Article 55 Providing additional information, instructions or documents to carrier

1. The controlling party, on request of the carrier or a performing party, shall provide in a timely manner information, instructions or' documents relating to the goods not yet

provided by the shipper and not otherwise reasonably available to the carrier that the carrier may reasonably need to perform its obligations under the contract of carriage.

2. If the carrier, after reasonable effort, is unable to locate the controlling party or the controlling party is unable to provide adequate information, instructions or documents to the carrier, the shipper shall provide them. If the carrier, after reasonable effort, is unable to locate the shipper, the documentary shipper shall provide such information, instructions or documents.

Article 56 Variation by agreement

The parties to the contract of carriage may vary the effect of articles 50, subparagraphs 1 (*b*) and (*c*), 50, paragraph 2, and 52. The parties may also restrict or exclude the transferability of the right of control referred to in article 51, subparagraph 1 (*b*).

Chapter 11 Transfer of rights

Article 57 When a negotiable transport document or negotiable electronic transport record is issued

1. When a negotiable transport document is issued, the holder may transfer the rights incorporated in the document by transferring it to another person:
   (a) Duly endorsed either to such other person or in blank, if an order document; or
   (b) Without endorsement, if: (i) a bearer document or a blank endorsed document; or (ii) a document made out to the order of a named person and the transfer is between the first holder and the named person.
2. When a negotiable electronic transport record is issued, its holder may transfer the rights incorporated in it, whether it be made out to order or to the order of a named person, by transferring the electronic transport record in accordance with the procedures referred to in article 9, paragraph 1.

Article 58 Liability of holder

1. Without prejudice to article 55, a holder that is not the shipper and that does not exercise any right under the contract of carriage does not assume any liability under the contract of carriage solely by reason of being a holder.
2. A holder that is not the shipper and that exercises any right under the contract of carriage assumes any liabilities imposed on it under the contract of carriage to the extent that such liabilities are incorporated in or ascertainable from the negotiable transport document or the negotiable electronic transport record.
3. For the purposes of paragraphs 1 and 2 of this article, a holder that is not the shipper does not exercise any right under the contract of carriage solely because:
   (a) It agrees with the carrier, pursuant to article 10, to replace a negotiable transport document by a negotiable electronic transport record or to replace a negotiable electronic transport record by a negotiable transport document; or
   (b) It transfers its rights pursuant to article 57.

Chapter 12 Limits of liability

Article 59 Limits of liability

1. Subject to articles 60 and 61, paragraph 1, the carrier's liability for breaches of its obligations under this Convention is limited to 875 units of account per package or other shipping unit, or 3 units of account per kilogram of the gross weight of the goods that are the subject of the claim or dispute, whichever amount is the higher, except when the value of the goods has been declared by the shipper and included in the contract particulars, or when a higher amount than the amount of limitation of liability set out in this article has been agreed upon between the carrier and the shipper.
2. When goods are carried in or on a container, pallet or similar article of transport used to consolidate goods, or in or on a vehicle, the packages or shipping units enumerated in the contract particulars as packed in or on such article of transport or vehicle are deemed packages or shipping units. If not so enumerated, the goods in or on such article of transport or vehicle are deemed one shipping unit.
3. The unit of account referred to in this article is the Special Drawing Right as defined by the International Monetary Fund. The amounts referred to in this article are to be converted into the national currency of a State according to the value of such currency at the date of judgement or award or the date agreed upon by the parties. The value of a national currency, in terms of the Special Drawing Right, of a Contracting State that is a member of the International Monetary Fund is to be calculated in accordance with the method of valuation applied by the International Monetary Fund in effect at the date in question for its operations and transactions. The value of a national currency, in terms of the Special Drawing Right, of a Contracting State that is not a member of the International Monetary Fund is to be calculated in a manner to be determined by that State.

Article 60 Limits of liability for loss caused by delay

Subject to article 61, paragraph 2, compensation for loss of or damage to the goods due to delay shall be calculated in accordance with article 22 and liability for economic loss due to delay is limited to an amount equivalent to two and one-half times the freight payable on the goods delayed. The total amount payable pursuant to this article and article 59, paragraph 1, may not exceed the limit that would be established pursuant to article 59, paragraph 1, in respect of the total loss of the goods concerned.

Article 61 Loss of the benefit of limitation of liability

1. Neither the carrier nor any of the persons referred to in article 18 is entitled to the benefit of the limitation of liability as provided in article 59, or as provided in the contract of carriage, if the claimant proves that the loss resulting from the breach of the carrier's obligation under this Convention was attributable to a personal act or omission of the person claiming a right to limit done with the intent to cause such loss or recklessly and with knowledge that such loss would probably result.
2. Neither the carrier nor any of the persons mentioned in article 18 is entitled to the benefit of the limitation of liability as provided in article 60 if the claimant proves that the delay in delivery resulted from a personal act or omission of the person claiming a

right to limit done with the intent to cause the loss due to delay or recklessly and with knowledge that such loss would probably result.

Chapter 13 Time for suit

Article 62 Period of time for suit

1. No judicial or arbitral proceedings in respect of claims or disputes arising from a breach of an obligation under this Convention may be instituted after the expiration of a period of two years.
2. The period referred to in paragraph 1 of this article commences on the day on which the carrier has delivered the goods or, in cases in which no goods have been delivered or only part of the goods have been delivered, on the last day on which the goods should have been delivered. The day on which the period commences is not included in the period.
3. Notwithstanding the expiration of the period set out in paragraph 1 of this article, one party may rely on its claim as a defence or for the purpose of set-off against a claim asserted by the other party.

Article 63 Extension of time for suit

The period provided in article 62 shall not be subject to suspension or interruption, but the person against which a claim is made may at any time during the running of the period extend that period by a declaration to the claimant. This period may be further extended by another declaration or declarations.

Article 64 Action for indemnity

An action for indemnity by a person held liable may be instituted after the expiration of the period provided in article 62 if the indemnity action is instituted within the later of:

(a) The time allowed by the applicable law in the jurisdiction where proceedings are instituted; or

(b) Ninety days commencing from the day when the person instituting the action for indemnity has either settled the claim or been served with process in the action against itself, whichever is earlier.

Article 65 Actions against the person identified as the carrier

An action against the bareboat charterer or the person identified as the carrier pursuant to article 37, paragraph 2, may be instituted after the expiration of the period provided in article 62 if the action is instituted within the later of:

(a) The time allowed by the applicable law in the jurisdiction where proceedings are instituted; or

(b) Ninety days commencing from the day when the carrier has been identified, or the registered owner or bareboat charterer has rebutted the presumption that it is the carrier, pursuant to article 37, paragraph 2.

Chapter 14 Jurisdiction

Article 66 Actions against the carrier

Unless the contract of carriage contains an exclusive choice of court agreement that complies with article 67 or 72, the plaintiff has the right to institute judicial proceedings under this Convention against the carrier:

(a) In a competent court within the jurisdiction of which is situated one of the following places:
   (i) The domicile of the carrier;
   (ii) The place of receipt agreed in the contract of carriage;
   (iii) The place of delivery agreed in the contract of carriage; or
   (iv) The port where the goods are initially loaded on a ship or the port where the goods are finally discharged from a ship; or

(b) In a competent court or courts designated by an agreement between the shipper and the carrier for the purpose of deciding claims against the carrier that may arise under this Convention.

Article 67 Choice of court agreements

1. The jurisdiction of a court chosen in accordance with article 66, subparagraph *b*), is exclusive for disputes between the parties to the contract only if the parties so agree and the agreement conferring jurisdiction:
   (a) Is contained in a volume contract that clearly states the names and addresses of the parties and either (i) is individually negotiated or (ii) contains a prominent statement that there is an exclusive choice of court agreement and specifies the sections of the volume contract containing that agreement; and
   (b) Clearly designates the courts of one Contracting State or one or more specific courts of one Contracting State.
2. A person that is not a party to the volume contract is bound by an exclusive choice of court agreement concluded in accordance with paragraph 1 of this article only if:
   (a) The court is in one of the places designated in article 66, subparagraph (*a*);
   (b) That agreement is contained in the transport document or electronic transport record;
   (c) That person is given timely and adequate notice of the court where the action shall be brought and that the jurisdiction of that court is exclusive; and
   (d) The law of the court seized recognizes that that person may be bound by the exclusive choice of court agreement.

Article 68 Actions against the maritime performing party

The plaintiff has the right to institute judicial proceedings under this Convention against the maritime performing party in a competent court within the jurisdiction of which is situated one of the following places:

(a) The domicile of the maritime performing party; or

(b) The port where the goods are received by the maritime performing party, the port where the goods are delivered by the maritime performing party or the port in which the maritime performing party performs its activities with respect to the goods.

Article 69 No additional bases of jurisdiction

Subject to articles 71 and 72, no judicial proceedings under this Convention against the carrier or a maritime performing party may be instituted in a court not designated pursuant to article 66 or 68.

Article 70 Arrest and provisional or protective measures

Nothing in this Convention affects jurisdiction with regard to provisional or protective measures, including arrest. A court in a State in which a provisional or protective measure was taken does not have jurisdiction to determine the case upon its merits unless:

(a) The requirements of this chapter are fulfilled; or
(b) An international convention that applies in that State so provides.

Article 71 Consolidation. and removal of actions

1. Except when there is an exclusive choice of court agreement that is binding pursuant to article 67 or 72, if a single action is brought against both the carrier and the maritime performing party arising out of a single occurrence, the action may be instituted only in a court designated pursuant to both article 66 and article 68. If there is no such court, such action may be instituted in a court designated pursuant to article 68, subparagraph (*b*), if there is such a court.
2. Except when there is an exclusive choice of court agreement that is binding pursuant to article 67 or 72, a carrier or a maritime performing party that institutes an action seeking a declaration of non-liability or any other action that would deprive a person of its right to select the forum pursuant to article 66 or 68 shall, at the request of the defendant, withdraw that action once the defendant has chosen a court designated pursuant to article 66 or 68, whichever is applicable, where the action may be recommenced.

Article 72 Agreement after a dispute has arisen and jurisdiction when the defendant has entered an appearance

1. After a dispute has arisen, the parties to the dispute may agree to resolve it in any competent court.
2. A competent court before which a defendant appears, without contesting jurisdiction in accordance with the rules of that court, has jurisdiction.

Article 73 Recognition and enforcement

1. A decision made in one Contracting State by a court having jurisdiction under this Convention shall be recognized and enforced in another Contracting State in accordance with the law of such latter Contracting State when both States have made a declaration in accordance with article 74.

2. A court may refuse recognition and enforcement based on the grounds for the refusal of recognition and enforcement available pursuant to its law.
3. This chapter shall not affect the application of the rules of a regional economic integration organization that is a party to this Convention, as concerns the recognition or enforcement of judgements as between member States of the regional economic integration organization, whether adopted before or after this Convention.

Article 74 Application of chapter 14

The provisions of this chapter shall bind only Contracting States that declare in accordance with article 91 that they will be bound by them.

Chapter 15 Arbitration

Article 75 Arbitration agreements

1. Subject to this chapter, parties may agree that any dispute that may arise relating to the carriage of goods under this Convention shall be referred to arbitration.
2. The arbitration proceedings shall, at the option of the person asserting a claim against the carrier, take place at:
   (a) Any place designated for that purpose in the arbitration agreement; or
   (b) Any other place situated in a State where any of the following places is located:
      (i) The domicile of the carrier;
      (ii) The place of receipt agreed in the contract of carriage;
      (iii) The place of delivery agreed in the contract of carriage; or
      (iv) The port where the goods are initially loaded on a ship or the port where the goods are finally discharged from a ship.
3. The designation of the place of arbitration in the agreement is binding for disputes between the parties to the agreement if the agreement is contained in a volume contract that clearly states the names and addresses of the parties and either:
   (a) Is individually negotiated; or
   (b) Contains a prominent statement that there is an arbitration agreement and specifies the sections of the volume contract containing the arbitration agreement.
4. When an arbitration agreement has been concluded in accordance with paragraph 3 of this article, a person that is not a party to the volume contract is bound by the designation of the place of arbitration in that agreement only if:
   (a) The place of arbitration designated in the agreement is situated in one of the places referred to in subparagraph 2 (*b*) of this article;
   (b) The agreement is contained in the transport document or electronic transport record;
   (c) The person to be bound is given timely and adequate notice of the place of arbitration; and
   (d) Applicable law permits that person to be bound by the arbitration agreement.
5. The provisions of paragraphs 1, 2, 3 and 4 of this article are deemed to be part of every arbitration clause or agreement, and any term of such clause or agreement to the extent that it is inconsistent therewith is void.

Article 76 Arbitration agreement in non-liner transportation

1. Nothing in this Convention affects the enforceability of an arbitration agreement in a contract of carriage in non-liner transportation to which this Convention or the provisions of this Convention apply by reason of:
   (a) The application of article 7; or
   (b) The parties' voluntary incorporation of this Convention in a contract of carriage that would not otherwise be subject to this Convention.
2. Notwithstanding paragraph 1 of this article, an arbitration agreement in a transport document or electronic transport record to which this Convention applies by reason of the application of article 7 is subject to this chapter unless such a transport document or electronic transport record:
   (a) Identifies the parties to and the date of the charter party or other contract excluded from the application of this Convention by reason of the application of article 6; and
   (b) Incorporates by specific reference the clause in the charter party or other contract that contains the terms of the arbitration agreement.

Article 77 Agreement to arbitrate after a dispute has arisen

Notwithstanding the provisions of this chapter and chapter 14, after a dispute has arisen the parties to the dispute may agree to resolve it by arbitration in any place.

Article 78 Application of chapter 15

The provisions of this chapter shall bind only Contracting States that declare in accordance with article 91 that they will be bound by them.

Chapter 16 Validity of contractual terms

Article 79 General provisions

1. Unless otherwise provided in this Convention, any term in a contract of carriage is void to the extent that it:
   (a) Directly or indirectly excludes or limits the obligations of the carrier or a maritime performing party under this Convention;
   (b) Directly or indirectly excludes or limits the liability of the carrier or a maritime performing party for breach of an obligation under this Convention; or
   (c) Assigns a benefit of insurance of the goods in favour of the carrier or a person referred to in article 18.
2. Unless otherwise provided in this Convention, any term in a contract of carriage is void to the extent that it:
   (a) Directly or indirectly excludes, limits or increases the obligations under this Convention of the shipper, consignee, controlling party, holder or documentary shipper; or

(b) Directly or indirectly excludes, limits or increases the liability of the shipper, consignee, controlling party, holder or documentary shipper for breach of any of its obligations under this Convention.

Article 80 Special rules for volume contracts

1. Notwithstanding article 79, as between the carrier and the shipper, a volume contract to which this Convention applies may provide for greater or lesser rights, obligations and liabilities than those imposed by this Convention.
2. A derogation pursuant to paragraph 1 of this article is binding only when:
   (a) The volume contract contains a prominent statement that it derogates from this Convention;
   (b) The volume contract is (i) individually negotiated or (ii) prominently specifies the sections of the volume contract containing the derogations;
   (c) The shipper is given an opportunity and notice of the opportunity to conclude a contract of carriage on terms and conditions that comply with this Convention without any derogation under this article; and
   (d) The derogation is neither (i) incorporated by reference from another document nor (ii) included in a contract of adhesion that is not subject to negotiation.
3. A carrier's public schedule of prices and services, transport document, electronic transport record or similar document is not a volume contract pursuant to paragraph 1 of this article, but a volume contract may incorporate such documents by reference as terms of the contract.
4. Paragraph 1 of this article does not apply to rights and obligations provided in articles 14, subparagraphs (*a*) and (*b*), 29 and 32 or to liability arising from the breach thereof, nor does it apply to any liability arising from an act or omission referred to in article 61.
5. The terms of the volume contract that derogate from this Convention, if the volume contract satisfies the requirements of paragraph 2 of this article, apply between the carrier and any person other than the shipper provided that:
   (a) Such person received information that prominently states that the volume contract derogates from this Convention and gave its express consent to be bound by such derogations; and
   (b) Such consent is not solely set forth in a carrier's public schedule of prices and services, transport document or electronic transport record.
6. The party claiming the benefit of the derogation bears the burden of proof that the conditions for derogation have been fulfilled.

Article 81 Special rules for live animals and certain other goods

Notwithstanding article 79 and without prejudice to article 80, the contract of carriage may exclude or limit the obligations or the liability of both the carrier and a maritime performing party if:

(a) The goods are live animals, but any such exclusion or limitation will not be effective if the claimant proves that the loss of or damage to the goods, or delay in delivery, resulted from an act or omission of the carrier or of a person referred to in article 18, done with the intent to cause such loss of or damage to the goods or such loss due to delay or done recklessly and with knowledge that such loss or damage or such loss due to delay would probably result; or

(b) The character or condition of the goods or the circumstances and terms and conditions under which the carriage is to be performed are such as reasonably to justify a special agreement, provided that such contract of carriage is not related to ordinary commercial shipments made in the ordinary course of trade and that no negotiable transport document or negotiable electronic transport record is issued for the carriage of the goods.

Chapter 17 Matters not governed by this Convention

Article 82 International conventions governing the carriage of goods by other modes of transport

Nothing in this Convention affects the application of any of the following international conventions in force at the time this Convention enters into force, including any future amendment to such conventions, that regulate the liability of the carrier for loss of or damage to the goods:

(a) Any convention governing the carriage of goods by air to the extent that such convention according to its provisions applies to any part of the contract of carriage;
(b) Any convention governing the carriage of goods by road to the extent that such convention according to its provisions applies to the carriage of goods that remain loaded on a road cargo vehicle carried on board a ship;
(c) Any convention governing the carriage of goods by rail to the extent that such convention according to its provisions applies to carriage of goods by sea as a supplement to the carriage by rail; or
(d) Any convention governing the carriage of goods by inland waterways to the extent that such convention according to its provisions applies to a carriage of goods without transshipment both by inland waterways and sea.

Article 83 Global limitation of liability

Nothing in this Convention affects the application of any international convention or national law regulating the global limitation of liability of vessel owners.

Article 84 General average

Nothing in this Convention affects the application of terms in the contract of carriage or provisions of national law regarding the adjustment of general average.

Article 85 Passengers and luggage

This Convention does not apply to a contract of carriage for passengers and their luggage.

Article 86 Damage caused by nuclear incident

No liability arises under this Convention for damage caused by a nuclear incident if the operator of a nuclear installation is liable for such damage:

(a) Under the Paris Convention on Third Party Liability in the Field of Nuclear Energy 'of 29 July 1960 as amended by the Additional Protocol of 28 January 1964 and by the Protocols of 16 November 1982 and 12 February 2004, the Vienna Convention on Civil Liability for Nuclear Damage of 21 May 1963 as amended by the Joint Protocol Relating to the Application of the Vienna Convention and the Paris Convention of 21 September 1988 and as amended by the Protocol to Amend the 1963 Vienna Convention on Civil Liability for Nuclear Damage of 12 September 1997, or the Convention on Supplementary Compensation for Nuclear Damage of 12 September 1997, including any amendment to these conventions and any future convention in respect of the liability of the operator of a nuclear installation for damage caused by a nuclear incident; or

(b) Under national law applicable to the liability for such damage, provided that such law is in all respects as favourable to persons that may suffer damage as either the Paris or Vienna Conventions or the Convention on Supplementary Compensation for Nuclear Damage.

Chapter 18

Articles 87–98 [Omitted]

Section V

RULES AND MODEL LAWS

CMI Rules for Electronic Bills of Lading 1990

1 Scope of application

These rules shall apply whenever the parties so agree.

2 Definitions

(a) 'Contract of Carriage', means any agreement to carry goods wholly or partly by sea.
(b) 'EDI', means Electronic Data Interchange, that is, the interchange of trade data effected by teletransmission.
(c) 'UN/EDIFACT' means the United Nations Rules for Electronic Data Interchange for Administration, Commerce and Transport.
(d) 'Transmission' means one or more messages electronically sent together as one unit of dispatch which includes heading and terminating data.
(e) 'Confirmation' means a Transmission which advises that the content of a Transmission appears to be complete and correct, without prejudice to any subsequent consideration or action that the content may warrant.
(f) 'Private Key' means any technically appropriate form, such as a combination of numbers and/or letters, which the parties may agree for securing the authenticity and integrity of a Transmission.
(g) 'Holder' means the party who is entitled to the rights described in Article 7(a) by virtue of its possession of a valid Private Key.
(h) 'Electronic Monitoring System' means the device by which a computer system can be examined for the transactions that it recorded, such as a Trade Data Log or an Audit Trail.
(i) 'Electronic Storage' means any temporary, intermediate or permanent storage of electronic data including the primary and the back-up storage of such data.

3 Rules of procedure

(a) When not in conflict with these Rules, the Uniform Rules of Conduct for Interchange of Trade Data by Teletransmission, 1987 (UNCID) shall govern the conduct between the parties.
(b) The EDI under these Rules should conform with the relevant UN/EDIFACT standards. However, the parties may use any other method of trade data interchange acceptable to all of the users.
(c) Unless otherwise agreed, the document format for the Contract of Carriage shall conform to the UN Layout Key or compatible national standard for bills of lading.
(d) Unless otherwise agreed, a recipient of a Transmission is not authorised to act on a Transmission unless he has sent a Confirmation.
(e) In the event of a dispute arising between the parties as to the data actually transmitted, an Electronic Monitoring System may be used to verify the data received. Data concerning other transactions not related to the data in dispute are to be considered as trade secrets and thus not available for examination. If such data are unavoidably revealed as part of the examination of the Electronic Monitoring System, they must be treated as confidential and not released to any outside party or used for any other purpose.
(f) Any transfer of rights to the goods shall be considered to be private information, and shall not be released to any outside party not connected to the transport or clearance of the goods.

4 Form and content of the receipt message

(a) The carrier, upon receiving the goods from the shipper, shall give notice of the receipt of the goods to the shipper by a message at the electronic address specified by the shipper.
(b) This receipt message shall include –
    (i) the name of the shipper;
    (ii) the description of the goods, with any representations and reservations, in the same tenor as would be required if a paper bill of lading were issued;
    (iii) the date and place of the receipt of the goods;
    (iv) a reference to the carrier's terms and conditions of carriage; and
    (v) the Private Key to be used in subsequent Transmissions.
    (vi) The shipper must confirm this receipt message to the carrier, upon which Confirmation the shipper shall be the Holder.
(c) Upon demand of the Holder, the receipt message shall be updated with the date and place of shipment as soon as the goods have been loaded on board.
(d) The information contained in (ii), (iii) and (iv) of paragraph (b) above including the date and place of shipment if updated in accordance with paragraph (c) of this Rule, shall have the same force and effect as if the receipt message were contained in a paper bill of lading.

5 Terms and conditions of the contract of carriage

(a) It is agreed and understood that whenever the carrier makes a reference to its terms and conditions of carriage, these terms and conditions shall form part of the Contract of Carriage.

(b) Such terms and conditions must be readily available to the parties to the Contract of Carriage.
(c) In the event of any conflict or inconsistency between such terms and conditions and these Rules, these Rules shall prevail.

6 Applicable law

The Contract of Carriage shall be subject to any international convention or national law which would have been compulsorily applicable if a paper bill of lading had been issued.

7 Right of control and transfer

(a) The Holder is the only party who may, as against the carrier –
    (1) claim delivery of the goods;
    (2) nominate the consignee or substitute a nominated consignee for any other party, including itself;
    (3) transfer the Right of Control and Transfer to another party;
    (4) instruct the carrier on any other subject concerning the goods, in accordance with the terms and conditions of the Contract of Carriage, as if he were the holder of a paper bill of lading.
(b) A transfer of the Right of Control and Transfer shall be effected: (i) by notification of the current Holder to the carrier of its intention to transfer its Right of Control and Transfer to a proposed new Holder, and (ii) confirmation by the carrier of such notification message, whereupon (iii) the carrier shall transmit the information as referred to in article 4 (except for the Private Key) to the proposed new Holder, whereafter (iv) the proposed new Holder shall advise the carrier of its acceptance of the Right of Control and Transfer, whereupon (v) the carrier shall cancel the current Private Key and issue a new Private Key to the new Holder.
(c) If the proposed new Holder advises the carrier that it does not accept the Right of Control and Transfer or fails to advise the carrier of such acceptance within a reasonable time, the proposed transfer of the Right of Control and Transfer shall not take place. The carrier shall notify the current Holder accordingly and the current Private Key shall retain its validity.
(d) The transfer of the Right of Control and Transfer in the manner described above shall have the same effects as the transfer of such rights under a paper bill of lading.

8 The Private Key

(a) The Private Key is unique to each successive Holder. It is not transferable by the Holder. The carrier and the Holder shall each maintain the security of the Private Key.
(b) The carrier shall only be obliged to send a Confirmation of an electronic message to the last Holder to whom it issued a Private Key, when such Holder secures the Transmission containing such electronic message by the use of the Private Key.
(c) The Private Key must be separate and distinct from any means used to identify the Contract of Carriage, and any security password or identification used to access the computer network.

9 Delivery

(a) The carrier shall notify the Holder of the place and date of intended delivery of the goods. Upon such notification the Holder has a duty to nominate a consignee and to give adequate delivery instructions to the carrier with verification by the Private Key. In the absence of such nomination, the Holder will be deemed to be the consignee.
(b) The carrier shall deliver the goods to the consignee upon production of proper identification in accordance with the delivery instructions specified in paragraph (a) above; such delivery shall automatically cancel the Private Key.
(c) The carrier shall be under no liability for misdelivery if it can prove that it exercised reasonable care to ascertain that the party who claimed to be the consignee was in fact that party.

10 Option to receive a paper document

(a) The Holder has the option at any time prior to delivery of the goods to demand from the carrier a paper bill of lading. Such document shall be made available at a location to be determined by the Holder, provided that no carrier shall be obliged to make such document available at a place where it has no facilities and in such instance the carrier shall only be obliged to make the document available at the facility nearest to the location determined by the Holder. The carrier shall not be responsible for delays in delivering the goods resulting from the Holder exercising the above option.
(b) The carrier has the option at any time prior to delivery of the goods to issue to the Holder a paper bill of lading unless the exercise of such option could result in undue delay or disrupts the delivery of the goods.
(c) A bill of lading issued under Rules 10(a) or (b) shall include: the information set out in the receipt message referred to in Rule 4 (except for the Private Key); and (ii) a statement to the effect that the bill of lading has been issued upon termination of the procedures for EDI under the CMI Rules for Electronic Bills of Lading. The aforementioned bill of lading shall be issued at the option of the Holder either to the order of the Holder whose name for this purpose shall then be inserted in the bill of lading or 'to bearer'.
(d) The issuance of a paper bill of lading under Rule 10(a) or (b) shall cancel the Private Key and terminate the procedures for EDI under these Rules. Termination of these procedures by the Holder or the carrier will not relieve any of the parties to the Contract of Carriage of their rights, obligations or liabilities while performing under the present Rules nor of their rights, obligations or liabilities under the Contract of Carriage.
(e) The Holder may demand at any time the issuance of a print-out of the receipt message referred to in Rule 4 (except for the Private Key) marked as 'nonnegotiable copy'. The issuance of such a print-out shall not cancel the Private Key nor terminate the procedures for EDI.

11 Electronic data is equivalent to writing

The carrier and the shipper and all subsequent parties utilizing these procedures agree that any national or local law, custom or practice requiring the Contract of Carriage to be evidenced in writing and signed, is satisfied by the transmitted and confirmed electronic data residing on computer data storage media displayable in human language on a video screen or as printed out by a computer. In agreeing to adopt these Rules, the parties shall be taken to have agreed not to raise the defence that this contract is not in writing.

CMI Uniform Rules for Sea Waybills 1990

1 Scope of application

(i) These Rules shall be called the 'CMI Uniforms Rules for Sea Waybills'.
(ii) They shall apply when adopted by a contract of carriage which is not covered by a bill of lading or similar document of title, whether the contract be in writing or not.

2 Definitions

In these Rules –

'Contract of carriage' shall mean any contract of carriage subject to these Rules which is to be performed wholly or partly by sea.

'Goods' shall mean any goods carried or received for carriage under a contract of carriage.

'Carrier' and 'Shipper' shall mean the parties named in or identifiable as such from the contract of carriage.

'Consignee' shall mean the party named in or identifiable as such from the contract of carriage, or any person substituted as consignee in accordance with rule 6(i).

'Right of Control' shall mean the rights and obligations referred to in rule 6.

3 Agency

(i) The shipper on entering into the contract of carriage does so not only on his own behalf but also as agent for and on behalf of the consignee, and warrants to the carrier that he has authority so to do.
(ii) This rule shall apply if, and only if, it be necessary by the law applicable to the contract of carriage so as to enable the consignee to sue and be sued thereon. The consignee shall be under no greater liability than he would have been had the contract of carriage been covered by a bill of lading or similar document of title.

4 Rights and responsibilities

(i) The contract of carriage shall be subject to any International Convention or National Law which is, or if the contract of carriage had been covered by a bill of lading or similar document of title would have been, compulsorily applicable thereto. Such convention or law shall apply notwithstanding anything inconsistent therewith in the contract of carriage.
(ii) Subject always to subrule (i), the contract of carriage is governed by:
    (a) these Rules;
    (b) unless otherwise agreed by the parties, the carrier's standard terms and conditions for the trade, if any, including any terms and conditions relating to the non-sea part of the carriage;

(c) any other terms and conditions agreed by the parties.

(iii) In the event of any inconsistency between the terms and conditions mentioned under subrule (ii)(b) or (c) and these Rules, these Rules shall prevail.

5 Description of the goods

(i) The shipper warrants the accuracy of the particulars furnished by him relating to the goods, and shall indemnify the carrier against any loss, damage or expense resulting from any inaccuracy.

(ii) In the absence of reservation by the carrier, any statement in a sea waybill or similar document as to the quantity or condition of the goods shall:

(a) as between the carrier and the shipper be *prima facie* evidence of receipt of the goods as so stated;

(b) as between the carrier and the consignee be conclusive evidence of receipt of the goods as so stated, and proof to the contrary shall not be permitted, provided always that the consignee has acted in good faith.

6 Right of control

(i) Unless the shipper has exercised his option under subrule (ii) below, he shall be the only party entitled to give the carrier instructions in relation to the contract of carriage. Unless prohibited by the applicable law, he shall be entitled to change the name of the consignee at any time up to the consignee claiming delivery of the goods after their arrival at destination, provided he gives the carrier reasonable notice in writing, or by some other means acceptable to the carrier, thereby undertaking to indemnify the carrier against any additional expense caused thereby.

(ii) The shipper shall have the option, to be exercised not later than the receipt of the goods by the carrier, to transfer the right of control to the consignee. The exercise of this option must be noted on the sea waybill or similar document, if any. Where the option has been exercised the consignee shall have such rights as are referred to in subrule (i) above and the shipper shall cease to have such rights.

7 Delivery

(i) The carrier shall deliver the goods to the consignee upon production of proper identification.

(ii) The carrier shall be under no liability for wrong delivery if he can prove that he has exercised reasonable care to ascertain that the party claiming to be the consignee is in fact that party.

8 Validity

In the event of anything contained in these Rules or any such provisions as are incorporated into the contract of carriage by virtue of rule 4, being inconsistent with the provisions of any International Convention or National Law compulsorily applicable to the contract of carriage, such Rules and provisions shall to that extent but no further be null and void.

Hague Conference Principles on Choice of Law in International Commercial Contracts 2015

Article 1 Scope of the Principles

1. These Principles apply to choice of law in international contracts where each party is acting in the exercise of its trade or profession. They do not apply to consumer or employment contracts.
2. For the purposes of these Principles, a contract is international unless each party has its establishment in the same State and the relationship of the parties and all other relevant elements, regardless of the chosen law, are connected only with that State.
3. These Principles do not address the law governing –
   (a) the capacity of natural persons;
   (b) arbitration agreements and agreements on choice of court;
   (c) companies or other collective bodies and trusts;
   (d) insolvency;
   (e) the proprietary effects of contracts;
   (f) the issue of whether an agent is able to bind a principal to a third party.

Article 2 Freedom of choice

1. A contract is governed by the law chosen by the parties.
2. The parties may choose –
   (a) the law applicable to the whole contract or to only part of it; and
   (b) different laws for different parts of the contract.
3. The choice may be made or modified at any time. A choice or modification made after the contract has been concluded shall not prejudice its formal validity or the rights of third parties.
4. No connection is required between the law chosen and the parties or their transaction.

Article 3 Rules of law

The law chosen by the parties may be rules of law that are generally accepted on an international, supranational or regional level as a neutral and balanced set of rules, unless the law of the forum provides otherwise.

Article 4 Express and tacit choice

A choice of law, or any modification of a choice of law, must be made expressly or appear clearly from the provisions of the contract or the circumstances. An agreement between the parties to confer jurisdiction on a court or an arbitral tribunal to determine disputes under the contract is not in itself equivalent to a choice of law.

Article 5 Formal validity of the choice of law

A choice of law is not subject to any requirement as to form unless otherwise agreed by the parties.

Article 6 Agreement on the choice of law and battle of forms

1. Subject to paragraph 2 –
   (a) whether the parties have agreed to a choice of law is determined by the law that was purportedly agreed to;
   (b) if the parties have used standard terms designating two different laws and under both of these laws the same standard terms prevail, the law designated in the prevailing terms applies; if under these laws different standard terms prevail, or if under one or both of these laws no standard terms prevail, there is no choice of law.
2. The law of the State in which a party has its establishment determines whether that party has consented to the choice of law if, under the circumstances, it would not be reasonable to make that determination under the law specified in paragraph 1.

Article 7 Severability

A choice of law cannot be contested solely on the ground that the contract to which it applies is not valid.

Article 8 Exclusion of renvoi

A choice of law does not refer to rules of private international law of the law chosen by the parties unless the parties expressly provide otherwise.

Article 9 Scope of the chosen law

1. The law chosen by the parties shall govern all aspects of the contract between the parties, including but not limited to –
   (a) interpretation;
   (b) rights and obligations arising from the contract;
   (c) performance and the consequences of non-performance, including the assessment of damages;
   (d) the various ways of extinguishing obligations, and prescription and limitation periods;
   (e) validity and the consequences of invalidity of the contract;
   (f) burden of proof and legal presumptions;
   (g) pre-contractual obligations.
2. Paragraph 1 (e) does not preclude the application of any other governing law supporting the formal validity of the contract.

Article 10 Assignment

In the case of contractual assignment of a creditor's rights against a debtor arising from a contract between the debtor and creditor -

(a) if the parties to the contract of assignment have chosen the law governing that contract, the law chosen governs mutual rights and obligations of the creditor and the assignee arising from their contract;

(b) if the parties to the contract between the debtor and creditor have chosen the law governing that contract, the law chosen governs -
   (i) whether the assignment can be invoked against the debtor;
   (ii) the rights of the assignee against the debtor; and
   (iii) whether the obligations of the debtor have been discharged.

Article 11 Overriding mandatory rules and public policy (ordre public)

1. These Principles shall not prevent a court from applying overriding mandatory provisions of the law of the forum which apply irrespective of the law chosen by the parties.
2. The law of the forum determines when a court may or must apply or take into account overriding mandatory provisions of another law.
3. A court may exclude application of a provision of the law chosen by the parties only if and to the extent that the result of such application would be manifestly incompatible with fundamental notions of public policy (*ordre public*) of the forum.
4. The law of the forum determines when a court may or must apply or take into account the public policy (*ordre public*) of a State the law of which would be applicable in the absence of a choice of law.
5. These Principles shall not prevent an arbitral tribunal from applying or taking into account public policy (*ordre public*), or from applying or taking into account overriding mandatory provisions of a law other than the law chosen by the parties, if the arbitral tribunal is required or entitled to do so.

Article 12 Establishment

If a party has more than one establishment, the relevant establishment for the purpose of these Principles is the one which has the closest relationship to the contract at the time of its conclusion.

UNCITRAL Arbitration Rules (with New Article 1, Paragraph 4, as adopted in 2013)

Section I. Introductory Rules

*Scope of application**

Article 1

1. Where parties have agreed that disputes between them in respect of a defined legal relationship, whether contractual or not, shall be referred to arbitration under the UNCITRAL Arbitration Rules, then such disputes shall be settled in accordance with these Rules subject to such modification as the parties may agree.
2. The parties to an arbitration agreement concluded after 15 August 2010 shall be presumed to have referred to the Rules in effect on the date of commencement of the

* A model arbitration clause for contracts can be found in the annex to the Rules.

arbitration, unless the parties have agreed to apply a particular version of the Rules. That presumption does not apply where the arbitration agreement has been concluded by accepting after 15 August 2010 an offer made before that date.

3. These Rules shall govern the arbitration except that where any of these Rules is in conflict with a provision of the law applicable to the arbitration from which the parties cannot derogate, that provision shall prevail.
4. For investor-State arbitration initiated pursuant to a treaty providing for the protection of investments or investors, these Rules include the UNCITRAL Rules on Transparency in Treaty-based Investor-State Arbitration ("Rules on Transparency"), subject to article 1 of the Rules on Transparency.

Notice and calculation of periods of time

Article 2

1. A notice, including a notification, communication or proposal, may be transmitted by any means of communication that provides or allows for a record of its transmission.
2. If an address has been designated by a party specifically for this purpose or authorized by the arbitral tribunal, any notice shall be delivered to that party at that address, and if so delivered shall be deemed to have been received. Delivery by electronic means such as facsimile or e-mail may only be made to an address so designated or authorized.
3. In the absence of such designation or authorization, a notice is:
   (a) Received if it is physically delivered to the addressee; or
   (b) Deemed to have been received if it is delivered at the place of business, habitual residence or mailing address of the addressee.
4. If, after reasonable efforts, delivery cannot be effected in accordance with paragraphs 2 or 3, a notice is deemed to have been received if it is sent to the addressee's last-known place of business, habitual residence or mailing address by registered letter or any other means that provides a record of delivery or of attempted delivery.
5. A notice shall be deemed to have been received on the day it is delivered in accordance with paragraphs 2, 3 or 4, or attempted to be delivered in accordance with paragraph 4. A notice transmitted by electronic means is deemed to have been received on the day it is sent, except that a notice of arbitration so transmitted is only deemed to have been received on the day when it reaches the addressee's electronic address.
6. For the purpose of calculating a period of time under these Rules, such period shall begin to run on the day following the day when a notice is received. If the last day of such period is an official holiday or a non-business day at the residence or place of business of the addressee, the period is extended until the first business day which follows. Official holidays or non-business days occurring during the running of the period of time are included in calculating the period.

Notice of arbitration

Article 3

1. The party or parties initiating recourse to arbitration (hereinafter called the "claimant") shall communicate to the other party or parties (hereinafter called the "respondent") a notice of arbitration.

2. Arbitral proceedings shall be deemed to commence on the date on which the notice of arbitration is received by the respondent.
3. The notice of arbitration shall include the following:
   (a) A demand that the dispute be referred to arbitration;
   (b) The names and contact details of the parties;
   (c) Identification of the arbitration agreement that is invoked;
   (d) Identification of any contract or other legal instrument out of or in relation to which the dispute arises or, in the absence of such contract or instrument, a brief description of the relevant relationship;
   (e) A brief description of the claim and an indication of the amount involved, if any;
   (f) The relief or remedy sought;
   (g) A proposal as to the number of arbitrators, language and place of arbitration, if the parties have not previously agreed thereon.
4. The notice of arbitration may also include:
   (a) A proposal for the designation of an appointing authority referred to in article 6, paragraph 1;
   (b) A proposal for the appointment of a sole arbitrator referred to in article 8, paragraph 1;
   (c) Notification of the appointment of an arbitrator referred to in article 9 or 10.
5. The constitution of the arbitral tribunal shall not be hindered by any controversy with respect to the sufficiency of the notice of arbitration, which shall be finally resolved by the arbitral tribunal.

Response to the notice of arbitration

Article 4

1. Within 30 days of the receipt of the notice of arbitration, the respondent shall communicate to the claimant a response to the notice of arbitration, which shall include:
   (a) The name and contact details of each respondent;
   (b) A response to the information set forth in the notice of arbitration, pursuant to article 3, paragraphs 3 (c) to (g).
2. The response to the notice of arbitration may also include:
   (a) Any plea that an arbitral tribunal to be constituted under these Rules lacks jurisdiction;
   (b) A proposal for the designation of an appointing authority referred to in article 6, paragraph 1;
   (c) A proposal for the appointment of a sole arbitrator referred to in article 8, paragraph 1;
   (d) Notification of the appointment of an arbitrator referred to in article 9 or 10;
   (e) A brief description of counterclaims or claims for the purpose of a set-off, if any, including where relevant, an indication of the amounts involved, and the relief or remedy sought;
   (f) A notice of arbitration in accordance with article 3 in case the respondent formulates a claim against a party to the arbitration agreement other than the claimant.
3. The constitution of the arbitral tribunal shall not be hindered by any controversy with respect to the respondent's failure to communicate a response to the notice of arbitration, or an incomplete or late response to the notice of arbitration, which shall be finally resolved by the arbitral tribunal.

Representation and assistance

Article 5

Each party may be represented or assisted by persons chosen by it. The names and addresses of such persons must be communicated to all parties and to the arbitral tribunal. Such communication must specify whether the appointment is being made for purposes of representation or assistance. Where a person is to act as a representative of a party, the arbitral tribunal, on its own initiative or at the request of any party, may at any time require proof of authority granted to the representative in such a form as the arbitral tribunal may determine.

Designating and appointing authorities

Article 6

1. Unless the parties have already agreed on the choice of an appointing authority, a party may at any time propose the name or names of one or more institutions or persons, including the Secretary-General of the Permanent Court of Arbitration at The Hague (hereinafter called the "PCA"), one of whom would serve as appointing authority.
2. If all parties have not agreed on the choice of an appointing authority within 30 days after a proposal made in accordance with paragraph 1 has been received by all other parties, any party may request the Secretary-General of the PCA to designate the appointing authority.
3. Where these Rules provide for a period of time within which a party must refer a matter to an appointing authority and no appointing authority has been agreed on or designated, the period is suspended from the date on which a party initiates the procedure for agreeing on or designating an appointing authority until the date of such agreement or designation.
4. Except as referred to in article 41, paragraph 4, if the appointing authority refuses to act, or if it fails to appoint an arbitrator within 30 days after it receives a party's request to do so, fails to act within any other period provided by these Rules, or fails to decide on a challenge to an arbitrator within a reasonable time after receiving a party's request to do so, any party may request the Secretary-General of the PCA to designate a substitute appointing authority.
5. In exercising their functions under these Rules, the appointing authority and the Secretary-General of the PCA may require from any party and the arbitrators the information they deem necessary and they shall give the parties and, where appropriate, the arbitrators, an opportunity to present their views in any manner they consider appropriate. All such communications to and from the appointing authority and the Secretary-General of the PCA shall also be provided by the sender to all other parties.
6. When the appointing authority is requested to appoint an arbitrator pursuant to articles 8, 9, 10 or 14, the party making the request shall send to the appointing authority copies of the notice of arbitration and, if it exists, any response to the notice of arbitration.
7. The appointing authority shall have regard to such considerations as are likely to secure the appointment of an independent and impartial arbitrator and shall take into account the advisability of appointing an arbitrator of a nationality other than the nationalities of the parties.

Section II. Composition of the arbitral tribunal

Number of Arbitrators

Article 7

1. If the parties have not previously agreed on the number of arbitrators, and if within 30 days after the receipt by the respondent of the notice of arbitration the parties have not agreed that there shall be only one arbitrator, three arbitrators shall be appointed.
2. Notwithstanding paragraph 1, if no other parties have responded to a party's proposal to appoint a sole arbitrator within the time limit provided for in paragraph 1 and the party or parties concerned have failed to appoint a second arbitrator in accordance with article 9 or 10, the appointing authority may, at the request of a party, appoint a sole arbitrator pursuant to the procedure provided for in article 8, paragraph 2, if it determines that, in view of the circumstances of the case, this is more appropriate.

Appointment of arbitrators (Articles 8 to 10)

Article 8

1. If the parties have agreed that a sole arbitrator is to be appointed and if within 30 days after receipt by all other parties of a proposal for the appointment of a sole arbitrator the parties have not reached agreement thereon, a sole arbitrator shall, at the request of a party, be appointed by the appointing authority.
2. The appointing authority shall appoint the sole arbitrator as promptly as possible. In making the appointment, the appointing authority shall use the following list-procedure, unless the parties agree that the list-procedure should not be used or unless the appointing authority determines in its discretion that the use of the list-procedure is not appropriate for the case:
   (a) The appointing authority shall communicate to each of the parties an identical list containing at least three names;
   (b) Within 15 days after the receipt of this list, each party may return the list to the appointing authority after having deleted the name or names to which it objects and numbered the remaining names on the list in the order of its preference;
   (c) After the expiration of the above period of time the appointing authority shall appoint the sole arbitrator from among the names approved on the lists returned to it and in accordance with the order of preference indicated by the parties;
   (d) If for any reason the appointment cannot be made according to this procedure, the appointing authority may exercise its discretion in appointing the sole arbitrator.

Article 9

1. If three arbitrators are to be appointed, each party shall appoint one arbitrator. The two arbitrators thus appointed shall choose the third arbitrator who will act as the presiding arbitrator of the arbitral tribunal.
2. If within 30 days after the receipt of a party's notification of the appointment of an arbitrator the other party has not notified the first party of the arbitrator it has appointed, the first party may request the appointing authority to appoint the second arbitrator.

3. If within 30 days after the appointment of the second arbitrator the two arbitrators have not agreed on the choice of the presiding arbitrator, the presiding arbitrator shall be appointed by the appointing authority in the same way as a sole arbitrator would be appointed under article 8.

Article 10

1. For the purposes of article 9, paragraph 1, where three arbitrators are to be appointed and there are multiple parties as claimant or as respondent, unless the parties have agreed to another method of appointment of arbitrators, the multiple parties jointly, whether as claimant or as respondent, shall appoint an arbitrator.
2. If the parties have agreed that the arbitral tribunal is to be composed of a number of arbitrators other than one or three, the arbitrators shall be appointed according to the method agreed upon by the parties.
3. In the event of any failure to constitute the arbitral tribunal under these Rules, the appointing authority shall, at the request of any party, constitute the arbitral tribunal and, in doing so, may revoke any appointment already made and appoint or reappoint each of the arbitrators and designate one of them as the presiding arbitrator.

*Disclosures by and challenge of arbitrators*** *(Articles 11 to 13)*

Article 11

When a person is approached in connection with his or her possible appointment as an arbitrator, he or she shall disclose any circumstances likely to give rise to justifiable doubts as to his or her impartiality or independence. An arbitrator, from the time of his or her appointment and throughout the arbitral proceedings, shall without delay disclose any such circumstances to the parties and the other arbitrators unless they have already been informed by him or her of these circumstances.

Article 12

1. Any arbitrator may be challenged if circumstances exist that give rise to justifiable doubts as to the arbitrator's impartiality or independence.
2. A party may challenge the arbitrator appointed by it only for reasons of which it becomes aware after the appointment has been made.
3. In the event that an arbitrator fails to act or in the event of the de jure or de facto impossibility of his or her performing his or her functions, the procedure in respect of the challenge of an arbitrator as provided in article 13 shall apply.

Article 13

1. A party that intends to challenge an arbitrator shall send notice of its challenge within 15 days after it has been notified of the appointment of the challenged arbitrator, or within

** Model statements of independence pursuant to article 11 can be found in the annex to the Rules.

15 days after the circumstances mentioned in articles 11 and 12 became known to that party.

2. The notice of challenge shall be communicated to all other parties, to the arbitrator who is challenged and to the other arbitrators. The notice of challenge shall state the reasons for the challenge.
3. When an arbitrator has been challenged by a party, all parties may agree to the challenge. The arbitrator may also, after the challenge, withdraw from his or her office. In neither case does this imply acceptance of the validity of the grounds for the challenge.
4. If, within 15 days from the date of the notice of challenge, all parties do not agree to the challenge or the challenged arbitrator does not withdraw, the party making the challenge may elect to pursue it. In that case, within 30 days from the date of the notice of challenge, it shall seek a decision on the challenge by the appointing authority.

Replacement of an arbitrator

Article 14

1. Subject to paragraph 2, in any event where an arbitrator has to be replaced during the course of the arbitral proceedings, a substitute arbitrator shall be appointed or chosen pursuant to the procedure provided for in articles 8 to 11 that was applicable to the appointment or choice of the arbitrator being replaced. This procedure shall apply even if during the process of appointing the arbitrator to be replaced, a party had failed to exercise its right to appoint or to participate in the appointment.
2. If, at the request of a party, the appointing authority determines that, in view of the exceptional circumstances of the case, it would be justified for a party to be deprived of its right to appoint a substitute arbitrator, the appointing authority may, after giving an opportunity to the parties and the remaining arbitrators to express their views: (a) appoint the substitute arbitrator; or (b) after the closure of the hearings, authorize the other arbitrators to proceed with the arbitration and make any decision or award.

Repetition of hearings in the event of the replacement of an arbitrator

Article 15

If an arbitrator is replaced, the proceedings shall resume at the stage where the arbitrator who was replaced ceased to perform his or her functions, unless the arbitral tribunal decides otherwise.

Exclusion of liability

Article 16

Save for intentional wrongdoing, the parties waive, to the fullest extent permitted under the applicable law, any claim against the arbitrators, the appointing authority and any person appointed by the arbitral tribunal based on any act or omission in connection with the arbitration.

Section III. Arbitral proceedings

General provisions

Article 17

1. Subject to these Rules, the arbitral tribunal may conduct the arbitration in such manner as it considers appropriate, provided that the parties are treated with equality and that at an appropriate stage of the proceedings each party is given a reasonable opportunity of presenting its case. The arbitral tribunal, in exercising its discretion, shall conduct the proceedings so as to avoid unnecessary delay and expense and to provide a fair and efficient process for resolving the parties' dispute.
2. As soon as practicable after its constitution and after inviting the parties to express their views, the arbitral tribunal shall establish the provisional timetable of the arbitration. The arbitral tribunal may, at any time, after inviting the parties to express their views, extend or abridge any period of time prescribed under these Rules or agreed by the parties.
3. If at an appropriate stage of the proceedings any party so requests, the arbitral tribunal shall hold hearings for the presentation of evidence by witnesses, including expert witnesses, or for oral argument. In the absence of such a request, the arbitral tribunal shall decide whether to hold such hearings or whether the proceedings shall be conducted on the basis of documents and other materials.
4. All communications to the arbitral tribunal by one party shall be communicated by that party to all other parties. Such communications shall be made at the same time, except as otherwise permitted by the arbitral tribunal if it may do so under applicable law.
5. The arbitral tribunal may, at the request of any party, allow one or more third persons to be joined in the arbitration as a party provided such person is a party to the arbitration agreement, unless the arbitral tribunal finds, after giving all parties, including the person or persons to be joined, the opportunity to be heard, that joinder should not be permitted because of prejudice to any of those parties. The arbitral tribunal may make a single award or several awards in respect of all parties so involved in the arbitration.

Place of arbitration

Article 18

1. If the parties have not previously agreed on the place of arbitration, the place of arbitration shall be determined by the arbitral tribunal having regard to the circumstances of the case. The award shall be deemed to have been made at the place of arbitration.
2. The arbitral tribunal may meet at any location it considers appropriate for deliberations. Unless otherwise agreed by the parties, the arbitral tribunal may also meet at any location it considers appropriate for any other purpose, including hearings.

Language

Article 19

1. Subject to an agreement by the parties, the arbitral tribunal shall, promptly after its appointment, determine the language or languages to be used in the proceedings. This

determination shall apply to the statement of claim, the statement of defence, and any further written statements and, if oral hearings take place, to the language or languages to be used in such hearings.

2. The arbitral tribunal may order that any documents annexed to the statement of claim or statement of defence, and any supplementary documents or exhibits submitted in the course of the proceedings, delivered in their original language, shall be accompanied by a translation into the language or languages agreed upon by the parties or determined by the arbitral tribunal.

Statement of claim

Article 20

1. The claimant shall communicate its statement of claim in writing to the respondent and to each of the arbitrators within a period of time to be determined by the arbitral tribunal. The claimant may elect to treat its notice of arbitration referred to in article 3 as a statement of claim, provided that the notice of arbitration also complies with the requirements of paragraphs 2 to 4 of this article.
2. The statement of claim shall include the following particulars:
   (a) The names and contact details of the parties;
   (b) A statement of the facts supporting the claim;
   (c) The points at issue;
   (d) The relief or remedy sought;
   (e) The legal grounds or arguments supporting the claim.
3. A copy of any contract or other legal instrument out of or in relation to which the dispute arises and of the arbitration agreement shall be annexed to the statement of claim.
4. The statement of claim should, as far as possible, be accompanied by all documents and other evidence relied upon by the claimant, or contain references to them.

Statement of defence

Article 21

1. The respondent shall communicate its statement of defence in writing to the claimant and to each of the arbitrators within a period of time to be determined by the arbitral tribunal. The respondent may elect to treat its response to the notice of arbitration referred to in article 4 as a statement of defence, provided that the response to the notice of arbitration also complies with the requirements of paragraph 2 of this article.
2. The statement of defence shall reply to the particulars (b) to (e) of the statement of claim (art. 20, para. 2). The statement of defence should, as far as possible, be accompanied by all documents and other evidence relied upon by the respondent, or contain references to them.
3. In its statement of defence, or at a later stage in the arbitral proceedings if the arbitral tribunal decides that the delay was justified under the circumstances, the respondent may make a counterclaim or rely on a claim for the purpose of a set-off provided that the arbitral tribunal has jurisdiction over it.
4. The provisions of article 20, paragraphs 2 to 4, shall apply to a counterclaim, a claim under article 4, paragraph 2 (f), and a claim relied on for the purpose of a set-off.

Amendments to the claim or defence

Article 22

During the course of the arbitral proceedings, a party may amend or supplement its claim or defence, including a counterclaim or a claim for the purpose of a set-off, unless the arbitral tribunal considers it inappropriate to allow such amendment or supplement having regard to the delay in making it or prejudice to other parties or any other circumstances. However, a claim or defence, including a counterclaim or a claim for the purpose of a set-off, may not be amended or supplemented in such a manner that the amended or supplemented claim or defence falls outside the jurisdiction of the arbitral tribunal.

Pleas as to the jurisdiction of the arbitral tribunal

Article 23

1. The arbitral tribunal shall have the power to rule on its own jurisdiction, including any objections with respect to the existence or validity of the arbitration agreement. For that purpose, an arbitration clause that forms part of a contract shall be treated as an agreement independent of the other terms of the contract. A decision by the arbitral tribunal that the contract is null shall not entail automatically the invalidity of the arbitration clause.
2. A plea that the arbitral tribunal does not have jurisdiction shall be raised no later than in the statement of defence or, with respect to a counterclaim or a claim for the purpose of a set-off, in the reply to the counterclaim or to the claim for the purpose of a set-off. A party is not precluded from raising such a plea by the fact that it has appointed, or participated in the appointment of, an arbitrator. A plea that the arbitral tribunal is exceeding the scope of its authority shall be raised as soon as the matter alleged to be beyond the scope of its authority is raised during the arbitral proceedings. The arbitral tribunal may, in either case, admit a later plea if it considers the delay justified.
3. The arbitral tribunal may rule on a plea referred to in paragraph 2 either as a preliminary question or in an award on the merits. The arbitral tribunal may continue the arbitral proceedings and make an award, notwithstanding any pending challenge to its jurisdiction before a court.

Further written statements

Article 24

The arbitral tribunal shall decide which further written statements, in addition to the statement of claim and the statement of defence, shall be required from the parties or may be presented by them and shall fix the periods of time for communicating such statements.

Periods of time

Article 25

The periods of time fixed by the arbitral tribunal for the communication of written statements (including the statement of claim and statement of defence) should not exceed 45 days. However the arbitral tribunal may extend the time limits if it concludes that an extension is justified.

Interim measures

Article 26

1. The arbitral tribunal may, at the request of a party, grant interim measures.
2. An interim measure is *any* temporary measure by which, at any time prior to the issuance of the award by which the dispute is finally decided, the arbitral tribunal orders a party, for example and without limitation, to:
   (a) Maintain or restore the status quo pending determination of the dispute;
   (b) Take action that would prevent, or refrain from taking action that is likely to cause, (i) current or imminent harm or (ii) prejudice to the arbitral process itself;
   (c) Provide a means of preserving assets out of which a subsequent award may be satisfied; or
   (d) Preserve evidence that may be relevant and material to the resolution of the dispute.
3. The party requesting an interim measure under paragraphs 2 (a) to (c) shall satisfy the arbitral tribunal that:
   (a) Harm not adequately reparable by an award of damages is likely to result if the measure is not ordered, and such harm substantially outweighs the harm that is likely to result to the party against whom the measure is directed if the measure is granted; and
   (b) There is a reasonable possibility that the requesting party will succeed on the merits of the claim. The determination on this possibility shall not affect the discretion of the arbitral tribunal in making any subsequent determination.
4. With regard to a request for an interim measure under paragraph 2 (d), the requirements in paragraphs 3 (a) and (b) shall apply only to the extent the arbitral tribunal considers appropriate.
5. The arbitral tribunal may modify, suspend or terminate an interim measure it has granted, upon application of any party or, in exceptional circumstances and upon prior notice to the parties, on the arbitral tribunal's own initiative.
6. The arbitral tribunal may require the party requesting an interim measure to provide appropriate security in connection with the measure.
7. The arbitral tribunal may require any party promptly to disclose any material change in the circumstances on the basis of which the interim measure was requested or granted.
8. The party requesting an interim measure may be liable for any costs and damages caused by the measure to any party if the arbitral tribunal later determines that, in the circumstances then prevailing, the measure should not have been granted. The arbitral tribunal may award such costs and damages at any point during the proceedings.
9. A request for interim measures addressed by any party to a judicial authority shall not be deemed incompatible with the agreement to arbitrate, or as a waiver of that agreement.

Evidence

Article 27

1. Each party shall have the burden of proving the facts relied on to support its claim or defence.
2. Witnesses, including expert witnesses, who are presented by the parties to testify to the arbitral tribunal on any issue of fact or expertise may be any individual, notwithstanding

that the individual is a party to the arbitration or in any way related to a party. Unless otherwise directed by the arbitral tribunal, statements by witnesses, including expert witnesses, may be presented in writing and signed by them.

3. At any time during the arbitral proceedings the arbitral tribunal may require the parties to produce documents, exhibits or other evidence within such a period of time as the arbitral tribunal shall determine.
4. The arbitral tribunal shall determine the admissibility, relevance, materiality and weight of the evidence offered.

Hearings

Article 28

1. In the event of an oral hearing, the arbitral tribunal shall give the parties adequate advance notice of the date, time and place thereof.
2. Witnesses, including expert witnesses, may be heard under the conditions and examined in the manner set by the arbitral tribunal.
3. Hearings shall be held in camera unless the parties agree otherwise. The arbitral tribunal may require the retirement of any witness or witnesses, including expert witnesses, during the testimony of such other witnesses, except that a witness, including an expert witness, who is a party to the arbitration shall not, in principle, be asked to retire.
4. The arbitral tribunal may direct that witnesses, including expert witnesses, be examined through means of telecommunication that do not require their physical presence at the hearing (such as videoconference).

Experts appointed by the arbitral tribunal

Article 29

1. After consultation with the parties, the arbitral tribunal may appoint one or more independent experts to report to it, in writing, on specific issues to be determined by the arbitral tribunal. A copy of the expert's terms of reference, established by the arbitral tribunal, shall be communicated to the parties.
2. The expert shall, in principle before accepting appointment, submit to the arbitral tribunal and to the parties a description of his or her qualifications and a statement of his or her impartiality and independence. Within the time ordered by the arbitral tribunal, the parties shall inform the arbitral tribunal whether they have any objections as to the expert's qualifications, impartiality or independence. The arbitral tribunal shall decide promptly whether to accept any such objections. After an expert's appointment, a party may object to the expert's qualifications, impartiality or independence only if the objection is for reasons of which the party becomes aware after the appointment has been made. The arbitral tribunal shall decide promptly what, if any, action to take.
3. The parties shall give the expert any relevant information or produce for his or her inspection any relevant documents or goods that he or she may require of them. Any dispute between a party and such expert as to the relevance of the required information or production shall be referred to the arbitral tribunal for decision.

4. Upon receipt of the expert's report, the arbitral tribunal shall communicate a copy of the report to the parties, which shall be given the opportunity to express, in writing, their opinion on the report. A party shall be entitled to examine any document on which the expert has relied in his or her report.
5. At the request of any party, the expert, after delivery of the report, may be heard at a hearing where the parties shall have the opportunity to be present and to interrogate the expert. At this hearing, any party may present expert witnesses in order to testify on the points at issue. The provisions of article 28 shall be applicable to such proceedings.

Default

Article 30

1. If, within the period of time fixed by these Rules or the arbitral tribunal, without showing sufficient cause:
    (a) The claimant has failed to communicate its statement of claim, the arbitral tribunal shall issue an order for the termination of the arbitral proceedings, unless there are remaining matters that may need to be decided and the arbitral tribunal considers it appropriate to do so;
    (b) The respondent has failed to communicate its response to the notice of arbitration or its statement of defence, the arbi-tral tribunal shall order that the proceedings continue, without treating such failure in itself as an admission of the claimant's allegations; the provisions of this subparagraph also apply to a claimant's failure to submit a defence to a counterclaim or to a claim for the purpose of a set-off.
2. If a party, duly noti ed under these Rules, fails to appear at a hearing, without showing sufficient cause for such failure, the arbitral tribunal may proceed with the arbitration.
3. If a party, duly invited by the arbitral tribunal to produce documents, exhibits or other evidence, fails to do so within the established period of time, without showing sufficient cause for such failure, the arbitral tribunal may make the award on the evidence before it.

Closure of hearings

Article 31

1. The arbitral tribunal may inquire of the parties if they have any further proof to offer or witnesses to be heard or sub-missions to make and, if there are none, it may declare the hearings closed.
2. The arbitral tribunal may, if it considers it necessary owing to exceptional circumstances, decide, on its own initiative or upon application of a party, to reopen the hearings at any time before the award is made.

Waiver of right to object

Article 32

A failure by any party to object promptly to any non-compliance with these Rules or with any requirement of the arbitration agreement shall be deemed to be a waiver of the right of such party to make such an objection, unless such party can show that, under the circumstances, its failure to object was justified.

Section IV. The award

Decisions

Article 33

1. When there is more than one arbitrator, any award or other decision of the arbitral tribunal shall be made by a majority of the arbitrators.
2. In the case of questions of procedure, when there is no majority or when the arbitral tribunal so authorizes, the presiding arbitrator may decide alone, subject to revision, if any, by the arbitral tribunal.

Form and effect of the award

Article 34

1. The arbitral tribunal may make separate awards on different issues at different times.
2. All awards shall be made in writing and shall be final and binding on the parties. The parties shall carry out all awards without delay.
3. The arbitral tribunal shall state the reasons upon which the award is based, unless the parties have agreed that no reasons are to be given.
4. An award shall be signed by the arbitrators and it shall contain the date on which the award was made and indicate the place of arbitration. Where there is more than one arbitrator and any of them fails to sign, the award shall state the reason for the absence of the signature.
5. An award may be made public with the consent of all parties or where and to the extent disclosure is required of a party by legal duty, to protect or pursue a legal right or in relation to legal proceedings before a court or other competent authority.
6. Copies of the award signed by the arbitrators shall be communicated to the parties by the arbitral tribunal.

Applicable law, amiable compositeur

Article 35

1. The arbitral tribunal shall apply the rules of law designated by the parties as applicable to the substance of the dispute. Failing such designation by the parties, the arbitral tribunal shall apply the law which it determines to be appropriate.
2. The arbitral tribunal shall decide as amiable compositeur or ex aequo et bono only if the parties have expressly authorized the arbitral tribunal to do so.
3. In all cases, the arbitral tribunal shall decide in accordance with the terms of the contract, if any, and shall take into account any usage of trade applicable to the transaction.

Settlement or other grounds for termination

Article 36

1. If, before the award is made, the parties agree on a settlement of the dispute, the arbitral tribunal shall either issue an order for the termination of the arbitral proceedings or, if

requested by the parties and accepted by the arbitral tribunal, record the settlement in the form of an arbitral award on agreed terms. The arbitral tribunal is not obliged to give reasons for such an award.

2. If, before the award is made, the continuation of the arbitral proceedings becomes unnecessary or impossible for any reason not mentioned in paragraph 1, the arbitral tribunal shall inform the parties of its intention to issue an order for the termination of the proceedings. The arbitral tribunal shall have the power to issue such an order unless there are remaining matters that may need to be decided and the arbitral tribunal considers it appropriate to do so.
3. Copies of the order for termination of the arbitral proceedings or of the arbitral award on agreed terms, signed by the arbitrators, shall be communicated by the arbitral tribunal to the parties. Where an arbitral award on agreed terms is made, the provisions of article 34, paragraphs 2, 4 and 5, shall apply.

Interpretation of the award

Article 37

1. Within 30 days after the receipt of the award, a party, with notice to the other parties, may request that the arbitral tribunal give an interpretation of the award.
2. The interpretation shall be given in writing within 45 days after the receipt of the request. The interpretation shall form part of the award and the provisions of article 34, paragraphs 2 to 6, shall apply.

Correction of the award

Article 38

1. Within 30 days after the receipt of the award, a party, with notice to the other parties, may request the arbitral tribunal to correct in the award any error in computation, any clerical or typographical error, or any error or omission of a similar nature. If the arbitral tribunal considers that the request is justified, it shall make the correction within 45 days of receipt of the request.
2. The arbitral tribunal may within 30 days after the communication of the award make such corrections on its own initiative.
3. Such corrections shall be in writing and shall form part of the award. The provisions of article 34, paragraphs 2 to 6, shall apply.

Additional award

Article 39

1. Within 30 days after the receipt of the termination order or the award, a party, with notice to the other parties, may request the arbitral tribunal to make an award or an additional award as to claims presented in the arbitral proceedings but not decided by the arbitral tribunal.
2. If the arbitral tribunal considers the request for an award or additional award to be justified, it shall render or complete its award within 60 days after the receipt of the request.

The arbitral tribunal may extend, if necessary, the period of time within which it shall make the award.

3. When such an award or additional award is made, the provisions of article 34, paragraphs 2 to 6, shall apply.

Definition of costs

Article 40

1. The arbitral tribunal shall fix the costs of arbitration in the final award and, if it deems appropriate, in another decision.
2. The term "costs" includes only:
   (a) The fees of the arbitral tribunal to be stated separately as to each arbitrator and to be fixed by the tribunal itself in accordance with article 41;
   (b) The reasonable travel and other expenses incurred by the arbitrators;
   (c) The reasonable costs of expert advice and of other assistance required by the arbitral tribunal;
   (d) The reasonable travel and other expenses of witnesses to the extent such expenses are approved by the arbitral tribunal;
   (e) The legal and other costs incurred by the parties in relation to the arbitration to the extent that the arbitral tribunal determines that the amount of such costs is reasonable;
   (f) Any fees and expenses of the appointing authority as well as the fees and expenses of the Secretary-General of the PCA.
3. In relation to interpretation, correction or completion of any award under articles 37 to 39, the arbitral tribunal may charge the costs referred to in paragraphs 2 (b) to (f), but no additional fees.

Fees and expenses of arbitrators

Article 41

1. The fees and expenses of the arbitrators shall be reasonable in amount, taking into account the amount in dispute, the complexity of the subject matter, the time spent by the arbitrators and any other relevant circumstances of the case.
2. If there is an appointing authority and it applies or has stated that it will apply a schedule or particular method for determining the fees for arbitrators in international cases, the arbitral tribunal in fixing its fees shall take that schedule or method into account to the extent that it considers appropriate in the circumstances of the case.
3. Promptly after its constitution, the arbitral tribunal shall inform the parties as to how it proposes to determine its fees and expenses, including any rates it intends to apply. Within 15 days of receiving that proposal, any party may refer the proposal to the appointing authority for review. If, within 45 days of receipt of such a referral, the appointing authority finds that the proposal of the arbitral tribunal is inconsistent with paragraph 1, it shall make any necessary adjustments thereto, which shall be binding upon the arbitral tribunal.

4.
   (a) When informing the parties of the arbitrators' fees and expenses that have been fixed pursuant to article 40, paragraphs 2 (a) and (b), the arbitral tribunal shall also explain the manner in which the corresponding amounts have been calculated;
   (b) Within 15 days of receiving the arbitral tribunal's determination of fees and expenses, any party may refer for review such determination to the appointing authority. If no appointing authority has been agreed upon or designated, or if the appointing authority fails to act within the time specified in these Rules, then the review shall be made by the Secretary-General of the PCA;
   (c) If the appointing authority or the Secretary-General of the PCA finds that the arbitral tribunal's determination is inconsistent with the arbitral tribunal's proposal (and any adjustment thereto) under paragraph 3 or is otherwise manifestly excessive, it shall, within 45 days of receiving such a referral, make any adjustments to the arbitral tribunal's determination that are necessary to satisfy the criteria in paragraph 1. Any such adjustments shall be binding upon the arbitral tribunal;
   (d) Any such adjustments shall either be included by the arbitral tribunal in its award or, if the award has already been issued, be implemented in a correction to the award, to which the procedure of article 38, paragraph 3, shall apply.
5. Throughout the procedure under paragraphs 3 and 4, the arbitral tribunal shall proceed with the arbitration, in accordance with article 17, paragraph 1.
6. A referral under paragraph 4 shall not affect any determination in the award other than the arbitral tribunal's fees and expenses; nor shall it delay the recognition and enforcement of all parts of the award other than those relating to the determination of the arbitral tribunal's fees and expenses.

Allocation of costs

Article 42

1. The costs of the arbitration shall in principle be borne by the unsuccessful party or parties. However, the arbitral tribunal may apportion each of such costs between the parties if it determines that apportionment is reasonable, taking into account the circumstances of the case.
2. The arbitral tribunal shall in the final award or, if it deems appropriate, in any other award, determine any amount that a party may have to pay to another party as a result of the decision on allocation of costs.

Deposit of costs

Article 43

1. The arbitral tribunal, on its establishment, may request the parties to deposit an equal amount as an advance for the costs referred to in article 40, paragraphs 2 (a) to (c).
2. During the course of the arbitral proceedings the arbitral tribunal may request supplementary deposits from the parties.

3. If an appointing authority has been agreed upon or designated, and when a party so requests and the appointing authority consents to perform the function, the arbitral tribunal shall fix the amounts of any deposits or supplementary deposits only after consultation with the appointing authority, which may make any comments to the arbitral tribunal that it deems appropriate concerning the amount of such deposits and supplementary deposits.
4. If the required deposits are not paid in full within 30 days after the receipt of the request, the arbitral tribunal shall so inform the parties in order that one or more of them may make the required payment. If such payment is not made, the arbitral tribunal may order the suspension or termination of the arbitral proceedings.
5. After a termination order or final award has been made, the arbitral tribunal shall render an accounting to the parties of the deposits received and return any unexpended balance to the parties.

UNCITRAL Conciliation Rules 1980

Application of the Rules

Article 1

(1) These Rules apply to conciliation of disputes arising out of or relating to a contractual or other legal relationship where the parties seeking an amicable settlement of their dispute have agreed that the UNCITRAL Conciliation Rules apply.
(2) The parties may agree to exclude or vary any of these Rules at any time.
(3) Where any of these Rules is in conflict with a provision of law from which the parties cannot derogate, that provision prevails.

Commencement of conciliation proceedings

Article 2

(1) The party initiating conciliation sends to the other party a written invitation to conciliate under these Rules, briefly identifying the subject of the dispute.
(2) Conciliation proceedings commence when the other party accepts the invitation to conciliate. If the acceptance is made orally, it is advisable that it be confirmed in writing.
(3) If the other party rejects the invitation, there will be no conciliation proceedings.
(4) If the party initiating conciliation does not receive a reply within thirty days from the date on which he sends the invitation, or within such other period of time as specified in the invitation, he may elect to treat this as a rejection of the invitation to conciliate. If he so elects, he informs the other party accordingly.

Number of conciliators

Article 3

There shall be one conciliator unless the parties agree that there shall be two or three conciliators. Where there is more than one conciliator, they ought, as a general rule, to act jointly.

Appointment of conciliators

Article 4

(1) (a) In conciliation proceedings with one conciliator, the parties shall endeavour to reach agreement on the name of a sole conciliator;
(b) In conciliation proceedings with two conciliators, each party appoints one conciliator;
(c) In conciliation proceedings with three conciliators, each party appoints one conciliator. The parties shall endeavour to reach agreement on the name of the third conciliator.

(2) Parties may enlist the assistance of an appropriate institution or person in connexion with the appointment of conciliators. In particular –
(a) a party may request such an institution or person to recommend the names of suitable individuals to act as conciliator; or
(b) the parties may agree that the appointment of one or more conciliators be made directly by such an institution or person.

In recommending or appointing individuals to act as conciliator, the institution or person shall have regard to such considerations as are likely to secure the appointment of an independent and impartial conciliator and, with respect to a sole or third conciliator, shall take into account the advisability of appointing a conciliator of a nationality other than the nationalities of the parties.

Submission of statements to conciliator

Article 5

(1) The conciliator,* upon his appointment, requests each party to submit to him a brief written statement describing the general nature of the dispute and the points at issue. Each party sends a copy of his statement to the other party.

(2) The conciliator may request each party to submit to him a further written statement of his position and the facts and grounds in support thereof, supplemented by any documents and other evidence that such party deems appropriate. The party sends a copy of his statement to the other party.

(3) At any stage of the conciliation proceedings the conciliator may request a party to submit to him such additional information as he deems appropriate.

Representation and assistance

Article 6

The parties may be represented or assisted by persons of their choice. The names and addresses of such persons are to be communicated in writing to the other party and to the conciliator; such communication is to specify whether the appointment is made for purposes of representation or of assistance.

* In this and all following articles, the term 'conciliator' applies to a sole conciliator, two or three conciliators, as the case may be.

Role of conciliator

Article 7

(1) The conciliator assists the parties in an independent and impartial manner in their attempt to reach an amicable settlement of their dispute.
(2) The conciliator will be guided by principles of objectivity, fairness and justice, giving consideration to, among other things, the rights and obligations of the parties, the usages of the trade concerned and the circumstances surrounding the dispute, including any previous business practices between the parties.
(3) The conciliator may conduct the conciliation proceedings in such a manner as he considers appropriate taking into account the circumstances of the case, the wishes the parties may express, including any request by a party that the conciliator hear oral statements, and the need for a speedy settlement of the dispute.
(4) The conciliator may, at any stage of the conciliation proceedings, make proposals for a settlement of the dispute. Such proposals need not be in writing and need not be accompanied by a statement of the reasons therefor.

Administrative assistance

Article 8

In order to facilitate the conduct of the conciliation proceedings, the parties, or the conciliator with the consent of the parties, may arrange for administrative assistance by a suitable institution or person.

Communication between conciliator and parties

Article 9

(1) The conciliator may invite the parties to meet with him or may communicate with them orally or in writing. He may meet or communicate with the parties together or with each of them separately.
(2) Unless the parties have agreed upon the place where meetings with the conciliator are to be held, such place will be determined by the conciliator, after consultation with the parties, having regard to the circumstances of the conciliation proceedings.

Disclosure of information

Article 10

When the conciliator receives factual information concerning the dispute from a party, he discloses the substance of that information to the other party in order that the other party may have the opportunity to present any explanation which he considers appropriate. However, when a party gives any information to the conciliator subject to a specific condition that it be kept confidential, the conciliator does not disclose that information to the other party.

Co-operation of parties with conciliator

Article 11

The parties will in good faith co-operate with the conciliator and, in particular, will endeavour to comply with requests by the conciliator to submit written materials, provide evidence and attend meetings.

Suggestions by parties for settlement of dispute

Article 12

Each party may, on his own initiative or at the invitation of the conciliator, submit to the conciliator suggestions for the settlement of the dispute.

Settlement agreement

Article 13

(1) When it appears to the conciliator that there exist elements of a settlement which would be acceptable to the parties, he formulates the terms of a possible settlement and submits them to the parties for their observations. After receiving the observations of the parties, the conciliator may reformulate the terms of a possible settlement in the light of such observations.
(2) If the parties reach agreement on a settlement of the dispute, they draw up and sign a written settlement agreement.** If requested by the parties, the conciliator draws up, or assists the parties in drawing up, the settlement agreement.
(3) The parties by signing the settlement agreement put an end to the dispute and are bound by the agreement.

Confidentiality

Article 14

The Conciliator and the parties must keep confidential all matters relating to the conciliation proceedings. Confidentiality extends also to the settlement agreement, except where its disclosure is necessary for purposes of implementation and enforcement.

Termination of conciliation proceedings

Article 15

The conciliation proceedings are terminated –

(a) by the signing of the settlement agreement by the parties, on the date of the agreement; or

** The parties may wish to consider including in the settlement agreement a clause that any dispute arising out of or relating to the settlement agreement shall be submitted to arbitration.

(b) by a written declaration of the conciliator, after consultation with the parties, to the effect that further efforts at conciliation are no longer justified, on the date of the declaration; or
(c) by a written declaration of the parties addressed to the conciliator to the effect that the conciliation proceedings are terminated, on the date of the declaration; or
(d) by a written declaration of a party to the other party and the conciliator, if appointed, to the effect that the conciliation proceedings are terminated, on the date of the declaration.

Resort to arbitral or judicial proceedings

Article 16

The parties undertake not to initiate, during the conciliation proceedings, any arbitral or judicial proceedings in respect of a dispute that is the subject of the conciliation proceedings, except that a party may initiate arbitral or judicial proceedings where, in his opinion, such proceedings are necessary for preserving his rights.

Costs

Article 17

(1) Upon termination of the conciliation proceedings, the conciliator fixes the costs of the conciliation and gives written notice thereof to the parties. The term 'costs' includes only –
  (a) the fee of the conciliator which shall be reasonable in amount;
  (b) the travel and other expenses of the conciliator;
  (c) the travel and other expenses of witnesses requested by the conciliator with the consent of the parties;
  (d) the cost of any expert advice requested by the conciliator with the consent of the parties;
  (e) the cost of any assistance provided pursuant to articles 4, paragraph (2)(b), and 8 of these Rules.
(2) The costs, as defined above, are borne equally by the parties unless the settlement agreement provides for a different apportionment. All other expenses incurred by a party are borne by that party.

Deposits

Article 18

(1) The conciliator, upon his appointment, may request each party to deposit an equal amount as an advance for the costs referred to in article 17, paragraph (1) which he expects will be incurred.
(2) During the course of the conciliation proceedings the conciliator may request supplementary deposits in an equal amount from each party.
(3) If the required deposits under paragraphs (1) and (2) of this article are not paid in full by both parties within thirty days, the conciliator may suspend the proceedings or may make a written declaration of termination to the parties, effective on the date of that declaration.

(4) Upon termination of the conciliation proceedings, the conciliator renders an accounting to the parties of the deposits received and returns any unexpended balance to the parties.

Role of conciliator in other proceedings

Article 19

The parties and the conciliator undertake that the conciliator will not act as an arbitrator or as a representative or counsel of a party in any arbitral or judicial proceedings in respect of a dispute that is the subject of the conciliation proceedings. The parties also undertake that they will not present the conciliator as a witness in any such proceedings.

Admissibility of evidence in other proceedings

Article 20

The parties undertake not to rely on or introduce as evidence in arbitral or judicial proceedings, whether or not such proceedings relate to the dispute that is the subject of the conciliation proceedings –

(a) views expressed or suggestions made by the other party in respect of a possible settlement of the dispute;
(b) admissions made by the other party in the course of the conciliation proceedings;
(c) proposals made by the conciliator;
(d) the fact that the other party had indicated his willingness to accept a proposal for settlement made by the conciliator.

Model conciliation clause

Where, in the event of a dispute arising out of or relating to this contract, the parties wish to seek an amicable settlement of that dispute by conciliation, the conciliation shall take place in accordance with the UNCITRAL Conciliation Rules as at present in force.

(The parties may agree on other conciliation clauses.)

UNCITRAL Model Law on Electronic Commerce 1996, as amended 1998

Part One Electronic commerce in general

Chapter I General provisions

*Article 1 Sphere of application**

* The Commission suggests the following text for States that might wish to limit the applicability of this Law to international data messages:
'This Law applies to a data message as defined in paragraph (1) of article 2 where the data message relates to international commerce.'

This Law** applies to any kind of information in the form of a data message used in the context*** of commercial**** activities.

Article 2 Definitions

For the purposes of this Law –

(a) 'Data message' means information generated, sent, received or stored by electronic, optical or similar means including, but not limited to, electronic data interchange (EDI), electronic mail, telegram, telex or telecopy.
(b) 'Electronic data interchange (EDI)' means the electronic transfer from computer to computer of information using an agreed standard to structure the information.
(c) 'Originator' of a data message means a person by whom, or on whose behalf, the data message purports to have been sent or generated prior to storage, if any, but it does not include a person acting as an intermediary with respect to that data message.
(d) 'Addressee' of a data message means a person who is intended by the originator to receive the data message, but does not include a person acting as an intermediary with respect to that data message.
(e) 'Intermediary', with respect to a particular data message, means a person who, on behalf of another person, sends, receives or stores that data message or provides other services with respect to that data message.
(f) 'Information system' means a system for generating, sending, receiving, storing or otherwise processing data messages.

Article 3 Interpretation

(1) In the interpretation of this Law, regard is to be had to its international origin and to the need to promote uniformity in its application and the observance of good faith.
(2) Questions concerning matters governed by this Law which are not expressly settled in it are to be settled in conformity with the general principles on which this Law is based.

Article 4 Variation by agreement

(1) As between parties involved in generating, sending, receiving, storing or otherwise processing data messages, and except as otherwise provided, the provisions of chapter III may be varied by agreement.

** This Law does not override any rule of law intended for the protection of consumers.

*** The Commission suggests the following text for States that might wish to extend the applicability of this Law: This Law applies to any kind of information in the form of a data message, except in the following situations: [...].'

**** The term 'commercial' should be given a wide interpretation so as to cover matters arising from all relationships of a commercial nature, whether contractual or not. Relationships of a commercial nature include, but are not limited to, the following transactions: any trade transaction for the supply or exchange of goods or services; distribution agreement, commercial representation or agency; factoring; leasing; construction of works; consulting; engineering, licensing; investment; financing; banking; insurance; exploitation agreement or concession; joint venture and other forms of industrial or business cooperation; carriage of goods or passengers by air, sea, rail or road.

(2) Paragraph (1) does not affect any right that may exist to modify by agreement any rule of law referred to in chapter II.

Chapter II Application of legal requirements to data messages

Article 5 Legal recognition of data messages

Information shall not be denied legal effect, validity or enforceability solely on the grounds that it is in the form of a data message.

Article 5 bis Incorporation by reference

Information shall not be denied legal effect, validity or enforceability solely on the grounds that it is not contained in the data message purporting to give rise to such legal effect, but is merely referred to in that data message.

Article 6 Writing

(1) Where the law requires information to be in writing, that requirement is met by a data message if the information contained therein is accessible so as to be usable for subsequent reference.
(2) Paragraph (1) applies whether the requirement therein is in the form of an obligation or whether the law simply provides consequences for the information not being in writing.
(3) The provisions of this article do not apply to the following: [...].

Article 7 Signature

(1) Where the law requires a signature of a person, that requirement is met in relation to a data message if –
    (a) a method is used to identify that person and to indicate that person's approval of the information contained in the data message; and
    (b) that method is as reliable as was appropriate for the purpose for which the data message was generated or communicated, in the light of all the circumstances, including any relevant agreement.
(2) Paragraph (1) applies whether the requirement therein is in the form of an obligation or whether the law simply provides consequences for the absence of a signature.
(3) The provisions of this article do not apply to the following: [...].

Article 8 Original

(1) Where the law requires information to be presented or retained in its original form, that requirement is met by a data message if:
    (a) there exists a reliable assurance as to the integrity of the information from the time when it was first generated in its final form, as a data message or otherwise; and
    (b) where it is required that information be presented, that information is capable of being displayed to the person to whom it is to be presented.

(2) Paragraph (1) applies whether the requirement therein is in the form of an obligation or whether the law simply provides consequences for the information not being presented or retained in its original form.
(3) For the purposes of subparagraph (a) of paragraph (1) –
  (a) the criteria for assessing integrity shall be whether the information has remained complete and unaltered, apart from the addition of any endorsement and any change which arises in the normal course of communication, storage and display; and
  (b) the standard of reliability required shall be assessed in the light of the purpose for which the information was generated and in the light of all the relevant circumstances.
(4) The provisions of this article do not apply to the following: […].

Article 9 Admissibility and evidential weight of data messages

(1) In any legal proceedings, nothing in the application of the rules of evidence shall apply so as to deny the admissibility of a data message in evidence –
  (a) on the sole ground that it is a data message; or
  (b) if it is the best evidence that the person adducing it could reasonably be expected to obtain, on the grounds that it is not in its original form.
(2) Information in the form of a data message shall be given due evidential weight. In assessing the evidential weight of a data message, regard shall be had to the reliability of the manner in which the data message was generated, stored or communicated, to the reliability of the manner in which the integrity of the information was maintained, to the manner in which its originator was identified, and to any other relevant factor.

Article 10 Retention of data messages

(1) Where the law requires that certain documents, records or information be retained, that requirement is met by retaining data messages, provided that the following conditions are satisfied –
  (a) the information contained therein is accessible so as to be usable for subsequent reference; and
  (b) the data message is retained in the format in which it was generated, sent or received, or in a format which can be demonstrated to represent accurately the information generated, sent or received; and
  (c) such information, if any, is retained as enables the identification of the origin and destination of a data message and the date and time when it was sent or received.
(2) An obligation to retain documents, records or information in accordance with paragraph (1) does not extend to any information the sole purpose of which is to enable the message to be sent or received.
(3) A person may satisfy the requirement referred to in paragraph (1) by using the services of any other person, provided that the conditions set forth in subparagraphs (a), (b) and (c) of paragraph (1) are met.

Chapter III Communication of data messages

Article 11 Formation and validity of contracts

(1) In the context of contract formation, unless otherwise agreed by the parties, an offer and the acceptance of an offer may be expressed by means of data messages. Where a data message is used in the formation of a contract, that contract shall not be denied validity or enforceability on the sole ground that a data message was used for that purpose.
(2) The provisions of this article do not apply to the following: [...].

Article 12 Recognition by parties of data messages

(1) As between the originator and the addressee of a data message, a declaration of will or other statement shall not be denied legal effect, validity or enforceability solely on the grounds that it is in the form of a data message.
(2) The provisions of this article do not apply to the following: [...].

Article 13 Attribution of data messages

(1) A data message is that of the originator if it was sent by the originator itself.
(2) As between the originator and the addressee, a data message is deemed to be that of the originator if it was sent –
    (a) by a person who had the authority to act on behalf of the originator in respect of that data message; or
    (b) by an information system programmed by, or on behalf of, the originator to operate automatically.
(3) As between the originator and the addressee, an addressee is entitled to regard a data message as being that of the originator, and to act on that assumption, if –
    (a) in order to ascertain whether the data message was that of the originator, the addressee properly applied a procedure previously agreed to by the originator for that purpose; or
    (b) the data message as received by the addressee resulted from the actions of a person whose relationship with the originator or with any agent of the originator enabled that person to gain access to a method used by the originator to identify data messages as its own.
(4) Paragraph (3) does not apply:
    (a) as of the time when the addressee has both received notice from the originator that the data message is not that of the originator, and had reasonable time to act accordingly; or
    (b) in a case within paragraph (3)(b), at any time when the addressee knew or should have known, had it exercised reasonable care or used any agreed procedure, that the data message was not that of the originator.
(5) Where a data message is that of the originator or is deemed to be that of the originator, or the addressee is entitled to act on that assumption, then, as between the originator and the addressee, the addressee is entitled to regard the data message as received as being what the originator intended to send, and to act on that assumption. The addressee is not so entitled when it knew or should have known, had it exercised reasonable care or

used any agreed procedure, that the transmission resulted in any error in the data message as received.

(6) The addressee is entitled to regard each data message received as a separate data message and to act on that assumption, except to the extent that it duplicates another data message and the addressee knew or should have known, had it exercised reasonable care or used any agreed procedure, that the data message was a duplicate.

Article 14 Acknowledgement of receipt

(1) Paragraphs (2) to (4) of this article apply where, on or before sending a data message, or by means of that data message, the originator has requested or has agreed with the addressee that receipt of the data message be acknowledged.

(2) Where the originator has not agreed with the addressee that the acknowledgement be given in a particular form or by a particular method, an acknowledgement may be given by –
   (a) any communication by the addressee, automated or otherwise; or
   (b) any conduct of the addressee, sufficient to indicate to the originator that the data message has been received.

(3) Where the originator has stated that the data message is conditional on receipt of the acknowledgement, the data message is treated as though it has never been sent, until the acknowledgement is received.

(4) Where the originator has not stated that the data message is conditional on receipt of the acknowledgement, and the acknowledgement has not been received by the originator within the time specified or agreed or, if no time has been specified or agreed, within a reasonable time, the originator –
   (a) may give notice to the addressee stating that no acknowledgement has been received and specifying a reasonable time by which the acknowledgement must be received; and
   (b) if the acknowledgement is not received within the time specified in subparagraph (a), may, upon notice to the addressee, treat the data message as though it had never been sent, or exercise any other rights it may have.

(5) Where the originator receives the addressee's acknowledgement of receipt, it is presumed that the related data message was received by the addressee. That presumption does not imply that the data message corresponds to the message received.

(6) Where the received acknowledgement states that the related data message met technical requirements, either agreed upon or set forth in applicable standards, it is presumed that those requirements have been met.

(7) Except in so far as it relates to the sending or receipt of the data message, this article is not intended to deal with the legal consequences that may flow either from that data message or from the acknowledgement of its receipt.

Article 15 Time and place of dispatch and receipt of data messages

(1) Unless otherwise agreed between the originator and the addressee, the dispatch of a data message occurs when it enters an information system outside the control of the originator or of the person who sent the data message on behalf of the originator.

(2) Unless otherwise agreed between the originator and the addressee, the time of receipt of a data message is determined as follows –
   (a) if the addressee has designated an information system for the purpose of receiving data messages, receipt occurs:
      (i) at the time when the data message enters the designated information system; or
      (ii) if the data message is sent to an information system of the addressee that is not the designated information system, at the time when the data message is retrieved by the addressee;
   (b) if the addressee has not designated an information system, receipt occurs when the data message enters an information system of the addressee.

(3) Paragraph (2) applies notwithstanding that the place where the information system is located may be different from the place where the data message is deemed to be received under paragraph (4).

(4) Unless otherwise agreed between the originator and the addressee, a data message is deemed to be dispatched at the place where the originator has its place of business, and is deemed to be received at the place where the addressee has its place of business. For the purposes of this paragraph –
   (a) if the originator or the addressee has more than one place of business, the place of business is that which has the closest relationship to the underlying transaction or, where there is no underlying transaction, the principal place of business;
   (b) if the originator or the addressee does not have a place of business, reference is to be made to its habitual residence.

(5) The provisions of this article do not apply to the following: […].

Part Two Electronic commerce to specific areas

Chapter I Carriage of goods

Article 16 Actions related to contracts of carriage of goods

Without derogating from the provisions of part one of this Law, this chapter applies to any action in connection with, or in pursuance of, a contract of carriage of goods, including but not limited to –

(a)
   (i) furnishing the marks, number, quantity or weight of goods;
   (ii) stating or declaring the nature or value of goods;
   (iii) issuing a receipt for goods;
   (iv) confirming that goods have been loaded;

(b)
   (i) notifying a person of terms and conditions of the contract;
   (ii) giving instructions to a carrier;

(c)
   (i) claiming delivery of goods;
   (ii) authorizing release of goods;
   (iii) giving notice of loss of, or damage to, goods;

(d) giving any other notice or statement in connection with the performance of the contract;
(e) undertaking to deliver goods to a named person or a person authorized to claim delivery;
(f) granting, acquiring, renouncing, surrendering, transferring or negotiating rights in goods;
(g) acquiring or transferring rights and obligations under the contract.

Article 17 Transport documents

(1) Subject to paragraph (3), where the law requires that any action referred to in article 16 be carried out in writing or by using a paper document, that requirement is met if the action is carried out by using one or more data messages.
(2) Paragraph (1) applies whether the requirement therein is in the form of an obligation or whether the law simply provides consequences for failing either to carry out the action in writing or to use a paper document.
(3) If a right is to be granted to, or an obligation is to be acquired by, one person and no other person, and if the law requires that, in order to effect this, the right or obligation must be conveyed to that person by the transfer, or use of, a paper document, that requirement is met if the right or obligation is conveyed by using one or more data messages, provided that a reliable method is used to render such data message or messages unique.
(4) For the purposes of paragraph (3), the standard of reliability required shall be assessed in the light of the purpose for which the right or obligation was conveyed and in the light of all the circumstances, including any relevant agreement.
(5) Where one or more data messages are used to effect any action in subparagraphs (f) and (g) of article 16, no paper document used to effect any such action is valid unless the use of data messages has been terminated and replaced by the use of paper documents. A paper document issued in these circumstances shall contain a statement of such termination. The replacement of data messages by paper documents shall not affect the rights or obligations of the parties involved.
(6) If a rule of law is compulsorily applicable to a contract of carriage of goods which is in, or is evidenced by, a paper document, that rule shall not be inapplicable to such a contract of carriage of goods which is evidenced by one or more data messages by reason of the fact that the contract is evidenced by such data message or messages instead of by a paper document.
(7) The provisions of this article do not apply to the following: [...].

UNCITRAL Model Law on Electronic Signatures, 2001

Article 1 Sphere of application

This Law applies where electronic signatures are used in the context* of commercial** activities. It does not override any rule of law intended for the protection of consumers.

* The Commission suggests the following text for States that might wish to extend the applicability of this Law: This Law applies where electronic signatures are used, except in the following situations: [...]. '.

** The term 'commercial' should be given a wide interpretation so as to cover matters arising from all relationships of a commercial nature, whether contractual or not. Relationships of a commercial nature include, but are

Article 2 Definitions

For the purposes of this Law:

(a) 'Electronic signature' means data in electronic form in, affixed to or logically associated with, a data message, which may be used to identify the signatory in relation to the data message and to indicate the signatory's approval of the information contained in the data message;
(b) 'Certificate' means a data message or other record confirming the link between a signatory and signature creation data;
(c) 'Data message' means information generated, sent, received or stored by electronic, optical or similar means including, but not limited to, electronic data interchange (EDI), electronic mail, telegram, telex or telecopy; and acts either on its own behalf or on behalf of the person it represents;
(d) 'Signatory' means a person that holds signature creation data and acts either on its own behalf or on behalf of the person it represents;
(e) 'Certification service provider' means a person that issues certificates and may provide other services related to electronic signatures;
(f) 'Relying party' means a person that may act on the basis of a certificate or an electronic signature.

Article 3 Equal treatment of signature technologies

Nothing in this Law, except article 5, shall be applied so as to exclude, restrict or deprive of legal effect any method of creating an electronic signature that satisfies the requirements referred to in article 6, paragraph 1, or otherwise meets the requirements of applicable law.

Article 4 Interpretation

1. In the interpretation of this Law, regard is to be had to its international origin and to the need to promote uniformity in its application and the observance of good faith.
2. Questions concerning matters governed by this Law which are not expressly settled in it are to be settled in conformity with the general principles on which this Law is based.

Article 5 Variation by agreement

The provisions of this Law may be derogated from or their effect may be varied by agreement, unless that agreement would not be valid or effective under applicable law.

Article 6 Compliance with a requirement for a signature

1. Where the law requires a signature of a person, that requirement is met in relation to a data message if an electronic signature is used that is as reliable as was appropriate for the

---

not limited to, the following transactions: any trade transaction for the supply or exchange of goods or services; distribution agreement; commercial representation or agency; factoring; leasing; construction of works; consulting; engineering; licensing; investment; financing; banking; insurance; exploitation agreement or concession; joint venture and other forms of industrial or business cooperation; carriage of goods or passengers by air, sea, rail or road.

purpose for which the data message was generated or communicated, in the light of all the circumstances, including any relevant agreement.

2. Paragraph 1 applies whether the requirement referred to therein is in the form of an obligation or whether the law simply provides consequences for the absence of a signature.
3. An electronic signature is considered to be reliable for the purpose of satisfying the requirement referred to in paragraph 1 if:
   (a) The signature creation data are, within the context in which they are used, linked to the signatory and to no other person;
   (b) The signature creation data were, at the time of signing, under the control of the signatory and of no other person;
   (c) Any alteration to the electronic signature, made after the time of signing, is detectable; and
   (d) Where a purpose of the legal requirement for a signature is to provide assurance as to the integrity of the information to which it relates, any alteration made to that information after the time of signing is detectable.
4. Paragraph 3 does not limit the ability of any person:
   (a) To establish in any other way, for the purpose of satisfying the requirement referred to in paragraph 1, the reliability of an electronic signature; or
   (b) To adduce evidence of the non-reliability of an electronic signature.
5. The provisions of this article do not apply to the following: [...].

Article 7 Satisfaction of article 6

1. *[Any person, organ or authority, whether public or private, specified by the enacting State as competent]* may determine which electronic signatures satisfy the provisions of article 6 of this Law.
2. Any determination made under paragraph 1 shall be consistent with recognized international standards.
3. Nothing in this article affects the operation of the rules of private international law.

Article 8 Conduct of the signatory

1. Where signature creation data can be used to create a signature that has legal effect, each signatory shall:
   (a) Exercise reasonable care to avoid unauthorized use of its signature creation data;
   (b) Without undue delay, utilize means made available by the certification service provider pursuant to article 9 of this Law, or otherwise use reasonable efforts, to notify any person that may reasonably be expected by the signatory to rely on or to provide services in support of the electronic signature if:
      (i) The signatory knows that the signature creation data have been compromised; or
      (ii) The circumstances known to the signatory give rise to a substantial risk that the signature creation data may have been compromised;
   (c) Where a certificate is used to support the electronic signature, exercise reasonable care to ensure the accuracy and completeness of all material representations made by the signatory that are relevant to the certificate throughout its life cycle or that are to be included in the certificate.
2. A signatory shall bear the legal consequences of its failure to satisfy the requirements of paragraph 1.

Article 9 Conduct of the certification service provider

1. Where a certification service provider provides services to support an electronic signature that may be used for legal effect as a signature, that certification service provider shall:
   (a) Act in accordance with representations made by it with respect to its policies and practices;
   (b) Exercise reasonable care to ensure the accuracy and completeness of all material representations made by it that are relevant to the certificate throughout its life cycle or that are included in the certificate;
   (c) Provide reasonably accessible means that enable a relying party to ascertain from the certificate:
      (i) The identity of the certification service provider;
      (ii) That the signatory that is identified in the certificate had control of the signature creation data at the time when the certificate was issued;
      (iii) That signature creation data were valid at or before the time when the certificate was issued;
   (d) Provide reasonably accessible means that enable a relying party to ascertain, where relevant, from the certificate or otherwise:
      (i) The method used to identify the signatory;
      (ii) Any limitation on the purpose or value for which the signature creation data or the certificate may be used;
      (iii) That the signature creation data are valid and have not been compromised;
      (iv) Any limitation on the scope or extent of liability stipulated by the certification service provider;
      (v) Whether means exist for the signatory to give notice pursuant to article 8, paragraph 1(b), of this Law;
      (vi) Whether a timely revocation service is offered;
   (e) Where services under subparagraph (d)(v) are offered, provide a means for a signatory to give notice pursuant to article 8, paragraph 1(b), of this Law and, where services under subparagraph (d)(vi) are offered, ensure the availability of a timely revocation service;
   (f) Utilize trustworthy systems, procedures and human resources in performing its services.
2. A certification service provider shall bear the legal consequences of its failure to satisfy the requirements of paragraph 1.

Article 10 Trustworthiness

For the purposes of article 9, paragraph 1(f), of this Law in determining whether, or to what extent, any systems, procedures and human resources utilized by a certification service provider are trustworthy, regard may be had to the following factors:

(a) Financial and human resources, including existence of assets;
(b) Quality of hardware and software systems;
(c) Procedures for processing of certificates and applications for certificates and retention of records;
(d) Availability of information to signatories identified in certificates and to potential relying parties;

(e) Regularity and extent of audit by an independent body;
(f) The existence of a declaration by the State, an accreditation body or the certification service provider regarding compliance with or existence of the foregoing; or
(g) Any other relevant factor.

Article 11 Conduct of the relying party

A relying party shall bear the legal consequences of its failure:

(a) To take reasonable steps to verify the reliability of an electronic signature; or
(b) Where an electronic signature is supported by a certificate, to take reasonable steps:
    (i) To verify the validity, suspension or revocation of the certificate; and
    (ii) To observe any limitation with respect to the certificate.

Article 12 Recognition of foreign certificates and electronic signatures

1. In determining whether, or to what extent, a certificate or an electronic signature is legally effective, no regard shall be had:
    (a) To the geographic location where the certificate is issued or the electronic signature created or used; or
    (b) To the geographic location of the place of business of the issuer or signatory.
2. A certificate issued outside *[the enacting State]* shall have the same legal effect in *[the enacting State]* as a certificate issued in *[the enacting State]* if it offers a substantially equivalent level of reliability.
3. An electronic signature created or used outside *[the enacting State]* shall have the same legal effect in *[the enacting State]* as an electronic signature created or used in *[the enacting State]* if it offers a substantially equivalent level of reliability.
4. In determining whether a certificate or an electronic signature offers a substantially equivalent level of reliability for the purposes of paragraph 2 or 3, regard shall be had to recognized international standards and to any other relevant factors.
5. Where, notwithstanding paragraphs 2, 3 and 4, parties agree, as between themselves, to the use of certain types of electronic signatures or certificates, that agreement shall be recognized as sufficient for the purposes of cross-border recognition, unless that agreement would not be valid or effective under applicable law.

UNCITRAL Model Law on International Commercial Arbitration, 1985

Chapter I General provisions

*Article 1 Scope of application**

(1) This Law applies to international commercial** arbitration, subject to any agreement in force between this State and any other State or States.

* Article headings are for reference purposes only and are not to be used for purposes of interpretation.

** The term 'commercial' should be given a wide interpretation so as to cover matters arising from all relationships of a commercial nature, whether contractual or not. Relationships of a commercial nature include,

(2) The provisions of this Law, except articles 8, 9, 35 and 36, apply only if the place of arbitration is in the territory of this State.

(3) An arbitration is international if –

  (a) the parties to an arbitration agreement have, at the time of the conclusion of that agreement, their places of business in different States; or

  (b) one of the following places is situated outside the State in which the parties have their places of business:

    (i) the place of arbitration if determined in, or pursuant to, the arbitration agreement;

    (ii) any place where a substantial part of the obligations of the commercial relationship is to be performed or the place with which the subject – matter of the dispute is most closely connected; or

  (c) the parties have expressly agreed that the subject-matter of the arbitration agreement relates to more than one country.

(4) For the purposes of paragraph (3) of this article –

  (a) if a party has more than one place of business, the place of business is that which has the closest relationship to the arbitration agreement;

  (b) if a party does not have a place of business, reference is to be made to his habitual residence.

(5) This Law shall not affect any other law of this State by virtue of which certain disputes may not be submitted to arbitration or may be submitted to arbitration only according to provisions other than those of this Law.

Article 2 Definitions and rules of interpretation

For the purposes of this Law –

(a) 'Arbitration' means any arbitration whether or not administered by a permanent arbitral institution.

(b) 'Arbitral tribunal' means a sole arbitrator or a panel of arbitrators.

(c) 'Court' means a body or organ of the judicial system of a State.

(d) Where a provision of this Law, except article 28, leaves the parties free to determine a certain issue, such freedom includes the right of the parties to authorize a third party, including an institution, to make that determination.

(e) Where a provision of this Law refers to the fact that the parties have agreed or that they may agree or in any other way refers to an agreement of the parties, such agreement includes any arbitration rules referred to in that agreement.

(f) Where a provision of this Law, other than in articles 25(a) and 32(2)(a), refers to a claim, it also applies to a counter-claim, and where it refers to a defence, it also applies to a defence to such counter-claim.

---

but are not limited to, the following transactions: any trade transaction for the supply or exchange of goods or services; distribution agreement; commercial representation or agency; factoring; leasing; construction of works; consulting; engineering; licensing; investment; financing; banking; insurance; exploitation agreement or concession; joint venture and other forms of industrial or business co-operation; carriage of goods or passengers by air, sea, rail or road.

Article 3 Receipt of written communications

(1) Unless otherwise agreed by the parties –
   (a) any written communication is deemed to have been received if it is delivered to the addressee personally or if it is delivered at his place of business, habitual residence or mailing address; if none of these can be found after making a reasonable inquiry, a written communication is deemed to have been received if it is sent to the addressee's last-known place of business, habitual residence or mailing address by registered letter or any other means which provides a record of the attempt to deliver it;
   (b) the communication is deemed to have been received on the day it is so delivered.

(2) The provisions of this article do not apply to communications in court proceedings.

Article 4 Waiver of right to object

A party who knows that any provision of this Law from which the parties may derogate or any requirement under the arbitration agreement has not been complied with and yet proceeds with the arbitration without stating his objection to such non-compliance without undue delay or, if a time-limit is provided therefor, within such period of time, shall be deemed to have waived his right to object.

Article 5 Extent of court intervention

In matters governed by this Law, no court shall intervene except where so provided in this Law.

Article 6 Court or other authority for certain functions of arbitration assistance and supervision

The functions referred to in articles 11(3), 11(4), 13(3), 14, 16(3) and 34(2) shall be performed by… [Each State enacting this model law specifies the court, courts or, where referred to therein, other authority competent to perform these functions.]

Chapter II Arbitration agreement

Article 7 Definition and form of arbitration agreement

(1) 'Arbitration agreement' is an agreement by the parties to submit to arbitration all or certain disputes which have arisen or which may arise between them in respect of a defined legal relationship, whether contractual or not. An arbitration agreement may be in the form of an arbitration clause in a contract or in the form of a separate agreement.

(2) The arbitration agreement shall be in writing. An agreement is in writing if it is contained in a document signed by the parties or in an exchange of letters, telex, telegrams or other means of telecommunication which provide a record of the agreement, or in an exchange of statements of claim and defence in which the existence of an agreement is alleged by one party and not denied by another. The reference in a contract to a document containing an arbitration clause constitutes an arbitration agreement provided that the contract is in writing and the reference is such as to make that clause part of the contract.

Article 8 Arbitration agreement and substantive claim before court

(1) A court before which an action is brought in a matter which is the subject of an arbitration agreement shall, if a party so requests not later than when submitting his first statement on the substance of the dispute, refer the parties to arbitration unless it finds that the agreement is null and void, inoperative or incapable of being performed.
(2) Where an action referred to in paragraph (1) of this article has been brought, arbitral proceedings may nevertheless be commenced or continued, and an award may be made, while the issue is pending before the court.

Article 9 Arbitration agreement and interim measures by court

It is not incompatible with an arbitration agreement for a party to request, before or during arbitral proceedings, from a court an interim measure of protection and for a court to grant such measure.

Chapter III Composition of arbitral tribunal

Article 10 Number of arbitrators

(1) The parties are free to determine the number of arbitrators.
(2) Failing such determination, the number of arbitrators shall be three.

Article 11 Appointment of arbitrators

(1) No person shall be precluded by reason of his nationality from acting as an arbitrator, unless otherwise agreed by the parties.
(2) The parties are free to agree on a procedure of appointing the arbitrator or arbitrators, subject to the provisions of paragraphs (4) and (5) of this article.
(3) Failing such agreement –
    (a) in an arbitration with three arbitrators, each party shall appoint one arbitrator, and the two arbitrators thus appointed shall appoint the third arbitrator; if a party fails to appoint the arbitrator within thirty days of receipt of a request to do so from the other party, or if the two arbitrators fail to agree on the third arbitrator within thirty days of their appointment, the appointment shall be made, upon request of a party, by the court or other authority specified in article 6;
    (b) in an arbitration with a sole arbitrator, if the parties are unable to agree on the arbitrator, he shall be appointed, upon request of a party, by the court or other authority specified in article 6.
(4) Where, under an appointment procedure agreed upon by the parties –
    (a) a party fails to act as required under such procedure; or
    (b) the parties, or two arbitrators, are unable to reach an agreement expected of them under such procedure; or
    (c) a third party, including an institution, fails to perform any function entrusted to it under such procedure,
    (d) any party may request the court or other authority specified in article 6 to take the necessary measure, unless the agreement on the appointment procedure provides other means for securing the appointment.

(5) A decision on a matter entrusted by paragraph (3) or (4) of this article to the court or other authority specified in article 6 shall be subject to no appeal. The court or other authority, in appointing an arbitrator, shall have due regard to any qualifications required of the arbitrator by the agreement of the parties and to such considerations as are likely to secure the appointment of an independent and impartial arbitrator and, in the case of a sole or third arbitrator, shall take into account as well the advisability of appointing an arbitrator of a nationality other than those of the parties.

Article 12 Grounds for challenge

(1) When a person is approached in connection with his possible appointment as an arbitrator, he shall disclose any circumstances likely to give rise to justifiable doubts as to his impartiality or independence. An arbitrator, from the time of his appointment and throughout the arbitral proceedings, shall without delay disclose any such circumstances to the parties unless they have already been informed of them by him.

(2) An arbitrator may be challenged only if circumstances exist that give rise to justifiable doubts as to his impartiality or independence, or if he does not possess qualifications agreed to by the parties. A party may challenge an arbitrator appointed by him, or in whose appointment he has participated, only for reasons of which he becomes aware after the appointment has been made.

Article 13 Challenge procedure

(1) The parties are free to agree on a procedure for challenging an arbitrator, subject to the provisions of paragraph (3) of this article.

(2) Failing such agreement, a party who intends to challenge an arbitrator shall, within fifteen days after becoming aware of the constitution of the arbitral tribunal or after becoming aware of any circumstance referred to in article 12(2), send a written statement of the reasons for the challenge to the arbitral tribunal. Unless the challenged arbitrator withdraws from his office or the other party agrees to the challenge, the arbitral tribunal shall decide on the challenge.

(3) If a challenge under any procedure agreed upon by the parties or under the procedure of paragraph (2) of this article is not successful, the challenging party may request, within thirty days after having received notice of the decision rejecting the challenge, the court or other authority specified in article 6 to decide on the challenge, which decision shall be subject to no appeal; while such a request is pending, the arbitral tribunal, including the challenged arbitrator, may continue the arbitral proceedings and make an award.

Article 14 Failure or impossibility to act

(1) If an arbitrator becomes de jure or de facto unable to perform his functions or for other reasons fails to act without undue delay, his mandate terminates if he withdraws from his office or if the parties agree on the termination. Otherwise, if a controversy remains concerning any of these grounds, any party may request the court or other authority specified in article 6 to decide on the termination of the mandate, which decision shall be subject to no appeal.

(2) If, under this article or article 13(2), an arbitrator withdraws from his office or a party agrees to the termination of the mandate of an arbitrator, this does not imply acceptance of the validity of any ground referred to in this article or article 12(2).

Article 15 Appointment of substitute arbitrator

Where the mandate of an arbitrator terminates under article 13 or 14 or because of his withdrawal from office for any other reason or because of the revocation of his mandate by agreement of the parties or in any other case of termination of his mandate, a substitute arbitrator shall be appointed according to the rules that were applicable to the appointment of the arbitrator being replaced.

Chapter IV Jurisdiction of arbitral tribunal

Article 16 Competence of arbitral tribunal to rule on its jurisdiction

(1) The arbitral tribunal may rule on its own jurisdiction, including any objections with respect to the existence or validity of the arbitration agreement. For that purpose, an arbitration clause which forms part of a contract shall be treated as an agreement independent of the other terms of the contract. A decision by the arbitral tribunal that the contract is null and void shall not entail ipso jure the invalidity of the arbitration clause.

(2) A plea that the arbitral tribunal does not have jurisdiction shall be raised not later than the submission of the statement of defence. A party is not precluded from raising such a plea by the fact that he has appointed, or participated in the appointment of, an arbitrator. A plea that the arbitral tribunal is exceeding the scope of its authority shall be raised as soon as the matter alleged to be beyond the scope of its authority is raised during the arbitral proceedings. The arbitral tribunal may, in either case, admit a later plea if it considers the delay justified.

(3) The arbitral tribunal may rule on a plea referred to in paragraph (2) of this article either as a preliminary question or in an award on the merits. If the arbitral tribunal rules as a preliminary question that it has jurisdiction, any party may request, within thirty days after having received notice of that ruling, the court specified in article 6 to decide the matter, which decision shall be subject to no appeal, while such a request is pending, the arbitral tribunal may continue the arbitral proceedings and make an award.

Article 17 Power of arbitral tribunal to order interim measures

Unless otherwise agreed by the parties, the arbitral tribunal may, at the request of a party, order any party to take such interim measure of protection as the arbitral tribunal may consider necessary in respect of the subject-matter of the dispute. The arbitral tribunal may require any party to provide appropriate security in connection with such measure.

Chapter V Conduct of arbitral proceedings

Article 18 Equal treatment of parties

The parties shall be treated with equality and each party shall be given a full opportunity of presenting his case.

Article 19 Determination of rules of procedure

(1) Subject to the provisions of this Law, the parties are free to agree on the procedure to be followed by the arbitral tribunal in conducting the proceedings.
(2) Failing such agreement, the arbitral tribunal may, subject to the provisions of this Law, conduct the arbitration in such manner as it considers appropriate. The power conferred upon the arbitral tribunal includes the power to determine the admissibility, relevance, materiality and weight of any evidence.

Article 20 Place of arbitration

(1) The parties are free to agree on the place of arbitration. Failing such agreement, the place of arbitration shall be determined by the arbitral tribunal having regard to the circumstances of the case, including the convenience of the parties.
(2) Notwithstanding the provisions of paragraph (1) of this article, the arbitral tribunal may, unless otherwise agreed by the parties, meet at any place it considers appropriate for consultation among its members, for hearing witnesses, experts or the parties, or for inspection of goods, other property or documents.

Article 21 Commencement of arbitral proceedings

Unless otherwise agreed by the parties, the arbitral proceedings in respect of a particular dispute commence on the date on which a request for that dispute to be referred to arbitration is received by the respondent.

Article 22 Language

(1) The parties are free to agree on the language or languages to be used in the arbitral proceedings. Failing such agreement, the arbitral tribunal shall determine the language or languages to be used in the proceedings. This agreement or determination, unless otherwise specified therein, shall apply to any written statement by a party, any hearing and any award, decision or other communication by the arbitral tribunal.
(2) The arbitral tribunal may order that any documentary evidence shall be accompanied by a translation into the language or languages agreed upon by the parties or determined by the arbitral tribunal.

Article 23 Statements of claim and defence

(1) Within the period of time agreed by the parties or determined by the arbitral tribunal, the claimant shall state the facts supporting his claim, the points at issue and the relief or remedy sought, and the respondent shall state his defence in respect of these particulars, unless the parties have otherwise agreed as to the required elements of such statements. The parties may submit with their statements all documents they consider to be relevant or may add a reference to the documents or other evidence they will submit.
(2) Unless otherwise agreed by the parties, either party may amend or supplement his claim or defence during the course of the arbitral proceedings, unless the arbitral tribunal considers it inappropriate to allow such amendment having regard to the delay in making it.

Article 24 Hearings and written proceedings

(1) Subject to any contrary agreement by the parties, the arbitral tribunal shall decide whether to hold oral hearings for the presentation of evidence or for oral argument, or whether the proceedings shall be conducted on the basis of documents and other materials. However, unless the parties have agreed that no hearings shall be held, the arbitral tribunal shall hold such hearings at an appropriate stage of the proceedings, if so requested by a party.
(2) The parties shall be given sufficient advance notice of any hearing and of any meeting of the arbitral tribunal for the purposes of inspection of goods, other property or documents.
(3) All statements, documents or other information supplied to the arbitral tribunal by one party shall be communicated to the other party. Also any expert report or evidentiary document on which the arbitral tribunal may rely in making its decision shall be communicated to the parties.

Article 25 Default of a party

Unless otherwise agreed by the parties, if, without showing sufficient cause –

(a) the claimant fails to communicate his statement of claim in accordance with article 23(1), the arbitral tribunal shall terminate the proceedings;
(b) the respondent fails to communicate his statement of defence in accordance with article 23(1), the arbitral tribunal shall continue the proceedings without treating such failure in itself as an admission of the claimant's allegations;
(c) any party fails to appear at a hearing or to produce documentary evidence, the arbitral tribunal may continue the proceedings and make the award on the evidence before it.

Article 26 Expert appointed by arbitral tribunal

(1) Unless otherwise agreed by the parties, the arbitral tribunal –
    (a) may appoint one or more experts to report to it on specific issues to be determined by the arbitral tribunal;
    (b) may require a party to give the expert any relevant information or to produce, or to provide access to, any relevant documents, goods or other property for his inspection.
(2) Unless otherwise agreed by the parties, if a party so requests or if the arbitral tribunal considers it necessary, the expert shall, after delivery of his written or oral report, participate in a hearing where the parties have the opportunity to put questions to him and to present expert witnesses in order to testify on the points at issue.

Article 27 Court assistance in taking evidence

The arbitral tribunal or a party with the approval of the arbitral tribunal may request from a competent court of this State assistance in taking evidence. The court may execute the request within its competence and according to its rules on taking evidence.

Chapter VI Making of award and termination of proceedings

Article 28 Rules applicable to substance of dispute

(1) The arbitral tribunal shall decide the dispute in accordance with such rules of law as are chosen by the parties as applicable to the substance of the dispute. Any designation of the law or legal system of a given State shall be construed, unless otherwise expressed, as directly referring to the substantive law of that State and not to its conflict of laws rules.
(2) Failing any designation by the parties, the arbitral tribunal shall apply the law determined by the conflict of laws rules which it considers applicable.
(3) The arbitral tribunal shall decide *ex aequo et bono* or as amiable compositeur only if the parties have expressly authorized it to do so.
(4) In all cases, the arbitral tribunal shall decide in accordance with the terms of the contract and shall take into account the usages of the trade applicable to the transaction.

Article 29 Decision making by panel of arbitrators

In arbitral proceedings with more than one arbitrator, any decision of the arbitral tribunal shall be made, unless otherwise agreed by the parties, by a majority of all its members. However, questions of procedure may be decided by a presiding arbitrator, if so authorized by the parties or all members of the arbitral tribunal.

Article 30 Settlement

(1) If, during arbitral proceedings, the parties settle the dispute, the arbitral tribunal shall terminate the proceedings and, if requested by the parties and not objected to by the arbitral tribunal, record the settlement in the form of an arbitral award on agreed terms.
(2) An award on agreed terms shall be made in accordance with the provisions of article 31 and shall state that it is an award. Such an award has the same status and effect as any other award on the merits of the case.

Article 31 Form and contents of award

(1) The award shall be made in writing and shall be signed by the arbitrator or arbitrators. In arbitral proceedings with more than one arbitrator, the signatures of the majority of all members of the arbitral tribunal shall suffice, provided that the reason for any omitted signature is stated.
(2) The award shall state the reasons upon which it is based, unless the parties have agreed that no reasons are to be given or the award is an award on agreed terms under article 30.
(3) The award shall state its date and the place of arbitration as determined in accordance with article 20(1). The award shall be deemed to have been made at that place.
(4) After the award is made, a copy signed by the arbitrators in accordance with paragraph (1) of this article shall be delivered to each party.

Article 32 Termination of proceedings

(1) The arbitral proceedings are terminated by the final award or by an order of the arbitral tribunal in accordance with paragraph (2) of this article.

(2) The arbitral tribunal shall issue an order for the termination of the arbitral proceedings when –
   (a) the claimant withdraws his claim, unless the respondent objects thereto and the arbitral tribunal recognizes a legitimate interest on his part in obtaining a final settlement of the dispute;
   (b) the parties agree on the termination of the proceedings;
   (c) the arbitral tribunal finds that the continuation of the proceedings has for any other reason become unnecessary or impossible.

(3) The mandate of the arbitral tribunal terminates with the termination of the arbitral proceedings, subject to the provisions of articles 33 and 34(4).

Article 33 Correction and interpretation of award; additional award

(1) Within thirty days of receipt of the award, unless another period of time has been agreed upon by the parties –
   (a) a party, with notice to the other party, may request the arbitral tribunal to correct in the award any errors in computation, any clerical or typographical errors or any errors of similar nature;
   (b) if so agreed by the parties, a party, with notice to the other party, may request the arbitral tribunal to give an interpretation of a specific point or part of the award.
   (c) If the arbitral tribunal considers the request to be justified, it shall make the correction or give the interpretation within thirty days of receipt of the request. The interpretation shall form part of the award.

(2) The arbitral tribunal may correct any error of the type referred to in paragraph (1)(a) of this article on its own initiative within thirty days of the date of the award.

(3) Unless otherwise agreed by the parties, a party, with notice to the other party, may request, within thirty days of receipt of the award, the arbitral tribunal to make an additional award as to claims presented in the arbitral proceedings but omitted from the award. If the arbitral tribunal considers the request to be justified, it shall make the additional award within sixty days.

(4) The arbitral tribunal may extend, if necessary, the period of time within which it shall make a correction, interpretation or an additional award under paragraph (1) or (3) of this article.

(5) The provisions of article 31 shall apply to a correction or interpretation of the award or to an additional award.

Chapter VII Recourse against award

Article 34 Application for setting aside as exclusive recourse against arbitral award

(1) Recourse to a court against an arbitral award may be made only by an application for setting aside in accordance with paragraphs (2) and (3) of this article.

(2) An arbitral award may be set aside by the court specified in article 6 only if –
   (a) the party making the application furnishes proof that:
      (i) a party to the arbitration agreement referred to in article 7 was under some incapacity; or the said agreement is not valid under the law to which the parties have subjected it or, failing any indication thereon, under the law of this State; or

(ii) the party making the application was not given proper notice of the appointment of an arbitrator or of the arbitral proceedings or was otherwise unable to present his case; or

(iii) the award deals with a dispute not contemplated by or not falling within the terms of the submission to arbitration, or contains decisions on matters beyond the scope of the submission to arbitration, provided that, if the decisions on matters submitted to arbitration can be separated from those not so submitted, only that part of the award which contains decisions on matters not submitted to arbitration may be set aside; or

(iv) the composition of the arbitral tribunal or the arbitral procedure was not in accordance with the agreement of the parties, unless such agreement was in conflict with a provision of this Law from which the parties cannot derogate, or, failing such agreement, was not in accordance with this Law; or

(b) the court finds that:

(i) the subject-matter of the dispute is not capable of settlement by arbitration under the law of this State; or

(ii) the award is in conflict with the public policy of this State.

(3) An application for setting aside may not be made after three months have elapsed from the date on which the party making that application had received the award or, if a request had been made under article 33, from the date on which that request had been disposed of by the arbitral tribunal.

(4) The court, when asked to set aside an award, may, where appropriate and so requested by a party, suspend the setting aside proceedings for a period of time determined by it in order to give the arbitral tribunal an opportunity to resume the arbitral proceedings or to take such other action as in the arbitral tribunal's opinion will eliminate the grounds for setting aside.

Chapter VIII Recognition and enforcement of awards

Article 35 Recognition and enforcement

(1) An arbitral award, irrespective of the country in which it was made, shall be recognized as binding and, upon application in writing to the competent court, shall be enforced subject to the provisions of this article and of article 36.

(2) The party relying on an award or applying for its enforcement shall supply the duly authenticated original award or a duly certified copy thereof, and the original arbitration agreement referred to in article 7 or a duly certified copy thereof. If the award or agreement is not made in an official language of this State, the party shall supply a duly certified translation thereof into such language.***

Article 36 Grounds for refusing recognition or enforcement

(1) Recognition or enforcement of an arbitral award, irrespective of the country in which it was made, may be refused only:

*** The conditions set forth in this paragraph are intended to set maximum standards. It would, thus, not be contrary to the harmonization to be achieved by the model law if a State retained even less onerous conditions.

(a) at the request of the party against whom it is invoked, if that party furnishes to the competent court where recognition or enforcement is sought proof that:
   (i) a party to the arbitration agreement referred to in article 7 was under some incapacity; or the said agreement is not valid under the law to which the parties have subjected it or, failing any indication thereon, under the law of the country where the award was made; or
   (ii) the party against whom the award is invoked was not given proper notice of the appointment of an arbitrator or of the arbitral proceedings or was otherwise unable to present his case; or
   (iii) the award deals with a dispute not contemplated by or not falling within the terms of the submission to arbitration, or it contains decisions on matters beyond the scope of the submission to arbitration, provided that, if the decisions on matters submitted to arbitration can be separated from those not so submitted, that part of the award which contains decisions on matters submitted to arbitration may be recognized and enforced; or
   (iv) the composition of the arbitral tribunal or the arbitral procedure was not in accordance with the agreement of the parties or, failing such agreement, was not in accordance with the law of the country where the arbitration took place; or
   (v) the award has not yet become binding on the parties or has been set aside or suspended by a court of the country in which, or under the law of which, that award was made; or

(b) if the court finds that:
   (i) the subject-matter of the dispute is not capable of settlement by arbitration under the law of this State; or
   (ii) the recognition or enforcement of the award would be contrary to the public policy of this State.

(2) If an application for setting aside or suspension of an award has been made to a court referred to in paragraph (1)(a)(v) of this article, the court where recognition or enforcement is sought may, if it considers it proper, adjourn its decision and may also, on the application of the party claiming recognition or enforcement of the award, order the other party to provide appropriate security.

UNCITRAL Model Law on International Commercial Conciliation, 2002

Article 1 Scope of application and definitions

(1) This Law applies to international[1] commercial[2] conciliation.

1 States wishing to enact this Model Law to apply to domestic as well as international conciliation may wish to consider the following changes to the text:Delete the word 'international' in paragraph (1) of article 1; andDelete paragraphs (4), (5) and (6) of article 1.

2 The term 'commercial' should be given a wide interpretation so as to cover matters arising from all relationships of a commercial nature, whether contractual or not. Relationships of a commercial nature include, but are not limited to, the following transactions: any trade transaction for the supply or exchange of goods or services; distribution agreement; commercial representation or agency; factoring; leasing; construction of works; consulting; engineering; licensing; investment; financing; banking; insurance; exploitation agreement or concession; joint venture and other forms of industrial or business cooperation; carriage of goods or passengers by air, sea, rail or road.

(2) For the purposes of this Law, 'conciliator' means a sole conciliator or two or more conciliators, as the case may be.

(3) For the purposes of this Law, 'conciliation' means a process, whether referred to by the expression conciliation, mediation or an expression of similar import, whereby parties request a third person or persons ('the conciliator') to assist them in their attempt to reach an amicable settlement of their dispute arising out of or relating to a contractual or other legal relationship. The conciliator does not have the authority to impose upon the parties a solution to the dispute.

(4) A conciliation is international if:
   (a) The parties to an agreement to conciliate have, at the time of the conclusion of that agreement, their places of business in different States; or
   (b) The State in which the parties have their places of business is different from either:
      (i) The State in which a substantial part of the obligations of the commercial relationship is to be performed; or
      (ii) The State with which the subject matter of the dispute is most closely connected.

(5) For the purposes of this article:
   (a) If a party has more than one place of business, the place of business is that which has the closest relationship to the agreement to conciliate;
   (b) If a party does not have a place of business, reference is to be made to the party's habitual residence.

(6) This Law also applies to a commercial conciliation when the parties agree that the conciliation is international or agree to the applicability of this Law.

(7) The parties are free to agree to exclude the applicability of this Law.

(8) Subject to the provisions of paragraph (9) of this article, this Law applies irrespective of the basis upon which the conciliation is carried out, including agreement between the parties whether reached before or after a dispute has arisen, an obligation established by law, or a direction or suggestion of a court, arbitral tribunal or competent governmental entity.

(9) This Law does not apply to:
   (a) Cases where a judge or an arbitrator, in the course of judicial or arbitral proceedings, attempts to facilitate a settlement; and
   (b) [...].

Article 2 Interpretation

(1) In the interpretation of this Law, regard is to be had to its international origin and to the need to promote uniformity in its application and the observance of good faith.

(2) Questions concerning matters governed by this Law which are not expressly settled in it are to be settled in conformity with the general principles on which this Law is based.

Article 3 Variation by agreement

Except for the provisions of article 2 and article 6, paragraph (3), the parties may agree to exclude or vary any of the provisions of this Law.

Article 4 Commencement of conciliation proceedings[3]

(1) Conciliation proceedings in respect of a dispute that has arisen commence on the day on which the parties to that dispute agree to engage in conciliation proceedings.
(2) If a party that invited another party to conciliate does not receive an acceptance of the invitation within thirty days from the day on which the invitation was sent, or within such other period of time as specified in the invitation, the party may elect to treat this as a rejection of the invitation to conciliate.

Article 5 Number and appointment of conciliators

(1) There shall be one conciliator, unless the parties agree that there shall be two or more conciliators.
(2) The parties shall endeavour to reach agreement on a conciliator or conciliators, unless a different procedure for their appointment has been agreed upon.
(3) Parties may seek the assistance of an institution or person in connection with the appointment of conciliators. In particular:
   (a) A party may request such an institution or person to recommend suitable persons to act as conciliator; or
   (b) The parties may agree that the appointment of one or more conciliators be made directly by such an institution or person.
(4) In recommending or appointing individuals to act as conciliator, the institution or person shall have regard to such considerations as are likely to secure the appointment of an independent and impartial conciliator and, where appropriate, shall take into account the advisability of appointing a conciliator of a nationality other than the nationalities of the parties.
(5) When a person is approached in connection with his or her possible appointment as conciliator, he or she shall disclose any circumstances likely to give rise to justifiable doubts as to his or her impartiality or independence. A conciliator, from the time of his or her appointment and throughout the conciliation proceedings, shall without delay disclose any such circumstances to the parties unless they have already been informed of them by him or her.

Article 6 Conduct of conciliation

(1) The parties are free to agree, by reference to a set of rules or otherwise, on the manner in which the conciliation is to be conducted.
(2) Failing agreement on the manner in which the conciliation is to be conducted, the conciliator may conduct the conciliation proceedings in such a manner as the conciliator considers appropriate, taking into account the circumstances of the case, any wishes that the parties may express and the need for a speedy settlement of the dispute.

3 The following text is suggested for States that might wish to adopt a provision on the suspension of the limitation period:

Article X. Suspension of limitation period

1. When the conciliation proceedings commence, the running of the limitation period regarding the claim that is the subject matter of the conciliation is suspended.
2. Where the conciliation proceedings have terminated without a settlement agreement, the limitation period resumes running from the time the conciliation ended without a settlement agreement.

(3) In any case, in conducting the proceedings, the conciliator shall seek to maintain fair treatment of the parties and, in so doing, shall take into account the circumstances of the case.
(4) The conciliator may, at any stage of the conciliation proceedings, make proposals for a settlement of the dispute.

Article 7 Communication between conciliator and parties

The conciliator may meet or communicate with the parties together or with each of them separately.

Article 8 Disclosure of information

When the conciliator receives information concerning the dispute from a party, the conciliator may disclose the substance of that information to any other party to the conciliation. However, when a party gives any information to the conciliator, subject to a specific condition that it be kept confidential, that information shall not be disclosed to any other party to the conciliation.

Article 9 Confidentiality

Unless otherwise agreed by the parties, all information relating to the conciliation proceedings shall be kept confidential, except where disclosure is required under the law or for the purposes of implementation or enforcement of a settlement agreement.

Article 10 Admissibility of evidence in other proceedings

(1) A party to the conciliation proceedings, the conciliator and any third person, including those involved in the administration of the conciliation proceedings, shall not in arbitral, judicial or similar proceedings rely on, introduce as evidence or give testimony or evidence regarding any of the following:
    (a) An invitation by a party to engage in conciliation proceedings or the fact that a party was willing to participate in conciliation proceedings;
    (b) Views expressed or suggestions made by a party in the conciliation in respect of a possible settlement of the dispute;
    (c) Statements or admissions made by a party in the course of the conciliation proceedings;
    (d) Proposals made by the conciliator;
    (e) The fact that a party had indicated its willingness to accept a proposal for settlement made by the conciliator;
    (f) A document prepared solely for purposes of the conciliation proceedings.
(2) Paragraph (1) of this article applies irrespective of the form of the information or evidence referred to therein.
(3) The disclosure of the information referred to in paragraph (1) of this article shall not be ordered by an arbitral tribunal, court or other competent governmental authority and, if such information is offered as evidence in contravention of paragraph (1) of this article, that evidence shall be treated as inadmissible. Nevertheless, such information may be disclosed or admitted in evidence to the extent required under the law or for the purposes of implementation or enforcement of a settlement agreement.

(4) The provisions of paragraphs (1), (2) and (3) of this article apply whether or not the arbitral, judicial or similar proceedings relate to the dispute that is or was the subject matter of the conciliation proceedings.
(5) Subject to the limitations of paragraph (1) of this article, evidence that is otherwise admissible in arbitral or judicial or similar proceedings does not become inadmissible as a consequence of having been used in a conciliation.

Article 11 Termination of conciliation proceedings

The conciliation proceedings are terminated:

(a) By the conclusion of a settlement agreement by the parties, on the date of the agreement;
(b) By a declaration of the conciliator, after consultation with the parties, to the effect that further efforts at conciliation are no longer justified, on the date of the declaration;
(c) By a declaration of the parties addressed to the conciliator to the effect that the conciliation proceedings are terminated, on the date of the declaration; or
(d) By a declaration of a party to the other party or parties and the conciliator, if appointed, to the effect that the conciliation proceedings are terminated, on the date of the declaration.

Article 12 Conciliator acting as arbitrator

Unless otherwise agreed by the parties, the conciliator shall not act as an arbitrator in respect of a dispute that was or is the subject of the conciliation proceedings or in respect of another dispute that has arisen from the same contract or legal relationship or any related contract or legal relationship.

Article 13 Resort to arbitral or judicial proceedings

Where the parties have agreed to conciliate and have expressly undertaken not to initiate during a specified period of time or until a specified event has occurred arbitral or judicial proceedings with respect to an existing or future dispute, such an undertaking shall be given effect by the arbitral tribunal or the court until the terms of the undertaking have been complied with, except to the extent necessary for a party, in its opinion, to preserve its rights. Initiation of such proceedings is not of itself to be regarded as a waiver of the agreement to conciliate or as a termination of the conciliation proceedings.

Article 14 Enforceability of settlement agreement[4]

If the parties conclude an agreement settling a dispute, that settlement agreement is binding and enforceable… *[the enacting State may insert a description of the method of enforcing settlement agreements or refer to provisions governing such enforcement].*

4 When implementing the procedure for enforcement of settlement agreements, an enacting State may consider the possibility of such a procedure being mandatory.

UNCITRAL Model Law on International Commercial Mediation and International Settlement Agreements Resulting from Mediation, 2018 (amending the UNCITRAL Model Law on International Commercial Conciliation, 2002)

Section 1 – General provisions

Article 1. Scope of application of the Law and definitions

1. This Law applies to international commercial[1] mediation[2] and to international settlement agreements.
2. For the purposes of this Law, "mediator" means a sole mediator or two or more mediators, as the case may be.
3. For the purposes of this Law, "mediation" means a process, whether referred to by the expression mediation, conciliation or an expression of similar import, whereby parties request a third person or persons ("the mediator") to assist them in their attempt to reach an amicable settlement of their dispute arising out of or relating to a contractual or other legal relationship. The mediator does not have the authority to impose upon the parties a solution to the dispute.

Article 2. Interpretation

1. In the interpretation of this Law, regard is to be had to its international origin and to the need to promote uniformity in its application and the observance of good faith.
2. Questions concerning matters governed by this Law which are not expressly settled in it are to be settled in conformity with the general principles on which this Law is based.

Section 2 – International commercial mediation

Article 3. Scope of application of the section and definitions

1. This section applies to international[3] commercial mediation.
2. A mediation is "international" if:

1 The term "commercial" should be given a wide interpretation so as to cover matters arising from all relationships of a commercial nature, whether contractual or not. Relationships of a commercial nature include, but are not limited to, the following transactions: any trade transaction for the supply or exchange of goods or services; distribution agreement; commercial representation or agency; factoring; leasing; construction of works; consulting; engineering; licensing; investment; financing; banking; insurance; exploitation agreement or concession; joint venture and other forms of industrial or business cooperation; and carriage of goods or passengers by air, sea, rail or road.

2 In its previously adopted texts and relevant documents, UNCITRAL used the term "conciliation" with the understanding that the terms "conciliation" and "mediation" were interchangeable. In preparing this Model Law, the Commission decided to use the term "mediation" instead in an effort to adapt to the actual and practical use of the terms and with the expectation that this change will facilitate the promotion and heighten the visibility of the Model Law. This change in terminology does not have any substantive or conceptual implications.

3 States wishing to enact this section to apply to domestic as well as international mediation may wish to consider the following changes to the text:

- Delete the word "international" in paragraph 1 of articles 1 and 3; and
- Delete paragraphs 2, 3 and 4 of article 3, and modify references to paragraphs accordingly.

   (a) The parties to an agreement to mediate have, at the time of the conclusion of that agreement, their places of business in different States; or
   (b) The State in which the parties have their places of business is different from either:
      (i) The State in which a substantial part of the obligations of the commercial relationship is to be performed; or
      (ii) The State with which the subject matter of the dispute is most closely connected.
3. For the purposes of paragraph 2:
   (a) If a party has more than one place of business, the place of business is that which has the closest relationship to the agreement to mediate;
   (b) If a party does not have a place of business, reference is to be made to the party's habitual residence.
4. This section also applies to commercial mediation when the parties agree that the mediation is international or agree to the applicability of this section.
5. The parties are free to agree to exclude the applicability of this section.
6. Subject to the provisions of paragraph 7 of this article, this section applies irrespective of the basis upon which the mediation is carried out, including agreement between the parties whether reached before or after a dispute has arisen, an obligation established by law, or a direction or suggestion of a court, arbitral tribunal or competent governmental entity.
7. This section does not apply to:
   (a) Cases where a judge or an arbitrator, in the course of judicial or arbitral proceedings, attempts to facilitate a settlement; and
   (b) [...].

Article 4. Variation by agreement

Except for the provisions of article 7, paragraph 3, the parties may agree to exclude or vary any of the provisions of this section.

Article 5. Commencement of mediation proceedings[4]

1. Mediation proceedings in respect of a dispute that has arisen commence on the day on which the parties to that dispute agree to engage in mediation proceedings.
2. If a party that invited another party to mediate does not receive an acceptance of the invitation within 30 days from the day on which the invitation was sent, or within such other period of time as specified in the invitation, the party may elect to treat this as a rejection of the invitation to mediate.

4 The following text is suggested for States that might wish to adopt a provision on the suspension of the limitation period:

Article X. Suspension of limitation period

1. When the mediation proceedings commence, the running of the limitation period regarding the claim that is the subject matter of the mediation is suspended.
2. Where the mediation proceedings have terminated without a settlement agreement, the limitation period resumes running from the time the mediation ended without a settlement agreement.

Article 6. Number and appointment of mediators

1. There shall be one mediator, unless the parties agree that there shall be two or more mediators.
2. The parties shall endeavour to reach agreement on a mediator or mediators, unless a different procedure for their appointment has been agreed upon.
3. Parties may seek the assistance of an institution or person in connection with the appointment of mediators. In particular:
   (a) A party may request such an institution or person to recommend suitable persons to act as mediator; or
   (b) The parties may agree that the appointment of one or more mediators be made directly by such an institution or person.
4. In recommending or appointing individuals to act as mediator, the institution or person shall have regard to such considerations as are likely to secure the appointment of an independent and impartial mediator and, where appropriate, shall take into account the advisability of appointing a mediator of a nationality other than the nationalities of the parties.
5. When a person is approached in connection with his or her possible appointment as mediator, he or she shall disclose any circumstances likely to give rise to justifiable doubts as to his or her impartiality or independence. A mediator, from the time of his or her appointment and throughout the mediation proceedings, shall without delay disclose any such circumstances to the parties unless they have already been informed of them by him or her.

Article 7. Conduct of mediation

1. The parties are free to agree, by reference to a set of rules or otherwise, on the manner in which the mediation is to be conducted.
2. Failing agreement on the manner in which the mediation is to be conducted, the mediator may conduct the mediation proceedings in such a manner as the mediator considers appropriate, taking into account the circumstances of the case, any wishes that the parties may express and the need for a speedy settlement of the dispute.
3. In any case, in conducting the proceedings, the mediator shall seek to maintain fair treatment of the parties and, in so doing, shall take into account the circumstances of the case.
4. The mediator may, at any stage of the mediation proceedings, make proposals for a settlement of the dispute.

Article 8. Communication between mediator and parties

The mediator may meet or communicate with the parties together or with each of them separately.

Article 9. Disclosure of information

When the mediator receives information concerning the dispute from a party, the mediator may disclose the substance of that information to any other party to the mediation. However, when a party gives any information to the mediator, subject to a specific condition that it be kept confidential, that information shall not be disclosed to any other party to the mediation.

Article 10. Confidentiality

Unless otherwise agreed by the parties, all information relating to the mediation proceedings shall be kept confidential, except where disclosure is required under the law or for the purposes of implementation or enforcement of a settlement agreement.

Article 11. Admissibility of evidence in other proceedings

1. A party to the mediation proceedings, the mediator and any third person, including those involved in the administration of the mediation proceedings, shall not in arbitral, judicial or similar proceedings rely on, introduce as evidence or give testimony or evidence regarding any of the following:
   (a) An invitation by a party to engage in mediation proceedings or the fact that a party was willing to participate in mediation proceedings;
   (b) Views expressed or suggestions made by a party in the mediation in respect of a possible settlement of the dispute;
   (c) Statements or admissions made by a party in the course of the mediation proceedings;
   (d) Proposals made by the mediator;
   (e) The fact that a party had indicated its willingness to accept a proposal for settlement made by the mediator;
   (f) A document prepared solely for purposes of the mediation proceedings.
2. Paragraph 1 of this article applies irrespective of the form of the informati on or evidence referred to therein.
3. The disclosure of the information referred to in paragraph 1 of this article shall not be ordered by an arbitral tribunal, court or other competent governmental authority and, if such information is offered as evidence in contravention of paragraph 1 of this article, that evidence shall be treated as inadmissible. Nevertheless, such information may be disclosed or admitted in evidence to the extent required under the law or for the purposes of implementation or enforcement of a settlement agreement.
4. The provisions of paragraphs 1, 2 and 3 of this article apply whether or not the arbitral, judicial or similar proceedings relate to the dispute that is or was the subject matter of the mediation proceedings.
5. Subject to the limitations of paragraph 1 of this article, evidence that is otherwise admissible in arbitral or judicial or similar proceedings does not become inadmissible as a consequence of having been used in a mediation.

Article 12. Termination of mediation proceedings

The mediation proceedings are terminated:

(a) By the conclusion of a settlement agreement by the parties, on the date of the agreement;

(b) By a declaration of the mediator, after consultation with the parties, to the effect that further efforts at mediation are no longer justified, on the date of the declaration;
(c) By a declaration of the parties addressed to the mediator to the effect that the mediation proceedings are terminated, on the date of the declaration; or
(d) By a declaration of a party to the other party or parties and the mediator, if appointed, to the effect that the mediation proceedings are terminated, on the date of the declaration.

Article 13. Mediator acting as arbitrator

Unless otherwise agreed by the parties, the mediator shall not act as an arbitrator in respect of a dispute that was or is the subject of the mediation proceedings or in respect of another dispute that has arisen from the same contract or legal relationship or any related contract or legal relationship.

Article 14. Resort to arbitral or judicial proceedings

Where the parties have agreed to mediate and have expressly undertaken not to initiate during a specified period of time or until a specified event has occurred arbitral or judicial proceedings with respect to an existing or future dispute, such an undertaking shall be given effect by the arbitral tribunal or the court until the terms of the undertaking have been complied with, except to the extent necessary for a party, in its opinion, to preserve its rights. Initiation of such proceedings is not of itself to be regarded as a waiver of the agreement to mediate or as a termination of the mediation proceedings.

Article 15. Binding and enforceable nature of settlement agreements

If the parties conclude an agreement settling a dispute, that settlement agreement is binding and enforceable.

Section 3 – International settlement agreements[5]

Article 16. Scope of application of the section and definitions

1. This section applies to international agreements resulting from mediation and concluded in writing by parties to resolve a commercial dispute ("settlement agreements").[6]
2. This section does not apply to settlement agreements:
   (a) Concluded to resolve a dispute arising from transactions engaged in by one of the parties (a consumer) for personal, family or household purposes;
   (b) Relating to family, inheritance or employment law.
3. This section does not apply to:
   (a) Settlement agreements:

5 A State may consider enacting this section to apply to agreements settling a dispute, irrespective of whether they resulted from mediation. Adjustments would then have to be made to relevant articles.
6 A State may consider enacting this section to apply only where the parties to the settlement agreement agreed to its application.

(i) That have been approved by a court or concluded in the course of proceedings before a court; and

(ii) That are enforceable as a judgment in the State of that court;

(b) Settlement agreements that have been recorded and are enforceable as an arbitral award.

4. A settlement agreement is "international" if, at the time of the conclusion of the settlement agreement:[7]

(a) At least two parties to the settlement agreement have their places of business in different States; or

(b) The State in which the parties to the settlement agreement have their places of business is different from either:

(i) The State in which a substantial part of the obligations under the settlement agreement is to be performed; or

(ii) The State with which the subject matter of the settlement agreement is most closely connected.

5. For the purposes of paragraph 4:

(a) If a party has more than one place of business, the relevant place of business is that which has the closest relationship to the dispute resolved by the settlement agreement, having regard to the circumstances known to, or contemplated by, the parties at the time of the conclusion of the settlement agreement;

(b) If a party does not have a place of business, reference is to be made to the party's habitual residence.

(c) A settlement agreement is "in writing" if its content is recorded in any form. The requirement that a settlement agreement be in writing is met by an electronic communication if the information contained therein is accessible so as to be useable for subsequent reference.

Article 17. General principles

1. A settlement agreement shall be enforced in accordance with the rules of procedure of this State, and under the conditions laid down in this section.
2. If a dispute arises concerning a matter that a party claims was already resolved by a settlement agreement, the party may invoke the settlement agreement in accordance with the rules of procedure of this State, and under the conditions laid down in this section, in order to prove that the matter has already been resolved.

Article 18. Requirements for reliance on settlement agreements

1. A party relying on a settlement agreement under this section shall supply to the competent authority of this State:

(a) The settlement agreement signed by the parties;

7 A State may consider broadening the definition of "international" settlement agreement by adding the following subparagraph to paragraph 4: "A settlement agreement is also 'international' if it results from international mediation as defined in article 3, paragraphs 2, 3 and 4."

(b) Evidence that the settlement agreement resulted from mediation, such as:
   (i) The mediator's signature on the settlement agreement;
   (ii) A document signed by the mediator indicating that the mediation was carried out;
   (iii) An attestation by the institution that administered the mediation; or
   (iv) In the absence of (i), (ii) or (iii), any other evidence acceptable to the competent authority.

2. The requirement that a settlement agreement shall be signed by the parties or, where applicable, the mediator, is met in relation to an electronic communication if:
   (a) A method is used to identify the parties or the mediator and to indicate the parties' or mediator's intention in respect of the information contained in the electronic communication; and
   (b) The method used is either:
      (i) As reliable as appropriate for the purpose for which the electronic communication was generated or communicated, in the light of all the circumstances, including any relevant agreement; or
      (ii) Proven in fact to have fulfilled the functions described in subparagraph (a) above, by itself or together with further evidence.
3. If the settlement agreement is not in an official language of this State, the competent authority may request a translation thereof into such language.
4. The competent authority may require any necessary document in order to verify that the requirements of this section have been complied with.
5. When considering the request for relief, the competent authority shall act expeditiously.

Article 19. Grounds for refusing to grant relief

1. The competent authority of this State may refuse to grant relief at the request of the party against whom the relief is sought only if that party furnishes to the competent authority proof that:
   (a) A party to the settlement agreement was under some incapacity;
   (b) The settlement agreement sought to be relied upon:
      (i) Is null and void, inoperative or incapable of being performed under the law to which the parties have validly subjected it or, failing any indication thereon, under the law deemed applicable by the competent authority;
      (ii) Is not binding, or is not final, according to its terms; or
      (iii) Has been subsequently modified;
   (c) The obligations in the settlement agreement:
      (i) Have been performed; or
      (ii) Are not clear or comprehensible;
   (d) Granting relief would be contrary to the terms of the settlement agreement;
   (e) There was a serious breach by the mediator of standards applicable to the mediator or the mediation without which breach that party would not have entered into the settlement agreement; or
   (f) There was a failure by the mediator to disclose to the parties circumstances that raise justifiable doubts as to the mediator's impartiality or independence and such failure to disclose had a material impact or undue influence on a party without which failure that party would not have entered into the settlement agreement.

2. The competent authority of this State may also refuse to grant relief if it finds that:
   (a) Granting relief would be contrary to the public policy of this State; or
   (b) The subject matter of the dispute is not capable of settlement by mediation under the law of this State.

Article 20. Parallel applications or claims

If an application or a claim relating to a settlement agreement has been made to a court, an arbitral tribunal or any other competent authority which may affect the relief being sought under article 18, the competent authority of this State where such relief is sought may, if it considers it proper, adjourn the decision and may also, on the request of a party, order the other party to give suitable security.

UNIDROIT Principles of International Commercial Contracts, 2010

Preamble

(Purpose of the Principles)

These Principles set forth general rules for international commercial contracts.

They shall be applied when the parties have agreed that their contract be governed by them.
They may be applied when the parties have agreed that their contract be governed by general principles of law, the *lex mercatoria* or the like.
They may be applied when the parties have not chosen any law to govern their contract.
They may be used to interpret or supplement international uniform law instruments.
They may be used to interpret or supplement domestic law.
They may serve as a model for national and international legislators.

Chapter 1 General provisions

Article 1.1 Freedom of contract

The parties are free to enter into a contract and to determine its content.

Article 1.2 No form required

Nothing in these Principles requires a contract, statement or any other act to be made in or evidenced by a particular form. It may be proved by any means, including witnesses.

Article 1.3 Binding character of contract

A contract validly entered into is binding upon the parties. It can only be modified or terminated in accordance with its terms or by agreement or as otherwise provided in these Principles.

Article 1.4 Mandatory rules

Nothing in these Principles shall restrict the application of mandatory rules, whether of national, international or supranational origin, which are applicable in accordance with the relevant rules of private international law.

Article 1.5 Exclusion or modification by the parties

The parties may exclude the application of these Principles or derogate from or vary the effect of any of their provisions, except as otherwise provided in the Principles.

Article 1.6 Interpretation and supplementation of the principles

(1) In the interpretation of these Principles, regard is to be had to their international character and to their purposes including the need to promote uniformity in their application.
(2) Issues within the scope of these Principles but not expressly settled by them are as far as possible to be settled in accordance with their underlying general principles.

Article 1.7 Good faith and fair dealing

(1) Each party must act in accordance with good faith and fair dealing in international trade.
(2) The parties may not exclude or limit this duty.

Article 1.8 Inconsistent behaviour

A party cannot act inconsistently with an understanding it has caused the other party to have and upon which that other party reasonably has acted in reliance to its detriment.

Article 1.9 Usages and practices

(1) The parties are bound by any usage to which they have agreed and by any practices which they have established between themselves.
(2) The parties are bound by a usage that is widely known to and regularly observed in international trade by parties in the particular trade concerned except where the application of such a usage would be unreasonable.

Article 1.10 Notice

(1) Where notice is required it may be given by any means appropriate to the circumstances.
(2) A notice is effective when it reaches the person to whom it is given.
(3) For the purpose of paragraph (2) a notice 'reaches' a person when given to that person orally or delivered at that person's place of business or mailing address.
(4) For the purpose of this article 'notice' includes a declaration, demand, request or any other communication of intention.

Article 1.11 Definitions

In these Principles

- "court" includes an arbitral tribunal;
- where a party has more than one place of business the relevant "place of business" is that which has the closest relationship to the contract and its performance, having regard to the circumstances known to or contemplated by the parties at any time before or at the conclusion of the contract;
- "long-term contract" refers to a contract which is to be performed over a period of time and which normally involves, to a varying degree, complexity of the transaction and an ongoing relationship between the parties;
- "obligor" refers to the party who is to perform an obligation and "obligee" refers to the party who is entitled to performance of that obligation;
- "writing" means any mode of communication that preserves a record of the information contained therein and is capable of being reproduced in tangible form.

Article 1.12 Computation of time set by parties

(1) Official holidays or non-business days occurring during a period set by parties for an act to be performed are included in calculating the period.
(2) However, if the last day of the period is an official holiday or a non-business day at the place of business of the party to perform the act, the period is extended until the first business day which follows, unless the circumstances indicate otherwise.
(3) The relevant time zone is that of the place of business of the party setting the time, unless the circumstances indicate otherwise.

Chapter 2 Formation and authority of agents

Section 1 Formation

Article 2.1.1 Manner of formation

A contract may be concluded either by the acceptance of an offer or by conduct of the parties that is sufficient to show agreement.

Article 2.1.2 Definition of offer

A proposal for concluding a contract constitutes an offer if it is sufficiently definite and indicates the intention of the offeror to be bound in case of acceptance.

Article 2.1.3 Withdrawal of offer

(1) An offer becomes effective when it reaches the offeree.
(2) An offer, even if it is irrevocable, may be withdrawn if the withdrawal reaches the offeree before or at the same time as the offer.

Article 2.1.4 Revocation of offer

(1) Until a contract is concluded an offer may be revoked if the revocation reaches the offeree before it has dispatched an acceptance.
(2) However, an offer cannot be revoked
  (a) if it indicates, whether by stating a fixed time for acceptance or otherwise, that it is irrevocable; or
  (b) if it was reasonable for the offeree to rely on the offer as being irrevocable and the offeree has acted in reliance on the offer.

Article 2.1.5 Rejection of offer

An offer is terminated when a rejection reaches the offeror.

Article 2.1.6 Mode of acceptance

(1) A statement made by or other conduct of the offeree indicating assent to an offer is an acceptance. Silence or inactivity does not in itself amount to acceptance.
(2) An acceptance of an offer becomes effective when the indication of assent reaches the offeror.
(3) However, if, by virtue of the offer or as a result of practices which the parties have established between themselves or of usage, the offeree may indicate assent by performing an act without notice to the offeror, the acceptance is effective when the act is performed.

Article 2.1.7 Time of acceptance

An offer must be accepted within the time the offeror has fixed or, if no time is fixed, within a reasonable time having regard to the circumstances, including the rapidity of the means of communication employed by the offeror. An oral offer must be accepted immediately unless the circumstances indicate otherwise.

Article 2.1.8 Acceptance within a fixed period of time

A period of acceptance fixed by the offeror begins to run from the time that the offer is dispatched. A time indicated in the offer is deemed to be the time of dispatch unless the circumstances indicate otherwise.

Article 2.1.9 Late acceptance. Delay in transmission

(1) A late acceptance is nevertheless effective as an acceptance if without undue delay the offeror so informs the offeree or gives notice to that effect.
(2) If a communication containing a late acceptance shows that it has been sent in such circumstances that if its transmission had been normal it would have reached the offeror in due time, the late acceptance is effective as an acceptance unless, without undue delay, the offeror informs the offeree that it considers the offer as having lapsed.

Article 2.1.10 Withdrawal of acceptance

An acceptance may be withdrawn if the withdrawal reaches the offeror before or at the same time as the acceptance would have become effective.

Article 2.1.11 Modified acceptance

(1) A reply to an offer which purports to be an acceptance but contains additions, limitations or other modifications is a rejection of the offer and constitutes a counter-offer.
(2) However, a reply to an offer which purports to be an acceptance but contains additional or different terms which do not materially alter the terms of the offer constitutes an acceptance, unless the offeror, without undue delay, objects to the discrepancy. If the offeror does not object, the terms of the contract are the terms of the offer with the modifications contained in the acceptance.

Article 2.1.12 Writings in confirmation

If a writing which is sent within a reasonable time after the conclusion of the contract and which purports to be a confirmation of the contract contains additional or different terms, such terms become part of the contract, unless they materially alter the contract or the recipient, without undue delay, objects to the discrepancy.

Article 2.1.13 Conclusion of contract dependent on agreement on specific matters or in a particular form

Where in the course of negotiations one of the parties insists that the contract is not concluded until there is agreement on specific matters or in a particular form, no contract is concluded before agreement is reached on those matters or in that form.

Article 2.1.14

(Contract with terms deliberately left open)

(1) If the parties intend to conclude a contract, the fact that they intentionally leave a term to be agreed upon in further negotiations or to be determined by one of the parties or by a third person does not prevent a contract from coming into existence.
(2) The existence of the contract is not affected by the fact that subsequently
    (a) the parties reach no agreement on the term;
    (b) the party who is to determine the term does not do so; or
    (c) the third person does not determine the term,

provided that there is an alternative means of rendering the term definite that is reasonable in the circumstances, having regard to the intention of the parties.

Article 2.1.15 Negotiations in bad faith

(1) A party is free to negotiate and is not liable for failure to reach an agreement.

(2) However, a party who negotiates or breaks off negotiations in bad faith is liable for the losses caused to the other party.
(3) It is bad faith, in particular, for a party to enter into or continue negotiations when intending not to reach an agreement with the other party.

Article 2.1.16 Duty of confidentiality

Where information is given as confidential by one party in the course of negotiations, the other party is under a duty not to disclose that information or to use it improperly for its own purposes, whether or not a contract is subsequently concluded. Where appropriate, the remedy for breach of that duty may include compensation based on the benefit received by the other party.

Article 2.1.17 Merger clauses

A contract in writing which contains a clause indicating that the writing completely embodies the terms on which the parties have agreed cannot be contradicted or supplemented by evidence of prior statements or agreements. However, such statements or agreements may be used to interpret the writing.

Article 2.1.18 Modification in a particular form

A contract in writing which contains a clause requiring any modification or termination by agreement to be in a particular form may not be otherwise modified or terminated. However, a party may be precluded by its conduct from asserting such a clause to the extent that the other party has reasonably acted in reliance on that conduct.

Article 2.1.19 Contracting under standard terms

(1) Where one party or both parties use standard terms in concluding a contract, the general rules on formation apply, subject to Articles 2.1.20–2.1.22.
(2) Standard terms are provisions which are prepared in advance for general and repeated use by one party and which are actually used without negotiation with the other party.

Article 2.1.20 Surprising terms

(1) No term contained in standard terms which is of such a character that the other party could not reasonably have expected it, is effective unless it has been expressly accepted by that party.
(2) In determining whether a term is of such a character regard shall be had to its content, language and presentation.

Article 2.1.21 Conflict between standard terms and non-standard terms

In case of conflict between a standard term and a term which is not a standard term the latter prevails.

Article 2.1.22 Battle of forms

Where both parties use standard terms and reach agreement except on those terms, a contract is concluded on the basis of the agreed terms and of any standard terms which are common in substance unless one party clearly indicates in advance, or later and without undue delay informs the other party, that it does not intend to be bound by such a contract.

Section 2 Authority of agents

Article 2.2.1 Scope of the section

(1) This Section governs the authority of a person ('the agent'), to affect the legal relations of another person ('the principal'), by or with respect to a contract with a third party, whether the agent acts in its own name or in that of the principal.
(2) It governs only the relations between the principal or the agent on the one hand, and the third party on the other.
(3) It does not govern an agent's authority conferred by law or the authority of an agent appointed by a public or judicial authority.

Article 2.2.2 Establishment and scope of the authority of the agent

(1) The principal's grant of authority to an agent may be express or implied.
(2) The agent has authority to perform all acts necessary in the circumstances to achieve the purposes for which the authority was granted.

Article 2.2.3 Agency disclosed

(1) Where an agent acts within the scope of its authority and the third party knew or ought to have known that the agent was acting as an agent, the acts of the agent shall directly affect the legal relations between the principal and the third party and no legal relation is created between the agent and the third party.
(2) However, the acts of the agent shall affect only the relations between the agent and the third party, where the agent with the consent of the principal undertakes to become the party to the contract.

Article 2.2.4 Agency undisclosed

(1) Where an agent acts within the scope of its authority and the third party neither knew nor ought to have known that the agent was acting as an agent, the acts of the agent shall affect only the relations between the agent and the third party.
(2) However, where such an agent, when contracting with the third party on behalf of a business, represents itself to be the owner of that business, the third party, upon discovery of the real owner of the business, may exercise also against the latter the rights it has against the agent.

Article 2.2.5 Agent acting without or exceeding its authority

(1) Where an agent acts without authority or exceeds its authority, its acts do not affect the legal relations between the principal and the third party.

(2) However, where the principal causes the third party reasonably to believe that the agent has authority to act on behalf of the principal and that the agent is acting within the scope of that authority, the principal may not invoke against the third party the lack of authority of the agent.

Article 2.2.6 Liability of agent acting without or exceeding its authority

(1) An agent that acts without authority or exceeds its authority is, failing ratification by the principal, liable for damages that will place the third party in the same position as if the agent had acted with authority and not exceeded its authority.
(2) However, the agent is not liable if the third party knew or ought to have known that the agent had no authority or was exceeding its authority.

Article 2.2.7 Conflict of interests

(1) If a contract concluded by an agent involves the agent in a conflict of interests with the principal of which the third party knew or ought to have known, the principal may avoid the contract. The right to avoid is subject to Articles 3.2.9 and 3.2.11 to 3.2.15.
(2) However, the principal may not avoid the contract:
    (a) if the principal had consented to, or knew or ought to have known of, the agent's involvement in the conflict of interests; or
    (b) if the agent had disclosed the conflict of interests to the principal and the latter had not objected within a reasonable time.

Article 2.2.8 Sub-agency

An agent has implied authority to appoint a sub-agent to perform acts which it is not reasonable to expect the agent to perform itself. The rules of this Section apply to the sub-agency.

Article 2.2.9 Ratification

(1) An act by an agent that acts without authority or exceeds its authority may be ratified by the principal. On ratification the act produces the same effects as if it had initially been carried out with authority.
(2) The third party may by notice to the principal specify a reasonable period of time for ratification. If the principal does not ratify within that period of time it can no longer do so.
(3) If, at the time of the agent's act, the third party neither knew nor ought to have known of the lack of authority, it may, at any time before ratification, by notice to the principal indicate its refusal to become bound by a ratification.

Article 2.2.10 Termination of authority

(1) Termination of authority is not effective in relation to the third party unless the third party knew or ought to have known of it.

(2) Notwithstanding the termination of its authority, an agent remains authorised to perform the acts that are necessary to prevent harm to the principal's interests.

Chapter 3 Validity

Section 1 General provisions

Article 3.1.1 Matters not covered

This Chapter does not deal with lack of capacity.

Article 3.1.2 Validity of mere agreement

A contract is concluded, modified or terminated by the mere agreement of the parties, without any further requirement.

Article 3.1.3 Initial impossibility

(1) The mere fact that at the time of the conclusion of the contract the performance of the obligation assumed was impossible does not affect the validity of the contract.
(2) The mere fact that at the time of the conclusion of the contract a party was not entitled to dispose of the assets to which the contract relates does not affect the validity of the contract.

Article 3.1.4 Mandatory character of the provisions

The provisions on fraud, threat, gross disparity and illegality contained in this Chapter are mandatory.

Section 2 Grounds for avoidance

Article 3.2.1 Definition of mistake

Mistake is an erroneous assumption relating to facts or to law existing when the contract was concluded.

Article 3.2.2 Relevant mistake

(1) A party may only avoid the contract for mistake if, when the contract was concluded, the mistake was of such importance that a reasonable person in the same situation as the party in error would only have concluded the contract on materially different terms or would not have concluded it at all if the true state of affairs had been known, and
   (a) the other party made the same mistake, or caused the mistake, or knew or ought to have known of the mistake and it was contrary to reasonable commercial standards of fair dealing to leave the mistaken party in error; or

  (b) the other party had not at the time of avoidance reasonably acted in reliance on the contract.
(2) However, a party may not avoid the contract if:
  (a) it was grossly negligent in committing the mistake; or
  (b) the mistake relates to a matter in regard to which the risk of mistake was assumed or, having regard to the circumstances, should be borne by the mistaken party.

Article 3.2.3 Error in expression or transmission

An error occurring in the expression or transmission of a declaration is considered to be a mistake of the person from whom the declaration emanated.

Article 3.2.4 Remedies for non-performance

A party is not entitled to avoid the contract on the ground of mistake if the circumstances on which that party relies afford, or could have afforded, a remedy for non-performance.

Article 3.2.5 Fraud

A party may avoid the contract when it has been led to conclude the contract by the other party's fraudulent representation, including language or practices, or fraudulent non-disclosure of circumstances which, according to reasonable commercial standards of fair dealing, the latter party should have disclosed.

Article 3.2.6 Threat

A party may avoid the contract when it has been led to conclude the contract by the other party's unjustified threat which, having regard to the circumstances, is so imminent and serious as to leave the first party no reasonable alternative. In particular, a threat is unjustified if the act or omission with which a party has been threatened is wrongful in itself, or it is wrongful to use it as a means to obtain the conclusion of the contract.

Article 3.2.7 Gross disparity

(1) A party may avoid the contract or an individual term of it if, at the time of the conclusion of the contract, the contract or term unjustifiably gave the other party an excessive advantage. Regard is to be had, among other factors, to
  (a) the fact that the other party has taken unfair advantage of the first party's dependence, economic distress or urgent needs, or of its improvidence, ignorance, inexperience or lack of bargaining skill, and
  (b) the nature and purpose of the contract.
(2) Upon the request of the party entitled to avoidance, a court may adapt the contract or term in order to make it accord with reasonable commercial standards of fair dealing.
(3) A court may also adapt the contract or term upon the request of the party receiving notice of avoidance, provided that that party informs the other party of its request

promptly after receiving such notice and before the other party has reasonably acted in reliance on it. Article 3.2.10(2) applies accordingly.

Article 3.2.8 Third persons

(1) Where fraud, threat, gross disparity or a party's mistake is imputable to, or is known or ought to be known by, a third person for whose acts the other party is responsible, the contract may be avoided under the same conditions as if the behaviour or knowledge had been that of the party itself.

(2) Where fraud, threat or gross disparity is imputable to a third person for whose acts the other party is not responsible, the contract may be avoided if that party knew or ought to have known of the fraud, threat or disparity, or has not at the time of avoidance reasonably acted in reliance on the contract.

Article 3.2.9 Confirmation

If the party entitled to avoid the contract expressly or impliedly confirms the contract after the period of time for giving notice of avoidance has begun to run, avoidance of the contract is excluded.

Article 3.2.10 Loss of right to avoid

(1) If a party is entitled to avoid the contract for mistake but the other party declares itself willing to perform or performs the contract as it was understood by the party entitled to avoidance, the contract is considered to have been concluded as the latter party understood it. The other party must make such a declaration or render such performance promptly after having been informed of the manner in which the party entitled to avoidance had understood the contract and before that party has reasonably acted in reliance on a notice of avoidance.

(2) After such a declaration or performance the right to avoidance is lost and any earlier notice of avoidance is ineffective.

Article 3.2.11 Notice of avoidance

The right of a party to avoid the contract is exercised by notice to the other party.

Article 3.2.12 Time limits

(1) Notice of avoidance shall be given within a reasonable time, having regard to the circumstances, after the avoiding party knew or could not have been unaware of the relevant facts or became capable of acting freely.

(2) Where an individual term of the contract may be avoided by a party under Article 3.2.7, the period of time for giving notice of avoidance begins to run when that term is asserted by the other party.

Article 3.2.13 Partial avoidance

Where a ground of avoidance affects only individual terms of the contract, the effect of avoidance is limited to those terms unless, having regard to the circumstances, it is unreasonable to uphold the remaining contract.

Article 3.2.14 Retroactive effect of avoidance

Avoidance takes effect retroactively.

Article 3.2.15 Restitution

(1) On avoidance either party may claim restitution of whatever it has supplied under the contract, or the part of it avoided, provided that the party concurrently makes restitution of whatever it has received under the contract, or the part of it avoided.
(2) If restitution in kind is not possible or appropriate, an allowance has to be made in money whenever reasonable.
(3) The recipient of the performance does not have to make an allowance in money if the impossibility to make restitution in kind is attributable to the other party.
(4) Compensation may be claimed for expenses reasonably required to preserve or maintain the performance received.

Article 3.2.16 Damages

Irrespective of whether or not the contract has been avoided, the party who knew or ought to have known of the ground for avoidance is liable for damages so as to put the other party in the same position in which it would have been if it had not concluded the contract.

Article 3.2.17 Unilateral declarations

The provisions of this Chapter apply with appropriate adaptations to any communication of intention addressed by one party to the other.

Section 3 Illegality

Article 3.3.1 Contracts infringing mandatory rules

(1) Where a contract infringes a mandatory rule, whether of national, international or supranational origin, applicable under Article 1.4 of these Principles, the effects of that infringement upon the contract are the effects, if any, expressly prescribed by that mandatory rule.
(2) Where the mandatory rule does not expressly prescribe the effects of an infringement upon a contract, the parties have the right to exercise such remedies under the contract as in the circumstances are reasonable.
(3) In determining what is reasonable regard is to be had in particular to:
    (a) the purpose of the rule which has been infringed;
    (b) the category of persons for whose protection the rule exists;

(c) any sanction that may be imposed under the rule infringed;
(d) the seriousness of the infringement;
(e) whether one or both parties knew or ought to have known of the infringement;
(f) whether the performance of the contract necessitates the infringement; and
(g) the parties' reasonable expectations.

Article 3.3.2 Restitution

(1) Where there has been performance under a contract infringing a mandatory rule under Article 3.3.1, restitution may be granted where this would be reasonable in the circumstances.
(2) In determining what is reasonable, regard is to be had, with the appropriate adaptations, to the criteria referred to in Article 3.3.1(3).
(3) If restitution is granted, the rules set out in Article 3.2.15 apply with appropriate adaptations.

Chapter 4 Interpretation

Article 4.1 Intention of the parties

(1) A contract shall be interpreted according to the common intention of the parties.
(2) If such an intention cannot be established, the contract shall be interpreted according to the meaning that reasonable persons of the same kind as the parties would give to it in the same circumstances.

Article 4.2 Interpretation of statements and other conduct

(1) The statements and other conduct of a party shall be interpreted according to that party's intention if the other party knew or could not have been unaware of that intention.
(2) If the preceding paragraph is not applicable, such statements and other conduct shall be interpreted according to the meaning that a reasonable person of the same kind as the other party would give to it in the same circumstances.

Article 4.3 Relevant circumstances

In applying Articles 4.1 and 4.2, regard shall be had to all the circumstances, including:

(a) preliminary negotiations between the parties;
(b) practices which the parties have established between themselves;
(c) the conduct of the parties subsequent to the conclusion of the contract;
(d) the nature and purpose of the contract;
(e) the meaning commonly given to terms and expressions in the trade concerned;
(f) usages.

Article 4.4 Reference to contract or statement as a whole

Terms and expressions shall be interpreted in the light of the whole contract or statement in which they appear.

Article 4.5 All terms to be given effect

Contract terms shall be interpreted so as to give effect to all the terms rather than to deprive some of them of effect.

Article 4.6 Contra proferentem rule

If contract terms supplied by one party are unclear, an interpretation against that party is preferred.

Article 4.7 Linguistic discrepancies

Where a contract is drawn up in two or more language versions which are equally authoritative there is, in case of discrepancy between the versions, a preference for the interpretation according to a version in which the contract was originally drawn up.

Article 4.8 Supplying an omitted term

(1) Where the parties to a contract have not agreed with respect to a term which is important for a determination of their rights and duties, a term which is appropriate in the circumstances shall be supplied.
(2) In determining what is an appropriate term regard shall be had, among other factors, to:
    (a) the intention of the parties;
    (b) the nature and purpose of the contract;
    (c) good faith and fair dealing;
    (d) reasonableness.

Chapter 5 Content and third party rights

Section 1 Content

Article 5.1.1 Express and implied obligations

The contractual obligations of the parties may be express or implied.

Article 5.1.2 Implied obligations

Implied obligations stem from:

(a) the nature and purpose of the contract;
(b) practices established between the parties and usages;
(c) good faith and fair dealing;
(d) reasonableness.

Article 5.1.3 Co-operation between the parties

Each party shall cooperate with the other party when such co-operation may reasonably be expected for the performance of that party's obligations.

Article 5.1.4 Duty to achieve a specific result. Duty of best efforts

(1) To the extent that an obligation of a party involves a duty to achieve a specific result, that party is bound to achieve that result.
(2) To the extent that an obligation of a party involves a duty of best efforts in the performance of an activity, that party is bound to make such efforts as would be made by a reasonable person of the same kind in the same circumstances.

Article 5.1.5 Determination of kind of duty involved

In determining the extent to which an obligation of a party involves a duty of best efforts in the performance of an activity or a duty to achieve a specific result, regard shall be had, among other factors, to:

(a) the way in which the obligation is expressed in the contract;
(b) the contractual price and other terms of the contract;
(c) the degree of risk normally involved in achieving the expected result;
(d) the ability of the other party to influence the performance of the obligation.

Article 5.1.6 Determination of quality of performance

Where the quality of performance is neither fixed by, nor determinable from, the contract a party is bound to render a performance of a quality that is reasonable and not less than average in the circumstances.

Article 5.1.7 (Price determination)

(1) Where a contract does not fix or make provision for determining the price, the parties are considered, in the absence of any indication to the contrary, to have made reference to the price generally charged at the time of the conclusion of the contract for such performance in comparable circumstances in the trade concerned or, if no such price is available, to a reasonable price.
(2) Where the price is to be determined by one party and that determination is manifestly unreasonable, a reasonable price shall be substituted notwithstanding any contract term to the contrary.
(3) Where the price is to be fixed by one party or a third person, and that party or third person does not do so, the price shall be a reasonable price.
(4) Where the price is to be fixed by reference to factors which do not exist or have ceased to exist or to be accessible, the nearest equivalent factor shall be treated as a substitute.

Article 5.1.8 Termination of a contract for an indefinite period

A contract for an indefinite period may be terminated by either party by giving notice a reasonable time in advance. As to the effects of termination in general, and as to restitution, the provisions in Articles 7.3.5 and 7.3.7 apply.

Article 5.1.9 Release by agreement

1 An obligee may release its right by agreement with the obligor.
2 An offer to release a right gratuitously shall be deemed accepted if the obligor does not reject the offer without delay after having become aware of it.

Section 2 Third party rights

Article 5.2.1 Contracts in favour of third parties

(1) The parties (the 'promisor' and the 'promisee') may confer by express or implied agreement a right on a third party (the 'beneficiary').
(2) The existence and content of the beneficiary's right against the promisor are determined by the agreement of the parties and are subject to any conditions or other limitations under the agreement.

Article 5.2.2 Third party identifiable

The beneficiary must be identifiable with adequate certainty by the contract but need not be in existence at the time the contract is made.

Article 5.2.3 Exclusion and limitation clauses

The conferment of rights in the beneficiary includes the right to invoke a clause in the contract which excludes or limits the liability of the beneficiary.

Article 5.2.4 Defences

The promisor may assert against the beneficiary all defences which the promisor could assert against the promisee.

Article 5.2.5 Revocation

The parties may modify or revoke the rights conferred by the contract on the beneficiary until the beneficiary has accepted them or reasonably acted in reliance on them.

Article 5.2.6 Renunciation

The beneficiary may renounce a right conferred on it.

Section 3 Conditions

Article 5.3.1 Types of condition

A contract or a contractual obligation may be made conditional upon the occurrence of a future uncertain event, so that the contract or the contractual obligation only takes effect if the event occurs (suspensive condition) or comes to an end if the event occurs (resolutive condition).

Article 5.3.2 Effect of conditions

Unless the parties otherwise agree:

(a) the relevant contract or contractual obligation takes effect upon fulfilment of a suspensive condition;
(b) the relevant contract or contractual obligation comes to an end upon fulfilment of a resolutive condition.

Article 5.3.3 Interference with conditions

(1) If fulfilment of a condition is prevented by a party, contrary to the duty of good faith and fair dealing or the duty of co-operation, that party may not rely on the non-fulfilment of the condition.
(2) If fulfilment of a condition is brought about by a party, contrary to the duty of good faith and fair dealing or the duty of co-operation, that party may not rely on the fulfilment of the condition.

Article 5.3.4 Duty to preserve rights

Pending fulfilment of a condition, a party may not, contrary to the duty to act in accordance with good faith and fair dealing, act so as to prejudice the other party's rights in case of fulfilment of the condition.

Article 5.3.5 Restitution in case of fulfilment of a resolutive condition

(1) On fulfilment of a resolutive condition, the rules on restitution set out in Articles 7.3.6 and 7.3.7 apply with appropriate adaptations.
(2) If the parties have agreed that the resolutive condition is to operate retroactively, the rules on restitution set out in Article 3.2.15 apply with appropriate adaptations.

Chapter 6 Performance

Section 1 Performance in General

Article 6.1.1 Time of performance

A party must perform its obligations:

(a) if a time is fixed by or determinable from the contract, at that time;
(b) if a period of time is fixed by or determinable from the contract, at any time within that period unless circumstances indicate that the other party is to choose a time;
(c) in any other case, within a reasonable time after the conclusion of the contract.

Article 6.1.2 Performance at one time or in instalments

In cases under Article 6.1.1(b) or (c), a party must perform its obligations at one time if that performance can be rendered at one time and the circumstances do not indicate otherwise.

Article 6.1.3 Partial performance

(1) The obligee may reject an offer to perform in part at the time performance is due, whether or not such offer is coupled with an assurance as to the balance of the performance, unless the obligee has no legitimate interest in so doing.
(2) Additional expenses caused to the obligee by partial performance are to be borne by the obligor without prejudice to any other remedy.

Article 6.1.4 Order of performance

(1) To the extent that the performances of the parties can be rendered simultaneously, the parties are bound to render them simultaneously unless the circumstances indicate otherwise.
(2) To the extent that the performance of only one party requires a period of time, that party is bound to render its performance first, unless the circumstances indicate otherwise.

Article 6.1.5 Earlier performance

(1) The obligee may reject an earlier performance unless it has no legitimate interest in so doing.
(2) Acceptance by a party of an earlier performance does not affect the time for the performance of its own obligations if that time has been fixed irrespective of the performance of the other party's obligations.
(3) Additional expenses caused to the obligee by earlier performance are to be borne by the obligor, without prejudice to any other remedy.

Article 6.1.6 Place of performance

(1) If the place of performance is neither fixed by, nor determinable from, the contract, a party is to perform:
    (a) a monetary obligation, at the obligee's place of business;
    (b) any other obligation, at its own place of business.
(2) A party must bear any increase in the expenses incidental to performance which is caused by a change in its place of business subsequent to the conclusion of the contract.

Article 6.1.7 Payment by cheque or other instrument

(1) Payment may be made in any form used in the ordinary course of business at the place for payment.
(2) However, an obligee who accepts, either by virtue of paragraph (1) or voluntarily, a cheque, any other order to pay or a promise to pay, is presumed to do so only on condition that it will be honoured.

Article 6.1.8 Payment by funds transfer

(1) Unless the obligee has indicated a particular account, payment may be made by a transfer to any of the financial institutions in which the obligee has made it known that it has an account.

(2) In case of payment by a transfer the obligation of the obligor is discharged when the transfer to the obligee's financial institution becomes effective.

Article 6.1.9 Currency of payment

(1) If a monetary obligation is expressed in a currency other than that of the place for payment, it may be paid by the obligor in the currency of the place for payment unless:
  (a) that currency is not freely convertible; or
  (b) the parties have agreed that payment should be made only in the currency in which the monetary obligation is expressed.

(2) If it is impossible for the obligor to make payment in the currency in which the monetary obligation is expressed, the obligee may require payment in the currency of the place for payment, even in the case referred to in paragraph (1)(b).

(3) Payment in the currency of the place for payment is to be made according to the applicable rate of exchange prevailing there when payment is due.

(4) However, if the obligor has not paid at the time when payment is due, the obligee may require payment according to the applicable rate of exchange prevailing either when payment is due or at the time of actual payment.

Article 6.1.10 Currency not expressed

Where a monetary obligation is not expressed in a particular currency, payment must be made in the currency of the place where payment is to be made.

Article 6.1.11 Costs of performance

Each party shall bear the costs of performance of its obligations.

Article 6.1.12 Imputation of Payments

(1) An obligor owing several monetary obligations to the same obligee may specify at the time of payment the debt to which it intends the payment to be applied. However, the payment discharges first any expenses, then interest due and finally the principal.

(2) If the obligor makes no such specification, the obligee may, within a reasonable time after payment, declare to the obligor the obligation to which it imputes the payment, p rovided that the obligation is due and undisputed.

(3) In the absence of imputation under paragraphs (1) or (2), payment is imputed to that obligation which satisfies one of the following criteria in the order indicated:
  (a) an obligation which is due or which is the first to fall due;
  (b) the obligation for which the obligee has least security;
  (c) the obligation which is the most burdensome for the obligor;
  (d) the obligation which has arisen first.
  (e) If none of the preceding criteria applies, payment is imputed to all the obligations proportionally.

Article 6.1.13 Imputation of non-monetary obligations

Article 6.1.12 applies with appropriate adaptations to the imputation of performance of non-monetary obligations.

Article 6.1.14 Application for public permission

Where the law of a State requires a public permission affecting the validity of the contract or its performance and neither that law nor the circumstances indicate otherwise:

(a) if only one party has its place of business in that State, that party shall take the measures necessary to obtain the permission;
(b) in any other case the party whose performance requires permission shall take the necessary measures.

Article 6.1.15 Procedure in applying for permission

(1) The party required to take the measures necessary to obtain the permission shall do so without undue delay and shall bear any expenses incurred.
(2) That party shall whenever appropriate give the other party notice of the grant or refusal of such permission without undue delay.

Article 6.1.16 Permission neither granted nor refused

(1) If, notwithstanding the fact that the party responsible has taken all measures required, permission is neither granted nor refused within an agreed period or, where no period has been agreed, within a reasonable time from the conclusion of the contract, either party is entitled to terminate the contract.
(2) Where the permission affects some terms only, paragraph (1) does not apply if, having regard to the circumstances, it is reasonable to uphold the remaining contract even if the permission is refused.

Article 6.1.17 Permission refused

(1) The refusal of a permission affecting the validity of the contract renders the contract void. If the refusal affects the validity of some terms only, only such terms are void if, having regard to the circumstances, it is reasonable to uphold the remaining contract.
(2) Where the refusal of a permission renders the performance of the contract impossible in whole or in part, the rules on non-performance apply.

Section 2 Hardship

Article 6.2.1 Contract to be observed

Where the performance of a contract becomes more onerous for one of the parties, that party is nevertheless bound to perform its obligations subject to the following provisions on hardship.

Article 6.2.2 Definition of hardship

There is hardship where the occurrence of events fundamentally alters the equilibrium of the contract either because the cost of a party's performance has increased or because the value of the performance a party receives has diminished, and

(a) the events occur or become known to the disadvantaged party after the conclusion of the contract;
(b) the events could not reasonably have been taken into account by the disadvantaged party at the time of the conclusion of the contract;
(c) the events are beyond the control of the disadvantaged party; and
(d) the risk of the events was not assumed by the disadvantaged party.

Article 6.2.3 Effects of hardship

(1) In case of hardship the disadvantaged party is entitled to request renegotiations. The request shall be made without undue delay and shall indicate the grounds on which it is based.
(2) The request for renegotiation does not in itself entitle the disadvantaged party to withhold performance.
(3) Upon failure to reach agreement within a reasonable time either party may resort to the court.
(4) If the court finds hardship it may, if reasonable:
    (a) terminate the contract at a date and on terms to be fixed; or
    (b) adapt the contract with a view to restoring its equilibrium.

Chapter 7 Non-performance

Section 1 Non-performance in general

Article 7.1.1 Non-performance defined

Non-performance is failure by a party to perform any of its obligations under the contract, including defective performance or late performance.

Article 7.1.2 Interference by the other party

A party may not rely on the non-performance of the other party to the extent that such non-performance was caused by the first party's act or omission or by another event for which the first party bears the risk.

Article 7.1.3 Withholding performance

(1) Where the parties are to perform simultaneously, either party may withhold performance until the other party tenders its performance.
(2) Where the parties are to perform consecutively, the party that is to perform later may withhold its performance until the first party has performed.

Article 7.1.4 Cure by non-performing party

(1) The non-performing party may, at its own expense, cure any non-performance, provided that:
   (a) without undue delay, it gives notice indicating the proposed manner and timing of the cure;
   (b) cure is appropriate in the circumstances;
   (c) the aggrieved party has no legitimate interest in refusing cure; and
   (d) cure is effected promptly.
(2) The right to cure is not precluded by notice of termination.
(3) Upon effective notice of cure, rights of the aggrieved party that are inconsistent with the non-performing party's performance are suspended until the time for cure has expired.
(4) The aggrieved part y may withhold performance pending cure.
(5) Notwithstanding cure, the aggrieved party retains the right to claim damages for delay as well as for any harm caused or not prevented by the cure.

Article 7.1.5 Additional period for performance

(1) In a case of non-performance the aggrieved party may by notice to the other party allow an additional period of time for performance.
(2) During the additional period the aggrieved party may withhold performance of its own reciprocal obligations and may claim damages but may not resort to any other remedy. If it receives notice from the other party that the latter will not perform within that period, or if upon expiry of that period due performance has not been made, the aggrieved party may resort to any of the remedies that may be available under this Chapter.
(3) Where in a case of delay in performance which is not fundamental the aggrieved party has given notice allowing an additional period of time of reasonable length, it may terminate the contract at the end of that period. If the additional period allowed is not of reasonable length it shall be extended to a reasonable length. The aggrieved party may in its notice provide that if the other party fails to perform within the period allowed by the notice the contract shall automatically terminate.
(4) Paragraph (3) does not apply where the obligation which has not been performed is only a minor part of the contractual obligation of the non-performing party.

Article 7.1.6 Exemption clauses

A clause which limits or excludes one party's liability for non-performance or which permits one party to render performance substantially different from what the other party reasonably expected may not be invoked if it would be grossly unfair to do so, having regard to the purpose of the contract.

Article 7.1.7 Force majeure

(1) Non-performance by a party is excused if that party proves that the non-performance was due to an impediment beyond its control and that it could not reasonably be

expected to have taken the impediment into account at the time of the conclusion of the contract or to have avoided or overcome it or its consequences.

(2) When the impediment is only temporary, the excuse shall have effect for such period as is reasonable having regard to the effect of the impediment on the performance of the contract.

(3) The party who fails to perform must give notice to the other party of the impediment and its effect on its ability to perform. If the notice is not received by the other party within a reasonable time after the party who fails to perform knew or ought to have known of the impediment, it is liable for damages resulting from such non-receipt.

(4) Nothing in this Article prevents a party from exercising a right to terminate the contract or to withhold performance or request interest on money due.

Section 2 Right to performance

Article 7.2.1 Performance of monetary obligation

Where a party who is obliged to pay money does not do so, the other party may require payment.

Article 7.2.2 Performance of non-monetary obligation

Where a party who owes an obligation other than one to pay money does not perform, the other party may require performance, unless

(a) performance is impossible in law or in fact;
(b) performance or, where relevant, enforcement is unreasonably burdensome or expensive;
(c) the party entitled to performance may reasonably obtain performance from another source;
(d) performance is of an exclusively personal character; or
(e) the party entitled to performance does not require performance within a reasonable time after it has, or ought to have, become aware of the non-performance.

Article 7.2.3 Repair and replacement of defective performance

The right to performance includes in appropriate cases the right to require repair, replacement, or other cure of defective performance. The provisions of Articles 7.2.1 and 7.2.2 apply accordingly.

Article 7.2.4 Judicial penalty

(1) Where the court orders a party to perform, it may also direct that this party pay a penalty if it does not comply with the order.

(2) The penalty shall be paid to the aggrieved party unless mandatory provisions of the law of the forum provide otherwise. Payment of the penalty to the aggrieved party does not exclude any claim for damages.

Article 7.2.5 Change of remedy

(1) An aggrieved party who has required performance of a non-monetary obligation and who has not received performance within a period fixed or otherwise within a reasonable period of time may invoke any other remedy.
(2) Where the decision of a court for performance of a non-monetary obligation cannot be enforced, the aggrieved party may invoke any other remedy.

Section 3 Termination

Article 7.3.1 Right to terminate the contract

(1) A party may terminate the contract where the failure of the other party to perform an obligation under the contract amounts to a fundamental non-performance.
(2) In determining whether a failure to perform an obligation amounts to a fundamental non-performance regard shall be had, in particular, to whether:
  (a) the non-performance substantially deprives the aggrieved party of what it was entitled to expect under the contract unless the other party did not foresee and could not reasonably have foreseen such result;
  (b) trict compliance with the obligation which has not been performed is of essence under the contract;
  (c) the non-performance is intentional or reckless;
  (d) the non-performance gives the aggrieved party reason to believe that it cannot rely on the other party's future performance;
  (e) the non-performing party will suffer disproportionate loss as a result of the preparation or performance if the contract is terminated.
(3) In the case of delay the aggrieved party may also terminate the contract if the other party fails to perform before the time allowed it under Article 7.1.5 has expired.

Article 7.3.2 Notice of termination

(1) The right of a party to terminate the contract is exercised by notice to the other party.
(2) If performance has been offered late or otherwise does not conform to the contract the aggrieved party will lose its right to terminate the contract unless it gives notice to the other party within a reasonable time after it has or ought to have become aware of the offer or of the non-conforming performance.

Article 7.3.3 Anticipatory non-performance

Where prior to the date for performance by one of the parties it is clear that there will be a fundamental non-performance by that party, the other party may terminate the contract.

Article 7.3.4 Adequate assurance of due performance

A party who reasonably believes that there will be a fundamental non-performance by the other party may demand adequate assurance of due performance and may meanwhile withhold its own performance. Where this assurance is not provided within a reasonable time the party demanding it may terminate the contract.

Article 7.3.5 Effects of termination in general

(1) Termination of the contract releases both parties from their obligation to effect and to receive future performance.
(2) Termination does not preclude a claim for damages for non-performance.
(3) Termination does not affect any provision in the contract for the settlement of disputes or any other term of the contract which is to operate even after termination.

Article 7.3.6 Restitution with respect to contracts to be performed at one time

(1) On termination of a contract to be performed at one time either party may claim restitution of whatever it has supplied under the contract, provided that such party concurrently makes restitution of whatever it has received under the contract.
(2) If restitution in kind is not possible or appropriate, an allowance has to be made in money whenever reasonable.
(3) The recipient of the performance does not have to make an allowance in money if the impossibility to make restitution in kind is attributable to the other party.
(4) Compensation may be claimed for expenses reasonably required to preserve or maintain the performance received.

Article 7.3.7 Restitution with respect to long-term contracts

(1) On termination of a long-term contract restitution can only be claimed for the period after termination has taken effect, provided the contract is divisible.
(2) As far as restitution has to be made, the provisions of Article 7.3.6 apply.

Section 4 Damages

Article 7.4.1 Right to damages

Any non-performance gives the aggrieved party a right to damages either exclusively or in conjunction with any other remedies except where the non-performance is excused under these Principles.

Article 7.4.2 Full compensation

(1) The aggrieved party is entitled to full compensation for harm sustained as a result of the non-performance. Such harm includes both any loss which it suffered and any gain of which it was deprived, taking into account any gain to the aggrieved party resulting from its avoidance of cost or harm.
(2) Such harm may be non-pecuniary and includes, for instance, physical suffering or emotional distress.

Article 7.4.3 Certainty of harm

(1) Compensation is due only for harm, including future harm, that is established with a reasonable degree of certainty.

(2) Compensation may be due for the loss of a chance in proportion to the probability of its occurrence.
(3) Where the amount of damages cannot be established with a sufficient degree of certainty, the assessment is at the discretion of the court.

Article 7.4.4 Foreseeability of harm

The non-performing party is liable only for harm which it foresaw or could reasonably have foreseen at the time of the conclusion of the contract as being likely to result from its non-performance.

Article 7.4.5 Proof of harm in case of replacement transaction

Where the aggrieved party has terminated the contract and has made a replacement transaction within a reasonable time and in a reasonable manner it may recover the difference between the contract price and the price of the replacement transaction as well as damages for any further harm.

Article 7.4.6 Proof of harm by current price

(1) Where the aggrieved party has terminated the contract and has not made a replacement transaction but there is a current price for the performance contracted for, it may recover the difference between the contract price and the price current at the time the contract is terminated as well as damages for any further harm.
(2) Current price is the price generally charged for goods delivered or services rendered in comparable circumstances at the place where the contract should have been performed or, if there is no current price at that place, the current price at such other place that appears reasonable to take as a reference.

Article 7.4.7 Harm due in part to aggrieved party

Where the harm is due in part to an act or omission of the aggrieved party or to another event for which that party bears the risk, the amount of damages shall be reduced to the extent that these factors have contributed to the harm, having regard to the conduct of each of the parties.

Article 7.4.8 Mitigation of harm

(1) The non-performing party is not liable for harm suffered by the aggrieved party to the extent that the harm could have been reduced by the latter party's taking reasonable steps.
(2) The aggrieved party is entitled to recover any expenses reasonably incurred in attempting to reduce the harm.

Article 7.4.9 Interest for failure to pay money

(1) If a party does not pay a sum of money when it falls due the aggrieved party is entitled to interest upon that sum from the time when payment is due to the time of payment whether or not the non-payment is excused.

(2) The rate of interest shall be the average bank short-term lending rate to prime borrowers prevailing for the currency of payment at the place for payment, or where no such rate exists at that place, then the same rate in the State of the currency of payment. In the absence of such a rate at either place the rate of interest shall be the appropriate rate fixed by the law of the State of the currency of payment.

(3) The aggrieved party is entitled to additional damages if the non-payment caused it a greater harm.

Article 7.4.10 Interest on damages

Unless otherwise agreed, interest on damages for non-performance of non-monetary obligations accrues as from the time of non-performance.

Article 7.4.11 Manner of monetary redress

(1) Damages are to be paid in a lump sum. However, they may be payable in instalments where the nature of the harm makes this appropriate.

(2) Damages to be paid in instalments may be indexed.

Article 7.4.12 Currency in which to assess damages

Damages are to be assessed either in the currency in which the monetary obligation was expressed or in the currency in which the harm was suffered, whichever is more appropriate.

Article 7.4.13 Agreed payment for non-performance

(1) Where the contract provides that a party who does not perform is to pay a specified sum to the aggrieved party for such non-performance, the aggrieved party is entitled to that sum irrespective of its actual harm.

(2) However, notwithstanding any agreement to the contrary the specified sum may be reduced to a reasonable amount where it is grossly excessive in relation to the harm resulting from the non-performance and to the other circumstances.

Chapter 8 Set-off

Article 8.1 Conditions of set-off

(1) Where two parties owe each other money or other performances of the same kind, either of them ('the first party') may set off its obligation against that of its obligee ('the other party') if at the time of set-off:

   (a) the first party is entitled to perform its obligation;

   (b) the other party's obligation is ascertained as to its existence and amount and performance is due.

(2) If the obligations of both parties arise from the same contract, the first party may also set off its obligation against an obligation of the other party which is not ascertained as to its existence or to its amount.

Article 8.2 Foreign currency set-off

Where the obligations are to pay money in different currencies, the right of set-off may be exercised, provided that both currencies are freely convertible and the parties have not agreed that the first party shall pay only in a specified currency.

Article 8.3 Set-off by notice

The right of set-off is exercised by notice to the other party.

Article 8.4 Content of notice

(1) The notice must specify the obligations to which it relates.
(2) If the notice does not specify the obligation against which set-off is exercised, the other party may, within a reasonable time, declare to the first party the obligation to which set-off relates. If no such declaration is made, the set-off will relate to all the obligations proportionally.

Article 8.5 Effect of set-off

(1) Set-off discharges the obligations.
(2) If obligations differ in amount, set-off discharges the obligations up to the amount of the lesser obligation.
(3) Set-off takes effect as from the time of notice.

Chapter 9 Assignment of rights, transfer of obligations, assignment of contracts

Section 1 Assignment of rights

Article 9.1.1 Definitions

'Assignment of a right' means the transfer by agreement from one person (the 'assignor') to another person (the 'assignee'), including transfer by way of security, of the assignor's right to payment of a monetary sum or other performance from a third person ('the obligor').

Article 9.1.2 Exclusions

This Section does not apply to transfers made under the special rules governing the transfers:

(a) of instruments such as negotiable instruments, documents of title or financial instruments, or
(b) of rights in the course of transferring a business.

Article 9.1.3 Assignability of non-monetary rights

A right to non-monetary performance may be assigned only if the assignment does not render the obligation significantly more burdensome.

Article 9.1.4 Partial assignment

(1) A right to the payment of a monetary sum may be assigned partially.
(2) A right to other performance may be assigned partially only if it is divisible, and the assignment does not render the obligation significantly more burdensome.

Article 9.1.5 Future rights

A future right is deemed to be transferred at the time of the agreement, provided the right, when it comes into existence, can be identified as the right to which the assignment relates.

Article 9.1.6 Rights assigned without individual specification

A number of rights may be assigned without individual specification, provided such rights can be identified as rights to which the assignment relates at the time of the assignment or when they come into existence.

Article 9.1.7 Agreement between assignor and assignee sufficient

(1) A right is as signed by mere agreement between the assignor and the assignee, without notice to the obligor.
(2) The consent of the obligor is not required unless the obligation in the circumstances is of an essentially personal character.

Article 9.1.8 Obligor's additional costs

The obligor has a right to be compensated by the assignor or the assignee for any additional costs caused by the assignment.

Article 9.1.9 Non-assignment clauses

(1) The assignment of a right to the payment of a monetary sum is effective notwithstanding an agreement between the assignor and the obligor limiting or prohibiting such an assignment. However, the assignor may be liable to the obligor for breach of contract.
(2) The assignment of a right to other performance is ineffective if it is contrary to an agreement between the assignor and the obligor limiting or prohibiting the assignment. Nevertheless, the assignment is effective if the assignee, at the time of the assignment, neither knew nor ought to have known of the agreement. The assignor may then be liable to the obligor for breach of contract.

Article 9.1.10 Notice to the obligor

(1) Until the obligor receives a notice of the assignment from either the assignor or the assignee, it is discharged by paying the assignor.
(2) After the obligor receives such a notice, it is discharged only by paying the assignee.

Article 9.1.11 Successive assignments

If the same right has been assigned by the same assignor to two or more successive assignees, the obligor is discharged by paying according to the order in which the notices were received.

Article 9.1.12 Adequate proof of assignment

(1) If notice of the assignment is given by the assignee, the obligor may request the assignee to provide within a reasonable time adequate proof that the assignment has been made.
(2) Until adequate proof is provided, the obligor may withhold payment.
(3) Unless adequate proof is provided, notice is not effective.
(4) Adequate proof includes, but is not limited to, any writing emanating from the assignor and indicating that the assignment has taken place.

Article 9.1.13 Defences and rights of set-off

(1) The obligor may assert against the assignee all defences that the obligor could assert against the assignor.
(2) The obligor may exercise against the assignee any right of set-off available to the obligor against the assignor up to the time notice of assignment was received.

Article 9.1.14 Rights related to the right assigned

The assignment of a right transfers to the assignee:

(a) all the assignor's rights to payment or other performance under the contract in respect of the right assigned; and
(b) all rights securing performance of the right assigned.

Article 9.1.15 Undertakings of the assignor

The assignor undertakes towards the assignee, except as otherwise disclosed to the assignee, that:

(a) the assigned right exists at the time of the assignment, unless the right is a future right;
(b) the assignor is entitled to assign the right;
(c) the right has not been previously assigned to another assignee, and it is free from any right or claim from a third party;
(d) the obligor does not have any defences;
(e) neither the obligor nor the assignor has given notice of set-off concerning the assigned right and will not give any such notice;
(f) the assignor will reimburse the assignee for any payment received from the obligor before notice of the assignment was given.

Section 2 Transfer of obligations

Article 9.2.1 Modes of transfer

An obligation to pay money or render other performance may be transferred from one person (the 'original obligor') to another person (the 'new obligor') either:

(a) by an agreement between the original obligor and the new obligor subject to Article 9.2.3, or
(b) by an agreement between the obligee and the new obligor, by which the new obligor assumes the obligation.

Article 9.2.2 Exclusion

This Section does not apply to transfers of obligations made under the special rules governing transfers of obligations in the course of transferring a business.

Article 9.2.3 Requirement of obligee's consent to transfer

The transfer of an obligation by an agreement between the original obligor and the new obligor requires the consent of the obligee.

Article 9.2.4 Advance consent of obligee

(1) The obligee may give its consent in advance.
(2) If the obligee has given its consent in advance, the transfer of the obligation becomes effective when a notice of the transfer is given to the obligee or when the obligee acknowledges it.

Article 9.2.5 Discharge of original obligor

(1) The obligee may discharge the original obligor.
(2) The obligee may also retain the original obligor as an obligor in case the new obligor does not perform properly.
(3) Otherwise the original obligor and the new obligor are jointly and severally liable.

Article 9.2.6 Third party performance

(1) Without the obligee's consent, the obligor may contract with another person that this person will perform the obligation in place of the obligor, unless the obligation in the circumstances has an essentially personal character.
(2) The obligee retains its claim against the obligor.

Article 9.2.7 Defences and rights of set-off

(1) The new obligor may assert against the obligee all defences which the original obligor could assert against the obligee.
(2) The new obligor may not exercise against the obligee any right of set-off available to the original obligor against the obligee.

Article 9.2.8 Rights related to the obligation transferred

(1) The obligee may assert against the new obligor all its rights to payment or other performance under the contract in respect of the obligation transferred.

(2) If the original obligor is discharged under Article 9.2.5(1), a security granted by any person other than the new obligor for the performance of the obligation is discharged, unless that other person agrees that it should continue to be available to the obligee.
(3) Discharge of the original obligor also extends to any security of the original obligor given to the obligee for the performance of the obligation, unless the security is over an asset which is transferred as part of a transaction between the original obligor and the new obligor.

Section 3 Assignment of contracts

Article 9.3.1 Definitions

'Assignment of a contract' means the transfer by agreement from one person (the 'assignor') to another person (the 'assignee') of the assignor's rights and obligations arising out of a contract with another person (the 'other party').

Article 9.3.2 Exclusion

This Section does not apply to the assignment of contracts made under the special rules governing transfers of contracts in the course of transferring a business.

Article 9.3.3 Requirement of consent of the other party

The assignment of a contract requires the consent of the other party.

Article 9.3.4 Advance consent of the other party

(1) The other party may give its consent in advance.
(2) If the other party has given its consent in advance, the assignment of the contract becomes effective when a notice of the assignment is given to the other party or when the other party acknowledges it.

Article 9.3.5 Discharge of the assignor

(1) The other party may discharge the assignor.
(2) The other party may also retain the assignor as an obligor in case the assignee does not perform properly.
(3) Otherwise the assignor and the assignee are jointly and severally liable.

Article 9.3.6 Defences and rights of set-off

(1) To the extent that the assignment of a contract involves an assignment of rights, Article 9.1.13 applies accordingly.
(2) To the extent that the assignment of a contract involves a transfer of obligations, Article 9.2.7 applies accordingly.

Article 9.3.7 Rights transferred with the contract

(1) To the extent that the assignment of a contract involves an assignment of rights, Article 9.1.14 applies accordingly.
(2) To the extent that the assignment of a contract involves a transfer of obligations, Article 9.2.8 applies accordingly.

Chapter 10 Limitation periods

Article 10.1 Scope of the chapter

(1) The exercise of rights governed by the Principles is barred by the expiration of a period of time, referred to as 'limitation period', according to the rules of this Chapter.
(2) This Chapter does not govern the time within which one party is required under the Principles, as a condition for the acquisition or exercise of its right, to give notice to the other party or to perform any act other than the institution of legal proceedings.

Article 10.2 Limitation periods

(1) The general limitation period is three years beginning on the day after the day the obligee knows or ought to know the facts as a result of which the obligee's right can be exercised.
(2) In any event, the maximum limitation period is ten years beginning on the day after the day the right can be exercised.

Article 10.3 Modification of limitation periods by the parties

(1) The parties may modify the limitation periods.
(2) However they may not
    (a) shorten the general limitation period to less than one year;
    (b) shorten the maximum limitation period to less than four years;
    (c) extend the maximum limitation period to more than fifteen years.

Article 10.4 New limitation period by acknowledgement

(1) Where the obligor before the expiration of the general limitation period acknowledges the right of the obligee, a new general limitation period begins on the day after the day of the acknowledgement.
(2) The maximum limitation period does not begin to run again, but may be exceeded by the beginning of a new general limitation period under Article 10.2(1).

Article 10.5 Suspension by judicial proceedings

(1) The running of the limitation period is suspended:
    (a) when the obligee performs any act, by commencing judicial proceedings or in judicial proceedings already instituted, that is recognised by the law of the court as asserting the obligee's right against the obligor;

(b) in the case of the obligor's insolvency when the obligee has asserted its rights in the insolvency proceedings; or
(c) in the case of proceedings for dissolution of the entity which is the obligor when the obligee has asserted its rights in the dissolution proceedings.

(2) Suspension lasts until a final decision has been issued or until the proceedings have been otherwise terminated.

Article 10.6 Suspension by arbitral proceedings

(1) The running of the limitation period is suspended when the obligee performs any act, by commencing arbitral proceedings or in arbitral proceedings already instituted, that is recognised by the law of the arbitral tribunal as asserting the obligee's right against the obligor. In the absence of regulations for arbitral proceedings or provisions determining the exact date of the commencement of arbitral proceedings, the proceedings are deemed to commence on the date on which a request that the right in dispute should be adjudicated reaches the obligor.
(2) Suspension lasts until a binding decision has been issued or until the proceedings have been otherwise terminated.

Article 10.7 Alternative dispute resolution

The provisions of Articles 10.5 and 10.6 apply with appropriate modifications to other proceedings whereby the parties request a third person to assist them in their attempt to reach an amicable settlement of their dispute.

Article 10.8 Suspension in case of force majeure, death or incapacity

(1) Where the obligee has been prevented by an impediment that is beyond its control and that it could neither avoid nor overcome, from causing a limitation period to cease to run under the preceding Articles, the general limitation period is suspended so as not to expire before one year after the relevant impediment has ceased to exist.
(2) Where the impediment consists of the incapacity or death of the obligee or obligor, suspension ceases when a representative for the incapacitated or deceased party or its estate has been appointed or a successor has inherited the respective party's position. The additional one-year period under paragraph (1) applies accordingly.

Article 10.9 Effects of expiration of limitation period

(1) The expiration of the limitation period does not extinguish the right.
(2) For the expiration of the limitation period to have effect, the obligor must assert it as a defence.
(3) A right may still be relied on as a defence even though the expiration of the limitation period for that right has been asserted.

Article 10.10 Right of set-off

The obligee may exercise the right of set-off until the obligor has asserted the expiration of the limitation period.

Article 10.11 Restitution

Where there has been performance in order to discharge an obligation, there is no right of restitution merely because the limitation period has expired.

Chapter 11 Plurality of obligors and of obligees

Section 1 Plurality of obligors

Article 11.1.1 Definitions

When several obligors are bound by the same obligation towards an obligee:

(a) the obligations are joint and several when each obligor is bound for the whole obligation;
(b) the obligations are separate when each obligor is bound only for its share.

Article 11.1.2 Presumption of joint and several obligations

When several obligors are bound by the same obligation towards an obligee, they are presumed to be jointly and severally bound, unless the circumstances indicate otherwise.

Article 11.1.3 Obligee's rights against joint and several obligors

When obligors are jointly and severally bound, the obligee may require performance from any one of them, until full performance has been received.

Article 11.1.4 Availability of defences and rights of set-off

A joint and several obligor against whom a claim is made by the obligee may assert all the defences and rights of set-off that are personal to it or that are common to all the co-obligors, but may not assert defences or rights of set-off that are personal to one or several of the other co-obligors.

Article 11.1.5 Effect of performance or set-off

Performance or set-off by a joint and several obligor or set-off by the obligee against one joint and several obligor discharges the other obligors in relation to the obligee to the extent of the performance or set-off.

Article 11.1.6 Effect of release or settlement

(1) Release of one joint and several obligor, or settlement with one joint and several obligor, discharges all the other obligors for the share of the released or settling obligor, unless the circumstances indicate otherwise.
(2) When the other obligors are discharged for the share of the released obligor, they no longer have a contributory claim against the released obligor under Article 11.1.10.

Article 11.1.7 Effect of expiration or suspension of limitation period

(1) Expiration of the limitation period of the obligee's rights against one joint and several obligor does not affect:
   (a) the obligations to the obligee of the other joint and several obligors; or
   (b) the rights of recourse between the joint and several obligors under Article 11.1.10.
(2) If the obligee initiates proceedings under Articles 10.5, 10.6 or 10.7 against one joint and several obligor, the running of the limitation period is also suspended against the other joint and several obligors.

Article 11.1.8 Effect of judgment

(1) A decision by a court as to the liability to the obligee of one joint and several obligor does not affect:
   (a) the obligations to the obligee of the other joint and several obligors; or
   (b) the rights of recourse between the joint and several obligors under Article 11.1.10.
(2) However, the other joint and several obligors may rely on such a decision, except if it was based on grounds personal to the obligor concerned. In such a case, the rights of recourse between the joint and several obligors under Article 11.1.10 are affected accordingly.

Article 11.1.9 Apportionment among joint and several obligors

As among themselves, joint and several obligors are bound in equal shares, unless the circumstances indicate otherwise.

Article 11.1.10 Extent of contributory claim

A joint and several obligor who has performed more than its share may claim the excess from any of the other obligors to the extent of each obligor's unperformed share.

Article 11.1.11 Rights of the obligee

(1) A joint and several obligor to whom Article 11.1.10 applies may also exercise the rights of the obligee, including all rights securing their performance, to recover the excess from all or any of the other obligors to the extent of each obligor's unperformed share.
(2) An obligee who has not received full performance retains its rights against the co-obligors to the extent of the unperformed part, with precedence over co-obligors exercising contributory claims.

Article 11.1.12 Defences in contributory claims

A joint and several obligor against whom a claim is made by the co-obligor who has performed the obligation:

(a) may raise any common defences and rights of set-off that were available to be asserted by the co-obligor against the obligee;

(b) may assert defences which are personal to itself;
(c) may not assert defences and rights of set-off which are personal to one or several of the other co-obligors.

Article 11.1.13 Inability to recover

If a joint and several obligor who has performed more than that obligor's share is unable, despite all reasonable efforts, to recover contribution from another joint and several obligor, the share of the others, including the one who has performed, is increased proportionally.

Section 2 Plurality of obligees

Article 11.2.1 Definitions

When several obligees can claim performance of the same obligation from an obligor:

(a) the claims are separate when each obligee can only claim its share;
(b) the claims are joint and several when each obligee can claim the whole performance;
(c) the claims are joint when all obligees have to claim performance together.

Article 11.2.2 Effects of joint and several claims

Full performance of an obligation in favour of one of the joint and several obligees discharges the obligor towards the other obligees.

Article 11.2.3 Availability of defences against joint and several obligees

(1) The obligor may assert against any of the joint and several obligees all the defences and rights of set-off that are personal to its relationship to that obligee or that it can assert against all the co-obligees, but may not assert defences and rights of set-off that are personal to its relationship to one or several of the other co-obligees.
(2) The provisions of Articles 11.1.5, 11.1.6, 11.1.7 and 11.1.8 apply, with appropriate adaptations, to joint and several claims.

Article 11.2.4 Allocation between joint and several obligees

(1) As among themselves, joint and several obligees are entitled to equal shares, unless the circumstances indicate otherwise.
(2) An obligee who has received more than its share must transfer the excess to the other obligees to the extent of their respective shares.

The York-Antwerp Rules 2004

Rule of interpretation

In the adjustment of general average the following Rules shall apply to the exclusion of any Law and Practice inconsistent therewith.

Except as provided by the Rule Paramount and the numbered Rules, general average shall be adjusted according to the lettered Rules.

Rule Paramount

In no case shall there be any allowance for sacrifice or expenditure unless reasonably made or incurred.

Rule A

There is a general average act when, and only when, any extraordinary sacrifice or expenditure is intentionally and reasonably made or incurred for the common safety for the purpose of preserving from peril the property involved in a common maritime adventure.

General average sacrifices and expenditures shall be borne by the different contributing interests on the basis hereinafter provided.

Rule B

There is a common maritime adventure when one or more vessels are towing or pushing another vessel or vessels, provided that they are all involved in commercial activities and not in a salvage operation.

When measures are taken to preserve the vessels and their cargoes, if any, from a common peril, these Rules shall apply.

A vessel is not in common peril with another vessel or vessels if by simply disconnecting from the other vessel or vessels she is in safety; but if the disconnection is itself a general average act the common maritime adventure continues.

Rule C

Only such losses, damages or expenses which are the direct consequence of the general average act shall be allowed as general average.

In no case shall there be any allowance in general average for losses, damages or expenses incurred in respect of damage to the environment or in consequence of the escape or release of pollutant substances from the property involved in the common maritime adventure.

Demurrage, loss of market, and any loss or damage sustained or expense incurred by reason of delay, whether on the voyage or subsequently, and any indirect loss whatsoever, shall not be allowed as general average.

Rule D

Rights to contribution in general average shall not be affected, though the event which gave rise to the sacrifice or expenditure may have been due to the fault of one of the parties to the adventure, but this shall not prejudice any remedies or defences which may be open against or to that party in respect of such fault.

Rule E

The onus of proof is upon the party claiming in general average to show that the loss or expense claimed is properly allowable as general average.

All parties claiming in general average shall give notice in writing to the average adjuster of the loss or expense in respect of which they claim contribution within 12 months of the date of the termination of the common maritime adventure.

Failing such notification, or if within 12 months of a request for the same any of the parties shall fail to supply evidence in support of a notified claim, or particulars of value in respect of a contributory interest, the average adjuster shall be at liberty to estimate the extent of the allowance or the contributory value on the basis of the information available to him, which estimate may be challenged only on the ground that it is manifestly incorrect.

Rule F

Any additional expense incurred in place of another expense, which would have been allowable as general average shall be deemed to be general average and so allowed without regard to the saving, if any, to other interests, but only up to the amount of the general average expense avoided.

Rule G

General average shall be adjusted as regards both loss and contribution upon the basis of values at the time and place when and where the adventure ends.

This rule shall not affect the determination of the place at which the average statement is to be made up.

When a ship is at any port or place in circumstances which would give rise to an allowance in general average under the provisions of Rules X and XI, and the cargo or part thereof is forwarded to destination by other means, rights and liabilities in general average shall, subject to cargo interests being notified if practicable, remain as nearly as possible the same as they would have been in the absence of such forwarding, as if the adventure had continued in the original ship for so long as justifiable under the contract of affreightment and the applicable law.

The proportion attaching to cargo of the allowances made in general average by reason of applying the third paragraph of this Rule shall not exceed the cost which would have been borne by the owners of cargo if the cargo had been forwarded at their expense.

Rule I Jettison of cargo

No jettison of cargo shall be allowed as general average, unless such cargo is carried in accordance with the recognised custom of the trade.

Rule II Loss or damage by sacrifices for the common safety

Loss of or damage to the property involved in the common maritime adventure by or in consequence of a sacrifice made for the common safety, and by water which goes down a ship's hatches opened or other opening made for the purpose of making a jettison for the common safety, shall be allowed as general average.

Rule III Extinguishing fire on shipboard

Damage done to a ship and cargo, or either of them, by water or otherwise, including damage by beaching or scuttling a burning ship, in extinguishing a fire on board the ship, shall be allowed as general average; except that no allowance shall be made for damage by smoke however caused or by heat of the fire.

Rule IV Cutting away wreck

Loss or damage sustained by cutting away wreck or parts of the ship which have been previously carried away or are effectively lost by accident shall not be allowed as general average.

Rule V Voluntary stranding

When a ship is intentionally run on shore for the common safety, whether or not she might have been driven on shore, the consequent loss or damage to the property involved in the common maritime adventure shall be allowed in general average.

Rule VI Salvage remuneration

(a) Salvage payments, including interest thereon and legal fees associated with such payments, shall lie where they fall and shall not be allowed in general average, save only that if one party to the salvage shall have paid all or any of the proportion of salvage (including interest and legal fees) due from another party (calculated on the basis of salved values and not general average contributory values), the unpaid contribution to salvage due from that other party shall be credited in the adjustment to the party that has paid it, and debited to the party on whose behalf the payment was made.

(b) Salvage payments referred to in paragraph (a) above shall include any salvage remuneration in which the skill and efforts of the salvors in preventing or minimising damage to the environment such as is referred to in Article 13 paragraph 1(b) of the International Convention on Salvage 1989 have been taken into account.

(c) Special compensation payable to a salvor by the shipowner under Article 14 of the said Convention to the extent specified in paragraph 4 of that Article or under any other provision similar in substance (such as SCOPIC) shall not be allowed in general average and shall not be considered a salvage payment as referred to in paragraph (a) of this Rule.

Rule VII Damage to machinery and boilers

Damage caused to any machinery and boilers of a ship which is ashore and in a position of peril, in endeavouring to refloat, shall be allowed in general average when shown to have arisen from an actual intention to float the ship for the common safety at the risk of such damage; but where a ship is afloat no loss or damage caused by working the propelling machinery and boilers shall in any circumstances be allowed as general average.

Rule VIII Expenses lightening a ship when ashore and consequent damage

When a ship is ashore and cargo and ship's fuel and stores or any of them are discharged as a general average act, the extra cost of lightening, lighter hire and reshipping (if incurred), and any loss or damage to the property involved in the common maritime adventure in consequence thereof, shall be allowed as general average.

Rule IX Cargo, ship's materials and stores used for fuel

Cargo, ship's materials and stores, or any of them, necessarily used for fuel for the common safety at a time of peril shall be allowed as general average, but when such an allowance is made for the cost of ship's materials and stores the general average shall be credited with the estimated cost of the fuel which would otherwise have been consumed in prosecuting the intended voyage.

Rule X Expenses at port of refuge, etc.

(a)

(i) When a ship shall have entered a port or place of refuge or shall have returned to her port or place of loading in consequence of accident, sacrifice or other extraordinary circumstances which render that necessary for the common safety, the expenses of entering such port or place shall be allowed as general average; and when she shall have sailed thence with her original cargo, or a part of it, the corresponding expenses of leaving such port or place consequent upon such entry or return shall likewise be allowed as general average.

(ii) When a ship is at any port or place of refuge and is necessarily removed to another port or place of refuge because repairs cannot be carried out in the first port or place, the provisions of this Rule shall be applied to the second port or place of refuge as if it were a port or place of refuge and the cost of such removal including temporary repairs and towage shall be allowed as general average. The provisions of Rule XI shall be applied to the prolongation of the voyage occasioned by such removal.

(b)

(i) The cost of handling on board or discharging cargo, fuel or stores whether at a port or place of loading, call or refuge, shall be allowed as general average, when the handling or discharge was necessary for the common safety or to enable damage to the ship caused by sacrifice or accident to be repaired, if the repairs were necessary for the safe prosecution of the voyage, except in cases where the damage to the ship is discovered at a port or place of loading or call without any accident or other extraordinary circumstances connected with such damage having taken place during the voyage.

(ii) The cost of handling on board or discharging cargo, fuel or stores shall not be allowable as general average when incurred solely for the purpose of restowage due to shifting during the voyage, unless such restowage is necessary for the common safety.

(c) Whenever the cost of handling or discharging cargo, fuel or stores is allowable as general average, the costs of storage, including insurance if reasonably incurred, reloading and stowing of such cargo, fuel or stores shall likewise be allowed as general average. The provisions of Rule XI shall be applied to the extra period of detention occasioned by such reloading or restowing.

But when the ship is condemned or does not proceed on her original voyage, storage expenses shall be allowed as general average only up to the date of the ship's condemnation or of the abandonment of the voyage or up to the date of completion of discharge of cargo if the condemnation or abandonment takes place before that date.

Rule XI Wages and maintenance of crew and other expenses putting in to and at a port of refuge, etc.

(a) Wages and maintenance of master, officers and crew reasonably incurred and fuel and stores consumed during the prolongation of the voyage occasioned by a ship entering a port or place of refuge or returning to her port or place of loading shall be allowed as general average when the expenses of entering such port or place are allowable as general average in accordance with Rule X(a).

(b) For the purpose of this and the other Rules wages shall include all payments made to or for the benefit of the master, officers and crew, whether such payments be imposed by law upon the shipowners or be made under the terms of articles of employment.

(c)

- (i) When a ship shall have entered or been detained in any port or place in consequence of accident, sacrifice or other extraordinary circumstances which render that necessary for the common safety, or to enable damage to the ship caused by sacrifice or accident to be repaired, if the repairs were necessary for the safe prosecution of the voyage, fuel and stores consumed during the extra period of detention in such port or place until the ship shall or should have been made ready to proceed upon her voyage, shall be allowed as general average, except such fuel and stores as are consumed in effecting repairs not allowable in general average.
- (ii) Port charges incurred during the extra period of detention shall likewise be allowed as general average except such charges as are incurred solely by reason of repairs not allowable in general average.
- (iii) Provided that when damage to the ship is discovered at a port or place of loading or call without any accident or other extraordinary circumstance connected with such damage having taken place during the voyage, then fuel and stores consumed and port charges incurred during the extra detention for repairs to damages so discovered shall not be allowable as general average, even if the repairs are necessary for the safe prosecution of the voyage.
- (iv) When the ship is condemned or does not proceed on her original voyage, fuel and stores consumed and port charges shall be allowed as general average only up to the date of the ship's condemnation or of the abandonment of the voyage or up to the date of completion of discharge of cargo if the condemnation or abandonment takes place before that date.

(d) The cost of measures undertaken to prevent or minimise damage to the environment shall be allowed in general average when incurred in any or all of the following circumstances:

(i) as part of an operation performed for the common safety which, had it been undertaken by a party outside the common maritime adventure, would have entitled such party to a salvage reward;
(ii) as a condition of entry into or departure from any port or place in the circumstances prescribed in Rule X(a);
(iii) as a condition of remaining at any port or place in the circumstances prescribed in Rule XI(c), provided that when there is an actual escape or release of pollutant substances the cost of any additional measures required on that account to prevent or minimise pollution or environmental damage shall not be allowed as general average;
(iv) necessarily in connection with the discharging, storing or reloading of cargo whenever the cost of those operations is allowable as general average.

Rule XII Damage to cargo in discharging, etc.

Damage to or loss of cargo, fuel or stores sustained in consequence of their handling, discharging, storing, reloading and stowing shall be allowed as general average, when and only when the cost of those measures respectively is allowed as general average.

Rule XIII Deductions from cost of repairs

(a) Repairs to be allowed in general average shall not be subject to deductions in respect of "new for old" where old material or parts are replaced by new unless the ship is over fifteen years old in which case there shall be a deduction of one third. The deductions shall be regulated by the age of the ship from the 31st December of the year of completion of construction to the date of the general average act, except for insulation, life and similar boats, communications and navigational apparatus and equipment, machinery and boilers for which the deductions shall be regulated by the age of the particular parts to which they apply.
(b) The deductions shall be made only from the cost of the new material or parts when finished and ready to be installed in the ship. No deduction shall be made in respect of provisions, stores, anchors and chain cables. Drydock and slipway dues and costs of shifting the ship shall be allowed in full.
(c) The costs of cleaning, painting or coating of bottom shall not be allowed in general average unless the bottom has been painted or coated within the twelve months preceding the date of the general average act in which case one half of such costs shall be allowed.

Rule XIV Temporary repairs

(a) Where temporary repairs are effected to a ship at a port of loading, call or refuge, for the common safety, or of damage caused by general average sacrifice, the cost of such repairs shall be allowed as general average.
(b) Where temporary repairs of accidental damage are effected in order to enable the adventure to be completed, the cost of such repairs shall be allowed as general average without regard to the saving, if any, to other interests, but only up to the saving in expense

which would have been incurred and allowed in general average if such repairs had not been effected there. Provided that for the purposes of this paragraph only, the cost of temporary repairs falling for consideration shall be limited to the extent that the cost of temporary repairs effected at the port of loading, call or refuge, together with either the cost of permanent repairs eventually effected or, if unrepaired at the time of the adjustment, the reasonable depreciation in the value of the vessel at the completion of the voyage. exceeds the cost of permanent repairs had they been effected at the port of loading, call or refuge.

(c) No deductions "new for old" shall be made from the cost of temporary repairs allowable as general average.

Rule XV Loss of freight

Loss of freight arising from damage to or loss of cargo shall be allowed as general average, either when caused by a general average act, or when the damage to or loss of cargo is so allowed.

Deduction shall be made from the amount of gross freight lost, of the charges which the owner thereof would have incurred to earn such freight, but has, in consequence of the sacrifice, not incurred.

Rule XVI Amount to be allowed for cargo lost or damaged by sacrifice

(a) The amount to be allowed as general average for damage to or loss of cargo sacrificed shall be the loss which has been sustained thereby based on the value at the time of discharge, ascertained from the commercial invoice rendered to the receiver or if there is no such invoice from the shipped value. The value at the time of discharge shall include the cost of insurance and freight except insofar as such freight is at the risk of interests other than the cargo.

(b) When cargo so damaged is sold and the amount of the damage has not been otherwise agreed, the loss to be allowed in general average shall be the difference between the net proceeds of sale and the net sound value as computed in the first paragraph of this Rule.

Rule XVII Contributory values

(a)

(i) The contribution to a general average shall be made upon the actual net values of the property at the termination of the adventure except that the value of cargo shall be the value at the time of discharge, ascertained from the commercial invoice rendered to the receiver or if there is no such invoice from the shipped value.

(ii) The value of the cargo shall include the cost of insurance and freight unless and insofar as such freight is at the risk of interests other than the cargo, deducting therefrom any loss or damage suffered by the cargo prior to or at the time of discharge.

(iii) The value of the ship shall be assessed without taking into account the beneficial or detrimental effect of any demise or time charterparty to which the ship may be committed.

(b) To these values shall be added the amount allowed as general average for property sacrificed, if not already included, deduction being made from the freight and passage money at risk of such charges and crew's wages as would not have been incurred in earning the freight had the ship and cargo been totally lost at the date of the general average act and have not been allowed as general average; deduction being also made from the value of the property of all extra charges incurred in respect thereof subsequently to the general average act, except such charges as are allowed in general average or fall upon the ship by virtue of an award for special compensation under Art. 14 of the International Convention on Salvage, 1989 or under any other provision similar in substance.

(c) In the circumstances envisaged in the third paragraph of Rule G, the cargo and other property shall contribute on the basis of its value upon delivery at original destination unless sold or otherwise disposed of short of that destination, and the ship shall contribute upon its actual net value at the time of completion of discharge of cargo.

(d) Where cargo is sold short of destination, however, it shall contribute upon the actual net proceeds of sale, with the addition of any amount allowed as general average.

(e) Mails, passengers' luggage, personal effects and accompanied private motor vehicles shall not contribute to general average.

Rule XVIII Damage to ship

The amount to be allowed as general average for damage or loss to the ship, her machinery and/or gear caused by a general average act shall be as follows:

(a) When repaired or replaced:
The actual reasonable cost of repairing or replacing such damage or loss, subject to deductions in accordance with Rule XIII;

(b) When not repaired or replaced:

The reasonable depreciation arising from such damage or loss, but not exceeding the estimated cost of repairs. But where the ship is an actual total loss or when the cost of repairs of the damage would exceed the value of the ship when repaired, the amount to be allowed as general average shall be the difference between the estimated sound value of the ship after deducting therefrom the estimated cost of repairing damage which is not general average and the value of the ship in her damaged state which may be measured by the net proceeds of sale, if any.

Rule XIX Undeclared or wrongfully declared cargo

(a) Damage or loss caused to goods loaded without the knowledge of the shipowner or his agent or to goods wilfully misdescribed at time of shipment shall not be allowed as general average, but such goods shall remain liable to contribute, if saved.

(b) Damage or loss caused to goods which have been wrongfully declared on shipment at a value which is lower than their real value shall be contributed for at the declared value, but such goods shall contribute upon their actual value.

Rule XX Provision of funds

(a) The capital loss sustained by the owners of goods sold for the purpose of raising funds to defray general average disbursements shall be allowed in general average.
(b) The cost of insuring average disbursements shall also be allowed in general average.

Rule XXI Interest on losses allowed in general average

(a) Interest shall be allowed on expenditure, sacrifices and allowances in general average until three months after the date of issue of the general average adjustment, due allowance being made for any payment on account by the contributory interests or from the general average deposit fund.
(b) Each year the Assembly of the Comité Maritime International shall decide the rate of interest which shall apply. This rate shall be used for calculating interest accruing during the following calendar year.

Rule XXII Treatment of cash deposits

Where cash deposits have been collected in respect of cargo's liability for general average, salvage or special charges such deposits shall be paid without any delay into a special account in the joint names of a representative nominated on behalf of the shipowner and a representative nominated on behalf of the depositors in a bank to be approved by both. The sum so deposited together with accrued interest, if any, shall be held as security for payment to the parties entitled thereto of the general average, salvage or special charges payable by cargo in respect of which the deposits have been collected. Payments on account or refunds of deposits may be made if certified to in writing by the average adjuster. Such deposits and payments or refunds shall be without prejudice to the ultimate liability of the parties.

Rule XXIII Time bar for contributions to general average

(a) Subject always to any mandatory rule on time limitation contained in any applicable law:
    (i) Any rights to general average contribution, including any rights to claim under general average bonds and guarantees, shall be extinguished unless an action is brought by the party claiming such contribution within a period of one year after the date upon which the general average adjustment was issued. However, in no case shall such an action be brought after six years from the date of the termination of the common maritime adventure.
    (ii) These periods may be extended if the parties so agree after the termination of the common maritime adventure.
(b) This Rule shall not apply as between the parties to the general average and their respective insurers

York-Antwerp Rules 2016

Rule of interpretation

In the adjustment of general average the following Rules shall apply to the exclusion of any law and practice inconsistent therewith.

Except as provided by the Rule Paramount and the numbered Rules, general average shall be adjusted according to the lettered Rules.

Rule Paramount

In no case shall there be any allowance for sacrifice or expenditure unless reasonably made or incurred.

Rule A

1. There is a general average act when, and only when, any extraordinary sacrifice or expenditure is intentionally and reasonably made or incurred for the common safety for the purpose of preserving from peril the property involved in a common maritime adventure.
2. General average sacrifices and expenditures shall be borne by the different contributing interests on the basis hereinafter provided.

Rule B

1. There is a common maritime adventure when one or more vessels are towing or pushing another vessel or vessels, provided that they are all involved in commercial activities and not in a salvage operation.

   When measures are taken to preserve the vessels and their cargoes, if any, from a common peril, these Rules shall apply.
2. If the vessels are in common peril and one is disconnected either to increase the disconnecting vessel's safety alone, or the safety of all vessels in the common maritime adventure, the disconnection will be a general average act.
3. Where vessels involved in a common maritime adventure resort to a port or place of refuge, allowances under these Rules may be made in relation to each of the vessels. Subject to the provisions of paragraphs 3 and 4 of Rule G, allowances in general average shall cease at the time that the common maritime adventure comes to an end.

Rule C

1. Only such losses, damages or expenses which are the direct consequence of the general average act shall be allowed as general average.
2. In no case shall there be any allowance in general average for losses, damages or expenses incurred in respect of damage to the environment or in consequence of the escape or release of pollutant substances from the property involved in the common maritime adventure.
3. Demurrage, loss of market, and any loss or damage sustained or expense incurred by reason of delay, whether on the voyage or subsequently, and any indirect loss whatsoever, shall not be allowed as general average.

Rule D

Rights to contribution in general average shall not be affected, though the event which gave rise to the sacrifice or expenditure may have been due to the fault of one of the parties to the common maritime adventure, but this shall not prejudice any remedies or defences which may be open against or to that party in respect of such fault.

Rule E

1. The onus of proof is upon the party claiming in general average to show that the loss or expense claimed is properly allowable as general average.
2. All parties to the common maritime adventure shall, as soon as possible, supply particulars of value in respect of their contributory interest and, if claiming in general average, shall give notice in writing to the average adjuster of the loss or expense in respect of which they claim contribution, and supply evidence in support thereof.
3. Failing notification, or if any party does not supply particulars in support of a notified claim, within 12 months of the termination of the common maritime adventure or payment of the expense, the average adjuster shall be at liberty to estimate the extent of the allowance on the basis of the information available to the adjuster. Particulars of value shall be provided within 12 months of the termination of the common maritime adventure, failing which the average adjuster shall be at liberty to estimate the contributory value on the same basis. Such estimates shall be communicated to the party in question in writing. Estimates may only be challenged within two months of receipt of the communication and only on the grounds that they are manifestly incorrect.
4. Any party to the common maritime adventure pursuing a recovery from a third party in respect of sacrifice or expenditure claimed in general average, shall so advise the average adjuster and, in the event that a recovery is achieved, shall supply to the average adjuster full particulars of the recovery within two months of receipt of the recovery.

Rule F

Any additional expense incurred in place of another expense which would have been allowable as general average shall be deemed to be general average and so allowed without regard to the saving, if any, to other interests, but only up to the amount of the general average expense avoided.

Rule G

1. General average shall be adjusted as regards both loss and contribution upon the basis of values at the time and place when and where the common maritime adventure ends.
2. This rule shall not affect the determination of the place at which the average adjustment is to be prepared.
3. When a ship is at any port or place in circumstances which would give rise to an allowance in general average under the provisions of Rules X and XI, and the cargo or part thereof is forwarded to destination by other means, rights and liabilities in general average shall, subject to cargo interests being notified if practicable, remain as nearly as possible the same as they would have been in the absence of such forwarding, as if the common maritime adventure had continued in the original ship for so long as justifiable under the contract of carriage and the applicable law.

4. The proportion attaching to cargo of the allowances made in general average by reason of applying the third paragraph of this Rule shall be limited to the cost which would have been borne by the owners of cargo if the cargo had been forwarded at their expense. This limit shall not apply to any allowances made under Rule F.

Rule I – Jettison of cargo

No jettison of cargo shall be allowed as general average, unless such cargo is carried in accordance with the recognised custom of the trade.

Rule II – Loss or damage by sacrifices for the common safety

Loss of or damage to the property involved in the common maritime adventure by or in consequence of a sacrifice made for the common safety, and by water which goes down a ship's hatches opened or other opening made for the purpose of making a jettison for the common safety, shall be allowed as general average.

Rule III – Extinguishing fire on shipboard

Damage done to a ship and cargo, or either of them, by water or otherwise, including damage by beaching or scuttling a burning ship, in extinguishing a fire on board the ship, shall be allowed as general average; except that no allowance shall be made for damage by smoke however caused or by heat of the fire.

Rule IV – Cutting away wreck

Loss or damage sustained by cutting away wreck or parts of the ship which have been previously carried away or are effectively lost by accident shall not be allowed as general average.

Rule V – Voluntary stranding

When a ship is intentionally run on shore for the common safety, whether or not she might have been driven on shore, the consequent loss or damage to the property involved in the common maritime adventure shall be allowed in general average.

Rule VI – Salvage remuneration

(a) Expenditure incurred by the parties to the common maritime adventure in the nature of salvage, whether under contract or otherwise, shall be allowed in general average provided that the salvage operations were carried out for the purpose of preserving from peril the property involved in the common maritime adventure and subject to the provisions of paragraphs (b), (c) and (d).

(b) Notwithstanding (a) above, where the parties to the common maritime adventure have separate contractual or legal liability to salvors, salvage shall only be allowed should any of the following arise:

(i) there is a subsequent accident or other circumstances resulting in loss or damage to property during the voyage that results in significant differences between salved and contributory values,
(ii) there are significant general average sacrifices,
(iii) salved values are manifestly incorrect and there is a significantly incorrect apportionment of salvage expenses,
(iv) any of the parties to the salvage has paid a significant proportion of salvage due from another party,
(v) a significant proportion of the parties have satisfied the salvage claim on substantially different terms, no regard being had to interest, currency correction or legal costs of either the salvor or the contributing interest.

(c) Salvage expenditures referred to in paragraph (a) above shall include any salvage remuneration in which the skill and efforts of the salvors in preventing or minimising damage to the environment such as is referred to in Article 13 paragraph 1(b) of the International Convention on Salvage, 1989 have been taken into account.
(d) Special compensation payable to a salvor by the shipowner under Article 14 of the International Convention on Salvage, 1989 to the extent specified in paragraph 4 of that Article or under any other provision similar in substance (such as SCOPIC) shall not be allowed in general average and shall not be considered a salvage expenditure as referred to in paragraph (a) of this Rule.

Rule VII – Damage to machinery and boilers

Damage caused to any machinery and boilers of a ship which is ashore and in a position of peril, in endeavouring to refloat, shall be allowed in general average when shown to have arisen from an actual intention to float the ship for the common safety at the risk of such damage; but where a ship is afloat no loss or damage caused by working the propelling machinery and boilers shall in any circumstances be allowed as general average.

Rule VIII – Expenses lightening a ship when ashore, and consequent damage

When a ship is ashore and cargo and ship's fuel and stores or any of them are discharged as a general average act, the extra cost of lightening, lighter hire and reshipping (if incurred), and any loss or damage to the property involved in the common maritime adventure in consequence thereof, shall be allowed as general average.

Rule IX – Cargo, ship's materials and stores used for fuel

Cargo, ship's materials and stores, or any of them, necessarily used for fuel for the common safety at a time of peril shall be allowed as general average, but when such an allowance is made for the cost of ship's materials and stores the general average shall be credited with the estimated cost of the fuel which would otherwise have been consumed in prosecuting the intended voyage.

Rule X – Expenses at port of refuge, etc.

(a) (i) When a ship shall have entered a port or place of refuge or shall have returned to her port or place of loading in consequence of accident, sacrifice or other extraordinary circumstances which render that necessary for the common safety, the expenses of entering such port or place shall be allowed as general average; and when she shall have sailed thence with her original cargo, or a part of it, the corresponding expenses of leaving such port or place consequent upon such entry or return shall likewise be allowed as general average.

When a ship is at any port or place of refuge and is necessarily removed to another port or place because repairs cannot be carried out in the first port or place, the provisions of this Rule shall be applied to the second port or place as if it were a port or place of refuge and the cost of such removal including temporary repairs and towage shall be allowed as general average. The provisions of Rule XI shall be applied to the prolongation of the voyage occasioned by such removal.

(b) (i) The cost of handling on board or discharging cargo, fuel or stores, whether at a port or place of loading, call or refuge, shall be allowed as general average when the handling or discharge was necessary for the common safety or to enable damage to the ship caused by sacrifice or accident to be repaired, if the repairs were necessary for the safe prosecution of the voyage, except in cases where the damage to the ship is discovered at a port or place of loading or call without any accident or other extraordinary circumstances connected with such damage having taken place during the voyage.

(ii) The cost of handling on board or discharging cargo, fuel or stores shall not be allowable as general average when incurred solely for the purpose of restowage due to shifting during the voyage, unless such restowage is necessary for the common safety.

(c) Whenever the cost of handling or discharging cargo, fuel or stores is allowable as general average, the costs of storage, including insurance if reasonably incurred, reloading and stowing of such cargo, fuel or stores shall likewise be allowed as general average. The provisions of Rule XI shall apply to the extra period of detention occasioned by such reloading or restowing.

(d) When the ship is condemned or does not proceed on her original voyage, storage expenses shall be allowed as general average only up to the date of the ship's condemnation or of the abandonment of the voyage or up to the date of completion of discharge of cargo if the condemnation or abandonment takes place before that date.

Rule XI – Wages and maintenance of crew and other expenses putting in to and at a port of refuge, etc.

(a) Wages and maintenance of master, officers and crew reasonably incurred and fuel and stores consumed during the prolongation of the voyage occasioned by a ship entering a port or place of refuge or returning to her port or place of loading shall be allowed as general average when the expenses of entering such port or place are allowable in general average in accordance with Rule X(a).

(b) (i) When a ship shall have entered or been detained in any port or place in consequence of accident, sacrifice or other extra-ordinary circumstances which render that entry or detention necessary for the common safety, or to enable damage to the ship caused by sacrifice or accident to be repaired, if the repairs were necessary for the safe prosecution of the voyage, the wages and maintenance of the master, officers and crew reasonably incurred during the extra period of detention in such port or place until the ship shall or should have been made ready to proceed upon her voyage, shall be allowed in general average.

(ii) Fuel and stores consumed during the extra period of detention shall be allowed as general average, except such fuel and stores as are consumed in effecting repairs not allowable in general average.

(iii) Port charges incurred during the extra period of detention shall likewise be allowed as general average except such charges as are incurred solely by reason of repairs not allowable in general average.

(iv) Provided that when damage to the ship is discovered at a port or place of loading or call without any accident or other extraordinary circumstance connected with such damage having taken place during the voyage, then the wages and maintenance of master, officers and crew and fuel and stores consumed and port charges incurred during the extra detention for repairs to damages so discovered shall not be allowable as general average, even if the repairs are necessary for the safe prosecution of the voyage.

(v) When the ship is condemned or does not proceed on her original voyage, the wages and maintenance of the master, officers and crew and fuel and stores consumed and port charges shall be allowed as general average only up to the date of the ship's condemnation or of the abandonment of the voyage or up to the date of completion of discharge of cargo if the condemnation or abandonment takes place before that date.

(c) (i) For the purpose of these Rules wages shall include all payments made to or for the benefit of the master, officers and crew, whether such payments be imposed by law upon the shipowners or be made under the terms of articles of employment.

(ii) For the purpose of these Rules, port charges shall include all customary or additional expenses incurred for the common safety or to enable a vessel to enter or remain at a port of refuge or call in the circumstances outlined in Rule XI(b)(i).

(d) The cost of measures undertaken to prevent or minimise damage to the environment shall be allowed in general average when incurred in any or all of the following circumstances:

(i) as part of an operation performed for the common safety which, had it been undertaken by a party outside the common maritime adventure, would have entitled such party to a salvage reward;

(ii) as a condition of entry into or departure from any port or place in the circumstances prescribed in Rule X(a);

(iii) as a condition of remaining at any port or place in the circumstances prescribed in Rule XI(b), provided that when there is an actual escape or release of pollutant substances, the cost of any additional measures required on that account to prevent or minimise pollution or environmental damage shall not be allowed as general average;

(iv) necessarily in connection with the handling on board, discharging, storing or reloading of cargo, fuel or stores whenever the cost of those operations is allowable as general average.

Rule XII – Damage to cargo in discharging, etc.

Damage to or loss of cargo, fuel or stores sustained in consequence of their handling, discharging, storing, reloading and stowing shall be allowed as general average, when and only when the cost of those measures respectively is allowed as general average.

Rule XIII – Deductions from cost of repairs

(a) Repairs to be allowed in general average shall not be subject to deductions in respect of "new for old" where old material or parts are replaced by new unless the ship is over fifteen years old in which case there shall be a deduction of one third. The deductions shall be regulated by the age of the ship from the 31st December of the year of completion of construction to the date of the general average act, except for insulation, life and similar boats, communications and navigational apparatus and equipment, machinery and boilers for which the deductions shall be regulated by the age of the particular parts to which they apply.

(b) The deductions shall be made only from the cost of the new material or parts when finished and ready to be installed in the ship. No deduction shall be made in respect of provisions, stores, anchors and chain cables. Drydock and slipway dues and costs of shifting the ship shall be allowed in full.

(c) The costs of cleaning, painting or coating of bottom shall not be allowed in general average unless the bottom has been painted or coated within the 24 months preceding the date of the general average act in which case one half of such costs shall be allowed.

Rule XIV – Temporary repairs

(a) Where temporary repairs are effected to a ship at a port of loading, call or refuge, for the common safety, or of damage caused by general average sacrifice, the cost of such repairs shall be allowed as general average.

(b) Where temporary repairs of accidental damage are effected in order to enable the common maritime adventure to be completed, the cost of such repairs shall be allowed as general average without regard to the saving, if any, to other interests, but only up to the saving in expense which would have been incurred and allowed in general average if such repairs had not been effected there.

(c) No deductions "new for old" shall be made from the cost of temporary repairs allowable as general average.

Rule XV – Loss of freight

Loss of freight arising from damage to or loss of cargo shall be allowed as general average, either when caused by a general average act, or when the damage to or loss of cargo is so allowed.

Deduction shall be made from the amount of gross freight lost, of the charges which the owner thereof would have incurred to earn such freight, but has, in consequence of the sacrifice, not incurred.

Rule XVI – Amount to be allowed for cargo lost or damaged by sacrifice

(a) (i) The amount to be allowed as general average for damage to or loss of cargo sacrificed shall be the loss which has been sustained thereby based on the value at the time of discharge, ascertained from the commercial invoice rendered to the receiver or if there is no such invoice from the shipped value. Such commercial invoice may be deemed by the average adjuster to reflect the value at the time of discharge irrespective of the place of final delivery under the contract of carriage.

(ii) The value at the time of discharge shall include the cost of insurance and freight except insofar as such freight is at the risk of interests other than the cargo.

(b) When cargo so damaged is sold and the amount of the damage has not been otherwise agreed, the loss to be allowed in general average shall be the difference between the net proceeds of sale and the net sound value as computed in the first paragraph of this Rule.

Rule XVII – Contributory values

(a) (i) The contribution to a general average shall be made upon the actual net values of the property at the termination of the common maritime adventure except that the value of cargo shall be the value at the time of discharge, ascertained from the commercial invoice rendered to the receiver or if there is no such invoice from the shipped value. Such commercial invoice may be deemed by the average adjuster to reflect the value at the time of discharge irrespective of the place of final delivery under the contract of carriage.

(ii) The value of the cargo shall include the cost of insurance and freight unless and insofar as such freight is at the risk of interests other than the cargo, deducting therefrom any loss or damage suffered by the cargo prior to or at the time of discharge. Any cargo may be excluded from contributing to general average should the average adjuster consider that the cost of including it in the adjustment would be likely to be disproportionate to its eventual contribution.

(iii) The value of the ship shall be assessed without taking into account the beneficial or detrimental effect of any demise or time charterparty to which the ship may be committed.

(b) To these values shall be added the amount allowed as general average for property sacrificed, if not already included, deduction being made from the freight and passage money at risk of such charges and crew's wages as would not have been incurred in earning the freight had the ship and cargo been totally lost at the date of the general average act and have not been allowed as general average; deduction being also made from the value of the property of all extra charges incurred in respect thereof subsequently to the general average act, except such charges as are allowed in general average or fall upon the ship by virtue of an award for special compensation under Article 14 of the International Convention on Salvage, 1989 or under any other provision similar in substance.[1] Where payment for salvage services has not been allowed as general average by reason of

1 The underlined words of Rule XVII (b) were omitted by error from the text of the York-Antwerp Rules adopted in New York in May 2016. They were in previous versions, and were not intended to be excluded in the New York discussions. The CMI Assembly will be asked in Genoa in September 2017 to approve this correction to the published text of the York-Antwerp Rules 2016.

paragraph (b) of Rule VI, deductions in respect of payment for salvage services shall be limited to the amount paid to the salvors including interest and salvors' costs.

(c) In the circumstances envisaged in the third paragraph of Rule G, the cargo and other property shall contribute on the basis of its value upon delivery at original destination unless sold or otherwise disposed of short of that destination, and the ship shall contribute upon its actual net value at the time of completion of discharge of cargo.

(d) Where cargo is sold short of destination, however, it shall contribute upon the actual net proceeds of sale, with the addition of any amount allowed as general average.

(e) Mails, passengers' luggage and accompanied personal effects and accompanied private motor vehicles shall not contribute to general average.

Rule XVIII – Damage to ship

The amount to be allowed as general average for damage or loss to the ship, her machinery and/or gear caused by a general average act shall be as follows:

(a) When repaired or replaced,
The actual reasonable cost of repairing or replacing such damage or loss, subject to deductions in accordance with Rule XIII;

(b) When not repaired or replaced,
The reasonable depreciation arising from such damage or loss, but not exceeding the estimated cost of repairs. But where the ship is an actual total loss or when the cost of repairs of the damage would exceed the value of the ship when repaired, the amount to be allowed as general average shall be the difference between the estimated sound value of the ship after deducting therefrom the estimated cost of repairing damage which is not general average and the value of the ship in her damaged state which may be measured by the net proceeds of sale, if any.

Rule XIX – Undeclared or wrongfully declared cargo

(a) Damage or loss caused to goods loaded without the knowledge of the shipowner or his agent or to goods wilfully misdescribed at the time of shipment shall not be allowed as general average, but such goods shall remain liable to contribute, if saved.

(b) Where goods have been wrongfully declared at the time of shipment at a value which is lower than their real value, any general average loss or damage shall be allowed on the basis of their declared value, but such goods shall contribute on the basis of their actual value.

Rule XX – Provision of funds

(a) The capital loss sustained by the owners of goods sold for the purpose of raising funds to defray general average disbursements shall be allowed in general average.

(b) The cost of insuring general average disbursements shall be allowed in general average.

Rule XXI – Interest on losses allowed in general average

(a) Interest shall be allowed on expenditure, sacrifices and allowances in general average until three months after the date of issue of the general average adjustment, due allowance being made for any payment on account by the contributory interests or from the general average deposit fund.

(b) The rate for calculating interest accruing during each calendar year shall be the 12-month ICE LIBOR for the currency in which the adjustment is prepared, as announced on the first banking day of that calendar year, increased by four percentage points. If the adjustment is prepared in a currency for which no ICE LIBOR is announced, the rate shall be the 12-month US Dollar ICE LIBOR, increased by four percentage points.

Rule XXII – Treatment of cash deposits

(a) Where cash deposits have been collected in respect of general average, salvage or special charges, such sums shall be remitted forthwith to the average adjuster who shall deposit the sums into a special account, earning interest where possible, in the name of the average adjuster.

(b) The special account shall be constituted in accordance with the law regarding client or third party funds applicable in the domicile of the average adjuster. The account shall be held separately from the average adjuster's own funds, in trust or in compliance with similar rules of law providing for the administration of the funds of third parties.

(c) The sums so deposited, together with accrued interest, if any, shall be held as security for payment to the parties entitled thereto, of the general average, salvage or special charges in respect of which the deposits have been collected. Payments on account or refunds of deposits may only be made when such payments are certified in writing by the average adjuster and notified to the depositor requesting their approval. Upon the receipt of the depositor's approval, or in the absence of such approval within a period of 90 days, the average adjuster may deduct the amount of the payment on account or the final contribution from the deposit.

(d) All deposits and payments or refunds shall be without prejudice to the ultimate liability of the parties.

Rule XXIII – Time bar for contributing to general average

(a) Subject always to any mandatory rule on time limitation contained in any applicable law:

  (i) Any rights to general average contribution including any rights to claim under general average bonds and guarantees, shall be extinguished unless an action is brought by the party claiming such contribution within a period of one year after the date upon which the general average adjustment is issued. However, in no case shall such an action be brought after six years from the date of termination of the common maritime adventure.

  (ii) These periods may be extended if the parties so agree after the termination of the common maritime adventure.

(b) This rule shall not apply as between the parties to the general average and their respective insurers.

For Product Safety Concerns and Information please contact our EU
representative GPSR@taylorandfrancis.com
Taylor & Francis Verlag GmbH, Kaufingerstraße 24, 80331 München, Germany

www.ingramcontent.com/pod-product-compliance
Ingram Content Group UK Ltd.
Pitfield, Milton Keynes, MK11 3LW, UK
UKHW051934190926
475701UK00014B/1150
* 9 7 8 0 3 6 7 6 4 6 6 2 2 *